To two great pioneers in
parks development and recreation administration:

Robert F. Moses
of New York

and

Robert W. Crawford
of Philadelphia

Creative Management in Recreation, Parks, and Leisure Services

Creative Management in Recreation, Parks, and Leisure Services

Richard G. Kraus

Professor, Recreation and Leisure Studies,
College of Health, Physical Education,
Recreation, and Dance,
Temple University,
Philadelphia, Pennsylvania

Joseph E. Curtis

Commissioner of Parks, Recreation,
and Human Services,
City of New Rochelle,
New Rochelle, New York

Fourth Edition
Illustrated

TIMES MIRROR/MOSBY
COLLEGE PUBLISHING

ST. LOUIS • TORONTO • SANTA CLARA   1986

Editor: Nancy Roberson
Manuscript Editor: Idelle Winer
Cover Designer: Susan E. Lane
Production: Celeste Clingan, Jeanne Gulledge

Fourth Edition

Library of Congress Cataloging in Publication Data

Kraus, Richard G.
  Creative management in recreation, parks, and
leisure services.

  Rev. ed. of: Creative management in recreation and
parks. 3rd ed. 1982.
  Bibliography: p.
  Includes index.
  1. Recreation—Management. 2. Parks—Management.
3. Recreation—United States—Management. 4. Parks—
United States—Management. 5. Recreation—Canada—
Management. 6. Parks—Canada—Management. I. Curtis,
Joseph E., 1922-   . II. Kraus, Richard G. Creative
management in recreation and parks. III. Title.
  ISBN 0-8016-2749-4

1803460.

C/VH/VH 9 8 7 6 5 4 3 2 1   02/B/234

About the Authors

Richard G. Kraus, M.A., Ed.D.

Dr. Kraus is primarily known as an educator, having taught at the University of Utah and Cortland College, N.Y., and headed recreation and leisure-service curricula at Teachers College, Columbia University, Lehman College of the City University of New York, and Temple University. He has written over 30 textbooks and monographs, including several widely used texts in recreation fundamentals, program planning and leadership, and therapeutic recreation. Dr. Kraus has served as a consultant to many agencies, including the Job Corps, the Office of Economic Opportunity, the YWCA, and numerous colleges and public agencies. He has done planning studies for the cities of Pittsburgh and Philadelphia and has carried out national studies on urban recreation and parks. Dr. Kraus has received the Distinguished Fellow Award of the Society of Parks and Recreation Educators, was selected the Jay B. Nash Scholar of the American Association of Leisure and Recreation, and was given the National Literary Award of the National Recreation and Park Association.

Joseph E. Curtis, M.A.

Mr. Curtis is Commissioner of Human Services, including Parks and Recreation, for the City of New Rochelle, N.Y. During his 38 years of parks and recreation leadership, he has headed major leisure-service departments in Boston, White Plains, N.Y., Oceanside, N.Y., and Baltimore County, Md. He is the author of three texts and numerous articles. Mr. Curtis has served as president of the American Park and Recreation Society, as well as of state societies in Massachusetts, New York, and Maryland. He has taught recreation management at Columbia University, New York University, Northeastern University, the University of New Hampshire, City University of New York, Massachusetts Institute of Technology, and Harvard University. He has received 65 awards and honors, including the Healthy America Fitness Award, and is a Distinguished Fellow of the American Park and Recreation Society. He has served as a special consultant to many cities, government departments, and major corporations.

Preface

The fourth edition of *Creative Management in Recreation, Parks, and Leisure Services* has been designed to provide a comprehensive, contemporary text for courses in the management of various types of leisure agencies. It has been thoroughly revised based on major changes in American and Canadian society that have influenced professional preparation in the recreation, park, and leisure-service field. These include the following:

1. *Diversification of the leisure-service field.* In addition to public recreation and park departments, the leisure-service field now includes private, commercial, armed forces, campus, employee, and therapeutic recreation services as well. Expanded emphasis is given to these other types of agencies in Chapters 4 and 6 to present a full picture of different approaches to leisure-service management.

2. *Impact of the ''era of limits''—the marketing thrust.* Limited financial support in many types of recreation agencies has resulted in a need for innovative fiscal practices. These include aggressive marketing approaches, self-generated funding, and full accountability, with documentation of both benefits and costs of leisure-service programming. Chapters 10, 11, and 15 present useful guidelines in the areas of fiscal management and marketing practices.

3. *Goal-oriented, human-service programming.* Once regarded by many as a frill, organized recreation service today must be goal oriented to make a significant contribution to community life. In many agencies, leisure service includes various types of human-service or personnel-benefit functions, including health and morale. Examples of how recreation agencies meet important personal and social needs are provided in Chapter 9, which describes important new concepts and trends in program development.

4. *Management information systems and computer use.* With the development of more sophisticated planning approaches and evaluation methods, leisure-service professionals are now using computers to plan and implement programs and document their outcomes. Chapter 15 deals in detail with the evaluation process and shows how computers play a vital role in establishing management information systems in recreation, parks, and leisure-service agencies.

Other additions to the text

In preparing this edition of *Creative Management in Recreation, Parks, and Leisure Services,* we reduced chapters dealing with such routine management functions as program planning, facilities, and leadership, since they are often dealt with in other courses and textbooks. At the same time, we added fresh material on legal aspects, risk management, and public and community relations in Chapters 12 through 14. In Chapters 2 and 3, emphasis is given to newer concepts of management, including both theoretical and practical approaches to personnel management. A number of critical new ideas have been drawn from recent popular books on social change by John Naisbitt and Alvin Toffler and on successful business management by Thomas Peters, Robert Waterman, and others. Chapter 3 provides a discussion of innovative Japanese management approaches, including the use of quality circles, based on an extensive recent tour of Japan by one of the co-authors.

As in previous editions, the book presents practical guidelines for effective management drawn from the current literature and from manuals and reports submitted by dozens of recreation agencies of all types in the United States and Canada. Thus it is more than a simple how-to text or an ivory-tower, theoretical discussion. Instead it offers a comprehensive, complex overview of the total operation of leisure-service agencies, designed primarily for undergraduate courses but with sufficient advanced material to be challenging on the graduate level as well.

New pedagogical aids

Another important change in this edition is the addition of teaching aids designed to make the book a more effective pedagogical tool. These include the following:

1. *Introductory anecdotes or quotations* at the beginning of each chapter to capture the reader's interest or present key issues in capsule form
2. *Detailed introductions and summaries* in all chapters to assist students in comprehending the material by highlighting the major areas covered
3. *Case studies* (two in each of the 10 chapters that deal with specific management processes), which present problem situations in areas such as personnel management or facilities operation and which can be used in problem-solving or planning exercises or as student assignments; these case studies are fictional, and their characters are not based on real persons, living or dead
4. *Questions for class discussion and individual or group student projects* following each chapter, which can be used to promote an experiential approach to learning through active participation and presentations by students throughout the semester

Acknowledgments

We have sought to make this book readable and interesting and to provide numerous examples. In so doing, we have drawn on our own experience and observation and on the contributions of many practitioners who responded to our request for assistance. Although we do not have space to name all the individuals who sent useful materials, the following were especially helpful: Janet Pomeroy, San Francisco Recreation Center for the Handicapped; Steve Weeks, Napa State Hospital, Imola, Calif.; Kirsty Griffiths, Ontario, Canada, March of Dimes; Bill Lewis, Brainerd, Minn., Camp Confidence; Mary Douglas, Project SOAR, Portland Ore.; Betty Usher, Nepean, Ont., Canada,

Parks and Recreation Department; Terri Clark, Vancouver, B.C., Canada, Parks and Recreation Board; Laurie Halladay, Busch Entertainment Corporation; Anne Mattes, formerly of the Cigna Corporation and Temple University, Philadelphia; Pamela Crespi, Operations Division, Naval Material Command, Washington D.C.; and Ron Stamphill, Naval Air Station, Leemore, Calif. The contributions of many others are cited throughout the book.

We also express gratitude to the publisher's reviewers who analyzed the third edition of this text and provided perceptive comments and suggestions that were helpful in its revision. These were Susan D. Hudson, North Texas State University; Wayne F. Stormann, Ithaca College, N.Y.; Sam Bozzo, San Jose State University, Calif.; and Regina B. Glover, Southern Illinois University. The review process, as well as the overall task of coordinating the revision and production of this edition, was carried on most capably by our editor, Nancy Roberson, and to her must go much of the credit for the final product.

We hope that many professors and students in recreation, parks, and leisure-studies curricula throughout the United States and Canada will use and enjoy the fourth edition of this text. Knowledgeable, skilled practitioners are needed throughout all sectors of the leisure-service field, and we are happy to have made a contribution to their education.

Richard G. Kraus
Joseph E. Curtis

Contents

1 Role of managers in leisure-service agencies, 1

Growth of recreation in modern life, 1
Management, 3
Formulating a philosophy of service, 7
Summary, 15

2 Traditional concepts of management, 19

Understanding management, 19
Key elements and purposes of management, 20
Management as a professional discipline: science or art? 20
Theory and practice in management, 21
Summary, 31

3 Management science today, 35

New directions in management theory, 35
Modern management theory: authority, power, and delegation, 41
Summary, 54

4 Structure and governance in leisure-service agencies: the organizing function, 59

Role of organizations, 59
Organizational responsibilities of managers, 60
Legal basis for establishing leisure-service agencies, 61
Types of administrative structures, 63
Administrative placement within larger systems, 64
Role of boards and commissions, 65
Organizational patterns of leisure-service agencies, 67
Informal agency processes, 79
Organization as a dynamic process, 82
Summary, 83

5 Goals, objectives, and policy development: the planning process, 87

Planning in leisure-service agencies, 87
Developing a philosophy of service, 88
Nature of organizational goals, 88
Transforming goals into objectives, 91
Development of recreation and park policies, 95
Planning process in action, 103
Summary, 106

6 Personnel management: the directing function, 111

Employment practices in leisure-service agencies, 111
Employment standards in leisure-service agencies, 120
Process of personnel management, 121
Personnel policies, 131
Use of volunteer workers, 134
Summary, 137

7 Personnel management: the motivating function, 143

Challenges facing supervisors, 143
Effective supervisory styles, 144
Recognizing employees' needs, 145
Guidelines for supervisory action, 146
Job enrichment, 149
Working with labor unions, 158
Professional identification and commitment, 162
Summary, 163

8 Recreation and park facilities: the manager's role, 169

Facilities: the manager's role, 169
Planning principles and methods, 169
Current urban planning methods, 171
Recreation and park planning studies, 171
Facilities planning in other types of leisure-service agencies, 174
Acquisition of properties, 176
Acquisition by nonpublic agencies, 178
Design process, 178
Role of the manager in facilities design and construction, 180
Planning and design approaches in other types of agencies, 181
Facilities design for safe use, 182
Design to provide access for the disabled, 182
Maintenance and operation of facilities, 184

Economy and efficiency strategies, 186
Innovative leisure facilities: challenges and trends, 188
Manager's role: synergy and stewardship, 198
Summary, 199

9   Recreation program development, 205

Understanding the concept of "program," 205
Five program functions, 206
Process of program development, 208
Program planning model, 208
Classification of program activities, 211
Factors affecting choices of program activities, 212
Program formats for participation, 215
Diversity of formats within a single facility or activity, 216
Scheduling methods, 216
Program schedules in other settings, 225
Other program planning concepts, 226
Program life cycle, 229
Current trends in recreation programming, 230
Summary, 232

10   Budgets and fiscal management, 237

Nature of fiscal management, 237
Managers' expertise in fiscal matters, 238
Meaning of "budget," 239
Types of budget, 239
Legal aspects of budgets, 245
Budget process, 245
Financial accounting system, 251
Sources of funding for leisure-service agencies, 254
Summary, 264

11   Innovative fiscal management: marketing, productivity, and strategic planning, 269

Need for innovative fiscal management, 269
Fiscal strategies for the 1980s and 1990s, 270
Summary, 296

12   Public and community relations, 301

Goals of public relations, 301
Identifying audiences for public relations, 303

Channels for public relations, 303
Need for quality and creativity, 311
Guidelines for public relations, 314
Overall approach to public relations, 314
Community relations, 316
Role of volunteers, 318
Coordination and cooperation among agencies, 322
Cooperation with the private sector, 325
Summary, 327

13 Risk management and security control, 333

Need for risk management, 333
Scope of physical risk in outdoor recreation, 334
Developing risk management plans, 335
Accident prevention and control procedures, 335
Specific areas of safety concern, 338
Prevention of vandalism and crime in recreation settings, 345
Use of rangers and park police, 347
Summary, 349

14 Legal aspects of recreation and park management, 355

Liability as a management concern, 355
Prevention of negligence liability claims, 359
Elements in defense of liability suits, 359
Other aspects of liability, 360
Liability insurance, 361
Contractual liability, 362
Personnel management and the law, 364
Programming and access for special populations, 366
Law-enforcement policies and practices, 368
Summary, 369

**15 The controlling function: evaluation, management information
systems, and computers,** 373

Evaluation defined, 373
Methods of agency evaluation, 375
Evaluation of personnel, 380
General guidelines for evaluation, 384
Need for efficient management information systems, 387
Summary, 398

16   The effective manager, 401

Qualities and skills underlying managerial success, 401
Intelligent decision making, 407
Providing creative leadership, 411
Managing in the future tense, 415
Summary, 417

Bibliography, 421

Creative Management in Recreation, Parks, and Leisure Services

CHAPTER

1

Managers [are] quasi-mythical beings, frequently male, who live out their lives in boxlike spaces called offices. It is usually easy to differentiate managers from the other beings who also inhabit the office ecosystem. The managers are the ones with the most padding on their chairs and the largest desks.[1]

Role of Managers
in Leisure-Service Agencies

Who are managers in leisure-service agencies today? What are their roles, basic philosophies, and strategies? Since there are so many different types of leisure-service organizations in American and Canadian life—including public, voluntary, private, commercial, therapeutic, and other types of recreation agencies—is it possible to identify any single approach to the management process that is found in all such settings?

This chapter seeks to provide answers to many of these questions. After describing the growth of recreation in American society, it defines the term "management," showing how it differs from the concept of administration. It outlines the functions of managers and presents a number of the important societal trends that have influenced the role of leisure-service organizations in recent years. It concludes by showing how the managerial styles of administrators, division heads, and supervisors of leisure-service agencies are rapidly changing in response to these trends and to the challenges facing recreation as a field of professional service today.

Growth of Recreation in Modern Life

The popularity and diversity of recreation in modern society have been well documented. Millions of people engage in sports and fitness programs, cultural activities, outdoor recreation and travel, the arts, hobbies, and numerous other forms of leisure activities. On every level of government, recreation and park facilities and programs have captured popular interest and involvement. Within the private sphere, recreation expenditures have grown dramatically, from $83 billion in 1969 to $125 billion in 1974 to $310 billion in 1984.[2]

Some of the examples of increased participation and the social factors influencing them were highlighted in a report, "Demand for Recreation in America: An Overview," prepared by the Outdoor Recreation Policy Review Group in the mid-1980s. These included the following:

American adults had 10 percent more free time by 1975 than a decade earlier. And some of that new-found free time resulted in an increase in sports, outdoor recreation and walking for pleasure from an average of .9 hours weekly to 1.3 hours weekly.

Total participation in the 30 most popular sports and recreation activities increased nine percent from 1973 to 1982. Recent fitness studies found almost half of the adult population practicing some form of exercise on a regular basis, up from only 24 percent exercising in 1960.

A population shift to the South and the West will generate more spending for recreation

TABLE 1-1   Percentages of Survey Respondents Participating in Activities (Summer Only)

Activity	Summer 1960	Summer 1982
Bicycling	9	28
Horseback riding	6	7
Fishing	29	30
Canoeing or kayaking	2	8
Sailing	2	4
Swimming	45	51
Camping	8	19

From *Nationwide Recreation Survey, 1982-1983,* Washington, D.C., April 1984, National Park Service, U.S. Department of the Interior.

because people can be more active in climates conducive to outdoor recreation and where recreation in general is often a more important part of lifestyle.

The prime target group for active sports and outdoor recreation goods—those aged 25-34—will increase by 35 percent in the next 10 years.[3]

The changing role of women and recent federal rulings requiring schools to provide equal recreational equipment and opportunities for women have translated into a sharp rise in spending for women's sports and athletics. The study concluded:

> There is no doubt that participation in outdoor recreation and in many sports forms has increased during the past 50 years because of increased mobility, discretionary income, diminished class differences, changes in religious attitudes toward recreation, increasing levels of formal education and changes in the role of women. . . . Leisure has emerged as a separate social institution, which is the vehicle for self-improvement and expression no less than work.[4]

To illustrate the dramatic growth in participation in outdoor recreational activities, a nationwide recreation survey carried out by the National Park Service in the early 1980s revealed changes in specific activities over the preceding two decades (Table 1-1).[5]

Similarly, the American Hotel and Motel Association reported in 1984 that tourism alone had accounted for $204 billion in domestic and foreign revenues in the preceding year and that it had become the nation's second largest retail industry and the second largest employer.

RECREATION: AN IMPORTANT SOCIAL INSTITUTION

Along with the striking growth in participation on all levels, recreation has become an important and recognized form of social service provided by public and voluntary nonprofit agencies. After an extensive study of the nation's major metropolitan areas, the U.S. Department of the Interior concluded, ''People in all urban areas want a well-balanced system of urban recreation opportunities which includes close-to-home neighborhood facilities and programs for all segments of the population.''[6]

Increasingly, other types of social agencies are providing recreation programs. In organizations serving special populations, recreation is a recognized therapeutic or rehabilitative service. Thousands of companies, colleges and universities, and armed forces units provide recreation for their employees or the clientele they serve. Without question, as leisure continues to expand, recreational participation will grow in the United States and Canada, and there will be an increasing need for skilled, professional managers in all such organizations.

Managers play a critical role within all leisure-service agencies. They are the individuals who are responsible for conceptualizing, planning, organizing, implementing, and evaluating all agency efforts. They coordinate and direct the work of other program or facility-related personnel and provide leadership to the entire leisure-service enterprise.

Management

The term "management" is a relatively new one in its application to the operation of business, government, and other types of organizations. Until fairly recently, individuals who were responsible for directing recreation agencies were typically referred to as "administrators" both in their job titles and in college courses or textbooks concerned with leisure-service operations.

In the mid-1950s, for example, Meyer and Brightbill described recreation administration as "the act of planning, organizing, managing, and directing organized recreation." The recreation administrator, they wrote, was

> usually the highest executive in the administration, who is entrusted with the execution of the laws, policies and regulations and the superintendence of administrative affairs . . . . he organizes and plans for others, must enlist their cooperation, adheres to policies and principles; keeps subordinates well informed; reserves his energies for the most important, overall administrative issues, rather than department details.[7]

Similarly, in the mid-1960s, Rodney wrote that administration was "the process that mobilizes an organization's resources, human and material, to attain predetermined goals."[8] Hjelte and Shivers concluded that all forms of human association require some aspect of administration and stated that "administrative procedures are found wherever material, natural, fiscal, or human resources must be marshaled to achieve a predetermined goal."[9]

Leisure-service administrators were typically described at this time as individuals who were responsible for carrying out a number of specific functions related to developing policies, planning and executing budgets, employing and supervising personnel, and implementing recreation programs. Their function was to ensure that the job was done as efficiently and effectively as possible, and they were primarily thought of as agency or department executives in public recreation and park organizations.

A BROADER VIEW OF MANAGEMENT

Over the past two decades, however, fields such as business and public administration have shifted toward use of the term "management," implying that the process of organizing and directing any major business or governmental enterprise is not the responsibility of top executives alone (as suggested by use of the word "administration"). Instead, it often involves several layers of executives and their deputies, division heads, specialists, consultants, planners, and others, all of whom may play a vital role in the management process. As an illustration of this shift, many cities began to apply the title ''manager'' or ''general manager'' to the heads of their recreation and park departments rather than ''commissioner'' or ''superintendent.'' At the same time, they came to recognize that management is a process shared by individuals at several levels of job responsibility and that many managerial functions are carried out by lower-level personnel within a participative framework.

Today management is seen as a process that is carried on within all types of leisure-service agencies. It is concerned with the generic roles of planning, organizing, motivating, and controlling to develop meaningful goals and achieve the desired organizational outcomes.

Management is entrusted with the task of helping an organization develop meaningful directions to marshal its resources for effective action in a rapidly changing socioeconomic environment.

At the same time that it must define and enforce formal policies, procedures, and processes based on established structures and operations, management also seeks to develop a positive climate of staff participation in shared problem solving, decision making, and goal setting.

The emphasis in present-day management has shifted from enforcing to persuading, from directing to motivating, from commanding to coordinating, and from reliance on established goals, policies, and procedures rooted in the past to a future-oriented, flexible, and creative leadership style.

ROLES AND FUNCTIONS OF TODAY'S MANAGERS

Feldman and Arnold point out that modern organizational management is a difficult and complex task because of the many different roles managers have to play. Whatever the type of organization, these roles fit into the following three areas[10]:

1. *Coordinating the activities* of numerous other individuals, including staff members, clients or business associates, and suppliers or contractors.
2. *Processing information* relevant to the work of the organization by gathering and analyzing it and then disseminating it to appropriate individuals.
3. *Making key decisions,* in terms of resource allocation, problem solving and conflict resolution, and developing new agency products or services.

As Feldman and Arnold point out, these roles are not independent of each other. Instead, they interact to form an integrated whole. In an interpersonal sense, the manager serves as a figurehead, or symbolic leader of an organization, as well as a direct leader who guides the work of staff members. He or she also serves as a liaison with a network of outside individuals or groups and negotiates with them on behalf of the organization. The manager approves and enforces policies and makes needed operational decisions with respect to personnel and other agency functions.[11]

SPECIFIC TASKS OF LEISURE-SERVICE MANAGERS

In addition to these generic functions, which are shared by managers in all kinds of organizations, management personnel in leisure-service agencies have a number of specific areas of job responsibility. These include the following.

Agency goals and policies

Leisure-service agency managers must provide leadership in formulating the philosophy, goals, and policies that govern the operation of their organizations. Other staff members should be encouraged to participate in this process, and understanding and support for goals and policies should be developed among other department or agency heads or with those in related organizations or service units.

Organizational development

Managers are responsible for developing, reviewing, and improving the organization's structure in its divisions and levels of responsibility, decision-making powers, and channels of communication. This role encompasses not only the physical definition of titles and areas of responsibility but also the processes of coordination and cooperative action that are not often made explicit in organization charts.

Personnel management

In addition to playing the vital role of symbolic leader for all members of the organization, managers must make key determinations of personnel needs. They are responsible for planning and carrying out the recruitment, hiring, training, and supervision of all staff members. Beyond this, they are responsible for maximizing the productivity of all personnel through effective counseling, job enrichment, delegation, and similar procedures.

Program planning and implementation

This function is at the heart of the leisure-service manager's responsibility: to conceptualize, plan, and put into action a varied range of recreation program activities and services, including providing facilities and initiating programs with other organizations on a cosponsorship basis.

Fiscal management and marketing leadership

Leisure-service managers must formulate financial priorities and policies, develop and gain approval for budgetary plans, and maintain control of all revenues, expenditures, and other aspects of fiscal management. Today in public recreation and park departments and in other types of leisure-service agencies, there is new emphasis on the need to develop and promote funding sources. Managers are expected to stress productivity and economical operations and to ''market'' recreation programs and services as vigorously and imaginatively as possible.

Facilities development and maintenance

Leisure-service managers have the unique responsibility for planning the development of varied recreational facilities—both outdoor and indoor—and for contributing to their design and construction, as well as to their ongoing maintenance. Particularly for recreation and park managers with extensive outdoor resources, this task involves concern for environmental and esthetic issues, as well as direct leisure uses of the facilities.

Public and community relations

Effective leisure-service managers place a high priority on public relations processes that provide publicity and also enrich public or members' understanding and support of the agency. They also strive to achieve positive relations with community groups and to coordinate their programs with other organizations and service groups.

Risk management, liability, and law enforcement

Particularly in public and commercial recreation agencies, managers must institute effective risk management plans. Since many leisure activities, such as team sports and many outdoor recreation pursuits, involve potential dangers, safety, first aid, accident prevention, and insurance are all vital concerns. Avoidance of costly liability suits for negligence is critical. In addition, preventing vandalism or other criminal activity in recreation settings is important.

Legal aspects

With leisure-service management becoming increasingly complex, it is essential that managers become familiar with the varied legal aspects of their work. These include issues related to accidents and negligence claims, as well as contracts and fiscal practices, leasing and concessions agreements, affirmative action and hiring policies, occupational health and safety, and labor relations.

Evaluation and management information systems

The manager must take the lead in establishing procedures for evaluating all agency operations, including programs and leadership, facility maintenance, and similar functions. Beyond this, the manager should conduct feasibility and needs studies, cost-benefit analyses, and other types of applied research to provide a solid data base for departmental planning, decision making, and policy development. As this text points out, computers and electronic data-processing techniques are being used increasingly in such functions.

INFLUENCE OF SPECIAL SETTINGS ON THE MANAGER'S ROLE

While the basic functions of leisure-service managers remain the same in many different types of recreation agencies, their on-the-job responsibilties may vary greatly according to the type of organization in which they are employed. Within each major category of leisure service, there may be different types of legal authorization, goals and objectives, and approaches to fiscal management and program planning. The manager of a large commercial recreation operation will have responsibilities that differ sharply from those of a therapeutic recreation program specialist, just as a voluntary agency director's job will contrast with the work of an armed forces recreation director.

Influence of agency size and structure

In each different type of organization, the size and structure of the agency will also affect the manager's role. In large municipal or commercial recreation organizations, there may be many staff members and the need for managers to delegate many responsibilities. There will often be separate specialists or division heads in charge of planning and design, maintenance, budget and finance, and other specialized management functions.

In smaller organizations with fewer employees, responsibilities are usually more centralized. The director of a small employee recreation program is likely to do his or her own program planning, publicity, and budget development and to rely on volunteers or paid ''per session'' instructors to carry out direct program leadership. In many therapeutic recreation settings there are only one or two leisure-service professionals on the job, and management functions are carried out by their superiors within the overall agency structure.

Despite these differences, it must be emphasized that the basic management tasks remain the same in *all* leisure-service organizations.

It is the essential responsibility of managers on every level, including executives, division heads, center directors, area or activity supervisors, and program coordinators, to provide leadership to the overall enterprise and to enable other staff members to contribute as fully as possible to its success. As will be discussed in later chapters, managers' functions include both the generic tasks of planning, organizing, motivating, and controlling and the specialized tasks of directing programs, fiscal operations, facilities, and similar elements of leisure-service operations. Beyond this, they have the unique responsibility of formulating a significant philosophy of recreation and leisure and meeting the important personal and social needs of participants or organization members.

Formulating a Philosophy of Service

Recreation and leisure represent a vital aspect of life in modern society, and all organized programs in this field should be based on a positive and constructive set of values and goals. Thus, although recreation can and should be ''fun'' and provide participants with pleasure and personal satisfaction, it should also be designed to contribute other important benefits to participants and sponsoring organizations or communities.

Obviously, no single type of leisure-service agency will be able to meet this total need in the modern community. Thus managers must be selective in program and facility development according to their goals and available resources, while coordinating their efforts at all times with other community recreation sponsors. In so doing, they must be aware of and responsive to a number of important trends that have emerged in recent years, both within the larger society and within the specific field of recreation service.

SEVEN SOCIAL FACTORS INFLUENCING LEISURE-SERVICE MANAGEMENT

What are these important trends and changing social conditions? They range from dramatic shifts in the demographic makeup of society to the emergence of a new ''era of limits'' and the emphasis on documentation and accountability within agencies of every type. As such, they have critical implications for leisure-service managers and will be individually discussed.

WHAT CENSUS CLOCK SHOWS NOW

The U.S. Census Bureau's population clock struck 237 million as 1985 got under way. That is an increase of 2.1 million Americans in one year, based on estimates of 3.7 million births, 2 million deaths and the net migration of 499,000 into the country. Forecast: Americans will total 250 million by 1991 and 268 million by the time the 21st century begins—when the rate of growth will start to drop. The nation's median age, 30.6 in 1982, is expected to reach 36.3 by the year 2000.

From *U.S. News and World Report,* Jan. 14, 1985, p. 7.

Dramatic demographic changes

Despite a widely publicized decline in the birthrate since World War II, the population of the United States continues to climb steadily, as shown in the box above. Similarly, it is expected that the present population of Canada will grow to between 28 and 32 million by the end of the century based on projections of birthrate, mortality, and net migration totals.

Beyond the changes in numbers, the populations served by leisure-service agencies will continue to be transformed. With greater numbers of single parents, there will be increased need for day-care and related services. The needs of the handicapped and those with alternative life-styles, including sexual minorities, will pose new challenges for recreation planners. There will be a greatly increased proportion of older citizens, blacks, Hispanics, and other ethnic or racial minority populations to be served. With the revitalization of our older cities, neighborhoods are emerging in which many so-called Yuppies (young urban professionals) live side by side with economically and socially depressed residents, creating new priorities and service needs.

New emphasis on human-service programming

To serve such changing populations, leisure-service managers can no longer afford to restrict their offerings to activities that have been typically regarded as recreation: games and sports, arts and crafts, hobbies, and social and outdoor activities that are clearly recognizable as recreation.

The "fun and games" approach, or viewing recreation primarily as a housekeeping service designed to maintain facilities, will no longer be acceptable. Instead, it is clear that leisure services are becoming more tightly interwoven with human development and social and environmental concerns. There is a growing emphasis on health and fitness, noncompetitive forms of play, and leisure's contribution to the quality of life. Many leisure-service managers have assumed human service tasks, including health and fitness programs, specific forms of counseling or therapy, nutritional services, transportation, and vocational services.

Fiscal pressures

In addition to being a form of personal experience, recreation has been shown to make a vital contribution to the economy. Many cities and regions in the United States and Canada depend heavily on recreation spending to support their economies and provide a major source of local employment.

This means, however, that recreation must be understood as a product or service that *costs* money to provide. Organized recreation has typically been supported through taxes, contributions, grants, membership fees, or other self-generated revenues, such as admissions charges, rental or registration fees, or payment for instruction or the purchase of needed equipment or materials.

Recreation sponsorship has become a highly competitive area of economic activity. Different forms of entertainment or leisure attractions vie for the public's interest and economic support. As people spend more on commercial forms of recreation, which has been the case in recent years, they tend to be less willing to support public or voluntary nonprofit leisure-service agencies with taxes or voluntary giving. This problem has become more acute as a result of inflation, economic recession, and the cuts in public spending that took place in the late 1970s and early 1980s. Although voluntary agencies have not been as severely curtailed as public departments, their budgets have also suffered. Similarly, armed forces recreation personnel, therapeutic recreation specialists, and those in other areas of leisure service have been forced to face the harsh reality of an era of limits.

Marketing model of leisure-service management

Recreation and park agencies have become resourceful in seeking out innovative forms of program support, increasing fees and charges, expanding concessions of contracting arrangements, encouraging cooperative program sponsorship, and soliciting government, foundation, or business grants and special gifts. They have also learned not just to respond to the public's expressed needs and wishes but to develop new forms of service and to promote their leisure offerings as vigorously as commercial recreation organizations have done.

Bullaro summed up what has come to be known as the marketing approach to leisure-service management:

> Inflation, resource scarcity, and shifting social priorities are creating an unfavorable climate for the leisure service organization. To keep their organizations alive, successful leisure service managers must accept the fact that they have a business, and they must practice sound business strategies, however unglamorous they might be. Marketing techniques, such as forecasting, pricing, advertising, selling, and distribution, are vital strategies if leisure service organizations intend to match their services with client needs and their cash flow with expenses.[12]

New emphasis on accountability and productivity

Closely related to the trend toward marketing has been a greater emphasis on fiscal accountability and employee productivity at all levels of leisure service. New planning and monitoring procedures have made it possible for recreation and park managers to measure and document the performance of their agencies.

Electronic data processing, systems planning, and cost-benefit analyses, as well as more rigorous efforts to define agency goals and objectives and to measure outcomes, provide both a challenge and an opportunity for leisure-service professionals. In voluntary, commercial, armed forces, and other types of recreation programs, efforts are being made to assess client or consumer needs and interests more systematically, to monitor employee performance, and to evaluate leisure service *during* the delivery process rather than at the end. Productivity is the keynote, and in specialized fields such as therapeutic recreation service, stricter standards and expectations are being applied to justify third-party reimbursement for services provided to patients and clients.

Continuing environmental concerns

Another important concern for leisure-service managers in the 1980s has been the environmental and energy-related problems that have affected all areas of American and Canadian life. Acid rain and other types of environmental pollution have affected our forests and trails, lakes, and seashores, limiting outdoor recreational opportunities. Fortunately, federal open-space and reclamation programs in both the United States and Canada have reversed this trend, although many such programs suffered from a lack of governmental support in the United States during the early 1980s, and acid rain continues to present a serious threat.

We have come to recognize that outdoor recreation, although socially desirable, is not always compatible with environmental needs and values. Careless or uncontrolled boating, hunting, or use of off-road vehicles may be extremely destructive of waterways, wildlife, and the natural environment. Recreation and park managers must give serious thought to the environmental impact of their programs and services. Furthermore, they must sharply limit the uses of fuel and other forms of energy in facility operations and maintenance to conserve such resources and keep costs down.

Shifting public values and leisure interests

Major changes have occurred in the social values and leisure interests of the American and Canadian public in recent years. At the beginning of the recreation and park movement, there was widespread support for the social values it represented. Vigorous sports, games, and outdoor recreational activities were seen as desirable, ''character-building'' pursuits for young people and as a safeguard against juvenile delinquency. Within a conservative moralistic climate that condemned gambling, vice, alcohol, and drugs, organized recreation programs were encouraged to provide constructive leisure alternatives.

Today the moral climate has been transformed. A new wave of permissiveness and hedonism emerged in the 1960s and 1970s with the appearance of the so-called Me Generation. Traditional family-oriented values are much less widely accepted, and the dramatic increase in broken marriages has meant that great numbers of adults are now part of a new single life-style. Many formerly forbidden activities have become widely accepted, including various forms of sex, gambling, and the use of drugs and alcohol.

While we still value the fitness benefits of organized sports and outdoor recreation, many people are content to watch professional or college athletes compete on television rather than participate themselves. Indeed, television watching in the mid-1980s reached

> ## *NOW, IT'S THE "STAY-AT-HOME" SOCIETY*
>
> A nation of recluses? Hardly. Yet more people than ever before are relying on new technology for recreation, shopping, health care—without leaving the house.
>
> With each passing year, the American home is regaining bit by bit the role it played decades ago as the center of life's activities.
>
> Cross-country car trips are giving way to living-room videogames and other products offered through the rapidly expanding home-entertainment market . . . . This emerging "stay-at-home society" is described in a report released in mid-June by the National Science Foundation . . . . at the forefront of this change is a flurry of electronic products—videogames, videocassette recorders, big-screen TVs, color cameras and a variety of home computers—all selling briskly despite a troubled economy.
>
> From *U.S. News and World Report,* June 28, 1982, p. 64.

a new high, averaging 6 hours and 48 minutes a day in the typical American home. We have become increasingly dependent on electronic entertainment, with television becoming "the new American hearth—a center for family activities, conversation, and companionship." Inevitably, we are becoming a home-centered society (see box above).

CHALLENGES TO LEISURE-SERVICE MANAGERS

Clearly such social trends present serious challenges and problems to leisure-service managers within each specialized area of recreation and park programming. They must develop new approaches and service-delivery techniques to ensure that all citizens of the United States and Canada receive full opportunity to use their leisure in creative and enriching ways. In part, the task will be one of helping individuals of all ages—from children in the early elementary grades to adults in senior centers—better understand and value the meaning of recreation and leisure in their lives. In part, it will be a matter of developing intra-agency cooperation in program delivery to prevent duplication and provide a fuller range of activities and services.

In the years ahead there will be a continuing growth of concern about the quality of life, environmental values, and the nature of leisure experience, along with a fuller sense of community. In a sense, we are at a crossroads in determining our popular leisure values and interests. We can move into greater reliance on technological forms of entertainment, as represented by television, electronic games, and other home entertainment, or we can stress more active, creative, and personally involving forms of leisure. We can accept as inevitable the growing dependence on alcohol, drugs, gambling, and commercialized sex as part of the hedonistic approach to leisure, or we can vigorously promote a new national outlook in which individuals will be encouraged to seek their "highs" through less destructive or demeaning recreational activity.

Beyond this, we need to help people understand that recreation need not be lush, gaudy, loud, glamorous, expensive, or passive. Local parks, beaches, sports fields, and entertainment centers often offer the best for the least cost. Crafts, games, hobbies, skills, and sports carried on in one's neighborhood offer lasting values far beyond the small investment of money and time involved. The glories of the vast state and national park systems, the museums, aquariums, hiking trails, woodlands, deserts, and mountains are all part of this basic, wholesome approach to recreation. Moreover, for the millions of people who cannot afford elaborate and expensive equipment, vacation trips, or second homes, the strengths and simplicity that marked our earlier concept of recreation should be appealing.

New concepts of service

How can leisure-service managers meet these changing needs and challenges? First, they must accept the realities of a society that exists within an "era of limits" and the shifts in life-styles that have come about, often with the awareness that small is beautiful and less is more. Social scientists predict that we will move increasingly into a conserver rather than a consumer society, and recreation and park programs will need to reflect these changes. Second, they will need to face the need for advocacy and community leadership to become a more significant function for leisure-service managers.

Foley and Benest urge that leaders in this field embark on a set of initiatives to accomplish the following[13]:

1. Redefine leadership, advocating more risk-taking and innovation
2. Transform recreation and park activities into human development experiences
3. Better define the needs of communities through social planning
4. Take a leadership role in liveability and life-style issues
5. Develop multi-service projects through interagency cooperation and integration
6. Organize people to develop more self-help programs and organize clients to support recreation and human-service programs

How critical are such needs? To cite a single example, it is clear that the American family is undergoing a dramatic transformation and that its stability and health are being seriously threatened (see box on opposite page).

Obviously, recreation and related leisure services cannot be expected to provide a total solution to such deep-rooted problems and social trends. Yet recreation clearly plays a vital role in helping to meet the physical, social, and psychological needs of people of all ages and can make an important contribution to strengthening family life and helping children and youth resist self-destructive impulses and leisure activities.

New management leadership styles

If leisure-service managers are to assume such responsibilities successfully, they must develop new and more effective leadership styles. They will need to become more skilled in organizational and interpersonal communications and decision-making processes, reflecting a humanistic and participative approach within each area of professional responsibility.

THE FAMILY IN TRANSITION

Families—The divorce rate has jumped 121 percent in the last 20 years. By 1990, the combined stepfamilies and single-parent families will exceed the number of "intact" families.

Working Mothers—This is the first time in our history that the typical school-age child has a mother in the work force.

Unattended Children—An estimated 50,000 children under the age of 6 are left home alone most of the day.

Television—Pre-school children spend a fourth of their waking time watching TV. Elementary-school children spend less time reading, doing chores and doing homework than they spend watching TV.

Mortality—Teens are killing themselves at three times the rate of 30 years ago. Children ages 5 to 14 are being killed at triple the rate of 1950. Among Western countries, the U.S. ranks first in childhood deaths by firearms and poisoning.

Child Abuse—If current trends continue, 30 percent of girls in the U.S. and 10 percent of boys probably will be sexually abused before age 18.

Runaways—The average age of a runaway 10 years ago was 15; today it is 12. A third are kicked out by their parents.

Sex—The number of teens engaging in sex increased by two-thirds in the last decade. Illegitimate births among teens 15 to 19 has jumped 33 percent since 1960. Abortions among unmarried girls in that age group more than tripled from 1971 to 1979.

From *Tampa Tribune and Times*, Oct. 21, 1984, p. 1-A.

Managers must also become more familiar with the current approaches to scientific management, including such accountability systems as management by objectives, zero-based budgeting, systems analysis, and similar models of modern planning and control. At the same time, managers must recognize that their task can be regarded as both an art and a science. They should avoid becoming too narrow in their approaches or becoming obsessively dependent on ''hardware.'' Instead, they should possess broad, eclectic intellectual interests. Bannon writes:

> The manager should . . . acquire an overall knowledge of all equipment and systems in an organization without gaining a specialist's or technician's comprehension of such technologies. The tendency to become an administrative technician should be resisted, as knowledge of machinery draws us away from concern with people, the prime administrative task.[14]

Finally, leisure-service managers in every type of agency must develop a new sense of the possible, of innovation, and of the potential role of recreation and park programs in urban and suburban society. They will no longer be able to sit back and wait for participants to come to them, taking the attitude, ''Here, I offer these fine programs and facilities to you. Use them or do not, at your convenience. I will be here whenever you need me.'' Instead, leisure-service managers must recognize that ''participants'' have become ''consumers.'' They are demanding and cost conscious. To attract and involve them, managers must become proactive in offering attractive and meaningful new programs and in providing high-quality service and painstaking care in serving the public.

If recreation is to become more highly regarded and influential in community life, its professional practitioners must have a greater understanding of their functions. They must generate a sense of mission and enthusiasm. They must become ''movers and shakers,'' the kinds of people who are able to communicate and work with business executives, religious leaders, civic officials, university and school system administrators, and people from every walk of life.

Only if its leaders are able to move forcefully in such directions will the recreation and park profession, including managers in every type of setting, be able to gain the support needed to promote leisure-service programs fully in community life.

In meeting these challenges, leisure-service managers must understand and come to grips with the remarkable shifts that have taken place in our society. As described by Naisbitt,[15] these include the following:

1. From an industrial to an information society
2. From forced technology to high tech/high touch
3. From a national economy to a world economy
4. From North to South in the United States
5. From short term to long term
6. From an either/or society to a multiple option society
7. From centralization to decentralization
8. From hierarchies to networking
9. From institutional help to self-help
10. From representative democracy to participatory democracy

At the 1983 National Congress for Recreation and Parks in Kansas City, Mo., Michael Annison, chief operating officer of the Naisbitt Group (a leading social forecasting organization), made the point that 30 years ago society was stable, with everything having a ''name and place'' and with major societal institutions and values fixed. Annison pointed out that now, with institutions undergoing rapid change, change no longer comes from ''the top'' or from major centralized organizations in society. Instead, he said,

> Basically, what's going to happen in parks and recreation and the quality of life in the communities where you live will be decided by you, your friends, and neighbors. ''They'' aren't going to fix it, whoever ''they'' were in Washington or in New York boardrooms. The ''they'' we used to look to are simply gone . . . .
>
> You are going to decide whether you can design a new set of services to meet the needs of your community. You are going to decide whether you can . . . work with state agencies or [nonprofit groups] or the private sector. You are going to spend your time and energy building up what's going to be, or you are going to pass up the opportunity. Now is the single most extraordinary moment that we'll get in our lives. The window is open to build what we think is important with people that we can help and serve and work with to shape our community.[16]

If they are to represent the leisure-service field effectively, managers must have as a primary concern the viability, productivity, and morale of their *own* organizations. They must be skilled in conflict resolution, in the process of job enrichment, and in the techniques of enabling all staff members to make the maximum possible contribution, often within organizations whose bureaucratic structure and past administrative practices have inhibited such efforts.

Perhaps the most difficult task for many organization executives, division heads, and supervisors is channeling their own time and energies in directions that will yield the maximum contribution and the most desirable and rewarding outcomes for themselves. The challenge of *being* an effective manager is a critical one. It is dealt with throughout this text in terms of appropriate strategies, goals, and on-the-job techniques. In the final chapter, it is discussed in a *personal* sense, as we examine the qualities and special skills that make some managers outstandingly successful as professional leaders.

Summary

This chapter describes the growth of recreation in modern life and its acceptance as an important social institution with several different types of community agencies that provide organized leisure opportunities today.

The chapter defines management and presents its major roles and functions, both in a generic sense and its specific applications to leisure-service organizations. It stresses the need for managers to have a positive and constructive philosophy of service and summarizes a number of major social changes that have influenced recreation and park agencies' policies and programs. It also describes a number of new concepts of service, including the emphasis on "human-service" programming and marketing approaches that strengthen the accountability of leisure-service agencies.

Concluding with a discussion of changing management styles, the chapter emphasizes the need for recreation and park professionals to play a vital, proactive role in their communities and to apply effective new, scientifically based management techniques in meeting the challenges confronting their agencies.

STUDY QUESTIONS

1. The text presents two contrasting emphases in leisure-service today: (1) the marketing model and (2) the human-service model. Discuss these, showing how they are influenced by current socioeconomic trends. What are their strengths and weaknesses for leisure-service managers, and can they both be applied within the same agency?
2. John Naisbitt's book *Megatrends* identifies 10 key trends in modern, postindustrial society. Which of these are most important for recreation agencies to consider, and what are their direct implications for managers?
3. Discuss what you see as the key roles of leisure-service managers today. How do they vary according to different types of recreation agencies, such as public, voluntary, commercial, therapeutic, or other types of specialized programs?

REFERENCES

1. Mescon, Michael H., Albert, Michael, and Khedouri, Franklin: *Management: Individual and Organizational Effectiveness,* New York, 1981, Harper & Row, Publishers, p. 4.
2. "Business Gets Healthy from Athletics Too," *U.S. News and World Report,* Aug. 13, 1984, p. 27.
3. *Demand for Recreation in America: An Overview,* Alexandria, Va., Feb. 1983, National Recreation and Park Association and Outdoor Recreation Policy Review Group.
4. *Ibid.*
5. *Nationwide Recreation Survey, 1982-1983,* Washington, D.C., April 1984, National Park Service, U.S. Department of Interior.
6. *National Urban Recreation Study, Executive Report,* Washington, D.C., Feb. 1978, National Park Service, U.S. Department of Interior, p. 10.
7. Meyer, Harold D., and Brightbill, Charles K.: *Recreation Administration: A Guide to Its Practice,* Englewood Cliffs, N.J., 1956, Prentice-Hall, Inc., pp. 25-26.
8. Rodney, Lynn S.: *Administration of Public Recreation,* New York, 1964, The Ronald Press Co., p. 19.

9. Hjelte, George, and Shivers, Jay S.: *Public Administration of Recreational Services,* Philadelphia, 1972, Lea & Febiger, Publishers, p. 3.

10. Feldman, Daniel C., and Arnold, Hugh J.: *Managing Individual and Group Behavior in Organizations,* New York, 1983, McGraw-Hill Book Co., p. 3.

11. *Ibid.*

12. Bullaro, John J.: "The Business of Survival: Developing a Marketing Strategy," *Journal of Physical Education, Recreation and Dance,* April 1982, p. 64.

13. Foley, Jack, and Benest, Frank C.: "Proposition 13 Aftermath—A Crisis in Recreation and Park Leadership," *Parks and Recreation,* Jan. 1980, p. 87.

14. Bannon, Joseph J.: "Challenges of Management," *Parks and Recreation,* July 1980, p. 31.

15. Naisbitt, John: *Megatrends: Ten New Directions Transforming Our Lives,* New York, 1982, 1984, Warner Books, Chapter 1.

16. Annison, Michael, cited in "Leisure in Transition: A Search for Trends," *Parks and Recreation,* Jan. 1984, p. 38.

CHAPTER 2

Of all management notions, classical theory has had the greatest impact on shaping the organizational character of recreation and park service agencies . . . . In large measure this was due to the fact that recreation and park services formed part of the larger public bureaucratic structure which already conformed to formal organizational ideas. The municipal recreation and park movement underwent its greatest period of growth during the late 1940s and 1950s. Classical theory, riding the crest of its popularity, was by that time firmly established as the prevailing public administration organization model.[1]

Traditional Concepts
of Management

*I*s management an art or a science? What are its basic theoretical models and structures? Although people have held the roles of business entrepreneurs, government officials, or directors of other types of organizations for many centuries, it was only in the latter half of the nineteenth century and the early twentieth century that management became a specialized field of professional practice that was scientifically studied and in which precise rules were laid down.

It was at this time, just at the height of the Industrial Era, that a number of basic concepts evolved regarding the ideal internal structure of organizations, the design of work functions, and the assignment of authority, which were widely adopted in the world of business and public administration. These concepts, stemming from the so-called classical period of management theory, still influence us today.

Understanding Management

Exactly what *is* management, and how is it carried on? Is it a mysterious, arcane craft or simply a common-sense, down-to-earth area of professional practice?

Management is a process or function that is common to all human organizations and institutions. Large hospitals, public-service agencies, the armed forces, educational systems, and businesses of every type are only a few of the settings in which it must operate. Whenever people join together to accomplish specific goals, the management process is at work. Although much of the impetus for developing professional management approaches has come from private industry, it would be false to assume that the only place management skills are needed is in profit-making enterprises. Instead, whenever two or more people become involved in cooperative efforts, the process of management comes into play.

The key to successful performance in any organization is the efficient use of human and physical resources. Therefore the basic element of management is the dynamic and changing process by which the activities and material resources of the group are set in motion, organized, and coordinated toward accomplishing selected objectives.

Management is more than just a set of job titles or a division of an organization that has been assigned administrative or supervisory responsibilities. Rather, it is a process that relates to and is part of all other organizational functions. In a sense, it is like the brain of a person or the steering mechanism of a car; it coordinates and directs all other operations.

Key Elements and Purposes of Management

Successful management is totally dependent on the *human element*. Divisional directors or program unit heads do not get the job performed by themselves, regardless of their individual talents or drive. Instead, they must work with and through others to achieve organizational goals and objectives.

The manager's essential purpose is to make *things happen* and to *achieve results*. No matter how great the effort, it is worth little unless it is meaningfully directed to improving the organization's performance. Therefore managers must concentrate on creating innovation and taking positive action rather than simply responding to crisis or challenge.

Management is a *dynamic process*. It is not stiff, rigid ''bossism'' or bureaucracy by the book. Circumstances, agency needs and priorities, and available resources are constantly changing. Therefore managers must remain alert to shifts in the surrounding environment to plan future developments with vision and perspective.

Management as a Professional Discipline: Science or Art?

In recent years, management has been widely recognized as a professional discipline requiring special knowledge and expertise. Many schools and special institutes of management have been established, and extensive research has explored every aspect of management performance in various types of organizations. Yet its essential character is still debatable, and authorities have described it both as a form of science and as an art.

The justification of management as a *science* is based on the growing body of empirically gathered knowledge and theories that has developed over the past several decades in various academic fields, including social psychology, economics, urban planning, sociology, and business administration. It is held that, whenever possible, managerial policies and decisions should be based on principles that have been verified through sound research procedures.

Yet it must be recognized that many aspects of agency management or organizational life cannot be precisely quantified, measured, and analyzed. Interpersonal relationships and outcomes do not lend themselves to easily proven cause-and-effect research studies. Indeed, many highly successful managers feel that scientific theories of management belong in the ivory towers of academia rather than in the real, everyday world of organizations.[2]

On the other hand, those who argue that management is an *art* point out that it depends heavily on the judgment, sensitivity, intuition, and leadership qualities of the practitioner. Particularly in dealing with other persons, managers must be highly flexible and responsive to individual temperaments and capabilities.

The truth is that management is both a science and an art. Torgerson and Weinstock[3] point out that science may provide the manager with facts regarding his or her professional mission and the probable effects of alternative courses of action. Within the constraints imposed by individual circumstances, managers must then blend the requirements of the situation with the resources available in arriving at a decision. Torgerson and Weinstock write "The application of knowledge (scientifically derived or otherwise) toward the achievement of human objectives is an *art*. Management may therefore be described as a science and an art, the former seeking knowledge and the latter applying it."[3]

Theory and Practice in Management

The manager must be familiar with both the theory and practice of modern management. For example, the practical responsibilities of recreation and park managers include such elements as setting up specific organizational structures, hiring and supervising full- or part-time leaders or maintenance personnel, planning and marketing new leisure programs and services, or formulating and administering fiscal plans. Theoretical approaches to management may present conceptual models of such functions based on validated research. These two contrasting ingredients of management must be blended in a harmonious relationship.

In fields such as government or business management, a number of theoretical approaches to effective practice have been developed over the past several decades. The most influential of these approaches are often referred to as part of classical management theory.

DEVELOPMENT OF CLASSICAL MANAGEMENT THEORY

The traditional approach to conceptualizing the administrative process came from the contributions of a number of pioneering thinkers in this field. Among these were Frederick Taylor, Max Weber, Luther Gulick and his associate Lyndall Urwick, and Henri Fayol. Their management principles and recommendations for the organization and operation of businesses and other forms of bureaucratic structures were immensely influential throughout the industrialized world.

Scientific management and the machine model: Frederick Taylor

In the United States during the early decades of the twentieth century, the "scientific management" approach was gradually developed. This approach consisted of a formal, highly structured management style, in which work responsibilities were divided so that each task was highly specialized and in which there was a clearly established assignment of authority and the power to demand conformity and obedience from subordinate employees. Within this framework, executive power was highly centralized, and there was a precise and orderly chain of command from the top to the bottom of the enterprise.

One of the leading contributors to this approach was Frederick Taylor, an engineer and steel company executive noted for his efforts to introduce a high level of efficiency into factory production. Taylor's famous text, *Scientific Management*,[4] gave rise to the movement itself and to what was often called the "machine model" approach to industrial management.

Taylor was convinced that most factories and other industrial enterprises were marked by a continuing conflict between management and employees, with many workers systematically resisting efforts to increase production. In addition, he believed that work assignments were wasteful and poorly designed. To overcome these problems, Taylor carried out time-and-motion studies that identified the most efficient and productive ways of streamlining work methods and eliminating unnecessary effort. These approved methods were to be standardized throughout an industrial plant and work-output rates established. Kelly describes Taylor's approach as

> specifying a "standard time" for each separate motion necessary to perform a task by timing tasks with a stopwatch; selecting the right person for the job; carefully planning the balance of machines, men, speed of working, and payment (usually on a piece basis); and developing line and staff management. Taylor invented a piecework system, which typically led to a threefold increase in productivity for a 50 percent increase in wages.[5]

The scientific management model was designed primarily for business enterprises, although it had strong implications for other large bureaucracies. Orderliness was its primary focus, and workers were seen as a component that had to be carefully assigned and supervised within the overall system. Taylor believed that there had to be a commonality of purpose for management and workers and that the key element in effective management was gaining the full cooperation of employees. His views were summarized as follows: "Management was interested in high profits and workers were interested in high wages; both would be able to reach their goals through cost reductions resulting from increased productivity."[6]

Max Weber and the bureaucratic ideal

The scientific management school drew many of its ideas from a school of philosophical and sociological analysis that promoted respect for highly organized, depersonalized bureaucratic management. Max Weber, a leading German sociologist during the late nineteenth and early twentieth centuries, was greatly impressed by the way in which Bismarck had unified Germany and transformed its government into a modern and technically efficient organization. Today we tend to regard bureaucracy as cumbersome and excessively controlled by red tape. Weber, however, believed that bureaucratic management systems were technically far superior to other management approaches: "Precision, speed, unambiguity . . . continuity, discretion, unity, strict subordination, reduction of friction and of material and personal cost—these are raised to the optimum point in the strictly bureaucratic administration."[7]

Weber viewed employees as emotional and often unpredictable, characteristics that tended to interfere with efficient organizational processes. Therefore in his view the depersonalized form of organization represented by bureaucracies with precisely defined, mechanistic roles, functions, divisions, and regulations would minimize the negative effect of dysfunctional or inefficient human behavior. He urged the adoption of "rational" administrative structures in which persons holding managerial posts would be subject to the following policies:

1. There would be a division of labor, in which authority and responsibility would be defined for each employee and all official duties would be clearly detailed. Strict rules, controls, and disciplinary procedures would be applied to ensure uniform, efficient performance of such tasks.

2. Managers would be selected on the basis of their demonstrated expertise, which would be determined by formal examinations and education or on-the-job training rather than by favoritism or other personal qualities.

3. All positions within the organization would be organized according to a vertical chain of command or hierarchy of authority, which came to be known as the "scalar" principle. Each lower office would fall under the command of a higher one, and the relationships among different departments and managers would be clearly specified.

Fayol's principles of management

Another major contribution to the evolving school of management theory was made by Henri Fayol, a leading French industrialist. Fayol held that five managerial processes or functions were critical in the entire administrative process, whether in business, military, government, or other types of organizations. These were planning, organizing, commanding, coordinating, and controlling. In his book, *Administration Industrielle et Generale,* published in 1929, Fayol[8] presented 14 key principles, which extended Weber's ideas and made them operational (see box on p. 24).

Fayol's principles had a strong international impact in that a number of other management theorists combined his views with those of Taylor and Weber and began to develop a number of management concepts that were widely adopted in schools of public administration or business and other training programs.

Luther Gulick and Lyndall Urwick: administrative functions

Focusing on the process of effective management, Luther Gulick and Lyndall Urwick[9] published a major work that used the term "POSDCORB" as a memory device to summarize the chief administrative functions of managerial personnel in public agencies. The letters represented words descriptive of these key tasks: planning, organizing, staffing, directing, coordinating, reporting, and budgeting. As interpreted by Lynn Rodney in a leading text on public recreation administration, several of these functions were applied to the leisure-service field as follows:

1. *Planning.* What are the objectives of the department? What programs and activities should be provided to meet the objectives? What policies should be formulated? What should be the scope of operation?

2. *Organizing.* How should the plans be carried out? How will the work be allocated or divided? What organizational units should be established to carry out basic functions? What relationships should exist between units of operation?

3. *Staffing and resources.* Who is to perform the many and varied tasks? What human and material resources are available? How are they to be allocated?

4. *Directing.* Who is to oversee how the work is being carried out? How are orders to be issued to get the organization operating and carrying out its function? Who will direct general operations? How will this direction be given?

5. *Coordinating.* How will the various units of work be fused together in a team effort? What means should be used to ensure that divisions of work are functioning in harmony and are synchronized in effort?[10]

FAYOL'S 14 PRINCIPLES

1. *Division of work.* Work assignments should be highly specialized and concentrated on narrower functions, in order to produce more and better work with the same time and effort.
2. *Authority and responsibility.* Authority is the right to give orders and to demand obedience and responsibility.
3. *Discipline.* Discipline implies respect for the agreements between the company and its employees, and is essential for the smooth operation of the organization. Without it, enterprises cannot prosper, and it must be enforced if necessary by judiciously applied sanctions.
4. *Unity of command.* An employee should receive orders from one superior only.
5. *Unity of direction.* There should be one plan and one head for each group of activities having the same objectives.
6. *Subordination of individual interest to general interest.* The interests of any employee or group of employees should not prevail over those of the company or overall organization.
7. *Remuneration of personnel.* Personnel compensation should be fair and satisfactory both to employees and to the organization, to maintain the loyalty and support of employees.
8. *Centralization.* Centralized management authority is a natural consequence of organizing, although the appropriate degree of centralization will vary according to the particular organization.
9. *Scalar chain.* The scalar chain is the chain of superior-subordinate relationships, ranging from the highest authority to the lowest rank of employees.
10. *Order.* The organization should provide an orderly place for each individual; a place for everyone and everyone in his place.
11. *Equity.* Equity, consisting of balanced fairness and a sense of justice, is found throughout the organization.
12. *Stability of tenure of personnel.* Time is needed for the employee to adapt to his work and perform efficiently. Since high turnover increases inefficiency, a mediocre manager who stays is preferable to a highly competent manager who comes and goes.
13. *Initiative.* At all organizational levels, employee initiative is augmented by zeal and energy.
14. *Esprit de corps.* Teamwork marked by the harmonious interpersonal relationship of employees provides strength to the organization.

Modified from Fayol, H.: *General and Industrial Management*, London, 1949, Pitman & Sons, Ltd.

This list of functions has gradually been consolidated. Today many management texts suggest that there are four key tasks: planning, organizing, motivating (or directing), and controlling. Throughout this text these generic functions are discussed in day-by-day leisure-service management.

FOUR BASIC PRINCIPLES OF MANAGEMENT

Based on these early contributions to the theory of management, four basic principles of management became broadly accepted and put into practice. They dealt with such elements as the nature of work and work assignments and the structure of organizations. A brief discussion of each follows.

Division of labor and task specialization

Under this principle the operational functions of an organization must be sharply identified and placed in separate departments. Departments in turn are subdivided into separate units or sections, reflecting different areas of work responsibility. New departments or units are added and older ones subdivided as the organization expands.

Based on the principles of Taylor and Fayol, work assignments are differentiated according to specialized functions, and exact procedures and standards are applied.

Assignment of authority and accountability

The overall administrative structure is generally dependent on the principle that authority is legitimated; that is, superiors have the right to command others to take certain actions and subordinates must obey their commands. Accompanying this principle is the tenet of accountability; once given an assignment, a person must carry it out and is responsible for its successful completion.

Within the "machine model" framework, the higher-level employee clearly had the right to impose orders on subordinates, provided that these did not violate personnel policies, labor union contractual agreements, or other departmental regulations.

Scalar principle and unity of command

According to this principle, authority is established at the top of the organization and flows in a vertical line down to the lower levels of the structure. This was often referred to as a "ladder," with each rung representing a level of authority or administrative responsibility. Linked to this is the concept of *unity of command*, which held that each subordinate employee should be directly responsible to only one superior. A related principle is that of *centralized decision making*, which held that decision-making powers in all important areas of concern must be tightly restricted to those at the upper end of the chain of command or to the heads of departments or subdivisions.

Span of control

This principle refers to the number of immediate subordinates that a supervisor or other manager can effectively direct. This may be shown diagrammatically by having a "narrow" or "tall" span of control contrasted with a "broad" or "flat" span of control. In the narrow structure, with several layers, each manager is able to exert a high degree of supervision and control over a limited number of subordinates. In the broad structure, with fewer layers but more employees in each layer, the manager is able to supervise more individuals, but cannot give them as much attention and control.

Some authorities have suggested that the maximum number of employees that a manager can supervise directly is between six and 10. However, no rigid standard may be applied in this area. Instead, the optimal span of control is influenced by: (1) the capability of the supervisor; (2) the skills and commitment of the employees being supervised; (3) the level of difficulty and degree of uniformity of the tasks assigned; and (4) the overall managerial approach and the extent to which it is willing to trust subordinate employees with a degree of independent authority in making routine decisions.

STRUCTURE OF ORGANIZATIONS

In addition to these principles, classical management theory was concerned with the *structure* of organizations. The term ''structure'' refers to the tangible framework of operational units, functions, work assignments, job titles, and relationships through which an organization is managed. Structure may be regarded as the established arrangement of the components and subsystems of an organization; it provides the channels of communication, coordination, and decision making.

Formal and informal structures

A logically organized structure is essential to effective operations, while a poorly designed one hampers performance at every level. The ultimate purpose of an organization's structure is to ensure smooth operation in day-to-day functioning. While the chief emphasis was given to the *formal* structure of organizations, it was recognized that there was also an *informal* system at work.

The formal structure of an organization consists of explicitly stated rules, operating policies, work procedures, and other devices that are put into effect by management to organize all the components of the work enterprise to meet established goals. It may be based not only on administrative decisions but also on union contracts that regulate hours, leaves, disciplinary action, arbitration of disputes, and even work output. It is usually reflected in organization charts, job descriptions, personnel manuals or regulations, and similar written documents.

In contrast, the informal structure of organizations does not appear in writing; it represents a fluid and dynamic process of interpersonal behavior and decision making. It is the way in which the formal code of operations is realistically adapted to the day-to-day problems of management and in which personnel on all levels actually carry out their functions, communicate with each other, and contribute to organizational goals.

Use of organization charts

Under the scientific management approach, businesses, government departments, and other organizations typically developed charts that presented pictorial models of their formal structures, showing each level of managerial responsibility, as well as the various departments or administrative divisions holding specialized functions. Each position or department normally has a title and placement on the chart indicating its specific area of responsibility. In some organization charts, dotted lines and arrows indicate structural relationships, such as who reports to whom. In others, the actual names of individuals holding specific positions are shown, along with the number of employees in each job slot.

Examples of several organization charts in representative leisure-service agencies are presented in Chapter 4. They show how administrative structures may be viewed in both vertical and horizontal subsystems.

VERTICAL ORGANIZATION   The vertical division of personnel reflects the basic hierarchy of power, or chain of command. Position within the structure usually identifies the status and responsibilities of each employee, with the climb up the career ladder typically representing a struggle for increased power and greater rewards.

HORIZONTAL ORGANIZATION   The horizontal division of organization charts is usually based on having separate departments side by side, which are generally identified according to one of three factors: function, product, or location.

Function is used as a basis for departmentalization when divisions or administrative units are established to carry out specialized assignments. In a public recreation and park department, for example, they might typically be assigned functions such as facility operation and maintenance, fiscal management, personnel, programs, and public relations.

Product specialization would be illustrated when different departments are assigned responsibility for developing and marketing different products. Within a large conglomerate in the commercial recreation field, one department might produce phonograph records and tapes, while another might operate a chain of lodges in the national parks, and still another might be in the cable television business. In a larger and more complex structure, each of these specialized products would be represented not by a separate department but by a separate subsidiary company.

Location departmentalization occurs when all the administrative responsibilities within a geographical area are brought into a single unit for effective management. It would be illustrated in the division of a large state park system into several districts or service areas, each under the direction of a regional supervisor.

· · ·

Organization charts should be as simple and understandable as possible rather than cluttered with myriad titles and excessive detail. If a chart is too complicated, it suggests that the organization itself is chaotic or confused. Charts should be updated regularly and should be displayed in appropriate places or publications to be most useful in providing needed information about the organization.

Differentiation of line and staff functions

In emerging management theory, a distinction was made between two types of personnel: line and staff.

Line employees are generally regarded as those responsible for carrying out the central function or mission of the agency. In a large voluntary organization, for example, they would be the administrator or executive, the heads of program departments, and the actual leaders or program specialists who direct activities. The line structure is usually perceived as a set of direct vertical relationships, or a chain of command, through which authority flows, such as the scalar principle.

Staff employees are not responsible for carrying out the central mission. In military units, for example, staff members are generally aides to executive officers rather than attached to fighting units. Staff personnel are often given advisory or consultative functions in tasks related to public relations, research, systems analysis, budget development, or simply as staff assistants to line administrative managers.

CHALLENGES TO THE SCIENTIFIC MANAGEMENT APPROACH

Many aspects of the scientific management approach proved to be distasteful to employees. For example, reducing jobs to highly specialized and routinized tasks made them mechanical and monotonous. The "speed-up" system in many industrial plants that was based on time-and-motion studies with extremely high rates of worker output frequently caused tension and stress on the assembly line.

Further, Scanlan and Keys[11] comment that the machine model approach to management reduced the worker to the status of a machine. Neglecting the human element, it falsely assumed that money-based incentive systems alone would be enough to motivate workers. There often was open resistance to such systems, involving job slowdowns and even sabotage. The highly organized, depersonalized management system visualized by Weber, who had been influenced by the efficiency of nineteenth century Prussian bureaucracy, was not as acceptable to twentieth century workers.

Bypassing formal processes

As organizations became more complex in their operations, it became increasingly difficult to provide the needed combination of various services within the vertical hierarchy.

For example, a recreation and park agency might wish to initiate a major new program in a large community center. Several administrative divisions might be involved in this process, including: (1) the recreation program department through its leaders or supervisors; (2) the maintenance department through its building custodians; (3) the personnel department, which would have to assign full- and part-time personnel to the center; (4) the budget or fiscal management department, which would have to approve funding for the center; and (5) public relations personnel, who would be involved in publicizing the program.

If full reliance were placed on the formal vertical structure, each person responsible for any of these functions would have to go up the chain of command to obtain approval of all specific plans involving assignment of individuals or financial allocations. Decisions would then flow—or creep—down the vertical chain of command to the line personnel responsible for taking action. If there were problems in the operation, the process would have to be repeated.

Realistically, within this tangled web of relationships, the vertical line of authority and the unity of command concepts might have to give way to a more flexible approach. In some cases there might be "diagonal" or even "horizontal" relationships, in which staff members function in cooperation with managerial personnel in administrative units *other* than their own.

Thus it became apparent that there was a need to develop more effective coordinating mechanisms between the separate divisions of an organization rather than to rely exclusively on the vertical chain of command within a rigidly departmentalized agency structure. This was particularly true in new kinds of companies or government organizations that were faced with the need for creative, rapid responses to changing environmental conditions, in contrast to industries in which the manufacturing process could be easily routinized and repeated.

Growing tension among employees

It was also evident that the scientific management approach was resulting in increased alienation and hostility on the part of many employees. The rigid application of authority within the chain of command often led to conflicts and labor-management unrest in major companies and other bureaucratic organizations.

Although the scientific management approach held appeal for industrialists and the heads of other large corporations and institutions, it did not represent a complete and consistent body of theory based on scientific research and empirical evidence. Beyond this, its major weakness was that it failed to consider the human factor in organizational life. People were regarded as cogs in a machine, with little concern for their feelings or the important elements of group process, human motivation, or individual creativity.

HUMAN-RELATIONS ERA

As a consequence of problems with scientific management, a new wave of exploration and concept-building emerged in the management field. What came to be called the "human-relations era" was concerned primarily with the nature of individual and group interactions within the work setting and the impact of different styles of management behavior on worker motivation and productivity.

Linked to the expanding scholarly field of social psychology, the human-relations approach began during the 1920s and had its greatest influence from about 1930 to the 1950s. The view that effective management could be based on rigid laws and principles that ignored the human element or that saw monetary pay as the only meaningful incentive was challenged.

Elton Mayo and the Hawthorne studies

The human-relations approach was strongly influenced by a famous study of working conditions and productivity that was carried out by Elton Mayo,[12] a psychologist, and Fritz Roethlisberger, a sociologist, at the Hawthorne branch of the Western Electric Company in Cicero, Ill., during the late 1920s (see box on p. 30).

Rather than focus on a mechanical analysis of work assignments, the human-relations approach stressed such elements as communication, leadership, interpersonal processes, and their effect on closely knit groups of employees. For the first time the human substructure within management systems was recognized, and supervisory and managerial human-relations skills were developed.

HAWTHORNE STUDIES

Heading a group of Harvard researchers, Mayo conducted a lengthy series of experiments that explored the effect of different changes in working conditions (including location and scheduling of work hours, rest periods, lighting, ventilation, and similar factors) on the output of teams of women workers on an assembly line. As various changes were introduced, it was found that absenteeism was reduced, and both the morale and the productivity of the employees increased. Even when working conditions were made less favorable, such as by reduced lighting, the elimination of rest periods, or lengthening of the work day, output continued to rise.

The key factor was that, when employees thought their needs were being considered, they responded with a higher level of individual and group motivation. The experimenters found that workers within any organization tended to coalesce into groups that developed their own values and codes of approved behavior. These in turn influenced the extent to which each worker would cooperate with management and the effort the worker would make to meet production goals. For example, when industrial engineers at the Hawthorne plant established an output standard of 7312 terminal connections per day for the bank wiring room, workers were unwilling to accept this figure and established their own informal output goal. Despite the pay inducements offered by the company, group pressures kept workers in line. Those who sought to exceed the group's self-imposed work limits "were controlled by a rigorously enforced code of conduct established by the closely knit work group. Group-applied sanctions such as social ostracism, name-calling, and ridicule brought about compliance to informal group norms."

In subsequent years a number of other social scientists explored group dynamics and the effect of different leadership styles. During the late 1930s, Kurt Lewin, Ronald Lippitt, and Ralph White[13] conducted a number of studies at the University of Iowa designed to measure the effects of three leadership styles—autocratic, democratic, and laissez-faire—on group behavior. They found that most group members preferred democratic leadership and reacted either aggressively or passively to authoritarian leadership. Other studies, conducted at Ohio State University and by the University of Michigan Survey Research Center, explored situational variables affecting leadership and the effect of different leadership approaches on group productivity.

Later developments: industrial humanism

In the 1950s and 1960s, a number of other behavioral scientists, including Douglas McGregor, Abraham Maslow, Rensis Likert, and Chris Argyris, continued to explore the ways in which leadership approaches and management styles affected work productivity and satisfaction.

Their approach, which came to be called the *industrial humanism model*, represented an extension of the human-relations approach. It stressed the need to consider all aspects of human personality in the design of job functions and the work environment. Some of the basic tenets of this management theory follow[10]:

1. Work must be made psychologically acceptable, rather than threatening or boring to the individual.
2. Work must permit employees to develop their individual faculties, creativity, and sense of responsibility. It must allow the opportunity for self-determination and must provide a sense of achievement and self-satisfaction.
3. The worker must have the possibility of controlling, in a meaningful way, the environment in which he or she functions. Personal commitment can be fostered and strengthened through participation and involvement by employees.
4. The organization should no longer be the sole and final decision-making agent; instead, this power should be shared more widely, and both the organization and the individual should be subject to an external code of values and moral order.
5. Since the human element is the key factor in determining the success or failure of achieving objectives, patterns of supervision and management must be built on the basis of an overall positive philosophy about people and their feelings about their work.[10]

As Chapter 3 indicates, there has been a continuous stream of research into leadership and supervisory styles in recent years, with considerable attention given to McGregor's "Theory X" and "Theory Y," to various theories of human motivation, and to Japanese management approaches. The management approaches that have evolved tended to reject many of the principles of classical management theory. Nonetheless, the traditional approaches outlined in this chapter continue to be influential in many public and business organizations today.

Summary

Management is described in this chapter as a process or function common to all human organizations and institutions. Its key element is the efficient and intelligently planned use of human and physical resources. The practice of management constitutes both a science and an art.

Historically, the major contributors to classical management theory included Frederick Taylor, Max Weber, Luther Gulick, and Henri Fayol. Taylor developed the "machine model" approach to management, which emphasized careful analysis and standardization of work tasks through time-and-motion studies. Max Weber promoted the bureaucratic structure as an impersonal, carefully defined management system, with a vertical chain of command and explicit job functions and responsibilities. Fayol identified the five processes of planning, organizing, commanding, coordinating, and controlling as the key elements in management and developed 14 key principles that widely influenced management thinking. Gulick developed the term "POSDCORB," which identified and analyzed the major elements in the management process.

The chapter also describes several basic principles of classical management theory, including division of labor and task specialization, assignment of authority and accountability, the scalar principle and unity of command, and span of control. It analyzes the use of organization charts, describes line and staff functions, and concludes with a review of the human-relations approach and the industrial humanism model of personnel management.

STUDY QUESTIONS

1. Summarize the major principles underlying the classical school of management theory as presented in Taylor's machine model, Weber's view of organizational bureaucracy, and Fayol's 14 principles. What elements made them appropriate for their time in a period of heavy industrialization in assembly-line factories?

2. Examine several concepts established in this period, such as: (1) division of labor and task specialization, (2) the scalar principle and unity of command, (3) span of control, and (4) the assignment of authority and accountability. In what kinds of organizations would they work effectively? In what kinds might they *not* be as effective?

3. What were the reasons for the human-relations and industrial humanism approaches gaining popularity? What was their basic message?

REFERENCES

1. Howard, Dennis R., and Crompton, John L.: *Financing, Managing and Marketing Recreation and Park Resources,* Dubuque, Iowa, 1980, William C. Brown Co., p. 199.

2. Mescon, Michael H., Albert, Michael, and Khedouri, Franklin: *Management: Individual and Organizational Effectiveness,* New York, 1981, Harper & Row, Publishers, p. 48.

3. Torgerson, Paul E., and Weinstock, Irwin T.: *Management: An Integrated Approach,* Englewood Cliffs, N.J., 1972, Prentice-Hall, Inc., p. 4.

4. Taylor, Frederick W.: *Scientific Management,* New York, 1911, Harper & Row, Publishers.

5. Kelly, Joe: *How Managers Manage,* Englewood Cliffs, N.J., 1980, Prentice-Hall, Inc., Chapter 2.

6. Johnson, Richard A., Monsen, R. Joseph, Knowles, Henry B., and Saxberg, Borje O.: *Management, Systems, and Society: An Introduc-tion,* Pacific Palisades, Calif., 1976, Goodyear Publishing Co., pp. 26-27.

7. *Ibid.,* p. 32.

8. Fayol, Henri: *General and Industrial Management,* London, 1949, Pitman & Sons, Ltd., pp. 20-41.

9. Gulick, Luther, and Urwick, Lyndall (Editors): *Papers on the Science of Administration,* New York, 1937, Institute of Public Administration.

10. Rodney, Lynn S.: *Administration of Public Recreation,* New York, 1964, The Ronald Press Co., pp. 26-53.

11. Scanlan, Burt, and Keys, J. Bernard: *Management and Organizational Behavior,* New York, 1979, John Wiley & Sons, Inc., p. 27.

12. Mayo, Elton: *The Human Problems of an Industrial Civilization,* New York, Macmillan Publishing Co., 1933, Chapters 3-5.

13. Lewin, Curt, Lippett, R., and White, R.K.: "Patterns of Aggressive Behavior in Experimentally Created Social Climates," *Journal of Social Psychology,* **10:**271-301, 1939.

Bureaucracy is a form of social organization that isolates people from any real human interaction while chaining them to the half-empty categories of organizational roles, rules, and language. If people simply lived, interacted with others as whole persons, engaged in common projects, they could learn the skills of self-assertion and communication that these categories attempt to capture.[1]

Management Science Today

Beginning in the 1950s, there was a wave of new theory development in public and business management. One focus was on employee-centered management approaches. Investigators sought to blend psychologically based studies of human needs and motivations with studies of leadership and managerial techniques. Other researchers examined the structure and processes of organizations within the total societal context.

A powerful new thrust came from computer-based systems models concerned with planning and controlling management processes. As society shifted from an industrial-based economy to the provision of services and the analysis and transmission of information as the basis for economic expansion, management techniques became increasingly dependent on sophisticated forms of analysis and evaluation. Finally, as we found ourselves competing on the world market with an increasingly successful Japan, researchers turned to an examination of that nation's management theories and practices as a source of new ways to strengthen America's productive capability.

New Directions in Management Theory

How has management theory changed in the Western world over the past three decades? Essentially, it has moved in two contrasting directions. The first, which may be characterized as the *behavioral science* approach, is an extension of the human-relations and industrial humanism eras. It is deeply concerned with organizational structure and processes, employee motivation, job enrichment, conflict resolution, and similar functions. The second, which is often referred to as *operations management,* emphasizes a systems-based, highly technological, and analytical approach to planning and controlling functions of management.

Together, these two trends comprise the modern *management science* approach, a powerful and diversified field of professional practice supported by numerous university curricula, training institutes, publications, and professional societies. Today management science has immense influence in business and government operations.

BEHAVIORAL SCIENCE

One of the major thrusts in the study of behavioral science in modern management was the analysis of organizational structure and processes. On the basis of earlier work by Elton Mayo and Kurt Lewin, behavioral scientists carried out intensive studies of human relationships in work situations and various forms of organizational behavior.

Organizational structure and behavior

Instead of the simplistic view of the large organization as a two- or three-level enter-prise, essentially composed of managers and workers, new management theorists began to see it as a much more complex structure. Roethlisberger and Dickson, for example, wrote that the human organization of an industrial plant included executives, technical specialists, supervisors, factory workers, and office employees, all of whom interact daily and form consistent patterns of relationships.

> Some relationships fall into routine patterns, such as the relationship between superior and subordinate or between office worker and shop worker . . . . The worker, for exam-ple, behaves toward his foreman in one way, toward his first-line supervisor in another way, and toward his fellow worker in still another . . . . Just as each employee has a particular physical location, so he has a particular social place in the total social environ-ment . . . . From this point of view the behavior of no one person in an industrial orga-nization, from the very top to the very bottom, can be regarded as motivated by strictly economic or logical considerations. Routine patterns of action involve strong sentiments.[2]

Based on this new awareness, behavioral scientists examined work environments and the effect of traditional management concepts that had evolved in the earlier period of theoretical development. They concluded that the bureaucratic structures and principles that had long been in vogue were no longer functional and that the human-relations and industrial humanism approaches needed to be extended and strengthened.

Douglas McGregor: the human side of management

An early major spokesman for the new wave in behavioral science was Douglas McGregor. McGregor was concerned with problems of human motivation and incentive and the effects of different types of reward and punishment systems on productivity and morale.

McGregor developed two sharply contrasting sets of assumptions, which he called Theory X and Theory Y. The traditional but essentially negative concept of human motivation, Theory X, holds that people tend to be lazy and unmotivated and that they need to be carefully supervised in their work and driven by clear-cut punishments and rewards. Theory Y holds that people have a much greater capacity for becoming inter-ested in their work and assuming responsibility in it, assuming that they are not dis-couraged or inhibited by traditional approaches to management control and leadership.

Unlike earlier adherents to the human-relations approach, McGregor held the view that conventional organization theory was meaningless:

> It would not, in any sense, be an exaggeration to assert that any large organization would come to a grinding halt within a month if all its members began behaving strictly in accordance with the structure of responsibility and authority defined by the formal organi-zation chart, the position descriptions, and the formal controls.[3]

Instead, McGregor held that the working of large organizations involves many more complex relationships and roles, realistic accommodations, problem solving, and forms of cooperative behavior on various levels than is implied in the simplistic models of formal organizational structure. He urged managers to develop higher levels of sensitiv-

---

McGREGOR'S KEY PRINCIPLES

1. *Understanding, mutual agreement, and identification with respect to the primary task.* It is essential that members of the team agree on their priorities and fundamental responsibilities.

2. *Open communications.* It is essential that sound decisions be based on full awareness of all the relevant facts—including not only information or logistical knowledge but also feelings and emotions. Genuinely open expression of ideas *and* feelings—what is often referred to as "leveling"—is a necessary condition for effective functioning in a managerial team.

3. *Mutual trust.* Recognizing that trust is a delicate property of human relationships, McGregor held that it must exist among all members of a managerial team if it is to be successful. Essentially, he argued that people needed to have confidence in each other and willingness to rely on each other for support in matters of crucial self-concern. Trust, he said, was best built by consistent action over a period of time, rather than by words.

4. *Mutual support.* Closely related to the need for open communication and trust, mutual support implies that members of a managerial unit should be freed from the need to defend or protect themselves and able to contribute their abilities more fully to the overall task of the team.

5. *Management of human differences.* Inevitably, in any group effort, there will be disagreements and conflicts, based on different points of view or perceptions of self-interest, or personality clashes. Successfully resolving such disagreements, rather than simply attempting to suppress them, is essential if decisions are to be reached that can be carried out without being sabotaged by dissatisfied members of the group.

---

ity and openness and rely less on the formal authority invested in them or on technical management skills. Instead, he advocated the principles above.

Emergence of the contingency approach

Michael Mescon and associates point out that the behavioral science approach, with its emphasis on participative management and organizational democracy, became so popular that it almost took over the field of management during the 1960s. However, since it advocated a "one best way" approach, with the assumption that job redesign and participative management methods would apply to *all* situations, it was not fully accepted.[4]

Gradually, some management experts began to argue for a *contingency approach,* in which various situational factors would have to be considered in selecting appropriate management models for an organization.[5] These factors would include the internal dynamics of the organization, its interchange with its environment, and other broader influences in the society at large. The nature of an organization's mission, the composition of its work force, the challenges facing it, and the overall climate in which it functions would influence the choice of management strategies on a short- and long-range basis.

For example, it might be difficult to suddenly impose McGregor's humanistic approach to management on an organization that had traditionally operated on an autocratic, highly structured, "carrot-and-stick" supervisory policy. At the same time, it might be possible to gradually develop appropriate attitudes and understandings through group development workshops, sensitivity training, and similar techniques so that the Theory Y approach *would* become accepted and effective.

Other emphases in behavioral science

In an effort to understand the other forces that influenced worker behavior and the success or failure of different styles of management, researchers have examined elements such as (1) employee motivation; (2) authority, power, and the delegation of responsibility; (3) communication processes; (4) conflict resolution; (5) decision-making techniques; and (6) the measurement of managerial effectiveness.

THEORIES OF MOTIVATION

A key element in the management process is understanding the nature of human motivation. Obviously, managing personnel so that they live up to their fullest potential becomes much easier if one understands their needs and the kinds of stimuli or encouragement that will help them become fully motivated in their job performance.

Maslow's needs hierarchy

In a pioneer investigation of motivation during the 1940s, Abraham Maslow concluded that, while people have many diverse needs, these may logically be grouped within five basic categories that fall within a hierarchy or ranked order of importance. The lowest-level needs are physiological, survival-related needs; the highest-level needs are those related to self-actualization and creative development. They are described as follows:

1. *Physiological.* These include food, water, shelter, rest, sex, relief from pain, and other needs concerned with human survival.
2. *Safety and security.* These include needs for freedom from environmental threats of a physical, psychological, or economic nature.
3. *Social and affiliation needs.* These include the needs for friendship, social interaction, being accepted by others, affection, and love.
4. *Esteem.* These include feelings of self-respect, recognition by others, and a sense of achievement and competence.
5. *Self-actualization.* These needs include fulfillment of a person's fullest potential and growth by maximizing talents and abilities.[6]

Maslow held that these needs are arranged in a hierarchy, with survival needs at the base and self-actualization needs at the top. It has been assumed that, as each level of need is recognized and satisfied, beginning with the most critical needs, the next needs in the hierarchy emerge and press for satisfaction.[7]

The most important messages of Maslow's theory for management theorists were that (1) people are motivated by a wide variety of needs and, if these needs are recognized and satisfied on the job, they will have a higher level of work motivation, and (2) unmet needs, or deficiencies, are more likely to exist on the esteem and self-actualization levels and can be met by intelligent managerial strategies.

McClelland's learned needs theory

One of the weaknesses of Maslow's theory was that it did not sufficiently take into account the differences among individual employees. While one person might have strong safety or security needs, another might have powerful social and affiliation needs:

> Managers must be aware of individual differences in reward preferences. What will motivate one subordinate will not work with another individual. Different people want different things, and managers must be sensitive to these needs if they want to motivate their subordinates.[8]

Such distinctions were the concern of David McClelland, a Harvard psychologist who proposed a theory of motivation based on three needs that are ''learned'' from the culture: power, achievement, and affiliation. He saw *power* as the desire to influence others, *achievement* as the satisfaction gained from carrying work to its successful completion, and *affiliation* as the need to be involved in a friendly way with others. In each case, an individual who was placed in a job situation that met that person's particular pattern of higher-level needs would be more likely to function well than if the job was *not* keyed to them.

McClelland[9] conducted research and concluded that few employees are challenged by opportunity and willing to work hard to achieve significant results, whereas most have a much lower level of initiative and enterprise. He suggested that this minority of highly motivated individuals possessed the need to achieve, which he designated as *n ACH motive*. Individuals with this drive tend to seek and assume a high degree of personal responsibility, take calculated risks, and set challenging but attainable goals for themselves.

Based on McClelland's theory, Mescon and associates[10] conclude that, to motivate employees in this group, managers should give them tasks involving a moderate degree of risk or failure, along with the needed authority, and should provide regular, specific performance feedback.

Herzberg's two-factor theory

Another behavioral psychologist, Frederick Herzberg, developed a two-factor theory of motivation. In this theory one set of factors, known as *hygiene* factors, was described as leading to job dissatisfaction. In this set, if the factors that were extrinsic conditions of the job, such as pay, fringe benefits, company procedures, or other working conditions, were poor or inadequate, workers would be dissatisfied and would have a low level of motivation. If they were acceptable, they would bring workers only to a neutral state of feeling.

The second set of factors was termed *motivators* or satisfiers. These consisted of intrinsic conditions of the job, such as the opportunity for achievement, recognition, responsibility, advancement, and the possibility for growth or pleasure taken in the work itself. Herzberg found that, when these factors were present on the job, they helped to build strong levels of motivation and good job performance. However, if they were not present, their absence did not lead to dissatisfaction.

Herzberg's theory led to a strong thrust in management toward job enrichment. Many companies and other organizations sought to challenge employees' needs for *motivators* by redesigning or diversifying work functions so they would provide one or more of the following: autonomy, challenge, responsibility, variety, and a sense of having completed a "whole" project or unit of work.

Process theories of motivation

Several other theories of motivation have been described as process theories, dealing with how individual behavior is stimulated, directed, continued, or stopped. Three examples of such theories are the *expectancy, equity,* and *reinforcement* theories.

VROOM'S EXPECTANCY THEORY This complex theory, developed by Victor Vroom,[11] assumes that motivation to direct behavior toward a given goal must be based on the individual's expectation that the behavior will in fact lead to satisfaction or achieve a desired outcome. Based on three factors (the employee's expectancy that successful performance of the task is possible, expectancy that a given reward will result, and the *valence* or satisfaction to be gained from the probable reward), it is possible to design tasks so that they fit the employee's expectancy pattern and thus result in a higher level of motivation to accomplish a given assignment. If any of the three elements is low, it is assumed that motivation and resultant performance will be poor.

LOCKE'S EQUITY THEORY Equity theory argues that employees are motivated by a desire to be treated fairly at work and that they make careful comparisons of their efforts and rewards with those of others in similar jobs.[12] If the comparison indicates imbalance (inequity), the other workers are perceived as gaining greater rewards for equivalent efforts, and the employee experiences tension, may decrease his or her efforts on the job, and as an extreme measure may quit.

Although most research on equity theory, carried out by Edwin Locke and others, focused on pay as a cause of feelings of inequity, another source of dissatisfaction is perceived job discrimination, such as being expected to do more work or less prestigious work than other employees, not being given the job for which one is qualified, not being accepted in informal job-related social activities or not having access to informal sources of communication related to the job, and not being encouraged or permitted to participate in in-house training programs.[13]

REINFORCEMENT THEORY Reinforcement theory deals with the effects of various forms of positive and negative reinforcements on motivation. The rewards or punishments that are used, as well as their frequency or timing, have significant influences on employee behavior. For example, the effectiveness of *continuous* reinforcement (applied each time a given behavior occurs) has been compared with that of *intermittent* reinforcement (applied only occasionally). It has been found that they produce important differences in performance:

During the initial development of a response (e.g., learning and applying a new job skills), continuous reinforcement is preferred because it accelerates early performance. Second, when trying to sustain a response (e.g., good performance) intermittent schedules are more effective.[14]

Modern Management Theory: Authority, Power, and Delegation

Traditional management systems were based on the assignment of authority and the development of a chain of command in which individuals at the upper levels of an organization issue orders, which must be obeyed by their subordinates. Two concepts inherent in this relationship are *authority* and *power*. Although they are obviously related, they are not the same.

Scanlan and Keys describe authority as "legitimate power," conferred by the organization on an individual who holds a particular position within the hierarchical structure: "Presumably, whoever occupied that same position would automatically be accorded the same degree of authority."[15]

In contrast, power represents the ability to exert influence over others, *with* or *without* legitimate authority. There are essentially five sources of power:

1. *Coercive power,* rooted in the ability to apply sanctions or punishment
2. *Reward power,* consisting of the ability to offer or deny rewards for employee performance
3. *Legitimate power,* based on the official position one holds within the organization
4. *Expert power,* derived from employee recognition of a manager's expertise, which promotes respect and willingness to follow his or her leadership
5. *Referent power,* stemming from a general sense of admiration or respect for the manager

Harold Leavitt and others[16] point out that authority is essential because it (1) provides predictability and regularity of employee behavior in conforming to the needs and expectations of the organization; (2) ensures continuity and stability in organizational life so that, although the individual holding a particular position may change, the authority remains and is passed on to the new manager or supervisor; and (3) provides a means for settling disputes and resolving conflicts.

At the same time, modern management philosophy generally supports the sharing of managerial authority and power through organizational democracy and participative planning and problem-solving processes.

Delegation of broader work responsibilities is one of the surest ways of contributing to the growth and development of subordinate employees. Assigning additional tasks or a higher level of decision-making powers is important in helping employees grow and gain needed competencies. It strengthens their sense of reward and challenge and intensifies their degree of commitment to their work, thus contributing to a favorable job climate and employee motivation. In addition, delegation of job responsibilities and functions helps free managers to deal with other, more critical concerns on a policy-making or conceptual level of responsibility.

Many managers hesitate to delegate powers broadly, particularly those involving matters of judgment. They often rationalize that subordinate employees lack the necessary experience or judgment to do the job or that it would be done more quickly and efficiently if they did it themselves. Joseph Bannon[17] points out other common reasons why managers do not or cannot delegate problem-solving responsibilities:

1. Lack of agreement among managers and workers on the specifics of delegation; lack of standards and guidelines
2. Lack of training to help subordinate employees accomplish delegated tasks
3. Lack of understanding of organizational objectives
4. Lack of confidence by managers in workers
5. Lack of confidence by managers in themselves, and unwillingness to take risks
6. Managers' fear that workers will ''outshine'' them and an unwillingness to delegate tasks they enjoy

Despite these reservations, current management theory holds that there should be broad participation in the planning process and in policy and decision making. The implication is that, by sharing personal power and thus creating a more highly motivated and efficient work force, the manager will ultimately be given more authority and power. Indeed, the performance of subordinates often reflects directly on how their supervisors are perceived and rated; therefore power should be perceived as a two-way flow between upper- and lower-level employees.[18]

COMMUNICATION AS A FOCUS OF MANAGEMENT THEORY

Closely linked to the preceding concept is the need to have effective communication processes. Meaningful two-way communication is essential to all manager-worker relationships. The term ''two-way'' implies that there must be an upward as well as a downward flow of information. In traditional management structures, all orders, statements of policy or procedures, criticism, and announcements flow from higher-level employees to lower-level ones. Contemporary management theory holds that managers must be willing to listen to their subordinates, and communication channels should be established to facilitate a healthy exchange of ideas, expressions of need, and program suggestions.

Communication is the process of expressing, transmitting, and receiving messages in verbal, written, or visual form. In leisure-service agencies, as in all types of organizations, communication is constantly at work. It occurs in staff meetings, personnel conferences, training workshops, formal speeches, annual reports and newsletters, meetings with citizen groups, and policy statements. It may even take place through acts, such as the firing or transfer of an employee, that deliver a message to other employees. It may be transmitted silently through gestures or body language that express feelings or ideas in forms that are often more eloquent than words.

It has been estimated that managers spend between 50% and 90% of their time communicating. Managers must communicate to carry out their various interpersonal, informational, and decisional tasks and to work with others in planning, organizing, motivating, and controlling. Within each such function, communication provides vital links.

As indicated, communication may be carried out in various formal and informal

TABLE 3-1   Stages of Communication

Stage Number	Stage	Explanation
1	Formulation of message	Determining what the communicator wants to say, and what its impact or effect should be
2	Encoding information	Translating information into language or symbols for effective communication; need for clarity, nonthreatening, and constructive impact
3	Transmitting	Using appropriate channel (speech, conversation, telephone call, memorandum, newsletter, etc.), plus method of delivery (style and efficiency of presentation)
4	Reception	Ensuring that those receiving the message are in a situation where it will reach them accurately and where they will be attentive to it
5	Decoding	Checking that all elements in the message are clearly understood, by follow-up questions, discussions, or monitoring methods

ways. However, it is in verbal and written communication that most managers need to be skilled. To ensure that they express their views, ideas, requests, and orders clearly and concisely, managers must recognize that communication involves more than simply *transmitting* information; if information is not comprehended by those who must understand it, it is useless.

The process of communication has been carefully analyzed in recent years, and its component parts have been clearly identified. It requires four basic elements: (1) a *sender*, who originates and transmits the information; (2) a *message*, which is the information, transformed or encoded into language or other symbols for transmission; (3) a *channel*, which is the physical means through which the message is transmitted; and (4) a *receiver*, the person who receives and interprets the message. This process may be shown in a five-step model (Table 3-1).

Communication may have various purposes, and these should be clearly understood by the sender so that each message is framed in the most appropriate way to achieve its special purpose.

Many messages are intended simply to *inform*. For example, employees in an agency may be informed about the success of a completed program, a new organization policy or rule, or the appointment of an individual to a new position. Other messages may have the purpose of *teaching* or *counseling* others, *blaming* or *warning* them, *influencing* them, or providing *praise* and *positive stroking*. Still other messages may *ask for information* or *request help*. Thus communication may have numerous purposes and may often have emotional or psychological overtones that should be carefully considered by the sender to ensure that they have the desired effect.

Several other aspects of current management theory are discussed in later chapters. These include personnel-related processes such as job enrichment, problem solving, and the task of assessing organization performance and productivity.

OPERATIONS MANAGEMENT

Operations management, a further major aspect of modern management science, has the following characteristics:

1. It places a heavy emphasis on *systems theory* and the interaction among varied units within an organization or between the organization and its total environment.

2. It stresses the need for decision making on every level to be as factually based and analytical as possible and therefore relies heavily on the use of *mathematical* and *statistical* techniques and *computer data processing* methods as the basis for making judgments.

3. It relies heavily on the development of *models,* or theoretical formulations of relationships and processes that are usually expressed in diagrammatic form, throughout the goal-setting and planning process.

To illustrate this approach, several examples of operations-management concepts and strategies are provided in the following section of this chapter. They demonstrate how systems theory is used to describe internal and external behavior of organizations and to develop innovative ways of planning and controlling agency functions.

Systems theory applied to management

The concept of system has many possible interpretations. Almost anything made up of a number of separate parts that in some way are related or connected to each other may be called a system. Arthur Laufer writes:

> Any group of things which are interrelated and combined so as to form an integrated whole can be called a system. It is not the individual parts that are important, but it is the connecting together or the interrelationship of these parts which is important to the making of a system.[19]

Richard Johnson and others point out that the term "system" may be used in a variety of different ways, as in *systems philosophy, systems management,* or *systems analysis.* It refers to a way of thinking or developing theories and concepts based on scientific principles. They write that it is "an array of essential principles or facts arranged in a rational dependence or connection; a complex of ideas, principles and laws forming a coherent whole."[20]

TYPES OF SYSTEMS   Systems may be classified in the following ways:

1. *Natural versus human-made systems.* Natural systems are those that come about through the action of nature, such as human beings themselves, composed of elements such as the nervous and circulatory systems and similar subsystems. In contrast, human-made systems are those that humans create and operate, such as the social or economic systems. Modern science has sometimes made it difficult to distinguish between these two types, since human intervention has radically affected many natural systems.

2. *Physical versus abstract systems.* A physical system consists of tangible, real objects, such as machinery, tools, or raw materials, whereas an abstract system consists

of ideas, such as statements of goals or strategic plans.

3. *Open versus closed systems*. An open system is one in which there is a significant degree of interaction between a system and its environment. A closed system, which is much rarer, is closed off and self-sufficient.

CHARACTERISTICS OF SYSTEMS   Systems are considered to have three principal elements: input, process, and output.

Input. Input is the generating function or initiating force that starts a system (such as the continuation of a previous system or process or the decision to initiate a new program), along with the human and material resources that are fed into the process.

Process. Process refers to the ongoing action of the system, which is carried out to achieve stated objectives. It includes both internally generated efforts and interaction with environmental forces.

Output. Output is the result, or what actually happens, in the transformation of the input during the process. It typically includes specific products, information, services, or ways in which clients or participants themselves are transformed or satisfied within the system.

•   •   •

Since systems theory emphasizes the influences of all subsystems and external forces on a given organization or process, models are often constructed to demonstrate these relationships. Two key aspects of such models are equilibrium and feedback.

Equilibrium. The concept of equilibrium implies that most human or natural processes tend to achieve a state of relative balance or steadiness. This centers around a fixed point or level of balance, which is the normal state. When external forces are brought to bear on the system, modifications occur. If the system is a highly stable one, the forces needed to create change must be powerful. If it is unstable or precarious, even small outside forces may affect the equilibrium.

Feedback. The concept of feedback refers to the process through which diagnostic information is gathered about the effects of various inputs or influences on the system. It also describes the reactions of the environment to the process that is in effect or to its products. In highly automated systems, feedback may be used as a self-regulating device to control the rate or volume of production, as in the simple example of a home-heating thermostat, or as a way to provide flow of information used in modifying a model or actual on-the-job performance.

Gibson and associates point out that feedback provides organizations with important information regarding the environment's acceptance or rejection of their outputs. Therefore they must be able to respond to such messages promptly and effectively:

USE OF SYSTEMS ANALYSIS IN FACILITIES MAINTENANCE

Traditionally, many small parks or playground complexes in large leisure-service systems have been assigned to a single custodian or gardener for year-round maintenance. Would a network of parks and other recreation facilities maintained on this basis (with larger parks divided into discrete tracts or units, each with its own gardener) be efficiently managed?

The systems analysis method would suggest that alternative approaches should be examined. A model of the maintenance process would be developed, identifying the different tasks that must be carried out, the effect of the different seasons of the year, and the work or output capabilities of employees and machines. Each element in the process of park maintenance would be analyzed: seeding, weeding, cutting, and watering lawns; planting and pruning trees and shrubs; and litter control and similar tasks. The rate of growth of each form of vegetation, the effects of use by city residents, and similar factors would be fully quantified.

It would probably be found that the different maintenance tasks would vary greatly. Some might have to be done on a daily basis, some weekly or monthly, and some only once a year or less often. Some might best be carried out by roving teams of employees using heavy equipment or carrying out rehabilitation tasks, others might best be performed by automated equipment (daily lawn-watering), and still others might continue to be carried out by single workers.

All such factors would be examined, as well as the effect of imposing a different type of work assignment on employees (along with possible complications with the union) or the agency's relationship with community or neighborhood advisory groups. Ultimately, however, the final maintenance model would be developed, and it would presumably provide more effective maintenance on a year-round basis at less cost to the department.

In business organizations, market research is an important feedback mechanism. In a more general sense, feedback is the dynamic process by which any organism learns from its experiences with its environment . . . . Systems theory emphasizes the importance of responding to the content of the feedback information.[21]

SYSTEMS MANAGEMENT   The term "systems management" refers to the design and operation of organizations as systems. It is based first on the idea that any company or institution represents a complex arrangement of subsystems with independent parts and variations, all of which influence or depend on each other. In turn, the organizations themselves must be perceived as integral parts of large societal, governmental, or economic systems that they influence and that have an impact on them.

Systems analysis takes the position that to make intelligent plans or decisions or carry out the controlling functions of management, business, or public agency managers must develop careful analyses of all the elements within the system and their relationships with and effects on each other. All parts of the operation must be integrated into a functional whole. Different courses of action that the manager is considering must be analyzed systematically regarding their relative costs and benefits, how they affect or are affected by the larger environment, and the likelihood of their success.

Use of models. This is often done by developing an analytical sequence or *model,* based on the problem or process being analyzed. A model is a representation of reality, which simplifies it by reducing the number of variables to a manageable number or which represents it in abstract form. The advantage of models is that they allow managers to explore possible solutions to a problem or the consequences of a given course of action without the risks that might result from a faulty plan put into effect without sufficient preliminary analysis.

Systems theory is increasingly being applied to certain aspects of recreation and park management. Edginton and Williams,[22] for example, point out that leisure-service managers function within two basic kinds of environments: the *external* or *macro* environment and the *internal* or *micro* environment. The macro environment includes elements such as the physical, social, economic, or political setting in which the agency operates. The micro environment includes variables such as managerial behavior, formal and informal operational structures, the behavior of individual employees, agency goals and objectives, and specific work activities.

Any disturbance or shift in these elements (such as demands for increased or modified services by the clientele) will affect the other elements. In developing new policies or programs, systems analysis provides a means through which needed resources or the probable outcomes of different strategies can be determined. The box on the opposite page shows how systems analysis methods may be applied to facilities maintenance.

A second example of how systems planning may be applied to leisure-service management is found in a computer-based approach to the prescriptive planning of therapeutic recreation service programs developed by Carol Peterson.[23] Peterson's model was based on fundamental principles of systems analysis, although it was intended to provide a flexible planning tool rather than a fixed procedure. It included seven steps that might readily be applied to any therapeutic recreation setting (see box on p. 48).

OTHER SYSTEMS-BASED PLANNING APPROACHES: NETWORK MODELS   Within the broad field of operations research and management science, a number of systems-based planning approaches were developed and widely publicized during the 1960s and 1970s. These were essentially *network models,* a term used to describe a method of planning programs or projects that are carried out over a period of time.

Network models involve three phases: (1) identifying and/or planning a project's essential *events* and *activities* (defined as the tasks that must be accomplished and the work required to do this) and arranging them in a logical sequence; (2) scheduling the *estimated period of time* it will take to accomplish each activity and cumulatively the entire project; and (3) *controlling* or *monitoring* the network of events step by step, including possible delays, changes of plans, or modifications as they occur.[24]

USE OF SYSTEMS ANALYSIS IN THERAPEUTIC RECREATION

1. *Conceptualization and formulation.* The planner or analyst identifies the components in the process (agency, clients, resources, current status of program, and purposes or objectives).
2. *Investigation.* This stage involves fuller study of the clients, the agency, and the environment in relation to program goals and identification of the most promising alternative program elements or strategies to achieve objectives.
3. *Analysis of alternatives.* The planner analyzes the probable outcomes of each alternative program element or strategy based on known factors in the situation or overall system. In some types of systems, this is done with computer analysis; this approach tends to be used less frequently in therapeutic recreation service.
4. *Determination of strategy or course of action.* The planner selects an appropriate course of action and identifies needed service components, resources, leadership, facilities, and so forth.
5. *Design of program.* In this key stage, the planner formulates specific goals and objectives of the program (usually stated in clearly measurable and quantifiable behavioral terms). He or she designs the actual program sequence, activities, schedules, and so on and constructs criteria and evaluation methods for each element of service.
6. *Operations planning.* As a continuation of the previous stage, detailed schedules, staff assignment and training, preparation of facilities, acquisition of needed supplies or equipment, and similar operations are planned and put in motion.
7. *Implementation.* The plan is put into action. As in all systems operations, it is continually reviewed and needed improvements or changes are carried out. If feedback indicates that elements need to be redesigned, or objectives rethought, this is done. Full evaluation would be carried out after a period of time in order to give the operation sufficient time to achieve its stated goals.

Modified from Peterson, C.A.: "Application of Systems Analysis Procedures to Program Planning in Therapeutic Recreation Service," in Avedon, Elliott M.: *Therapeutic Recreation Service: An Applied Behavioral Science Approach,* Englewood Cliffs, N.J., 1974, Prentice-Hall, Inc.,

---

PERT and CPM. Program Evaluation Review Technique (PERT) provides an excellent example of the use of systems planning and network models in management science. It is a system of planning and control that uses mathematical concepts and computers to identify all key activities that must be carried out to accomplish a given project successfully.

These are outlined in advance through the Critical Path Method (CPM) approach, which arranges each activity in a complicated flow sequence, showing the amount of time, kinds of resources, and human performance that will be required to accomplish each task. Dearden sums up PERT as "the science of using network techniques for the maximum utilization of manpower, machinery, and time in the accomplishment of a project."[25]

To accomplish this, starting and completion times for each task or "event" are plotted to present a pictorial description of the time sequence of the total projects. A system of arrows shows which activities can be begun, based on which earlier ones have been completed. Each event is assigned a number to simplify references to specific activities. The entire sequence is designed for mathematical and computer analysis, and estimates are made regarding its time demands (PERT-TIME) and financial requirements (PERT-COST).

The chief purpose of PERT-TIME analysis is to keep management informed about the progress of a project. By sharply identifying each activity and its expected time of accomplishment, as well as those activities that must be completed before others are begun, it provides a means of efficiently monitoring and planning projects throughout their entire sequence, making adjustments as necessary.

Both PERT-TIME and PERT-COST make it possible for managers to carefully plan all the elements of a project well in advance, to gain immediate feedback of its progress at each stage, and to divert resources from activities that have "slack time" to others under greater pressure.

PPBS. Another specific method of applying systems theory, Planning-Program-Budgeting Systems (PPBS), was developed in the early 1960s by the U.S. Department of Defense. It represents an attempt to build a planning mechanism that integrates information of all kinds into a single, coherent management system, with special emphasis on budgetary planning. PPBS requires the careful and precise development of goals and objectives, the preliminary evaluation of each program intended to meet these goals (measuring the projected benefits against the estimated costs), and the shaping of budget requests based on these analyses. Fuller justifications for budget requests are thus provided within the context of a long-range program and fiscal plan.

More broadly, PPBS may be used to deal with any aspect of organizational responsibility. Its key aspect is a systematic analysis of alternative courses of action, consisting of:

1. Careful identification and description of governmental or other organizational objectives and projection of needs on both a short- and long-range basis
2. Explicit, systematic identification of alternative ways of reaching these objectives
3. Estimation of total costs implications (including capital, personnel, and other operational costs) of each alternative and the probable results of each alternative approach, given certain environmental conditions
4. Presentation of the major cost and benefit trade-offs among the alternatives, along with identification of major assumptions and uncertainties over the period of time ahead

In some cases PPBS may be used to analyze possible courses of action that depend on factors or conditions that cannot be positively predicted, such as economic growth or recession or given population trends. Although PPBS represents a costly and complex process, depending on sophisticated computer analysis, it is believed that in the end the efficiency and rational basis it provides for planning make it worth the cost.

Systems such as PERT-TIME and PERT-COST, CPM, and PPBS are used by few recreation and park agencies. However, their basic principles may be adapted to planning and carrying out many types of recreation programs or facility development projects.

OTHER APPROACHES TO MANAGEMENT

Other applications of current management science methods may be found in systems such as management by objectives (MBO), zero-based budgeting (ZBB), or techniques used in problem solving, conflict resolution, personnel or program evaluation, and similar tasks. These are described later in this text.

Japanese management models

The striking success of Japan in recovering from the devastation of World War II and becoming a leading world manufacturing and marketing power has had a strong impact on management thinking in the Western world. Yoshioka, Nilson, and Edginton[26] point out that Japan is already leading all nations in the production of motorcycles, cars, watches, cameras, ships, electronics equipment, and steel, and that it is estimated that by the year 2000 the gross national product of Japan will be the highest in the world, despite limited natural resources, a tiny home base, and a relatively small population.

Yet for most of this century, Americans have taken great delight in ridiculing all things Japanese. We derided the output of their craft shops and factories. The product label ''Made in Japan'' was for us synonymous with cheap, junky, malfunctioning, and short lived, and Japanese products were seen as poor imitations of higher-quality Western goods. Over the past three decades, things have changed radically. Japanese products have come to mean precision, strength, efficiency, and low price and have gained their nation a leading place in the world trade market.

How did this come about? How did the Japanese become such a dominant economic force in such a short period of time? What Japanese management techniques and strategies are responsible for this striking success story? Numerous American study teams and management experts have traveled to Japan to determine the answers to these questions, including one of the coauthors of this text, who carried out an intensive study of Japanese management practices and leisure-service programs during the spring of 1984.

Management experts have discovered a number of unique differences and approaches, some of which stem from traditional, deeply implanted Japanese social values and cultural traditions and others from newly adopted management styles and techniques. These include broad management functions such as problem-solving and decision-making approaches, job design and satisfaction efforts, career patterns, and communication processes. Yoshioka, Nilson, and Edginton write:

> Although social and cultural differences between American and Japanese societies may affect the applicability of a given management strategy, decision-making by consensus, lifetime employment, quality circle, nonspecialized career paths, bottom-up organizational design, creation of collective values, and holistic concern for the individual are tools applicable to leisure service management.[27]

MANAGEMENT STYLES AND STRATEGIES   David Gray points out that there are marked differences between Japanese and American management styles. American executives are perceived as active, energetic, aggressive, and hard driving, whereas their Japanese counterparts are contemplative, reflective, low-key, and unaggressive. While both groups are interested in efficiency, productivity, and "bottom-line" results, the American chain-of-command approach in which power is concentrated at the top differs sharply from the Japanese approach, which stresses sharing of opinions and consensus among a wide group of employees. Gray writes: "The American style, with the "boss" in command, decision-making concentrated in a few people at the top, and commitment to short-term goals, contrasts with the Japanese, based on a strong corporate philosophy, decision-making by consensus, and long-range planning."[28]

Japanese employees are typically committed to strong collective values and an intense sense of loyalty to their organizations, while Americans value competition, individuality, and striving for personal advancement.

EMPLOYMENT PATTERNS AND BENEFITS   One of the unique aspects of Japanese management practice, which would be extremely difficult to transfer to the Western world, involves the intense loyalty and commitment of employees to their companies or institutions, as well as the virtual guarantee of lifetime employment. Japanese companies are highly paternalistic in that housing, recreational, educational, health, and other benefits are provided for employees, who accept these gratefully.

On the job, the relationship between subordinates and supervisors is extremely close, with frequent socialization among employees on different status levels. Beyond this, employees are intensively involved with each other:

> Every employee [in large organizations] from top to bottom, is simultaneously a member of as many as eight or a dozen work groups, each with a different task. These groups work very closely together, and although their membership changes periodically, all know that through a career, each person will continue to function in many such groups.[29]

When an important decision needs to be made in a Japanese organization, such as the choice of location for a new plant or a major modification in a product line, as many as 60 to 80 people may be carefully consulted, many again and again, until a true consensus is reached. Ouchi writes: "Making a decision this way takes a very long time, but once a decision is reached, everyone affected by it will be likely to support it."[30]

QUALITY CONTROL AND JOB REDESIGN   Some of the ideas that have shaped Japanese management approaches were originally borrowed from Western industry. In the mid-1950s, for example, the idea of developing stronger quality control standards and practices spread rapidly throughout Japanese companies. However, Cole writes, all persons in the organizational hierarchy, from top management to lower-level employees, were given training in quality control knowledge and methods:

This is . . . both a simple and a most profound twist to the original ideas [of] Western experts. Quality control shifted from being the prerogative of the minority of engineers with limited shop experience (''outsiders'') to being the responsibility of each employee. Instead of adding additional layers of inspectors and reliability assurance personnel . . . each worker, in concert with his or her workmates, is expected to take responsibility for solving quality problems.[31]

Quality circles. This highly publicized aspect of present-day Japanese management involves the practice of having voluntary groups of employees (usually from five to 10) meet on a regular basis, usually led by a foreman or senior worker, within each work unit. Members are taught group communication and decision-making skills and undergo training in evaluation and problem solving. Cole writes that the quality circle is a relatively autonomous, spontaneously formed study group, which concentrates on

solving job-related quality problems, broadly conceived as improving methods of production as part of company-wide efforts. At the same time, it focuses on the self-development of workers. This includes: development of leadership abilities of foremen and workers, skill development among workers, identification of natural leaders with supervisory potential, improvement of worker morale and motivation, and the stimulation of teamwork within work groups.[32]

Members of quality circles are encouraged to use the company's resources fully. They generate and evaluate their own feedback and are responsible for the quality of intragroup communications and statistical analyses. Henderson and Goode write:

Quality circles do not exist for ''gripe'' sessions. The structure provides a ''process'' or a system through which to define a problem, set priorities for working on it, find causes, propose solutions, and, where possible, implement solutions . . . . The effect of quality circles on worker attitudes and behavior may be one of the most important aspects of the technique . . . .
Employees develop increased awareness of ''quality.'' Creativity and ''brain power'' are encouraged. Worker morale improves, while the managerial ability of the circle leaders is enhanced . . . . Projects tackled by employees relate directly to the individual's work; each person has a stake in the outcome of investigations . . . . Circles have been shown to increase a supervisor's respect for his or her workers and to increase workers' understanding of the difficulties supervisors face.[33]

IMPLICATIONS OF JAPANESE MANAGEMENT APPROACHES As indicated earlier, many American management experts have studied Japanese methods intensively and have developed management systems that embody key Japanese principles. Their approach has been identified by William Ouchi as ''Theory Z'' (an extension of McGregor's Theory X and Y).

Yet when applied to American companies, these methods have frequently failed to work. Gray points out that the basic premises of Japanese management run counter to American perceptions of management prerogatives and employee relationships. Such techniques as quality circles are often seen as a fad. He writes:

They do not become an integral part of the organization; companies insist on instant results; there is inadequate training of personnel in group dynamics, human behavior, and problem-solving techniques; and, most important, there is a lack of management support for such groups and timely response to their recommendations. Middle managers are frequently hostile to quality circles because they fear they will lose control or lose their jobs.[34]

Beyond this, many of the conditions that help support the Japanese system do not apply to American organizations. The homogeneous makeup of the Japanese people, their ready acceptance of highly paternalistic management practices, their willingness to accept long-range goals rather than emphasize immediate achievement, and their subordination of individual needs and drives to the overall needs of the organization are not typically American characteristics.

NEGATIVE ASPECTS OF JAPANESE MANAGEMENT   In addition, it is clear that some of the specific aspects of Japanese management are not as appealing as their adherents would suggest. There is strong evidence that employees work long hours without question, including a 6-day week in most companies, and that vacations for average employees are only 5 days a year. Workers are often reluctant to leave work early because it is considered "bad form," and much of their social life becomes necessarily centered around company groups. A 1983 poll revealed widespread dissatisfaction with jobs in Japan:

> The report showed that 81 percent of the American workers were "somewhat" or "very" satisfied with their jobs, compared with 53 percent of the Japanese. Moreover, 67 percent of the Americans would take their present jobs again, compared with 20 percent of the Japanese; 68 percent of the American workers were found willing to help their companies succeed, compared with 44 percent of the Japanese.[35]

Two other elements of the Japanese system raise important concerns. First, Japanese manufacturers are increasingly turning to the use of robots in so-called manless factories; Japanese industry, as a whole, is believed to have more robots in use than the rest of the world combined. The implications of this trend with respect to replacing human workers and creating technological unemployment are obvious. Second, Japanese companies are extremely sexist, with few female university graduates hired for upper-level professional positions. In Japan, women hold only 1.7% of managerial posts compared with 17.8% in the United States.[36]

It is obvious then that while numerous elements in the Japanese management approach provide useful models for the United States and indeed are closely related to the practices promoted in the "behavioral science" management movement in the United States, the overall system does not lend itself to an easy transfer. For the foreseeable future, it seems likely that American and Canadian governmental and business management systems will continue to be influenced primarily by the two major lines of development outlined in this chapter: the "behavioral science" and "operations management" approaches.

Summary

During the 1950s and 1960s, the management science approach in the United States and Canada took two broad directions: behavioral science and operations management. Behavioral science was concerned with organizational structure and behavior and the effects of different management techniques on employee productivity. Douglas McGregor's Theory Y presented a new set of beliefs that promoted the "human side" of management and argued for participatory leadership methods. Other behavioral scientists, including Abraham Maslow, David McClelland, and Frederick Herzberg, developed theories of motivation that stressed meeting the psychosocial needs of employees to improve their motivation and resultant productivity. Other theories of motivation included Vroom's expectancy theory, Locke's equity theory, and reinforcement theory.

Other aspects of management research included analyses of authority and power, the delegation of responsibility, and communication as a key aspect of management behavior. Based on the "contingency" approach, it is apparent that no single management style or technique is likely to be effective in all types of organizations.

The second half of the chapter is concerned with the operations management approach. This places a heavy emphasis on sytems theory and the development of computer-based statistical analyses, simulation studies, and models that depict organizational processes. Examples of the application of systems planning to leisure-service agencies are provided, and several major planning approaches, such as PPBS, PERT, and CPM, are presented. Finally, many of the innovative approaches used by Japanese companies today are reviewed; these clearly have direct links to many of the behavioral science principles developed in American personnel management studies over the past three decades. However, given the differences between the two societies in their life-styles and social values, it does not appear likely that the Japanese approach can be easily applied in U.S. business and governmental settings.

STUDY QUESTIONS

1. Douglas McGregor made a major contribution to the developing field of behavioral science and industrial psychology. Summarize it, and then show how the research findings and theories of Maslow, McClelland, and Herzberg extended his views. Based on these, develop a statement on how to strengthen employee motivation.

2. Participative management styles and the delegation of responsibility are key elements in modern behavioral science management thinking. How would these apply specifically to management practices in leisure-service agencies? Give concrete examples, and then show how they might have limitations in actual practice.

3. Summarize the key principles underlying the operations management approach in terms of systems analysis and planning and control models described in this chapter.

4. The Japanese quality circle approach has captured the interest of many management experts. What are its essential features? How might it contribute to productivity in American work settings, and what would be some of its limitations?

REFERENCES

1. Ferguson, Kathy: *The Feminist Case Against Bureaucracy,* Philadelphia, 1984, Temple University Press, p. 76.
2. Roethlisberger, F.J., and Dickson, W.J.: *Management and the Worker,* Cambridge, Mass., 1939, Harvard University Press, n.p.
3. McGregor, Douglas, in Bennis, Warren, and McGregor, Caroline (Editors): *The Professional Manager,* 1967, McGraw-Hill Book Co.
4. Mescon, Michael H., Albert, Michael, and Khedouri, Franklin: *Management: Individual and Organizational Effectiveness,* New York, 1981, Harper & Row, Publishers, p. 45.
5. *Ibid.,* pp. 59-62.
6. Maslow, Abraham: *Motivation and Personality,* New York, 1954, Harper & Row, Publishers.
7. Edginton, Christopher R., Compton, David M., and Hanson, Carole J.: *Recreation and Leisure Programming: A Guide for the Professional,* Philadelphia, 1980, Saunders College Publishing, pp. 86-87.
8. Mitchell, Terence. In Mescon et al., *op. cit.,* p. 318.
9. McClelland, David C.: *The Achievement Motive,* New York, 1953, Appleton-Century-Crofts, Inc.
10. Mescon et al., *op cit.,* p. 319.
11. Vroom, Victor H.: *Work and Motivation,* New York, 1964, John Wiley & Sons, Inc., pp. 14-15.
12. Locke, Edwin A., "The Nature and Causes of Job Satisfaction," in Dunnette, M. (Editor): *Handbook of Industrial and Organizational Psychology,* Chicago, 1976, Rand McNally & Co., pp. 1297-1349.
13. *Ibid.*
14. Gibson, James L., Ivancevich, John M., and Donnelly, James H. Jr.: *Organizations: Behavior, Structure, Processes,* Plano, Texas, 1982, Business Publications, Inc., p. 100.
15. Scanlan, Burt, and Keys, J. Bernard: *Management and Organizational Behavior,* New York, 1979, John Wiley & Sons, Inc., p. 105.
16. Leavitt, Harold J., Oill, William R., and Eyring, Henry B.: *The Organization World,* New York, 1973, Harcourt Brace Jovanovich, Inc., pp. 32-39.
17. Bannon, Joseph J.: "Reduce Stress and Increase Effectiveness Through Time Management," *Parks and Recreation,* Nov. 1982, p. 41.
18. Gibson et al., *op. cit.,* p. 233.

19. Laufer, Arthur C.: *Operations Management*, Cincinnati, Ohio, 1975, South-Western Publishing Co., p. 19.

20. Johnson, Richard A., Monsen, R. Joseph, Knowles, Henry R., and Eyring, Henry B.: *Management, Systems, and Society: An Introduction*, Pacific Palisades, Calif., 1976, Goodyear Publishing Co., p. 31.

21. Gibson et al., *op. cit.*, p. 28.

22. Edginton, Christopher R., and Williams, John G.: *Productive Management of Leisure Service Organizations*, New York, 1978, John Wiley, Chapter 1.

23. Peterson, Carol A.: "Application of Systems Analysis Procedures to Program Planning in Therapeutic Recreation Service," in Avedon, Elliott M.: *Therapeutic Recreation Service: An Applied Behavioral Science Approach*, Englewood Cliffs, N.J., 1974, Prentice-Hall, Inc., pp. 80-103.

24. Edginton and Williams, *op. cit.*, p. 36.

25. Dearden, John: *Computers in Business Management*, Homewood, Ill., 1966, Dow Jones-Irwin, Inc., p. 203.

26. Yoshioka, Carlton F., Nilson, Ralph A., and Edginton, Christopher R.: "What Park and Leisure Service Managers Can Learn from Japanese Managers," *Leisure Today, Journal of Physical Education, Recreation and Dance*, April 1982, p. 61.

27. *Ibid*.

28. Gray, David E.: "American Management Lessons from the Japanese," *Journal of Park and Recreation Administration*, Jan. 1983, p. 2.

29. Ouchi, William G.: *Theory Z: How American Business Can Meet The Japanese Challenge*, New York, 1981, Avon Books, pp. 24-25.

30. *Ibid.*, p.37.

31. Cole, Robert: "Work Reform and Quality Circles in Japanese Industry," in Fischer, Frank, and Sirianni, Carmen (Editors): *Critical Studies in Organization and Bureaucracy*, Philadelphia, 1984, Temple University Press, pp. 424-425.

32. *Ibid.*, pp. 423-424.

33. Henderson, Karla, and Goode, Virginia: "Employee Participation Through Quality Circles," *Parks and Recreation*, Jan. 1984, p. 74.

34. Gray, *op. cit.*, p. 3.

35. "Poll Contrasts Workers Views," Chicago Tribune Service, *Philadelphia Inquirer*, Dec. 8, 1983, p. 20-C.

36. "Goodbye Kimono: Opportunities in Foreign Firms," *Time*, Dec. 12, 1983, p. 46.

Any leisure service organization is far more varied and complex than abstract organizational theories or hierarchical charts suggest. Informal relationships, subgroups, and grapevines often provide more satisfaction and efficiency than the more formal structure permits. Furthermore, although staff in a leisure service organization expect and appreciate an operational framework and directives, they are also quite capable of self-direction and imaginative problem-solving.[1]

Structure and Governance in Leisure-Service Agencies

The Organizing Function

*A*t the heart of leisure-service management is the nature of the organization itself. One of the key functions of recreation and park managers is to help develop the kinds of organizational structures and processes that will blend all elements in the system—staff members, participants, physical resources, and program activities—into a productive and efficient enterprise. Both the formal structure of an agency (including its vertical ranks or layers of authority and its horizontal division into separate functional departments) and its informal network of relationships and channels for decision making and planning are essential aspects of this process.

Moving from a consideration of the key principles of modern management, we now examine the first step in the management process—the establishment of organizational structures and operational codes in leisure-service agencies. This chapter examines the place of organizing in the sequence of managerial tasks and then presents the legal basis for the operation of recreation, park, and leisure-service organizations. It discusses the role of boards, commissions, and other advisory citizens' or members' councils and analyzes the various types of structures through which recreational organizations are governed. Finally, it reviews a number of key principles of contemporary management as they actually influence the operation of leisure-service organizations today.

Role of Organizations

In modern society many of the functions that were formerly carried out by the individual citizen or the family have become the responsibility of organizations. These organizations, whether governmental, business, educational, or social service, provide instruments through which the needs of people are met. Organizations build the homes we live in, provide us with food, clothing, and entertainment, preserve law and order, help to care for the disadvantaged, and protect us from foreign aggression, among many other functions.[2]

Exactly what *is* an organization? Simply stated, it may be defined in the following terms: "An organization is a group of people whose activities are consciously coordinated toward a common objective or objectives."[3]

Other definitions of the word "organization" include:

> State or manner of being organized; organic structure; purposive systematic arrangement; constitution . . . . The executive structure of a business; the personnel of management, with its several duties and places in administration; the various persons who conduct a business, considered as a unit.[4]

Taking the definition a step further, the verb "to organize" has the following meanings: "To arrange or constitute in interdependent parts, each having a special function, act, office or relations with respect to the whole; to systematize; to get into working order; as, to *organize* an army; to *organize* recruits."[5]

Applied to leisure-service agencies, the organizing function includes the task of establishing an overall structure of divisions, departments, or other operating units, which carry out needed tasks to fulfill the organization's purposes. This structure may be viewed in two ways: (1) as a *formal* arrangement of parts that have prescribed relationships to each other in a structured chain of command and (2) as an *informal* set of operating procedures and relationships through which planning, decision making, and other forms of teamwork take place.

Such organizational arrangements are not fixed in a permanent mold. While such key principles as departmentalization, span of control, and the scalar principle continue to be observed in most areas of public or business management, there is a new flexibility in their application. Organizations must be able to respond to changing environments and circumstances, new needs and goals, and shifting patterns of agency service. Instead of the carefully planned but rigid structures recommended by the early management theorists, many experts today believe that large organizations must permit more frequent changes in employee roles and responsibilities, as well as more dynamic interaction among personnel on all levels. Within such flexible structures, which some authorities have described as "adaptive-organic" agencies, executives may play a less commanding role and may instead become coordinators or links between different departments or other project teams. They tend to view conflict as an opportunity for creative growth and are able to mediate effectively among different interests using a participative management approach.

In part, the organizing function includes developing the initial structure of organizations or developing major new structures over time. It also consists of making ongoing modifications in the system or developing new ways of working together in carrying out the organization's functions.

Organizational Responsibilities of Managers

Managers play a key role within this overall process. Edginton and Griffith[6] point out that the essential elements in the process of organizing include the following: (1) defining goals and objectives; (2) determining the work or task to be accomplished; (3) determining and acquiring the resources (human, physical, and fiscal) needed to accomplish organizational goals; (4) clustering functions within the organization; (5) assigning responsibilities to individuals and granting authority; and (6) establishing and implementing a structure of control and accountability.

Summing up the responsibilities of recreation and leisure-service managers with respect to the organizing function, they write:

> He or she must have the ability to organize the human, physical, and fiscal resources of the organization. A manager should understand how organizations function, the factors that influence people within organizations, and the organizational structures that best achieve

organizational goals. The process of organization is essential wherever people work collaboratively.[7]

To illustrate these principles, we will now examine a number of key aspects of the organizing process, including the legal basis through which leisure-service agencies are established and the forms of control or supervision that govern them, the formal structures through which they are organized, and the way in which these structures are translated into action through joint planning, decision making, program implementation, and controlling processes.

Legal Basis for Establishing Leisure-Service Agencies

How do recreation, park, and other types of leisure-service agencies come into existence? What is the legal basis for their establishment, and how does this influence the forms they take and the functions they carry out?

First, it should be understood that different types of recreation providers have widely varying origins. For example, a therapeutic recreation program may simply be carried out as a unit of functional service within a larger department or division of medical or rehabilitative service. A commercial recreation venture will typically be established as a business, subject to the laws that govern private, profit-making enterprises. A campus recreation program is usually initiated as a responsibility of a college or university department of student life or intramural program sponsored by a department or school of physical education.

LOCAL PUBLIC RECREATION AND PARK AGENCIES

Of the various types of leisure-service organizations, local recreation and park departments are usually regarded as having a key responsibility for providing recreational facilities and programs to meet community needs.

Such agencies must normally function within a framework of enabling legislation provided by state government. Under the American form of government, states have the authority to regulate governmental programs and various areas of human activity within their territories, except as limited by the federal Constitution or their own constitutions. This regulatory power is commonly known as "police power" and provides authorization to enact laws necessary for the health, safety, morals, and general welfare of the citizens of each state. Although police power belongs exclusively to the states, Lutzin and Storey write that it

> may be delegated by appropriate state legislative and constitutional provisions to local units of government. A municipality, as a subdivision and creature of a state, can exercise police powers only to the extent that the power is delegated to it and only in the manner expressed in enabling legislation. This direct authorization is necessary before local units of government can conduct recreation programs.[8]

In the early days of the recreation and park movement, as local governments began to assume the responsibility for operating recreation programs and facilities, they often did so on the basis of the police powers granted to them by their states. Providing local government the right to frame and enforce reasonable measures for the protection of health, life, property, and morals, these were used to justify a broad range of governmental functions intended to serve the common good.

As recreation became a more widely recognized form of government responsibility, the following types of legislation were developed.

Special recreation and park laws

One approach to state legislation supporting local recreation and park agencies was the *special law*. These laws, many of which are operative today, were passed by state legislatures and empowered cities or towns to sponsor recreation and park facilities and programs. They usually dealt with specific types of facilities (such as auditoriums, community buildings, stadiums, swimming pools, or golf courses) and provided legal authorization for taxing, floating bonds, or otherwise funding such ventures.

Regulatory laws

A second type of state legislation affecting recreation was the *regulatory law*. These are laws that seek to control, license, censor, or supervise recreation programs to protect the public health, safety, and general well-being. They usually apply not only to governmental agencies but also to voluntary, commercial, private, educational, and other organizations.

Enabling laws

The major type of state legislation affecting recreation and parks is the *enabling law*. These state laws empower local branches of government to acquire, develop, and maintain recreation and park areas and facilities and to operate programs under leadership. They usually specify the types of local governmental units that may operate such programs, as well as their specific permissible functions, including fiscal practices, cosponsorship activities, and other operational processes. State enabling laws usually stipulate whether a recreation and park board or commission must be established to oversee the local public leisure-service agency and if so the manner of its appointment, the number of members, and its powers and responsibilities.

State law is usually *permissive* rather than *mandatory* in this area; it permits local communities to establish recreation and park programs, but it does not compel them to do so. In some cases enabling provisions may be found as part of the state education code, in which local school districts are authorized to sponsor community education and recreation programs and tax specifically for such purposes.

Special district laws

In some states special enabling legislation has been passed that permits two or more municipalities or other political subdivisions to establish joint park or recreation programs. This is normally done by setting up independent districts that function in this area of government alone. Such laws may include provisions giving special districts the right to impose taxes on residents within their borders, as well as the power to acquire, develop, and maintain recreation areas and facilities, sponsor programs, and employ personnel.

Home rule legislation

Many states encourage a high level of local self-determination by permitting municipalities and counties to develop their own charters for home rule. If provision for recreation and parks is not made in the original charter, it may be added in the form of an amendment that provides general authority for this function, to be followed by more specific ordinances outlining the responsibilities and powers of government in this area.

VOLUNTARY NONPROFIT ORGANIZATIONS

Other types of leisure-service agencies, such as voluntary nonprofit organizations, may also be required to be established on a legal basis to gain tax exempt status and carry out their programs with a degree of public recognition and stability. For example, Young Men's Christian Association (YMCA) and Young Women's Christian Association (YWCA), Boys' Clubs and Girls' Clubs, Boy and Girl Scout organizations, and similar groups are typically chartered or approved as nonprofit corporations—in some cases through recognition by Congress and in others by registration under state law governing such bodies.

COMMERCIAL LEISURE-SERVICE ORGANIZATIONS

Profit-oriented recreation businesses fall into three categories of ownership and management practices: (1) *sole proprietorship,* in which one individual owns the business fully and is in total charge of its operation; (2) *partnerships,* in which two or more persons own and operate a business with shared financial responsibilities and management functions; and (3) *corporations,* which are legal entities with all the rights and powers of individuals. Corporations represent only 20% of all types of businesses, but they carry on about 80% of the total dollar volume of annual sales. They are typically owned by shareholders (either publicly or privately), who are represented by a board of directors who oversee the corporation's overall goals and policies and hire the management team that puts these into action.

OTHER TYPES OF ORGANIZATIONS

The formal structures of other types of leisure-service agencies may vary greatly. They often are established as part of the ongoing operation of a larger institution or program. For example, employee recreational activities within a large corporation might function as a service unit within an overall department of personnel management and services. In some cases it might be established as a separate employee association, attached to the company, but operating under its own financing and leadership.

As indicated earlier, a campus recreation program might be conducted under the administrative supervision of a dean of student life or a director of a large student union organization, or it might consist primarily of intramurals and sports club programs under the direction of a physical education or athletic department administrator.

Types of Administrative Structures

Within each type of agency there are many different types of administrative structures. For example, local, public recreation and park agencies may fit into the following categories: (1) separate recreation departments operating under their own boards or commissions or reporting directly to mayors or city managers; (2) separate park departments similarly structured; (3) school-sponsored programs, often linked to adult education activities; (4) combined recreation and park departments; or (5) other municipal or county agencies, such as youth boards, housing authorities, welfare departments, or police, which may operate or assist leisure-service programs.

JOINT OPERATIONS

Sometimes several governmental units that overlap geographically make contractual agreements for jointly sponsored recreation programs. To illustrate, the city of Pasadena, Calif., the Los Angeles County Board of Supervisors, and the Pasadena Board of Education share responsibility for operating recreational facilities and programs in the county and school district area. All school facilities are made available without charge, and city-owned facilities, including 22 parks, a civic auditorium, and the Rose Bowl, are also used. Similar joint operations have been developed in numerous California communities. In other cases several different units of local government may jointly sponsor a single program, although they do *not* overlap geographically.

COOPERATION BETWEEN LOCAL GOVERNMENT AND VOLUNTARY AGENCY

In some cases local government recreation agencies operate in a cooperative relationship with a private or voluntary organization. For example, the village of Mt. Kisco, N.Y., entered into a cooperative agreement with the Mt. Kisco Boys' Club. Both organizations contribute to the overall budget of several hundred thousand dollars, share the use of facilities, and employ a common staff. Through this arrangement the jointly operated program is able to take advantage of the strength and stability of the affiliation with local government and the flexibility and relative independence of the Boys' Club.

Similarly, in the Canadian city of Peterborough, Ont., the public recreation and park department and the Peterborough Family YMCA have a contractual agreement to share the use of the Y's excellent facilities, which were improved through a capital development grant of $500,000 from the Ontario Ministry of Culture and Recreation. This arrangement amounts to a joint operation in serving the city.

Administrative Placement within Larger Systems

In examining the structure of leisure-service agencies, it should be pointed out that many organizations operate as units within larger systems. For example, hundreds of parks, forests, seashores, historic sites, and recreation areas are part of federal agencies such as the National Park Service or Forest Service. To a degree, they operate independently, although they are subject to nationally determined budget allocations, policies, and personnel procedures.

Many voluntary nonprofit organizations are part of larger federations that provide direction and technical assistance and that establish basic governance policies under which they must operate. For example, the local YMCA is usually affiliated with a metropolitan or regional YMCA board, which in turn is part of a larger national organization that establishes goals, policies and programs, and personnel guidelines.

In the therapeutic recreation field, many programs are provided as a specialized form of treatment service within a larger institution that has varied rehabilitative functions, such as a general hospital, mental health center, or special school for the retarded. In such situations the recreation program is generally determined by the agency's own professional staff, subject to the supervision and input of the agency supervisor or other members of the treatment team.

In some therapeutic recreation settings a national or regional structure may dictate program elements, staffing arrangements and other operational procedures. For example, in the Veterans Administration, more than 170 different hospitals serve over 30 million veterans and their dependents throughout the United States. The overall Veterans Administration establishes personnel and program guidelines, which in turn are implemented in the separate institutions, with recreation classified as a treatment modality within the Physical Medicine and Rehabilitation Service of the Department of Medicine and Surgery.

Role of Boards and Commissions

A key element in the management of leisure-service organizations is the role of boards and commissions. Such groups are established to oversee and direct the work of the agency either in general policy matters or in specifically reviewing and approving all major plans and decisions.

PUBLIC AGENCY BOARDS AND COMMISSIONS

In local public recreation and park departments, the composition and function of supervising boards and commissions are usually defined by law. They fall into three categories: (1) completely independent bodies with full authority for establishing and overseeing policy, (2) semi-independent bodies with the power to make policy, but dependent on a higher governmental body that provides funding and to which they must report, and (3) advisory boards or commissions with limited powers.

Boards and commissions may be either elected or appointed. Appointment is generally made by the mayor, city manager, or county executive officer, sometimes with the approval of the city council or county board of supervisors. Special park and recreation districts usually elect their board members, just as school districts do. Boards normally have between five and seven members, although they may have as few as three or as many as 11 or more members. They usually serve for overlapping 3-year terms, so some members with experience and some new members are on the board each year. Ideally, board membership should reflect the socioeconomic, religious, or ethnic components of the community. They may also be selected to represent different community agencies or special-interest groups, such as the school system or business community.

Functions

Such groups serve to interpret the work of local public departments to the community and to develop both the moral and financial support of citizens and political groups. Their task is to review and approve all policies and work with the professional agency's managers to develop plans for meeting the present and future leisure needs of the community.

Operating under a civil service structure in most cases, boards and commissions consider and approve all personnel appointments or promotions and determine personnel policies, although many of these are governed by overall policies within the local governmental structure. They should be involved in all facility planning or rehabilitation projects and should carry out long-range planning in cooperation with other community organizations to meet public recreational needs.

It is important to draw a sharp distinction between the role of recreation and park boards and commissions in *determining* policy and their role in *administering* policy. As a general rule, they should not interfere with the functions of the departmental administrator by attempting to dictate how the details of administration should be carried out, meddling with department routines, or developing unofficial but close relationships with subordinates. Although a board's approval is normally required for many specific administrative acts, such as hiring and firing, the acts themselves should be clearly regarded as within the administrator's domain.

Once the board or commission has defined the objectives of the department and established written policies or shared in these processes, it must be prepared to delegate real responsibility for implementing these guidelines to the director and staff of the agency. On the other hand, the administrator must be open with the board, providing it with all important or relevant information, seeking its advice on all controversial matters, conscientiously adhering to its policy directives, and weighing its views seriously. It helps greatly for board members to be tolerant, tactful, and willing to work hard and support the agency director before the public and community groups.

Role of advisory groups

Many public recreation and park departments also encourage the formation of communitywide or neighborhood advisory councils, recreation center committees, or similar groups. Although such groups do not usually have legal status, they play an invaluable role in making the views of the community known to the professional staff and in other concrete ways, such as assisting in program planning, raising funds for specific projects, and providing volunteer leadership. Examples of such advisory groups, which often supplement the work of more formal boards and commissions, are provided in Chapter 12.

BOARDS OF VOLUNTARY AND THERAPEUTIC AGENCIES

Other types of leisure-service organizations also operate under the direction of policy-making or advisory boards, usually referred to as boards of directors or trustees. In general, they seek to attract individuals who represent influential elements of the community, who have sound judgment, and who can assist in fund raising or recruiting other forms of support. Several examples of the administrative structure and boards or supervising bodies of voluntary and therapeutic agencies follow.

Boys' Clubs of America

Typical of many such organizations, the Boys' Clubs of America has published a constitution and set of bylaws to assist local chapters or units in developing their own structure and operating procedures.

An individual Boys' Club may choose to be structured as a corporation, association, or administrative committee, although the national organization generally recommends that it be incorporated under existing state law. This arrangement ensures that a large group of representative citizens will be closely associated with the organization and have responsibility for its development. The overall membership elects a board of directors, who directly oversee club operations.

The suggested Boys' Club constitution includes name, purpose, membership rules, meetings, board of directors, officers, executive director, and similar elements. Under the bylaws, specific recommendations are made regarding the function of officers of the board and the establishment of committees for finance, program, personnel, public relations, nominations, and property management. Within this structure, individual Boys' Clubs may operate in a highly autonomous way, provided that they carry out the goals and objectives of the Boys' Clubs of America.

Girl Scouts of the U.S.A.

This extensive national youth organization has a somewhat more tightly structured system of government. Founded through congressional charter, the Girl Scouts of the U.S.A. operates under a constitution that identifies three major levels of governance: the national council, the national board of directors, and local Girl Scout councils.

The membership of the national council is constituted by the members of the Girl Scout Corporation, who are elected delegates from local councils (up to 2000), members of the national board of directors, and other elected persons. The council serves as the coordinating head of the Girl Scout movement in the United States. More specific powers are assigned to the national board of directors. This body has the responsibility for establishing requirements for membership, local council charters, standards, and other major operating procedures. Finally, local Girl Scout councils directly administer and supervise programs implemented in individual troops based on the goals and policies that have been established by the national council and board of directors.

San Francisco Recreation Center for the Handicapped

This unique voluntary agency, serving the comprehensive recreation and social needs of the disabled was founded in 1952. Today it provides varied programs for all age groups in an outstanding new facility. It operates under the guidance of a board of directors whose members are broadly representative of the health and welfare field, including physicians, educators, business executives, and recreation specialists, as well as the parents of handicapped individuals served by the center.

The board delegates formal administrative responsibility to the center director and business manager, who in turn work closely with board members in 18 standing committees. These committees have responsibility for such areas of management as budget, building construction, camping, insurance, medical and technical programs, parents' auxiliary, personnel, program planning, publicity, and transportation.

Organizational Patterns of Leisure-Service Agencies

As preceding chapters have indicated, leisure-service organizations must have carefully designed structures that reflect the hierarchy of authority on several levels and facilitate carrying out the key functions of management. These structures are illustrated through a number of organization charts (Figs. 4-2 to 4-9), which represent the formal organizational patterns of many government, voluntary agency, and business groups. They are influenced by several concepts developed during the earlier period of management theory: (1) levels of authority, (2) division of labor and departmentalization, (3) span of control, and (4) delegation of responsibility.

LEVELS OF AUTHORITY

In public recreation and park departments, three levels of authority have been customary: (1) the executive or top managerial level, (2) the supervisory or middle management level, and (3) the leadership or direct service level. In many leisure-service agencies today, this would represent an extreme oversimplification of the hierarchy of authority.

In a large commercial recreation enterprise, for example, major influence would be wielded by a board of directors, headed by a chief executive officer. Reporting directly to the board of directors are several individuals who comprise the top management of the organization and whose primary function is to develop corporate plans and make major policy decisions. Below the top management level are middle management individuals who may be known as department or division heads, superintendents, or project managers. Their task is to implement the policy and plans that have been established by top management; they do this by developing intermediate plans and maintaining control over aspects of company performance such as production and sales figures. Below middle management are first-level managers, such as section managers or supervisors, who are responsible for developing and implementing more short-range operating plans and day-to-day production or marketing activities. Similar patterns may be found in other types of leisure-service organizations.

DIVISION OF LABOR AND DEPARTMENTALIZATION

Traditional management theory stressed the need to divide work into a number of sharply defined, specialized tasks both to ensure that each individual knows precisely what he or she must accomplish and to standardize the way of carrying out the work. Thus, within any organization, people are typically assigned to certain roles, such as laborers or maintenance personnel, bookkeepers, leaders, or program specialists.

Departmentalization consists of identifying the major functional areas within an organization and using them as a basis for grouping jobs and determining the lines of managerial control and communication. This may be done in several ways: according to the assigned area of responsibility within the organization, the geographical location or district, or the specific product or program service provided.

SPAN OF CONTROL

Span of control, described in Chapter 2, is concerned with the height and width of organizational structures and the number of subordinate employees a supervisor or other manager is expected to supervise. For example, in a wide span of control, there would be few horizontal layers, with each manager expected to supervise a large number of

	Highly structured, formal, centralized		Unstructured, informal, decentralized
		Degree of specialization	
Division of labor:	High		Low
		Basis	
Departmentalization:	Homogeneous		Heterogeneous
		Number supervised	
Span of control:	Few		Many
		Delegation of authority	
Authority:	Centralized		Decentralized

FIG. 4-1   Contrasts in organizational structure. (From Gibson, J.L., Ivancevich, J.M., and Donnelly, J.H., Jr.: *Organizations: Behavior, Structure, Processes,* Plano, Tex., 1982, Business Publications, Inc.)

subordinate employees. In a narrow span of control, there would be a greater number of horizontal layers of employees within the organizational structure, and each supervisor would be expected to oversee the work of a smaller number of subordinates. In general, a wide span of control is appropriate for organizations in which work is clearly defined and systematized and the work force is relatively homogeneous. A narrow span of control is more useful when work tasks vary greatly, requiring flexibility in job performance, and the work force is likely to be more heterogeneous.

DELEGATION OF AUTHORITY

Delegation of authority is concerned with the extent to which individuals up and down the chain of command are permitted to make their own decisions without having to seek the approval of managers on higher levels. An organization that favors the delegation of authority is generally thought of as *decentralized*. Here, managers are encouraged to assume problem-solving responsibilities and develop their own creativity and ingenuity, which in turn leads to the effective performance of the entire agency. In a sense, this approach requires managers to develop broad rather than highly specialized skills, since they often are called on to deal with a wide range of problems that are not covered by agency policies.

CONTRASTS IN ORGANIZATIONAL STRUCTURE

Several of the factors just described help define the managerial style of an organizational structure. Fig. 4-1 shows how organizations might fall along a continuum ranging

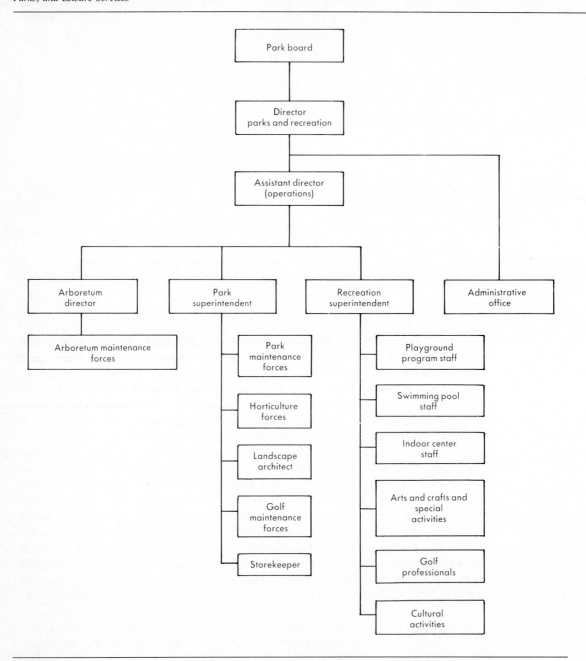

FIG. 4-2   Organization of Spokane, Wash., Park Department.

from highly formal and structured on the left to informal and unstructured on the right.[9] Differentiating these approaches, Gibson, Ivancevich, and Donnelly write:

> Generally speaking, organizational structures will tend toward one extreme or the other along each continuum. Structures tending to the left are characterized by a number of terms including formalistic, structured, bureaucratic . . . and mechanistic. Structures tending to the right are termed informalistic, unstructured, nonbureaucratic . . . and organic.[10]

EXAMPLES OF ORGANIZATION CHARTS
Public recreation and park departments

SPOKANE, WASH., PARK BOARD   Fig. 4-2 is an illustration of a fairly simple structure in which a director of parks and recreation is responsible for administering three major functional units: an arboretum, a park division, and a recreation division. Each of these is under the control of its own director or superintendent.

The park and recreation divisions are in turn divided into a number of functional units related to their major areas of responsibility. As shown on the right side of the chart, the administrative office staff is attached directly to the central office of the director and assistant director, who are responsible for overseeing all programs.

OMAHA, NEB., DEPARTMENT OF PARKS, RECREATION, AND PUBLIC PROPERTY   As in Spokane, in Omaha both park and recreation functions are placed under a joint departmental structure. However, as Fig. 4-3 makes clear, this agency also has a major responsibility for operating municipally owned properties, including civic waterways and docks, a huge auditorium and stadium, and various other public buildings. The chart is a simplified one, stressing major areas of job responsibility rather than the detailed functions of specific positions.

VANCOUVER, B.C., BOARD OF PARKS AND PUBLIC RECREATION   Fig. 4-4 shows how the work of a public recreation and park department may be divided into several functional areas involving both program service and facilities operation. Three of these areas—zoos, works and buildings, and grounds, construction, and maintenance—are the responsibility of a deputy superintendent, whereas beaches and pools, administration (controller), income operations, and supervised recreation fall directly under the superintendent. It should be noted that this chart is organized and presented horizontally, whereas most charts are vertical, with the chain of command illustrated on successively higher levels of management.

These organization charts of public recreation and park departments show how the major functional areas of management responsibility, such as fiscal management, personnel supervision, or facilities planning, design, and maintenance, are usually assigned to separate divisions. They also show how specific areas of departmental responsibility, such as zoos, golf courses, or municipal marinas, may be established as separate administrative divisions. As a common practice, recreation service divisions may also house a number of separate program units, such as "inner-city" programs, performing and creative arts, golden age programs, municipal camps, summer playgrounds, aquat-

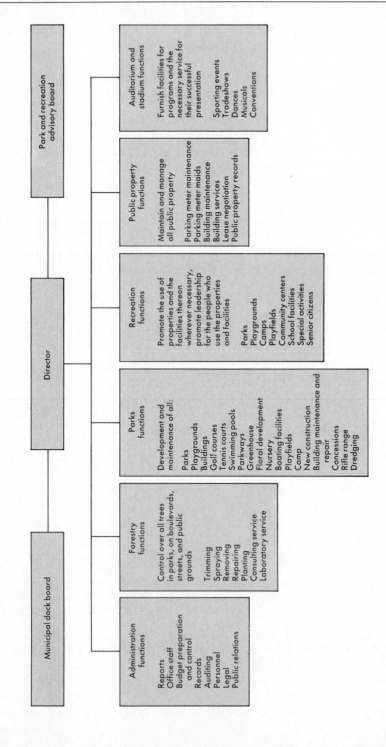

FIG. 4-3   Organization of Omaha, Neb., Parks, Recreation and Public Property Department.

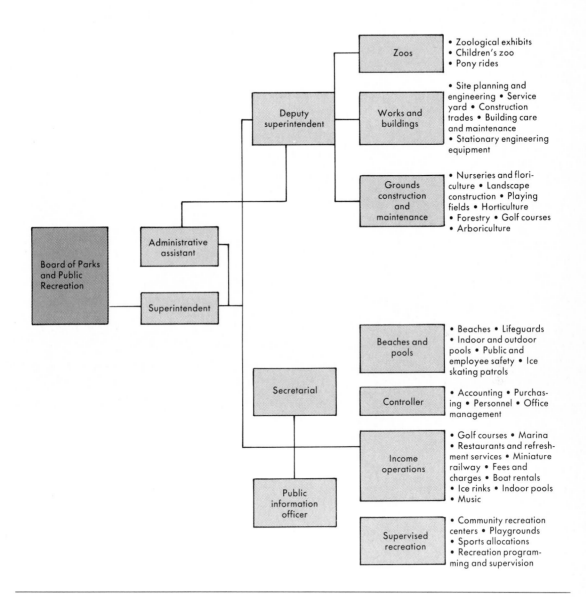

FIG. 4-4   Organization of Vancouver, Canada, Department of Parks Public Recreation.

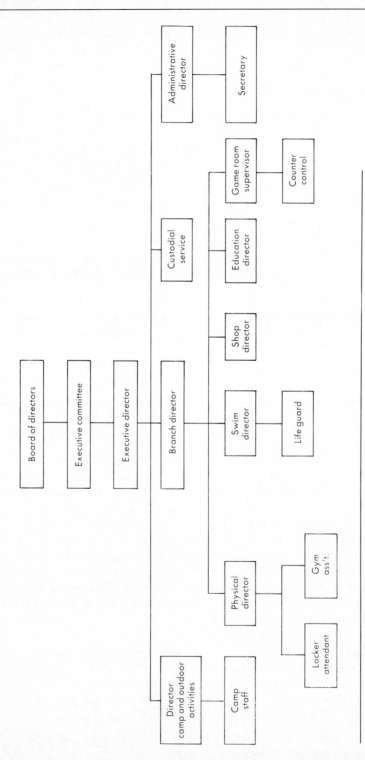

FIG. 4-5   Organization of Boys' Clubs of Dallas, Inc.

ics, and municipal athletics. In the past, many departments had separate program divisions based on gender, such as Divisions of Girls' and Womens' Sports, or Boys' and Mens' Sports. Today, however, such sex-related program divisions are rare.

Other types of agencies

BOYS' CLUB OF DALLAS, INC. The Boys' Club of Dallas, Tex., places major responsibility for administering the Boys' Club building and its program on the agency's branch manager. Other managers, such as the director of camping and outdoor programs, are directly responsible to the executive director of the organization for the operation of citywide services (Fig. 4-5).

RECREATION CENTER FOR THE HANDICAPPED, INC. This community-based organization serving special populations has a relatively simple and functional organization chart (Fig. 4-6). Program service managers represent a major administrative division and report directly to the center's director. In addition to a unit responsible for support services, such as transportation or food, a separate administrator carries out resource development (primarily fund-raising) and arranges special events.

ARMED FORCES Military recreation programs in the United States and abroad are under the direction of the Assistant Secretary of Defense for Manpower, Reserve Affairs and Logistics, in Washington, D.C. Within each of the major branches of the service, a different office is responsible for coordinating leisure-service programming. For example, in the Department of the Army, it is directed by the Morale, Welfare and Recreation Coordinator, headquartered in Alexandria, Va. In the Department of the Navy, it is coordinated by the Director of the Recreational Services Division of the Naval Military Personnel Command, in Washington, D.C. Within each branch, special coordinating units plan and assist in implementing programming in specific areas such as: (1) arts and crafts; (2) child care; (3) post exchanges; (4) libraries; (5) military entertainment; (6) motion picture services; (7) recreation services; and (8) sports and outdoor activities. Other units in each of the armed forces branches are responsible for training materials, audiovisual aids, fund procurement, and personnel services.

The actual responsibility for hiring personnel, maintaining facilities, and directing programs lies with military and civilian personnel on specific bases, subject to regulations and policies enacted by the Department of Defense and other offices within the military chain of command. Specific program areas are assisted in training, publicity, and other management functions by staff members who coordinate such activities. This is illustrated in Fig. 4-7, which shows the breakdown of service units for the Recreation Services Agency in Korea.

COMMERCIAL RECREATION For-profit leisure-service agencies may take an immense variety of forms, ranging from tiny, ''mom and pop'' campgrounds, dance studios, or video game centers to huge, complex structures. Two examples are presented here: a medium-size health and fitness center in Philadelphia and the Disney World operation in Orlando and Lake Buena Vista, Fla.

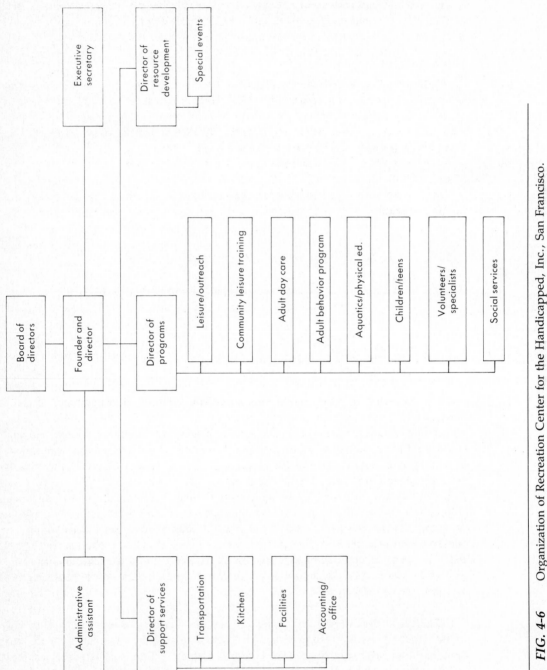

FIG. 4-6   Organization of Recreation Center for the Handicapped, Inc., San Francisco.

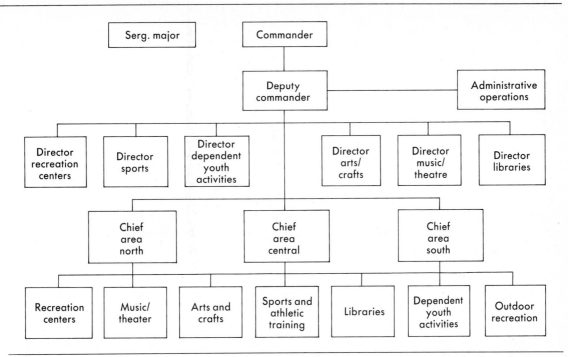

FIG. 4-7   Organization of U.S. Army Recreation Service Agency, Korea (USARSAK). Within each of the three geographical areas, programs in all seven activity elements are provided.

Northeast Health Spa. Health and fitness centers became a popular form of recreation-related commercial enterprise in the United States during the late 1970s. These centers typically offer elements such as weight training and exercise equipment rooms; pools, whirlpools, and saunas; racquetball or squash courts; indoor tracks; gyms with exercise classes, aerobic dancing, or Jazzercise; and similar facilities or programs. More elaborate ones might include more specialized facilities, classes or individualized instruction, or guidance, as well as social lounges, restaurants, bars, and special events.

The organization chart of the Northeast Health Spa in Philadelphia is shown in Fig. 4-8. It represents a simple structure, in which the director and assistant director supervise four types of employees: (1) program instructors, who direct classes, supervise the use of exercise equipment, provide individualized exercise programs for members, and supervise the pool and other aquatic activities; (2) sales staff, representing a key element in such agencies; (3) the receptionist and clerical staff; and (4) maintenance personnel. The instructors and marketing personnel are divided by sex, although the program is essentially coeducational.

Disney World and EPCOT Center. In the field of commercial recreation, an outstanding example is Disney World in Lake Buena Vista, Fla. This enterprise, which was expanded in 1982 with the addition of the EPCOT Center (Experimental Prototype

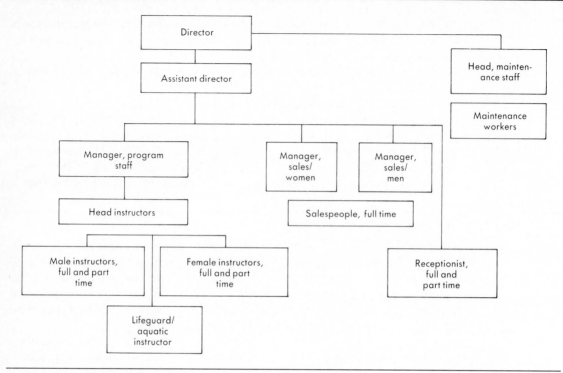

FIG. 4-8   Organization of Northeast Health Spa, Philadelphia.

Community of Tomorrow), has a structure that is too complicated to depict in a single organization chart. It may be briefly described as consisting of both internal functional divisions and external or subsidiary companies. To illustrate, it has the following major functional subunits:

1. *Finance:* handles the business side of the operation: budgets, financial planning, statistics, etc.
2. *Food:* responsible for food outlets, restaurants, and special sales
3. *General services:* provides essential services such as wardrobe, safety, warehousing, and staff development and training
4. *Administration:* coordinates, plans, and directs the entire operation
5. *Employee relations:* supervises all personnel functions, such as hiring, personnel records, job assignment, compensation, benefits, relocation, and employee relations
6. *Entertainment:* produces all special live shows and provides entertainment groups
7. *Facilities:* responsible for maintaining and operating facilities with safety, efficiency, and cleanliness
8. *Operations:* supervises guest relations, security, and fire prevention; operates the actual program attractions and rides

9. *Marketing:* a communications and promotional unit that coordinates various business and industry group trips and events and does research to measure consumer interest and characteristics

10. *Merchandising:* designs and sells souvenirs and other specialty merchandise in Disney World

11. *Hotel:* operates major hotels for visitors

In addition, this impressive enterprise has established a number of other companies to perform specialized services, provide utilities, or meet other needs. These in-house or wholly owned subsidiaries are responsible for such functions as construction, engineering, land development and master planning, general insurance, advertising, outside merchandising, gift shops, and electric, gas, water, incinerator, and sewage facilities.

Informal Agency Processes

The preceding section of this chapter describes the formal structure of several different kinds of leisure-service agencies. Without question, having such formal patterns of organization, along with standardized operating procedures, directives, and policies, tends to encourage order, predictability, and stable relationships. Bannon[1] suggests that without organization charts that designate areas of responsibility or the chain of command, confusion, inefficiency, and irresponsibility might result.

At the same time, it has been pointed out that often overly rigid organizational structures may constrict an agency's ability to respond promptly and creatively to sudden challenges or opportunities. Bureaucratic red tape may prove a serious stumbling block in attempting to solve problems or develop cooperative relationships within an organization. Therefore all organizations tend to develop informal structures or processes through which the formal lines of communication or segregated policy-making and decision-making powers may be bypassed. Such arrangements often represent a realistic way of accomplishing tasks and bringing freshness and creativity to the overall operation.

STRENGTHS AND WEAKNESSES OF INFORMAL PROCESSES

The influence of informal structures and processes on the work of an organization may be both beneficial and detrimental. On the one hand, they may improve planning and problem-solving functions and reduce the amount of time it takes to develop projects by encouraging lateral relationships between separate departments or divisions of an organization. On the other hand, Edginton and Griffith write:

> The informal organization can also impede the work of an organization. Informally organized groups can be a powerful force within the organization, disrupting its work and challenging the formal organizational structure. They often operate covertly and can undermine the manager's authority.[11]

Ideally, the functions of the informal structure can be incorporated in the actual design and operations of a leisure-service agency. This may be demonstrated through a number of organizational concepts and models that have emerged in recent years, which seek to break down the rigidity of formal, inflexible structures. They include ''linking-pin,'' ''modular,'' ''matrix'' and ''free-form'' approaches to organizational processes.

LINKING-PIN CONCEPT

This organizational model, developed by Rensis Likert, is based on the concept that individuals within the hierarchy of an agency serve as ''linking-pins'' or means of connecting with work groups both above and below their own units. The linking-pin structure tends to promote open communication and decision making between groups, with an easier flow of ideas up and down the chain of command.

MODULAR APPROACHES

Here the work of a larger department or division is divided into sharply identified tasks or projects, which are made the direct responsibility of smaller personnel units with needed functional skills. Each such group, or modular unit, has clearly assigned, specific functions to carry out, with their varied activities coordinated by a higher authority that has been made responsible for the overall enterprise. This represents a form of decentralization, in which the members of each modular unit can be given a fuller degree of responsibility for decision making and carrying out their assigned tasks.

MATRIX ORGANIZATION APPROACHES

Another way of breaking down the barriers to organizational efficiency that are often found in rigid structures is through the ''matrix'' approach. Individuals may continue to function within their regular department, but also be assigned to another agency project on a short- or long-term basis. Thus they report to two managers, one in their functional department and one in the special project unit.

Matrix structures are particularly useful in organizations that face rapidly changing market conditions demanding rapid information processing and decision making. Such structures may lead to (1) improved flexibility in conditions of change and uncertainty; (2) better technical performance through cross-fertilization of expertise by specialists in different areas; (3) freedom of top management for long-range planning; and (4) greater opportunity for personal development of employees, and improving motivation and commitment.

A simple example of using the matrix organization approach in leisure-service agencies would be in large municipal recreation and park departments, in which staff members may have managerial responsibilities within a given recreation center or district and also be assigned to a citywide task force to work on major athletic programs or other special projects.

To illustrate how an organization may develop a structure that is deliberately designed to facilitate such interactive processes, Fig. 4-9 shows the structure of a voluntary agency known as Shared Outdoor Adventure Recreation (SOAR) in Portland, Ore. SOAR's mission is to promote and sponsor challenging outdoor adventure programs for handicapped individuals. As a nonprofit community organization, it must work with many civic groups and individuals, coordinating their efforts in joint projects. In such a situation a formal agency structure with rigid lines of authority would probably be self-defeating.

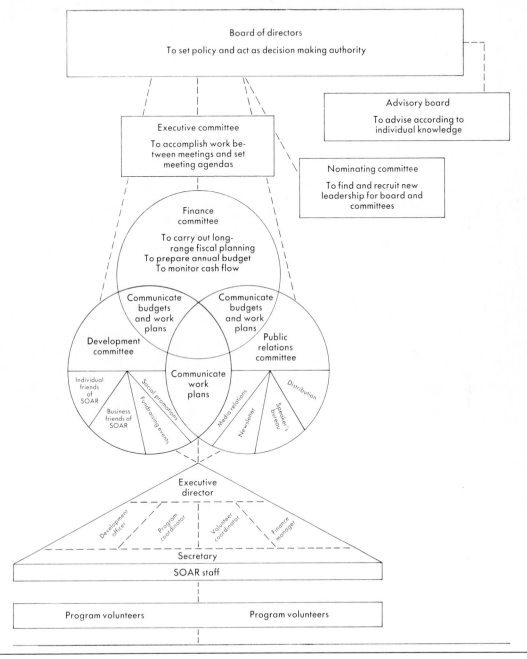

FIG. 4-9   Organization of Shared Outdoor Adventure Recreation (SOAR), Portland, Ore.

Instead, SOAR has developed a flexible plan in which various committees, volunteers, and staff members work together with shared or overlapping functions. These shared areas, in which the circles of committee responsibility overlap, show very clearly how the matrix approach may be applied in linking various agency functions. Although the SOAR structure might not be readily applicable to larger or more formal or bureaucratic organizations, it shows how the informal approach to management may be used for maximum productivity.

FREE-FORM APPROACHES

A final example of informal organizational models may be found in organizations in which all structural arrangements are highly adaptable and flexible.

> There is no rigid role definition, and the internal structure is not fixed. There is no one way of organizing. The structure is fixed to particular needs at a particular time (through) self-contained centers that encourage participation, individual initiative, open communication, and sensitivity.[12]

Obviously, such organizations are able to respond rapidly and creatively to external changes and new needs or approaches within the field of operations. By minimizing centralized decision making and breaking down departmental or divisional lines of authority, it should be possible to bring an organization's resources to bear more effectively and productively. At the same time, such "free-form" approaches represent a high level of risk and are likely to be strongly resisted in many public, commercial, or other types of leisure-service agencies.

RESISTANCE TO INFORMAL STRUCTURES AND PROCESSES

One of the key elements of informal approaches is that they offer lower-level personnel the opportunity to share meaningfully in agency planning and problem solving and break down rigid divisional or departmental lines. In a discussion of the barriers that restrict such forms of "organizational democracy" in government agencies, Smith comments that delegating decision making and related functions to middle- or lower-level personnel may be strongly resisted for political reasons:

> Politics constrain public administrators. In the interdependent political environment of public bureaucracy, high-level career officials are likely to develop strategies designed to protect their power and affirm their independence from other sources of power.[13]

They are often reluctant to share their power simply because they feel the need to play their cards "close to their vest" to maintain a tightly organized structure that does not permit cliques or dissension and because any change may be seen as threatening turbulence or uncertainty compared with the reassuring "order" of the complacent, if ineffective, bureaucratic structure.

Organization as a Dynamic Process

No matter how it is structured, the organization is not just an assemblage of people, places, and financial or other resources. Instead, it is an ongoing system—a living enterprise. If managed effectively, it will achieve its goals, whether they be employee satisfaction, public support, or a more positive image and level of participation. However, Mescon and associates conclude that there is no one best way to structure an organization or carry on its operations. "What works for one organization in a particular time and place," they write, "may not work for another. What failed in one situation may work in another."[2] Thus even the most successful structure and management processes may need to be modified over time to respond to changing circumstances and needs.

Summary

A key function of modern management is organizing—the establishing of organizational structures and processes that are designed to accomplish the agency's goals as effectively as possible. This chapter examines this process, beginning with an overview of the legal basis for the establishment of public recreation and park departments and voluntary and commercial leisure-service agencies. It describes the various administrative structures under which public departments operate, including joint programs with voluntary agencies.

Many voluntary and therapeutic organizations are established as part of larger systems or federations that provide a framework for action, as well as policies and other operational guidelines. Boards and commissions play this role for public departments; similarly, boards of directors or trustees usually provide direction for nonprofit and therapeutic agencies.

Organizational patterns of leisure-service agencies are reviewed, with illustrations of several principles derived from traditional management theory: (1) levels of authority; (2) division of labor and departmentalization; (3) span of control; and (4) delegation of authority. These principles tend to be applied less rigidly in informal, decentralized agency structures than in formal, centralized structures. Eight examples of organization charts of public, voluntary, therapeutic, armed forces, and commercial recreation agencies are presented, with a discussion of informal agency processes that often accompany more formal management arrangements. Several alternative ways of developing flexibility in leisure-service organizations are presented, including "linking-pin," "modular," "matrix," and "free-form" approaches. In conclusion, it is stressed that organizing must be seen as a dynamic process, with the need for constant adaptation and creative responses to meet changing agency and environmental conditions.

STUDY QUESTIONS

1. Visit selected community leisure-service agencies, gather information, and report to the class on each agency's legal basis or the steps through which it was established; its organization chart, including structure of its board, commission, or other governing authority; and its allocation of work functions and levels of responsibility.

2. With other students, prepare a debate or other class presentation that argues the relative merits of highly centralized, formal, and traditional agency structures compared with decentralized, informal, and innovative structures. Illustrate with examples where possible.

3. With other students, prepare organization charts for specific types of leisure-service agencies (public, voluntary, and so on). Incorporate several of the key principles of management and show how flexible channels of communication or cooperation may be developed with linking-pin, matrix, or modular approaches. Present them to the class and discuss.

REFERENCES

1. Bannon, Joseph J.: ''The Organizational Chart: The Manager's Toy,'' *Leisure Today, Journal of Physical Education, Recreation and Dance,* April 1982, p. 47.
2. Mescon, Michael H., Albert, Michael, and Khedouri, Franklin: *Management: Individual and Organizational Effectiveness,* New York, 1981, Harper & Row, Publishers, p. 11.
3. *Ibid.,* p.13.
4. Neilson, William A. (Editor): *Webster's New International Dictionary,* Springfield, Mass., 1956, G. & C. Merriam Co., p. 1719.
5. *Ibid.*
6. Edginton, Christopher R., and Griffith, Charles A.: *The Recreation and Leisure Service Delivery System,* Philadelphia, 1983, Saunders College Publishing, p. 112.
7. *Ibid.,* p. 111.
8. Lutzin, Sidney G., and Storey, Edward H.: *Managing Municipal Leisure Services,* Washington, D.C., 1973, International City Management Association, p. 71.
9. Gibson, James L., Ivancevich, John M., and Donnelly, James H. Jr.: *Organizations: Behavior, Structure, Processes,* Plano, Texas, 1982, Business Publications, Inc., p. 291.
10. *Ibid.*
11. Edginton and Griffith, *op. cit.,* p. 114.
12. *Ibid.,* p. 130.
13. Smith, Michael P.: ''Barriers to Organizational Democracy in Public Administration,'' in Fischer, Frank, and Sirianni, Carmen: *Critical Studies in Organizational and Bureaucracy,* Philadelphia, 1984, Temple University Press, p. 460.

CHAPTER 5

We are proceeding further into the era of discontinuous change brought on by energy problems, finite resources . . . and [an] economy which does not function effectively or efficiently. In this context, we encounter ever increasing organizational complexity. . . . Public service organizations such as hospitals, schools, and welfare agencies are enmeshed in conflicting federal, state, county, and city planning systems, brought on by various government requirements and by the diversity of planning sources. Organizations facing these increasingly turbulent and often hostile environments will need more systematic and informed means of making the major strategic changes required for organizational survival and viability.[1]

Goals, Objectives, and Policy Development

The Planning Process

*T*his chapter is concerned with the second major function of leisure-service managers today: planning. It examines the process of determining an organization's basic philosophy and the fundamental mission or goals statements that stem from this. It then discusses the development of objectives, policies, and standards that serve to implement the goals statements in direct action.

Agency planning may take many forms, ranging from land-use planning, which is usually part of a community or regional comprehensive planning study concerned primarily with physical or resource-based factors, to the development of short- and long-range goals for programs, facilities, fiscal support, or similar elements in leisure-service management. Moving from a broad consideration of the goal-setting process, the chapter then shows how specific policy and standards may serve as operational guidelines through which to plan concrete actions for an organization. It concludes with a suggested step-by-step model of the planning process that is useful in carrying out managerial functions.

Planning in Leisure-Service Agencies

The word "planning" is widely used in discussions of the functions of managers in many types of organizations. Generally, it is used to describe the initial stages of determining goals and ways of achieving them. A dictionary definition of the term suggests that a plan is "a method or scheme of action; a way proposed to carry out a design; project; as, a plan of campaign."[2]

Plans precede action but are essential to carrying it out efficiently and purposefully; they imply a careful weighing of all factors and a determination of the most logical course of action or strategy to achieve desired outcomes. Planning may be done on a large scale, such as the example of a 5-year plan for a recreation and park department, which includes projections of future needs, major property acquisitions, or the development of major new program elements. Planning may also refer to much more sharply focused actions, such as designing a single facility or meeting the needs of a given neighborhood or population group.

NEED TO BASE PLANS ON SOLID FOUNDATION

Planning that is done based on whim or on the spur of the moment is likely to be ineffective. Instead, it should be based on a solid foundation of shared purposes and philosophical beliefs that underlies all planning efforts. Without a clear statement of its mission, including both its goals and objectives, any organization, whether government, business, or social service, is like a ship without a rudder, subject to every passing breeze or current.

It is therefore essential that leisure-service managers develop systematic statements of their goals, objectives, and policies that will assist them in steering an intelligent and consistent course and directing their agencies effectively. The first step in this process is to formulate a meaningful philosophy of service.

Developing a Philosophy of Service

Too often the term ''philosophy'' is taken to mean a remote, ivory tower, intellectual exercise. Instead, it should be correctly understood as an ideology or system of human values and beliefs that helps shape the planning process. To illustrate, philosophy is defined as

> the body of principles or general conceptions underlying a major discipline, a religious system, a human activity, or the like, and the application of it . . . . an integrated and consistent personal attitude toward life or reality, or toward certain phases of it, especially if this attitude is expressed in beliefs or principles of conduct.[3]

In general, the philosophy of leisure-service managers stems from the societal acceptance of recreation and leisure as important aspects of life in the modern community and as forms of applied service that meet significant human needs. Beyond this broad view, however, there may be a number of contrasting ideological views of recreation and leisure (see box on opposite page).

In developing an appropriate philosophy of leisure service, managers are likely to begin with the premise that leisure is growing steadily in modern life and that government and other major social agencies have an obligation to provide varied opportunities for creative and constructive recreation to improve the quality of life. Beyond this, a number of more specific goals or values may be expressed, relating to desired outcomes such as promoting health and physical fitness, enriching culture and the arts, reducing juvenile delinquency or other forms of social deviancy, or protecting the natural environment.

Nature of Organizational Goals

In general, goals represent broad statements of purpose or value, which are based on an organization's fundamental philosophy, as well as other situational factors that may affect it. For example, public recreation and park agencies are typically influenced in their goal setting by the following factors: (1) the legal mandate empowering them to function, which sets guidelines or limits under which they must operate; (2) the political framework of service in a given community; (3) the wishes of residents, both communitywide and as representatives of different socioeconomic, ethnic, or age groups; (4) the practical realities presented by human and material resources; and (5) the background and personal views of the agency managers.

Beyond such factors, public leisure-service agencies are also obviously influenced by

---

SIX LEISURE-SERVICE ORIENTATIONS TODAY

1. *The quality-of-life or amenity approach.* This approach sees recreation as an important community service that is carried on both for its own sake and because it contributes to the physical and mental health of participants. The role of recreation in providing pleasurable, constructive leisure outlets is emphasized.

2. *The marketing approach.* In the marketing approach recreation is viewed as a service or product that has economic value and that should be designed and aggressively promoted to yield the maximum financial return—and thus to be relatively independent as a form of community service.

3. *The human-services approach.* The human services approach is based on a holistic and humanistic view of human life. The important role of recreation in meeting individual and social needs of participants is emphasized. Seeing leisure involvement as a means to an end, human-service adherents strive to make all recreation programs highly purposeful and to link them to other community-based programs of a health-related, vocational, counseling, or other social-service nature.

4. *The prescriptive approach.* Similar to the human-services approach, the prescriptive approach sees recreation not as an activity carried on for its own sake, free of extrinsic purpose, but as designed to accomplish specific goals. Prescriptive planners, who usually work in therapeutic recreation settings, urge that recreation be applied as a distinct form of therapy, carefully formulated to achieve treatment outcomes for patients and clients.

5. *The environmental/aesthetic/preservationist approach.* This approach links several groups in society who are concerned with preserving the natural environment and the nation's historic heritage with others who see natural beauty and visually appealing man-made environments as a critical aspect of government's responsibility. It is found chiefly among recreation and park managers who serve in resource-based agencies.

6. *The hedonist/individualist approach.* Stemming from the dramatic shift in social values that occurred during the past two decades with the emergence of the "me generation," this approach stresses the pursuit of excitement and pleasure as a primary focus of leisure programs. In addition, it seeks to promote individual forms of creative expression, rather than mass programming in familiar, stereotyped activities.

Modified from Kraus, Richard: *Recreation Program Planning Today,* Glenview, Ill., 1985, Scott, Foresman & Co.

---

national trends in recreation and emerging program trends. In contrast, other types of sponsors tend to have more sharply focused purposes. For example, an employee recreation program will seek to contribute to the health of workers on various levels, reduce absenteeism and the accident rate, and build a sense of loyalty and identification with the company's management.

A therapeutic recreation agency will have goals of contributing to the rehabilitation process and reeducation or normalization of its clients or patients. A voluntary agency usually has specific human-service goals for its membership, which may also, particularly in the case of religious-affiliated groups, have spiritual or other values-oriented purposes. A commercial recreation business obviously has efficient management and making a substantial profit as its primary goals.

TYPES OF GOALS

Goals themselves may be divided logically into two types: *internal* or *operational* goals, and *external* or *outcome* goals.

The first kind of goal relates to the effort of an organization to define its own role and to function as effectively as possible as an operating agency. For example, Edginton[4] has defined several such internal goals:

1. *Management goals.* These represent internal efforts within an organization to use its resources most wisely or make effective decisions in problem areas.
2. *Adaptation goals.* These relate to an organization's effort to relate or adapt to changing environmental circumstances and challenges.
3. *Positional goals.* These include efforts to strengthen an organization's acceptance and support within the community or to gain a higher level of resources or participation.

Internal goals are concerned chiefly with what an organization does and how it *mobilizes itself* for effective effort, including setting targets for program services. In contrast, *external* goals consist of those outcomes that an agency seeks to *achieve* by offering programs. These may be stated in the numbers of participants served, the strengthening of positive intergroup relationships in a community, or specific behavioral changes that may be brought about through recreation.

EXAMPLES OF GOAL STATEMENTS
Public agencies

In a recent annual report, the recreation division of the Milwaukee public schools stated the following basic philosophy:

> In Milwaukee, the Recreation Division seeks to promote the well-rounded development of all boys, girls, men and women, and to meet the needs and desires of all individuals it serves. By emphasizing educational as well as entertainment values of recreation, the varied activities of the different programs conducted by the Recreation Division contribute to increased learning, better social adjustment, and needed relaxation for all participants. Programs are planned by professional recreation personnel, to meet neighborhood interests and needs, providing suitable facilities, adequate equipment, and qualified leadership are available.[5]

Armed Forces

A recent mission statement of the morale, welfare and recreation program of the U.S. Department of Defense included the following purposes:

> Recognizing that quality morale, welfare and recreation (MWR) programs contribute significantly to the quality of life in the military community and directly relate to recruitment and retention of military personnel, the Department of Defense, as mandated by law, advocates a comprehensive MWR program with program activities that:
> 1. Maintain a high level of *esprit de corps;* enhance job proficiency; contribute to military

effectiveness; aid in recruitment and retention by making military service an attractive career; and aid service personnel in the transition from civilian to military life.

2. Promote and maintain the physical, mental and social well being of military members, their families, and other eligible members of the military community.

3. Encourage constructive use of off-duty leisure time with opportunities for acquiring new talents and skills that contribute to the military and civilian community.

4. Provide community support programs and activities for military families, particularly when the service member is on an unaccompanied tour or involved in armed conflict.

It is the responsibility of military commands to create, maintain, and support comprehensive, quality MWR programs, services, and activities that meet the changing needs and interests of the military establishment; that are flexible to meet unique geographic requirements; and that take into consideration the evolving social and economic environment.[6]

Therapeutic recreation

The staff manual of the therapeutic recreation program of the Piersol Rehabilitation Center of the Hospital of the University of Pennsylvania cites the following purposes:

The purpose of the Therapeutic Recreation program is to provide recreational activities and experiences which are modified to meet an individual's physical, emotional, mental and/or social limitations and abilities. Activities are aimed at promoting the functional independence of the individual and aiding in the total rehabilitation process of the patient.

Recreational activities are directed toward maintaining and/or improving the physical and mental health of the patient. The overall goals of the Therapeutic Recreation program are:

1. To facilitate favorable adjustment to treatment and to the hospital environment.
2. To stimulate socialization and interaction.
3. To promote optimal psychomotor, cognitive and affective functioning through adapted activities.
4. To provide leisure education.
5. To encourage a constructive, meaningful and independent leisure lifestyle.
6. To prepare the patient for participation in community recreation programs upon discharge.

The activities are geared toward teaching skills and hobbies that can be taken back to the home/community environment. The Therapeutic Recreation program works in conjunction with the rehabilitation therapy team, establishing goals that complement the patient's therapy programs in occupational therapy, physical therapy, speech, and other modalities.[7]

Transforming Goals into Objectives

The terms "goals" and "objectives" are often used interchangeably, since they both represent purposes or outcomes that an organization is seeking to achieve. However, they are *not* the same.

As illustrated, goals express rather broad philosophical intentions or values. It may often be impossible to achieve them fully; yet they serve to remind staff members and the public of the essential purposes and priorities of an organization.

In contrast, objectives represent statement of intent that *are* attainable, specific in nature, and measurable. In effect, they are goals that are transformed into a program of intended actions designed to take place over a period of time. In general, goals may be thought of as long-range, whereas objectives are usually short-range. Graham and Klar write:

> Objectives which are specific, measurable, and expected to be attained within a predetermined time period give clear direction to the leisure service practitioner. In fact, the success of a given program then rests upon the attainment of those objectives. Programs cannot be said to be successful according to any type of objective criteria *unless* objectives are specified, evaluated, and attained.[8]

WAYS OF STATING OBJECTIVES

Objectives may be stated in several ways. They often express desired *behavioral change* for participants. This would be particularly true in a therapeutic or human-service program, which seeks to improve the emotional health, physical fitness, or social functioning of participants. Examples of behavioral change objectives might be:

1. To have participants successfully perform specific skills in motor activities, such as sports or games
2. To have participants learn and practice specific social skills as part of ongoing group membership without demonstrating past negative behaviors, such as hostility, aggression, or reliance on drugs or alcohol as social facilitators
3. To have teenagers in an after school work-study program improve their academic attitudes and performance

Objectives may also be expressed as *program implementation,* that is, to initiate specific projects or activities, attract a given number of participants, or develop new forms of services that meet important community needs. Examples of program implementation objectives might be:

1. To successfully establish six multiservice senior centers, one in each district of the city, with average memberships of 150 men and women over the age of 65
2. To conduct a series of sports workshops in basketball, field hockey, and volleyball in cooperation with women's physical education or athletic departments in nearby colleges
3. To provide day-care programs serving a minimum of 200 children of service personnel on a military base

Other objectives represent desired *management directions* in areas such as staff in-service education, productivity or economy, personnel performance, maintenance targets, or planning and evaluation. They are intended to achieve the internal or operational goals of agencies in these areas by providing specific tasks to be carried out.

In *all* cases, objectives should be based on the broader values and priorities expressed within the agency's philosophy and goals statement. They provide a target at which to aim and help motivate employees at all levels. They should be realistic and yet demanding enough to provide a significant challenge.

MANAGEMENT BY OBJECTIVES

The development of appropriate objectives represents an important element in the planning process in leisure-service agencies. If objectives are determined solely by top administrative personnel, they are unlikely to be as widely accepted and supported as they would if they were the result of meaningful discussions and joint planning efforts by a wide range of agency employees.

Based on this principle, a popular management strategy known as management by objectives (MBO) has emerged in recent years. It emphasizes the joint involvement of supervisors and subordinate employees in the careful establishment of agency objectives at four levels: department, divisional, unit, and staff. Performance and success in meeting these objectives are regularly and carefully evaluated, and lower-level employees are given much more responsibility and opportunity for initiative than in traditional job settings.

Glover comments that MBO is "one example of an increasingly popular management concept that has improved efficiency and organization in various types of public and private sector organizations, and which should prove to be similarly useful in . . . leisure service organizations."[9] He suggests a number of guidelines for setting objectives, interlocking them in an organizational network, and measuring their attainment:

1. Objectives must be quantifiable so they can be used as criteria for future evaluation.
2. Each objective should be given a precise time limit for accomplishment.
3. Although objectives must fit within the framework of overall department philosophy and policy, personnel at each level should play a role in setting their own objectives.
4. A limited number of major objectives, such as three or four, are appropriate for each unit or individual rather than too many.

Example of MBO in Dallas

In applying an MBO process in the Recreation Division of the Dallas Parks and Recreation Department, Chambliss and Clegg focused specifically on recreation center programs. A set of goals were developed and approved by the agency head, and an implementation calendar was designed. Two training seminars were then held to prepare center directors and supervisors for the MBO process.

Among the subjects covered in the first seminar were an introduction to the MBO approach, methods of writing objectives and action plans, techniques for evaluation, and potential benefits to be derived from the system. The second seminar showed how performance reviews would be part of the MBO approach; center directors and supervisors were also given materials to use in teaching the system to their subordinates. Clegg and Chambliss write:

> After the training sessions, the difficult job of writing specific objectives began. First, recreation leaders at each center developed a personal set of objectives. Once approved by the center director, these objectives were combined with the center director's to create a set of objectives for that particular recreation center. This process was used at each management level, following the chain of command up the hierarchy until final approval was given each sub-division head by [the] division director. . . . During this process, personal objectives for improving employee performances were also developed. These objectives included: enrolling in a training course, improving public relations skills, developing certain new management skills, and becoming more involved in a civic activity.[10]

The performance review process involved regular meetings between supervisors and subordinates and between supervisors and higher-level administrators up the chain of command to examine progress and difficulties encountered. At the end of the year a formal performance appraisal based on common objectives was conducted for each subordinate, both to review the impact on programs and to serve as input in the personnel review process concerned with merit raises, promotions, or other actions. Although reactions to MBO were generally favorable, with agreement that it promoted creativity and work commitment on the job, divison members concluded that it was a long, difficult process demanding strong administrative support and effective staff training. Beyond this, they felt that MBO should not be expected to be a panacea and that it should be introduced in limited ways at the outset.

MBO Combined with PERT and CPM in New Rochelle, N.Y.

In an adaptation of MBO that combined it with two systems approaches described in Chapter 3, program evaluation review technique (PERT) and critical path method (CPM), one of the authors of this text has had his staff members go through the process described in the box below.

In sum, MBO is not a substitute for hard work or a cure-all for poor management techniques, but rather a systematic method of establishing priorities, clarifying job expectations, evaluating unit and individual performance, and coordinating the work of employees in a complex organization. It can also be useful in measuring output, reducing role conflict, and quickly identifying problems and ways of solving them. In this sense it is similar to the Japanese quality circle approach described in Chapter 3.

SEQUENCE APPROACH TO USING MBO
IN PROJECT PLANNING

1. Staff members are directed to place themselves at START (beginning point of major department project).
2. From START, they are asked to transport themselves mentally to FINISH, or "goal."
3. At FINISH, they must visualize all the conditions that were required to complete the journey successfully. (In PERT and CPM terms, these might be described as "events.")
4. Working backward, they must identify the conditions that existed at point 9 (the last one before FINISH).
5. Taking the step backward to 9, they must write down all the necessary actions that must have been completed before it could have been reached, as the forerunner to FINISH.
6. This sequence is repeated; they take another step backward to 8 and write down the actions or tasks required to reach 8.
7. This process is continued, until staff members take the final step backward from 2 to START. Based on this sequence approach, they have identified a precise, reliable, step-by-step route from START to FINISH, with each of the important conditions that must have been met along the way.

To provide a management framework in which objectives can be achieved, it is necessary to formulate policies that confirm the intention of the agency and that provide the basis for day-by-day planning and action.

Development of Recreation and Park Policies

Exactly what are policies? McMaster describes them as management's expression of how organizational objectives or goals should be achieved and how certain circumstances should be handled without lower-level employees having constantly and unnecessarily to refer all matters to higher levels for decisions. He writes:

> Policy statements are designed to provide general courses of action with regard to the achievement of organizational goals or objectives. Procedures, by comparison, provide the detailed, step-by-step means for achieving these goals. Ordinarily, policy statements are used instead of procedures when situations are fluid, somewhat unpredictable, or are never or rarely the same. They should be written to allow for a certain amount of judgment on the part of the individual given the authority to act under stated circumstances.[11]

Applied to leisure-service agencies, policies should be viewed as *management guidelines that reflect major departmental principles in the provision of service, operation of facilities, management of personnel, or similar areas of management concern.*

Policies are more than procedures in that they give direction to the overall process of directing and controlling an agency's operation. They tend to be broad in their scope and application, whereas procedures are the specific actions, rulings, or approved steps required to carry them out.

Policies are not irreversible. They may be changed at any time when either circumstances or departmental philosophy changes or when the need arises for a more flexible or different course of action. However, such changes should not be made on a whim, but only after careful deliberation.

BASIS FOR POLICYMAKING IN PUBLIC AGENCIES

Managers in public recreation and park departments, in cooperation with their boards or commissions or other relevant groups, may determine effective policies in several ways. The following factors usually come into play:

1. *Professional literature.* Recreation and park administrators, college educators, board members, officers of professional organizations, and other influential individuals may publish articles or study findings that influence the development of policies in the field.
2. *Recommendation of professional societies.* Professional organizations, such as the National Recreation and Park Association or its member branches, the American Association for Leisure and Recreation, the National League of Cities, and the International City Management Association, frequently hold conferences or appoint task forces that lead to the formulation of policies within key areas of administrative practice.
3. *Expectations of funding agencies.* Federal or state agencies, private foundations, or other funding organizations may establish guidelines that must be met by mu-

nicipal departments receiving assistance from them. For example, such guidelines may deal with the need for nondiscriminatory practices or special services for a particular population.

4. *Departmental factors.* In addition to the preceding influences, the opinions of board members, the judgment of legal counsel, the advice of other officials in municipal government, political considerations, and the expression of public opinion are likely to play an important role in determining policy.

When a recreation and park board or commission determines policy in a given area, it must take all of the preceding factors into account. The ultimate good of the community and the success of the program in meeting its stated objectives should be key factors in arriving at official policies.

When they are put into effect for the first time, particularly if they have a significant effect on the work life of employees or the services the public will receive, policies should be appropriately publicized through newsletters, meetings, or news releases, as well as being placed in policy manuals. If they are at all controversial, special meetings with leaders and supervisors to explain and discuss new policies and their applications may be desirable to avoid distortion or misunderstanding.

POLICIES IN OTHER SETTINGS

Similar practices are likely to prevail in other types of leisure-service agencies. In the case of voluntary organizations that are part of national federations, such as the Boy or Girl Scouts or YMCA or YWCA, major goals and purposes are likely to be defined on the national level, along with key policies. However, local councils or centers are often free to determine their own specific management policies based on local circumstances.

Similarly, private, commercial, employee, and armed forces organizations customarily develop their own operational guidelines, subject to the approval of their executive directors or divisional heads. Therapeutic agencies increasingly are adopting programming policies that reflect guidelines published by national professional societies or that meet the recommended standards of accrediting bodies.

PREPARATION OF A POLICY MANUAL

All policies should be put in writing as soon as they have been formulated. They may be distributed down the chain of command in the form of bulletins, newsletters, or handbooks. Written, official policy statements are essential so that they are available to everyone in the same form and can readily be checked for an exact interpretation of their meaning. Most efficient managers keep records of policies by putting them into a policy book or manual with the date when they were adopted or revised. Such policy manuals are usually organized so that specific policies fit into a major set of categories of managerial responsibility, all coded for easy reference. Policy manuals can be bound in loose-leaf form so that additions or revisions can be easily inserted in the appropriate locations, following a numbering system according to categories.

For example, in the case of public, local recreation and park departments, James McChesney and Richard Tappley[12] suggest that each policy be listed on a separate page, with

---

EXAMPLES OF POLICY AREAS OF RECREATION
AND PARK DEPARTMENTS

1. *Policies pertaining to people.* People-related services include recreational opportunities, accessibility, dissemination of information, nondiscrimination, and leisure education.
   Examples: Special populations—program for handicapped, migrant workers, prisoners, and elderly. Human services—create one-stop shopping centers for recreation and human services, in schools, shopping malls, or other centers. Sports and athletics—provide facilities rather than sponsor teams; provide lifetime sports activities as main focus.
2. *Policies pertaining to planning.* These include new approaches to scope of planning efforts, interagency planning, and cooperative planning with federal, state, and local authorities.
   Examples: Involve people in decisions affecting the acquisition, master planning, and development of areas and facilities. Provide more facilities closer to people's homes; give priority to urban needs; offer more passive parks, rather than traditional active parks.
3. *Policies pertaining to physical resources and support.* Such policies involve the provision of areas and facilities, preservation of historical and cultural heritage, increased opportunity for the handicapped, environmental and interpretive education, cooperative school-park programs, and increased user fees.
   Examples: Establish and utilize local park and recreation councils for development and programs, with matching funds arrangements. Reclaim land for park use—use of landfills, rights-of-way, water rights, and other unconventional sources of property.
4. *Policies pertaining to a balanced system.* These policies include working with federal, state, and local agencies; investment opportunities with private entrepreneurs; links to private foundations and trusts; and consideration of transportation and utilities.
   Examples: Examine possible consolidation of services. Utilize concepts of regional or metropolitan government. Improve public visibility and public relations methods to reach community groups and private agencies or groups.

Modified from Cryder, R.S.: Presentation to Washington State Park and Recreation Conference, November 1979.

legal references (such as state, city, or county law or ordinance, or resolution of local managing authority) and the date of adoption of the policy listed at the bottom of the page. They suggest that a manual be divided into several basic parts in the following manner:

   1000   Administration
   2000   Community relations
   3000   Finances
   4000   Personnel
   5000   Participants
   6000   Program
   7000   Maintenance

NASSAU COUNTY

Department of Recreation and Parks

Administrative Directive 101

SUBJECT: Scheduling of personnel

PURPOSE: To prescribe a uniform system for the scheduling of personnel
to ensure adequate supervision and coverage of public-use Facilities

IMPLEMENTATION

SS-1   Responsibility for personnel scheduling
It is the responsibility of all Division Heads to insure that work
schedules are developed for all personnel assigned to public-use
Facilities. It is recommended that all levels of supervision within
these Facilities formulate schedules for their respective units with
the understanding that they will be reviewed and approved by the
next level in the chain of command within the Facility. It is recommended, but not mandatory, that personnel schedules be utilized by
administrative offices and within other areas of the Department.

SS-2   Scheduling procedure
Personnel schedules are to be made out on Department Form PK-5027.
The schedule is to be signed by the Facility Head indicating that
the schedule meets the criteria established for Department personnel
schedules and then forwarded to the level of supervision established
by the Division Head as the Approving Authority for personnel schedules. When reviewed and signed by this individual, it then becomes
an approved, official schedule.

Approved schedules are to be posted, two weeks prior to the
commencement of the schedule, on Personnel Bulletin Boards in the
main administrative offices of the Facilities. Additional schedules may be posted at other locations within a Facility if a sufficient number of personnel report to a location other than the main
administrative office.

Form PK-5027 is to be filled in completely, indicating the name
of the Facility. The schedule week will begin on Friday and end on
the following Thursday. The exact dates should appear in the area
on which the days of the week have been pre-printed. When listing
the names of personnel on the schedule, group similar functions together and skip a line between each function; e.g., supervisory personnel, cashiers, rink guards, museum attendants, greens-keepers,
etc. This will assist in the review of the schedule to determine
adequate coverage.

The time that the individual is to work is to be indicated by
writing in the exact hours; e.g., 9:00-4:45, 8:30-4:30, etc. If an
individual is not scheduled to work due to personal entitlements,
the payroll symbol for that entitlement should be entered in the
scheduled hours space.

If overtime is required, the hours to be worked must also be
indicated and circled in red in the scheduled hours space.

FIG. 5-1

NASSAU COUNTY

Department of Recreation and Parks

Administrative Directive 101 Continued

SS-3 Criteria for scheduling
Every effort should be made to make the scheduling of personnel as equitable as possible. This includes dividing evening, weekend, and holiday assignments as evenly as is practical. The major portion of the staff should be scheduled during peak load periods and the appropriate skill level of staff must be available to provide the service offered.

The following guidelines should be used in developing work schedules:

The following guidelines should be used in developing work schedules:

    a. Provide adequate staff to insure facilities are manned during the days and hours facilities are open to the public.

    b. Avoid assigning personnel to positions which vary greatly from their own job descriptions.

    c. Recognize the personal needs and desires of employees for scheduling preferences.

    d. Normally, a five-day work week is to be followed.

SS-4 Changes to approved schedules
Personnel schedule changes must be approved by the designated Approving Authority or notification given as soon as possible after an emergency schedule change has occurred. In the former case, all copies of the schedule are to be corrected after approval is secured, and the printed initials of the Approving Authority are to be noted next to the change.

FIG. 5-1

Within each section, major subclassifications would have a prefix beginning with 100. For example, the following areas might be included under Personnel:

4000   Personnel
4100   Personnel organization chart
4200   Employment
4300   Duties and qualifications
4400   Rules of conduct
4500   In-service training
4600   Travel
4700   Compensation and related benefits

On the third level of detailed policies, specific guidelines might be presented, covering such subheadings as: 4710, Salary classification and guidelines; 4720, Time reports and paychecks; 4730, Insurance; and 4740, Sick leave. In general, policy manuals of this type tend to emphasize routine procedural approaches. Other types of policies may deal with more controversial managerial issues or areas of concern. For example, Ralph Cryder,[13] director of the Los Angeles County Department of Parks and Recreation, suggests that the policies of municipal and county recreation and park departments be classified under four major headings: People, Planning, Physical Resources, and Balanced System. Brief examples of these categories, and the concerns with which they deal, are described in the box on p. 97.

EXAMPLES OF POLICY STATEMENTS

The following examples show how policies may provide precise administrative directives (Nassau County, N.Y.) and somewhat broader guidelines for administrative operations (Oak Park, Ill.).

Nassau County, N.Y., Department of Recreation and Parks

An administrative directive on scheduling of personnel is shown in Fig. 5-1; it indicates the department's approach to having a uniform system for the scheduling of personnel and lists specific procedures that must be followed with respect to this process.

Oak Park, Ill., Recreation Department

A detailed statement of departmental policy with respect to renting recreation department facilities to community groups and organizations is provided in Fig. 5-2. Later sections of this policy statement cover schedule of rental charges, storage of equipment or materials, insurance and liability, rental procedures (reservations and cancellations), and rules for use of facilities.

Policies in voluntary agency: Girl Scouts of the U.S.A.

Voluntary organizations such as the Girl Scouts of the U.S.A. must also formulate policies to govern the operations of local programs. For example, the National Board of Directors of the Girl Scouts has developed a list of 22 policies that each local or regional council must agree to enforce in its application for a Girl Scout Charter.

These policies are intended to uphold the values of the Girl Scout movement and

```
                    OAK PARK, ILLINOIS
                   Recreation Department
              Manual of Policies and Procedures

                       Administration


RENTAL OF FACILITIES                                    204.3
    The Recreation Department facilities are available on a rental
    basis under the following policies:
    1.  Recreation Department facilities are available to resident
        groups and organizations for reservation from the hours of
        6:00 P.M. through 11:30 P.M. when the facility is not sched-
        uled for department supervised or sponsored programs.  Facil-
        ities will normally not be available on Sunday mornings or
        holidays.
    2.  Rental Categories and Priority:
        Recognizing that the Department facilities will provide only
        minimum space and time for the many individuals, clubs, and
        organizations that desire its use, the following priorities
        by category will be followed in scheduling a facility.
        a.  Recreation Department supervised programs
        b.  Recreation Department sponsored organizations and
            activities
        c.  Educational, cultural or civic meetings or programs of
            Oak Park organizations (Oak Park organizations must con-
            sist of at least 50% Oak Park residents)
        d.  Meetings sponsored by political or other special inter-
            est organizations in Oak Park
        e.  Oak Park groups and/or individuals requesting the facil-
            ity for such activities as parties, teas, meetings, wed-
            ding receptions, etc. where no admission is charged
        f.  Groups and/or individuals renting the facilities for ac-
            tivities that are of a commercial nature or that require
            an admission fee
        g.  Non-resident groups in any of the above categories sub-
            ject to Board approval
```

FIG. 5-2

protect it against exploitation or misuse. They deal with such subjects as admission qualifications for membership; the selection of adult members and boards of directors; the place of religion in the Girl Scout movement; health and safety; political and legislative activity; restricted use of membership and mailing lists; fund-raising methods; and permissions for commercial endorsements or use of Girl Scouting. Examples of such national policies follow:

Place of religion in the Girl Scout program. Girls are encouraged and helped through the Girl Scout program to become better members of their own religious group, but every

Girl Scout group must recognize that religious instruction is the responsibility of parents and religious leaders.

Political and legislative activity. Girl Scouts of the U.S.A. and any council or other organization holding a Girl Scouts of the U.S.A. credential may not, nor may they authorize anyone on their behalf to participate or intervene directly or indirectly in any political campaign on behalf of or in opposition to any candidate for public office; or participate in any legislative activity or function which contravenes the laws governing tax exempt organizations.

Permissions for commercial endorsement. Permission to endorse commercial products or services or to give endorsement of such by implication must be obtained from Girl Scouts of the United States of America and shall be granted only when such endorsement is in keeping with Girl Scout principles and activities.[14]

In addition to such policies, the National Board of Directors of the Girl Scouts has also formulated a set of highly detailed and specific guidelines within major operational areas. Under health and safety, for example, a nationally distributed manual presents a number of important principles and standards that govern practices in local councils throughout the nation. In each case, mandatory or recommended procedures are presented, along with useful leadership resources.

In most cases policies are used to guide regular, ongoing agency operations and are rather explicit and direct in their implications. In some cases, however, when unique problems or emergencies arise, a degree of managerial flexibility is needed and creative problem-solving approaches must be applied that take into account the special circumstances involved. This is particularly the case when recreation and park managers in leisure-service agencies must respond to sudden emergencies, political demands, or similar pressures.

This does not mean that the firm policy statement is an obsolete tool or should be abandoned. This would be a grave error. A well thought out and philosophically sound policy provides a solid base for departmental action; it can accommodate occasional expedient decisions or compromises under fire. However, it may also be necessary at times to use a flexible approach to problem solving within existing policy guidelines. Rather than develop rigid procedures within such areas, leisure-service managers and their boards or advisory councils may choose to develop appropriate positions that emphasize goals and desirable strategies, but that allow a degree of choice in meeting individual problem situations as they occur.

Various groups should be represented in hearings or planning sessions that lead to policymaking in such areas. These might include board or commission members, different levels of personnel in the agency itself, community residents with a stake in the problem, other government officials or community agency representatives, and experts in the field who may offer technical advice or useful information. Although policymaking is ultimately the responsibility of recreation and park boards and commissions, it should be democratically shared with those who will be affected by it and who must carry it out.

POLITICAL IMPLICATIONS OF POLICYMAKING

Particularly in government-sponsored leisure-service agencies, the recreation and park manager may be subjected to strong political pressures. He or she may be expected to hire only the "right" summer workers or provide special programs only to neighborhoods that have been loyal to the party in power. The question of political and professional integrity is discussed more fully in Chapter 16. However, it should be stressed here that public recreation and park professionals must face and live with the reality of political life in their communities.

Recognizing this, they must strive whenever possible to base policies and decisions on what is best for the community as a whole. Many managers who have done this rather than go "down the line" for the party in power have gained such a high level of community respect and support that they have been able to survive successive turnovers of power in city hall. On the other hand, the recreation and park director who is an ardent loyalist and has played the political game to the hilt may be fired the moment a new administration takes over.

Invisible power structure

The perceptive recreation and park manager will recognize that goal setting and policy determination must be carried on with consideration not only for the visible political forces in the community, but also for the invisible power structure that exists in many cities, counties, and towns. Many organizations and special-interest groups may wield greater influence on governmental affairs than elected officials and their traditional hierarchy of support. Examples of such forces include the League of Women Voters, American Legion, Knights of Columbus, Rotary Clubs, Parent-Teacher Association, legal and medical societies, police associations, sports leagues, religious bodies of various denominations, and a host of other business or social groups.

Recreation managers must have a working knowledge of the philosophy and programs of such groups and must accurately perceive the power clusters and alliances in the community. There is no substitute for regular contacts with such organizations, either as a scheduled speaker or simply as an informal visitor at monthly meetings or events. Without such contacts, recreation professionals may inadvertently make policy decisions that oppose strongly held community opinions or undermine their support among civic groups.

Although the aforementioned examples are drawn from public recreation and park departments, managers of other types of agencies, such as voluntary, therapeutic, or commercial recreation programs, should also be acutely aware of the public relations risks that come from inappropriate policy decisions in sensitive areas of concern.

Planning Process in Action

This chapter has focused on the initial phase of the planning process, which is concerned with developing a basic philosophy or mission statement, as well as related goals, objectives, and agency policies. Beyond this, planning is a process that continues throughout the life of any leisure-service organization and is a key element in each functional area of management responsibility. It is not something that happens only at the inception of a yearly program or when a new program is begun. Instead, the planning process enters into the development of budget proposals or into the consideration of new revenue sources or marketing schemes.

Planning is obviously an important part of program development and facilities design and maintenance. At every level of operations—public relations, risk management, and various other points in the ongoing operation of leisure-service agencies—planning plays a vital role.

EXAMPLE OF PLANNING MODEL

Although many approaches to the planning process are possible, it is helpful to examine a model that incorporates a number of the most commonly found elements (see box below).

YOUNG/ALLEN PLANNING MODEL*

Planning is a continuous process of obtaining, organizing, and using information systematically to make agency or community decisions. The following questions must be considered in the planning process:
1. What is the scope of the planning effort and who will be involved?
2. What outcomes are desired?
3. What resources will help the effort, and what restraints will hinder the effort?
4. What specific objectives must be achieved to accomplish the overall goals?
5. How many methods may be used to accomplish each specific objective?
6. Which method or methods are best?
7. Who is going to implement these methods and when?
8. How will the success of the planning effort be measured; if it is not successful, what changes will need to be made?

Basic Steps of Planning
Step I. Focus Planning Effort

In planning, the scope and dimensions of what is to be done should be described so that all who are involved fully understand:
1. What is to be planned.
2. What type of process will be used to plan.
3. Who is to be involved or affected by the planning effort.
4. Whether the planning effort is for immediate or long-range purposes.
Focusing helps ensure that planning is done *with* people rather than *for* people.

Step II. Conduct Community/Agency Assessment and Needs Assessment

Community or agency assessment is conducted to provide the planners with a comprehensive understanding of the resources, value system, norms, and other aspects of the community or agency involved. This, combined with information gathered from the needs assessment of community residents or agency clientele, will enable the planner to establish appropriate goals for the planning effort.

Step III. Determine Priorities and Long-Range Goals

Goal statements that reflect the needs and desires of participants or potential participants are developed within the framework of the overall mission and goals of the sponsoring leisure-service agency. These may include both immediate (short-range) goals and appropriate long-range goals.

YOUNG/ALLEN PLANNING MODEL—cont'd

Step IV. Identify Resources and Restraints

Based on the community or agency assessments, this step consists of listing and categorizing the human, physical, fiscal, and other resources of the agency, as well as the specific restraints or barriers related to the achievement of each of the goals.

Step V. Generate Alternative Methods

Methods or approaches to fulfill each short- and long-range goal can be generated in the following ways:
1. Brainstorming sessions
2. Current practices approach using methods found elsewhere
3. Authoritative approach, in which professional staff members (particularly managers) make key suggestions and decisions
4. Using neighborhood or membership advisory councils
5. Developing cooperative or interagency programs in conjunction with the planning and method-generating process

Step VI. Analyze and Select the Best Methods

Through discussion, model-building or simulation approaches are used to weigh the pros and cons of each method and to select the best method for achieving each goal, given the available resources. This may involve projecting future trends (population, economic, environmental, or other) and identifying appropriate methods to use if different future trends occur. The best methods are selected on the basis of the most accurate projections possible and the community or agency's needs and capabilities.

Step VII. Implement the Plan

The recommended actions are carried out according to the time frame developed in the plan. In program planning, for example, daily, weekly, monthly, seasonal, and special events activities will be placed within a schedule, assigned needed staff and other resources, and carried out. In facilities development planning, each of the steps in acquiring property, designing facilities, and constructing and maintaining them will be initiated.

Step VIII. Evaluate Process and Results

Process evaluation involves analyzing the full planning sequence, with emphasis on the implementation phase, to determine if the steps were carried out efficiently and effectively. Results evaluation provides information regarding the outcomes of the planning effort, mostly whether its objectives were achieved. Both types of evaluation provide feedback to the planner and serve as a means of modifying procedures and continuing to evolve new goals as needed.

*This approach is based on a model developed by Ken M. Young for Community Collaborators, Charlottesville, Va., and modified by Dr. Larry Allen at the University of Wyoming.

Other examples of planning approaches are found in later chapters of this text. It should be made clear that none of the key functions of managers, such as organizing, planning, motivating, and controlling, can be understood in isolation. They must be examined in relation to each other as part of the total effort of agency management, just as elements such as program planning, facilities design, and fiscal operations are also closely integrated tasks.

Summary

Planning is presented in this chapter as the initial process of determining a logical course of action or strategy to achieve desired outcomes. It must be based on a solid foundation, which consists of both a sound philosophy or system of values and more sharply defined goals and objectives that help an agency determine its appropriate mission. Six such philosophical approaches are presented here, including the quality-of-life, marketing, human-services, prescriptive, environmental/aesthetic/preservationist, and hedonist/individualist emphases.

Organizational goals represent broad statements of agency purpose, of which there are two types: internal or operational goals and external or outcome goals. Examples of goals statements of public, armed forces, and therapeutic recreation agencies are provided, followed by examples of objectives, which spell out goals in concrete, measurable, and usually short-term target statements.

The final section of this chapter deals with policies, which are major operational guidelines that reflect department principles and define appropriate courses of action in various areas of agency performance. Policy manuals are described, and examples of policy statements are presented. In conclusion, the political implications of policy statements are reviewed, and the point is made that the fullest possible consultation is desirable in controversial areas of policy-making.

STUDY QUESTIONS

1. Select any two of the philosophical orientations presented in the chapter (for example, quality-of-life approach) and show how they would influence programming in a specific type of leisure-service agency, such as armed forces or employee recreation program. Indicate the specific goals that would be developed for each orientation, as well as their strengths and weaknesses.
2. Explore the use of management by objectives (MBO) in the literature, including the Clegg and Chambliss article. Then develop a plan for using it in managing a specific leisure-service agency or in carrying out a major program project.
3. Select a management problem area based on the topics suggested on p. 97. Narrow down the area to identify a significant problem or difficulty facing a leisure-service manager. Then develop an appropriate policy statement to apply to this situation with valid arguments to support it.

Case 1   *Boating or Birds: A Philosophical Issue*

YOU ARE BRIAN DOLAN, managing director of a county recreation and park department. Your agency operates a small marina and boat-launching site on Bluefield Lake, a popular area for public boating and fishing. Most of the lake's perimeter is privately owned, and there is constant pressure for more access to the water.

The county also owns considerable frontage on Bluefield Creek, a somewhat marshy stream that flows into the lake. You have carried out a planning study that shows it would be feasible to dredge and widen the mouth of the creek to construct a large new extension to the marina with as many as 100 new slips and moorings and additional launching ramps. With the likelihood of supplemental funding from private, state, and federal sources, you are about to submit a proposal for building the marina addition to your county board of supervisors.

Suddenly, objections are heard from several environmental groups. They claim that the creek and the marshland surrounding it provide an irreplaceable habitat for wildlife, particularly birds. They are strongly opposed to dredging the area and building the marina addition. The board hearing is tomorrow, and the environmental groups plan to show up in force to fight your proposal.

Questions for Class Discussion and Analysis

1. As managing director of the recreation and park department, what is your philosophical position with respect to maintaining and protecting the natural environment?
2. What are your most potent, practical arguments in favor of the marina proposal?
3. What could you have done in terms of strategy to anticipate or forestall the opposition of the environmental groups?

Case 2   *Gambling for Seniors: Permissible or Prohibited?*

YOU ARE KATHY GRANDOLFI, director of a large multiservice senior center that meets daily in the parish hall of a church in your community. Among your various program activities, which include both human-service and recreational opportunities, you regularly hold bingo sessions, which are used for fund-raising purposes. You also schedule occasional "casino" nights, in which gambling games are played for small stakes. Both of these programs are popular with many participants.

The center council recommends that you plan a charter bus trip to Las Vegas over a spring weekend. Since you are in a nearby southwestern location, this would be a trip of reasonable length. You are going ahead to make arrangements, when suddenly the minister of the church and several elders call you in for a meeting. They want to discuss the gambling aspect of your program. While they have not previously objected to the bingo games or casino nights, they now have two concerns. Should gambling be a prominent part of a senior center program that meets in a church, and, if members of the senior center go to Las Vegas, will some of them lose substantial sums of money that they cannot afford?

Continued.

Case 2 cont'd	*Gambling for Seniors: Permissible or Prohibited?*

You are at the point of negotiating a new 3-year lease for your center with the church's governing board, and the gambling issue is on everybody's mind. The minister, Harold Porter, asks you to begin by giving your point of view with regard to the appropriateness of gambling as a senior center activity.

Questions for Class Discussion and Analysis

1. Define the basic goals of your senior center and then indicate the kinds of policies that might flow from these with respect to gambling as part of the program.
2. You find yourself in a somewhat hostile, even adversary relationship with the church minister and board. The gambling issue threatens to damage your formerly close and friendly relationship. How could this have been avoided or made less confrontational?
3. As the senior center director, what course of action would you recommend to deal with this situation?

REFERENCES

1. Tichy, Noel M.: *Managing Strategic Change: Technical, Political, and Cultural Dynamics,* New York, 1983, John Wiley & Sons, Inc., p. 5.

2. Neilson, William A. (Editor): *Webster's New International Dictionary,* Springfield, Mass., 1956, G. & C. Merriam Co., p. 1879.

3. *Ibid.,* p. 1842.

4. Edginton, Christopher R.: ''Organizational Goals—What Directors Think They Should Be, and Are,'' *Recreation Canada,* May 1978, p. 33.

5. *Statement of Philosophy,* Milwaukee, Wis., n.d., Department of Municipal Recreation and Adult Education.

6. *Morale, Welfare and Recreation Program Overview,* Washington, D.C., March 1982, Office of Assistant Secretary of Defense, p. 3.

7. *Therapeutic Recreation Program, Philosophy Statement,* Phildelphia, 1983, Piersol Rehabilitation Center, Hospital of University of Pennsylvania, n.p.

8. Graham, Peter J., and Klar, Lawrence, R. Jr.: *Planning and Delivering Leisure Services,* Dubuque, Iowa, 1979, William C. Brown Co., p. 25.

9. Glover, James M.: ''MBO: A Tool for Leisure Service Management,'' *Parks and Recreation,* March 1979, p. 26.

10. Clegg, Charles C., and Chambliss, George: ''Management by Objectives: A Case Study,'' *Leisure Today, Journal of Physical Education, Recreation and Dance,* April 1982, p. 45.

11. McMaster, John B.: *Optimum Management,* New York, 1980, Petrocelli Books, Inc., p. 29.

12. McChesney, James C., and Tappley, Richard A.: *Administrative Policy Manual,* Arlington, Va., 1966, National Recreation and Park Association Management Aids Bulletin No. 61, p. 5.

13. Cryder, R.S.: Presentation to Washington State Park and Recreation Conference, November 1979.

14. *''Leader's Digest of Documents,'' Policies and Procedures,* New York, n.d., Girl Scouts of the U.S.A., pp. 8-10.

Since it is ultimately people who perform the work of the organization, another essential aspect of the organizing function is deciding who is to accomplish each of the many tasks of the organization. . . . The manager matches people with work by delegating tasks and the authority, or right, to use the organization's resources to individuals. . . . The concept of organizing work and people systematically can be extended . . . to create a structure for the entire organization.[1]

Personnel Management
The Directing Function

*P*ersonnel management is a key factor in the success of all types of organizations; it is essential in maintaining a smoothly functioning, productive enterprise. Although some leisure-service agencies may have hundreds of employees and others may have only a few, the task of hiring, training, supervising, and motivating personnel is a critical responsibility of managers. These functions are described in detail in this chapter, with emphasis on the actual procedures and guidelines followed in most agencies. It presents the formal, "by-the-book" approach to personnel management and is therefore subtitled "the *directing* function."

In contrast, Chapter 7 provides a fuller analysis of job enrichment, delegation of functions, conflict resolution, and similar processes that reflect the contemporary "behavioral science" concepts described earlier in this text. Since it is concerned with a less formal approach to personnel management and ways of encouraging employee productivity through participative management approaches, it is subtitled "the *motivating* function."

Employment Practices in Leisure-Service Agencies

Any examination of personnel practices in governmental, business, or other social agencies must begin with the conditions of employment. What kinds of jobs do people hold? How are they hired and trained to do their work? What is the nature of supervision, how are employees evaluated, and how do they advance within the agency structure?

In all types of leisure-service agencies, classification and standardization of job titles are essential to effective organization. They provide the basis for defining job responsibilities clearly, having comparable salary levels for similar qualifications or job demands, and establishing a career ladder with opportunity for promotion within the system.

PUBLIC AGENCIES
Personnel classification systems

In public leisure-service agencies, positions are frequently grouped into classes and series within a civil service structure that applies to almost all government employment. The term "class" refers to a group of positions that have roughly comparable responsibilities and qualifications, which may be stated in terms of education, previous experience, and specific knowledge or job skills. Positions on the same class level may be found in different departments and are usually subject to the same policies regarding pay, fringe benefits, promotions, and similar personnel matters.

A *series* represents a form of vertical classification of employees, usually found within a particular department or specialization, but with a gradation of skill and qualifications, as well as different levels of salary and status. For example, a series of titles within a recreation department might run from recreation trainee or assistant through several grades of recreation leader, ultimately moving up to recreation supervisor or center director.

Classification systems provide an overall structure through which jobs are defined and fitted onto an organization chart and a civil service plan. Each position is identified as to class or grade and is assigned a salary range, specific work responsibilities, required qualifications (usually meaning education and experience and sometimes including an examination), and personnel benefits such as holidays, vacations, leave, hospitalization, retirement plan, and similar benefits.

Job categories

Large municipal or county recreation and park departments employ a wide variety of workers. For example, the civil service positions in a large municipal department include such titles as administrative analyst, architect, building maintenance superintendent, brick mason, camp director, carpenter, cement finisher, city planner, civil engineer, clerk stenographer, and construction project technician.

It would be a mistake to think that all these job categories represent specialized professional employment in recreation and parks. However, every effort should be made to imbue employees who are nonprofessional leisure-service workers with a sense of the mission and purpose of the agency. Through meetings, house publications, and training, they should gain an awareness of the department's work and a sense of pride and loyalty that increases their effectiveness and pays rewards in improved public relations.

Customarily, positions in public recreation and park departments have been assigned to three levels: *administrative, supervisory,* and *leadership.* Although both administrative and supervisory positions are thought of as part of management, administrative positions are considered executive or top level, while supervisory positions are described as secondary or middle management level.

Administrative positions

Depending on the community, regional practices, or civil service codes, the specific title of the individual who is the chief administrative officer of a public recreation and park department may be general manager, director, administrator, superintendent, or commissioner. Persons at this level are mainly responsible for planning and implementing a recreation and park program to meet the needs and interests of the total population of a community.

Specific responsibilities of chief administrators include (1) coordinating and directing the overall work of the department; (2) directing the acquisition, planning, construction, and maintenance of facilities; (3) recruiting, selecting, assigning, and supervising all department personnel; (4) preparing and administering an annual budget; (5) planning, organizing, and implementing programs; (6) maintaining an effective public relations and community relations program; (7) initiating a systematic risk management and accident prevention program; (8) evaluating the department's overall effectiveness; and (9) providing inspirational and creative leadership to all staff members.

Supervisory positions

These represent a secondary or middle level of management. Supervisors are normally responsible for overseeing operations within a geographical area or district of a community or are in charge of a major facility or area of program service. They have a degree of administrative authority, particularly over line personnel who work directly under them. They also serve as representatives of the chief administrative officer, carrying out his or her directives and promoting overall department policies. They typically have all of the responsibilities that chief administrators have *within* their districts, such as coordinating activities, managing facilities, supervising personnel, contributing to the preparation and supervision of budgets, and planning and carrying out programs.

Leadership positions

Leadership positions are full-time professional-level jobs in which individuals are responsible for planning, organizing, and directly supervising recreation programs in one or more facilities. They may also involve being a specialist in a given area of activity, such as sports and games or the performing arts, or working with a special population, such as the aged or handicapped.

Typically departments have several grades of recreation leader, such as leader I, II, and III or senior leader or in other cases recreation aide or assistant leader. Such positions normally involve a lower level of job responsibility and expertise and more limited management functions than more advanced positions.

NEWER APPROACHES TO POSITION ANALYSIS

The preceding section of this chapter presented a traditional approach to defining job levels, titles, and functions. It applies chiefly to public recreation and park departments and less so to voluntary, therapeutic, private, or commercial agencies. With this in mind, attempts have been made to analyze positions within the broad field of leisure services in a more generic way. The New York State Recreation and Park Society, for example, offers an alternative way of identifying job levels and responsibilities in a publication entitled "Guide to Personnel Criteria and Personnel Standards."[2]

Functional classification

In a functional classification, three levels of responsibility are identified: managerial, logistical, and operational.

Managerial units include top and middle management positions with such titles as administrator, commissioner, director, manager, superintendent, and assistant superintendent.

Logistical units usually comprise *staff* personnel, with titles such as budget officer, planner, designer, personnel officer, or public relations officer.

Operational units involve the *line* personnel directly responsible for program execution and plant operation. Titles may be classified as generalist (supervisor, senior leader, etc.), specialist (aquatics director, dramatics instructor, etc.), or facilities-related (caretaker, engineer, groundskeeper, etc.).

Whatever method of job classification is used, thorough and accurate job description sheets must be prepared for each position in a recreation and park department. These typically include *title, civil service grade* (if governmental), *listing of responsibilities and functions, required knowledge and skills, minimum acceptable education and previous experience,* and *physical or medical standards.*

To assist in this process, it is important that each position be carefully analyzed to determine exactly what is required of those who fill it. Feldman and Arnold point out that no one "right" way of doing a job applies to all different agencies. What is best or most appropriate for one organization may be inappropriate for another. Therefore each leisure-service agency should develop its own job analyses. These must be *behavior centered,* focusing on the actual behaviors needed for effective on-the-job performance, and *reliable,* in the sense that different job analysts will agree on their components. They should be *updated regularly,* since job requirements tend to change over time.[3]

JOB DESCRIPTIONS IN OTHER AGENCIES

In addition to local public recreation and park departments, many other types of leisure-service agencies develop job classification systems and descriptions to standardize and simplify their personnel operations. Several examples follow.

National Park Service

Like most major government employers, the National Park Service in the U.S. Department of the Interior provides a systematic set of job descriptions for civil service positions on various levels. For example, it outlines the position of park ranger with respect to duties, location, training, career potential, application procedures, and basic qualifications.

Duties of park rangers in the National Park Service include the following: (1) planning and carrying out conservation efforts to protect plant and animal life; (2) planning and conducting programs of public safety, including law enforcement and rescue work, (3) setting up and directing interpretive programs, such as slide shows and tours; (4) coordinating environmental education programs; (5) planning recreation programs; and (6) performing administrative, community relations, and other related tasks.

To qualify for appointment as a park ranger at civil service grade GS-5, applicants must meet one of the following three basic requirements:

1. Complete a full 4-year program in an accredited college or university leading to a bachelor's degree with at least 24 semester hours in one or not more than two of the following fields: park and recreation management, field-related natural science, history, archaeology, police science, business administration, behavioral sciences, or closely related subjects.

2. Complete 3 years of park or conservation experience providing a good general understanding of systems, methods, and administrative practice; have the ability

to analyze and solve problems and communicate effectively, and similar skills.

3. Attain appropriate combinations of education and experience as defined in items 1 and 2, with an academic year of study comprising 30 semester hours being considered equivalent to 9 months of experience.

On higher levels of employment in the National Park Service, such as park ranger grade GS-7, graduate study in park and recreation management or related fields or acceptable performance on the Federal Professional and Administrative Career Examination (PACE) represent acceptable alternatives for qualifying.

Veterans Administration

Within the U.S. Veterans Administration, career lines are established for entry-level professional positions in five specialized areas, beginning at grade GS-5. These are: recreation therapist and creative arts therapist (with specialization in art, dance, music, or psychodrama). National job descriptions identify the following work descriptions and statement of qualifications:

> Recreation Therapists perform professional work requiring application of a knowledge of the concepts, principles, and practices of recreation therapy, and the use of recreational modalities to maintain the physical and/or mental health or to achieve the physical and/or mental rehabilitation of patients. . . . They evaluate the history, interests, aptitudes, and skills of patients by interviews, inventories, tests, and measurements, and use such findings, along with medical records, and the therapy orders of physicians or nurses, to develop and implement recreation therapy . . . for individual patients [which are] directed toward achieving such therapeutic objectives as diminishing emotional stress of patients, providing a sense of achievement, channeling energies and interests into acceptable forms of behavior, aiding physical and mental rehabilitation, and promoting successful community reentry.

As an example of current personnel staffing patterns in this agency, the St. Louis, Mo., Veterans Administration Medical Center offers a comprehensive recreation treatment program in the bed sections of psychiatry, chemical dependency, spinal cord injury, cardiac rehabilitation, nursing home care, and rehabilitation. Job requirements are as follows:

> Entry level for the professional therapeutic recreation specialist requires at least a minimum of a bachelor's degree in therapeutic recreation or recreation with a therapeutic emphasis plus a clinical internship experience in a therapeutic setting. . . . All therapists are clinically privileged yearly by the St. Louis VAMC and currently hold American Red Cross Senior Lifesaving, CPR and First Aid certifications.
>
> Salaries (1984) currently range from $13,837 to $20,965 for therapeutic recreation specialists . . . from the entry level of GS-5 ($13,837) depending on paid work experience in therapeutic recreation, up to GS-9 ($20,965). Each year, federal employees receive a cost-of-living increase in salary. In addition, the federal system has a sick leave policy, annual leave policy, health and life insurance coverage.[4]

Armed forces: U.S. Navy personnel openings

Similarly, the various branches of the U.S. armed forces regularly advertise a wide range of positions for recreation specialists both in the United States and abroad. To illustrate, in 1984 the Naval Military Personnel Command in Washington, D.C., announced numerous management positions at Navy bases or on shipboard, including many that involved the operation of clubs, messes, or other special facilities. As the following examples show, these positions often involve special management skills in marketing, facilities operations, public relations, or different activity areas[5]:

Naval Air Station, Brunswick, ME is recruiting for an Outdoor Recreation Area Manager, UA-188-07 to run a 45 acre outdoor recreation area. It includes a 9 hole golf course, driving range, pro shop, ski slope, cross country ski trails, equipment rental and archery. Applicant should have prior golf course management experience, skiing and retail. SF-171's should go to MWR Dept., Personnel Div., Naval Air Station, Box 34, Brunswick, ME 04011.

Naval Air Station, Fallon, NV is recruiting for a Recreation Specialist (Special Interest Coordinator), a Recreation Specialist, UA-188-07 to run the ticket and tours, youth and family special events and marketing. SF-171's should go to Recreation Services Department, Bldg. 394, Naval Air Station, Fallon, NV 89406. Ann # NAF-06-84.

Naval Air Station Barbers Pt, HI is recruiting for a Recreation Services Director, UA-1101-12. Directs planning, promoting, organizing and administering the athletic and Recreation Programs at the station and provides a well rounded continuing program designed to serve the needs of military personnel and their dependents. Directs and supervises preparation and execution of budget annually which included appropriated and nonappropriated funds. Send SF-171's to: Personnel Office, Recreational Services Department, Bldg. 55, Naval Air Station Barbers Pt, HI 96862.

Naval Construction Battalion Center, Port Hueneme, CA is recruiting for a Visual Information Specialist, UA-1084-7 to conduct a complete marketing program to promote the visibility of Recreation Services Division and encourage maximum participation by the base community. SF-171's to Civilian Personnel Office, Code 231 NAF, Naval Construction Battalion Center, Port Hueneme, CA 93043.[5]

POSITIONS IN VOLUNTARY AGENCIES

In the federal agencies described, job titles, grades, and eligibility requirements are developed nationally, although hiring in a particular region, hospital, or base may reflect local needs and priorities. In the voluntary agency field, various national organizations develop personnel guidelines and hiring criteria, although hiring on the local level is influenced by regional practices or priorities. Several examples of the job descriptions and qualifications found in such agencies follow.

Boys' Clubs of America

Any individual employed on a full-time basis in a managerial or program leadership role in a Boys' Club affiliated with the national organization or on the national professional staff is eligible for certification as a professional worker, provided that the following requirements are met:

1. *Education.* A degree in an appropriate field from an accredited four-year college.
2. *Training.* A total of ten training credits to be gained according to an approved formula from such sources as: (a) events sponsored by the National Manpower Development

Committee or Regional Manpower Development Committees of Boys' Clubs of America; (b) attendance at a Boys' Clubs of America National Conference; (c) participation in administrative conferences; or (d) involvement in other forms of non–Boys' Club training, to be approved by the National Board of Certification.

3. *Experience.* At least two years of full-time paid experience in a managerial or program position in a Boys' Club affiliated with the national organization or on the National Staff, including current employment in such a setting, with an acceptable record of performance.

Young Men's Christian Association

Professional positions within the YMCA include the following:

General Director. Directs the work of the local YMCA within the framework of general policies determined by the Board of Directors; acts as executive officer of the Board of Directors; guides the process by which policies are developed, and carries them out; is responsible for budgetary management, personnel functions, program direction and facilities operation.

Executive Director. Directly assists the General Director in administering the total operation of the branch, including interpreting and executing established policies, maintaining an adequate staff, evaluating the program, develop short- and long-range goals and objectives, producing and carrying out budget plans, developing job descriptions, employing and supervising personnel.

Youth Director. Assists boys and girls through organized groups and informal education to develop attitudes and social habits consistent with Christian principles; integrates programs with school, church, family and other community concerns; guides the Youth Program Committee of the Board of Directors; identifies youth needs and develops programs to meet them; interprets YMCA to public; manages business aspects of youth department, and operates day camp and sometimes resident camp programs.

Other specialized professional positions within the modern YMCA include the youth outreach director, physical education director, program director, and membership director.

In addition to personal qualifications, professional staff members should have as a basic requirement an undergraduate degree or equivalent in a field such as religion, philosophy, history, psychology, or other behavioral or social sciences. This should be supplemented by specialized professional training in group leadership, counseling, community organization, organizational leadership, and the study of YMCA history, objectives, programs, administration, and financing.

These examples are fairly typical of employment practices and required qualifications in many voluntary agencies throughout the United States and Canada today.

THERAPEUTIC AND COMMERCIAL RECREATION

The trend in recent years has been to screen leisure-service job applicants not only regarding their education or experience, but also with respect to the specialized competencies needed for on-the-job success.

Therapeutic recreation

A major influence in therapeutic recreation has been the national registration/certification plan established by the National Therapeutic Recreation Society, which has developed national standards for hiring personnel on different levels of professional responsibility. In addition to this approach, there has been a strong effort to determine the skills and knowledge essential to successful job performance. A study at Temple University determined that master's degree curricula in this field should provide high-level competency in the following functions (placed in rank order of importance):

1. Recruiting and hiring staff
2. Formulating a department philosophy
3. Functioning on treatment team
4. Conducting therapeutic recreation activities
5. Preparing treatment plans
6. Implementing basic recreation programs
7. Doing functional assessment of patients
8. Promoting community integration of clients
9. Supervising paid staff
10. Leisure counselling
11. Developing departmental philosophy
12. Developing policies and procedures
13. Conducting in-service training
14. Maintaining supplies and equipment
15. Doing activity analysis
16. Writing clinical reports
17. Conducting program evaluations
18. Preparing and supervising budget
19. Doing interagency coordination
20. Supervising volunteers
21. Recruiting and hiring personnel
22. Supervising practicum students
23. Taking part in administrative meetings
24. Doing administrative reports
25. Carrying out public relations
26. Monitoring relevant legislation
27. Consultation[6]

These task functions were found to be the most important competencies for therapeutic recreation specialists working in disability areas such as mental health, mental retardation, geriatrics, physical disability, corrections, and drug and alcohol rehabilitation.

Commercial recreation

A similar approach is found in the employment practices of commercial recreation organizations. Normally, those who hire employees for profit-oriented businesses such as amusement complexes, travel agencies, outdoor sports centers, fitness spas, entertainment centers, dance or music studios, bowling alleys or billiard halls, or other types of companies, are less concerned with the formal education of candidates than they are with their past employment experience, personality, and ability to do the job.

In some cases they may stipulate college degrees or specific technical course background as important qualifications. Normally, however, commercial employers are not convinced that a degree in recreation and parks is essential for most employees.

As a specific example of qualifications needed by employees in the field of commercial recreation, a research report published at Michigan State University outlined the job specifications and skills needed by ski area managers. Based on a study of over 50 ski centers in a number of states, the following areas were identified as essential, ranked in order of importance:

1. General administration and management techniques
2. Control ticket sales
3. Labor cost control
4. Apply safety regulations and understand liability
5. Determine types of tickets (to be sold)
6. Select lift equipment
7. Personnel management
8. Carry out lift preventative maintenance
9. Accounting
10. Institute ticket and traffic control
11. Public relations
12. Apply safety checking procedures
13. Design and develop ski hills
14. Utilize the ski school and accident prevention program
15. Install lifts
16. Marketing
17. Develop ski packages
18. Finance
19. Liability insurance
20. Carry out evacuation and first aid
21. Operate or integrate ski school activities
22. Apply theory of snow grooming and snow textures
23. Operate ground lifts
24. Carry out mechanical maintenance
25. Operate aerial lifts
26. Do advertising and promotion
27. Use various types of snow grooming equipment[7]

A great deal of employment in commercial recreation concerns is part-time or seasonal. At theme parks, for example, weekends, holidays, and special vacation periods markedly expand the need for employees, which may then slacken off abruptly at other times. The Old Country, Busch Gardens, in Williamsburg, Va., requires hundreds of employees to operate the park's 22 restaurants and 29 shops and staff numerous rides, stage shows, and other attractions. As many as 7500 applications are received in a year, chiefly from high school and college students. Desaulniers writes:

> Qualifications vary for the different seasonal jobs. For example, many of the seasonal
> employees deal with the public on a day-to-day basis. They may be chosen for their friend-

liness and ability to communicate with others. Another important qualification is availability. Working at a theme park is not a nine-to-five job, but one that requires a flexible schedule with the ability to work weekends and evenings. Age is also a consideration. Most of the jobs require that employees be 18 years of age or older. Yet there are some positions available for 16- and 17-year-olds. Qualifications for behind-the-scenes jobs . . . emphasize the desire and ability to work.[8]

Employment Standards in Leisure-Service Agencies

Although patterns vary among different types of agencies, there has been a steady drive toward professionalization in the leisure-service field. This has included the development of statewide or national standards for employment, particularly in public and therapeutic recreation agencies. Such standards include certification, registration, and civil service job requirements.

CERTIFICATION AND REGISTRATION

Certification and registration are closely related procedures, and the two terms are frequently used interchangeably. For example, in fields such as occupational or physical therapy, certification usually means to be registered or approved by a state or national body responsible for qualifying individuals within a given area of service. It makes an individual eligible for employment within a professional field and is customarily based on such elements as education, job experience, examinations, and personal recommendations.

In a number of states, formal certification procedures for recreation and park employment have been established by legislation, and in such cases the process of screening and approving candidates is a legal one and mandated for employment. The most common pattern, however, has been for state or provincial recreation and park societies to develop registration plans through which qualified professionals might have their credentials reviewed and approved. In the early 1970s a National Registration Board was established in the United States, through which the National Recreation and Park Association (NRPA) might review and approve the registration plans of various state societies and encourage reciprocal recognition of plans by the different states. In addition, the National Therapeutic Recreation Society (NTRS) developed a national registration system that screens workers in this field.

Several thousand therapeutic recreation workers were registered within this system, making a strong impact on professionalization in this field. In the early 1980s it was transformed into a certification process with two levels of job titles (professional and paraprofessional) to be administered by the National Council for Therapeutic Recreation Certification, administratively affiliated with the NRPA.[9]

ACCREDITATION

Approximately 350 colleges and universities offer degree programs in recreation, parks, and leisure studies. In the late 1970s, the NRPA and the Society of Park and Recreation Educators, in cooperation with the American Association for Leisure and Recreation, set in motion an accreditation process, designed to establish appropriate standards for professional education in this field. By the mid-1980s approximately 50 baccalaureate degree programs had been approved by this plan.

In the early 1980s the NRPA Board of Trustees approved a plan designed to link the three elements of certification, accreditation, and continuing education. This new Model Certification Plan for Recreation, Park Resources and Leisure-Services Personnel was designed to provide a national means of upgrading the educational and experiential qualifications of individuals working in the recreation and parks field.

The NRPA plan included a stipulation that individuals seeking national certification after Nov. 1, 1986 would be required to hold a degree from a college or university approved by the National Council on Accreditation. In addition, it required that approved practitioners be awarded a minimum of two Continuing Education Units (CEUs) every 24 months from their date of certification. Such efforts have been designed to upgrade the qualifications of personnel working in the leisure-service field, although they depend on the voluntary compliance of leisure-service agencies for enforcement.

CIVIL SERVICE

At present, most governmental recreation and park departments rely on civil service procedures to screen applicants. These are based on a system of examinations and eligibility lists, which may be applied on a countywide or statewide basis or through municipal civil service commissions. Although their original intention was to provide hiring procedures that ensure a merit-based system of appointments and promotions that would not be subject to political interference, there is widespread discontent with the way civil service has operated in the recreation and park field.

Cumbersome hiring procedures make it difficult to hire personnel when needed or when available. The relevance of the examinations themselves is challenged. Too often civil service officials and examiners are almost totally ignorant of the recreation and park field and the demands made of its practitioners; their examinations reflect this lack of understanding. Fortunately, within the past several years, a number of state recreation and park societies have succeeded in upgrading civil service requirements and providing input that has helped examinations and other hiring procedures become more relevant to actual professional needs.

In nongovernmental agencies, civil service standards obviously do not apply. However, organizations such as the National Employee Services and Recreation Association (NESRA) have established personnel standards for individuals who seek certification in the employee recreation field. State departments of health frequently set minimum standards for recreation or activity therapy personnel working in nursing homes or other residential care settings.

Process of Personnel Management

We now examine the process of personnel management, including recruitment and hiring of personnel; orientation and in-service training; establishing sound personnel policies; effective supervision leading to positive departmental relationships and personal development of employees; and use of volunteers.

RECRUITMENT, SELECTION, AND HIRING OF PERSONNEL

Recruitment, selection, and hiring constitute key elements in the entire personnel process. The goal is to employ the best-qualified men and women to fill openings in the department. The process has several distinct phases.

Recruitment

JOB DESCRIPTION   A written job description should be prepared giving essential information about the responsibilities, salary, personnel benefits, and hiring qualifications and procedures of the position to be filled. It should be concise and attractive, completely accurate, and approved by the department's personnel office or the community's personnel director.

PUBLICIZING THE POSITION   Announcement of the job opening should be carried out with the use of newsletters, mailing of brochures, announcements at professional meetings, direct correspondence, or placement of the opening with the personnel placement service of professional organizations. State or regional recreation and park societies frequently maintain listings of job openings.

CONSIDERATION OF PAST EMPLOYEES   Frequently recruitment may be carried out directly by considering past employees for positions. Many recreation and park departments employ college students during the summer or on a part-time basis during the winter and spring. When they have graduated, they may be considered for full-time employment, with the obvious advantage of having the department familiar with their work and vice versa.

Selection and hiring

SELECTION PROCEDURE   Normally the selection procedure includes (1) having the candidate fill out a detailed job application form; (2) detailed consideration of the candidate's background, past performance, and references; (3) a personal interview with the candidate; (4) a written examination, usually part of a state, county, or municipal civil service series; (5) a physical examination; (6) a character investigation; and (7) in some cases a performance test in specific skill areas.

JOB APPLICATION FORM   An example of a job application form developed by the Nassau County, N.Y., Department of Recreation and Parks (Fig. 6-1) includes (1) personal details about the applicant; (2) educational background; (3) employment history; (4) personal references; (5) recreational interests and involvement; and (6) listing of specific skills in administrative, supervisory, or leadership areas. This form is used as the basis for interviewers to make hiring recommendations and as a convenient reference source through which department administrators can locate a wide variety of needed skills among staff members.

Customarily, based on performance on examinations, the applicant is placed on an eligibility list, with the appointment made from the three highest-ranking candidates. Appointment may then be made when the opening occurs. In some cases a candidate

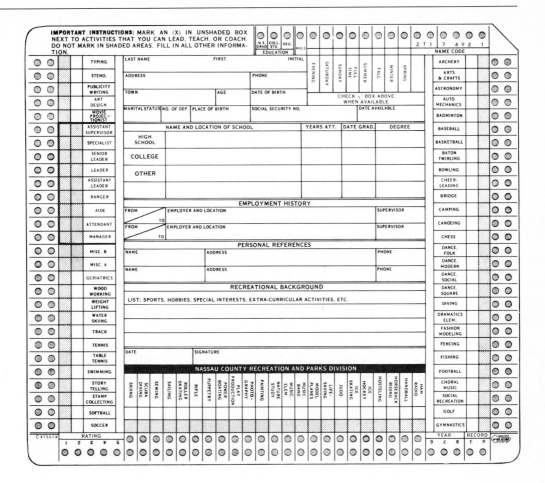

FIG. 6-1   Job application form, Nassau County, N.Y.

may be appointed on a provisional basis because no examination that applies to the position in question has been scheduled. At a later point, he or she would be required to take the examination.

SELECTION PROCESS   Depending on the level of the position to be filled, the selection and screening process may be relatively brief or may be complex and drawn out. For example, in a search for an outstanding new superintendent of recreation for the Peoria, Ill., Park District, more than 5 months elapsed between the resignation of the previous superintendent and the selection of a new one. In this process, representatives of five separate public agencies in Illinois joined together to develop the state's first personnel assessment center in the recreation and parks field.

James Brademas described the personnel assessment center as an innovative method of employee selection, which seeks to provide more complete data under standardized conditions about an individual's capability for performing a job than can normally be gained from personal interviews, supervisory ratings, letters of reference, or written or oral tests alone. Brademas writes:

> An assessment center puts six final candidates through a series of group and individual exercises and interviews designed to simulate the conditions of a supervisory/managerial job, and determines if they have the skills and abilities necessary to perform the job. It brings out the candidates' job related behavior which is observed, recorded, and evaluated by a team of trained assessors (usually managers one or two steps above the position to be filled). The assessors conduct the interviews and observe all scheduled exercises. . . . All six candidates go through the center at the same time. While it may be feasible to work with fewer candidates, six provides an ideal level of interaction in the group process.[10]

INTERVIEW TECHNIQUES   Too often, selection methods such as the personal interview are carried out poorly and provide ineffective results. DeAnne Rosenberg writes:

> Interviewing is a great guessing game—perhaps the greatest yet invented. If you have ever interviewed and then hired a person who looked and sounded as if he or she were perfect for the job and then turned out to be a real disaster, you know the problems. More than 90 percent of the people who perform at an unsatisfactory level because of low motivation, poor attitude, or poor interpersonal skills could have been easily spotted in the interview if the interviewer had known what to look for. It doesn't take a personnel expert to have that clarity of vision.[11]

Preparatory work should be done before an interview is scheduled. The candidate's references should be carefully checked by either mail or telephone, with the confidentiality of responses assured. Psychological tests are sometimes given. The individual's background should be thoroughly examined to determine the appropriateness of his or her experience or education and to identify possible unexplained gaps in employment, too frequent job changes, or other signals of personal or professional instability or difficulty.

The goals of the actual interview are several: (1) to gather fuller information about the relevance of the applicant's experience and education to the position; (2) to assess the applicant's personality and character, including apparent levels of motivation, achievement drive, leadership quality, and personal style; and (3) to evaluate the applicant's overall intelligence, adaptability, and problem-solving or analytical ability. Interviews may range from structured question and answer sessions, in which employers ask exactly the same questions of each candidate, to much more flexible and unstructured sessions in which the candidate is encouraged to "run with the ball."

In general, interviews should be carried out in a comfortable and private setting and should be as pleasant and unpressured as possible. Candidates should be put at ease. The interviewer should permit them to respond fully and should show a sincere interest in all responses. The employer should avoid arguing or disagreeing with the interviewee and should seek to be as positive and objective as possible throughout while remaining fully in control of the session. Questions may be direct, such as eliciting specific information, attitudes, or ideas, or they may be open-ended.

EQUAL EMPLOYMENT OPPORTUNITY A final important aspect of the screening and selection process involves the need to comply with equal employment opportunity regulations for both moral and legal reasons. In all types of agencies or businesses today, avoiding any form of discrimination based on religion, sex, national origin, race, marital status, age, disability, or character is essential. Questions in these areas may be asked only when there is a clear need to determine a bona fide occupational qualification. Numerous local, state, and federal regulations deal with this problem, and before embarking on the hiring process, employers or department heads should check with their personnel managers, municipal officials, or lawyers regarding these regulations and the procedures that have been designed to satisfy them. (See Chapter 14 for a fuller discussion of legal aspects of hiring practices.)

MAKING THE DECISION In making the final decision about hiring a candidate, Feldman and Arnold point out that two basic options are available for combining information to arrive at a sound selection. The first, which they describe as the *intuitive judgment* or *clinical* approach, relies on a manager within the organization to review all the information on an applicant and then to make a hiring decision based on his or her best judgment and influenced by the overall impression that the applicant has created. The second method, known as the *statistical approach,* requires that all of the applicant's qualities and skills be rated numerically, with those most critical in job performance being given heavier weight. Hiring decisions are based on the final scores of all applicants.[12]

The vast majority of selection decisions in organizations are made by intuitive judgment. Thus it is essential that as many involved persons as possible be consulted in the process and have input into the final judgment.

The practice of "trial periods" (not to be confused with probationary periods) is being experimented with, particularly in hiring for middle management posts. The candidate is asked to spend a period of time—a half or full day, for example—observing the job setting, discussing the new position, and interacting with potential coworkers. This brief "trial period" can be very helpful in reaching the final decision on whether to hire an applicant.

APPOINTMENT AND PROBATION

After being hired, candidates normally undergo a 3- to 6-month probationary period. New employees should be carefully observed and evaluated during this period. If their performance is satisfactory, they are then eligible for permanent employment and may not be discharged except for cause, according to the personnel procedures or union contracts that normally govern such actions.

The entire process of recruitment and selection is a key one in selecting the best candidates to fill open positions. Often the vigor, efficiency, and overall image of a recreation and park agency are dependent on its ability to hire the best-qualified and most capable individuals for entry-level positions. In part this is dependent on freedom from political dictation and manipulation in hiring, and every administrator should strive for the freedom to hire the best candidates, regardless of political influence.

ORIENTATION AND IN-SERVICE EDUCATION
Orientation

The first weeks or months of an employee's job experience must provide a thorough orientation. This might include such elements as a tour of the department and exposure to its various divisions and functions, a careful outlining of all responsibilities and procedures, and a period of thorough supervision, with in some cases the individual working directly as an assistant in a center or other facility before being given more independent responsibility.

A key element in the orientation should be giving the worker a departmental personnel manual that includes detailed descriptions of the legal structure and organization of the department, personnel practices and obligations, guides for leaders in various settings, and a statement of the objectives of the department.

As an illustration of the orientation process, the program for therapeutic recreation field-placement students in the Patient Activities Department of the Clinical Center of the National Institutes of Health in Bethesda, Md. includes the following elements. The first 2 weeks of the student's internship is devoted to a general orientation to the department, with visits to each program area, meetings with program area supervisors, and sessions within each of the Clinical Center's ancillary service areas.[13]

In-service education

After the orientation period, there should be a well-organized program of in-service education that heightens employees' understanding of their work, improves their skills, and generally enhances professional growth. In too many departments, insufficient attention is paid to this need. This is the most sensitive and impressionable period for a new employee, but often, even in apparently sophisticated departments, new workers are given only a brief orientation and left to fend for themselves. In-service education includes several key elements.

INDIVIDUAL CONFERENCES WITH SUPERVISORS Workers should be regularly observed and should have the opportunity to meet with their supervisors to discuss their work in a nonthreatening, constructive fashion.

STAFF MEETINGS At various levels, staff meetings contribute to in-service training. The staff of a large center or district or even the entire recreation staff of a department may meet monthly to be informed of departmental plans, policies, and similar matters and to take part in problem-solving discussions or project planning. Individual members of the staff may be asked to report on aspects of their work, or committees may be appointed to study special problems and present them to the group. Individuals who have attended professional conferences may be asked to report back to the staff on these meetings.

SPECIAL INSTITUTES These are short-term training workshops, usually dealing with a special activity within the recreation program, such as theater, arts and crafts, sports, or camping and nature activities. They may also deal with special programs, such as

Charles Russo

R.T. Miller

Clifford R. Yeich

Staff training programs of Reading, Pa., Recreation and Park Department include first aid and outdoor games workshops. Leaders conduct games festival in the town's main square.

activities for the mentally retarded or the development of golden age clubs. Institutes may last for only a day or two or may extend over a period of several days. Such institutes may be staffed by experts from the department itself or from neighboring departments or professional organizations, or they may be conducted in cooperation with nearby colleges or universities.

PRESEASON TRAINING INSTITUTES Customarily, preseason institutes are held before the summer season and train seasonal employees for work on playgrounds and other special programs. In some cases several municipal departments may join together to sponsor such a training institute. Topics assigned might include the following:

1. Goals and objectives of recreation programs
2. Orientation to the recreation and parks department in terms of major personnel, divisions, officials, and so on
3. Guidelines for scheduling activities
4. Responsibilities of playground leaders, personnel practices, rules of employment, and characteristics of effective leadership
5. Specific training sessions in program areas
6. Guidelines for maintaining safe programs, basic first aid methods, and instructions on steps to take in case of an accident

IN-SERVICE TRAINING COURSES In-service training courses are comparable to institutes, except that they usually are extended over a period of time, with perhaps one morning or early afternoon a week devoted to attendance. In small cities one such course might also be offered during the winter session. In large cities several such courses might be offered simultaneously in different districts of the city. The same topics might be covered in each district, but on a rotating basis. Normally, in-service training programs are compulsory when scheduled during work hours although the department administrator may designate them for certain personnel only. In some departments they may be given as weekend or evening classes and attended voluntarily.

OTHER IN-SERVICE EDUCATION METHODS In addition to the preceding approaches, staff members may be encouraged, given brief leaves, and even assisted financially to attend national or regional conferences in recreation and parks.

They may also be encouraged to attend college or university courses in recreation and parks leadership and administration or to work toward appropriate degrees, with adjustments made in their schedules to make this possible.

A library may be maintained with books and magazines in the recreation field, and staff members should be encouraged to read and make use of these.

Staff members may be encouraged to join professional organizations and participate in their activities, in part because of their value in professional development. Visits may be arranged for staff members to see recreation and park departments in neighboring communities as a form of in-service education.

In any recreation department or agency, in-service training must be recognized as a key aspect of personnel administration. It is not enough to schedule several meetings and clinics throughout the year almost at random and then conclude that the job has been done. Instead, Dimock suggests that the training program should be carefully worked out with as many staff members as possible participating in its planning. He identifies six key steps to developing in-service education programs:

1. Collecting information on staff needs and interests
2. Establishing specific objectives for training
3. Planning a training design with sequence and continuity
4. Preparing specific training activities and events
5. Conducting the training program
6. Evaluating the program[14]

TRAINING IN OTHER SETTINGS The content and organization of in-service education programs may vary widely in different types of agencies, depending on the needs and capabilities of each organization. For example, the Boy Scouts of America operates with a relatively small core of paid professionals and many thousands of volunteer adult leaders. The national headquarters of the organization therefore develops an extensive training program for leaders with national and regional training events, clearly stated standards and goals, training manuals, and award certificates. Such programs, which are carried out by many other youth organizations, ensure a constant staff development process for both new and veteran volunteer leaders.

In a commercial organization such as The Old Country, Busch Gardens, job training may include slide presentations, practicing ride operations without people, operating cash registers, and learning basic food preparation and cleanliness. At appropriate times the Old Country may hold a practice day for employees' friends and families, which may serve as a ''dress rehearsal'' for park employees. As employees gain experience in such tasks as being ride operators, zoo attendants, or food service workers, they may move on to managerial positions. Desaulniers writes:

> As an employee advances in the organization to the position of unit supervisor, area supervisor, or lead, he or she receives additional training in the form of three 4-hour sessions, or leadership modules, which cover the following subjects: (1) The Old Country business philosophies, including leadership styles, supervisor responsibilities, and employee welfare; (2) communication; (3) motivation or building a productive working climate.[15]

Many hospitals and other treatment centers conduct effective in-service educational programs. In some cases these are specially designed to meet the needs of college fieldwork students who are assigned to their recreational therapy departments. For example, Beatty Memorial Hospital, a large psychiatric hospital in Westville, Ind., has designed an extensive training program for fieldwork students to provide: (1) an understanding of the causes, development, and treatment of mental illness; (2) an understanding of the role of recreation in the treatment of the mentally ill; (3) clinical experience under close supervision in a psychiatric treatment program; and (4) an understanding of professional ethics and responsibility.

In Beatty Memorial Hospital these objectives are achieved through a 480-hour training program, including the following:

1. Orientation—tour of hospital areas, facilities, and clinical and administrative staff (20 hours)
2. Clinical psychopathology—operational definitions, classification, and introduction to mental disorders (130 hours)
3. Orientation to recreation philosophy, objectives, functions, and organization (20 hours)
4. Music, occupational therapy, and volunteer services (40 hours)
5. Observation and assistance experience in recreation programs (126 hours)
6. Conducting own program (80 hours)
7. Diagnostic and disposition staffings, case histories, and patient evaluation (12 hours)
8. Administrative duties, records, and reports (40 hours)
9. Supervisory conferences with director—counseling, discussion, and self-evaluation (12 hours)

EXPERIENTIAL TRAINING APPROACHES In-service training should combine factual knowledge and theoretical understanding with very practical guidelines for carrying out assigned tasks effectively. Whenever possible, it should be *experiential,* based on "hands-on" involvement in group situations, role playing, or actual settings. Problem solving, brainstorming, project planning, and similar assignments may be used to facilitate the learning process.

Example of training in campus recreation. In many campus recreation programs, staff members must deal with situations that involve problems in human relationships. In a Temple University training program for resident assistants (RAs) (graduate students who work with students and advise on dormitory programs and activities), such situations constituted the basis for a role-playing exercise entitled "Behind Closed Doors." RAs were asked to play out the following problem situations and then discuss the ways in which they reacted to them:

1. You (the RA) have noticed that Mary's boyfriend, John, is around the floor a lot. You have even noticed him in the bathroom in the mornings. Mary's roommate, Cathy, has been sleeping in the dormitory lounge. You, the RA, talk to Mary and Cathy about the situation.
2. You are the RA on duty for the building. It is Thursday night. On your rounds of each floor, you hear a lot of noise and see people going in and out of two adjacent rooms. You knock on one of the doors and see cases of beer on the floor with everyone drinking. There is a "no-alcohol" policy in the dormitory. You ask for IDs, and the residents refuse to show them.
3. A father finds an RA in the hallway. He says he must talk to the RA about his daughter immediately; she needs to change to another room. He beats around the bush to explain why she doesn't really like the room: She needs to be closer to her friends, the cafeteria, classes, etc. Finally, he tells the RA that the problem is racial. The wife and daughter spot them and join the conversation. They are all very stubborn and insist that the daughter cannot live with her assigned roommate and must be moved.[16]

SHARING IN-SERVICE EDUCATION RESOURCES   In some cases smaller agencies or departments that are not able to mount their own in-service education programs because of limited numbers of staff and training resources have joined with other organizations to cosponsor in-service activities. Several such public departments may cooperate on a countywide level to establish summer leadership-training institutes. Not infrequently, state professional societies develop special courses and workshops for their members in addition to their regular conferences. Such efforts are extremely important in providing training opportunities for recreation and park personnel on all levels.

In addition to generalized efforts, it is essential that employees be encouraged to evaluate their own progress and evolve a personal professional development plan.

Personnel Policies
PUBLIC AGENCIES

A key aspect of personnel management is the development of sound, up-to-date, and attractive personnel policies. Customarily, these must be consistent with personnel policies prevailing through all municipal employment. However, in some respects they may be adapted to the special requirements within a given field of service.

McChesney has written an excellent manual describing personnel policies in recreation and park departments, based on the practices followed in a number of outstanding departments. This manual includes the following major categories of personnel policies:

    I. General regulations
        Responsibility
        Adoption
        Revision
   II. Classification plan
        Contents
        Maintenance of plan
        Employee review
  III. Definitions
        Full-time
        Seasonal
        Salaried
  IV. Employment
        Application
        Recruitment and selection
        Appointment
        Probation
        Seasonal
        Evaluation and ratings
        Promotions
        Assignment and transfer
        Disciplinary actions
        Separation and resignation
        Reinstatement

    V. Hours of work
          Workweek
          Full-time salaried employees
          Full-time hourly employees
          Work schedules
   VI. Compensation and related benefits
          Salary classification and guides
          Pay periods and time reports
          Deductions
          Holidays
          Overtime
          Vacations
          Insurance
          Retirement
          Credit union
  VII. Absences and leaves
          Absences
          Health or hardship leave
 VIII. Travel and vehicle use
          Departmental vehicles
          Private vehicles
   IX. In-service training
          Purpose
          Conference attendance
          Staff meetings and conferences
    X. Rules of conduct
          Dress and appearance
          Employee cooperation
          Reporting for duty
   XI. Relations between employees—department—community
          Employee-administrator relations
          Employee-community relations
          Gifts
          Solicitation of funds
          Management of funds
          Publicity releases
          Employee-patron relations
          Accidents to patrons[17]

In the typical large city personnel manual, detailed policies are stated with regard to each of these areas of practice, as well as many others not listed here. As a single example, however, typical personnel policies with respect to disciplinary action and personnel evaluations are summarized as follows.

Disciplinary action

Departmental personnel manuals should clearly specify the required behavior of employees in areas such as dress, smoking or drinking, persistent lateness, acts of dishonesty or pilferage, refusal to perform assigned tasks, violence or verbal abuse of patrons or coworkers, unauthorized absence, use of departmental vehicles, or general attitude. Both informal and formal disciplinary actions should be set forth in the manual. Depending on the nature and degree of the infraction, disciplinary actions should include the following procedures:

1. *Reprimands,* either verbal or formal, which are entered in the service record
2. *Suspensions,* or temporary separations without pay, for specified periods
3. *Demotions,* involving placing employee on a lower job classification at a lower rate of pay
4. *Dismissals,* which are discharges or separations for cause

Usually such procedures are implemented only in serious cases in which there is clear evidence of the employee's unsatisfactory performance or violation of department requirements. The department should provide opportunity for a hearing or grievance proceedings in the case of such disciplinary actions when the demoted or discharged employee wishes to resist the departmental action. Increasingly, municipal labor unions are playing a role in such proceedings.

As an example of how policies must be flexible and responsive to changing circumstances, a form of employee misconduct such as sexual harassment, which in the past probably would not have been regarded as a serious offense, today must be regarded as such and should be specifically identified as one in policy handbooks.

Personnel evaluations

The use of service ratings has already been mentioned with respect to promotion and disciplinary actions. Recreation and park departments should provide for regular and systematic evaluation of the work of *all* employees. Such evaluation may be carried out through on-the-job observations and ratings made by departmental supervisors, which may be required at stated intervals to be placed in the employee's service record, and general appraisals of the employee's work, including elements of overall personality, as well as specific performance on the job. Usually, such ratings are most efficient when they cover specific categories of performance and provide a gradation of specific descriptions of behavior rather than a general reaction to the employee.

NONPUBLIC ORGANIZATIONS

Detailed personnel policies are found most often in public agencies, in which they have been developed over time through civil service processes or labor union agreements that apply to all governmental employees. Large voluntary agencies and therapeutic recreation programs are also likely to have carefully detailed personnel procedures and manuals that apply to all their staff members.

In contrast, many smaller leisure-service programs in private or commercial settings have rudimentary personnel plans. Often hours of work and leaves are treated flexibly, as are disciplinary actions and evaluation procedures. In many such programs there are no retirement plans and limited health and welfare benefits.

In some commercial recreation settings, however, such as large theme parks, there are elaborate personnel plans, with several categories of full- and part-time employees, systematic training programs, and carefully defined policies for employee evaluation.

As an example, there may be overall policies dealing with performance elements that are extremely important to the employing agency. To illustrate, in Florida's Disney World, the employee's image in meeting the public is of crucial concern; precise guidelines are established for appearance in areas such as hair grooming and coloring, sideburns, mustaches, wigs, cosmetics, perfume, fingernails, jewelry, and accessories. The employee's ''presenteeism'' (management's term for total appearance and manner before the public) is strictly regulated, with rigid taboos governing behavior with ''guests,'' use of narcotics or intoxicants, gambling, dishonesty, and similar matters.

Use of Volunteer Workers

It should be stressed again that the preceding personnel guidelines tend to be geared to the needs and capabilities of larger departments or agencies with many full-time employees who must be recruited, selected, trained, and supervised.

However, there are many smaller leisure-service agencies of all types that have limited numbers of staff members. A community with several thousand residents or an industry with a similar population of employees might have only one or two professional recreation staff members, along with clerical and maintenance employees. Such agencies often rely heavily on volunteers. The effective direction of volunteer services is therefore an important aspect of leisure-service personnel management.

The motivation to contribute time and effort to a leisure-service agency may stem from a variety of reasons. Graham and Klar write:

> Parents often become actively involved in those activities and programs which are of direct benefit to their children such as Boy or Girl Scouts and organized youth sports leagues. In addition to academic credits, student interns gain valuable professional experience through their association with a community leisure service program. Elder citizens often believe it their civic responsibility to donate their services. Some persons perceive their contribution as a means of ''getting a foot in the door'' with respect to future salaried employment, while others become involved to gain personal recognition, publicity, and prestige within the community. For many individuals, the chance to be of voluntary help is in itself a form of recreation.[18]

Volunteers can assist recreation and park departments and organizations in a variety of ways, including the following:

1. Assisting in administrative, promotional, or advisory activities
2. Working with specific groups or activities, in playgrounds, community centers, and similar facilities, or providing adult direction for teenage or golden age clubs
3. Mounting special community projects, particularly in areas related to the arts, ecology, or social service, in which special expertise and interest are needed
4. Providing clerical assistance and helping with mailings, preparation of reports, and similar assignments
5. Offering special technical assistance (as in the case of residents who are architects, lawyers, or planners) with studies, films, or other projects designed to promote the work of the department

Of these, the largest area of use is in direct leadership of groups or assisting professional leaders at work. Four elements are necessary for this process to be successful: recruitment, training, supervision, and recognition.

RECRUITMENT

It is necessary to seek out volunteers in a systematic way because they usually will not appear on their own volition. The most useful techniques for enlisting volunteers are through appeal to organizations with an interest in recreation, such as church groups, parent-teacher associations, or special-interest organizations whose members are interested in promoting their hobby or interest. Hospitals frequently employ coordinators of volunteer programs, who develop contacts for reaching potential volunteers. In some cases there may be a community council of social agencies, which serves to publicize the need for volunteers and channels volunteers to appropriate agencies for work assignments.

In general, the most effective kinds of volunteers are those with special training or interest, such as parents, schoolteachers, those with previous recreation leadership experience, or hobbyists who have special skills they enjoy teaching to others. Many departments use large numbers of college students as volunteers. Often these are students who are majoring in education or recreation, in which case the volunteer assignment may constitute a fieldwork course for college credit.

A number of large municipal recreation and park departments have made concerted efforts to mobilize large numbers of volunteers, sometimes in specially organized and funded projects carried out in cooperation with neighborhood councils or other citizen groups. The Heritage Conservation and Recreation Service has published a useful handbook that documents such programs, showing how they have provided departments with many thousands of hours of volunteer service and suggesting guidelines for effective recruitment and use of volunteers.

TRAINING

Volunteers should be carefully screened and trained before being assigned to specific tasks. Those who are unstable, have unrealistic expectations of the volunteer assignment, or lack the potential for making a real contribution should be weeded out by the coordinator or supervisor of volunteers. Next, there should be a series of orientation sessions or meetings designed to familiarize the volunteers with the objectives and philosophy of the department, departmental rules and policies, principles of recreation leadership, and the specific responsibilities they are expected to assume. If sufficient numbers are involved, special training institutes may be held for the orientation of volunteers.

SUPERVISION

The function of supervising volunteers is similar to that of supervising paid personnel, except that they tend to require closer attention and more technical assistance and advice. Supervisors must help them realize that the department counts on their regular involvement just as it does that of paid employees and that their attendance must be consistent and dependable. If they are given meaningful assignments that challenge their capabilities, their involvement *will* be more consistent than if they are given trivial or mechanical jobs to perform.

RECOGNITION

Finally, it is necessary to make clear to volunteers that their work does make a major contribution to the department. This can be done through simple verbal appreciation, recognition of volunteers in reports and publicity, department meetings in which their work is singled out for praise, special dinners or meetings (sometimes on an annual basis) designed to recognize the work of volunteers and promote fuller volunteer involvement, or awards, plaques, or other tangible expressions of appreciation.

• • •

The real potential of volunteer leadership in recreation work has yet to be explored. Many recreation and park executives tend to take the position, "Volunteers are OK, but they take too much of my time, and they're not reliable." In truth, few executives give sufficient attention to the screening, training, and supervision of volunteer workers, and thus their success or failure is left largely to chance. That there are so many successes in the use of volunteers despite this is proof of the dedication, persistence, and skill of many residents who are determined to contribute to recreation programs in their communities.

A final important value of volunteer services in many community or therapeutic agencies is the bridge they help to build between the program and the community at large. At the Penetanguishene Mental Health Centre in Ontario, Canada, hospital authorities recognize the contribution made by volunteers not only with respect to leadership services they provide within the hospital itself, but also in their external role. Volunteers who work in the hospital with patients are seen as an important means of educating those in the outside community about the nature of mental illness. They help to break down the isolation that occurs in mental institutions, and this makes it easier for patients to enter community programs and activities either during hospitalization or after discharge. In addition, many volunteers who begin by doing hospital work later take on responsibilities with the Canadian Mental Health Association, both in its office operation and in promoting its programs and goals in the community.

For all these reasons, the successful conduct of volunteer services must become an important part of recreation and park management. In addition to workers who volunteer for unpaid service as individuals, many men and women contribute their services as part of neighborhood task forces or special committees. In some cases they serve through special funding arrangements on a part-time basis. For example, in the city of Revere, Mass., eight of the city's largest parks have been maintained by Revere senior citizens with special funding from the Urban Parks and Recreation Recovery Program (UPARR) of the U.S. Department of Interior. Known as the Senior Citizen Park Maintenance Corps, these men and women have been employed as part-time landscapers and maintenance personnel on the city's outdoor recreation areas with outstanding results.[19]

While they are not volunteers in a strict sense, such special groups of part-time employees also require careful orientation and supervision and must be considered important elements in a community's leisure-service system. With continuing growth in the number of senior citizens and the probability that tax funds allocated to the maintenance of park resources will continue to be limited, it seems likely that such practices will expand in the future.

Summary

This chapter has provided a picture of the overall personnel process that is responsible for productive operations in all types of recreation, park, and leisure-service organizations.

These processes include the development of personnel classification systems and job descriptions and the specific tasks of recruiting, selecting, hiring, orienting, and providing in-service education for employees. The preparation of personnel manuals and detailed personnel policies is an important part of this process, as is the evaluation of employees on all levels. Increasingly, the effective supervision of volunteers is an important part of the personnel management process.

As indicated in the introduction, this chapter emphasizes the establishment of formal procedures that provide rules and official channels through which personnel are employed and supervised. The use of the term ''directing'' in the subtitle implies an authority-based, traditional relationship between managers and subordinate personnel in leisure-service agencies. In contrast, Chapter 7 is more concerned with job enrichment, the participative approach to management, conflict resolution, and similar interpersonal processes that contribute to positive motivation on the part of employees.

STUDY QUESTIONS

1. Visit a large leisure-service agency, such as a major commercial recreation facility, large state hospital, or armed forces base, and examine its personnel structure and processes. Report to the class with an analysis of its job classification system, functions of various positions, hiring methods, and overall personnel practices.
2. As a class exercise, prepare a plan for in-service training of personnel in a specific recreation setting. Present the entire plan to the class and involve students in a number of the activities as a workshop project.
3. Develop an instrument, such as a rating scale, check list, or other evaluation form, that can be used to assess employee performance in a given type of leisure-service agency. Make sure that it is not just a general personnel evaluation form, but applies specifically to this type of setting and personnel role.

Case 3   A Supervisor's Right to Suspend

YOU ARE MARK SCHMIDT, district supervisor of a large municipal recreation and park agency. Within your district, there is one major recreation center. The custodian of this center, John Figgins, has occasionally been reported to be drinking on the job by Mary Cartier, the center manager. You have warned him about it informally but have not put the warnings in his personnel folder, since you like John and feel he could overcome the problem.

Late one afternoon you get a call from Mary. John Figgins has been drinking heavily. You hurry over to the center and find John in a drunken stupor in the boiler room. The next day you call him to a meeting in your office at Mary's urgent request. She feels that she can no longer put up with his behavior. You inform him that you are suspending him and bringing his name before the recreation and park board for consideration of possible job termination.

When you confer with the city's personnel director, he informs you that you may have difficulty in making the charges stick, since there is no official written record of his past misconduct or your warnings. In addition, the head of the municipal maintenance employees' union has informed the personnel director that John Figgins has diabetes and is prepared to claim that he was having an attack and that his medication caused the apparent drunkenness. The union head indicates that his organization may secure legal assistance claiming that John is being discriminated against because of his disability. In any case they are prepared to fight the possible firing, since they have been looking for a possible test case in this area.

It looks as if you may not be able to impose the suspension and bring him up on charges. Mary Cartier is upset and indicates that she may ask for a job transfer.

Questions for Class Discussion and Analysis

1. How sound a case do you feel you have for imposing the suspension and bringing John Figgins before the board?
2. Exactly what should you have done before this incident to put yourself in a more solid position for dealing with John's problem?
3. Apart from warning John or taking strong punitive action, what could you and Mary Cartier have done to deal positively with this situation?

Case 4   Member of the Board

YOU ARE ELLIOT SIMON, a member of the board of trustees of a Young Men's–Young Women's Hebrew Association (YM-YWHA) in your community, and you have many ideas about program activities that would be successful. However, you find that the center director, Harry Goldfarb, tends to be slow in accepting or acting on your suggestions. While you like Harry, you do not feel that he is creative or aggressive enough in promoting Y programs.

Therefore you have developed a practice of initiating contacts with the different program specialists or division heads in the YM-YWHA and giving them advice

Case 4
cont'd

Member of the Board

regarding new program activities or events. Since you are friendly with many business people in the community, you have also been able to get them to make contributions or provide volunteer services to assist these programs. While you have bypassed Harry Goldfarb in taking these steps, you feel that it has been justified because it has helped make the Y's program more successful.

At a monthly meeting of the board, Harry accuses you of going beyond your prerogatives and making his position as agency director untenable. Either you stop your direct contacts with members of his staff and work through him, he says, or he will consider resigning. As it happens, he has the offer of a business position that is tempting. How do you respond?

Questions for Class Discussion and Analysis

1. How valid are Harry's charges? Do you feel that you have done anything wrong in bypassing Harry? After all, you had nothing to gain and only had the Y's interests at heart.
2. Regarding your relationship with other staff members, what kinds of policies could have prevented this crisis from developing?
3. Is there any way in which you could have provided creative input to the program other than the approach you used?

REFERENCES

1. Mescon, Michael H., Albert, Michael, and Khedouri, Franklin: *Management: Individual and Organizational Effectiveness,* New York, 1981, Harper & Row, Inc., p. 52.
2. *Guide to Personnel Criteria and Personnel Standards,* Peekskill, N.Y., 1975, New York State Recreation and Park Society.
3. Feldman, Daniel C., and Arnold, Hugh J.: *Managing Individual and Group Behavior in Organizations,* New York, 1983, McGraw-Hill Book Co., p. 40.
4. *Job Opportunities in the Veterans Administration,* Washington, D.C., 1984, Brochure of the Veterans Administration.
5. *Executive Referral Listings, Naval Military Personnel Command,* Washington, D.C., Aug. 1984, U.S. Department of the Navy.
6. *Bureau of Education for the Handicapped Project Update in Therapeutic Recreation,* Newsletter of Temple University, Department of Recreation and Leisure Studies, Philadelphia, Feb. 1980, p. 1.
7. Christie-Mill, Robert, and Seid, Bradford: *Job Specifications and Skills Necessary for Ski Area Managers,* Research Report No. 408, East Lansing, Mich., Oct. 1980, Michigan State University.
8. Desaulniers, Connie: "Theme Park Employment," in *Trends: The Park and Recreation Employee,* Heritage Conservation and Recreation Service, and National Recreation and Park Association, Summer 1980, pp. 17-18.

9. Kraus, Richard: *Recreation and Leisure in Modern Society,* Glenview, Ill., 1984, Scott, Foresman & Co., Chapters 12-13.

10. Brademas, James: "The Personnel Assessment Center: Peoria Puts the Right Person With the Right Job," *Parks and Recreation,* Oct. 1979, pp. 46-51.

11. Rosenberg, DeAnne: "Take the Guesswork out of Job Interviewing," *California Parks and Recreation,* Dec.-Jan. 1978-1979, p. 22.

12. Feldman and Arnold, *op. cit.,* p. 53.

13. *Therapeutic Recreation Field Placement Program, Activities Department,* Bethesda, Md., Jan. 1984, Clinical Center, National Institutes of Health.

14. Dimock, Hedley G.: "How to Train Successful Camp Leaders," *Social Agency Management,* March 1975, p. 27.

15. Desaulniers, *op. cit.,* p. 18.

16. Locklin, Susan: *Staff Training Workshop Plan,* Philadelphia, 1984, Office of Cocurricular and Leisure Programs, Temple University.

17. McChesney, James C.: *Personnel Policies,* Washington, D.C., 1966, National Recreation and Park Association, Management Aids Bulletin No. 66.

18. Graham, Peter J., and Klar, Lawrence R., Jr.: *Planning and Delivering Leisure Services,* Dubuque, Iowa, 1979, William C. Brown Co., p. 164.

19. Feeney, Robert E.: "Revere's Senior Citizen Park Maintenance Corps," *Parks and Recreation,* Feb. 1983, pp. 52-55.

CHAPTER 7

In the context of understanding motivation in work organizations...what causes a person to report regularly for work each day rather than frequently calling in sick? What causes one person to attack difficult problems head-on, while someone else avoids and procrastinates for long periods? What causes some people to choose to engage in the activities encouraged by the organization, while others seem bent on doing just those things which have been discouraged or prohibited?[1]

Personnel Management
The Motivating Function

Modern leisure-service management is deeply concerned with ways of promoting the maximum productivity and commitment on the part of its employees. Based on current theories of motivation and effective management styles, this chapter presents a number of useful guidelines for supervisors in various types of recreation agencies.

Its primary emphasis is on working with employees in different job settings to bring out their fullest energies and creative abilities and achieve a climate of highly motivated participation in the work of the organization. Linked to this task are such issues as appropriate leadership styles on the part of supervisors, as well as specific techniques used in problem solving, decision making, and conflict resolution. The coaching and counseling roles of supervisors are examined, along with the task of assisting employees suffering from job-related stress and burnout. Finally, the chapter deals with supervisory problems related to labor-union relationships.

Challenges Facing Supervisors

Beyond the traditional personnel management functions described in Chapter 6, there is a key need today to improve employee morale and motivation, strengthen positive work attitudes, and promote job productivity.

In the 1960s and 1970s, increased absenteeism and industrial accidents and decreased productivity suggested that employees needed to be dealt with not as cogs in a machine, but as real people, with hopes, ambitions, and needs. Boredom and lack of job motivation became evident in many organizations.

This problem is probably more acute in large industries where work tends to be highly standardized and monotonous than in a professional field such as organized recreation. Recreation leaders or therapists deal with a variety of tasks and challenges and must work creatively to succeed. Nonetheless, it is necessary to face the problem of employee morale, attitude, and productivity in recreation and park agencies. Hatcher and Lamke suggest that ''demotivators'' such as reduced job security (real or imagined), low salaries and job status, and lack of opportunity for promotion have reduced the job incentive of many leisure-service professionals. They comment:

> Recreation was once a profession in which employees were willing to work hard, take pride in personal achievements, and seek personal growth and development as well as recognition and responsibility. It is now dominated by a new breed of individuals. The hallmark of this new breed of the 70's and 80's appears to be a preoccupation with

self. . . . Employers today are perplexed by employees who don't subscribe to the traditional value system in which work provides life's major satisfactions and the type and quality of one's work reflects what kind of person you are.[2]

Essentially, this is the challenge that faces supervisory personnel in recreation and park agencies. As middle-level managers, these individuals are directly responsible for assigning work and ensuring that it is carried out properly, as well as for the broader task of making sure the complex structure of an organization is functioning smoothly.

Although supervisors are sometimes thought of primarily as "technical" specialists, their real role with employees is far broader and may be described under three headings: interpersonal, informational, and decision-making.

> *Interpersonal* roles encompass the development of a set of interpersonal relationships between the manager (or supervisor) and his or her subordinates and superiors. These include such roles as figurehead or symbol of authority, leader and motivator, and liaison among different individuals and groups. *Informational* roles involve receiving and sending information; the manager acts as monitor, disseminator and spokesperson for the organization. Finally, *decision-making* has the manager act as entrepreneur, promoter of change in the organization, disturbance-handler or conflict-resolver, resource-allocator and negotiator.[3]

Within each of these sets of roles, the supervisor should seek to establish a constructive climate of human relationships and promote favorable work attitudes on the part of employees toward their job, each other, and the organization itself. The supervisor interprets and applies company policies and work orders, trains new employees, counsels and disciplines employees (where necessary), initiates or recommends personnel actions, and plans and puts into action time and work schedules, subject to limitations on his or her authority. Thus the supervisor may be viewed as a leader and trainer of others, an implementer of fresh ideas and approaches, a superior to lower-level employees, a coworker with others, and an aide to top management. He or she must be able to understand and effectively express and respond to the needs of those on all levels and where necessary mediate employee complaints or requests or enforce management policy.

Supervisors must not be regarded narrowly as overseers whose primary task is to determine that individuals are not loafing on the job. Instead, they should be seen as helpful and sympathetic coworkers who are interested primarily in helping workers reach their full potential to make life within the organization more satisfying and the daily routine more interesting and ego fulfilling.

Effective Supervisory Styles

What personal qualities or behavioral styles characterize effective supervisors? While hundreds of empirical studies of leadership have been conducted, there is no single, universally acceptable answer to this question. One way to approach the issue is to point out that leadership is not simply a one-way process, in which leaders seek to get others to perform as they wish them to do. Instead, leadership must be perceived as a *mutual influence* process, in which both superiors and subordinates (in the agency hierarchy) interact with each other and influence their behavior.

While supervisors obviously have certain kinds of power that they can use to *force* employees to perform in certain ways, this approach is usually not as effective as the kind of behavior that genuinely gains support of subordinate employees and is successful in motivating them. In general, research has identified two primary styles of supervisory behavior: *employee-oriented* and *production-oriented*.

EMPLOYEE-ORIENTED

Employee-oriented supervisory behavior has great consideration for employees. The employee-oriented supervisor is concerned with the well-being of subordinates, engages in two-way communication with them, is generally supportive and nonpunitive, and encourages a participative approach to planning and decision making, with considerable delegation of responsibility and authority to lower-level employees.

PRODUCTION-ORIENTED

In contrast, production-oriented supervisors are task oriented. They emphasize careful planning, goal setting, and meeting schedules and deadlines. They are more likely to give their subordinates precise instructions, maintain a high degree of control over them, stress the importance of output, and delegate responsibility less frequently.

For a time it was thought that employee- and production-oriented leadership approaches were at opposite ends of a continuum and that supervisors might follow one approach or the other, but not both. However, Feldman and Arnold point out that research has disproved this assumption:

> It appears that the two dimensions are independent of each other; the extent to which a person is high or low on one dimension does not determine where that person stands on the other dimension. As a result, a leader may simultaneously be high or low on either or both of the dimensions.[4]

Thus, ideally, a supervisor in a leisure-service agency might combine both behavioral styles—being supportive and caring with subordinates and generally following the guidelines implied in McGregor's Theory Y, while at the same time pressing hard to be as creative and productive as possible in accomplishing work objectives. Indeed, based on the contingency model of leadership, it is believed today that leadership style that will be most effective in a given situation will depend on the difficulty of the task, the manager's position of power, the relationship between the manager and subordinates, and similar factors. In general, employees will respond more favorably to supervisors who are friendly, accepting, helpful, enthusiastic, and supportive than to supervisors who have the opposite traits.

Recognizing Employees' Needs

Beyond these qualities, supervisors should be able to recognize the needs of employees and the kinds of on-the-job factors that will motivate them positively. In a study of recreation and park employees in Sunnyvale, Calif., leaders were asked to rank the factors that motivated them the most and the least. At the same time, their supervisors

TABLE 7-1 Median Ranking of Motivators by Park and Recreation Supervisors and Subordinates Using Herzberg's Motivation/Hygiene Typology

Motivator Description	Rank Order Subordinates	Superiors
Doing work you feel is important and worthwhile (M)	1	1
Chance to do quality work (M)	2	2
Chance to learn new things, to develop your skills (M)	3	4
Chance to do interesting work (M)	4	5
Feeling involved in decision-making (M)	5	3
Chance to achieve personal work-related goals (M)	6	6
Being part of a team and not letting them down (H)	7	12
Full appreciation by supervisor for work you've done (M)	8	7
Desire to help your agency attain its goal (H)	9	11
Getting along with your supervisor (H)	10	14
Job security and steady work (H)	11	16
Good working conditions: hours, discipline, fair assignments, understanding of personal problems (H)	12	8
Getting along with co-workers (H)	13	9
Possibility of increased freedom on the job (H)	14	10
Good wages (H)	15	13
Amount of information and feedback you get about job performance (H)	16	15
Good benefits package: vacation, pension and insurance (H)	17	17
Chance for promotion (H)	18	18
Opportunities for raises and other rewards (H)	19	19
Being appointed leader of your group (M)	20	20

From Neal, L.L., Williams, J.G., and Beech, S.A.: "How Managers Perceive Subordinates," *Leisure Today, Journal of Physical Education, Recreation and Dance,* April 1982, p. 57.

were asked to rank the factors as they thought the leaders would. Strikingly, there was a high degree of similarity between the two lists, as shown in Table 7-1. Both groups saw *motivator* factors (identified as M, according to Herzberg's theory) as more influential than *hygiene* factors (identified as H).[5] The key elements in motivating employees appeared to be providing opportunities for growth and self-improvement, meaningful involvement, and recognition.

Guidelines for Supervisory Action

While supervisory styles vary widely, with different situations calling for different approaches, the guidelines on the opposite page are broadly applicable to most situations. The successful supervisor typically demonstrates these behaviors.

BEHAVIORS OF EFFECTIVE SUPERVISORS

1. Establishes high but attainable expectations for staff in terms of work standards and goals, and makes sure that these are designed to achieve the goals of the department itself.
2. Places staff members in jobs in which their individual abilities are most likely to be fully utilized.
3. Recognizes the universal need for approval, and helps staff members meet this need by (a) bestowing credit and praising accomplishments, (b) showing consideration toward staff members, and (c) acknowledging their share in the total enterprise and their contribution in making it a success.
4. Seeks to help staff members become more effective, and removes obstacles to success by providing technical assistance and emotional support.
5. Avoids ego-threatening behavior, and uses the mistakes of subordinates as a basis for counseling and improving performance rather than as an opportunity for threats and punishment.
6. Clearly defines the responsibilities and accountability of staff members and shows confidence in their ability to carry out these tasks.
7. Encourages staff members to participate in policy-planning, decision-making and program development, not as a "token" gesture but with serious weight being given to their contributions.
8. Exercises leadership when necessary, asserting rank, making decisions and exerting force to achieve departmental goals.
9. Is an effective link between management and leadership, communicating information helpful to their psychological well-being and morale and to their awareness of total departmental developments.
10. Appraises employees on the basis of objective and measurable performance elements, taking into account differences in the qualities of individual workers and different levels of task difficulty.
11. Does not play favorites, but seeks to reward all workers equally and to provide tangible rewards and status symbols, particularly for high-level performance.
12. Is friendly, sympathetic and approachable, yet also maintains a sense of dignity based on the rank he or she has been assigned and the authority vested by the department.

COACHING AND COUNSELING APPROACHES

Some personnel experts point out that two of the most important elements of supervision include *coaching* and *counseling*. Both of these involve a close relationship between the supervisor and the subordinate employee. Buzzotta, Lefton, and Sherberg point out that, whereas formal training programs, seminars, or courses may occasionally take place, along with staff meetings devoted to agency business, other, more personal contacts occur more frequently, as often as several times a day in many situations. They describe the two key aspects of such one-to-one supervisory-employee relationships in the following way:

Coaching and counseling is (1) the use of *managerial power* (2) to elicit *self-analysis* by the subordinate which (3) combines with the manager's *own* insights and knowledge (4) to produce *self-understanding* on the part of the subordinate, *commitment* to mutually acceptable goals, and a *plan of action* for achieving them.[6]

Although they are closely related, the two methods differ in that coaching focuses on improving job skills and knowledge, whereas counseling is concerned with problems of attitude and motivation or difficulties with interpersonal relationships that may hamper an individual's job performance. Both methods are applied in various ways, including daily or periodic contact of an informal nature, which is concerned with immediate problems and solutions, as well as semiformal efforts carried out over a period of time or periodic appraisals of a more formal nature.

It is important for supervisors to recognize developing problems, such as increased accidents, absenteeism or lateness, withdrawal, irritability, or fatigue, or similar evidence of personal difficulty. In working with employees showing such symptoms, managers should seek to reassure them that their purpose is not to "nail" them or have them fired, but rather to help them in both a personal and a professional sense. In the counseling process, in contrast to teaching job skills, which is a less sensitive task, Landahl[7] suggests the following guidelines.

1. Listen patiently to what employees say before making any comment.
2. Refrain from criticizing or offering hasty advice on the problem.
3. Never argue with employees while counseling them.
4. Give undivided attention to employees while they are talking.
5. Look beyond the mere words of what employees say—listen to see if they are revealing something deeper than what appears on the surface.

If the problem is relatively minor, simply helping the employee unburden himself or herself may lead to a solution. Discussing the matter with a helpful and supportive supervisor may suggest commonsense courses of action to take or at least may pinpoint the areas of difficulty and the need to take action. If the problem is more severe or the employee shows a significant level of personal disturbance, the supervisor should recommend a counselor or clinic. At the same time that the counseling effort is friendly and supportive, it must also be realistic in that the employee must come to grips with the consequences of the difficulty he or she is experiencing. For example, if drinking is the problem, the agency's rules and policies must be made explicit and the problem person must recognize that, if improvement is not shown, suspension or job termination is a real possibility. If the policy mandates such penalties for the employee's behavior, the supervisor has no choice and must carry them out.

USE OF BEHAVIOR MODIFICATION

Apart from the application of such general guidelines for improving supervisory skills, some organizations have used recently developed behavior modification techniques to achieve objectives. The basic premise underlying this approach is that almost all behavior is operant or learned behavior. Therefore it can be modified or changed by deliberate supervisory action.

Typically, behavior modification is based on the principle that the appropriate use of reinforcers will support desired changes in employee behavior. Reinforcers tend to be of two types: (1) *positive* reinforcers, which add something good, such as a bonus, a "stroke," or a desired change in work assignment, to the employee's life and (2) *negative* reinforcers, which consist of removing something unpleasant, such as a distasteful task or schedule, from the employee's life. So-called *punishers,* or *deterrents,* may also be positive or negative. They are positive when they involve low ratings or extra work because of poor performance, and negative when they consist of taking away something good from the employee's environment. Reinforcement techniques are usually far superior to punishment techniques in producing lasting behavioral changes.

In addition to such strategies, many other important principles and techniques can be used to motivate employees and improve productivity. These include specific approaches such as job enrichment and participative management techniques.

NEED FOR ORGANIZATIONAL COMMITMENT

An important outcome of effective supervision is to develop a sense of organizational commitment on the part of employees. Nogradi points out that this term generally refers to the "relative strength of an individual's identification with and involvement in a particular organization," with the assumption that more highly committed employees perform better and make a stronger contribution to organizational effectiveness. Linked to this is the element of *job involvement,* which describes the degree to which "the person identifies with his job, actively participates in it, and considers his performance important to his self-worth. Persons with a high degree of job involvement tend to have strong growth needs and a history of job success; they are satisfied with their jobs and are less likely to leave their organizations."[8]

The issue of employee commitment can be broadened to include several different kinds of attachment: (1) to the individual's specific agency or organization, (2) to the overall leisure-service profession, and (3) to the community the employee serves. Based on a study of 49 recreation and park departments in Illinois, London and Howat found that various procedures were used to strengthen each of these kinds of commitment:

> Many organizations attempt to induce organizational commitment by "locking" employees in. Strategies include nontransferable pension plans, good salaries and benefits, [and] early promotions. . . .
>
> Possible methods to enhance professional commitment include encouraging attendance at professional meetings, subsidizing journal subscriptions and memberships in professional organizations, and making an effort to regularly discuss recent advances in the field. Commitment to the community might be increased by holding regular meetings with local residents and encouraging involvement in community organizations (e.g., Rotary). In general, prompting employees to behave in ways that are typical of those committed to the organization, profession or community may cause them to actually feel more committed [and] may in turn influence future behavior.[9]

Job Enrichment

Job enrichment provides a useful means of strengthening employees' commitment to their agencies and work roles. Recognizing that poor morale may result from monotonous, highly specialized, routine work assignments, a number of companies have experimented with more flexible assignments and schedules. In many cases workers have responded favorably; in one case the personnel officer of a large industrial concern reported that employees responded to "flextime" with greater punctuality, improved efficiency, and better attitudes.

> Flextime has helped to bring about increased cooperation, more exchange of information, greater delegation by the supervisor, less supervisory control and more informality. Employees also report that flextime has improved group...communication, motivation and job satisfaction.[10]

Recent studies have shown that the fears of executives that employees will exploit their companies by showing up and leaving at odd hours are groundless. Analysis of flextime in several U.S. government agencies in different states showed that workers typically stayed fairly close to their original schedules and in fact actually worked more hours than were required.

CHANGING ASSIGNMENTS

In the past, many large public recreation and park agencies assigned leaders to the same facility on a full-time, year-round basis. For several reasons, this approach has shifted toward using personnel in more diversified ways. Today few large cities have enough full-time professional leaders to staff all their facilities on a permanent basis. In addition, because of the nature of recreation scheduling and program changes during the year, assigning a person to one location throughout all seasons is neither economical nor logical. Many departments have therefore changed their personnel assignment policies in the following ways:

1. They are rotating assignments at different seasons, so a given individual might work at various times in a golden age center, in a youth center, on a playground, or in a camp, depending on where he or she can be most productive at a given time.

2. In addition to their regular assignments, leaders may be assigned to other district-wide or citywide roles, which they can carry on in slack periods during the day or week. For example, a playground director may be given the responsibility of supervising a satellite after school program during the winter season, may serve as district chairperson for a particular tournament or program, or may be a member of a committee planning a citywide special event, such as a bicycle rodeo or soapbox derby. Such assignments ensure that staff members are used to their fullest potential and that adequate staffing is given to these special programs.

3. In many cases leaders who were formerly assigned full-time to face-to-face leadership in a facility have been given greater responsibility for coordinating and directing programs, with the actual leadership tasks being given to part-time workers or seasonal leaders with special skills that they can use in a rotating way in several locations.

A strong case can be made for applying job rotation on all levels of an organization. For example, the notion that having the same superintendent or executive director in the top position of an agency for 15, 20, or even 30 years is comfortable and desirable can be seriously challenged. Instead, one might make the case that such positions should "turn over" at least every 5 years or absolutely every 10 years. Such rotations need not require brutal firings. They can be accomplished by reorganizing the structure of an organization, shifting functions, and other techniques that ensure fresh, dynamic leadership while at the same time retaining the advantages of the training and experience of senior managers.

Another radical approach to job diversification involves breaking away from the familiar model in many public and voluntary agencies of having a fixed number of full-time, year-round employees supplemented by a limited number of specialists during the year and an influx of summer workers for playground or camping programs. Many commercial recreation organizations operate in a much more fluid manner so they can be responsive to immediate surges or slumps in program demands. Disney World, for example, has three basic types of personnel classifications:

Permanent—employment in an established job on a permanent basis for four days and at least 20 hours per week

Casual regular—employment under which an individual is regularly scheduled at least one day but less than four days per week

Casual temporary—employment designed to accommodate a specific period of expanded activity, such as summer or winter seasons, holiday weeks, etc.

This type of personnel plan makes it possible to tailor the supply of workers to fit the exact needs of the job situation, day by day and week by week. Although it poses a threat to the traditional job pattern found in most public agencies, it is particularly useful given the nature of recreation and park program operations. It explains why many public departments choose to have private concessionaires operate restaurants and similar facilities in parks rather than manage them themselves. Private operators are able to run such ventures at a profit, partly because of their flexibility in personnel hiring and assignment procedures, whereas public adminstrators are constrained by civil service personnel contracts and union agreements.

The second way to achieve job enrichment is by developing managerial styles that give employees the fullest possible opportunity to share in the decision-making process and increase levels of communication, trust, and mutual support. In a manual on job enrichment prepared for the American Management Association, Yorks identified several characteristics of positions designed to build employee motivation:

1. The job should be a complete piece of work in the sense that the worker can identify a series of tasks or activities which result in a definable product for the receiver (client) or receivers of the work. . . .

2. The worker should have as much decision-making control as possible over how he or she executes that complete piece of work [and] given a certain level of competence, is . . . permitted to deviate from prescribed methods and procedures. . . .

3. Workers should be provided with direct information on how well they are doing their jobs . . . through customer (client) reactions, the immediate outcome of decisions, and performance criteria.[11]

Workers must be given the fullest possible opportunity to function at their highest level of capability, and specific obstacles that tend to block effective performance must be overcome. Edginton and Williams identify a number of such barriers:

There are conditions that block an employee's performance and make it impossible or difficult to work at a high level of performance. Some of the common obstacles to performance are red tape, organizational policies and procedures, bottlenecks in the work load, lack of money, lack of manpower, improper instructions, faulty job descriptions, sudden change in the goal of a supervisor, lack of communication, too many programs for the number of employees, and lack of authority.[12]

Finally, the personal style of managers must be carefully examined if they are to develop a favorable job climate and enrich employee motivation. In a discussion of the "OK boss," James uses the system of behavioral analysis known as Transactional Analysis (TA) to show how people tend to feel and act in one of three ways that are essentially derived from patterns of behavior experienced while growing up. These three patterns may best be described as *child, adult,* and *parent ego states.* James suggests that in any of these states it is possible to function effectively toward oneself and one's subordinates.

> In the parental state, you can be an OK boss—one who brings out the best in people— if you give critiques rather than criticism, don't interfere too much, and know how to be supportive. Or, you can be an OK boss in the adult state by being responsive and analytical. Or, you can be an OK boss in the child state by being cooperative, ready to negotiate, or creative.[13]

On the other hand, it is possible to be a "parent" who is negative and opinionated or overprotective and controlling. A poor "adult" boss may be mechanical and uncreative. A "child" boss may be sullen, apologetic, or even scatterbrained. The ultimately preferable boss has a mature, adult, positive view of himself or herself, and of subordinates—in other words, an "I'm OK, you're OK" stance. Such a manager tends to get along well with others and feel confident and constructive. He or she seeks out and gives a loose rein to confident, capable employees and encourages anxious or insecure workers to operate to their fullest potential.

DELEGATION OF AUTHORITY

A key aspect of the participative management approach involves the delegation of authority by managers to lower-level employees. As described in Chapter 3, this helps employees face new challenges, sharpen their skills, and become more productive staff members. When delegation is done, it should involve careful consideration of the level of difficulty of the task and whatever briefing or orientation is necessary to ensure that the individual knows exactly what is expected of him or her and how the assignment is to be performed. The supervisor should be ready to assist at all times and should be alert to signs of difficulty.

Once the task has been successfully completed, the manager may gradually permit the subordinate employee to proceed with increasing independence. As the employee's confidence grows, more and more tasks can be delegated, freeing the manager from a burden of many daily tasks and concerns, minor details, and deadlines. Bannon writes of the manager who refuses to delegate such responsibilities:

> Such a style of management becomes a relentless cycle of ceaseless work, little or no time for reflection, and not a thought to work delegation. Not only is problem solving neglected, such a manager gives little thought to long-range planning, coordination of

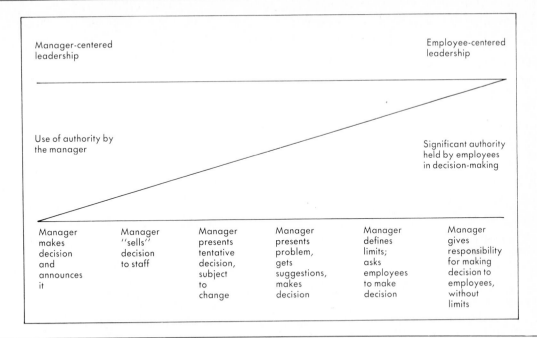

Manager-centered leadership

Employee-centered leadership

Use of authority by the manager

Significant authority held by employees in decision-making

| Manager makes decision and announces it | Manager "sells" decision to staff | Manager presents tentative decision, subject to change | Manager presents problem, gets suggestions, makes decision | Manager defines limits; asks employees to make decision | Manager gives responsibility for making decision to employees, without limits |

FIG. 7-1   Continuum of management styles in decision-making. (Modified from Tannenbaum, R., and Schmitt, W.H.: Harvard Business Review, March-April 1958, p. 9.)

work, or in-service training of employees which can aid in effectively sharing work. . . .Managers who do not delegate effectively become more workers than managers. They work harder, yet produce less than those who delegate effectively.[14]

SHARED DECISION MAKING AND PROBLEM SOLVING

Similarly, the managerial style that emphasizes widely shared decision making and planning participation by lower-level personnel will result in a higher level of work motivation and commitment to the goals of the organization.\The discussion of the Japanese approach to company management, including the use of quality circles, illustrates this principle. Actually, shared decision making and planning do not represent an *either/or* proposition. There can be a continuum of approaches, ranging from a highly autocratic, manager-centered approach to one that places a high degree of responsibility in the hands of employees (Fig. 7-1).[15]

The term "decision making" is often used interchangeably with "problem solving." Although they are similar, since the problem-solving process often results in decisions being made, a distinction should be made between them.

Decision making tends to be routine, involving the application of basic departmental policies and sound judgment in choosing among alternatives. When it is at this level, lengthy consultation should not be necessary to arrive at an appropriate decision. When the decision is more complex or significant in its costs or outcomes, it usually benefits from a joint consultation process, shared by managers and subordinate employees with a stake in the matter.

Problem solving approaches

The term "problem solving" suggests that there are serious barriers to arriving at an easy solution or decision or that there have been difficulties within the area of concern over a period of time that have had serious negative outcomes for the organization. Often a problem cannot be solved simply by making a decision; instead it may require a series of remedial actions over a period of time. There are several typical ways of dealing with problems of this type[16]:

1. *Authoritarian action.* The administrator or supervisor makes a decision alone, without consulting subordinates or program participants.
2. *Group-centered problem solving.* In direct contrast is the approach in which the members of the team become involved in a process of group discussion and analysis that examines alternatives and ultimately decides on an appropriate course of action. Such team-oriented approaches to problem solving have become increasingly popular in recent years.
3. *Analysis by planning specialists.* In some recreation and park departments, problems of a special nature or of a high level of importance are assigned to special teams of planners or experts in systems analysis. Such teams carefully analyze the problem and recommend solutions.
4. *Decisions by higher authorities.* One way of dealing with difficult problems is to "pass the buck" by moving them up the chain of command. This may be done either because lower-level employees do not want responsibility for handling more serious problems or because administrators have made clear that they *wish* to be consulted on all such matters.
5. *Avoidance.* A final approach is simply to avoid the problem and hope it will go away. Although there is some justification for letting difficulties work themselves out and for not making an emergency out of every problem, this ostrichlike approach is obviously not a desirable course of action.

It is generally believed today that the most effective approach to problem solving stresses group participation in the problem-solving process. With techniques such as group discussion, brainstorming, or role playing it is possible to get at the roots of the problem and understand opposing points of view or alternative solutions. The problem-solving process usually includes several steps (see box on opposite page).

CONFLICT RESOLUTION

A closely related task is conflict resolution. Here the assumption is that two or more staff members or groups of staff members, participants, or other concerned individuals are in sharp disagreement with each other. Johnson and Johnson, for example, describe *conflicts of interest* as "incompatible activities desired by group members based upon (1) differences in needs, values, and goals; (2) scarcities of certain resources such as power, influence, money, time, space, and position; or (3) competition or rivalry among group members."[17]

PROBLEM-SOLVING PROCESS

1. Recognize the problem, including not only its symptoms but also its apparent causes. This may involve varied types of difficulties such as: (1) problems of staff functioning or interpersonal relationships; (2) problems of interdepartmental or interagency relationships; (3) problems of community relationships; (4) problems between staff members and participants; or (5) problems of inadequate finances or other difficulties in the agency's environment.

2. Assign responsibility for solving the problem; this may be the task of a single program leader or supervisor or may be assigned to a small group or "task force" of staff members, depending on its severity and the resources required. At the same time, the desired objectives of the problem solution should be defined.

3. Investigate the problem and gather all relevant data. This may involve the examination of records, direct observation of a program or facility, interviews with concerned parties, or even formal hearings or other investigative sessions.

4. Identify alternative solutions. Here, several different strategies for solving the problem may be identified and balanced with each other both in their probable degree of success and in the difficulty that might be experienced in implementing them.

5. The solution that appears most logical and most likely to be successful, as well as the most feasible in administration, should be selected and put into action. When this is done, it is usually wise to inform all parties of the decision that has been reached or ideally to have this occur as part of the shared problem-solving effort.

6. When the problem-solving solution has been implemented, it must be carefully monitored and its success evaluated. If it is *not* working, or if new difficulties appear, reviewing the strategy that has been chosen and trying a new solution may be necessary.

The traditional view of conflict within any governmental or business organization was that it was harmful and should be avoided or prevented at all costs. Any employee who caused conflict was thought to be a troublemaker, and authoritarian or legal means were used to deal with such workers. *Preventing* conflict was a widely shared purpose of administrators.

In modern management theory a somewhat different view prevails. Many experts believe not only that conflict is inevitable, but that it is desirable and may be used to constructive ends. This is based on the conviction that organizations must adapt and change to survive. Conflict, which often stems from sharply contrasting points of view or from individuals or groups who refuse to accept traditional or establishment approaches, may lead to problem solving or other adjustments that help the organization move more effectively toward its goals.

The effort must *not* simply be to reduce or eliminate conflicts when they appear. Instead, the creative manager may actually encourage them to some degree and should certainly seek to use them to benefit and support the goals of the organization. Seen in this light, conflict management and resolution become important responsibilities in modern management practice.

Group processes usually involve negotiation, which focuses on the concrete issues to be resolved and seeks to arrive at an agreement that will be acceptable to both parties. Typically, most parties enter negotiations with an aggressive frame of mind, in which they want to come out with an agreement that is as close as possible to their original position and in which they expect, or hope, that the other party will yield on all important points. Such attitudes often result in a stalemate, hard feelings, or dissatisfaction, even when an agreement is finally reached.

Obviously, there are a number of different ways of dealing with conflict. One of these is through the use of "clout" in an authoritarian way. For example, after one series of heated exchanges regarding the feasibility of a project under consideration, the chairman concluded the discussion by saying, "Now we have everyone's point of view. Those who are not in favor of going ahead with this project may signify by saying 'I resign.' " This may be described as the "win-lose" approach, in which either the power figure or most of the group impose their will without concessions from the others. They *win,* and the others *lose.* Another approach may be described as a "lose-lose" tactic. Here, through compromise or arbitration, neither side attains what it really wants and considers important and thus both sides lose.

Conflict is resolved most productively when a strong effort is made to involve all members of the group, who are helped by bringing their underlying needs and values out into the open and discussing them in the honest effort to arrive at a consensus. In the "win-win" approach, all participants feel that their thinking has been properly presented and given full consideration by all members of the group. Each member recognizes the rights of other members to have feelings, values, and ideas and strives to respect these rather than fight in a determined way for the alternative that he or she considers to be unilaterally best. Ultimately, through this kind of open confrontation and discussion, decisions can be made that all members recognize are in the best interests of the organization. Rather than avoid conflict by repressing it or seeking to impose a quick solution by a managerial decision "rocking the boat" may actually lead to uniting, healing, and stimulating organizational activity.

A positive problem-solving orientation, which avoids threats, hostility, deception, or the arbitrary exercise of power, will help solve such conflicts in the most constructive way. Techniques such as group discussion, role-reversal psychodrama exercises, or the use of third-party mediators are helpful in resolving conflicts.

STRESS MANAGEMENT IN LEISURE-SERVICE AGENCIES

Closely related to the problem of conflict resolution in many leisure-service organizations is concern about stress management. Many employees on all levels in both business and government agencies may be suffering from a degree of personal stress that limits their effectiveness on the job. Stress—which may be defined as a state of pressure and anxiety that may lead to heart attacks or other illness, depression, alcoholism, or drug dependence and to a breakdown in normal relations with friends, family, and colleagues—has grown markedly in recent years. Today many companies and other organizations recognize that it is responsible for the loss of key employees, poor performance, sloppy decision making, low morale, and decreased production. They are developing courses in stress management or ''wellness'' and physical fitness programs in an effort to deal constructively with this problem.

Stress is not necessarily bad. Hans Selye, a pioneer in this field, has commented that without stress life would be boring. In moderate amounts it is a healthy and natural phenomenon; it contributes to the tension and energy that are necessary for an individual to perform well. However, when it is excessive because of a high level of frustration, continuing conflicts within an individual or among individuals, or excessive pressures on employees, it can clearly undermine confidence and efficiency. Individuals under excessive stress tend to feel highly pressured about time, to overemphasize work in their lives, and to give inadequate attention to leisure pursuits. They are easily irritated, show impatience with other people, and often have serious problems in adjusting to setbacks or difficult situations on the job or in their personal lives.

Beyond striving to recognize when stress is hampering employees' job performance and personal lives and counseling them in dealing with this problem, managers should consider sponsoring special staff meetings or workshops aimed at stress management. Such programs include physical examinations, lectures, seminars, and supervised sessions that teach employees to substitute positive behavior patterns for harmful ones.

Today authorities recognize the importance of varied forms of recreation in helping to reduce stress. Cleaver and Eisenhart point out that many physical activities achieve a state of relaxation and help reduce stress:

> Following periods of extended exertion the body systems slow, bringing on a state of deep relaxation. Attaining this relaxed state is essential to lessening the stress reaction. . . .From the reports of thousands of joggers and runners we know that their daily mileage has become one of the most important activities in their lives. Many other physical and recreational activities, done regularly, provide a comparable reduction in stress.[18]

At the same time, they also point out that passive activities such as hobbies or crafts may also lower blood pressure, relax the nervous system, and help reduce stress, partly enabling participants to ''lose'' themselves in the activities and thereby ease external pressures or other stress factors. Given the value of recreation in helping reduce stress, it is a curious comment that many recreation agency employees themselves experience a high level of stress.

Grossman and Heywood point out some of the reasons for this situation. Leisure-service employees, they suggest, often work when others are playing—on evenings, weekends, holidays, and summer vacations. They write:

> Not only do most employees work . . . when others have free time, they usually work under the constraint of tight budgets. Furthermore, they may experience many stress factors with which individuals in other [human-service] professions have to cope, e.g., competitiveness, hostility, meeting time constraints, and nonproductive meetings, as well as self-determined high expectations, standards, and personal demand.[19]

They comment that, just as the cobbler's children often go without shoes, many leisure-service managers have not recognized the need to reduce the work-related stress of their employees. If there are signs of pressure and anxiety among staff members, managers should consider implementing stress management programs. Stress can be alleviated by providing effective problem-solving and conflict resolution processes, as well as making employee role expectations clear through accurate and meaningful position descriptions and agency policies. Participative management techniques and improved communication methods, along with careful concern given to employee workload, improving the work environment, and similar steps will also help reduce tensions.

Dealing with burnout

An extreme form or result of stress is *burnout,* which is increasing in human-service fields such as education, social work, and leisure-service programming. This phenomenon is generally described as a feeling of extreme emotional exhaustion and a sense of personal devastation or disillusionment that occurs over time in response to continuous work-related stress or frustration. It is marked by negative self-concept, poor work patterns, and fatigue and irritability. One psychiatrist defines it as a "progressive loss of idealism, energy and purpose experienced by people in the helping professions as a result of the conditions of their work."[20]

Shank points out that some common factors in the work of human-service professionals add to the threat of burnout, such as: (1) inadequate pay; (2) lack of input into decision making in bureaucratic institutions; (3) overloads through inadequate staffing; (4) role conflict and lack of role clarity; and (5) lack of administrative or supervisory support, often linked to the limited understanding and support of recreation itself. Pointing out that this is a gradual process with recognizable symptoms in the early warning stages, Shank writes:

> The initial stages of burnout can be used as a stimulus for making changes, for rearranging priorities, and perhaps most importantly, for re-introducing the self to the self. Negative stress can be turned into positive energy if the individual is willing to let go of some "emotional garbage" and fill the vacated space with coping techniques that can be tapped whenever the alarm signals are allowed to be heard.[21]

This suggests that an important responsibility of managers is to attempt to create a healthy emotional environment for their employees, which helps build positive self-concepts and satisfactions and overcomes the built-in factors that tend to create stress and frustration. Beyond this, managers should be sensitive to the emotional state of co-workers or subordinates and should be supportive and helpful, assisting them personally when appropriate or suggesting that they seek professional help to deal with severe pressures or early stages of burnout.

Working with Labor Unions

A final important aspect of the personnel-related responsibilities of leisure-service managers consists of their role in dealing with the powerful unions that represent employees in public, voluntary, commercial, and therapeutic agencies. In general, unionization has affected public recreation and park departments more than other types of leisure-service organizations.

TABLE 7-2 Issues Negotiated in Park and Recreation Labor Union
Contractual Agreements

Issue	Percentage of Agencies in Which Issues are Negotiated
Fringe benefits	95.8
Wages and salaries	94.4
Grievance procedures	91.7
Overtime	88.9
Vacation time	85.9
Working conditions	84.7
Holidays	83.3
Hours of work	77.8
Seniority provisions	76.4
Leaves of absence	71.2
Discipline and discharge	65.3
Retirement plans	61.1
Safety regulations	52.8
Selection and promotion criteria	47.2
Work load standards	33.3
Contracting work out	18.1

From Culkin, D., and Howard, D.: "Collective Bargaining and Recreation and Parks Operation," *Parks and Recreation,* Oct. 1982, p. 58.

In 1982, Culkin and Howard[22] reported the findings of a study of unionization among public recreation and park departments. Using a population of 200 agencies selected randomly from a list provided by the National Recreation and Park Association, they achieved a response rate of 92%. Of these, almost 43% had established bargaining units, with departments in the Northeast, Mid-Atlantic, and Pacific Coast regions having the highest percentage of unionization. In general, larger cities or counties were more likely to have unionized recreation and park departments, with more than 90% of those with populations over 500,000 being unionized.

Culkin and Howard also found that almost two thirds of the employee bargaining units were affiliated with major national or international unions such as the American Federation of State, County and Municipal Employees (AFSCME) or the Teamsters; the remaining units were often identified as employee associations. Bargaining units typically dealt with a wide range of issues in labor negotiations and contractual agreements (Table 7-2).

More than one fourth of the agencies with labor unions or associations reported having had at least one strike, with the average length being 16.7 days.

Strikes can be extremely serious in their consequences for public leisure-service agencies. For example, in Vancouver, B.C., a strike by all Park Board unionized employees in 1972 continued from April 27 to June 19 with the following effects:

> The parks suffered most as all maintenance of grass areas, gardens and landscaped areas ceased during our most intensive growing period. Emergency and essential work was performed by a handful of officials and union-excluded staff members who fed zoo animals,

cut golf greens at six golf courses to prevent them from being put out of use for a year, and performed essential office duties including answering thousands of telephone calls by the public who were greatly inconvenienced because of the closure of most facilities, including the zoo, community centres, swimming pools, restaurants, golf courses, refreshment booths, etc.[23]

In 1978, the city of Calgary, Alberta, experienced a strike of outside workers and foremen for 55 days during March and April, which resulted in 375 recreation and park employees joining the picket lines. All 11 municipal arenas and all 12 swimming pools were closed down, with only limited service being provided for numerous other facilities, including zoos, where without care numerous animals might have quickly died. During the strike, there were many incidents of violence and one case of suspected arson.

Clearly, strikes and work stoppages can be highly destructive. Most grievances concerning unsatisfactory working conditions, disciplinary actions, or alleged contract violations or violations of work rules can be settled without the threat of strike. However, this imposes constraints on recreation and park administrators in their ability to assign personnel appropriately or change working conditions according to the needs of a given situation. The demotion of an individual or in some cases failure to promote may readily become the subject of a union grievance procedure.

Union contracts have posed particular difficulties for recreation and park departments through rigid and inflexible controls over the use of personnel, including possible scheduling at odd hours or on weekends, as well as through limitations on the managers' ability to transfer employees or exert specific forms of discipline or control. However, it should also be noted that, particularly in larger cities, labor unions have been instrumental in markedly upgrading the status and pay of recreation and park employees, improving their working conditions, and giving them a stronger sense of dignity and self-worth. Typically, these have been a mixed blessing for department managers in the sense that the numerous fringe benefits that employees have gained, such as extra paid holidays, sick time, personal days, sabbaticals, conference days, pregnancy leaves, and time off for giving blood or voting, have represented the loss of available employee time and sharply rising personnel costs.

The mixed impact of unionization and collective bargaining units on public recreation and park agencies is shown in Table 7-3, which summarizes the views of department heads on specific outcomes.

In dealing with this important aspect of personnel management, recreation and park department heads must work as effectively as possible with public employee unions. Buechner suggests that the ''line official'' is at the front when it comes to supervision, handling grievances and disciplinary action, and adhering to other terms of labor agreements. He offers several labor relations ''rules of the game'' that should be helpful to administrators in working constructively with employees:

1. Develop complete job descriptions and duties including pay grades.
2. Familiarize yourself with the collective bargaining laws of your state and local jurisdiction and keep current on new legislation.
3. Train your supervisors on how to deal with union complaints and grievances and

TABLE 7-3   Effects of Unionization and Collective Bargaining, as Perceived
by Agency Heads

Statement	Percentage Agree	Percentage Disagree
Improved the welfare of the employees by gaining for them higher salaries and benefits than they would have otherwise received	81.7	18.3
Forced the organization to reduce the quantity of services it provides for the public	31.0	69.0
Enhanced the organization's ability to offer programs and services on the days and at the times when they are most desired by the public	10.5	89.5
Hurt employee morale	22.4	77.6
Improved the quality of services we provide the community	19.7	80.3
Restricted management's ability to enforce proper conduct and discipline in the work force	50.7	49.3
Enhanced management's ability to hire well qualified personnel	27.5	72.5
Forced the organization to seek alternative revenue sources in order to meet union pressures for greater wages and benefits	33.3	66.7

From Culkin, D., and Howard, D.: "Collective Bargaining and Recreation and Park Operations," *Parks and Recreation*, Oct. 1982, p. 58.

be sure that they are familiar with the terms of the agreement.

4. Establish a grievance procedure—even if you don't have unions.
5. Employ or retain a qualified labor relations director.
6. Remember that unions are not the enemy. They are a group of your own employees.
7. Do not put union relationship on a once-a-year, contract-time basis. It is a full-time job.
8. If supervisors cannot be discouraged from unionizing, at least separate them from the bargaining unit of the employees that they supervise.
9. If possible, determine the bargaining unit through a secret election rather than a show of cards, or other means.
10. Do not panic or fear union leaders or concede to their every demand. When you feel you are justified, say no!
11. The union should be prohibited from conducting union activities during working hours, except for presentation of grievances—and even this should have a supervisor's approval.
12. Always bargain in good faith, learn to control emotions, and develop patience. Don't give the union cause or opportunity for criticism.
13. Do not underestimate union organizers. They are experts in their field, well trained and knowledgeable in labor-relations matters.
14. Take disciplinary action as required and provided for under the agreement. If you let one employee off the hook others will expect the same treatment.[24]

To these guidelines one might add the following advice. It is important to keep in regular touch with the union rather than wait for emergencies. Union members should be kept well informed about personnel plans and developments and should be involved in major policy discussions, although not in the decision-making process. In confrontations, the recreation and park administrator should insist on courtesy, comfortable surroundings, and orderly procedures. He or she will be wise to listen rather than speak, to acknowledge the sound points of union representatives, to avoid harangues or hot arguments, and finally to withhold *all* decisions until they have been thoroughly reviewed after the meeting.

When recreation and park managers are involved in formal bargaining sessions as part of the bargaining team, their function is usually to provide technical information about the operation of their department or the probable effects of contract points under consideration to the other management representatives and negotiators.

Managers should seek to avoid unnecessarily hostile situations with labor unions. Probably the best advice is that of W.D. Heisel, director of the Institute of Governmental Research of the University of Cincinnati, who comments:

> You can create an atmosphere of hostility, or an atmosphere of harmony. You can deal with union leaders as interlopers, or as equals. You can make or break the labor relations directors' efforts. Unions are here to stay; I suggest that we learn to live with them in peace.[25]

In other types of leisure-service agencies, labor unions also represent an important element of the personnel management function. In many large voluntary and social service agencies, such as the network of Jewish community centers throughout the United States and Canada, employees in both professional and clerical categories are unionized, and many serious strikes have taken place in recent years. Increasingly, hospitals and other settings for therapeutic recreation have also become unionized, and in 1984 a major labor conflict took place at Walt Disney World and the EPCOT Center in Florida. To a great degree the resolution of such problems is not the responsibility of recreation managers but is the function of labor relations specialists who are responsible directly to the board or executive directors of the agency.

Professional Identification and Commitment

A final concern facing personnel managers in recreation and park service is the need to seek ways to build or reinforce a sense of personal identification with the field and a commitment to its goals.

It has sometimes been said of the leisure-service field that "we have achieved a profession, but we have lost a movement." This suggests that over the past several decades, in the process of becoming established as professionals in governmental, voluntary, therapeutic, and other types of agencies, many workers in the field have lost the sense of dedication and purpose that once characterized leaders in recreation and park agencies. Concern about professional techniques and functions or job status, fringe benefits, and promotional opportunities has to some degree replaced the wholehearted philosophy that pioneers in leisure service had—the sense of mission and purpose.

As managers in recreation and parks seek to make effective use of contemporary techniques for human resource development, they must also strive to imbue their staff members with a continuing commitment to the field and its goals and to the public whose needs must be the paramount concern of all professional practitioners.

Summary

Beyond the task of developing and applying appropriate personnel policies as described in Chapter 6, managers are responsible for establishing a climate for the supervision of employees that promotes positive motivation and job productivity.

Two primary styles of supervisory behavior have been identified: employee-oriented and production-oriented. These are not necessarily diametrically opposed and may be combined within a single effective manager. Recognizing employees' needs and satisfying them by providing ''motivator'' factors such as opportunities for growth and self-improvement, involvement, and recognition are essential. Coaching and counseling elements of supervision, the need to develop a sense of commitment to the agency through job enrichment, and a participative approach to management are also described in this chapter.

The delegation of authority and shared decision making and problem solving are described, as are methods of conflict resolution and stress management approaches in leisure-service agencies. The chapter concludes with a discussion of the task of working with labor unions in larger public, voluntary, and commercial recreation organizations.

STUDY QUESTIONS

1. Which type of supervisory approach is most suitable for leisure-service agencies—production-oriented or employee-oriented? Hold a class debate on this issue with reference to a particular type of leisure-service setting, such as a company recreation program or an armed forces base.
2. Experiment in class with the participative management approach and the delegation of authority by taking full responsibility with other class members for a session on this chapter. (The instructor should relinquish all authority for supervising or grading work during this session.)
3. Identify a recreation organization that is unionized within your region. Interview its director to determine the impact of unionization on the program and the approaches he or she uses in working with the union.

Case 5   Morale on the Treatment Team

YOU ARE CHARLES BECKER, the new director of activity therapies in a large state-sponsored mental health center. You have been successful in having several recreation therapists placed on the treatment team, along with other medical, nursing, social service, and adjunctive therapy personnel.

However, the therapeutic recreation specialists feel that they are not given the same degree of status or respect as the others. Their advice is seldom sought; they are not expected to keep detailed case records or provide input at treatment team meetings. A second problem involves the need to provide regular staff for selected weekend or evening assignments, which are currently handled by part-time personnel. The recreation therapists are reluctant to work at these times, even on a rotating basis. In fact, they cite the examples of other therapists and make it clear that, although there is no formal contract or other stipulation of work schedules, they are not willing to give up their "free" hours to do this job. You have concluded that both their morale and sense of professional commitment are low.

Questions for Class Discussion and Analysis

1. What are the fundamental causes of the difficulties you are facing in working with the recreation therapists?
2. Are the two problems cited in the case study connected in your opinion?
3. What specific steps could you take to deal with the overall problem of morale? How could you improve both situations, and particularly how could you make the evening and weekend work assignment acceptable to staff members?

Case 6   Modernizing the Y's Management System

YOU ARE EDNA STEVENS, the middle-aged director of a suburban YWCA. Based on numerous courses in administration that you took years ago, you have developed what you regard as an extremely efficient system, which follows the principles you learned then and in which you have always believed.

For example, you have a formal organization chart that defines the lines of authority, responsibility, and communication very clearly. The chain of command operates at all times. Power in the agency is tightly centralized, and you do not encourage your division heads to delegate authority. If they do and if things go wrong, you hold them responsible. Although this bureaucratic approach has worked well in the past, in the last few years you have hired several staff members who have resented and resisted it. Three have resigned, and the others, you feel, are not working up to the level of their ability.

Recently you attended a workshop in modern management approaches, in which you were exposed to ideas such as job enrichment, delegation of authority, participative management, and matrix or linking-pin organizational structures. However, you have never seen these approaches tried in practice. How could you experiment with them and yet not risk too much?

Case 6
cont'd

Modernizing the Y's Management System

Questions for Class Discussion and Analysis

1. Do you feel that the conflict between you and some of the newer staff members is basically an issue of subordinate employees challenging the power structure or youth versus age, or is there more to it?
2. What *might* be the value of adopting more participative management approaches, and what are the *real* risks that you would encounter?
3. If you decided to loosen up the formal structure of your agency, what would be a good way to begin?

REFERENCES

1. Feldman, Daniel C., and Arnold, Hugh J.: *Managing Individual and Group Behavior in Organizations,* New York, 1983, McGraw-Hill Book Co., Inc., p. 107.
2. Hatcher, Marilyn, and Lamke, Gene: "Job Status and Work Incentive: Developing a Current Picture," *California Parks and Recreation,* July 1979, p. 18.
3. Mescon, Michael H., Albert, Michael, and Khedouri, Franklin: *Management: Individual and Organizational Effectiveness,* New York, 1981, Harper & Row, p. 19.
4. Feldman and Arnold, *op. cit.,* pp. 300-301.
5. Neal, Larry L., Williams, John G., and Beech, Stephen A.: "How Managers Perceive Subordinates," *Leisure Today, Journal of Physical Education, Recreation and Dance,* April 1982, p. 57.
6. Buzzotta, V.R., Lefton, R.E., and Sherberg, Mannie: "Coaching and Counseling: How You Can Improve the Way It's Done," *Training and Development Journal,* Nov. 1977, p. 50.
7. Landahl, William: "Help Employees Help Themselves," *Parks and Recreation,* Feb. 1980, p. 45.
8. Nogradi, George S.: "Managerial Activities, Organizational Commitment and Job Involvement: A Study of Recreation Personnel in Mental Health Centers," *Therapeutic Recreation Journal,* 1st Q. 1981, p. 37.
9. London, Manuel, and Howat, Gary: "Employee Commitment in Park and Recreation Agencies," *Journal of Leisure Research,* 3rd Q. 1979, p. 205.
10. "Flexible Hours Work for Pitney Bowes," *Recreation Management,* May 1978, pp. 8-9.
11. Yorks, Lyle: *Job Enrichment Revisited,* American Management Association, 1979, pp. 8-9.
12. Edginton, Christopher R., and Williams, John G.: *Productive Management of Leisure Service Organization,* New York, 1978, John Wiley & Sons, Inc., p. 86.
13. James, Muriel: "The OK Boss in All of Us," *Psychology Today,* Feb. 1976, p. 32.

14. Bannon, Joseph J.: *Problem Solving in Recreation and Parks,* Englewood Cliffs, N.J., 1981, Prentice-Hall, Inc., p. 11.

15. Tannenbaum, Robert, and Schmitt, Warren H.: "How to Choose a Leadership Pattern," *Harvard Business Review,* March-April 1958, p. 96.

16. Kraus, Richard G., Carpenter, Gaylene, and Bates, Barbara J.: *Recreation Leadership and Supervision: Guidelines for Professional Development,* Philadelphia, 1981, Saunders College Publishing, p. 320.

17. Johnson, David W., and Johnson, Frank P.: *Joining Together: Group Theory and Group Skills,* Englewood Cliffs, N.J., 1982, Prentice-Hall, Inc., p. 280.

18. Cleaver, Vicki, and Eisenhart, Henry: "Stress Reduction Through Effective Use of Leisure," *Leisure Today, Journal of Physical Education, Recreation and Dance,* Oct. 1982, p. 33.

19. Grossman, Arnold H., and Haywood, Lloyd A.: "Stress Management in Leisure Services," *Leisure Today, Journal of Physical Education, Recreation and Dance,* Oct. 1982, p. 37.

20. Shank, Patricia Ann: "Anatomy of Burnout," *Parks and Recreation,* March 1983, p. 53.

21. *Ibid.,* p. 57.

22. Culkin, David, and Howard, Dennis: "Collective Bargaining and Recreation and Park Operations," *Parks and Recreation,* Oct. 1982, pp. 58-65.

23. Annual Report, Vancouver, B.C., Park and Recreation Department, 1972, pp. 5-6.

24. Buechner, Robert D.: *Public Employee Unions—Organizations,* Arlington, Va., 1969, National Recreation and Park Association, Management Aids Bulletin, No. 81, pp. 39-40.

25. Heisel, W.D., and Hallihan, J.D.: *Questions and Answers on Public Employee Negotiation,* Public Personnel Association, 1967.

CHAPTER 8

By far the most objectionable flotsam and jetsam on the County's beaches is caused by the inconsiderate littering of daily patrons. On a peak day Haulover attracts some 14,000 visitors, Crandon Park as many as 40,000, and the shores along Miami Beach just as many. These patrons leave behind cans, paper, pop-tops, cigarette and cigar butts, cups, straws, bottles, plastic bags and a number of other assorted kinds of refuse. . . . Because the public is allowed onto the beaches during their posted hours of 6 A.M. to 12 Midnight, clean-up is hindered; personnel must maneuver their machinery around the patrons, and many people refuse to move out of the way. [It] was doubly important in the light of Dade County's ever expanding areas of responsibility that the Department establish the most appropriate [beach maintenance] techniques and obtain additional equipment and personnel.[1]

Recreation and Park Facilities
The Manager's Role

*T*his chapter is concerned with a key aspect of leisure-service management: the planning, design, construction, and maintenance of recreation and park facilities.

Its primary emphasis is on public, municipally owned and operated areas and facilities, since local governmental agencies tend to sponsor the greatest variety of different types of recreational facilities, as well as the most extensive land and water areas. However, it also examines the planning principles involved in developing leisure facilities for voluntary, commercial, therapeutic, and other types of agencies. In addition to presenting specific guidelines and standards for planning, designing, constructing, and maintaining facilities, it gives essential information with respect to providing access for physically disabled and other special populations.

The concluding section of the chapter focuses on innovative types of recreational facilities, new approaches for sharing the development and operation of areas and structures, and the important role of managers in ensuring the effective stewardship of open space and environmental quality.

Facilities: The Manager's Role

Facilities operation is an important responsibility of leisure-service managers in American and Canadian communities. Public recreation and park departments in particular operate extensive networks of indoor and outdoor facilities, including playgrounds and parks, community centers of various types, sports complexes, swimming pools and beaches, ice rinks, and numerous other types of specialized leisure-service areas.

Although other staff members may be directly responsible for designing, constructing, or maintaining such facilities, it is the manager who must provide leadership in determining community needs for leisure facilities and making sure these needs are met. The manager must also be aware of current trends in leisure-service facilities and should be ready to pursue cooperative relationships with other organizations in planning innovative areas and structures.

Planning Principles and Methods

How does the modern community meet the needs of its citizens for park and recreational facilities through systematic, comprehensive planning? Several approaches have been used: (1) planning based on concepts of the neighborhood and community;

(2) recommended standards for open space and facilities based on population, service radius, or percentage of total acreage; and (3) urban planning methods based on land-use principles, analysis of community needs, and related economic and social factors.

NEIGHBORHOOD AND COMMUNITY PLANNING

This traditional planning approach identified two key units of local government and residential living patterns as the basis for providing recreational and park facilities: *neighborhoods* and *communities*.

Neighborhoods are generally regarded as residential sections of a larger city or town, usually about three quarters of a mile to a mile square, with fairly homogeneous populations. The term "community" is usually applied to larger residential areas, comparable in size to high school districts, just as neighborhoods are comparable to elementary school districts. Many basic leisure-service facilities are developed according to neighborhood and community needs, including: (1) neighborhood play lots or tot lots; (2) neighborhood playgrounds; (3) community playfields and parks; and (4) recreation centers of various types, designed to meet either level of need for indoor programming. Planning intended to serve neighborhoods or communities may assign such facilities to areas based on population numbers or so that individuals on different age levels will have access to them within a stipulated travel distance.

OPEN SPACE AND FACILITY STANDARDS

Closely linked to the preceding approach, open space and recreation facility standards have served for the past several decades as a means of identifying community needs for specific types of recreation spaces and facilities. These have usually been expressed as the ratio of needed recreation and park acreage to the total population, with the most common figure cited 10 acres of recreation space per 1000 community residents. In the mid-1960s the National Recreation and Parks Association revised this expectation to include property owned by local authorities, nearby counties, park districts, or state agencies, amounting to a total of 25 acres per 1000 residents.

In addition, standards for different types of facilities were developed, indicating the types of facilities that should be provided according to population totals in the community being served.[2] Another approach has been to determine needs on the basis of percentage of land area devoted to recreation and park uses or remaining as undeveloped land. Still another approach has been to identify a maximum service radius for each type of recreational facility. For example, there should be a neighborhood playground within a quarter mile of each elementary school child's home, or there should be a neighborhood center within a half mile of each high school–age youth's home.

LIMITATIONS OF STANDARDS APPROACH

Because communities differ widely in population density and residential housing patterns, fiscal capability, and recreational needs and interests, no single set of standards can apply equally well to all cities, towns, or counties. This point was recognized by the members of a National Recreation and Park Task Force on Standards, which recently published a compilation of current recreation park and open space standards. Pointing out that their publication should be used as a *guide,* they state:

> Without expensive and extensive long-term research, there is no way to apply the standards in the same manner in all locations. The uniqueness of every village, town, city and county—with their differing socioeconomic, climatic, geographic, and cultural characteristics—makes it impossible, and undesirable, to apply all of the standards in every community.[3]

Current Urban Planning Methods

There are essentially three levels of planning that relate to recreation and park facilities and services. These are (1) total master planning that considers all aspects of municipal growth, including industrial and residential development, transportation, education, housing, health, and other major aspects of community life; (2) planning that focuses solely on recreation and park development within a total community, sometimes as a separate portion of a total master plan; and (3) planning that is concerned with the development of a particular facility or the needs of a single neighborhood.

IDEAL MODELS OF THE COMMUNITY

One approach to urban planning has been to develop "ideal" models of what the "good" community would be like in physical terms. Planners assumed that each type of land use (such as heavy industry, shopping areas, residential areas, or public service facilities) could be placed in a logical juxtaposition to the others. Thus it would be in the most convenient location for efficient operation (heavy industry, for example, would be close to major highways or railroad lines) and at the same time would be so located that housing would be screened from unattractive or unpleasant land uses.

USER-ORIENTED APPROACHES

Other planners have adopted a user-oriented approach, which seeks to begin with the goals of the community and its citizens and then develop programs and facilities that represent the best means of achieving these goals within realistic financial constraints.

NEEDS INDEX MODELS

Other planning studies have used the criterion of social needs as the basis for planning urban leisure-service facilities. Typically, cities such as New York and Los Angeles have developed "needs index" approaches, in which they have identified areas of the city that have the highest degree of social pathology, such as poverty, poor housing, and crime. Using a complex formula that includes an analysis of each area's present recreational facilities and programs, these planners have identified *high, medium,* and *low* priority areas for recreation and park development.

Recreation and Park Planning Studies

Planning studies that seek to develop meaningful recommendations for recreation and park areas and facilities in a community must take the following into account:

1. Quantity and quality of existing public, private, commercial, and voluntary agency lands and recreation resources
2. Demographic and socioeconomic profiles of those to be served (age, sex, family size, income education, cultural, and ethnic characteristics)
3. Geographic location, climate, and special topographic conditions
4. Local traditions and customs or regional trends or patterns in recreation
5. Expressed desires and leisure needs of the citizenry

Planning studies usually include a general statement of the present status of the community's recreation and park resources and a statement of what those resources should consist of by a given date to serve the anticipated population satisfactorily. This requires an estimate of *demand projections,* which would be arrived at by measuring the present and anticipated uses of various types of facilities and by projecting population trends, developing forecasts of ultimate use when population has reached its maximum density in a given area.

Normally, three types of recommendations may be presented: (1) a *long-term* statement of needs and recommended acquisition (this might outline a total program of development for a 15-year period); (2) a *short-term* plan, covering action to be taken over the next 3 to 5 years; and (3) *immediate* recommendations for land acquisition and development.

GUIDELINES FOR URBAN RECREATION AND PARK PLANNING

A number of guidelines for urban recreation and park planning follow. They are primarily concerned with the development of facilities but also relate to program planning and fiscal management, since all these functions are closely interrelated.

1. Recreation and park systems should be established to meet varied community needs and should provide equal recreational opportunity to all, as far as possible.
2. Planning should reflect the needs and wishes of all citizens and should involve them in systematic assessment processes.
3. Each recreation facility should be centrally located within the area it is intended to serve and should provide safe and convenient access for all residents.
4. The design of each facility should be done individually to ensure that it is adapted to the specific needs of the area it will serve. Beauty, functional efficiency, economy, and safety are important design considerations.
5. Planning decisions must take into account the capability of the recreation and park agency to operate the facility under consideration (see Chapters 10 and 11 for a fuller discussion of fees and charges as a key factor).
6. Communities should have a long-range plan for site acquisition with a regularly updated master plan to ensure that properties are acquired while still available.
7. Intergovernmental planning with other public agencies is a must; in addition, the resources provided by other nonpublic organizations should also be considered in developing leisure-service facilities.
8. Recreational facilities should be designed and developed to permit the fullest possible use by different groups on a year-round and round-the-clock basis. Planning must consider not only physical sites and structures but also program operations.

EQUITY IN THE DISTRIBUTION OF FACILITIES

Crompton argues that the concept of *equality* in the distribution of urban recreation and park facilities and services is not as useful today as the concept of *equity*. By this he means that, while equal opportunity is the goal of planning, given the widely varying interests and capabilities of different socioeconomic groups within the community, simply providing equal amounts of facilities and services will not ensure equal levels of participation. Instead, planning must be based on fairness and justice—which are the essential thrust of equity. To illustrate, Crompton points out that equal expenditures for maintenance in parks having varying amounts of litter and vandalism will be unlikely to result in equally clean parks. Instead, equality of results commonly will require inequality of resources in different areas of a jurisdiction. He writes:

> Distribution concerned with achieving equal results would allocate bigger and better parks to poorer neighborhoods whose citizens have less private recreational space, and more maintenance personnel to high litter and vandalism parks, to achieve equal maintenance levels in all parks.
> Perfect equality of results in the distribution of leisure services is probably not a realistic goal. . . .Hence, the operational objective frequently is to increase the compensatory role of public recreation and park services to improve the opportunity of the underprivileged, while recognizing that complete equality may be non-feasible.[4]

Using a different model, which Crompton refers to as "market equity," the assumption would be that facilities and services would be distributed to areas or neighborhoods in proportion to the tax or fee revenues they produce. While this approach, which is typically used in the private sector of the leisure-service field, might not be accepted by the public as a fair way of distributing services, it is often applied indirectly when facilities or programs that are heavily dependent on fees or other special revenues are located within a community's overall recreation and park plan.

Although traditional planning guidelines have urged that facilities be distributed equally throughout the community being served, this has rarely been achieved in actual practice. However, every effort should be made to meet the special priorities or needs of each neighborhood or district within the larger area in order to serve different groups of residents appropriately. This relates to the issue of equity, or fairness, in providing recreation and park facilities (box above).

Instead of relying on the traditional open space and facility standards, many communities today have developed their own formulas for identifying facility needs and priorities. For example, the city of Chesapeake, Va., has systematically projected community needs for facilities for softball, football, soccer, basketball, and tennis. Since existing resources and participation needs varied widely throughout the city, Wade developed a personalized method of calculating needs among each of the five recreation service districts in Chesapeake, based on activity participation load for all facilities.[5]

Facilities Planning in Other Types of Leisure-Service Agencies

Planning considerations for facilities development in other types of recreation organizations vary greatly according to the special needs and capabilities of each category of sponsor.

VOLUNTARY AGENCIES

Nonprofit organizations, such as the YMCA or YWCA, or Boys' or Girls' Clubs, often combine recreation with other educational or social service functions, and their facilities must be designed to serve these purposes. Typically, they tend to operate buildings for varied indoor programs, but have limited outdoor facilities for special recreational use. Funds to support property acquisition or construction are raised not through taxes or bond issues, but usually by means of fund-raising drives in the community.

SCHOOLS AND COLLEGES

Recreational facilities in schools and colleges are generally constructed to meet multiple program needs, with instruction the primary concern. Typically in many colleges, gymnasiums, pools, or other athletic facilities have the following order of priorities of use: (1) formal academic program use; (2) use in intercollegiate practice sessions or competition; (3) use in intramural or campus recreational programming; and (4) use by community residents. In addition to such facilities, many campus unions or student activity center buildings have extensive social rooms, auditoriums, lounges, bowling alleys, game rooms, and similar areas designed for general recreational use or for special-interest groups or clubs.

THERAPEUTIC AGENCIES

Many hospitals, nursing homes, and rehabilitation centers or special schools have recreation rooms, lounges, arts and crafts shops, and in some cases gymnasiums, pools, and other special facilities. This is particularly true of psychiatric institutions or other residential facilities housing people who are physically in reasonably healthy condition and thus able to take part in active forms of recreation. On the other hand, smaller agencies, including nursing homes, tend to have limited facilities. Increasingly, guidelines for the operation of therapeutic recreation programs and accreditation standards for specialized treatment facilities are including recommended standards with respect to needed facilities and equipment.

COMMERCIAL RECREATION

In profit-oriented organizations, one tends to find an extremely broad range of facilities, some of which are highly diversified; for example, resort hotels or conference centers may offer various sports and aquatic, social, entertainment, and other areas for special activities. The key thrust in designing such facilities is economic viability, which includes the need to estimate the market or projected need for the facility accurately and plan it to be most attractive to the public as well as operable at an acceptable profit level. Guidelines for planning such commercial attractions are becoming increasingly

Outstanding facilities for the disabled provided at the San Francisco Recreation Center for the Handicapped include a fleet of vans with hydraulic lifts for transporting clients in wheelchairs and a pool with ramps for convenient participation.

sophisticated, particularly for amusement centers or theme parks, which represent very heavy investments and must be based on sound feasibility studies.

Donnelly[6] outlines the steps and considerations involved in planning a major commercial recreational facility of this type:

1. *At the beginning—an idea.* All recreation attractions that develop into large and successful business ventures must start with an idea that has drawing power for large numbers of people. This appeal may consist of (a) filling an existing need, such as the development of a year-round ski and recreation resort, or (b) creating a market and interest based on a new, novel concept.

2. *Testing its appeal.* The next step is to determine the idea's potential to a broad spectrum of the population, including both sexes, all ages, and all nationalities. Four types of potential visitors must be considered: (a) tourists and vacationers from more than one day's travel away; (b) local area residents; (c) special interest groups who may attend in large charter or special-trip packages; and (d) "spin-off" participants who have visited another nearby attraction and are able to visit adjacent vacation places.

3. *Location.* In the selection of an area in which to locate a facility, key elements are a heavily populated region, and accessibility by road and air. Other important factors are having a mild or moderate climate, a major airport, and large parcels of available, undeveloped, and reasonably inexpensive land.

4. *Weather.* As indicated, weather is an important factor, either with the possibility of year-round attendance of the same basic program, or with an alternating program based on seasonal changes, such as a ski resort in the winter that is converted to a camp in the summer and convention lodge in other seasons.

5. *Government controls and regulations.* Another significant factor in recent years has been the nature of federal and state laws that have affected taxes, fees and charges, pricing, labor practices, and the ecological impact of new developments.

Within each specialized area of recreation service, considerations similar to these must be taken into account in the facilities planning process.

Acquisition of Properties

Once planning decisions have been made and appropriate sites selected for facilities development, the next step is to acquire the needed areas. The selection of sites for recreational and park use must be carried out in a systematic way. The size and exact location of each area should be part of an overall community plan that provides balanced opportunity to all neighborhoods within a city. In cities that have already been heavily developed with a minimum of available open space, it is difficult to accomplish this goal. Often in such circumstances, it is necessary to *create* open space through urban renewal programs that involve the demolition of blighted tenement areas or razing of old factory or railroad yard areas. In many cities, parks, playgrounds, plazas, and other recreation areas have been created in this way.

In general, the methods through which municipalities may acquire land for recreation and parks are as follows.

PURCHASE

Direct purchase of property from its owner is the most common method of land acquisition. Through the right of eminent domain, government may acquire property by means of condemnation, with the court fixing a fair purchase price if the owner is unwilling to sell his or her land directly.

TRANSFER

Recreation lands may be acquired by transferring or exchanging properties from one government department to another. As suggested earlier, dumps, warehouses, river frontage properties, and even tax-delinquent lands may become available. Although such land may appear inappropriate for recreation development, through landfill and other engineering methods it often can be converted to outstanding recreational and park use.

Other types of marginal properties that may be acquired include the following: (1) railroad rights-of-way for hiking trails; (2) utility rights-of-way for hiking, biking, or horseback riding; (3) flood plains for seasonal use as linear parks, with picnic areas and trails; (4) properties surrounding water supply reservoirs; (5) airport buffer lands; (6) power generation sites, which may provide useful boating, swimming, and fishing close to hydroelectric plants; and (7) atop municipal underground parking facilities.

LEASING

Long-term leasing arrangements are sometimes used to make land available for park use. These are best applied between government agencies or departments. If the intention is to use the property for recreation on a permanent basis, the temporary nature of the lease poses a special risk when the arrangement is with a private owner.

GIFTS

Many cities and counties have been able to acquire substantial park properties through gifts and bequests from public-spirited citizens. Although this is obviously the least expensive form of land acquisition, such properties should be accepted only when free from narrow use restrictions and suitable in location and topography for recreational use.

DEDICATION BY SUBDIVIDERS

A growing practice in many suburban communities is to require a land developer or subdivider to set aside a certain percentage of property for recreational and park use. In some cases this land is deeded to an organization of persons who have bought houses in the development. In others, the land is given directly to the town or other government in which the land has been developed.

As an example of such mandatory dedication, Anne Arundel County, Md., has an ordinance that states, ''The developer of a single family or duplex subdivision . . . shall provide 1,000 square feet of recreational land per each or every lot or dwelling unit . . . within the proposed subdivision.'' For multifamily subdivision areas, a scale of percentage of property that must be given has been developed.

EASEMENTS

In some cases land may be made available for recreation without direct acquisition. This may involve an agreement between government and private-property owners that permits specified recreational use of the land. In some cases flood control lands or property adjoining highways or airports is made available for recreation on this basis, without the land being transferred to the public recreation and park department. In others, owners of undeveloped land are given a reduced tax rate as compensation for keeping the land as open space rather than developing it.

Kershaw points out that many special kinds of arrangements have been worked out involving exchange of properties or permitting people to retain a portion of their land or use it during their lifetimes with major tax advantages. He concludes:

> It is the obligation of every parks and recreation director who has the responsibility of acquiring park-land to explore and become fully knowledgeable about the broad implications of tax loopholes, negotiations procedures, and other incentives that will expedite or enhance his jurisdiction's ability to efficiently acquire park property.[7]

Acquisition by Nonpublic Agencies

Acquisition of recreation and park properties by nongovernmental organizations is generally a simpler process. Therapeutic and industrial agencies usually do not purchase separate properties for recreational purposes, but instead include this function as part of the overall facility development effort. In some cases companies or associations of employees separately acquire properties for development as camps or sports areas, usually through a regular purchasing procedure. Similarly, voluntary agencies typically buy properties for development, although they may also rely on gifts or in some urban centers on rebuilding older structures or unused school buildings that have been made available to them.

Commercial organizations must also buy properties through a normal purchasing process, although, particularly when they are assembling a large area for a major new attraction, they may have to acquire land from a number of different owners and do it with a degree of secrecy, purchasing options through agents or subsidiaries to avoid suddenly inflating land values.

Design Process

Once land has been acquired for recreational and park use through any of the methods described, it is necessary to determine exactly how it is to be developed and to have designs prepared.

The design process usually involves the following steps: (1) selecting and employing a qualified architect, based on a legal contract that outlines all responsibilities and commitments of the task; (2) providing all relevant information regarding the purpose and function of the facility, as well as input from community groups or other potential users; (3) preparing preliminary drawings; and (4) reviewing and revising successive designs until the plan is acceptable to all concerned.

COST CONTROL AND FACILITY LIFE CYCLE

In planning any new recreational facility, it is essential that the costs of labor and materials over time, energy demands, and possible changes in community needs and user requirements be considered. Shipman, Forsyth, and Lerman[8] point out that careful analysis of operating costs, as well as initial capital costs, is becoming standard in the decision to construct a facility and in the design process and choice of types of mechanical equipment to be used. Since in many cases facility operating costs for ice arenas or similar structures are equaling capital costs in 10 years or less, the design process must give emphasis to efficient design to minimize heating or cooling costs and permit other economies.

Finally, if specific expertise is needed to design an appropriate kind of facility, the architect or engineer should make sure to secure this. In planning an artificial skating rink, similar facilities in the same climate belt should be explored to determine the relative value of different types of construction, freezing systems, and design layouts. No designer is likely to be an expert in all phases of construction, but when undertaking a specialized project of this kind, the designer must become, for a time at least, an authority on its special problems and needs.

DESIGNING SPECIAL FACILITIES

Numerous articles and special manuals provide guidelines for the design of various types of recreational and park facilities. For example, Eckhoff and Kershaw[9] have presented principles and methods for the planning and design of golf courses, including the need for feasibility studies, effective site selection processes, development costs and financing methods, architect selection, design and contouring features, landscaping, and maintenance. Recreation and park managers who are considering the development of any major facility of this type should obviously become as familiar as possible with the background literature and should also make a point of visiting similar facilities in their region and interviewing the individuals involved in the design process to learn from their experiences.

As another example, Ribble describes the process of planning a multiservice community center in Costa Mesa, Calif. The facility was designed to host the city's large senior citizen club 4 days a week, but also to accommodate conventions, conferences, banquets, community meetings, and wedding receptions and in so doing provide substantial revenue to offset its operational costs. The design therefore emphasized flexibility, with a large banquet room that could seat as many as 1100 in several arrangements or that might also be divided into four individual rooms for smaller meetings or event.

Among the special considerations in designing this type of facility, Ribble includes the following: (1) the need for sophisticated staging and lighting facilities for special programs; (2) planning for portable bars and a special wooden dance floor, marketable elements that generate substantial revenue; (3) adequate parking space for large groups, with special arrangements for "overflow" events when two or more organizations are scheduled at the same or overlapping times; (4) a safe pedestrian drop-off and pickup location; (5) accurate control of heating and air conditioning, particularly in rooms serving elderly or younger participants. Ribble writes:

You must be prepared for a real "wear and tear" on your carpet in a multi-purpose facility. We serve beer and wine. In addition to the wear from the heavy foot traffic and table and chair setups, we can expect food and drink spillage. Dark fabric hides dirt and damage more effectively. Some modern carpets are laid in 2' by 2' sections, allowing replacement of sections instead of the entire carpet.[10]

Since it is unlikely that the architect will be familiar with such special needs or conditions, the recreation and park professionals staff should provide input to ensure that the facility's design is realistic and practical. If *they* are not thoroughly familiar with the program factors affecting the facility that is being planned, they should visit other facilities—if necessary in other communities—to make sure that they are well informed on key details.

Role of the Manager in Facilities Design and Construction

What is the role of the recreation and park manager in the process of developing new leisure-service facilities? As this chapter has indicated, in most situations an outside architectural or engineering firm is employed to design recreation and park projects, although in some cases government employees may perform such tasks.

In smaller communities the manager is likely to be intimately involved and may work closely with the designer, participating in laying out excavation lines, making decisions regarding materials, and even instituting change orders directly at the construction site.

In larger cities, however, the recreation and park manager tends to be less involved, either because his or her own responsibilities are too demanding or because departmental lines are more sharply drawn. Instead, the major responsibility for selecting the architectural firm, approving the design, and following up on the construction process falls to the city or town engineer. There are certain advantages to this. The municipal engineer, who is usually a well-qualified professional, may regard the recreational facility as a personal project and give it full attention and support. On the other hand, many municipal engineers are narrow in their thinking and fail to understand recreation and park needs, particularly programs and people-oriented factors.

For this reason, recreation and park administrators should seek to become as fully involved as possible in each construction project, according to the following guidelines:

1. The recreation and park director should become familiar with all background information related to the facility plan and should be actively involved in all public hearings and planning sessions about it.
2. He or she should meet and discuss the project with all public officials or civic leaders, such as city council members, members of planning boards, or school administrators, who have a stake in it. He or she should be thoroughly familiar with their views and wishes and consider their suggestions seriously.
3. He or she should insist on being involved in the selection of the architectural or engineering firm that is to do the plan, pressing strongly for the selection of a designer who is highly qualified by experience and performance rather than the lowest bidder or the firm with political connections.
4. He or she should strive to be present at all design and modification conferences

to make sure that program needs are considered.

5. When construction begins, he or she should visit the site regularly either with staff members or with the architect on inspection visits. He or she should study the construction process carefully and note all problems. It is important to follow up on these immediately to correct errors that might be much more expensive and difficult to remedy later.

6. He or she should insist, through channels if necessary, that all construction details or standards be carried out or followed exactly as specified.

Planning and Design Approaches in Other Types of Agencies

Similar guidelines apply in nonpublic leisure-service agencies. Examples of two such approaches to facilities construction follow.

BOYS' CLUBS OF AMERICA

National organizations such as the Boys' Clubs of America usually offer advice and technical assistance to local chapters or agencies with respect to planning and designing facilities. This body in particular has a national task force on building design and has sponsored clinics for its member agencies on building design and construction. The following guidelines are adapted from a statement of "do's and don'ts" for club executives and boards planning a building program:

1. Define exactly what you expect of the new building before you start to design it: i.e., number of boys, types of programs, girls' participation, other special uses.

2. Establish how much money can be spent, and do not make any detailed designs until you have obtained cost estimates from a competent builder that will give a general picture of the kind of building you can construct within your budget. It is more effective to start designing under the proper restraints, than to try to cut costs from a completely designed building which turned out to be too expensive.

3. The Boys' Club director should take the lead in designing the structure, with an architect or competent builder's help. An experienced director knows what is needed and what not to have in a Boys' Club, and it is more effective to let the architect design the building around his concepts than to try to modify an architect's design to meet a Club's needs.

4. Don't hire an architect unless he or she is willing to minimize the cost of the building within the limits of durability and low maintenance, and maximize its useful space. The architect should be the practical engineer type who is an expert of materials of construction, cost-saving techniques, and other practical concerns. A good builder can provide helpful input during the design process.

5. A major building project requires a good deal of attention—perhaps 10 hours a week—from a member of the Boys' Club management and a representative of the Board of Directors. Make sure this assistance is provided.[11]

SENIOR CENTER FACILITIES

Another important type of recreation structure is the senior center, a building designed to house varied social, recreation, health-related, and other programs and services for older participants. Although many senior centers or golden age clubs meet on a part-time basis in churches or other community buildings, the trend is toward designing or developing new structures that will provide optimal facilities for the specialized programs needed by senior citizens.

Certain key concepts present themselves as critical in the design of such facilities, including problems of location and access, ability to serve specific program functions, safety, attractiveness, low-cost maintenance, and similar problems. Based on a study of senior center facilities carried out for the National Institute of Senior Centers, a number of key architectural guidelines and checklists for multipurpose centers have been identified. The study found that

> certain problems in planning . . . occur again and again. They include a failure to provide a variety of lounge spaces adequate to serve the conflicting demands of quiet conversation, television watching, reading and card playing. They require an understanding of the importance of a well planned and equipped kitchen together with adequate storage for refrigerated and dry foodstuffs. They point out the need for better design and selection of mechanical systems for heating, ventilating and air conditioning.[12]

A properly designed senior center building must normally provide each of the following types of areas, with special features that make them safe, convenient, and useful for older participants: hallways, multipurpose rooms, entry areas, quiet lounge, library, noisy lounge, auditorium, dining room, kitchen, craft room, meeting rooms, consultation rooms, first-aid rooms, storage rooms, offices, bathrooms, parking, and outdoor recreation or relaxation areas.

The arrival and departure area outside the center must provide adequate space and access for pickup cars, minibuses, emergency vehicles, and delivery trucks. Specific design elements should include a sheltered and illuminated approach; storage for car or bus; automatic doors or levered-door hardware with easy movement; an entry without steps; a vestibule to accommodate wheelchairs; slip-proof pavement; a car and bus turnabout; parking area; service entry; loading dock; and concealed garbage and refuse storage and pickup area.

Other specialized types of facilities have similar unique design considerations that recreation managers and architects must take into account in planning them.

Facilities Design for Safe Use

Another important consideration in all design of physical areas and facilities is to analyze the possible safety hazards of the facility and eliminate these in the planning process. Examples of such problem areas appear in the box opposite.

Design to Provide Access for the Disabled

Another extremely important trend in designing recreational and park facilities is the need to make them accessible for physically handicapped children and adults. In the past, there was little concern about such populations, and it was taken for granted that they would not be involved in normal recreational activities, particularly in active sports

---

> ## *EXAMPLES OF SAFETY DESIGN FEATURES*
>
> 1. Laying out all aquatic areas, whether swimming pools or beach of lakefront areas, to facilitate careful supervision and efficient emergency procedures and (in the case of natural sites) avoid built-in dangers, such as hidden rocks, low diving areas or dangerous currents, or conflict with boating uses
> 2. Using safety surfacing in playgrounds under climbing or swinging apparatus and equipment that has a minimum of inherent risk in the play experiences it offers
> 3. Laying out contiguous areas so one does not impose possible accidents on the other (for example, a baseball field immediately next to an outdoor area for senior citizens)
> 4. Using guard rails or similar barriers next to steep inclines or natural hazards, such as those found in some national or state parks
> 5. Providing needed safety equipment or approved features in all crafts and construction areas, particularly those using power equipment or tools, electrical units such as kilns, or acids or other possibly dangerous substances
> 6. Appropriately designing all high-risk sports or outdoor recreational facilities, such as ski slopes, to eliminate possible physical hazards

or outdoor pastimes. Today in both the United States and Canada, public and voluntary agencies must accept the responsibility for providing a full range of leisure opportunities for disabled populations of all sorts. In addition, through programs of modified sports or Wheelchair or Special Olympics, we have come to realize that the blind, the deaf, those with cerebral palsy, the orthopedically disabled, the aging, and the mentally retarded and ill can take part in camping, swimming, various sports, and even relatively high-risk activities such as snow skiing.

A key problem over the past several years has been to make facilities available for use by the disabled. In the past, little consideration was given to the needs of physically handicapped persons in designing recreational facilities; therefore it was often impossible or at least extremely difficult for them to gain access to such leisure areas.

Today almost all federal, state, or provincial governments require that public facilities be made fully accessible to the physically handicapped. The National Society for Park Resources, the National Research Council, and numerous organizations concerned with architectural standards have developed guidelines for facilitating access to recreational and park facilities and improving opportunities for successful participation. These include:

1. Logical design of walks and trails, with minimum widths and grades, appropriate surfaces for wheelchair use, elimination of expansion joints, and appropriate resting and pickup places for the handicapped and elderly
2. Picnic tables, fishing areas, specially designed nature trails, golf putting areas, and similar facilities that permit use by the blind or those in wheelchairs
3. Redesign of ramps, doors, vestibules, dressing rooms, swimming pools, toilets, drinking fountains, showers, and similar areas to facilitate use by the disabled

Once the determination to serve disabled persons more fully is made, the removal of physical barriers results in a much more comfortable, enjoyable, and dignified experience for them and their families. The U.S. Department of Housing and Urban Development has published an extensive bibliography on barrier-free design, including both theoretical and practical guidelines, cost-benefit analysis, and detailed recommendations for different populations and types of settings.[13] The Canadian Rehabilitation Council for the Disabled in Toronto provides similar materials and technical assistance in various areas of service, including recreation.

Maintenance and Operation of Facilities

Once a leisure facility has been completed, it is ready for operation. At this point the maintenance function becomes all important in promoting full and effective utilization of a facility by the public. Although they may not be directly concerned in supervising this function, agency managers must be sure that it is carried out thoroughly and efficiently both from a fiscally sound perspective and because it bears so heavily on the overall productivity and public image of the organization.

Owens describes the important role of park maintenance in community preservation and beautification:

> When you go to visit a park and find an inviting entrance—verdant, well-kept lawns; full, vigorous shrubs and trees that complement the landscape . . . clean, wide, smooth, and direct walkways and roadways; convenient, accessible parking areas; automobile barriers confining traffic to roadways and parking areas that are readily seen . . . and adequate receptacles for refuse; and neatly dressed employees who are informed and answer questions courteously—then you know that management recognized the important role that maintenance holds.[14]

This task goes beyond keeping park areas and facilities in the most attractive, clean, sanitary, safe, and convenient condition possible. It is also linked, Owens writes, to encouraging esthetic values in our communities:

> We must speak for beauty. We must take the lead in opposing moves to deface and scar our landscape. We must speak out against junkyards, litter, and the pollution of our atmosphere and airways. Acceptance of these challenging concepts can lead a park district to many exciting facets for its maintenance personnel.[15]

The basic task of maintenance is to keep an indoor facility bright, clean, and cheerful; an outdoor facility should be regularly and carefully cleaned, watered, weeded, or fed, according to its special needs. Good maintenance will earn respect for a recreational and park facility, encourage participation, and lengthen the life of a facility and the equipment in it. Poor maintenance practices will do just the opposite. In addition, through regular inspections and prompt repair of broken equipment or dangerous conditions, accidents will be prevented and lawsuits avoided.

In developing an effective maintenance plan, it is necessary to establish goals or basic principles and then to categorize the types of services, or functions that must be performed. For example, in the Texas state park system the maintenance management program is divided into three parts. Each year all maintenance requirements and needs of the various parks in the system are determined through a "current condition" inspection. This visual, on-site inspection is performed by the regional maintenance specialists in the company of the superintendent of the park being inspected, often with the involvement of key maintenance-oriented rangers. The information gathered is used to determine maintenance repair tasks, fully described with preliminary estimates, which in turn are entered onto budget control forms, one sheet per task.[16]

Tasks are then classified according to three levels of importance and difficulty and compiled into a prioritized list to be either carried out by regular maintenance staff or assigned to other operations and maintenance divisions within the state park system.

USE OF WRITTEN MAINTENANCE PLANS

Routine maintenance operations can be greatly facilitated with the use of written plans that interpret all responsibilities to field personnel in simple, clear terms. Sternloff[15] suggests that the plan used should list essential details for each facility under the following headings:

1. *Maintenance standards*—the minimum acceptable level of maintained condition for an area, facility, or equipment item
2. *Routine maintenance tasks*—these include tasks such as cleaning, lubricating, painting, litter and trash removal, planting, fertilizing, watering, weeding, and mowing
3. *Procedures for maintaining*—concise descriptions of how to do the tasks in the most effective and efficient manner possible
4. *Frequency*—daily, weekly, monthly, biannually, annually, or other guidelines for when work must be done, including seasonal variations
5. *Materials, supplies, and tools*—detailed statement of all materials and equipment needed to perform tasks
6. *Personnel*—minimum number of personnel required to carry out task, with identification of technical skills required and standardized statement of time needed to carry out task

Such a written maintenance plan is best presented in a format with several vertical columns and the wording as short and simple as possible. Sternloff comments:

> Keeping it short and simple certainly applies to the park/recreation maintenance manager who is anxious to institute a new routine maintenance plan. Unfortunately, the history of parks and recreation is replete with examples of meticulously written but lengthy plans going unused, simply because they are difficult to interpret and do not capture and hold the attention of the supervisor or worker quickly enough.[17]

Fisher[16] outlines an overall approach to developing a maintenance management plan that includes four elements: (1) defining goals and objectives of the maintenance plan; (2) taking a detailed inventory of the park and recreation system, resulting in an accurate listing of all the features, facilities, buildings, and equipment at each department-operated site; (3) defining maintenance tasks and developing standards for carrying these out; and (4) creating a format for scheduling maintenance work. As a final step that

helps organize the work effectively, it is necessary to develop a form for daily maintenance work and assignments. This form should reflect departmental priorities, should
divide the day into logical work segments, and should include information such as the
title of the task, location, person assigned to do it, and concise instructions if needed.
When displayed at an appropriate location in the maintenance building or office, it gives
direction to the maintenance crew and facilitates supervision of their work.

Finally, work order request forms should be developed for nonroutine, nonrecurring
maintenance tasks—specific, isolated jobs that are not part of the regular schedule.
These, Fisher writes, "should be funneled to the head of the maintenance division for
review and approval. The requests must be worked into the maintenance schedule. As
much lead time as possible and a measure of flexibility are vital."[18]

DEVELOPING WORK STANDARDS

Some departments have carried out time-and-motion studies in which each job function is clearly described, with standards developed, work assignments specified as to
frequency and duration, and the entire assignment carefully systematized. Functions are
grouped together and instruments and methods carefully developed to measure the cost
of job performance and assist in evaluating employee work output and assigning tasks
or planning budgets.

Within this overall process, park and recreation managers constantly strive to improve maintenance standards while reducing maintenance costs. One approach is to use
a systems technique to categorize maintenance levels by area. Donahue, a Canadian
parks maintenance specialist, describes how this is done:

> A downtown formal garden would be classified as an "A" area, demanding that the
> grass be cut three or four times per week, the garbage collected twice per day, and the area
> kept at a high fertility level. Such grounds would be automatically irrigated and the flower
> and planting beds would receive daily attention. At the other end of the scale would be
> "D" or "E" areas such as utility rights-of-way which require only an annual cleanup, and
> the grass cut once or twice per year. This categorizing of maintenance is invaluable in
> determining operating costs and in forecasting for accurate budgets.[19]

To illustrate such a schedule, the San Jose, Calif., Parks Division uses a maintenance
plan that itemizes the individual tasks that must be performed at two frequency levels,
one for optimum care and the second for minimum care, during active and inactive
seasons of the year (Table 8-1).[20]

Economy and Efficiency Strategies

Maintenance managers are constantly seeking new ways of achieving greater economy and efficiency. For example, the use of growth retardants may result in significant
cost savings in turf care over the traditional use of a standard rotary mower with a
walking groundskeeper. Similarly, the use of herbicides may be more effective and
cheaper as a means of keeping down roadside vegetation, particularly poison ivy or
other objectionable weeds. However, the use of herbicides will raise other questions

TABLE 8-1   Tasks Performed by Grounds Maintenance Personnel, and Frequency by Seasons and Levels of Care (Partial List)

Task List	Optimum Care Level On-Season	Optimum Care Level Off-Season	Minimum Care Level On-Season	Minimum Care Level Off-Season
1. Litter pickup	D	D	D	D
2. Clean restrooms/drinking fountains	D	D	D	D
3. Rake tanbark/sand areas	D	D	D	3W
4. Sweep perimeter of building	D	4W	D	3W
5. Set out refuse	3W	2W	2W	2W
6. Irrigate turf	2W	W2	2W	W2
7. Check trees/ties/stakes	D	D	3W	2W
8. Rake bleacher areas	4W	3W	3W	W
9. Irrigate flower beds	D	W2	4W	W2
10. Clean picnic areas	2W	W	W	W2
11. Mow turf areas	W	W	W	W2
12. Remove spent flowers	W	M	W	M
13. Edge ground-cover	M	M2	M	M3
14. Prune/trim hedges	M	M2	M	M2
15. Spray flowers/insect control	M	0	M	0
16. Fertilize flowers	M3	0	M3	0
17. Rake leaves, shrub/turf areas	M4	W	M4	W
18. Mulch shrub areas	M6	M6	M6	M6

Column header note: Frequencies* — Optimum Care Level (On-Season, Off-Season), Minimum Care Level (On-Season, Off-Season).

Modified from Mills, A.S., Harris, R.W., and Conway, K.L.: "Case Report—San Jose," *Parks and Recreation*, Jan. 1980, p. 89.
*D, Daily; W, weekly; 2W, 3W, 4W, two, three, four times weekly; W2, every other week; M, monthly; M2, M3, M4, M6, once every two, three, four and six months. On-Season is the eight-month period from March 1 through October. Off-Season is the four-month period from November 1 through February.

related to environmental impact or possible health dangers affecting people or animals using the area. Such considerations must be taken into account, along with esthetic and other concerns.

USE OF SPECIAL MAINTENANCE TEAMS

As indicated earlier, many recreation and park departments now use mobile teams to carry out routine or special maintenance procedures more efficiently than through the use of regularly assigned personnel. For example, the New Mexico State Park and Recreation Division has assigned a marina repair and maintenance team to its lakes and reservoirs, which has saved the state several hundred thousand dollars based on repair costs in years before the program was initiated. This team, formed from volunteers from the state park service, has had intensive training by qualified diving instructors and has acquired the necessary equipment, marina data, and technical skills to carry out routine and preventive maintenance of marina underwater structures and to do a number of major emergency repair jobs.

CONTRACTING OF MAINTENANCE FUNCTIONS

Another approach has been to subcontract maintenance to private companies or services. This is being done because commercial concerns can often carry out maintenance functions more economically than public agencies. Cryder points out that bureaucratic structures and similar political influences may make it difficult for those in the public sector to perform their tasks effectively and efficiently. He writes:

> In view of the recent upsurge in taxpayer revolts, a mechanism is needed to reduce costs and preserve the level and quality of the public services provided by local agencies. Contract services, which is the performance by private business of functions previously handled by public employees, has emerged as a good means for achieving cost savings, which in turn helps the public sector continue to perform many of its vital responsibilities.[21]

Sometimes referred to as "privatization," this policy is being applied to areas such as security services, park maintenance, and golf course starter operations. Garbage collection, building maintenance, and tree trimming have also been carried out by private concerns, frequently resulting in substantial savings (see Chapter 11).

Donahue argues that contractors should not be used as a last resort management option, but instead should be seen as a legitimate tool to improve productivity or upgrade quality. He stresses the importance of defining the work to be done with a contract that clearly specifies the quantity, quality, and price of the work:

> Unmeasurable work standards, open-ended expense features, and a lack of quality standards can lead to constant combat over provisions of the contract, conflict that will ultimately only benefit lawyers. The work should not require such complex day-to-day work variation that no one can write an accurate list of duties that can reasonably dictate the work schedule.[22]

Innovative Leisure Facilities: Challenges and Trends

In addition to being responsible for overseeing the planning, design, and maintenance of traditional types of recreation and park facilities, managers must be aware of trends in leisure facilities. The concluding section of this chapter examines these trends, as well as the social and economic forces that helped bring them about.

The primary problem that has affected many urban recreation and park systems over the past 15 years has been tight budget allocations, linked to the inflationary spiral, which raised the cost of land acquisition and construction sharply and reduced the availability of federal and state or provincial funds for recreation and park projects. Inflation has also greatly increased the costs of energy needed to heat, cool, and maintain large facilities, as well as personnel costs for staffing recreation areas.

At the same time, in many large cities the existing network of small parks and playgrounds has become largely nonfunctional. With reduced maintenance budgets, maintaining such facilities has become almost impossible. Often they are physically deteriorated and dominated and vandalized by youth gangs, drug addicts, or alcoholics. Blighted parks with slatless benches, broken shrubs, dying trees, vandalized restrooms, and weed-infested playing fields are becoming all too familiar.

Sports and fitness activities are found in many settings. *Upper left,* Adult employees take part in "fitness" events sponsored by the Honeywell Corporation. *Upper right,* Marines use fitness trail at Charleston, S.C., Naval Weapons Station. *Lower left and right,* Youngsters compete strenuously in Hershey Track and Field Youth Program.

Numerous studies during the 1970s revealed that many small urban parks and playgrounds were seriously underused. A leading planner, Seymour Gold, commented that most neighborhood parks were no longer meeting changing urban needs and life-styles. Increasingly, he wrote, upper- and middle-income families were abandoning local parks as leisure outlets.

To make neighborhood parks more attractive and useful for typical urban dwellers, Gold[23] suggests that the following design and management techniques or program elements be included in the development or revitalization of all parks: (1) use of *directional signs* and *maps* to tell the public where the parks are; (2) fuller *pedestrian access* from all sides and in as many places as possible to encourage entry and maximum use; (3) safe, convenient, and well-marked *bicycle access* to extend the service radius of parks; (4) simple concessions, vending machines, or use of street vendors to provide *food service* in neighborhood parks both as a form of leisure activity and to encourage social interaction; (5) use of *water features,* such as fountains, ponds, lagoons, or spray pools to attract and satisfy park users; (6) simple *labels* or *pamphlets* to describe the *flora* and *fauna* of each park; (7) providing *community gardens*—both flower and vegetable—to encourage community participation and a social focus for integrating neighborhood groups; and (8) replacing stereotyped children's play areas with *challenging* and *imaginative* designs linked to the adventure playground concept.

Casual observers of neighborhood playgrounds in large cities are likely to see many little-used facilities. Some critics have concluded that they are too fixed and static and allow no opportunity for creative exploration. Dattner[24] comments that the basic fault of traditionally designed playgrounds is that they lack anything to inspire interest and curiosity. After a little swinging, sliding, and seesawing, the built-in opportunities for play are exhausted.

What innovative solutions have designers found to meet this need? One approach is to use new and novel kinds of equipment that challenge the child's imagination and foster creative play. Typically, these may include huge animals made out of concrete or metal and new kinds of climbing apparatus or slides, brightly colored and designed in a contemporary style. They may often be based on a theme that appeals to the child's imagination, such as storybook characters, ''space age,'' ''prehistoric park,'' ''Western town,'' or similar themes.

ADVENTURE PLAYGROUNDS

Another approach is the ''adventure playground.'' Sometimes referred to as junk playgrounds or construction playgrounds, these may involve little more than an empty lot, a pile of scrap lumber, tools, a few sheets of canvas, and other waste materials. Under adult supervision, children are free to create playgrounds of their own design by building their own shacks and forts or creating different kinds of play apparatus and other structures. There may often be a small pond or stream nearby or simply a hose for water play or manufacturing mud. Adventure playgrounds may also include firebuilding and cooking activities, pet care and gardening, or even tunnel construction and cave digging—risky as many of these activities appear.

Although the adventure playground concept may seem revolutionary, it has been familiar to Europeans for several decades. Moreover, Vance writes that many of the objections to their appearance and their potential for accidents disappear once communities experiment with them:

> Studies by the American Adventure Play Association . . . have shown consistently that such playgrounds, where they have been established in the U.S., are extremely well accepted by both the community in general and by city officials involved in their formation and control. Additionally, it is not uncommon for such playgrounds to be frequented by many times the number of youngsters playing at more conventional playgrounds. The past

decade of experience in ongoing adventure play sites has also provided overwhelming evidence that such playgrounds can be conducted safely, without fear of undue hazard to children playing in them.[25]

In addition to the development of these facilities in the United States, a number of successful adventure playgrounds have been established in Canadian cities such as Toronto and Vancouver.

AIR-SUPPORTED STRUCTURES

A fairly recent innovation has been the use of air-supported structures, or "bubbles," to cover both large and small areas, such as tennis courts, swimming pools, track and field sites, and ice rinks. An air-supported structure, which basically consists of a balloonlike "skin" that serves as walls and roof, can be anchored in place, blown up, and made ready for use within a day. It can be deflated, untied, folded like a tent, and stored in even less time. Air-supported structures are comfortable and safe and are easily maintained; however, they have a life expectancy of only 5 to 7 years and are susceptible to vandalism. In many neighborhoods, zoning laws must be changed to permit their construction. Such bubbles provide great flexibility in that an area may be kept open during the warm months and then quickly enclosed during colder weather.

A number of schools, colleges, and commercial recreation enterprises have made use of air-supported structures. They are less fully accepted by public recreation and park departments.

MOBILE RECREATION UNITS

Many communities are making use of mobile recreation units to enrich program opportunities on play streets, in vacant lots, and in other improvised settings. Although they are not a new form of service, mobile units have expanded greatly in recent years. Many cities and towns in the United States and Canada have developed new mobile recreation units of the following types:

1. *Cultural units*—Band show wagons, portable stages and platforms, portable shells, puppet theaters, craftmobiles, bookmobiles, filmmobiles, historymobiles, and other units used for the performing arts and creative programs
2. *Sports and games*—Units with playground equipment, skatemobiles, boxingmobiles, circusmobiles, physical fitness trailers, portable swimming pools, and other sportsmobiles
3. *Nature and science units*—Naturemobiles, zoomobiles, sciencemobiles, starmobiles, etc.

ECOLOGICAL RECOVERY SITES

Another trend in publicly operated recreation and park facilities involves the recovery and improvement of the natural environment, either by reclaiming or protecting natural areas or by imaginative new uses of disposable wastes. This effort in turn may be linked to establishing nature centers, new wilderness habitats, or other environmentally based programs.

In addition, imaginative planners are actually using waste materials or the damaged environment to develop exciting new facilities. For example, one solution to a growing problem of urban ecologists—garbage disposal—has been found by the recreation and parks department of the borough of Etobicoke near Toronto. Instead of burying the town's refuse or dumping it elsewhere, it is being used to build a large ski hill. The hill is constructed by piling sanitary industrial wastes, covering it with additional fill, and planting trees to anchor it. Charges for dumping privileges are ordinarily higher than the cost of building the hill, so it is anticipated that a fine new winter sports facility will be made possible for Etobicoke without extra cost.

NATURE CENTERS

A closely related type of facility designed to conserve natural areas and promote environmental understanding is the nature center. Several hundred such facilities have been established in the United States and Canada over the past 10 years, and new ones are being added each year.

In some cases cities are developing new natural sites by ingenious methods. For example, in Foothills Park in Palo Alto, Calif., spring water seepage was dammed up to create a natural-looking marsh with a variety of wildlife and plants in an area where most of the natural terrain had been drained, filled, and reclaimed for housing and other commercial development. A marsh area of sizable dimensions was created through the work of youth crews and volunteer local residents. Plants were transplanted into the marsh, and Scout troops donated frogs, toads, salamanders, and turtles gathered on trips. Inevitably, other forms of wildlife appeared, ranging from microscopic life and insects to birds and mammals. Park visitors today delight in observing the unusual setting and ecological lessons displayed in this seemingly natural marsh.

It should be stressed that the facility itself will be incomplete unless it is staffed by a professional and creative interpretive division. Under such leadership, a variety of different kinds of programs can be initiated, including visiting school classes that seek to learn firsthand about trees, birds, animals, and historic or social science aspects of the environment. Learning should not be restricted to natural life itself but should embrace a general understanding and respect for the overall environment.

AQUATIC FACILITIES

One of the most popular recreational activities is swimming. Indeed, water-based activities in general, including swimming, boating, fishing, water skiing, and scuba diving, rank at the top of all outdoor recreation pastimes and are closely linked to camping, travel, and similar pursuits.

Swimming pools have undergone a variety of innovations in recent years, with technological advances making new forms of recreation, such as surfing, available to areas that would otherwise not have access to them.

Wave pools

The nation's first wave pool was developed at Point Mallard Aquatic Center in Decatur, Ala., in the Northern Mountain Lakes region of the state, adjoining the Wheeler National Wildlife Refuge.

The wave-making machinery, activated by time clocks, operates on 15-minute cycles, since the Point Mallard managers found that otherwise bathers were exhausted by the vigorous action of the waves. Unlike natural ocean beaches, there is no undertow, seaweed, or jellyfish or other ''varmints'' to sting the unwary swimmer. At the shallow end of the fan-shaped pool, swimmers walk down a sloping carpeted beach that leads into toe deep water and the edge of the gentler waves. The pool's whitecaps are liveliest at the 8-foot water level.

Other communities throughout North America have jumped on the ''wave pool'' bandwagon, with Calgary constructing the first indoor WaveTek pool in Canada—a huge, unique facility that can be easily converted to competition swimming. The popularity of this new design approach suggests that recreation and park managers are responding increasingly to the real leisure motivations of participants.

Water play parks

As an extension of the wave pool concept, some 30 water play parks have been built throughout the United States, Canada, and Mexico over the past 15 years. As described by Shedlock, a water play park

> consists of a major swimming pool equipped with wave-making machinery, one or more activity pools, often featuring diving platforms, pulley slides, and small ''waterfalls''; and a number of body flumes and slides. This often is augmented by special play areas for small children, and by non-water-play activity areas. A reasonable proportion of space allocated to rest and sunbathing also is available.[26]

Shedlock estimates that in the mid-1980s such an aquatic complex would cost approximately $6 million to build, if it were located on public land where no site cost would be incurred. Given a service area population of half a million residents or more, a park of this type (with its strong appeal for families and repeated visits) might anticipate drawing 300,000 to 400,000 patrons annually and clearing a substantial profit over its direct operating expenses.

Leisure pools

Even among smaller pool projects carried out by local communities or voluntary agencies, there has been a fundamental rethinking of pool design based on a new awareness of public leisure interests. Typically, pools have been built by communities that have relatively little knowledge of swimming needs and standards and that gather information from existing facilities, competitive aquatic organizations, pool builders or suppliers, and water safety and instruction organizations, such as the Red Cross, YMCAs, and similar bodies.

Customarily, such pools are designed primarily for exercise and competitive swimming, with a minimum of six or eight lanes, deep diving wells for competitive diving, and extensive bleachers for viewers. However, this sort of design is poorly suited for recreational use. Many cities in European countries such as Great Britain, Germany, and the Netherlands have recognized that a completely new model is needed to offer more possibilities for leisure swimming and related activities for the family as a unit.

Based on extensive studies of the needs and behavior patterns of visitors to existing conventional swimming pools, it was found that only 11% came primarily for physical exercise, while others were more leisure oriented, with the stay and play around the pool the most desired elements.

Based on these findings, more and more leisure pools have been constructed with certain design features in mind:

> the free form of the pools, water temperature, wide and spacious pool decks with sunbathing facilities, subtropical flora, such as palm trees, color, and other elements . . . . the roof should be transparent if possible . . . . its form should create the illusion of height and space and the sensation of being outdoors . . . . with solaria that give people an opportunity to get suntanned in the wintertime.[27]

ZOO DESIGN

Many cities are developing exciting new zoo facilities. The city of Los Angeles, for example, has built a modern multilevel zoo in which moats and natural barriers are used instead of fences and cages. This permits a close view of all specimens from safe positions; bridge spans provide exciting panoramas from above. So natural is the environment that a number of types of animals that have become increasingly scarce are now breeding successfully in this setting. Animals from a particular continent are in areas with settings depicting their typical native environment; each continental area is in effect a complete zoo in itself.

In part, such changes in zoo design are being made to provide animals and other creatures with more realistic, attractive, and natural surroundings than the restricted, barred cages of the past. However, they are also intended to make the experience of visiting the zoo far more participatory for visitors. Instead of serving as warehouses, the new designs provide settings for entertainment and involvement.

More and more major zoos today recognize that their real competition for public attendance comes not from art or natural history museums, but from family entertainment centers that offer active, diversified experiences in the outdoors. Accordingly, many zoos are undergoing large-scale remodeling that focuses on the visitor's experience. For example, the Philadelphia Zoo, the nation's oldest zoological garden, has now constructed a mile-long monorail that provides a 20-minute tour through the most interesting parts of the zoo, during which visitors listen to a taped commentary describing the animals and birds 15 feet below them. In addition, the zoo is now constructing a $2.4 million treehouse and other unique new settings:

> The children will explore a whole range of habitats from the animals' point of view . . . . They go under a pond and you hear the sounds you'd hear underwater. They get inside a [replica of a] frog and see what the frog would see. For the active children, we have the $5.7 million Primate Center, where there will be tests to see if you can swing like a primate does, or if you can walk along a log like a primate does.[28]

PHYSICAL FITNESS FACILITIES

A major new preoccupation of many leisure-service agencies has been to promote physical fitness within a broad new wellness concept of service. Industrial agencies, commercial health spas, public recreation and park departments, YMCAs, YWCAs, and YM/YWHAs have entered this arena vigorously. Jogging and running programs, racquetball and platform tennis, aerobic dancing, slim and trim programs, and a host of other special activities combine the physical fitness emphasis with recreational motivations and so have developed an enriched appeal for millions of Americans and Canadians of all ages.

As a result of the need to combine recreation and fitness in single activity packages, many recreation and park managers have sought out new program concepts and facilities. The European concept of self-guided exercise circuits, which first became popular in Switzerland, represents one such approach. The exercise circuit concept was introduced to North America in 1973 by Parcourse, Ltd., a San Francisco–based firm. Since then, more than 700 Parcourse circuits have been installed in parks, schools, and recreation centers; they are suited for any age level and may be used as a family activity for all members to enjoy safely and effectively. According to W. Brent Arnold, past president of the American Association of Fitness Directors in Business and Industry, at least 400 companies have initiated major fitness programs under professional direction. Many have developed elaborate facilities to house these programs. For example, the Goodyear Tire and Rubber Company has built a block-long, six-story, $3 million facility that serves as the center of the company's recreation and activity program. It houses a 1400-seat theater and a huge gymnasium that can accommodate three basketball or volleyball games simultaneously.[29] Similarly, many colleges and universities have built extensive physical fitness and sports facilities, some of which are used by community groups for recreation purposes.

LIGHTING

Another means of expanding community sports opportunities has been through the increased use of night lighting, which has lengthened the hours of use of many sports programs. For example, the city of Huntington Beach, Calif., recently installed an extensive new lighting system in Murdy Park, a 17-acre, year-round sports complex with football and softball fields, basketball and tennis courts, and a community center. In addition, pier and beach areas have also been lit to levels that now permit nighttime fishing, swimming, and even surfing. The volume of participation has increased greatly because of Huntington Beach's new capability for extending play well into the evening hours. In addition, the city recognizes several other values of night lighting: (1) it is a major deterrent to personal crime, vandalism, and theft; (2) it serves to distinguish various activities in the park, with various sports areas easily recognized by their unique lighting systems; and (3) it beautifies the park by enhancing plants, trees, and architectural features and helps integrate the park into a unified complex.

SPECIAL FACILITIES FOR THE DISABLED

As indicated earlier, there is growing recognition of the need to make recreation and park facilities accessible to disabled people of all ages. Numerous special facilities are being developed to meet such needs. Such facilities should not promote the segregation of the disabled but should permit their integration with the nondisabled.

For example, the University of New Orleans has developed a wheelchair fitness trail, which provides upper body exercise and practice at wheelchair balancing and maneuvering at 10 exercise stations running about 400 yards along a 1½-mile fitness course for able-bodied users. In many national and state parks, special facilities have been installed to serve blind or deaf users of nature trails through special tape-recorded messages, plaques, guidelines, and similar devices.

A number of communities have developed experimental playgrounds for disabled children, with modified equipment and apparatus that promote creative play and the development of needed movement skills. A most unusual facility for a special kind of disabled population—the socially disabled—was developed in Los Angeles with the establishment of a unique, controversial park for derelicts:

> The new 15,000-sq.ft. Skid Row Park, just east of downtown Los Angeles, is littered with drunks and derelicts. But no one minds. The place was designed for them. The designers of the park . . . have won an award from the American Society of Landscape Architects for their thoughtful and straightforward approach to a tough urban problem—combining a community park with a haven for bums.[30]

The rationale for developing Skid Row Park, which is next to a slum of about 10,000 to 15,000 people, is that derelicts from the area could be dissuaded from wandering downtown by being given patches of grass and benches to sleep on, a shelter for keeping dry, toilets, and freedom from harassment by police and teenage gangs.

COMMERCIAL RECREATION FACILITIES

Throughout this chapter, major emphasis has been given to facilities developed by public recreation and park agencies, which tend to operate the most diverse range of structures and special use areas. However, many recreation businesses operate extensive and imaginatively designed facilities. Typically, resorts and theme parks have incorporated exciting new design features based on sophisticated analyses of play behaviors and leisure motivations of participants.

DIVERSIFIED RESORT FACILITIES

Commercial recreation facilities cover a huge range of types of areas and structures, including bowling alleys, ski centers, riding trails, pools, health spas, and many others. Over the past two decades many new resorts have been built that combine dozens of different recreation program attractions within a single complex. A spin-off from the familiar tourist motel, these huge enterprises are designed to appeal both to individual or family vacationers and to organizations or business concerns that wish to combine a convention with a vacation stay for a large number of participants.

The Host Farm and Corral, a huge resort in the Pennsylvania Dutch Country, offers tours of the scenic countryside, tennis on both indoor and outdoor lighted courts, trails for jogging and running, card rooms, billiard parlors, game arcades, a ski slope and lifts, swimming pools, golf course, nightclubs and cabaret theatre, indoor and outdoor ice rinks, tobogganing and ski sledding, bicycling, horseback riding and carriage rides, and numerous other games and social events.

PARTICIPATORY PLAY PARKS

Still another innovative approach to building play areas has been initiated by Busch Gardens, operator of several major theme parks. In cooperation with the Children's Television Workshop, producers of "Sesame Street" and "The Electric Company," Busch Gardens has built a prototype, small-scale educational play park called Sesame Place, designed for families with children ages 3 to 12 years, in Oxford Valley Mall in Bucks County, Pa.

The concept underlying Sesame Place is to provide a variety of active play areas geared to the abilities of children of different age levels, including climbing, crawling through "caves," jumping and walking through "swamps," walking on stilts, shinnying up ropes, and swinging hand over hand across shallow pools of water. These activities are housed in three "regions," a land court, water court, and air court. In addition, Sesame Place has a science and game pavilion that offers educational challenges through a combination of specially adapted and designed computer games and hands-on science experiments.

Sesame Place is a unique example of how a commercial recreation enterprise can make use of ideas that have essentially come from educational and creative play designers around the United States and Canada and transform them into an economically viable operation.

In another innovative facility, Busch Gardens has opened a 22-acre water park called Adventure Island, a short distance from The Dark Continent in Tampa. This heavily landscaped park, with palm trees, tropical plants, white sand beaches, and a "trading village," provides an all-inclusive water experience, in which visitors slide down water chutes, ride the waves, dive from cliffs, or float in a peaceful lagoon. It is built on a myriad of levels, with waterfalls, cascades, slides, pools, cliffs, and rocks. Adventure Island also has a separate 17,000–square foot pool known as the Endless Surf, with a 3- to 5-foot wave for body and raft surfing.

TOTAL PLANNING: DISNEY'S EPCOT CENTER

Probably the most unusual example of a totally commercial recreation atraction is the most recent and ambitious addition to Walt Disney World in Florida—the EPCOT Center. The name stands for Experimental Prototype Community of Tomorrow; it represents a more serious foray into grown-up themes such as energy, food, technology, and communications in the world of tomorrow, along with international pavilions produced by Disney in cooperation with foreign governments.

This carefully designed 260-acre environment, which attracts up to 100,000 people a day, reflects the early influence of Disney's animated films, shifted from the flat screen to three-dimensional space. Visitors are typically moved past a succession of audio-animatronic figures, lifelike, computer-controlled dummies that depict history from the cavemen and early Egyptian periods through American life and ultimately the invention of complex high technology devices.

Such facilities can best be developed by commercial sponsors with substantial venture capital. Few public recreation and park agencies would be able to design and construct leisure attractions on this scale. However, they can learn from the concepts presented in the new Busch Gardens and Disney Enterprises parks and can incorporate these ideas, when feasible, in their designs for new facilities.

Manager's Role: Synergy and Stewardship

Beyond the tasks of facilities planning, design, and maintenance, leisure-service managers have two other important functions: synergy and stewardship.

BUILDING PARTNERSHIPS IN FACILITIES DEVELOPMENT

The term ''synergy'' refers to cooperative relationships in which partners can accomplish far more jointly than they could through independent efforts. Particularly since the fiscal crisis of the late 1970s, many recreation and park agencies have sought to develop such partnerships. Local departments have joined in synergetic programming and facilities development with national business organizations or with voluntary agencies and armed forces bases.

An excellent example of this trend may be found in the armed forces, in which military and civilian recreation and park managers have joined to share resources of various types. This process is discussed in a Department of the Interior manual that describes resource sharing as a give-and-take relationship through which recreation providers share or pool their facilities, equipment, personnel, land, or administrative support to promote public services and resolve common and overlapping problems:

> Resource sharing is also a form of barter. By bartering underutilized, temporarily idle, or [other] resources, recreation managers are able to secure resources needed for immediate priorities . . . . the balance of trade does not have to be equal. Resource sharing enables cooperative projects where each participant contributes and achieves gainful results.[31]

Numerous examples may be cited of public, voluntary agency, and armed forces units joining together to construct, rehabilitate, or operate recreation facilities. These patterns of cooperation appear to be growing steadily.

STEWARDSHIP OF NATURAL RESOURCES

Another issue that many recreation and park managers must face is that of stewardship and protection of publicly owned lands and waterfront areas. A growing population and residential and industrial development threaten to take over open spaces or damage parks and other natural resources. Kennedy writes:

> Even if the economy is not flourishing, Americans are still monied and mobile and have an enormous appetite for using our parks and engaging in outdoor recreation . . . . The continuing development of nearby roads, utilities, housing, factories, mines and agriculture impairs the aesthetics of adjacent lands and degrades the visitor's view from parklands.[32]

Because of such pressures, as well as other environmental threats, recreation and park managers must be vigilant in protecting the properties they hold as stewards and strive, where possible, to acquire new lands. Sound management practices, protective regulations, limited use of facilities, and appropriate planning policies will reduce threats to parks and other natural areas. Similarly, urban recreation and park managers must assume leadership in maintaining and protecting many parks and other recreational resources that have been permitted to deteriorate over the past decade. Inadequate funding and staff have resulted in serious decay in many urban facilities. Managers must bring such problems forcibly to the attention of their constituents and gain private and corporate support in "adopt-a-park" programs and other voluntary forms of assistance to preserve and protect these valuable community properties.

Thus on every level, facilities planning and operations must be regarded as key aspects of the leisure-service manager's responsibility. Although closely intertwined with other areas of management, such as personnel management, programming, and fiscal functions, they represent a vital, separate area of concern.

Summary

The design, construction, and maintenance of recreational and park facilities represent a critical function of leisure-service managers. The process begins with planning, which determines the community's or agency's needs for recreation areas and structures on the basis of open space standards or other relevant criteria. Short- and long-range planning studies lead to recommendations for acquiring or developing sites.

After outlining several familiar methods of acquiring properties, this chapter presents guidelines for designing facilities, emphasizing the manager's special role in providing expertise to the architect or other designer. Several key concerns in designing recreational facilities are outlined, including the need for critical safety features and providing access for the disabled. Guidelines for maintaining the facilities are described, with suggested use of systematic maintenance management plans at different levels of care.

Current trends in facilities development include innovative types of playgrounds and small parks, the use of air-supported structures, and mobile recreation units. Ecological recovery sites and nature centers are discussed, with new design trends in swimming pools and water play parks and zoos. Zoo design and the availability of fitness facilities, along with participatory and educational play parks, are also described. The chapter concludes by emphasizing the need for managers to promote cooperative relationships among agencies in developing and maintaining recreational facilities and to provide leadership in protecting the natural environment as a continuing responsibility.

STUDY QUESTIONS

1. With other students, carry out a survey of available recreational and park facilities within the community or region, mapping them by categories. Determine the extent to which they meet past or present National Recreation and Park Association standards for open space or specific types of activity areas. As part of this, rate the facilities with respect to access for the physically handicapped. This may be done as a slide presentation, with less emphasis on standards and more on the visual aspects of the facilities.

2. With other students, develop a design for a facility either to serve a particular population (such as the elderly) or within a major activity category, such as a swimming pool complex. This should not be approached from a technical engineering or architectural viewpoint, but rather with respect to managerial concerns for programming, supervision, staffing, and similar needs. If possible, this should be researched by visits to existing facilities of this type.

3. Develop a maintenance plan outlining the most economical and efficient means of caring for a large park or other outdoor facility. As an alternative, examine the issue of environmental protection for a major natural site and develop a set of policies and procedures to provide needed protection with respect to recreational uses.

Case 7 *Conflict on the Campus*

YOU ARE DAN JEFFERSON, assistant dean in charge of campus recreation programs at San Pedro State College and director of the College's student union building. You are responsible for campus social programs, entertainment events, clubs, and publications, along with counseling in the dormitory buildings.

As a separate responsibility, a recreation sports program is sponsored by the San Pedro Athletic Director, Will Nunez. This program includes intramurals, sports clubs, and outdoor recreation trips. You have gotten along fairly well with the recreational sports program in the past. However, friction has begun to develop between the two programs. For example, twice during the last year, there have been major conflicts when both the student union and the recreational sports program scheduled large-scale events on the same weekend. Attendance suffered, and students complained that they could not attend both events. Beyond this, there are now bad feelings with respect to the interchange of facilities. In the past you were able to use the gyms for dances, and the sports programs used your facilities for award ceremonies and banquets. However, lately it has been difficult to cooperate with Will Nunez. He has indicated that next year his schedule might not permit him to let your department use the regular gyms for social events.

You recognize that the real problem is in the arbitrary division of the campus recreation program into two separate units. However, no one seems willing to give up any authority, and the result is confusion and inefficiency.

Questions for Class Discussion and Analysis

1. Would it be a good idea for you to deny Will Nunez the use of your facilities in retaliation for his reluctance to let you use the gyms for your program?
2. From a program planning point of view, how could you combine your efforts, even if you continue to be administratively separate?
3. On the issue of program scheduling, would there be a simple way to avoid overlap or conflict? What is the *real* issue here?

Case 8 *The Mayor Cracks Down*

YOU ARE BARRY PARSONS, commissioner of a medium-sized municipal recreation and park department. For the past 3 years your budget has been frozen. With continuous inflation, your maintenance costs have risen, and despite this new facilities have been added, which stretch your capabilities to the limit.

This is an election year, and your mayor, Jeannine Day, is determined not to raise taxes. She has just announced her budget for the following fiscal year. Your department's budget has been frozen for the fourth straight year. You view this as the last straw and call a press conference, which reporters from the two city newspapers and several television and radio stations attend. You announce that, rather than operate a number of inadequate facilities with increasing complaints about poor maintenance and supervision, you are going to have to cut back on your program.

Continued.

Case 8   **The Mayor Cracks Down**
cont'd
Specifically, you have decided to close a large swimming pool, a golf course, and a nature center and withdraw all personnel from a large park. By doing this, you will be able to provide adequate maintenance for other parks and recreational areas, even with the limited budget. At the same time, you send a memorandum outlining your plan to the mayor and the city council.

Within an hour, Jeannine Day is on the phone. She is furious. Curtly she informs you, "I am not going to take complaints from all the families and neighborhood groups that want these facilities open. Politically, this move is a disaster, and I refuse to be blackmailed by you. You will open these facilities up or you will be fired. Period!"

Questions for Class Discussion and Analysis

1. Apart from resigning, which you do not want to do because you like your job and your family is comfortably settled in the community, what are your options?
2. Was your strategy a wise one? How could the problem have been handled differently?
3. If additional funds cannot be found in the budget for your department, what other kinds of approaches could you explore to ensure that maintenance and recreation programs are adequately staffed?

REFERENCES

1. *Beach Maintenance* (Report for National Association of Counties Award), Metro Dade County, Fla., Jan. 1977, Parks and Recreation Department, p. 3.
2. Lancaster, Roger (Editor): *Recreation, Parks and Open Space Standards and Guidelines,* Alexandria, Va., 1983, National Recreation and Park Association.
3. *Ibid.,* pp. 40-45.
4. Crompton, John L.: "Are Your Leisure Services Distributed Equitably?" *Leisure Today, Journal of Physical Education, Recreation and Dance,* April 1982, p. 67.
5. Wade, Glenn: "Projecting the Need for New Sports Facilities: A Case Report," *Parks and Recreation,* July 1982, pp. 40-43.
6. Donnelly, Kevin: "Current Trends in Commercial Recreation," *Leisure Today, Journal of Health, Physical Education and Recreation,* June 1973, pp. 32-33.

7. Kershaw, Warren M.: *Land Acquisition,* Arlington, Va., 1975, National Recreation and Park Association, p. 25.
8. Shipman, John, Forsyth, Brian, and Lerman, Maurice: "The Design of New Facilities," *Recreation Canada,* June 1980, pp. 36-40.
9. Eckoff, Harry C.: How to Plan a Golf Course," *Trends,* Summer 1978, pp. 12-17; and Kershaw, Frank E.: "Municipal Golf Design for Efficient Low-Cost Maintenance," *Recreation Canada,* April 1978, pp. 8-11.
10. Ribble, Jon: "Before You Build: A Check List of Community Center Considerations," *Parks and Recreation,* Oct. 1983, p. 40.
11. Oldach, Clarence, Savage, John, and Barisano, Richard: "Do's and Don'ts for Clubs Planning and Building Program," *Keynote,* Winter 1976-1977, pp. 13-14.
12. Jordan, Joe J.: *Senior Center Facilities,* Washington, D.C., Nov. 1975, National Institute of Senior Centers, p. 8.

Five Program Functions

Any agency that seeks to provide a rounded program of recreational services in the community must assume responsibility for the following functions: (1) providing facilities for self-directed leisure use or active play; (2) providing leadership for organized or supervised program activities; (3) coordinating other services and cosponsoring programs or cooperating with other recreation organizations; (4) providing education for leisure or leisure counseling where needed; and (5) sponsoring other forms of human or social services related to recreation participation. Each of these tasks is described in the following section.

PROVISION OF FACILITIES

Recreation and park agencies typically provide a wide range of facilities for public use in a self-directed way. This may include the use of parks for walking, enjoying nature, sunning, biking, jogging, or other informal outdoor activities. It may also include the operation of playgrounds, beaches, scenic areas, picnic grounds, ballfields of various types, and many other kinds of leisure facilities.

In some cases participation in tennis, golf, swimming, or similar activities involves scheduling, instruction, or other forms of supervision for safety purposes. Ballfields must normally be scheduled by permit for use by community leagues. However, the primary emphasis in this major program function is on providing facilities for unscheduled and unsupervised use.

PROVISION OF ORGANIZED OR SUPERVISED ACTIVITIES

Organized or supervised activities are conducted under direct leadership. Such activities usually require registration or formal group membership, which would not be true of free play or unsupervised use of a facility. Examples of organized activities include the following:

1. Summer day-camp or organized playground programs
2. Teenage canteens, lounge or coffeehouse programs, or work-study projects
3. Sports leagues, classes, tournaments, or instructional clinics
4. Adult social clubs or special-interest groups, such as little theater groups, choruses, or art groups
5. Senior citizens' clubs or golden age groups
6. Organized outings and trips
7. Community celebrations or special events
8. Mobile recreation programs, which send a portable facility to different areas of a community with program activities and equipment

COORDINATION AND ASSISTANCE FUNCTIONS

Although it is not as broadly recognized as the first two functions, many public recreation and park departments today have responsibility for coordinating community recreation service and providing assistance to other agencies. Since of all the different types of organizations in this field it is the only type that has *primary* responsibility for promoting communitywide participation, local public agencies should assist other sponsors by:

13. Steinfeld, Edward (Project Director): *Selected Bibliography on Barrier-Free Design,* Washington, D.C., April 1979, U.S. Department of Housing and Urban Development.
14. Owens, Rhodell: "The Role of Park Maintenance in Community Preservation and Beautification," *Parks and Recreation,* Feb. 1983, p. 37.
15. *Ibid.*
16. Hauser, R.C.: "Park Maintenance Management Program," *Trends,* Summer 1979, p. 39.
17. Sternloff, Robert E.: "The 'KISS' Approach to Routine Maintenance," *Parks and Recreation,* March 1982, p. 52.
18. Fisher, Carl: "A Maintenance Management Plan: It Can be Done," *Parks and Recreation,* March 1982, p. 51.
19. Donahue, Michael: "Low-Cost Maintenance—The Prime Concern in Parks Design," *Recreation Canada,* April 1977, pp. 27-29.
20. Mills, Allen S., Harris, Richard W., and Conway, Kenneth L.: "Case Report—San Jose," *Parks and Recreation,* Jan. 1980, p. 89.
21. Cryder, Ralph S.: "Contract Services for Public Parks and Recreation Agencies," *Parks and Recreation Resources,* Jan. 1982, p. 42.
22. Donahue, Ron: "Get More for Your Maintenance Dollar Through Contracting," *Parks and Recreation,* Feb. 1983, pp. 42-43.
23. Gold, Seymour: "Neighborhood Parks: The Nonuse Phenomenon," *California Parks and Recreation,* Feb.-March 1978, p. 18.
24. Dattner, Richard: *Design for Play.* Copyright 1969 by Litton Educational Publishing, Inc. Reprinted by permission of Van Nostrand Reinhold Co., pp. 44-45.23.
25. Vance, Bill: "Adventure Playgrounds: The American Experience," *Parks and Recreation,* Sept. 1982, p. 68.
26. Shedlock, Robert E.: "Water-Play Parks in Public Lands: A Revenue Source and a Public Benefit," *Parks and Recreation,* March 1983, p. 39.
27. Jasulak, Neil: "European Swimming Pool Designs Cross the Atlantic," *Parks and Recreation,* March 1983, p. 45.
28. Naedele, Walter: "Zoos Focus on Animals Outside the Cages," *Philadelphia Inquirer,* May 1, 1984, p. 4-BN.
29. Watts, Bernard A.: "Goodyear's Approach," *Trends,* Summer 1980, p. 20.
30. von Eckhardt, Wolf: "The Greening of Skid Row," *Time,* July 19, 1982, p. 81.
31. *Let's All Pull Together: Resource Sharing for Military and Civilian Park and Recreational Managers,* Washington, D.C., 1982, U.S. Department of the Interior, National Park Service, p. 1.
32. Kennedy, Bruce: "California's Stewardship Survey," *Parks and Recreation,* May 1984, p. 51.

CHAPTER 9

Recreation Program Developme

Although it would be easy to say that programming is the raison d'etre of any recreation and leisure service organization, such a statement would not be accurate. It is important to remember that people and their recreation and leisure needs are the reasons for an agency's existence and should be considered the focal point of its services. Programs are the tool of the recreation and leisure service professional—the vehicle for service delivery. Through the use of programs, values are formed, skills developed, and processes learned.[1]

*P*rogram planning and implementation are primary areas of responsib service managers and are actually the basis for their existence. All oth manager's work, including personnel supervision, facilities developme erations, are intended to contribute to the ultimate goal of leisure which is to provide diversified, appealing, and constructive recreation the public.

This chapter provides an overview of the programming proces definition of programs and a suggested model of planning methods a types of agencies. It then describes major categories of program a and presents several basic principles of program planning and sch by depicting a number of important new trends in leisure participa and several issues that confront recreation and park managers tod

Understanding the Concept of "Program"

Ask any child or adult on the street what recreation is all likely to reply, "It's the things we do for fun—games, sports, tainment."

A key responsibility of leisure-service managers is to pr for participation in such activities to the public at large or word *program* is usually taken to mean the specific acti agency offers to potential participants. However, this is a Instead, Farrell and Lundegren stress that the concept of resources that help make participation possible: "The wo stood to mean (1) the activity in which people participate the activity experience to take place, and (3) the leader for facilitating this experience."[2]

Extending this view, Edginton, Compton, and Hanso leisure-service agencies should include leisure-facilit broaden the public's understanding of recreation and lei this function should be considered part of programmin this text argues that the idea of program should include recreational opportunities and participation in commu

1. Working with other agencies to provide them with technical assistance, leadership training, the use of facilities, and sometimes equipment
2. Promoting overall coordination of community recreational activities by carrying out surveys and inventories of needs and services, developing community councils or planning committees, and encouraging joint projects
3. Assisting individuals or families with special needs or interests by publishing directories of varied opportunities within the community, making referrals to existing programs, helping neighborhood groups organize, or lending equipment
4. Acting as a strong citywide representative for recreation through the press, within municipal government, and other civic departments and agencies, with business and religious groups, and finally in cooperation with state or federal authorities in jointly sponsored or specially funded programs

Thus the public recreation and park department should act as a catalyst, flag bearer, promoter, and mobilizer of public interest and support and in any other role that promotes leisure services or related social programs.

EDUCATION FOR LEISURE

Closely related to the function of promoting overall community recreation is the role of helping educate community residents for the fullest and most satisfying and constructive use of leisure. In agencies that serve special populations, this may involve providing leisure education or leisure counseling to individuals who are reentering the community after a period of rehabilitation or who are approaching retirement. It may also be carried out by sponsoring events that strengthen and enrich public awareness of leisure needs and values.

PROVISION OF RELATED SERVICES

Particularly in agencies that have accepted a human-services role in the community, programs typically include many activities and functions that are not essentially recreational in character. Instead of seeking to provide pleasure or enjoyment as a primary focus, they offer services that meet the critical developmental needs of participants or assist them in problem areas of their lives. These services may include workshops, classes, individual counseling, or other forms of assistance that fit within the general sphere of responsibility of recreation professionals. For example:

> A public agency's youth program might include such elements as leadership training, vocational education and job placement, alcohol or drug abuse counseling, legal assistance, family services, and a variety of other forms of social assistance . . . .
> An employee recreation program might be administratively placed within a company unit responsible for other personnel services or benefits. Thus, the same staff member who is in charge of planning employee recreation activities might also coordinate car-pool schedules, plan stress-reduction or weight-loss workshops, conduct pre-retirement workshops, or administer a buying cooperative or employee discount purchasing program.[4]

In sum, the process of program development in a leisure-service agency is concerned with providing a wide range of activities, services, and other forms of education and assistance that contribute in a fully rounded way to recreational interests and participation by all members of the community.

Process of Program Development

How does a leisure-service agency decide which of these activities and services it will provide to the public at large or to its own constituency? Essentially, five primary approaches that tend to influence the way in which managers go about this process have been identified: (1) the *traditional approach,* in which the program is structured mostly on the basis of what has been presented in the past and has been successful; (2) the *current practices approach,* in which agency managers and program planners are on the alert to follow what seems to be in vogue or the most current trend in similar communities or organizations; (3) the *expressed desires* approach, which places reliance on surveys or checklists to determine what members of the public or the organization's membership would like to have offered; (4) the *authoritarian approach,* which relies chiefly on the judgment and preferences of the agency's director or program staff; and (5) the *sociopolitical approach,* which focuses on the need to provide programs that meet important social needs or are responsive to community pressures and political influence.

Other program approaches that have been identified include the *cafeteria approach,* in which participants are encouraged to choose their areas of participation from a broad range of activities, and the *prescriptive approach,* in which recreation is prescribed, usually as a form of therapy, for individual participants.

In most leisure-service agencies, no single approach is used. Instead, a program supervisor and his or her staff work closely together, building overall plans and schedules on the basis of all the methods described here.

In developing programs it is often helpful to use guidelines that have been formulated by professionals in the field and that have appeared in the literature. A number of widely accepted program planning principles that apply to public, local recreation and park agencies appear in the box on the opposite page.

Each of these principles should be carefully interpreted based on actual community situations. For example, the first guideline does not mean that all residents must be served equally—first because this is manifestly impossible and second because different groups have different needs. Instead, the principle suggests that all groups must be served but that this may be done in highly differentiated ways. Collectively, these principles provide a framework within which professionally sound and effective program planning can be performed.

Program Planning Model

The eight specific steps of planning and carrying out leisure-service programs are as follows.[5]

1. *Establish a philosophical framework.* The purpose of this initial stage is to provide an ideological base, or system of values and overall goals, for the program. Obviously, activities that are offered should be in harmony with the agency's philosophy and should be geared to meeting specific goals and objectives. A fuller discussion of this stage is provided in Chapter 5.

2. *Assess participant/community leisure needs and interests.* The purpose of this step

---

GUIDELINES FOR COMMUNITY RECREATION PROGRAMMING

1. Community recreation should serve all elements in the community without discrimination on the basis of age, sex, race, religion, or social or economic class.
2. Community recreation should meet significant social needs, should be couched within a framework of democratic social values, and should provide constructive and creative leisure opportunity for all.
3. Community recreation should provide a varied range of activities and provide diversity and balance to meet varied needs of participants.
4. Community recreation programs should involve residents in planning and carrying out activities through advisory councils, needs assessment studies, and volunteer service opportunities.
5. Special groups in the community, such as the mentally or physically disabled, should be served by recreation programs that meet their diverse social, emotional, creative, and physical needs for satisfying leisure activity.
6. Recreation programs should be flexibly scheduled to meet the needs of participants most effectively.
7. Recreation programs should be planned to make the fullest and most imaginative use of all community facilities, including those belonging to other agencies.
8. Recreation programs should be supervised and administered by full-time, qualified professionals whenever possible, although much of the direct, face-to-face leadership may be performed by seasonal, part-time, or volunteer employees.
9. Community recreation programs should be meaningfully interpreted to the public at large through effective public relations media and community relations activities.
10. Recreation program activities and events should be systematically evaluated to determine whether they have achieved their objectives and satisfied community wishes.
11. Dynamism is an essential part of programming; recreational activities should strive for novelty, excitement, and surprise whenever possible and should involve varied schedules, new locations, and fresh leadership to achieve a needed change of pace.

is to analyze the needs and interests of participants to ensure that they will be met through the program. Linked to the *expressed desires* approach described earlier, it may be carried out through needs assessment studies or surveys, town meetings or advisory group sessions, membership application forms, or program evaluation sheets that may be handed out at the end of a program unit or series. In therapeutic programs, treatment team members may make careful assessments of patient or client needs or leisure interests.

3. *Determine goals, objectives, and policies.* These represent a more concise and detailed statement of the program's mission, which is based on the philosophy outlined

in step 1, combined with the needs and interests of participants identified in step 2. It must also be based on an assessment of other available leisure services in the community to avoid overlap with programs sponsored by other agencies. Goals represent the broad statements of purpose, while objectives spell them out in more concrete and quantifiable terms. Policies, as described in Chapter 5, are administrative guidelines specifically directed to agency priorities or recommended courses of action.

4. *Identify range of possible activities and services.* At this point in the program planning process it is necessary to identify the major categories of activities and services that might be offered, along with the population groups they would serve. Both popular activities that are traditionally offered and newer or more innovative kinds of program elements are considered.

5. *Determine alternative approaches to program design.* Careful consideration is given to varied program activities based on their appeal and value and their potential for being self-supporting or requiring some subsidizing by the agency. Each possible program activity or service along with the format under which it might be offered (see p. 215) and its requirements with respect to staff, facilities, equipment, and similar needs, is examined.

6. *Develop program plan.* Based on the factors that have just been described, the program activities to be offered by the agency, as well as the groups to be served, the format of the activities, the use of specific facilities, the assignment of leadership personnel, and the actual scheduling of programs and events are formally selected. The program itself should be carefully reviewed by all concerned, and once formally approved, it should be confirmed and publicized in in-house memos and program schedules and externally through brochures, announcements, and program bulletins.

7. *Implement program plan.* The program plan is now put into action, with various center activities (classes, leagues, clubs, and special events) carried out under careful supervision. Program operations are usually governed by a set of guidelines or procedures, which define the correct ways to carry them out.

8. *Supervise, monitor, and evaluate program.* Finally, it is necessary to carefully supervise the program, monitor its progress, and evaluate its quality and degree of success in achieving its outcome. This process has several purposes: (1) to ensure that all goes as planned; (2) if problems occur, to detect them and take remedial action; (3) to measure the professional performance of staff members as a basis for counseling them or taking needed personnel actions; (4) to determine whether given programs should be repeated; and (5) to measure the effectiveness of program procedures or develop recommendations for carrying them out more effectively.

In using a program planning model of this kind, it should be recognized that few programs are really developed entirely from scratch. Instead, they often tend to be repeated from season to season or from year to year, with some degree of change as new program activities or services are introduced or as older ones may be modified or terminated. It should also be recognized that programs may have many different elements that tend to be at different stages. Thus, as one major program feature is being planned, another is being carried out, and a third is being evaluated.

Classification of Program Activities

Most large public and voluntary recreation organizations offer a wide range of leisure pursuits. Typically, these are classified in several different ways.

In some communities, they may be structured according to age levels and gender groupings, such as playground and after-school center programs for elementary school youth or evening center and weekend programs for teenagers and adults. In other cases programs may be classified according to their location or facility, such as sports field activities or pool and beach programs. It is also possible to classify activities according to their districts, funding support, or administrative responsibility.

However, the most common approach is to classify program activities by placing them within several familiar categories that describe their general nature. These include the following categories with a number of typical examples for each:

1. *Active sports*. These include popular team games such as baseball, basketball, football, soccer, softball, or field hockey, and other individual or dual sports, such as tennis, golf, fencing, archery, or combative activities, that is, wrestling, boxing, or karate.

2. *Active games*. These include variations of tag games, relays, dodgeball, kickball, and numerous other stunts and active contests.

3. *Equipment and table games*. Chess, checkers, card and board games, horseshoes, marbles, and shuffleboard fit within this category.

4. *Physical fitness activities*. Varied kinds of exercise classes, including slimnastics, aerobic dance, Jazzercise, and gymnastics or calisthenics, fit in this category, along with jogging, use of the trampoline, and similar conditioning activities.

5. *Outdoor recreation activities*. This category includes a wide range of nature-related activities, such as camping, bird walks, backpacking, mountaineering, and gardening, along with many sports that are best enjoyed in the outdoors, such as scuba diving, skiing, ice skating, hunting, and fishing.

6. *Aquatics*. Although this might be considered a form of sport or outdoor recreation, it is such a diverse and popular area that it is often identified as a separate category. It includes swimming, diving, boating, water skiing, synchronized swimming, and surfing.

7. *Arts and crafts*. One of the most popular and useful forms of program activity, this includes fine arts (drawing, painting, sculpture, and graphics) and craft activities (carving, ceramics, jewelry making, leather working, metal craft, needlework, and weaving).

8. *Music*. This aspect of the performing arts includes both participatory and spectator activity and ranges from community singing and rhythm bands to instrument instruction, orchestras, drum and bugle corps, choral groups, operettas, and rock and roll band competitions.

9. *Drama*. Dramatic activities include children's informal drama activities, dramatic games, puppetry and story telling, as well as one-act plays, play readings, adult theater programs, and variety shows.

10. *Dance*. Dance activities range from social dance, disco and rock and roll or

break dancing, to folk, square, and tap or clog dance, as well as to artistic forms of dance such as ballet or modern dance.

11. *Hobbies.* This category may include many of the activities already mentioned, such as card playing or craft activities, as well as collecting, model building, or other pastimes carried on individually or in clubs.

12. *Mental and linguistic activities.* This category involves literary pursuits, such as book clubs, creative writing groups, poetry clubs, or current events discussion groups, along with puzzles, word games, magic or mathematics tricks, and paper and pencil games.

13. *Social recreation.* Banquets, carnivals, fun nights, potluck suppers, progressive parties, treasure hunts, trips and outings, and other special events of an informal, participative nature fit in this group.

14. *Programs for the handicapped.* While they may include many of the activities just mentioned, special programs for the physically and mentally disabled tend to be organized as a separate area of program activity in many community leisure-service agencies.

15. *Volunteer programs.* Many voluntary agencies in particular offer structured opportunities for participants to provide unpaid leadership in public service programs. These placements represent a much needed leisure outlet for many residents and fulfill a personal need to be of service to others.

16. *Human-service activities.* Many agencies provide activities that are not really recreational, but meet related human needs, such as drug or alcohol abuse counseling, stress reduction workshops, fitness programs, health or nutrition service, or varied advocacy programs.

It should be noted that each of these categories includes only a few sample activities. Actually, there are hundreds of different activities that might be listed, including variations of the most popular activities. For example, variations of archery might include crossbow archery, archery golf, wheelchair archery, archery fishing, or fletching and bowmaking. Variations of basketball might include water basketball, donkey basketball, roller-skate basketball, low-basket basketball, one-handed basketball, and other basketball-related games.

Factors Affecting Choices of Program Activities

Obviously the problem is not one of being able to identify *enough* potential activities. Instead the challenge is to ensure that activities are appropriately matched with population groups and that they are also compatible with the resources, goals, and values of the agency. Each of the following five factors must be considered.

CHARACTERISTICS OF PARTICIPANTS

This includes the age of participants, their previous background or level of skill, the size of the group, their sex, physical condition, educational or socioeconomic level, expressed interests and needs, and relevant ethnic or other personal considerations. Tra-

Educational and play activities are combined at the innovative Sesame Place educational play park in Langhorne, Pa., a joint venture of Busch Entertainment Corporation and Children's Television Workshop. Children climb cargo nets, swim in a sea of plastic balls, play computer games, experience multiple images, and watch a pasta machine at work.

213

ditionally we have tended to use factors such as age or sex as key elements in designing programs, with the idea that certain activities are clearly suitable for certain sharply defined age levels and not for others or that certain activities are male oriented and appropriate only for them, whereas others are female oriented. Today there is much greater freedom and flexibility in these areas and reluctance to stereotype people or limit them because of such elements of personal identification. We tend to be much more aware of what disabled people *can* do, despite their disability, or to resist the idea that people should be restricted to limited programs because of socioeconomic or ethnic factors or past limitations in their own involvement and interests.

FACILITIES REQUIRED

What facilities are available to operate programs—neighborhood playgrounds, community centers, small parks, ballfields, courts, or other specialized facilities? Obviously, it is not possible to select or schedule certain activities that require specialized facilities unless those facilities are available. However, imaginative program modification may make it possible to offer activities that might otherwise appear highly unlikely. For example, skiing may be offered by giving preseason exercise programs or dry land skiing practice sessions and then by sponsoring trips to ski centers. Often a department that does not possess a given type of facility may rent it from another agency or work out a cooperative or cosponsorship arrangement with them.

PERSONNEL

What activities can be conducted without special leadership, simply by scheduling them and providing space? What activities require general supervision and what others require specially skilled leadership? It is important to do a personnel needs analysis of all activities in a program to ensure that the needed leadership is available for any given program feature and also that the talents of staff members are fully used. However, the lack of a given type of specialized competence on a recreation staff should not be a reason for automatically assuming that a given activity should not be offered. Instead, several options should be considered: (1) hiring special part-time or session workers with needed skills, (2) seeking out community volunteers with needed skills, and (3) using staff training or in-service education workshops or clinics to develop needed skills.

FUNDS REQUIRED

What will be the costs of specific programs with respect to leadership, maintenance of facilities, purchase of supplies and equipment, transportation, or other factors? Can fees be charged and if so to what degree will they offset program costs? Although there is a strong trend today toward relying on fees and charges to pay for programs to the fullest extent possible and operate facilities and programs on a "pay-as-you-go" basis, it must be recognized that some programs of a high social value simply cannot return substantial fees to an agency because they serve groups with limited financial capability. Thus it is important to use a cost-benefit analysis approach to determine the costs and values derived from given activities.

SCHEDULING

What are the time requirements of an activity? When is the best time to offer it, for how long, and how often? Once activities have been selected, they must be organized according to when, how, and where they will be made available to the public or to the agency's membership. The goal is to develop schedules that will serve the most people effectively within the resources and staff capabilities of the organization.

Program Formats for Participation

Before examining typical approaches to scheduling, it is helpful to understand the different ways in which various activities may be presented. There are at least eight such formats for participation, each of which will be briefly discussed.

INSTRUCTION

Instruction includes classes or practice sessions in various types of sports, aquatics, crafts, outdoor recreation skills, and similar program elements. Many leisure-service agencies offer extensive youth and adult recreation skills classes, often in cooperation with adult education departments. Other forms of instruction may be less formal on playgrounds or in community centers.

FREE PLAY

Free play involves unstructured participation without any direct instruction or super-vision within an informal setting. Examples might involve walking or hiking through a park, picnicking, or casual conversation at a senior center. Often youth groups or adults play informal games, such as basketball or volleyball, at a recreation center where there is some degree of supervision but no structure beyond that.

ORGANIZED COMPETITION

Organized competition is usually thought of as sports competition, with teams being formed and league play continuing over a period of time. However, other forms of leisure activity, such as music, dance, or art, may also involve competition in which awards are given for outstanding performances or creative products. There may also be gardening contests, debating competitions, and numerous other examples of this format.

PERFORMANCES AND EXHIBITIONS

A fourth important type of format is staging shows or performances such as art or hobby shows, choral or drama performances, or gymnastic or dance demonstrations. Almost any type of recreational pursuit lends itself to such exhibitions, which are usu-ally scheduled toward the end of a program unit or series and which serve as culminat-ing events that boost morale and provide incentive for participants.

LEADERSHIP TRAINING

While leadership training is not a form of recreational participation as such, many agencies offer it as a vital element in their leisure-service program. For example, they may sponsor courses in water or life safety, coaching or officiating, or similar leadership skills. Through such means, they help promote varied areas of recreational programming and assist other agencies in their staff development efforts.

CLUBS AND SPECIAL-INTEREST GROUPS

Another popular form of recreational involvement consists of clubs or special-interest groups that focus on a particular type of leisure pursuit. For example, many recreation agencies sponsor archery clubs, hiking clubs, poetry groups, theater groups, and other special-interest clubs that meet regularly to participate in events and activities related to their shared hobby.

SOCIAL EVENTS

Apart from performances and exhibitions, which are usually intended to display a given activity or performing group, programs may include parties, carnivals, play days, historical celebrations, banquets, festivals, and similar events that are primarily of a social nature. Festivities of this type help create a sense of belonging within a community or other organization and often become a tradition.

TRIPS AND OUTINGS

Away from home activities help promote and enrich the overall recreational experience. For example, a choral group may travel to a nearby city to hear an outstanding performance, or members of a senior center may take a short trip to a popular tourist attraction.

Diversity of Formats within a Single Facility or Activity

A fully rounded recreation program within a large recreation center or similar facility is likely to include many different formats, such as instructional classes, competition, social events, and special-interest groups. Within a single type of activity, different formats may be implemented simultaneously or in a logical sequence as people gain skills and deepen their interest. For example, within an arts and crafts medium such as ceramics, participants may take beginners' classes, engage in self-directed work in a studio, exhibit their work at craft fairs, and compete for prizes. The most talented participants might take part in a leaders' workshop and ultimately become leaders in the program themselves.

Scheduling Methods

Scheduling represents a key task in developing a program plan. Most public and voluntary agencies break down their year-round programs into three or four major time periods, usually based on the seasons of the year. Depending on climatic factors, which influence sports and other forms of outdoor recreational participation, the schedule might be divided into four seasons: winter, spring, summer, and fall.

To illustrate, winter programs would tend to place heavier emphasis on instructional

Above, New concepts of swimming pool design are reflected in the Herringthorpe Leisure Center, Rotherham, Great Britain. *Below*, The Shelly Ridge Girl Scout Center in Philadelphia has won awards for outstanding design, including extensive open space for special events and an esthetic layout that fits harmoniously into the environment.

CHICAGO PARK DISTRICT

PHYSICAL ACTIVITIES SCHEDULED PROGRAM

LOCAL PARK ACTIVITIES

JANUARY

4 Junior Boys' Indoor Volleyball (January thru March).
4 Plan Pinochle Tournaments.
5 Co-Rec Volleyball R-5 Reports Due.
5 Basketball School R-65 Reports Due.
5 Boys' Basketball Free Throw Tournament, R-5 and R-46 Reports Due.
8 Junior and Intermediate Boys' Basketball Reports R-5 and R-13 Reports Due Area Chairman.

FEBRUARY

4 Senior Men's Industrial Basketball R-5 and R-13 Reports Due.
6 Ice Skating R-5 Reports Due.

MARCH

1 Plan Local Chess Tournaments, complete by March 27.
2 March thru June, Plan Community Baseball Leagues School.
2 Plan Community Marble Tournaments, (March 2 to April 14).
2 Plan Community Baseball Leagues.
30 Chess Tournaments R-5 Reports Due.
31 Two-Tap Volleyball R-5 Reports Due.
31 Community Competitive Report R-5 for Novice Wrestling Due to Chairman.

APRIL

1 Basketball Schools (April thru June).
1 Boxing Shows (April thru May).
1 Plan Boys' and Girls' Track and Field Meets (April thru May 4).
1 Plan Junior and Intermediate Boys' and Girls' Softball Program (April thru June).
1 Hula "Hoop and Frisbee Contests (April thru June).
2 Plan "Let's Play Activities" Program (April thru June).
13 Marble Tournaments R-5 Reports Due.

MAY

1 Junior Boys' Softball Starts Local League Play (May thru June).
1 Senior Men's Softball (May thru June).
1 Cycling Community Education and Testing Programs (May and June).
1 Boys' and Girls' Achievement Tests - Softball, Track and Field.
3 Track and Field Tournaments for the Mentally Handicapped.
4 Plan Community Handball.
10 Junior Girls' Softball R-13 Reports Due.
14 Chicago Park District Inter-Club Tennis Association Entries Due.
21 Boys' Track and Field R-5 Reports Due.
21 Junior Boys' Softball R-5 and R-13 Reports and Schedules Due.
23 Local Kite Contests.
25 Junior Boys' Softball Declare Bracket Winner or All-Star Team. Special Team Roster Form and Birth Certificates Due to your Area Chairman. Draw for Area Play.

AREA ACTIVITIES

JANUARY

4 Junior and Intermediate Boys' Basketball Starts.
11 Women's One-Tap Volleyball Starts, North and South Divisions.
15 Co-Rec Volleyball Reports Due to the City-Wide Chairman.
15 Junior and Intermediate Boys' Basketball Special Community Competitive Reports Due.

FEBRUARY

4 Girls' and Women's One-Tap Volleyball Finals.
8 Area Pinochle Tournaments this Week.
9 Junior and Intermediate Boys' Basketball District Championships start all Areas (February 9, 10, 11).
15 Junior, Intermediate and Senior Area Two-Tap Indoor Volleyball Tournaments this Week.
15 Table Tennis R-5 Reports Due Area Chairman.
15 Pinochle R-4 Reports Due.
22 Table Tennis Area Tournaments this Week.

MARCH

8 Table Tennis Tournament Reports Due R-4.
8 Junior Boys' Indoor Volleyball Area Tournaments Start.

APRIL

5 Chess Area Tournaments this Week.
13 Chess R-4 Reports Due.
19 Marble Area Tournament this Week.
26 All Marble Reports Due.
26 Area Kite Contests (April 26 - 30)

NOVEMBER

2 Two-Tap Volleyball (November thru March).
2 Bowling Tournament for the Mentally Handicapped.
2 Junior and Intermediate Boys' Basketball (November thru January).
2 Plan Boys' and Girls' Indoor Volleyball (November thru January)
2 Women's Division One-Tap Volleyball (November thru December)
2 Synchronized Swimming, Indoor Natatoriums (November to December).
2 Wrestling Community R-5 Reports Due to Area Chairman.
3 Boys' and Girls' Checkers R-5 Reports Due.
3 Plan Local Ice Skating Meets.
13 Touch Football R-5 and R-13 Reports Due.

DECEMBER

1 Plan Community Table Tennis Tournaments (December thru February 11).
1 Football Achievement Tests R-5 Reports Due.
1 Local Ice Skating Meets (December thru January).
1 Conduct Physical Fitness Testing Programs (December thru January).

CITY-WIDE ACTIVITIES

JANUARY

9 Indoor Swim Meet #1 - Ida Crown.
23 Indoor Swim Meet #2 - Ida Crown.
28 Women's Division One-Tap Volleyball Championships Start this Week.
29 Novice City-Wide Wrestling Meet (January 29 & 30).

FEBRUARY

4 Women's Division One-Tap Volleyball Final Championship Game.
6 Indoor Swim Meet #3 - Ida Crown.
6 Scuba Course Starts.
13 Open Division City-Wide Wrestling Championships.
19 Junior and Intermediate Boys' Basketball Championships.
20 Indoor Swim Meet #4 - Ida Crown.

MARCH

6 Indoor Swim Meet #5 - Ida Crown.
13 Junior Girls' Two-Tap Volleyball Preliminaries and Championship Game.
13 Indoor Archery Championship - Gage Park
15 Intermediate and Senior Girls' Indoor Two-Tap Volleyball Championships Start.
19 G. P. R. A. Pinochle Tournament.
20 Indoor Swim Meet #6 - Ida Crown.
31 Intermediate and Senior Girls' Two-Tap Volleyball Finals.

APRIL

3 Indoor Club Meet #7 - Ida Crown
5 City-Wide Bowling Tournament for the Mentally Handicapped.
10 G. P. R. A. Bridge Tournament.
17 Junior Boys' Indoor Volleyball Championships.
17 Indoor Swim Meet #8 - Ida Crown.

JUNE

2 G. P. R. A. Women's Industrial Volleyball Clinic (June 2 thru 4).
5 Chicago Park District Inter-Club Tennis Play Begins (June 5 & 6)
5 City-Wide Track and Field Meets for the Mentally Handicapped.
5 Midget, Juvenal and Junior Boys' Track and Field Meets.
6 Roach Junior Archery Shoot - Riis Park.
9 G. P. R. A. Girls' Industrial Softball.
10 G. P. R. A. Women's Volleyball Tournament (June 10 thru August 5).
10 Youth Week (June 10 thru 16).
14 Clout and Team Archery Shoot - Washington Park.
19 Junior Boys' Softball Championships this Week.
19 Junior Girls' Softball City-Wide Championships.
28 Robin Hood Archery Tournament - Columbus Park.
28 Junior Tennis Instruction Center Begins C. P. D.
28 Junior Center Tournament.
29 G. P. R. A. Tennis Instruction (June 29 thru August 24).

FIG. 9-1

218

classes and social clubs or other group activities in community centers. They would include heavy emphasis on cultural activities, such as arts and crafts or the performing arts, and on sports such as basketball or hockey.

In contrast, summer programs would stress playground and day-camp activities and outdoor sports, aquatics, and special events. Generally, summer program schedules are greatly expanded, since summer is the time when children are on vacation and many adults are also free from work for extended periods.

EXAMPLES OF SEASONAL SCHEDULING

Fig. 9-1 shows in detail how program activities are organized during the winter and spring seasons in Chicago. This section of the original chart shows how a single area of program service consisting primarily of sports is carried out from January through June.

It should be noted that activity flows from competition on the local park or center level to larger areas or districts in the city and finally to citywide tournaments or performances. For example, Junior Boys Indoor Volleyball Tournaments begin on Jan. 4 on the local park level. On March 8, those teams that have won on the local level compete in area play-offs. Finally on April 17, the area winners compete for the city championship.

In another illustration of seasonal programming, Fig. 9-2 depicts the free indoor-outdoor winter program presented for residents of Detroit during the winter months in a recent year in 275 neighborhood locations throughout the city. The ''Wintercade'' program brochure lists outdoor winter activities such as ice skating, hockey, sledding, tobogganing, horse-drawn sleigh rides, nature trails and winter picnics. It also presents a wide range of popular indoor pursuits in the major program categories in recreation centers throughout the city.

MONTHLY SCHEDULING

Within the overall framework of seasonal programming, many departments also develop monthly calendars, which show all regularly scheduled activities in their appropriate time period and facility and which also give information about special events. Graham and Klar point out that monthly calendars assist in the assignment of supervisory and leadership personnel, payroll projection, and facility maintenance and repair. In addition, they may serve as valuable publicity instruments. They write:

> Monthly calendars are easily mass produced in a single color (the cost of multiple color reproductions is usually prohibitive) and may be distributed to the program participants. By providing periodic information regarding new activities, entry deadlines, and planned changes in the normal schedule of operations, the monthly calendar becomes an excellent public relations and communications vehicle.[6]

SCHEDULING OF WEEKLY PROGRAMS

In addition to seasonal planning, many leisure-service agencies plan their programs on a weekly basis, including both regular activities that are offered at the same time on given days from week to week and other special events offered on a one-time basis.

FIG. 9-2

Many centers, for example, develop weekly program charts that are posted in central locations to inform participants of available activities and events, changes in scheduling, or similar information. The following section provides several examples of weekly scheduling.

Frederick County, Md., Outdoor School

Fig. 9-3 shows the weekly schedule of a school camping program, at which children go away with their school classes for several days of living in a natural setting and learning about the environment, wildlife, and similar topics. Major morning and afternoon time blocks are suggested, along with a regular schedule of meals, meetings, cleanup, and other regular responsibilities each day.

Newark, N.J., YM/YWHA physical recreation schedule

The schedule for a voluntary agency, shown in Fig. 9-4, gives an extensive weekly program of sports, games, aquatics, and conditioning activities for children, teenagers,

Frederick County Outdoor School	. . . . Sample schedule, activities are flexible.

7:15   Reveille—If you get up earlier—6:30 earliest, please be quiet so you don't disturb the deer and bird life.

7:40   K.P. and flag raising bell (four campers raise the American and Maryland flags).

8:00   Breakfast—Followed by lively songs. Individuals or class groups lead them. Weather report.

8:45   Clean-up—Cabin and wash room, staff meeting.

Monday	Tuesday	Wednesday	Thursday	Friday
Cabin assignments	All day field trip	Compass-water-	Mountain view	Nature craft,
9:00 flag raising	Temp. changes	shed quest	Rock formation	sketching,
Camp tour of nature	Changes in plant	How to spot a fire	Study rocks: color,	tools
cabin, weather	growth	Use of compass	texture, hardness	Use of axes,
station, dining	Water's effect on	Maps: sketch and	Terms: Piedmont,	crosscuts,
hall, rec. hall,	rocks	topographic	Plateau, fault,	sledges
nature craft,		Discussion of a	inland seas	Sketch with
nurses cabin		watershed	Mountain form-	charcoal
			ation: age,	Whittle;
			volcanic action	totem-pole,
				pencil-holder

12:15   Lunch: Weather report, songs, K.P.'s report at 12:00 to set the tables. One K.P. per table. (Each class group has 4 or 5 meals.)

Lazy time: Whittle, crafts, nature cabin, rest in cabins.

1:30 Field note	Cook-out	Trout hatchery	Forestry—tree	Busses leave
hike	Each cooks his own	See 18" trout	planting	Catoctin
Hike in forest	in a mess kit.	Slides of trout	Types of trees	Furnace
Take field notes	Care of forest	View trout ponds	Age of trees	You may wish to
Use five senses	Compass hike	Pond study, fishing	Interesting growth	visit this
	Use of compass	Life in pond	Plant succession	historic area
3:30 Nature hunt	in woods	Temp. changes	Plant pine tree	enroute home
Teams of 4 and 5	Observation of	in water	Animal life	
children	plant and	Dissect frog, fish	What is a forest	
	animal life			

4:30   Shower and free time: Nature cabin, run on greentop, nature crafts, whittle, rest.

5:15   Supper: Skits, stunts, or jokes from boys and girls. Weather report.

6:15   Flag lowering: Four boys or girls.
      Vespers: Each class group has charge of one of these "nature" inspired 10 minutes (poems, readings, songs, original writings, choral readings).

6:30   Class meeting: Each of the class groups meet separately, the classroom teacher is in charge. They evaluate the day's activities and plan for the next.

7:30   Evening activities: Planned at the outdoor school by the council. Outdoor games, stunts, campfires, games, stories and songs, star study, night noises and beauty.

9:00   Taps: If you have a student that can play this or any of the other bugle calls, have him or her bring the instrument.

FIG. 9-3

\nbsp;		

Newark, New Jersey, Y.M.H.A. and Y.W.H.A.

PHYSICAL EDUCATION SCHEDULE FOR ALL AGE GROUPS

	SUNDAY	MONDAY	TUESDAY	WEDNESDAY	THURSDAY	FRIDAY
JUNIORS	1:00 Gym, Games, Scooters, Trampoline 1-3 General Swim	3:45 Learn to Swim 4:15 Fun Swim	3:45 Gym Games & Skills 3:45 Learn to Swim 4:15 Fun Swim	3:45 Learn to Swim 3:45 Gym Games & Skills 4:15 Fun Swim	3:45 Learn to Swim 4:15 Fun Swim	To Be Announced
NU-TEENS	2:00 Basketball, Trampoline 3-5 General Swim	3:45 Basketball Fun & Intramurals 3:45 Learn to Swim 4:15 Fun Swim 5:00 Varsity Basketball Practice 7-8 Fun Swim	3:45 Learn to Swim 4:15 Fun Swim 5:00 Varsity Basketball Practice	3:45 Learn to Swim 4:15 Fun Swim 5:00 Varsity Basketball Practice	3:45 Learn to Swim 3:45 Basketball Fun 5:00 Intramurals 4:15 Fun Swim 5-6 Varsity Basketball Practice 7-8 Fun Swim	To Be Announced
TEENS— COLLEGIATES	10-12:45 Coll. Men Paddleball & Basketball 11-1 Coll. Men General Swim 3-5 Teens—General Swim 3:15 Teens Basketball Fun	12-3 Gym Usage College Men 2:30 Teen Boys Basketball & Gym Skills 5-6 Varsity Basketball Practice 6:15-9:45 Teen & Coll. Men Basketball & Exercise Corner 7-10 Teen & Coll. Men—General Swim	12-3 Coll. Men—Full Gym 2:30 Teen Boys Basketball & Gym Skills 5-6 Varsity Basketball Practice 6:15-9:45 Teen Girls Gym Usage—Badminton, basketball, paddleball 8:30-10 Teen girls, general swim	12-3 Coll. Men—Gym 2:30 Teen Boys 2:30 Teen Boys Basketball & Gym Skills 5-6 Varsity Basketball Practice 6:15-9:45 Teen & Coll. Men—Full Gym Usage 8-10 Teen & Coll. Men General Swim	12-3 Coll. Men Full Gym Usage 2:30 Teen Boys Basketball & Gym Skills 5-6 Varsity Basketball Practice 6:15-9:45 Teen Girls Keep Fit Class; volleyball & coed recreation 8:30-10 Teen Girls—General Swim	12-3 Coll. Men Full Gym Usage 2:30-4 Teen Boys Full Gym
ADULTS	10-12:45 Adult Men Paddleball & Basketball 11:00 Adult Men Keep Fit Class 11-1 Adult Men General Swim 10:30-12:30 Karate	12-3 Adult Men Gym Usage 6:00 Coed Keep Fit Class 6:15-9:45 Adult Men Paddleball	10:00 Ladies Volley Ball & Paddleball 10:30 Ladies Keep Fit Class 11:10 Ladies Interviews and Measurings 11-12 Ladies Learn to Swim & Fun Swim 12-3 Adult Men Gym Usage 6:15-9:45 Coed Adult Full gym usage; badminton, basketball, paddleball 8-8:30 Coed Keep Fit Class 8-8:30 Adult Learn to Swim 8:30-10 Adult Coed General Swim 8:40 Recreation, coed	12-3 Adult Gym Usage 1:15 Adult Keep Fit Class, coed 1:45 Coed Adult General Swim	10:00 Ladies Volleyball & Paddleball 10:30 Ladies Keep Fit Class 11:10 Council Center Special Swim 11-12 Ladies Learn and Fun Swim 12-3 Adult Men Gym Usage 6:15-9:45 Coed Adult full gym usage—badminton, basketball, paddleball 8-8:30 Coed Keep Fit Class 8-8:30 Adult Learn to Swim 8:30-10 Adult Coed General Swim 8:40 Coed Volleyball and Recreation	12-3 Adult Men Gym Usage 1:00 Men Keep Trim Class

This activity schedule is subject to change on holidays and school vacations

FIG. 9-4

and adults. In general, this reflects the pattern found in most community centers of serving children of elementary age on weekday or weekend afternoons and school holidays, teenagers during the later afternoon and evenings, and adults during the evening and on weekends. In addition, in many centers, special groups of older adults, housewives, those who work during the night, or possibly groups of handicapped persons may be served in special programs during the morning or early afternoon.

Mt. Sinai Hospital, N.Y., weekly schedule

Fig. 9-5 shows how program activities are grouped in the weekly schedule of the Therapeutic Activities Division of the Department of Psychiatry of Mt. Sinai Hospital in New York City. Here, programs are classified under three main headings: *leisure-time groups* (activities that are clearly recreational), *prevocational groups* (activities that are seen as contributing to work readiness), and *rehabilitation groups* (programs intended to help a patient become ready for discharge). In a hospital situation, the nature of the patient's attendance may be designated: voluntary, by referral, or with a desig-

Therapeutic Activities Division

ACTIVITIES GROUPS AVAILABLE

LEISURE TIME GROUPS

Notes

POETRY
    Fri. 12:30-1:30   No referral required, voluntary.
                                      Music Room.

CURRENT EVENTS DISCUSSION GROUP
    Mon. 2:00-3:30   Voluntary. Music Room.
    Thurs. 2:30-4:00

MUSIC LISTENING
    Fri. 2:00-3:30   Voluntary. Music Room.

CRAFTS WORKSHOP
    Tues. thru Fri. 10:15-11:30   Maximum 4 patients per unit. Min.4 ses.
                                      By referral. Referrals start Tues. Rm.2

PAINTING
    10:00-11:30 Mon.   2 sessions a week. By referral.
     2:00-3:30 Tues.

CO-ED BODY MOVEMENT
    Wed., Thurs., Fri., 5:30-6:00   Voluntary. Gym.

MEN'S EXERCISE GROUP
    Tues., Fri., Sun.,   Voluntary. Gym.
      7:00, 6:00, 6:00.

SEWING GROUP
    Mon.+ Thurs. 10:15-11:15   4 sessions min. By referral. Room 2.
    Wed. + Fri.-2:00-4:00   Unit therapists supply wool + needles.

CLAY WORKSHOP
    Mon. + Thurs. 2:00-4:00   4 sessions min. By referral. Room 4.

SOCIAL DANCING
    Wed. 10:00-10:45   Gym. By referral.

PRE-VOCATIONAL GROUPS

FOOD A LA CARTE (COFFEE CART)
    Tues. + Thurs. 10:15-11:30   Pts. attend all 3 sessions. 2 wks. min.
    Fri. 2:00-3:30   By referral.

PRODUCTION LINES
    Tues. thru Fri. 10:15-11:30   2 separate groups--Tie-Dye workshop and
                                      Candle-Making workshop. By referral.
                                      Permanent assignment, until discharge.
                                      Room 4.

REHABILITATION GROUPS

PLANNING FOR LEISURE TIME
    Mon. 5:00 and Thurs. 12:00   2 meetings a week. By referral. Room 2.

FOOD AND NUTRITION
    Wed. + Fri. 10:15-11:15   4 sessions min. By referral. Room 5.

WOMEN'S DISCUSSION GROUP
    Thurs. 1:00   By referral. 7 South Dining Area.

FIG. 9-5

nated number of times he or she must attend or with the maximum number of patients permitted per activity.

DAILY SCHEDULING APPROACHES

In addition to weekly schedule plans, it is sometimes necessary to plan program activities on a daily basis. For example, a summer playground program would normally be planned in the following way.

Dividing day into major time blocks

Typically, the day is scheduled to incorporate major time periods. In addition to at least one time block of an hour during the morning and probably two such blocks in the afternoon, other shorter time periods would be scheduled to allow for activities that take shorter periods of time, free play, setting out or collection of equipment, and similar tasks.

Selecting activities for schedule

Activities would be selected on a summer playground on the basis of type, age level, and group size and then fitted into the schedule in appropriate time blocks. For example, activities of different types (games and sports, quiet activities, folk dancing, and arts and crafts) might be designated for different age levels in the playground population, such as children ages 6 to 8 and 9 to 12 years. The size of the group would determine how much supervision and what area of the playground it would require. Some activities, such as a baseball game, would normally require at least an hour to play and would thus be fitted into a major time block, whereas others, such as story telling, might be fitted into a shorter time slot.

Simultaneous scheduling

Assuming that there are enough children on the playground to justify dividing them, more than one group might be scheduled at the same time. This would have to be done so that those activities that require leadership are given it, while other are carried on under general supervision. For example, at the same time one group is taking part in arts and crafts or a quiet game without direct supervision (having already learned the activity), another is supervised, such as children using a wading pool or playground slides and swings, and still another is receiving direct leadership in an activity such as folk dancing or playground music.

Use of areas

Scheduling also depends on the areas available for participation. In a typical playground, there might be an area set aside for play equipment, a wading or spray pool, tables for arts and crafts, a shaded area or pavilion for story telling and quiet games, and a multiuse blacktop area for group games, volleyball, or tetherball. In addition, many playgrounds have an adjacent ballfield for baseball, softball, or other team games. The scheduling should ensure that these facilities are used properly and safely and that activities do not interfere with each other.

Time for playground responsibilities

In addition to setting aside time periods for activities, some time must be allowed for routines such as cleanup, staff meetings or in-service training, inspection of equipment, and similar functions.

Assigning activities to different time periods

Based on the preceding, daily and weekly playground schedules would be prepared. The most popular activities, such as ballgames or swimming trips, might be scheduled each day. Others might be scheduled only once or twice a week. Strenuous activities might be placed in a morning or late-afternoon time slot when the sun is less intense, with quiet activities scheduled for the middle of the day. Special events, trips, or other program features would be assigned to certain afternoons of the week.

Program Schedules in Other Settings

The examples of program schedules just discussed are drawn primarily from public, voluntary, and therapeutic recreation agencies. Each different type of leisure-service organization tends to have its own program emphasis and scheduling patterns, based on its goals, resources, and the work schedules or commitments of its clientele. For example, recreation programs for company employees tend to be scheduled primarily in the evening hours or on weekends, although some companies schedule fitness activities heavily during lunch hours on a staggered schedule. As a single example of program scheduling in a commercial setting, one might examine hotel or resort programs.

RESORT RECREATION PROGRAMS

Many large resorts operate varied facilities for recreational participation, along with scheduled sessions of instruction, social events, or other novel recreational activities. To illustrate, the Playboy Resort and Country Club at Lake Geneva, Wis., prepares a weekly schedule of guest activities, including the following listings:

Saturday, Nov. 3
10:00 AM	*Complimentary hayrides*—Hayrides depart approximately every ½ hour until 1 PM. Dress warmly to enjoy the beautiful scenery.
11:00 AM	*Blackjack*—In the Game Room; try your luck at beating a tough dealer!
1:00 PM	*Water volleyball*—In the indoor pool; join in the splash party.
3:00 PM	*Ping-pong tournament*—In the Activities Center; you must be on time to enter.

Monday, Nov. 5
11:00 AM	*Monday morning briefing*—In the Activities Center; a must attend activity for those staying the week; find out what is happening on and off property.
1:00 PM	*Parcourse fitness circuit explanation*—Station 1 is located on the Lakeside; exit from Building 4.

3:00 PM	Learn a new game or play an old.
5:00 PM	*Fitness program*—In the Health Club; get in shape for skiing or just to get in shape.
7:00 PM	*Wheel of Fortune*—In the Activities Center; it may seem easy on TV, but. . . .

Other activities scheduled throughout the week at specific times include the following: "Password Plus," a miniature golf tournament, disco lessons, a ski session at the Chalet, "Backgammon with a Bunny," "Bingo/Let's Make a Deal," bowling, "Casino Night," "Trivia Quiz Game," and "Grand Auction." These tend to be novel and amusing games and contests, often based on popular television shows, and are similar to many of the events scheduled on cruise ships or in other tourist settings.

Other Program Planning Concepts

As recreation programs are planned and presented, three additional concepts should be considered: (1) program structure and degree of centralization; (2) methods of program presentation; and (3) program life cycle.

PROGRAM STRUCTURE

In most of the kinds of settings that have been described, as well as in senior centers, youth centers, or other recreation programs serving different groups, some activities are likely to require fairly strong organization and direction, whereas others are performed by the participants themselves without direct supervision. For example, in a youth center, program activities might include lounge activities that are very spontaneous and casual, as well as arts and crafts instruction or dramatic activities that are carefully directed.

In summer camps, some camp programs are established within a highly organized framework that provides a minimum of choice and flexibility to campers. Other camps operate with completely free choice for campers in selecting the activities in which to participate. Five different types of program structures may be identified:

1. *Totally nonstructured.* Counselors and campers plan their own camp programs and activities with total flexibility and without any campwide expectations or schedules.
2. *Skeletal structures.* Meals, rising hour, and bedtime are planned, but other phases of the program are planned by counselors and campers.
3. *Semistructured.* Counselors and campers follow the skeletal structure, plus one or two scheduled activities that they are expected to take part in, and have the opportunity to plan the rest of their camp experiences.
4. *Scheduled with camper's choice.* All activities have been scheduled, but counselors and campers can choose which activities to take part in.
5. *Fully structured.* All activities and programs have been scheduled, and campers must take part in assigned activities, without individual choice.

Applying this model to community recreation programs, the issue is whether local programs in neighborhood centers or playgrounds should be expected to follow a highly

Innovative commercial recreation facilities include the fearsome Loch Ness Monster and the new Italian Village at the Old Country, Busch Gardens, in Williamsburg, Va., and the *African Queen*, cruising through a native village, and various water-based areas at Adventure Island, the new Busch water theme park in Tampa, Fla.

structured, standardized model developed by a central planning office or whether they should be free to be highly flexible. The advantage of a structured, centralized approach is that a set of clear-cut program guidelines and standards can be used to ensure that all local programs provide a core of needed activities and thus achieve the stated objectives of the agency. In contrast, the unstructured, decentralized approach may be most effective in responding to local neighborhood needs and special characteristics and in encouraging the creative imagination of staff members.

PROGRAM PRESENTATION: THE DIAGRAPH

A device that is particularly useful in planning and staffing programs within a complex community recreation and park department or other agency is the *diagraph*. This visual presentation combines elements of a diagram and graph to show all events or continuing activities in a convenient and easily understood form. As one large recreation and park department uses the device, it is a ¼-inch thick rectangular board, 4 by 6 feet, consisting of two skins of white gloss paper separated by fine Styrofoam and weighing approximately 3 pounds.

The program activity diagraph is mounted in a staff planning room, to provide a work board for program conferences. Twelve vertical columns represent the months of the year and are labeled as such. The activities themselves are organized under three types or headings:

1. *Scheduled sequence.* These are programs that concentrate on a specific skill, interest, or experience within a scheduled time frame, such as 10 weeks of square dance instruction one evening per week or 6 weeks of jazz concerts every Wednesday evening, 8:00 to 10:30 PM, July 1 to Aug. 15, etc.
2. *Sustained sequence.* These are programs that because of convenience, popularity, or heavy participation, operate throughout the calendar year, interrupted only for schedule changes, facility repairs, or other special reasons. Examples include golf course operation or ice skating, year-round, indoors.
3. *Special events.* These are shows, tournaments, or other spectacular events that are scheduled in advance for one big day or a weekend. All related preparations are aimed at that one date. Examples are outdoor art shows, playground Olympics, Christmas festival, or Thanksgiving Day parade. A special event is often used as the kickoff or culmination of a scheduled sequence.

Although miscellaneous smaller events or programs may occur, these three categories account for most scheduled activities. To set up the diagraph, a data collection process must be carried out in which all programs are identified, cross-referenced, and labeled with correct dates, staff assignments, and locations.

Activities in the form of scheduled and sustained sequences are applied horizontally from left to right on this 12-month format, covering the exact time periods. The material used is ½-inch tape, color-coded for identification. If there are other different types of activities than the 8 or 10 colors that are available, crosshatching or other markings may be used to distinguish additional tapes from each other. Tapes are marked by small white identification strips with hand lettering for easy reading, such as ''Tennis,'' or ''Swim Instruction.''

A scheduled sequence in archery instruction, for example, beginning April 1 and ending June 15, would be depicted as a colored tape starting at the April line and extending from left to right to a point halfway between June and July. Pertinent details regarding locations, instructors, or charges are penned onto the white label marker. This makes archery a highly visible and easily analyzed element within the annual program. Sustained sequences are shown in the same way. Special events are depicted by bright yellow disks of adhesive tape, 1 inch in diameter, placed at the date they occur.

The program activity diagraph can be used for budget planning sessions and to provide information about (1) various programs offered; (2) programs of greatest time extension; (3) months of greatest and least congestion; (4) conflicts among special events; and (5) areas of needed program service.

Two similar visual aids that may be used to help a department display its overall program efforts and as an aid in program planning and related managerial tasks are (1) a *flowchart,* which is used to show individual projects or programs laid out along a calendar, with specific tasks (such as initial planning, facility arrangements, publicity, registration, or similar functions) indicated for the dates on which they are to be begun and completed; and (2) a communitywide *map of program activities,* in which various major facilities and ongoing programs, whether short- or long-term, are identified on a map of the community using color-coded pins. The first of these is used as a tool in planning and carrying out specific programs. The second is helpful in viewing the communitywide availability of programs and particularly in detecting the underprovision or overprovision of different types of activities on a geographical basis.

Program Life Cycle

How long should specific programs be carried on? Clearly, some activities seem to have appeal year after year and attract large numbers of participants regularly. At the same time, others seem to spring into sudden popularity, flourish for a time, and then rapidly decline in interest and attendance.

Crompton suggests that the marketing concept that best describes this phenomenon is the idea of "product life cycle." Products (which is actually what recreation program activities are) are compared to human beings in that they pass through a period of stages: youth, maturity, and ultimately senescence and death. Crompton suggests that there are five actual stages to the recreation program life cycle:

> the *introduction,* in which consumer acceptance is slow; . . . the *take-off stage,* which is a period of rapid growth; . . . *maturity,* during which growth rate slows down; . . . *saturation,* in which no further growth takes place and consumer acceptance wanes; and . . . *decline,* resulting in . . . removal from the marketplace . . . or substantially reduced level of market acceptance remaining constant over a period of time.[7]

He points out that managers must be alert to detect signs of decline in the attractiveness of some recreation programs and should consider potential strategies for extending a program's life cycle, possibly by assigning new leadership, using different facilities, or developing fresh approaches or formats. They must recognize various possible causes for decline, such as new sources of satisfaction appearing or the reduced value of the familiar and the search for new experiences. If the management and promotional effort needed to attract new consumers or hold old ones becomes excessive, it may be necessary to terminate the program or at least to offer it less frequently.

Although commercial recreation organizations are probably the most active in responding to changing public tastes and indeed in creating *new* products or formats to intrigue and attract the public, public and voluntary agencies today must learn to be equally aggressive in measuring demand and marketing their products imaginatively.

Current Trends in Recreation Programming

What are the major trends and priorities in recreation programming? The concluding section of this chapter identifies numerous areas in which various types of leisure-service agencies have expanded their offerings or in which there is a high level of interest.

HEALTH, FITNESS, AND WELLNESS

Probably the most striking area of growth has been in the realm of physical activity designed to promote fitness. From being a fad of the 1970s, exercise has developed into a national phenomenon, described in *U.S. News and World Report* as a "big business of the '80s—as ingrained in the American way of life as mom and apple pie." Commercially sponsored health spas, corporation-sponsored employee fitness programs, Y's and community recreation departments, and armed forces and college physical education programs have begun such activities.

Major corporations such as the Atlantic Richfield Company, the Hershey Corporation, and Wells Fargo have initiated national campaigns to promote public fitness or established extensive programs for their employees. The President's Council on Physical Fitness and Sport and the National Recreation and Park Association have promoted public awareness of fitness needs. In addition to jogging, aerobics, and other exercise programs, many municipal departments have focused on the fitness needs of varied age groups, including the elderly. Many also sponsor fitness-related activities in areas such as nutrition, cardiopulmonary resuscitation training, weight reduction and smoking cessation workshops, and similar activities.

SPORTS PROGRAMMING

Traditionally, sports have represented a major area of public interest and involvement. Today, interest in team sports such as softball, baseball, football, basketball, and hockey continues to run high. However, the unique trend has been to expand sports participation to groups that have not been heavily served in the past, such as girls and women, the handicapped, or the aging. For example, women today freely engage in bodybuilding, high-risk sports, and even triathlons, probably the most grueling of all sports contests. As a single example of sports participation by seniors, several hundred older adults regularly participate in an annual Golden Olympics cosponsored by the Virginia Recreation and Park Society and the Blue Cross/Blue Shield of Virginia.

Beyond this trend, there is a growing concern about the emphasis on winning in high-level sports competition for children and youth. Numerous organizations such as the National Youth Sports Coaches Association seek to promote constructive value systems that emphasize the value of mass participation on a ''fun'' basis rather than high-pressure, win-at-all-costs play for a few.

CULTURAL ARTS PROGRAMMING

Popular involvement in the various cultural arts, including music, drama, dance, and different forms of arts and crafts, has continued to grow over the past three decades. Today numerous communities sponsor arts centers and annual arts festivals, and millions of individuals of all ages actively participate in such programs. Ideally, successful programs in the cultural arts involve the collaboration of public agencies, the schools, museums, and various civic groups concerned with the arts. Based on an extensive study of cultural arts programs, Manning and Williams report that in addition to having arts councils, task forces, or commissions to help promote the arts, it was necessary to have the person with a dream ''to make something unique happen in the arts. Without artistic direction from the arts community itself, local governments cannot 'manufacture' successful arts programs.''[8]

PROGRAMMING TO MEET FAMILY AND AGE-GROUP NEEDS

Beyond such trends in specific areas of leisure participation, there is growing interest in meeting the needs of different age groups and families as a unit in the modern community. Programs designed to promote the fitness of children and youth or provide alternatives to drug or alcohol abuse among young people have received increased attention. The dramatic shift in family structures with the great number of divorces in recent years and the increase in single parent families or the number of single adults in society has compelled attention to meeting these needs. Programs designed to meet the needs of the elderly will obviously continue to become more important as this age group becomes a larger segment of the population.

Public recreation and park departments, voluntary agencies (including religious agencies), and the armed forces have shown special concern in these areas. Many military morale, welfare, and recreation units in particular have initiated expanded services for families because of the special stresses found in military life and the problems affecting many armed forces bases stemming from family conflicts. Various types of leisure-service agencies offer counseling, day-care, and similar services to meet such needs.

COMPREHENSIVE HUMAN-SERVICE APPROACH

Linked to such emphases, a growing number of leisure-service organizations offer human-service programs. As described elsewhere in this text, such programs seek to meet the critical social and personal needs of participants through varied services. These may range from nutritional programming, transportation assistance, family counseling or legal advice, medical or dental clinics or workshops, assertive training or counseling for divorced persons, courses in finance and home repair activities, sex education classes for youth, stress management and weight reduction programs, alcohol and drug abuse activities, discount purchasing, and similar services to other forms of youth and adult classes and social groups.

This program trend is evidenced in two ways: (1) the inclusion of such activities in the ongoing activities of public, voluntary, or other leisure-service agencies, sometimes with special funding, and (2) a restructuring of the organizations themselves so that instead of being described as recreation agencies that happen to sponsor such activities as part of their overall offering, they become umbrella-like human-service organizations with a number of related community functions. The trend toward having multiservice agencies rather than independent recreation and park departments is particularly evident on the West Coast, where numerous recreation and park authorities have strongly promoted the human-service concept.

Summary

Program planning and implementation represent key responsibilities of leisure-service managers. From a broad perspective, program planning consists of more than simply providing activities for participation. As a concept, it also includes providing facilities for self-directed use, the coordination or cooperation with other community agencies, education for leisure, and sponsorship of related human or social services.

The process of program development involves a sequence of eight major steps, extending from developing a philosophical framework and assessing participant or community needs to implementing, supervising, and evaluating actual programs. Activities may be selected from a wide range of recreational pursuits and presented in various formats on the basis of the characteristics and needs of participants and the capability of the sponsoring organizations. This chapter presents guidelines for scheduling based on seasonal, weekly, and daily approaches in varied settings.

Several current trends in recreation programming are described, including the popular emphasis on health- and fitness-related activities, new emphases in sports programming, cultural arts trends, and concerns with the family and numerous age groups that have special needs. A comprehensive human-services approach to structuring leisure service is offered in the chapter's final section.

STUDY QUESTIONS

1. Survey a comprehensive recreation program, such as a large YMCA, YWCA, or community center. Using a checklist of activity categories drawn from this chapter, indicate which activities are offered and the formats in which they fall. Is there any major gap in programming, or is there an obvious area of overemphasis?

2. Prepare an assessment form to determine leisure needs and interests designed for a particular age level or other special population groups to be reviewed by members of the class.

3. With other students, select one of the program areas described in the text as currently popular and carry out an informal survey of the community or region to determine all the programs serving this need (for examples, fitness centers or high-risk, adventure programming). Indicate the special role that each agency or program fulfills in providing this activity or service.

Case 9   *Exercise Physiologist or Recreation Specialist?*

YOU ARE MARY WEBB, personnel director of a large pharmaceutical company. Through the years, your office has sponsored a successful employee recreation program, consisting chiefly of sports, social clubs, charter travel programs, and similar activities.

Employee health and fitness have become growing concerns. With the encouragement of the company president, you have had a fitness laboratory installed; it includes exercise machines, a weight room, treadmills, a small jogging track, and stress-testing equipment. When the former head of the recreation program retired, you replaced him with an exercise physiologist, Myron Porter, who is well qualified in the area of sports medicine. You felt that Myron would be the ideal person to supervise the recreation program with its heavy emphasis on cardiovascular fitness testing and activities.

However, over the last 3 months, you have found that Myron has little idea of how to develop and publicize programs, encourage volunteer leadership, or work with people generally. With the exception of a small group of fitness addicts, who work out daily, some of whom are training for a half marathon, most employees are no longer involved regularly in recreational activities. The bowling and softball teams are close to breaking up, and the last two charter trips have had to be canceled because of insufficient interest.

Questions for Class Discussion and Analysis

1. Where did you go wrong? What is the fundamental lesson that you have learned?
2. What can you do now? Myron Porter is considering taking a position at a commercial health spa. If he were to leave, what would be your next move?

Case 10   *State Park Policy on Skinny-Dipping*

YOU ARE JIM MARAVICH, director of a state park system in a southern state. For years there has been a problem with "skinny-dipping" at several of the rivers and lakes in or bordering your parks. Groups of adults have selected sites where they sunbathed and swam in the nude, with the location of these sites gradually becoming known and attracting other skinny-dipping enthusiasts.

At first you tried to prevent this by legal action, but found it was difficult to enforce the law, which was vague on the issue. Finally you decided to resolve the matter by setting aside two areas along somewhat remote rivers that have fairly secluded beach and swimming sites and letting it be known that persons swimming and sunbathing in the nude there would not be prosecuted, although ordinances against it would be strictly enforced elsewhere.

Initially this seemed to work. Growing numbers of nudists began to use the selected locations. However, new problems have developed. Numerous voyeurs are now hiking in to spy on and photograph the nude bathers. Families with children who boat or raft past these beaches are complaining of immoral behavior on them.

Case 10 **State Park Policy on Skinny-Dipping**
cont'd
You are receiving reports of heavy drinking or drug use at one of the locations, and worst of all, there have been several incidents of sexual assaults on isolated nude bathers.

Questions for Class Discussion and Analysis

1. Was your initial decision to set aside spots for "approved" nude bathing a sound one?
2. In establishing these sites, you did not clear the matter with state police officials. Your own state park rangers can give tickets but do not normally·have law enforcement authority for criminal acts. What can be done now to provide a safer environment?
3. What basic principles regarding the use of state park facilities should be observed? Is it your place to legislate morality, and is this a moral issue? Perhaps you had better do some research to determine exactly what the law is with respect to nudity in such locations and learn what policies are followed elsewhere.

REFERENCES

1. Edginton, Christopher R., Compton, David M., and Hanson, Carole J.: *Recreation and Leisure Programming: A Guide for the Professional*, Philadelphia, 1980, Saunders College Publishing, p. 25.
2. Farrell, Patricia, and Lundegren, Herberta M.: *The Process of Recreation Programming*, New York, 1978, John Wiley & Sons, Inc., p. 1.
3. Edginton, Compton, and Hanson, *op. cit.,* pp. 213-263.
4. Kraus, Richard: *Recreation Program Planning Today*, Glenview, Ill. 1985, Scott, Foresman & Co., p. 23.
5. *Ibid.,* Chapter 3.
6. Graham, Peter J., and Klar, Lawrence R., Jr.: *Planning and Delivering Leisure Services*, Dubuque, Iowa, 1979, William C. Brown Co., p. 253.
7. Crompton, John L.: "Recreation Programs Have Life Cycle, Too," *Parks and Recreation,* Oct. 1979, p. 52.
8. Manning, Susan, and Williams, John: "Sunnyvale's Guidelines for Cultural Arts Programming Success," *Parks and Recreation,* July 1982, p. 27.

CHAPTER 10

Definition of the Fiscal Management Process: *The administration, custody, protection, and control of all revenues received by the recreation system from all sources and properly expending funds for approved purposes. . . . The purpose of fiscal management is to handle and be responsible for all money matters (financial records, accounting, collections, protection, controls, investments, expenditures, conformance to laws and administrative directives, property inventories, debt services, and other items of value.)*[1]

Budgets and Fiscal Management

Probably no area of management responsibility is more critical or important today than budget and fiscal management.

Money—coming and going—is what makes programs and facilities; it pays for personnel, materials, heat and light, and all the other ingredients that permit an agency to function. Goal setting and program planning would be meaningless if they did not consider the financial implications of each strategy under consideration.

This chapter therefore focuses on the fiscal management process. It presents guidelines for the preparation and execution of budgets, including auditing and accounting procedures, and also describes the sources of recreation and park funding in various types of organizations.

Recognizing that most leisure-service agencies today must operate within a climate of fiscal austerity, Chapter 11 suggests a variety of innovative approaches that are being used by creative recreation and park managers to meet the challenge of the present "era of limits." Combining the two chapters, the reader should gain a full understanding both of tried-and-true methods in fiscal management and of new strategies that are gaining popularity in many community agencies today.

Nature of Fiscal Management

Leisure-service organizations of all kinds may be divided into two basic categories: profit oriented and nonprofit oriented. Profit-oriented organizations seek to bring in revenues that are greater than their expenditures. While nonprofit-oriented organizations are concerned primarily with providing a needed community service, they must ensure that their expenditures do not exceed their revenues. Edginton and Williams write:

> Both profit and nonprofit organizations are concerned with the manner in which their resources (assets) are utilized. Both types of organizations seek to maximize their operating efficiency. The profit-oriented organization does this to increase its profit margin; the nonprofit-oriented organization does this to maximize its impact regarding services [and to] increase the number of services available and reduce the cost of services.[2]

Fiscal management is the process of directing and controlling the use of money in every phase of the leisure-service operation. It should be an important function of fiscal management not simply to *receive* and *spend*, but aggressively to *seek out* funds; the marketing process is a key aspect of fiscal management in the modern leisure-service agency.

Managers' Expertise in Fiscal Matters

Calvin Coolidge once said, "The business of America is business." Certainly it is true that support for every form of public service, including recreation and parks, *must* come from adequate financial backing and intelligent fiscal management. The same principle applies in voluntary, private, commercial, therapeutic, and other types of leisure-service agencies.

The setting of departmental goals and the design of a budget intended to achieve these goals, the process of budget review and approval, and the actual administration of a fiscal program through the year constitute major responsibilities of recreation and park administrators.

It can be an extremely complicated process, involving expertise in the realm of bonds and indebtedness, credit management, working with private funds and foundations, expenditure and control systems, pension plans, and similar concerns. Typically, many recreation and park executives approach this responsibility with a mixture of fear and ignorance.

Yet it should not represent such a difficult hurdle. It is not necessary for administrators to become financial wizards. Provided that they have a basic understanding of the elements of budget making and fiscal management and that they continue to learn and grow in this field, they can operate effectively. In most cities, finance commissioners or comptrollers, city managers, budget analysts, or lay finance chairpersons have helped recreation and park executives develop the competence needed to function intelligently and effectively in this area.

It is a tribute to this competence and the support given to recreation and leisure service as a form of governmental responsibility that the gross value of publicly owned recreation and park resources—including ice rinks, marinas, parks, tennis courts, golf courses, sports centers, swimming pools, and other facilities—has climbed to many billions of dollars. It has been estimated that government on various levels in the United States spends approximately $6 billion a year on recreation and park facilities and programs. Billions more are spent by other types of leisure-service organizations. As a single example, Table 10-1 shows the scope of the Boys' Club movement in the United States during the early 1980s in facilities, personnel, participants, and budget.

Multiplying this pattern by the hundreds of national organizations and thousands of local agencies providing leisure services shows the fiscal importance of organized recreation in the national economy. In many states, tourism alone rates as one of the leading employers, and today commercial recreation represents an estimated expenditure of over $300 billion each year. According to *U.S. News and World Report,*[3] outlays for sports, recreation, and entertainment have increased rapidly:

    1969 $83 billion
    1974 $125 billion
    1984 $310 billion

Given these impressive totals, it is apparent that fiscal management is a key element in leisure-service agency operations. At the heart of this process is the budget, the major financial instrument used or misused by managers.

TABLE 10-1   Scope of Boys' Club Movement in 1982

Number of youth served	Over 1 million
Number of Boys' Club facilities	1,000, in 50 states, Puerto Rico and Virgin Islands
Number of full-time career professionals	3,200
Number of part-time professional staff	4,800
Number of youth members employed as part-time staff	5,000
Number of volunteer adult staff	55,000
Number of volunteer leaders on boards and auxiliaries	91,000
Total of operating budgets of all Boys' Clubs	$110 million
Estimated replacement value of all facilities	$260 million
Annual operating budget for national organization	$7.7 million

From *Annual Report*, New York, 1983, Boys' Clubs of America.

Meaning of "Budget"

The term "budget" comes from the French word *bougette*, meaning bag or wallet. This would suggest that many leisure-service managers think of their budgets primarily as bags full (or partly full) of money, which they use to purchase equipment, hire personnel, or pay department charges.

However, the word should have a broader meaning. The budget should be thought of as a management plan through which a work program or project is outlined, including the financial details and schedules necessary to achieve certain predetermined goals.

The well-conceived and effectively presented budget should do the following:

1. Provide a general statement of the financial needs, resources, and plans of the department, including an outline of all program elements and their costs and allocations for facilities and personnel.
2. Inform taxpayers and government officials (or in other types of organizations stockholders, boards of trustees, college officials, hospital directors, or company managers) of the amounts of money spent, the sources of revenue, and the costs of achieving departmental goals.
3. Help in promoting standardized and simplified operational procedures by classifying all expenditures and requiring systematic procedures for approving them.
4. Serve for evaluating the program and ensuring that objectives are met.

Whereas in the past a budget was often viewed as a 1-year financial plan, sound budgeting practice now requires that it be a continuous process with yearly revisions and changes to adjust to changing circumstances.

Types of Budget

The most common budget format is of the "line-item" type, in which each category of spending is itemized according to its anticipated expenditure for the fiscal year ahead.

Beyond this, budgets are usually identified according to the following types: object classification, function classification, organizational unit classification, or classification by fund.

OBJECT CLASSIFICATION

This type of budget classifies all proposed expenditures according to a systematic breakdown or classification by type. Typically, categories would include elements such as personal services, purchase of supplies and equipment, or contractual services. The major object groups in a widely used object classification system are as follows[5]:

1000	Services—personal: involves salaries and wages
2000	Services—contractual: involves work performed or services rendered or materials supplied on a contractual basis
3000	Commodities: supplies and materials
4000	Current charges: includes rent, insurance, licenses, etc.
5000	Current obligations: fixed expenses such as interest, taxes, loans, etc.
6000	Properties: cost of equipment, buildings, or land
7000	Debt payment

A more detailed explanation of the terms used in this system would include the following:

Personal services involve salaries and wages paid to persons employed by the government body.

Contractual services involve work performed for the government through agreement or contract by other than employees, as well as the provision of equipment and furnishing of commodities under agreement.

Communication and transportation expenses include the cost of telephone, postage, freight, express, drayage, and traveling expenses for transporting persons.

Printing, binding, and advertising expenses include all charges for printing, including advertising and publication of notices, and expenditures for mimeographing, photography, blueprinting, and binding.

A supply is a commodity that is consumed, impaired, or worn out in a reasonably short period of time. For example, stationery, food, fuel, ice, clothing, cleaning, and motor items are supplies.

Materials are items of a more permanent nature that may be combined or converted to other uses. Included here would be lumber, paints, iron, or other building materials, masonry and road materials, fiber products, leather, and repair parts.

Although object classification budgets offer a convenient means of looking at the major categories in which money is spent, they do not relate expenditures meaningfully enough to programs. Therefore some departments use budget classification systems that attempt to relate expenditures to the actual function being performed.

CLASSIFICATION BY FUNCTION

In one system, proposed expenditures are assigned to the specific departmental *function* they will serve, such as playground operations, indoor centers, or senior citizens' program. Although there is no single widely used classification system that illustrates this method, one common approach is to divide the budget into three major functional areas: administration, facilities, and special services.

CLASSIFICATION BY ORGANIZATIONAL UNITS

In another approach, expenditures are classified according to the organizational unit of the department that is responsible for them, such as division of recreation, personnel department, maintenance bureau, and so on. Thus the relative cost of each section of the department is illustrated rather than the item being purchased.

CLASSIFICATION BY FUND

Some departments that draw their revenues from several different sources classify all expenditures against the different funds that support them. In a recent Revenue Sources Management School, Stone outlined a number of major examples of different types of governmental funds and their uses. These included the following, among others:

1. *Special Revenue Fund*—to account for the proceeds of specific revenue sources (other than special assignments) or to finance specified activities as required by law or administrative regulation
2. *Debt Service Fund*—to account for the payment of interest and principal on long-term debt other than special assessment and revenue bonds
3. *Capital Project Funds*—to account for the receipt and disbursement of monies used for the acquisition of capital facilities other than those financed by special assessment and by enterprise fund
4. *Enterprise Funds*—to account for the financing of services to the general public where all or most of the costs involved are paid in the form of charges by the users of such services (examples might include golf courses, skating rinks, or sportsmens' centers)
5. *Intragovernmental Service Funds*—to account for the financing of special activities and services performed by the designated organization unit within a governmental jurisdiction for other organization units within the same governmental jurisdiction[6]

To illustrate fund classification, the Bureau of Naval Personnel in the U.S. Department of the Navy defines recreation funds as trust funds generated by Navy personnel and their dependents to help provide financial support for their recreation activities.
Specifically, they are

monies received from Navy exchange profits, fees and charges placed on the use of recreation facilities and services or other authorized sources for the support of Navy recreation programs. Unit Recreation Funds are those which serve the recreation needs of individual ships, shore stations and other Navy activities. Composite Recreation Funds are those which serve two or more activities which share the same recreation facilities. Consolidated Recreation Funds are those which serve the recreation needs of several separate installations within a geographical area.[7]

Since such funds operate outside of the normal sphere of tax-appropriated monies, it is extremely important that controls be established to ensure that they are not misused. The *Navy Special Services Manual* dealing with this function states:

The management of a Recreation Fund is a command responsibility. This responsibility may not be delegated to others. The Fund Administrator shall exercise precautions to ensure that funds are properly received, safeguarded and accounted for in accordance with existing Navy Department regulations.[8]

Rossman points out that since funds are handled as separate fiscal entities because of legal restrictions, regulations, limitations on use, or managerial policy, they can be more efficiently controlled and observed. If a particular agency activity is segregated as a self-balancing accounting entity, he writes:

> All of the usual accounting reports can be prepared for it. These include a balance sheet, statements of cash receipts and disbursements, and reconciliation of retained earnings. A fund flow statement can also be prepared for each fund which facilitates analysis of the fiscal resources used in the fund.[9]

PERFORMANCE BUDGET

The performance budget represents a combination of object and function classification methods. Expenditures are classified by listing the main expenditures by object or categories of objects to be purchased (including services, materials, or other charges) in the left-hand vertical column and the functions of the departmental operation horizontally across the top of the page. By examining such a budget, it is possible to tell more clearly just *how* money is to be spent. For example, the budget will show exactly what amounts are allocated for items such as staff salaries, rentals, supplies and equipment, and printing and postage for a specific aspect of the program, such as senior citizens' centers.

PROGRAM BUDGETING

Each of the types of budgets just described is essentially a *line-item* budget. As described earlier, this type of financial plan shows, line by line, specific amounts earmarked for specific items. The annual cost of each staff member, the amounts to be spent on charges for utilities, and so on are clearly laid out. Such instruments are easy to prepare and appear to be businesslike, orderly, and logical. Their major shortcoming is that they do not really explain the program they are intended to finance and do not carry a meaningful message for the reader.

For this reason, many business organizations and government departments have moved in the direction of program budgeting, an approach under which budgets are designed in such a way that large units of work, or special programs, are isolated, identified, and described in detail. Edginton and Williams write:

> The idea behind the program budget is to put more emphasis on dealing with programs that are desirable and on associating costs with each of these programs in terms of resources necessary to carry them out; in other words, to determine which programs the policymaking or governing boards want to offer and to permit the manager to determine how to finance these programs and assure accountability.[10]

An example of program budgeting is shown in Fig. 10-1. It is the annual budget for municipal camps of the Department of Parks and Recreation of Kansas City, Mo. Sim-

Department of Parks and Recreation

Program: RECREATION PROGRAMS
Sub-Program: MUNICIPAL CAMPS

Expenditures by Character	Actual 1977-78	Estimated 1978-79	Estimated 1979-80
Personal Services	$ 201,076	$ 224,200	$ 246,123
Contractual Services	28,675	45,900	58,675
Commodities	20,502	21,929	20,806
Capital Outlay	1,139	574	1,750
Total Expenditures	$ 251,392	$ 296,603	$ 327,354
Expenditures by Fund			
General	$ 219,814	$ 263,169	$ 291,703
Public Service Employment	31,578	33,434	35,651
Total Expenditures	$ 251,392	$ 296,603	$ 327,354
Regular Man Years	18.0	19.2	18.8
CETA Man Years	3.0	3.0	3.0
Total Man Years	21.0	22.2	21.8

Key Objectives

1. Conduct four ten-day sessions of resident camping and three ten-day sessions of day camping in accordance with the standards of the American Camping Association
2. Provide classes and informal learning experiences about the natural environment, ecology, archaeology and local history
3. Conduct a Learn-to-Ride program for children and adults

Performance Measures	Actual 1977-78	Estimated 1978-79	Estimated 1979-80
1. Daily attendance			
Resident campers	59	80	80
Day campers	91	125	125
2. Program participation			
Outdoor School	2,200	1,000	1,000
Nature Wagon/Outdoor Discovery	8,532	9,000	9,000
Lakeside Nature Center	30,680	35,000	40,000
Line Creek Museum	17,145	25,000	25,000
Heritage Village	10,494	14,866	28,000
Jerry Smith Park	820	1,250	2,500
Swope Interpretive Center	10,814	15,000	20,000
3. Horseback riding/weekly average	79	80	80

Highlights

In 1978-79, three seasonal positions were added to the Municipal Camps program to assist in the program development at Heritage Village. In 1979-80, program development will continue at this facility, as well as at Jerry Smith Park. Two seasonal cook positions at the resident camp have been eliminated from the 1979-80 budget as food service will now be provided through a contractual arrangement. Participation fees from this program's activities are expected to generate $20,875 in 1979-80.

FIG. 10-1   Program budget of Kansas City, Mo., Parks and Recreation Department.

ilar separate program budgets are prepared for neighborhood center programs, summer recreation programs, open-door school programs, and several other program elements.

Much more work and detailed preparation go into assembling a program budget than a conventional line-item budget. For this reason, most still rely on line-item budgets. However, the trend is toward program budgeting, and it may be expected that more and more municipalities will move toward a modified program budgeting technique. This trend is being facilitated by the rapid development of computer services, since program budgeting and unit cost analysis rely heavily on computer analysis.

Use of program budgets on cost-benefit analysis

Many community funding organizations (such as United Way or Community Chest) that provide funding to different agencies to carry out specific social-service programs require that they prepare contractual agreements that itemize specifically the long-range and immediate objectives of the program. This is linked to the tasks that are to be performed under the contract, along with costs of services and quantified statements of outcomes.

Program budgets make it possible to measure the projected costs of any active or program service, identify its expected benefits or outcomes, and thus develop an item-by-item "cost-benefit" analysis. However, cost efficiency should not be the only criterion through which program success or value is measured. Meserow, Pompel, and Reich point out that a costly program for disabled or culturally deprived individuals may have far greater value to society than a less expensive community center program. Nevertheless, they conclude:

> A cost-efficiency evaluation system is a tool which can be used in a variety of ways by park and recreation administrators. With benefit-cost analysis figures at their disposal to defend judicious and beneficial programs, administrators will have more freedom to innovate, to expand, and to attempt establishing new areas of service for their communities.[11]

OPERATING BUDGET VERSUS CAPITAL BUDGET

A distinction should be made between two basic types of budgets: operating and capital.

The *operating budget* is the document that contains detailed statements of all administrative costs in the form of personnel salaries, office rentals, gasoline, typing paper, baseballs, or paint brushes required to operate the department for the course of 1 year. In many cities the fiscal year is identified as July 1 to June 30, although it may be identical to the calendar year or any other legally authorized 1-year period. In a few cases, budgets may be set up for a 2-year period. Normally, a municipality assembles and reviews its entire budget, consisting of the separate budgets of each of its departments, such as police, fire, schools, and the like, at one time.

The *capital budget* is a separate document that includes plans and proposed expenditures for carrying out major purchases and construction projects of a substantial and long-term nature. These would include the purchase of heavy snow removal trucks or parkland or the construction of new golf courses, ice rinks, or recreation buildings. They might include major renovation projects but would not include routine maintenance charges.

Legal Aspects of Budgets

Unlike certain other elements of recreation and park management, in which there is no legal compulsion to operate in specific ways, fiscal management is usually a carefully defined process. The principle has long been accepted that the most appropriate method of financing recreation and park needs is through tax funds. State enabling laws and city charters usually assign this power to municipalities and specify regulations governing all public budget procedures.

Normally, these broad regulations are supplemented by local ordinances or administrative procedures that require that an itemized budget of appropriations be placed before the city council and that may also define the method of presentation, the calendar of presentation, required public hearings, the officials who must be consulted, or similar details. The budget process varies considerably among cities.

In the mayor-council form of municipal government, the mayor is usually designated as responsible; in other structures the city manager or a member of a city commission may be assigned the budget-making responsibility. In larger communities, special budget officers and staff are employed for this purpose.

Such regulations and procedures would not normally apply in nonpublic agencies. Instead, the laws governing commercial enterprises might require that stockholders of a corporation receive detailed financial statements or prospectuses, as well as all major fiscal plans, before their implementation. In other specialized forms of leisure service, such as employee recreation programs, the armed forces, or therapeutic recreation, budget processes might simply require advanced presentation of fiscal plans (including anticipated revenues and expenditures) for review by agency comptrollers, a finance committee, or other administrators.

Budget Process

The budget process is normally divided into three stages: preparation, authorization or approval, and execution.

BUDGET PREPARATION

The preparation of the budget is a job for the chief executive and his or her key staff members, and it must involve much more than merely making routine adjustments in the previous year's budget. A long-term and carefully thought-out program of budget development is essential unless the administrator enjoys chaos, confusion, and fiscal defeat. This implies the need for careful advance preparation of all program elements and costs and for a logical short-, medium-, and long-term construction program, tied to an intelligent plan for financial support.

No aspect of recreation management has changed as radically in recent years as the budget preparation function. A mere 10 to 15 years ago, most public department budgets were prepared as follows:

1. The chief executive or his deputy prepared an overall estimated budget, based on the past year, current practices, and indicated future trends and economic factors. This was usually done 2 to 3 months in advance of the budget submission deadline.

BUDGET PREPARATION SEQUENCE IN PUBLIC AGENCY

January   Department begins spending annual budget. Financial office requests outline of spending practices as seen by recreation chief executive for year ahead.

February   First monthly sheet of expenditures comes from finance officer to department head indicating its congruity or incongruity with spending schedule as outlined in approved budget (see later section on *accrual accounting*). Any overspending or underspending is brought to department head's attention.

March-April   Same pattern as February. Serious spending irregularities are brought in focus, with warnings of impoundment of funds if problems are not corrected. Projections on spending for the next 6 months are now assembled based on the spending patterns of the first 4. Revenue patterns are also reviewed and projected. Personnel problems (excessive absence, heavy overtime, and similar irregularities) are studied, and caution signals are sent up wherever dangers are indicated.

Timetable for long-term capital expenditure is triggered, and first steps are taken on projects requiring long lead times for specifications, advertising, bid taking, contract preparation, and similar tasks. Based on such factors, all relevant data for the budget are compiled.

---

2. Special-interest groups, district supervisors, or other divisional representatives were invited to submit their plans and needs for the coming year.

3. Headquarters staff and upper-level managers reviewed all proposals, checking their feasibility and congruence with the preliminary model assembled by the agency chief executive.

4. Trimming, adding, cutting, or trading-off items took place until about 6 weeks before the deadline.

5. A carefully prepared draft of the budget was presented by the agency head to the mayor, managing director, or other key fiscal officer of the community for a preliminary review.

6. The budget was returned to the agency with directions for changes as needed, which would normally be executed with some degree of negotiation if needed.

7. The budget was presented in its final form to the municipality's board, council, or other elected officials with responsibility for approving or rejecting it.

This process has been altered sharply in recent years as a result of tighter budgetary limits and increased sophistication in the art of agency and municipal management. It is far more demanding and painstaking than before and is heavily dependent on the office computer to rapidly and accurately accumulate and sort data concerning revenues, charges, deficits, and other financial elements. These can be retrieved, processed, and made available to those reviewing the budget in a matter of minutes. Below is shown what a current year of budget operations in a typical recreation agency might be.

BUDGET PREPARATION SEQUENCE IN PUBLIC AGENCY—cont'd

May-June   First work sessions are now held on the budget for the following year. Indicators for consumption of materials and supplies, repair and replacement of equipment, personnel charges, revenues, and similar elements are reviewed to develop recommendations for change in major areas of budget. Environmental factors such as economic trends, health needs, changing functions of other agencies, and similar concerns are assembled.

July   Work sessions on the future budget continue, along with careful review of current budget activity and agency operation. The end of the first 6-month period of the current budget triggers a flow of half-year reports and trends analysis by the overall municipal fiscal office. They may ask why certain budget accounts are *under* spent and whether fund transfers should be made while there is still time to do so. In a crisis situation, such changes may be made during the budget year from one department to another.

August   The budget planning process has now left the casual "workshop" level and has become a mass of attendance reports, revenue reports, inventory statements, and appraisals of goal accomplishments. Failures are noted, analyzed, and appropriately prepared for in the future budget. Hard-nosed meetings begin between the recreation agency director and the city's top administrative officer. These continue, usually on a weekly basis, through September.

Work desks typically include two piles of data. One consists of all current reports and information on the agency's *ongoing* operation and fiscal activity. The other involves projections and recommendations for the format of the *future* budget.

Over the next 4 months the budget plans are refined and go through a series of drafts and reviews, which result in the approval of a final budget in time for the cycle to begin again.

Guidelines for budget development

The budget development process does not assume that there is a ceiling figure imposed by the citywide administration that sets arbitrary limits for the budget of the recreation and park department. Nor are internal divisions of the department asked to frame their requests within specific budget limits. Such cautions or devices to prevent overspending prevent the development of an honest and meaningful budget. This does not imply that municipal funds are unlimited. However, it makes clear that a budget should reflect the legitimate needs of the constituency to be served and the justified program of the department rather than merely a listing of items that can be afforded under an arbitrary budget ceiling.

On the other hand, it is a mistake to inflate a budget request deliberately in the expectation that it will be reduced by a certain percentage to come out with a reasonable budget total. During the course of review by the city's financial analyst, hearings, and other means of examining budgets, each items will be carefully scrutinized and *must* be strongly justified.

Items must not be included simply because they were in earlier budgets. Pet projects, holdovers, and similar program features must be examined ruthlessly and with total objectivity. Every item should be examined as though it were under consideration for the first time. If it is weak, wishy-washy, and without clear goals or a reasonable promise of being productive, it should be rooted out. The budget must be lean, rugged, and as tight as possible. Legislators, city council members, mayors, and budget officials develop an uncanny ability to perceive the bloated budget. Like one's reputation for honesty, budget credibility can never be recovered by the recreation and parks executive once he or she has been exposed as a budget fraud.

BUDGET AUTHORIZATION OR APPROVAL

The municipal council or other county or town legislative body will usually schedule a series of public hearings on all of its proposed budget sections to provide the general public with an opportunity to voice pros and cons. Such hearings should be well publicized and attended.

Public hearings

Public hearings represent a crucial stage if the budget that has taken so much effort in preparation is to be carefully considered and fairly evaluated. Public hearings, whether on a village, town, county, or large city level, can be tense and sometimes extremely difficult. The introduction of pressure groups and political lobbying, the presence of committee chairpersons from the city's legislative body, and the presence of reporters and sometimes television cameras make it essential that the departmental administrator conduct himself or herself with maximum coolness and efficiency. The following guidelines will help ensure success during this stage of budget considerations.

CAREFUL PREPARATION   The recreation and park executive must be thoroughly familiar with the proposed budget, including each item and the justification for it. It can be extremely embarrassing for the administrator to fail to locate needed background materials or the documentation for items under sharp questioning by an appropriations committee chairperson. Statements such as "I'm sorry, I can't seem to locate it" give the impression of weakness or confusion.

OPENING STATEMENT   The administrator should make a brief opening statement that describes the prime thrust of the department, its goals, and some past successes. It should clarify the new directions and priorities found in the budget and should present a positive and optimistic picture of the work of the department. This statement should be delivered in a relaxed conversational manner rather than ponderously read.

RESPONSE TO QUESTIONS   Responses to questions raised at the hearing should be short and informative. Just as in a courtroom, it is a mistake to answer more than is asked and wander off into dangerous territory that may open up discussion points not within the area under questioning. Responses should be precise and factual, not philosophical.

DEMEANOR OF ADMINISTRATOR   At all times the administrator should strive to be affirmative and confident. He or she should not backpedal or vacillate under fire. It is a serious mistake to reply to challenges with such comments as, ''Well, I didn't really expect you would pass that item'' or ''I don't feel I can fight for this program.'' Such expressions of weakness may imperil the entire budget presentation.

The administrator must also strive to remain controlled and confident at all times and not be drawn into angry exchanges under sarcastic questioning or critical jibes frequently heard at public hearings. Instead, he or she must rely on facts and documentation. If questioning becomes illogical or wandering, it is best to remain silent; after a particularly unjustified tirade or attack, the executive may return with a statement such as: ''Now if we may return to the subject of the budget.''

After the series of budget hearings and behind-the-scenes meetings, it is likely that additional changes may be made in the budget. In some cases these may be the inevitable result of overall financial problems or policies of the municipal government with respect to the coming year. However, assuming that the budget is a sound one, it should be substantially accepted and authorized for the coming year.

It should also be noted that budgets that continue to climb annually may actually involve less *real* dollars being spent, if they do not keep up with the rate of inflation in buying power or escalating personnel costs.

BUDGET EXECUTION

This section deals with budget execution, which is the actual process of administering the disbursements, receipts, and other financial functions of the department that have been authorized by the budget. This process is designed to conform with state law as it governs the fiscal operations of municipalities within its borders. It may also be influenced by local administrative policies or simply by procedures that have developed through the years and that are generally recommended in training institutes or workshops or textbooks or other manuals.

Once a budget has been legally approved and adopted, it is in effect for the following fiscal year. It must then be carefully adhered to as a fiscal plan and as a guide to attain the goals and objectives of the department.

Effective budgetary controls

An essential element in executing an annual budget is a work program, which outlines tasks to be performed, standards of service and efficiency, and methods to be used. Such a program defines each task, how often it is to be carried out, how long it should take, and what staffing it requires. It thus breaks all departmental functions down into measurable units. Since overall costs have already been calculated in the budget, it is possible to measure the cost of each unit of service or activity and thus to control the amount of expenditures within each area of maintenance or program leadership.

With such a work program an allotment system may be set up to schedule expenditures on a monthly or quarterly basis. This provides a means of control through which all funds are spaced out properly through the year and in which it should not normally be necessary for any expenses to go beyond the allotted amount. Typically, Johnson describes the quarterly expenditure plan, which identifies the manner in which resources are to be used during a fiscal year. Under it, the department head gives key responsibility for planning and controlling the use of budget funds to line or divisional supervisors. Johnson writes:

> The department head . . . should charge the supervisor with the responsibility of operating within fiscal authority. The central budget office should review periodically the quarterly projections, along with actual expenditures, to make sure that the fiscal plan is legitimate. This system should establish the necessary control to prevent overexpenditures.[12]

The following three procedures ensure efficient and honest performance with respect to expenditure of funds.

PROCEDURES FOR PURCHASE OF SUPPLIES OR EQUIPMENT Customarily, items that cost less than a given amount such as $50 or $100 may be purchased directly without seeking special approval. Items or materials costing more than this but less than $1000, for example, may be purchased from an approved supplier. Items costing more than this amount may only be purchased from an approved supplier *after* the materials to be purchased are advertised and bids received from at least three suppliers. Although procedures in this area vary from department to department, there are usually controls to ensure that materials are purchased at the lowest possible cost from responsible suppliers.

Since fiscal management must be scrupulously careful to avoid the possibility of graft or ''kickbacks,'' these procedures must be adhered to exactly.

Smith[13] points out that a systematic, carefully planned purchasing program in any large organization must be based on the following elements: (1) advance planning, which allows for adequate lead time in making purchasing decisions and which ensures that vendors will have needed supplies in stock; (2) careful attention to corporate or agency policy regarding classification of purchases (such as expendable supplies, capital equipment, etc.), as well as required requests for bids and dollar limits on types of purchasing procedures; (3) compilation of an inventory of materials that your department will need during the coming year, including a careful forecast of repair and replacement requirements; (4) development of a list of approved suppliers, including an up-to-date record of their performance; and (5) familiarity with or access to sound legal advice on all legal considerations that come into play with respect to purchasing.

COST CONTROL PROCEDURES In addition to purchasing procedures, many agencies will define precise guidelines for carrying out inventories, pricing goods or services that are for sale, and maintaining efficient cost control procedures. For example, in the operation of U.S. Navy Clubs and Messes, which are part of the overall recreational services program, performance-based training procedures for managers include detailed inventory forms. These carry each "accountable unit," meaning items such as cheese slices, ground beef patties, or fish cakes, through a sequence from item size, beginning inventory, inventory after new "issues" or additions, through tallies of the per unit cost, the selling price, and the total sales.[14] Fig. 10-2 shows a form used to maintain such records. It includes projected income totals, actual sales totals from register tapes and guest checks, and records of "over/under" discrepancies on items and income.

Efficient procedures of this type are essential in maintaining businesslike operations in those leisure-service programs in which sales, fees and charges, or other revenue sources are part of the financial management responsibility.

In many other areas of program service, personnel must collect registration and admission fees, charges for supplies or equipment rental, permit fees, and similar items. It is essential that rules regarding the collection of money and turning it over to a central departmental office are precisely defined and exactly followed.

PROCEDURES FOR MAKING CONTRACTUAL AGREEMENTS   When individuals or outside firms are hired on a contractual basis to perform specific responsibilities for the department, there again must be clearly outlined procedures for selecting them and precise contractual agreements to define their task, the basis for payment, and the like.

•   •   •

The most important aspect of maintaining financial controls, however, is keeping adequate financial records and preparing and submitting monthly reports relating expenditures to the appropriate categories in the annual budget. It is therefore essential that there be an efficient accounting system to monitor every aspect of financial management.

Financial Accounting System

Accounting is concerned with systematically gathering, recording, and reporting all data related to the fiscal operations of an agency or business organization. It provides an accurate, up-to-date picture of all income and expenditures, payrolls, property inventories and requisitions, and other financial transactions. Basically, it represents the built-in watchdog or monitor that helps safeguard and control the fiscal management process.

Since most bookkeeping, computing, and record keeping are currently done through the use of the computer, often through a central financial office in municipal government or other large agencies, the task of the recreation and park department is to gather and submit all financial data according to prescribed procedures. In addition, the department's managers must regularly review computer printouts to ensure that periodic controls on spending are being maintained or to determine unexpended balances.

A related process is auditing, which is concerned with verifying and confirming the validity of fiscal transactions and determining whether they were appropriately carried out and accurately recorded. There are two kinds of audits: (1) *internal,* or concurrent, which involves daily checking by staff members before payments are made and (2) *external,* or post audits, which are generally made by an outside inspector (a separate

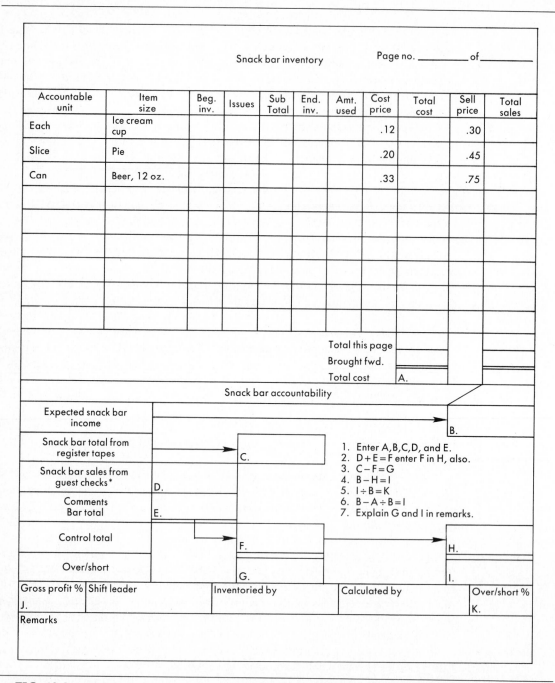

FIG. 10-2   U.S. Navy cost control form for clubs and messes. (From Cost control for clubs and messes [control snack bar], Washington, D.C., 1983, U.S. Navy Recreational Services, Manual F-7.)

agency of government or accounting firm) at regular intervals. An agency's records may be audited annually as part of a total fiscal overview of municipal government.

Accounting and auditing are important to maintain internal control of funds within a department. Normally, countercheck procedures must be used, so that more than one employee must verify information, sign checks, approve expenditures, or do similar tasks to prevent dishonesty.

A number of special methods or procedures are used to guarantee effective accounting systems. These include cost accounting, accrual accounting, the use of balance sheets, and concurrent auditing.

COST ACCOUNTING

This represents a form of recording financial expenditures so that they are keyed to work performed or services rendered. In essence, it is a way of following up on program or performance budgets. It involves keeping separate accounts for each function within a department, such as administration, facilities, or special services. Cost accounting is useful in the following ways:

1. It facilitates and promotes evaluation of departmental efficiency.
2. It can be used to evaluate individual personnel performance.
3. It is valuable in determining the feasibility of constructing facilities with either the agency's own labor force or on a contractual basis using outside firms.
4. It is helpful in determining the proper balance between different phases of departmental operation.

ACCRUAL ACCOUNTING

Accrual accounting is a widely used accounting system under which all encumbrances, or charges, against specified accounts are shown on reports of expenditures that are kept up to date. In most large municipalities today, computerized systems are used that feed out monthly reports showing total amounts authorized in each section of a budget, the amounts spent to date, and the balance remaining. This system is essential to efficient fiscal administration in that it gives an instant, up-to-date picture of all disbursements and obligations and the current status of each section of the budget.

BALANCE SHEETS

These represent a form of bookkeeping report showing the assets and liabilities in a given fund or budget. They illustrate the financial status of a department and its ability to finance future expenditures, particularly with respect to capital development or major rehabilitation or refurbishment projects. Balance sheets may be used to show the actual cost of programs by indicating the initial investment in a facility and the annual costs of operating the activities carried on in it. The information provided in the balance sheet is particularly useful in long-range planning of areas and facilities.

CONCURRENT AUDITING

Audits usually show expenditures only after they have been authorized and carried out. However, the procedure of concurrent auditing or control auditing takes place either before or during the expenditure of public funds. It represents a preaudit of expected income or disbursements and assists in preventing improper or inappropriate expenditures.

Customarily, municipal departments must issue financial statements or reports at stated intervals during the year, as well as year-end financial reports. Such reports typically describe the overall operations and revenue of a department. They usually present both operational costs and revenues in columnar form. Items presented under *operations* include the appropriation for each object, expenditures to date, outstanding encumbrances, the unencumbered balance, and the percentage of appropriations not yet spent or committed.

Auditors usually provide such financial statements at the end of each month and at the end of the fiscal year. They are obviously helpful in allowing administrators to adjust the operation of the program to the level of expenditures and revenues at any given time or throughout a given period.

AUDIT OF WORK PROGRAMS

A final form of financial control is exerted through a formal check, or audit, of specific administrative or program divisions of a department or construction or maintenance projects. Here, instead of an overall balance sheet or accrual accounting system, the emphasis is on checking to ensure that the work plan is up to date, that items paid for (in the form of materials or services) have actually been delivered, and that all projects are being carried on as efficiently as possible.

Sources of Funding for Leisure-Service Agencies

The sources of funding to support both operating and capital budgets of leisure-service agencies vary greatly. Examples of both public and private funding sources are provided in the following section of this chapter.

TAXES

Taxes represent the most common means of financing the ongoing operations of public recreation and park departments. They fall into four major categories: general, special, millage, and special assessment.

General taxes

These represent the most common form of tax revenues used to support recreation and parks. They consist of the local real estate or property taxes, which are the chief source of municipal funds or of local school district financing. These are derived by assessing industrial or residential property within the borders of the municipality at a given rate; this is usually expressed as a percentage ranging from 20% to 50% of market value. A tax rate is established by the municipality for a given fiscal year. When the assessed value of the property is multiplied by the tax rate, the resulting figure is the tax that must be paid by the property owner.

The general real estate tax normally provides support for services such as police, highways, health, sanitation, recreation and parks, and similar services. Not infrequently, in suburban areas individuals must pay separate taxes to the county, township, or village for different services provided by each of these units of government. Normally, however, all real estate taxes are paid into the general fund of a single municipality, and it is from this source that budget allocations are made to support municipal services.

Special taxes

In some cities and more commonly in areas that are served by a special park or recreation and park district, special taxes may be used to support public recreation. Thus taxes on liquor, amusement admissions, or items such as motorboat fuel may be assigned directly to the support of municipal recreation and park services.

Millage taxes

A millage tax represents a specific tax (usually low and therefore expressed in mills) leveled against the assessed value of residential or industrial property. Here too the amount derived is assigned directly to a recreation and park fund and used exclusively for that purpose. In some states, such as California, millage taxes are authorized in the state education code and assigned directly to the support of school recreation and other community-related programs. The advantage of special taxes of this type is that residents are taxed directly for the support of parks and recreation; if they value this service, they will normally support the tax, which is not lost within a total general fund appropriation.

Special assessment taxes

In some municipalities there is the custom of taxing only those residents who stand to benefit from a particular service for the support of that service. Special assessment taxes are frequently used to support highway and sewer construction programs; in some cases they are also used to support recreation and park developments for residents in separate districts of a community. As a recent trend, some communities have begun to impose recreation impact fees on residential developers, which require them to pay stipulated sums of money for the acquisition, design, and construction of needed recreational facilities. These impact fees represent a form of special assessment tax, collected primarily at the time of building permit issuance, and customarily may be used only to finance capital outlays for recreation and parks.

BONDS

Bonds represent a second major support of municipal recreation and park programs. They are normally applied only to the financial support of major capital development programs. With respect to recreation and park departments, they are used chiefly for the acquisition of land and the development of major facilities such as large parks, swimming pools, stadiums, ice rinks, sportsmen's centers, or golf courses. In some cases a municipality or large recreation and park district may float a substantial bond issue that includes a number of separate recreation and park development projects; in other cases a bond issue may be intended to support the development of a single major project.

Bonds represent a form of deferred payment by which the cost of any government enterprise can be spread over a period of years rather than applied to a single year's budget. In addition to recreational and park facilities, they also are used to pay for the development of schools, highways, sewer systems, and similar projects. Bonds are normally to be repaid within a 10- to 30-year period, thus ensuring that those who will use the facilities over this period will pay for them at a reasonable rate.

Although it is not essential for recreation and park administrators to be highly sophisticated about the different types of bond issues, it is helpful for them to know the fundamental features of each type. If a recreation and park bond issue is to be presented to the public for approval, the recreation and park administrator must build a strong case and gather all the documentation possible to convince the public that this is a desirable project for the municipality to undertake.

Types of bonds

There are several types of bonds, which vary according to their method of retirement: term bonds, callable bonds, and serial bonds.

TERM BONDS In this type of bond the government agency promises to pay off the entire principal at the end of a given period of time. Normally, it would use the *sinking fund* method, under which an annual sum is put aside each year, with the amount accumulating each year until the full principal has been set aside at the end of the term of the bond.

CALLABLE BONDS This is a special type of bond in which the government has the option of calling in bond issues for payment at a specified time before the end of its term or at any time it chooses. Since bond interest rates tend to fluctuate, it is thus possible for the issuer to call in a bond and reissue it at lower interest rates, depending on market conditions.

SERIAL BONDS Under this method of financing capital outlays, the government pays the bond purchaser a specified portion of the principal, plus interest, each year that the bond issue is in effect. Thus a percentage of the bond is reduced each year through payments of approximately equal sums. This is similar to the way in which homeowners normally pay off mortgage indebtedness over a period of years.

OTHER TYPES OF BONDS Bonds may also be classified according to their method of gathering funds for debt service. *General obligation bonds* are those in which the payment on interest and principal is drawn from the general tax revenues of the municipality. *Assessment bonds* are those in which the money is derived from special assessments on residents benefiting from whatever has been built, such as a golf course, marina, or cultural center.

GRANTS

A third major source of funding for local recreation and park departments has been federal and state grants. In the mid-1970s, a considerable share of funding for local recreation and parks was paid for by the federal government, as the following illustrates:

> Four major federal assistance programs—the Land and Water Conservation Fund (LWCF), the Community Development Block Grant program (CDBG), the Comprehensive Employment and Training Act program (CETA), and General Revenue Sharing (GRS)— provide about $1.2 billion to local park and recreation systems each year . . . about 35 percent of all dollars spent by cities and counties for parks and recreation in 1976.[15]

In addition, numerous other special grant programs were designed to meet the needs of certain population groups or assist in high-priority areas of concern. A broad range of federal funding assistance programs in the late 1970s included various sports and cultural programs for youth, arts and humanities assistance, delinquency prevention and conservation funds, and grants for urban recreation and park rehabilitation.[16] During the early 1980s many such programs were cut sharply or discontinued entirely.

FEES AND CHARGES

Fees and charges represent an increasingly important source of needed income for public recreation and park departments, as well as for other types of leisure-service sponsors. For several decades there was widespread acceptance of the view that public recreation and park services and facilities should be free or almost free to all potential users. However, as the facilities provided have grown more elaborate and expensive and the types of programs offered have become more diversified, it is clear that some system of imposing charges to support programs is increasingly necessary.

Types of fees and charges

Hines[17] categorized the most common types of fees and charges as follows:

1. *Entrance fees.* Charges made to enter large parks, botanical gardens, zoos, or other developed recreational areas, such as fairgrounds, game preserves, or historical sites
2. *Admission fees.* Charges for entering buildings offering exhibits or performances, such as grandstands or museums
3. *Rental fees.* Charges for the exclusive use of property that is not consumed or destroyed and that is returned, such as boats, cabins, canoes, checking facilities, skis, archery equipment, or parking
4. *User fees.* Charges made for the use of facilities or participation in activities usually carried on simultaneously with others, such as artificial ice rinks, ski lifts, driving ranges, swimming pools, or golf courses
5. *License and permit fees.* Charges for the right to carry out certain activities, such as hunting, fishing, or camping; vending or exhibition permits
6. *Special-service fees.* Charges for special or unusual services, such as entry fees for team competition, instruction in organized classes, summer camp enrollment, and workshops or clinics

Although for a time there was resistance to the increased use of fees and charges in public leisure-service agencies on the grounds that it discriminated against the poor, elderly, and handicapped and constituted a form of "double taxation," today it is widely accepted as a logical means of supporting public recreation and park programs.

Guidelines for establishing charges

In a study conducted by Economics Research Associates[18] in the mid-1970s, most citizens interviewed felt that more recreation services should be on a pay-as-you-go basis. The following levels of support from fee revenues were advocated: special facilities (52%); operations and maintenance (47%); and land acquisition (33%). Many administrators, according to the Economics Research Associates' study, have found that although there has been initial resistance to new or increased fees, reflected by *short-term* decline in usage, this effect has tended to disappear within 2 to 3 years. In some cases higher fees have been followed by increased attendance at facilities and programs.

In the past many municipal recreation and park departments were content to obtain approximately 10% of their operating funds from fees, charges, concessions, and similar revenue sources. This percentage has gradually risen, with a 1981 report indicating that public recreation and park agencies derived 22.5% of their operating budgets from user fees alone. In some areas, such as California, the figure is much higher, with an emphasis on programs that are completely self-sustaining through fees and charges.

Another study, reported in 1982, indicated that in a sample of 280 California park and recreation departments, budget self-sufficiency (percentage of total budget, including capital expenses, that is derived from fees and charges) was highest among recreation departments and lowest among park departments.[19] Table 10-2 shows the types of fees and charges in effect.

Public resistance to fees and charges will lessen if appropriate pricing methods are used (p. 276) and when it becomes apparent that they lead to improved leisure services. For example, research has shown that fee increases may result in better maintained facilities that support services of increased quality and diversity. The presence of fee collection personnel may provide a greater feeling of security for some participants.

The Economics Research Associates' study of fees and charges points out that fees may be used to reduce congestion during peak times of use, thus improving the recreational experience for all visitors. For example, in Santa Clara County, Calif., users are charged more during peak Saturday, Sunday, and holiday hours and less during nonpeak hours, thus spreading the demand for facilities throughout the week and reducing waiting lines.

Techniques that are useful in minimizing the impact that increased fees may have on the public include the following:

1. *Public relations.* Park and recreation facility users should be provided the courtesy of advance notice on fee changes, as well as an explanation of the need for the revenues collected and the basis for them.
2. *Gradual increases.* Gradual increases, clearly tied to rising costs, may be more acceptable to the constituency than sudden or drastic fee increases.
3. *Fee-by-fee consideration.* Each type of activity or facility should be separately

TABLE 10-2   Use of Revenue Sources by California Agencies

Type of Fee or Charge	Percentage of Departments Using*
Program/activity fees	87.9
User fees	63.2
Rental fees	52.1
Sales revenue	44.6
Lease revenue	41.4
Entrance/admission fees	40.0
Other fees and charges	18.5

From Crossley, J.: "Status Report on Commercialized Public Recreation," *California Parks and Recreation*, Dec. 1981-Jan. 1982, p. 16.

examined and an appropriate fee set according to the level of demand, cost of the activity, types of fees asked at competing opportunities, possible cosponsorship of the activity, or similar factors. In some cases activities or facilities that tend to yield a "profit" may be used to subsidize or partially subsidize the cost of others.

4. *Annual passes.* Agencies may also provide frequent visitors to parks with the opportunity to purchase annual passes or other special privileges. This method may be used to increase both visitation volume and user identification with the recreation and park system; it is typically used for community swimming pools.

The determination of the appropriate range of admissions or other fees is far more complex than simply asking what the traffic will bear. In a discussion of fees and charges in public zoos, Gobar points out that as admissions charges are raised, per capita revenue is increased, but attendance may decrease. Thus there is a price that would maximize revenue, beyond which all higher prices would reduce attendance so much that total revenues would be less. Gobar concludes that to determine an optimal admissions charge policy for a particular market area (referring to density of population) that will result in the attainment of defined financial and attendance level goals it is necessary to

have a proper understanding of the relationship between zoo size, admissions policy, attendance, revenues and costs, to make the most efficient use of public resources to attain the objectives sought . . . whether financial . . . or public service.[20]

Such calculations can be extremely complex, making use of multiple regression analysis techniques. They should also take into account the effects of reduced attendance levels on other forms of income, such as concessions volume.

Compensatory policies for special populations

A major problem with increased fees and charges is that they tend to exclude the poor, handicapped, and other special populations from important areas of recreational opportunity. There is a legitimate concern that the need for public agencies to generate more revenue will transform organizations that should have human service as a primary concern into "businesses" in which the profit motive is paramount.

What are the solutions to this problem? Special consideration is being given by many public recreation and park departments to children and the elderly, low-income groups, and the handicapped. Methods used to avoid their exclusion are (1) establishing differences in the fee structure for special populations; (2) waiving fees on an individual basis; (3) having local citizens, businesses, or service clubs provide scholarships or subsidize programs; (4) adjusting the fee structure according to the income level of the neighborhood; and (5) allowing for extended or deferred payment schedules.

Fee-charging policies vary considerably according to the type of community involved. In most affluent suburban areas or moderately well-to-do cities and towns, it is taken for granted that fees will be charged for all special facility programs, adult classes, or youth programs in which registration is charged or instruction provided. In contrast, in larger cities with substantial numbers of low-income residents, fee-charging policies and programs themselves are often much more limited.

USES OF SPECIAL REVENUES

One of the problems associated with the trend toward gaining increased revenues from fees and charges is that often they are simply deposited in the municipality's general fund rather than used to support recreation and park programs. Particularly if the fees have been imposed or increased to compensate for inadequate funding from tax sources, this may mean that leisure-service agencies must continue to suffer from fiscal restraints.

Some communities have adopted the approach of depositing sums derived from fees and charges into revolving funds (funds that are continually being replenished and drawn from, maintaining a minimum balance) that are used to support recreation and park operations. In other cases, they may be specifically assigned to recreation-related programs.

There are numerous examples of how special facilities such as golf courses, tennis complexes, skating rinks, and art centers have been put on a pay-as-you-go basis and in fact have maximized their revenues to the point that they are financially assisting other elements in the leisure-service system.

CONCESSIONS

A fifth major type of income source for public leisure-service agencies involves the use of concessions. Under such arrangements, public recreation and park managers authorize private individuals or businesses to sell merchandise or services in parks, stadiums, or other publicly owned facilities. Concessions are generally granted when the public department cannot provide a service efficiently or economically in comparison to the commercial organization. Some of the areas of service in which concessions are commonly granted are boat rentals, refreshment stands, equipment shops, and instructional services.

The use of concessionaires permits a recreation and park department to provide services, equipment, or refreshments that it might otherwise not be able to offer because of limited staffing. Since concessionaires are private businesspeople or companies, they are not restricted by civil service personnel requirements or other municipal bureaucratic regulations. Therefore they are able to provide the service while charging a reasonable fee and at the same time make a profit on the operation. Customarily, concessionaires pay a percentage of their gross revenue to the department and might also pay an annual fee for the concession privilege.

In Canada, for example, with the exception of Vancouver and Montreal, all major cities have made leasing arrangements for food service facilities with private concessionaires. Leasing agreements are usually for 5 years and provide a percentage of gross income payment to the municipality, which ranges between 10% and 18%. Cities such as Toronto make careful checks on the quality of concessionaires' performance and derive substantial income from leasing arrangements. In Montreal, where the city parks department used self-operated vending machines as an alternative, it was found that heavy vandalism occurred in unguarded refreshment facilities. Even Vancouver, which has derived as much as $1.5 million per year in income from food services, has begun to lease some facilities to concessionaires on a guaranteed fee or percentage of gross basis.

GIFTS AND BEQUESTS

A final important form of income benefiting many public recreation and park agencies consists of gifts and bequests from private sources, such as individual donors, foundations, or business contributors.

Many large city parks have been the personal gift of a public-spirited individual or family. Larger estates as well as smaller properties have often been bequeathed to municipalities, with the understanding that the land would be used solely for recreation and park purposes. Foundations have often contributed either to support a specific program element or project or more commonly to assist in developing a recreational facility to meet community needs. Just as wealthy philanthropists contribute money to private schools and colleges or to hospitals, so may they give funds to build a center, park, or other facility.

Finally, many cities are assisted by major industries or other business firms in sponsoring special events or programs, ranging from sports tournaments to concerts, mobile recreation units, or social-service activities sponsored by recreation agencies. Examples of such practices may be found in Chapter 11.

SOURCES OF INCOME FOR NONPUBLIC ORGANIZATIONS

This chapter has focused on budgetary procedures and sources of income of public recreation and park agencies. Other types of organizations vary somewhat in their funding approaches, with the primary difference being that they do not directly receive tax funds to support their overall program efforts.

Voluntary agencies

Nonprofit community organizations such as the YMCAs and YWCAs, Boy and Girl Scouts, Boys' and Girls' Clubs, or Police Athletic League tend to depend on a mix of different revenue sources including: (1) membership dues, which often vary according to the age or nature of membership; (2) special fees or charges for classes, courses, team or health club membership; (3) allocations from Community Chest, Red Feather, United Fund, or similar communitywide fund drives; (4) their own fund-raising efforts; or (5) special gifts or grants from private individuals or foundations.

Many voluntary organizations also obtain government grants for providing special services, such as senior center programs for the aging, or antidelinquency programs. They may also rely heavily on wealthy board members or business firms in the community for additional contributions. Typically, voluntary agencies in well-to-do neighborhoods, such as a YMCA in an upper-class suburb, are relatively self-sufficient based on membership and other fees, while the same type of organization in a disadvantaged inner-city community would be unable to charge such fees and would depend primarily on grants, contributions, and similar sources.

Employee recreation

Recreation and related personnel services often derive much of their financial support directly from the sponsoring company in the form of funds to build or maintain facilities or salaries for professional staff members. These expenditures are generally viewed as costs related to personnel management, such as other fringe benefits, which constitute an impressive portion of overall personnel costs.

However, many employee recreation programs are also supported fully or in part by annual dues for membership in an employee association or by fees for participating in specific activities. Substantial funding may be derived from cigarette, soft drink, canteen, or other vending machine profits, which many companies use to support employee activities. Increasingly, such programs are relying on their own efforts to provide financial support for their activities, with a self-sufficiency concept governing classes, clubs, sports competition, or travel activities. In addition, many employee services also include discount purchasing plans and similar activities, which may yield a margin of profit.

Campus programs

Recreation programs in colleges and universities are generally supported by three different types of sources: (1) the use of institutional funds to assist intramural or student union programs as an important student service; (2) the use of special student activity fees, which are charged on an annual or semester basis, usually at time of registration; and (3) specific fees paid by students, faculty members, or staff to take part in given activities. In addition to these sources, Colgate[21] suggests other ways of financing college intramural sports programs:

1. Entry fees and dues—either charged individually or for teams, when entering a league, tournament, or special events
2. Admissions fees—charged to attend or take part in sports nights, carnivals, professional shows or performances, exhibition games, showing of sports films, school dances, or similar events
3. Sales—arrangements made with companies that provide schools with catalogues and items to sell for fund-raising projects, such as magazine subscriptions, cookies, candy, school stationery, or similar products; students may sell these on a

voluntary basis, or for a percentage of sales income

4. Automatic vending machines—profit from income of vending machines placed in athletic or college union facilities, which sell cigarettes, snacks, soft drinks or similar products

5. One-day special projects—car washes, paper drives, cake sales, can and bottle recycling collections, volunteering for community service projects, marathons, and similar events

Military recreation

Funding support of armed forces morale, welfare, and recreation (MWR) programs is of two types: (1) *appropriated money,* which is allocated by Congress for general support of the armed forces, and (2) *nonappropriated money,* which includes revenues derived from post exchange profits, vending machines, military club profits, fees for participation in programs, and similar sources. The proportion of nonappropriated funding has risen steadily since the mid- and late 1970s, and many recreation programs in the armed forces are currently required to have a specified level of self-sufficiency. Indeed, Daniel points out that total exchange sales rose in the mid-1980s to $6.3 billion and that substantial nonappropriated funds were being used to "build and renovate commissaries, exchanges, clubs, and other morale, welfare and recreation activities. These programs are growing rapidly, and have almost doubled in size since 1983."[22]

Despite this trend, the core of armed forces recreation programs must be supported by appropriated funds that are used both to construct major facilities and to pay for the full-time military and civilian professional personnel who manage these operations.

Therapeutic recreation

Recreation services to special populations are provided in so many different kinds of settings—nursing homes, special schools for the retarded, mental health centers, physical rehabilitation or long-term care hospitals, camps for disabled children, or other community-based programs—that no single form of funding is provided. When it is provided in an institutional setting, recreation is typically supported as part of overall service to the patient or resident and is paid for as part of the total funding package. Since the late 1970s, however, there has been a strong push toward including recreation as a reimbursable service.

Essentially, recreation is regarded as an ancillary service, with third-party payments that are charged to Blue Cross or Blue Shield Plans, commercial insurance carriers, Medicaid, or other organizations that pay health or medical expenses on behalf of beneficiaries or recipients. The term "third party" refers to the distinction between the individual receiving the service (the first party), the individual or institution providing it (the second party), and the organization paying for it (the third party). Many therapeutic recreation specialists in treatment settings strive to meet the necessary standards and requirements needed to justify inclusion as part of the treatment team and to receive such reimbursement.

In other situations, therapeutic recreation programs may be supported by special fund drives, contributions, memberships and fees, or tax funds assigned to support specific programs. In this sense they are much like voluntary organizations, and indeed, many nonprofit community agencies sponsor therapeutic recreation, such as special camping or adapted sports programs for the handicapped, along with their other services. In some cases major foundations such as the Joseph P. Kennedy, Jr., Foundation support programs designed to assist a particular population, such as the mentally retarded.

Commercial recreation

Financial support of commercial recreation organizations is derived from a vast array of public spending on recreation. This includes all pleasure-oriented travel and tourism, commercial sports and entertainment, classes and special schools in a wide variety of hobby skills or other leisure activities, and even the purchase of recreational goods and equipment, such as clothes, boats, sports equipment, hunting and fishing supplies, and vacation homes.

Fiscal management in such settings is comparable to other types of businesses and essentially involves a marketing operation, in which consumer needs and interests are assessed, marketing conditions are analyzed, and products are designed, priced, and presented to the public. While all forms of recreation today are marketed in a true sense, if they are to be successful and economically viable, commercial recreational services and programs are the only ones that have profit making as their *primary* purpose. They have substantial capital sums at their command, as well as the flexibility to design ambitious and innovative facilities and programs. However, they must also function in the highly competitive environment of the business world, without the kinds of subsidies or special forms of support that public or voluntary programs may enjoy. As a result, the planning methods used to design and present many commercial recreation programs are often far more sophisticated than those used in other types of leisure-service operations.

Summary

Fiscal management is a key element in the operation of all types of leisure-service agencies. It is concerned with the planning and control of money in support of programs, facilities, and staffing expenditures and is usually formalized through the presentation and approval of annual budgets that describe anticipated revenues and expenses in detail.

Several types of budgets are described in this chapter, including line-item budgets, performance budgets, and program budgets. The use of special funds as a budgeting method is examined, and the differences between operating and capital budgets are explained. The entire process of budget formulation, presentation, approval, and execution is described with guidelines for effective managerial performance at each stage. Financial accounting systems involve various types of auditing of expenditures and work programs, as well as accrual accounting and the use of balance sheets.

The chapter outlines several major sources of funding for leisure-service agencies: (1) taxes of various types (general, special, and millage); (2) bonds, usually used for capital development; (3) grants for higher levels of government or foundations; (4) fees and charges; (5) concessions; and (6) gifts and bequests. Although primary emphasis is given to fiscal management of public recreation and park agencies, examples of funding sources or budget approaches of employee recreation, campus, armed forces, therapeutic recreation, and commercial recreation programs are also cited.

STUDY QUESTIONS

1. Visit nearby leisure-service agencies to obtain copies of their proposed and approved budgets or annual financial reports, along with procedural guidelines or manuals controlling purchasing, auditing, accounting and money-handling activities. Review and compare these in class.
2. With other students organize a mock budget hearing or bond proposal, to be held before a city council or county board of supervisors with members of the public present. In role-playing, criticize or defend specific aspects of the budget or bond proposal.
3. Conduct an informal survey of public and voluntary leisure-service agencies to determine the range of fee structures for basic instructional programs, memberships, or other recreational charges.

Case 11 Setting Up the Fund

YOU ARE BETTY BRUNSON, director of a neighborhood recreation center in a medium-sized community. By law, all of the revenues that come in from fees and charges must go into the city's general fund and cannot be used directly by your department.

Over the past 2 years you have developed a mechanism under which various community groups sponsor and take full charge of special-interest groups for adults, such as an aerobics class, ceramics workshops, sports leagues, and similar activities. They collect fees directly, pay the instructors, and are basically self-supporting. The department's fiscal officer now tells you that this procedure bypasses the intent of the law and cannot be continued. Since the funds are collected in the center for participation in activities carried on in the center, they represent center income that must be deposited in the public treasury.

Questions for Class Discussion and Analysis

1. How can you continue these special programs under the city's policy? For example, how could you pay the instructors if you do not have direct access to the registration income?
2. One staff member has suggested that you develop a special enterprise fund that would permit you to deposit and use the money directly. How would this work? Do some research and prepare a proposal to develop such a fund.
3. Prepare a proposal for the city council that shows the estimated revenues and costs of these special activities carried on by community groups, so that they will understand the arrangement and allocate the funding that will permit you to continue the programs while turning over the revenues to the general fund.

Case 12 Third-Party Payments

YOU ARE DOLORES JACKSON, director of therapeutic recreational activities in the Activity Therapies Department of the Hutchinson Center for Physical Rehabilitation.

In the past, several adjunctive modalities, such as occupational and physical therapy, have been designed as services receiving third-party reimbursement by Medicaid or Medicare or private hospitalization insurance programs. John Drinan, administrative director of the Hutchinson Center, now asks you to design the recreation programs so that this service can also be filed for special payment for services rendered to patients.

If you are to continue to receive administrative support and have your staff remain at its present level, it is clear that you will need to meet the eligibility requirements for third-party payments.

Questions for Class Discussion and Analysis

1. Based on a preliminary examination of present guidelines (you will need to do some research to determine these), what steps will you have to take to make the recreation program eligible for reimbursement?

Case 12
cont'd
Third-Party Payments

2. Since third-party programs must be designed to meet the needs of individual patients through a medically approved treatment plan, will this affect some of your general recreation programming within the rehabilitation hospital?

3. Present the pros and cons of the plan that John Drinan has asked you to carry out and develop guidelines, if possible, that might permit you to offer both kinds of programs.

REFERENCES

1. Hjelte, George, and Shivers, Jay S.: *Public Administration of Recreational Service,* Philadelphia, 1972, Lea & Febiger, p. 316.

2. Edginton, Christopher R., and Williams, John G.: *Productive Management of Leisure Service Organizations,* New York, 1978, John Wiley & Sons, p. 279.

3. "Business Gets Healthy from Athletics Too," *U.S. News and World Report,* Aug. 13, 1984, p. 27.

4. *Annual Report,* New York, 1983, Boys Clubs of America, n.p.

5. Original classification developed by A.E. Buck; see Rodney, Lynn S.: *Administration of Public Recreation,* New York, 1964, The Ronald Press Co., pp. 256-258.

6. Stone, Robert: *Outline of Non-Appropriated Fund Development,* 1980, National Recreation and Park Association Revenue Sources Management School.

7. "Administration of Recreation Funds," in *Special Services Manual, 1710-11,* U.S. Department of the Navy, March 1974, p. 6-2.

8. *Ibid.*

9. Rossman, J. Robert: "Fund Accounting," *Leisure Today, Journal of Physical Education, Recreation and Dance,* April 1982, p. 54.

10. Edginton and Williams, *op. cit.,* p. 216.

11. Meserow, L. Hale, Pompel, David T., and Reich, Charles M.: "Benefit-Cost Evaluation," *Parks and Recreation,* Feb. 1975, p. 29.

12. Johnson, Norman S., in Lutzin, Sidney G. (Editor): *Managing Municipal Leisure Services,* Washington, D.C., 1980, International City Management Association, p. 228.

13. Smith, Joseph A.: "Planned Purchasing," *Recreation Management,* Feb. 1979, pp. 11-13.

14. *Cost Control for Clubs and Messes (Control Snack Bar)* Washington, D.C., 1983, U.S. Navy Recreational Services, Manual F-7.

15. Benedict, Judith S., "Federal Support for Local Park and Recreation Systems," *Trends* (Park Practice System), Fall 1978, p. 39.

16. *Ibid.,* p. 42.

17. Hines, Thomas I.: *Budgeting for Public Parks and Recreation, Washington,* D.C., 1968, National Recreation and Park Association Management Aids Bulletin, No. 46, p. 23.

18. Heritage Conservation and Recreation Service: *Fees and Charges Handbook,* Washington, D.C., 1979, U.S. Department of Interior, p. 5.

19. Crossley, John: "Status Report on Commercialized Public Recreation," *California Parks and Recreation,* Dec. 1981-Jan. 1982, p. 16.

20. Gobar, Alfred J.: "Understanding the Zoo," *Parks and Recreation,* Oct. 1973, p. 32.

21. Colgate, John A.: *Administration of Intramural and Recreation Activities,* New York, 1978, John Wiley & Sons, p. 28.

22. Daniel, Dan: "A Time of Progress and Change: A Legislative View of the Military Re-Sale System," *InterService,* Fall 1984, p. 29.

CHAPTER 11

Many successful leisure executives consider marketing their top priority. The leisure service organization that has a sound marketing program is equipped for survival. The leisure service manager will be better able to assess needs, identify new markets (or, in business jargon, "user groups"), attract community leaders ("power brokers"), raise needed revenue, and identify new problems and opportunities. The manager cannot do it alone, however. The entire leisure service organizational staff must be actively involved in the marketing process if survival is to be assured.[1]

Innovative Fiscal Management
Marketing, Productivity, and Strategic Planning

*P*robably the most critical challenge facing recreation and park managers today and for the foreseeable future is the need to develop creative and innovative fiscal management techniques to cope with the budgetary limitations imposed by the "era of limits" that has emerged since the mid-1970s.

This chapter takes the position that appropriate planning strategies to achieve adequate support must be more than "band-aid" remedies that meet temporary crises or provide fragmented and unrelated solutions. It therefore outlines an approach that includes a critical review of the agency's philosophy and priorities, followed by redefinition of goals and priorities, if appropriate. It then presents the case for a vigorous marketing approach, which influences the development and presentation of programs and services on every level. The chapter then deals with other elements that contribute to fiscal self-sufficiency, including new approaches to contracting, concessions, and leasing, enhanced productivity measures, the use of zero-based budgeting and cost-benefit analysis, grantsmanship, and other synergetic techniques that draw on other community organizations and institutions.

The chapter concludes with a discussion of fund-raising methods and grantsmanship strategies. It emphasizes the principle that different aspects of management theory, such as philosophy and goal development, program planning, and fiscal management, cannot be seen as separate entities. Instead, they must be dealt with in an integrated, unified way.

Need for Innovative Fiscal Management

After World War II, most public leisure-service agencies expanded their services, developed new facilities, and added numerous staff members, supported by the nation's flourishing economy. Deppe and Sharpless[2] point out that the decade from 1967 to 1977 was an outstanding period for public recreation and parks, with total expenditures increasing by more than 200% from $1.24 billion to $3.75 billion. By the end of the 1970s, however, inflation and government budget cuts forced numerous agencies to cut back on their programs.

As a dramatic illustration, California's Jarvis-Gann Property Tax Initiative (commonly referred to as Proposition 13) was enacted in July 1978. It had the immediate effect of cutting local taxing powers and reducing property tax revenues to local governments by $7 billion. Although the impact was softened by the allocation of state surplus funds to municipalities in the first year, Proposition 13 nonetheless resulted in the elimination of thousands of local government jobs. All forms of municipal services were cut, with many recreation and park departments receiving particularly heavy budget slashes.

Similar pressures have been felt in Canada; in 1980, *Recreation Canada* reported:

> Direct government involvement in most municipal services has been increasingly questioned; increasing municipal taxes have been effectively challenged. . . . In recent years, municipal parks and recreation operating budgets and revenues have not kept pace with demand for services or actual operating costs for two-thirds of . . . municipalities.[3]

Kemp and Feliciano point out that the bedrock of local government services has traditionally been ''hard'' services such as police, fire, and public works, while museums, parks, community centers, and libraries have been viewed as ''soft.'' As the public's demand for such resources and programs has grown steadily over time, municipal governments have been able to meet the needs for leisure services. However, as

> funds become tighter . . . and politicians are forced to cut back, these services are subject to an increasing level of scrutiny during the difficult budget-cutting process. . . . [As] ever-dwindling resources are stretched even more, many recreational administrators are looking at ways to maintain services, and often even provide additional services, without requiring more public funds.[4]

Social-service, educational, and health-related institutions today must seek funds in a competitive economic environment. Tight budgets and the need for ''accountability'' are here to stay, with the emphasis on clearly documented productivity. Slush funds, contingency accounting, and fiscal latitude are things of the past.

Fiscal Strategies for the 1980s and 1990s

Even in the most economically depressed periods the public is willing to pay for the kinds of recreational programs and services it wants. During the early 1980s, spending on tourism rose to more than $200 billion a year; the U.S. Travel Data Center[5] reported that tourism was climbing at the rate of 11% a year in the mid-1980s. Spending on outdoor recreation has also been high; for example, in the mid-1980s the boating industry reached a new record of $9.4 billion.[6]

Spending on less desirable forms of recreation has also continued to climb dramatically; *Time*[7] reported that the underworld's profits from activities such as drug trafficking, prostitution, and illegal gambling are an estimated $170 billion annually.

Although some might dispute it, such unsavory activities are essentially leisure-related pastimes and represent a growing part of public recreation spending. They demonstrate that an immense amount of money is being spent on recreation; the challenge of governmental, voluntary, and other leisure-service agencies is to educate or persuade the public to use their facilities and programs and to do so on an economically sound basis.

In defining their options for the years ahead, leading recreation and park administrators have proposed a number of key strategies, including the following: (1) reviewing their missions and purposes and redefining their priorities; (2) reorganizing their structures and developing the capability for functioning effectively in present conditions; (3) adopting an aggressive marketing posture that will increase self-generated revenues and help make their agencies as self-sufficient as possible; (4) employing other management devices to promote efficiency and productivity; and (5) developing the fullest possible level of community understanding and support, including cosponsorship and synergetic relationships with other organizations.

REVIEWING AGENCY PHILOSOPHY AND PRIORITIES

The first step in meeting the challenges that lie ahead is to review the agency's philosophy and priorities in light of changing community needs and related social and economic factors. It is often difficult to accept the need for change. Gray points out that many agencies are bureaucratic, with hierarchical structures, narrowly defined functional roles, and routines that are difficult to break through. Such organizations "abhor surprises, control initiative, and punish failure." They "establish rules and stay in their comfort zones."[8] In contrast, Gray suggests:

> Entrepreneurial organizations support reasonable risk taking, learn from failure, and reward success. They do not punish failure. They realize that change creates opportunity and maintain an environmental scan to assess where opportunity exists. These groups work at the growing edge of practice in their field, bring collective intelligence to new ventures, and identify risk capital. . . .
>
> They tolerate ambiguity, encourage intuitive pathfindings, and look outward. They plan by working back from a preferred future. They honor their traditions, but are not bound by them.[8]

Changing model of service

To illustrate the difference between the two approaches, Gray argues that we are shifting from a traditional paradigm of public recreation service to a model with an entirely new set of assumptions.

TRADITIONAL APPROACH The familiar pattern of public recreation agencies assumes that they will (1) seek to provide equal services to all community residents; (2) offer programs selected from a restricted list of popular, accepted activities; (3) act primarily as direct service providers under staff leadership and in their own facilities; (4) fund all basic programs from tax allocations; (5) plan programs with the staff, chiefly by updating the past; (6) require financial accountability and justify budgets based on historical precedent; and (7) evaluate outcomes mainly through attendance figures.

FUTURE-ORIENTED APPROACH The model that has been influential for the past half century is gradually shifting to a new, future-oriented approach that assumes that public leisure-service agencies will (1) provide programs and services based on social and economic need that may go far beyond traditional recreational activities; (2) act in an enabling or catalyzing role in matching community resources to citizens' needs; (3) offer programs anywhere in the community, with staff resources helping residents develop their own leadership skills; (4) organize programs through a widely shared planning process, focusing on the needs of client groups and based on careful assessment of communitywide needs; (5) fund programs from varied sources, including taxes, fees and charges, barter, agency partnerships, and cooperation with the private sector; and (6) evaluate services in terms of human consequences.

This argument suggests *one* approach to rethinking a leisure-service agency's mission and modus operandi. Obviously, other models of service are possible within each of the different types of recreation-sponsoring organizations. What is essential is that managers are prepared to discard old assumptions and work consciously toward a preferred future.

REORGANIZING THE DEPARTMENT

The second important step in the process of meeting fiscal challenges is to reorganize the department or organization, assigning new roles to staff members, instituting in-service training programs where necessary, and establishing task forces or other work units that cut across traditional divisions or lines of authority to work on key problems and develop creative solutions. The quality circle approach and participative management method described in earlier chapters suggest ways that this can be accomplished. Often, it is not so much the structural change as the change in agency climate and leadership styles that makes the needed difference (see box on opposite page).[9]

ADOPTING AN AGGRESSIVE MARKETING POSTURE

Probably the most important element supporting innovative fiscal management in leisure-service agencies is the adoption of vigorous and aggressive marketing approaches. Practitioners in public and nonprofit agencies commonly complain that the public does not value and support their program. They are resigned to the fact that much greater amounts of discretionary money are spent on commercially provided leisure services than on those offered by government or nonprofit organizations. Yet they are often slow to recognize that the reason for this may be their failure to market their wares more effectively.

The term "marketing" may convey an image of hucksterism or cheap advertising gimmicks. This should not be the case; indeed, the true concept of marketing avoids a "hard sell" orientation that concentrates on "numbers through the door." Instead, it is deeply concerned with consumer needs and wants and seeks to achieve customer satisfaction through a coordinated set of marketing activities.

Defining "marketing"

What does the term "marketing" mean? Is it more than selling? In *Marketing for Nonprofit Organizations*, Philip Kotler[10] defines marketing as the effective management by an organization of its exchange relations with its various markets and publics. In a more detailed statement, Howard and Crompton write:

> Marketing is the analysis, planning, implementation and control of carefully formulated programs designed to bring about voluntary exchanges with target markets for the purpose of achieving agency objectives. It relies heavily upon designing offerings consistent with client's wants, and on using effective pricing, communication and distribution to inform, motivate, and service the markets.[11]

CHANGE IN THE TRAVEL AND TOURISM INDUSTRY: PEOPLE EXPRESS

Over the past several years, dozens of fledgling airlines have emerged, transforming America's travel habits with low-cost flights made possible by the federal deregulation of the air-transport business. By far the most successful of these new companies has been People Express, which exploded from a tiny airline with 250 employees and three planes in 1981 to a company with a half-billion dollars in assets, 4000 full-time employees, and more than 60 planes in 1984. Apart from new formulas for cut-rate travel without amenities, the secret of People Express's success has apparently been in the organizational approach and leadership style of the company's young founder, Don Burr. These include the following elements:

1. A financial stake in the company—employees of People Express hold a third of all the outstanding shares of company stock, and share in company profits
2. A chance to learn and hold a variety of jobs—employees are organized in teams of three or four that tend to move about from job to job, thus making the job more interesting and improving company efficiency
3. An organizational structure that allows workers to make large and small decisions based upon a company philosophy and tradition, with necessary limits based on safety factors and scheduling requirements
4. A sense of belonging not just to a company, but to a family, with many employees sharing apartments and houses, working and playing together, and unified by an elaborate communications system so that everyone knows what's going on in the company and has an opportunity to voice his or her opinion on it

Based on Rimer, S.: "The Airline that Shook the Industry," *New York Times Magazine,* Dec. 23, 1984, p. 18.

Customarily the marketing process is considered to have four key activities or tasks: (1) product or service, (2) price, (3) place or distribution, and (4) promotion. Together these comprise the marketing "mix." Essentially, it represents a systematic approach to planning programs or services that will appeal or be useful to specific audiences or target populations and then delivering these products in the most effective way. Each stage of the marketing process must involve systematic and objective analysis. In the business world this often requires extensive market research to gather critical information on consumer attitudes, opinions, and reactions to product offerings.

Kotler points out that although the marketing concept was developed in the 1950s to serve the business world, it is also relevant to many governmental and nonprofit voluntary agencies. He describes the generic approach as consisting of three important variables. If called into a nonprofit organization and asked to appraise its operations from a marketing point of view, a marketer would analyze three elements:

First, he would evaluate the marketing environment of the organization, specifically its markets, customers, competitors, and macroenvironment. Second, he would evaluate the marketing system within the organization, specifically the organization's objectives, programs, implementation, and organization. Third, he would evaluate the major marketing activities of the organization, specifically its products, pricing, distribution, personal contact, advertising, publicity, and sales promotion.[12]

Based on information about these variables and their interrelations, the marketer may recommend strategies to convert consumer demand from one direction to another, to create, develop, revitalize, maintain, or reduce it if necessary, and in some circumstances to eliminate it. Kotler concludes that managerial marketing deals not "just with an effort to build or maintain demand but also with a variety of problems that an organization might face in its relation to a market."[13]

Market analysis

Applying the marketing approach to the leisure-service field, one might begin by analyzing the environment in which the agency operates or in which it is considering a venture. What are the needs and interests of the public, and what are their present leisure behaviors? Who is providing leisure services and with what degree of success? What are the pricing policies, and what is the profit margin?

In the case of an organization that is considering establishing a particular recreational facility or program, such as a new amusement complex or theme park, the initial market analysis might represent a *feasibility study*. This seeks to determine the need and potential market for a given product or attraction, the target audience or audiences, appropriate factors of location and accessibility, the nature of the competition, projected attendance, and projected revenues.

Product analysis

Product analysis involves a systematic study of all the products, services, and auxiliary enterprises that might surround a proposed operation. If the facility under consideration were a ski center, not only would the slope itself—with chair lifts, snow-making equipment, needed utilities, and structures—be of concern, but also potential sources of revenue from ski classes, a lodge, restaurants, equipment shop, and similar ventures.

Again the potential markets for given products, along with pricing alternatives, the competition, and the possibility of off-season activities to provide maximum year-round usage, would come into play. In the case of a commercial agency, the issue of economic feasibility would be primary, and if the facility could not clearly be shown to have the potential for making a reasonable profit, it would not be explored further. In the case of government, it may well be that the other needs of the region, such as esthetic needs for a cultural arts center or a place for school sports or community organizations to hold festivals, would be important enough so that the facility would justify a given level of subsidy, if it could not pay for itself in annual revenue.

Management analysis

Analyzing the facts gathered in the preceding analyses, a picture can be developed of the kind of recreational product that might be developed and its probable acceptance by the surrounding population, along with the capability of the present organization for creating and delivering the product effectively. This does not simply mean "selling" the product, which represents a one-way street. Instead, effective marketing implies a "two-way street," meaning that there is constant sensitivity to consumer reactions, behavior, and changing needs, with a readiness on the part of management to change its operations or modify its products to respond to market conditions.

To be fully effective, a marketing plan must be both flexible and practical, able to deal with either a broad, complex operation, a single specialized service or product, or any single aspect of the organization's relationship with its public.

Market segmentation

A key element in successful marketing is determining the audiences or groups of consumers that might be served with leisure programs or facilities. Crompton defines such groups as "target markets," consisting of relatively homogeneous groups of people having relatively similar service needs or preferences. He writes:

> Target marketing is a key marketing concept. Every park and recreation agency has to decide *whose* needs should be served before deciding *what* needs to serve. The identification and selection of target market groups influences and often directly determines all the ensuing decisions regarding types of services and their distribution, pricing, and communication.[14]

As an illustration of the kind of analysis that may be done in identifying target market groups, two studies in Canada were concerned with analyzing elements of water-based outdoor recreation.

In a comprehensive study of the potential for expanding water-based recreational opportunity, Sustronk[15] conducted a marketing study to assist in planning a marina in the metropolitan Toronto area. It initially involved examining factors affecting demands such as (1) market area population, including growth trends; (2) travel distance to the facility; (3) service proposed to be provided, including alternative models such as summer berthing and storage with limited services compared with a complete marina facility offering boat and engine sales and repairs, winter boat storage, and food services; (4) competition from other facilities in the market area; and (5) past and present growth patterns in recreational boating.

Based on study of these factors, numerous alternative concept plans were developed for the basin itself, entrance protection, and back-up shore area layout. These concepts were evaluated for their environmental effects, operational costs, capacity, and development costs. An ultimate choice to develop was made based on all factors considered and taking into account the possibility of funding assistance from the Canadian federal government under the Marina Policy Assistance Program.

In a related marketing study, Matheusik and Mills[16] surveyed several hundred sport divers in Ontario and British Columbia to assist in planning "underwater parks" that might meet the needs of specific target markets (groups of divers characterized by relatively similar motives and preferences). This process identified key motives such as "risk taking/challenge" and "experiencing and learning about nature." It combined these with other characteristics and preferences of divers, including sociodemographic, behavioral, and related factors to develop marketing mixes that might be precisely tailored to the needs and preferences of sports divers in selected areas.

Planning recreation centers

The Fairfax County, Va., Park Authority has developed several large recreation centers with swimming pools, saunas, weight rooms, video game areas, handball/racquetball/squash courts, and numerous social or meeting rooms, workshops, and similar areas.

The planning process carried out to determine the need and appropriate program for each facility focused on the issue of site location with respect to population, transportation, utilities, and physical aspects of the land. Primary market areas for each center were considered to be within a 3-mile radius, with a secondary service area market within a 6-mile distance. These boundaries included most potential users for each site and provided a framework for demographic analysis. Downs identifies the factors examined in preliminary marketing analysis:

1. Area future trends, including population growth estimates, market planning, and economic stability.
2. Employment centers, their growth within the community, their effects on the project, and local sources of income.
3. Present and future needs, including adequacy of present recreational facilities, existing competition, and need versus market size.
4. Size and type of design for the purpose intended.
5. Income levels and economic capabilities of families in the area, need and desire for recreational facilities, and resultant financial support to the project.
6. Complete costs of the project.
7. Costs of operation based on local conditions, as well as analysis of income from all sources.
8. Methods of financing and debt reduction.
9. All factors determining whether the project will be self-liquidating or self-supporting in the future.[17]

PRICING STRATEGIES

A key consideration in all marketing planning involves pricing, which not only brings in revenue but also has the potential for either *excluding* potential patrons who cannot afford to pay the charge that has been established or *attracting* others who prefer the aura of exclusivity or value that a high price may convey. Crompton[18] identifies a number of different pricing approaches based on the costs of the product or service, as well as others that are not:

1. *Charges based on costs.* These may include the total cost of all fixed elements in the program or service (such as the hall, the overhead charges, or the leadership) and the variable costs (such as supplies or food), which increase with the number of participants. Variations may include basing the charge on variable costs only (divided by the number of participants) or on variable costs with some portion of overhead costs added.
2. *Charges not based on costs.* These may be based on the going rate, in which the

price reflects the average charges set by other, similar organizations, for similar services. They may also be based solely on consumer demand, in other words, what the traffic will bear.

Pricing approaches vary according to the nature of the sponsoring organization and its philosophy and social mandate. Public and voluntary agencies are generally more obligated to consider factors of social need than are private or commercial organizations. However, the latter providers must be aware that they can price themselves out of business by setting fees that are too high or that they can create ill will through unreasonable pricing tactics. In some cases pricing policies may be differentiated by client groups; a rental charge may be higher for a profit-oriented organization than a nonprofit group. A public agency may charge higher fees in wealthy neighborhoods than in poorer ones or may waive charges or provide ''scholarships'' for disadvantaged participants or those with other special needs.

OTHER FACTORS AFFECTING PRICING

Numerous other factors or conditions may influence pricing decisions as part of the overall marketing strategy. For example, in a detailed study of national parks in the United States, the General Accounting Office (GAO) concluded that the National Park Service probably could increase its entrance fees by an average of 150% without having a ''measurable impact on visitation levels at those Park Service units which have few close substitutes and for which the entrance fee is a small portion of the total recreation expense.''[19] However, the rate of increase or the initiation of an entrance fee for an individual Park Service site was dependent on a series of cost-effective fee variables, which might or might not make it logical to impose or increase fees. According to the GAO, the key variables were:

> the annual visitation level, the number of accesses to the area, the cost of capital improvements needed in order to collect entrance fees, the effect of entrance fees on visitation levels, property deed clauses prohibiting the collection of entrance fees, collection costs, and fee levels. At those 22 units where entrance fees were deemed uneconomical, the number of access points was the most commonly cited factor in the decision not to charge.[20]

MARKETING ATHLETIC PROGRAMS

Another example of marketing in the leisure-service field involves the packaging of school and college sports programs to increase revenue and improve relations with the student body and the alumni.

Don Canham, Director of Athletics at the University of Michigan, points out that it has become necessary to promote and market high school and college athletic programs more effectively and imaginatively than in the past. With budgeting for athletic programs being cut back in many regions, these efforts have various purposes such as arousing interest and support for the institution's entire athletic program, promoting attendance at specific events, or raising funds directly with which to support the program. Some of the specific methods being used to market and promote programs include the following:

Such things as swim-a-thons and jog-a-thons have been extremely successful on collegiate and high school levels.

A number of schools, such as Michigan State and Tennessee, run large-scale summer sports camps, both on a day camp basis or as live-in camps. Such camps are well-received because they keep dorms busy during the summer months, and provide continued employment for janitors, maintenance and food service workers, and athletic staff members who act as instructors.

Celebrity golf tournaments run both athletic departments during the summer help maintain relationships with alumni and provide revenue as well.

Some high schools and colleges sponsor ox roasts, pork days, or chicken frys to raise athletic funds, sometimes with raffles of merchandise donated by merchants. Weekly bingo games are also used as fund-raisers, along with concerts and sports exhibitions.

The University of Michigan sponsors a weekly cleanup in which a local Catholic high school's students and their families come to the stadium for Mass; the parishioners then go to work with their brooms to clean the huge structure thoroughly.

Other colleges sponsor huge pre-game band shows, with thousands of high school band members being admitted to the stadium free. Still other colleges, like the University of Wichita, sponsor novelty shows at football games, like camel races and turkey chases. Others sponsor cheerleading days, Boy or Girl Scout days and similar events with discounted or free tickets.

One college promotes non-revenue sports by selling a "Gold Key Card" for $25 that will let the purchaser and a guest into every athletic contest on campus except football, basketball and hockey.[21]

Such efforts not only raise revenue and promote attendance (often the person admitted free is accompanied by paying family members) but also contribute to alumni or fan interest and support of the school and its teams. The key ingredient in such marketing and promotional efforts is imagination and creativity, plus the ability to translate a novel idea into a practical reality.

POSSIBLE NEGATIVE IMPLICATIONS OF MARKETING APPROACH

It is important to recognize some possible negative aspects of the marketing approach, particularly for leisure-service agencies with a community service orientation. Inevitably, the bottom line from a marketing perspective is profitability.

Given this emphasis, leisure-service managers are likely to examine all possible ventures in terms of their attractiveness to consumers who will be able to pay for them. Those with a strong potential for yielding substantial income will clearly be favored over those that must be subsidized. Thus programs and services that have limited potential for economic return within a marketing framework are likely to atrophy and become nobody's business. Those that appeal to affluent residents and yield meaningful fees have no difficulty in finding sponsors.

MANAGEMENT TECHNIQUES TO ACHIEVE PRODUCTIVITY AND EFFICIENCY

In addition to the approaches cited thus far, many community leisure-service organizations have adopted other methods to achieve a high degree of productivity and efficiency and thus a better level of fiscal security. These include: (1) cost-cutting practices and other techniques designed to achieve a maximum level of agency productivity, (2) a fuller use of cost-benefit analysis methods, (3) zero-based budgeting, and (4) increased contracting, leasing, and concessions arrangements.

Cost cutting and productivity enhancement

While improved marketing may increase revenues to an agency, it is also essential that maximum effort be made to utilize existing funds as effectively and economically as possible. This means careful scrutiny of all expenditures to ensure that they are essential and that maximum value is derived from every dollar spent. It requires a hard look at every area of spending, including energy costs, uses of personnel, maintenance schedules, supplies and requisitions, and similar factors.

Terms such as accountability, austerity, and productivity have become popular on all levels. Recreation and park planners and managers who may have been influenced primarily by esthetic or human needs concerns in the past must now come to grips with the challenges posed by higher costs and the demands of city councils, boards of trustees, or aroused taxpayers. The need has grown for strong budget justifications, significant goals and objectives, and rigorous cost-benefit analysis of all program elements.

Budgets and budget processes are being monitored far more closely than ever before by fiscal officers in municipal and county governments. Hiring new staff members or replacing those who have left often requires extensive justification and detailed job specifications for *all* personnel working in the department. Comptrollers are slashing expenditures related to typical recreation and park budget items such as (1) gasoline consumption and number of vehicles in department pools; (2) purchase of consumable supplies (paper, paint, crayons, basketballs, etc.) that are dispensed to the public without a fee or accountability; (3) travel to conferences and related expenses, particularly when they are at a considerable distance; and (4) subscriptions, memberships, and purchase of books and training films.

Beyond such efforts, there is a new emphasis on achieving higher levels of productivity as a total departmental goal.

Meaning of "productivity"

Recently, it has been made a major economic goal of the United States to enhance technological innovation and stimulate capital investment, human-resources development, and labor-management and business-government cooperation, all designed to promote productivity as an important national priority. On a more basic level, the concept of productivity is deceptively simple:

> Productivity measures the relationship between the amount of goods or services produced (output) and the quantities of labor, capital, and material resources (inputs) used to produce that output. In order to compare productivity over time or among many different productive entities, it is usually stated as a ratio of output to input.[22]

It is important to recognize that any management approach that deals with productivity by examining *separate* agency or company functions misses the high potential for improvement in areas such as waste caused by unresolved conflicts in departmental priorities; duplication of effort, and rework caused by uncoordinated interdepartmental efforts and mismatched local systems and procedures.

It is time for top managements to broaden this definition of productivity to encompass the performance of their organizations as a whole in achieving strategic *business* objectives. All efforts, whether devoted to developing, producing, marketing, or delivering a product or service, and all support systems for information, communications, planning and bonus awards belong under the concept of productivity. . . . The senior executive must create and sustain a climate that makes productivity improvement everyone's business.[23]

Ways of monitoring productivity

Recognizing that it is difficult to measure the outcomes of recreation and park services precisely and objectively (it is usually easier to measure performance related to physical resources, such as maintenance operations, than it is to measure program-related accomplishments), there is general agreement that the key to productivity in both public and private sectors is the effective management of personnel. In a recent report of the National Center for Productivity and Quality of Working Life,[24] the conclusion was reached that public agencies fall significantly short of private industry in the management of employees.

Better procedures need to be established to monitor employee performance and document levels of productivity. Middle-level managers must be held more accountable for programs and employees under their supervision, with responsibility decentralized so that it rests with managers at every level and locality rather than solely with the central offices of the agency.

Productivity should be approached as a total departmental concern. For too many employees it is a suspect word, implying pressure tactics by supervisors, shortened lunch periods and elimination of relief or refreshment breaks, rigid conformity to time schedules, suspension of safety procedures, reduced overtime, and generally more work for less pay.

Viewed more positively, increased productivity means better work attitudes, more careful handling of materials and equipment, punctual arrival and departure of personnel, and a fuller effort to provide stronger levels of attendance and participation in all program events than in the past. The key to productivity lies in personnel attitudes and behavior. A number of suggestions for strengthening these include the following:

1. Include budget and cost discussions at regular staff meetings. Point out specific examples of how leadership and maintenance supervisory personnel can effect small but significant regular savings.
2. Establish a budget committee made up of several top management personnel in the department. Plan all budget planning through this committee to develop greater awareness of the problem and commitment to economy.
3. Train all key personnel to do program planning on a unit-cost basis, with emphasis on making program choices on the basis of objective measures of attendance and desirable outcomes rather than subjective judgments.
4. Recognize outstanding examples of time- and money-saving techniques by department personnel.

5. Request periodic reviews of department productivity by outside firms, agencies, or individuals to ensure that the public receives maximum value for every dollar spent.
6. On a cyclical basis, evaluate each bureau, division, or section of the department at least once a year by closely studying its operations for waste, time loss, public relations, and efficient storage, maintenance, transportation, etc.

Cost cutting, like budget planning, must be a year-round concern. There is nothing harsh, unethical, or antisocial about reducing costs and raising productivity in recreation.

Cost-benefit analysis

Cost-benefit analysis is a budget planning and control technique that seeks to evaluate the outcomes of programs by relating the benefits derived from them to the dollars invested in them.

Cost-benefit analysis can be used to: (1) foster valid comparisons within and between operational facilities and program units; (2) permit the assignment of priorities to specific programs and services; (3) provide targets and guidelines for management decision making and resource allocation; (4) assist in continual evaluation of agency objectives and procedures; (5) provide valuable support data for justifying budget requests; (6) identify high- and low-cost programs and services as related to maintenance, administration, and direct leadership costs per participant-hour of service rendered; and (7) provide essential data for policy formulation and revisions.

To compare programs and services purely according to cost efficiency would be questionable; some programs of high social priority may necessarily be much more costly than other, less significant programs. Are spectator-hours to be equated with participant-hours in calculating user totals? Is routine maintenance of a facility comparable to carrying out major rehabilitation? How are levels of user satisfaction or benefit to be determined?

Webster and Reich[25] suggest that it is best to approach the process gradually, building a model of data collection and analysis for continual cost-benefit evaluations of programs and services that will be appropriate to a given community or agency. As the process is improved, it will prove increasingly useful in budget-planning and budget-control procedures.

Obviously, cost-benefit analysis is closely linked to the process of program evaluation. If program objectives are clearly defined and outlined in the planning and budgeting sequence, it should be possible to determine the extent to which they are being met. This can be done quantitatively by measuring elements such as the number of clients served, percentage of participants satisfied with the program, and percentage of target populations participating within given time periods or by measuring behavioral change or other outcomes.

The cost factor may also be difficult to measure precisely, since in addition to the direct costs of running a program (for staff time, equipment and supplies, transportation, and similar costs), there are also costs related to the day-by-day operation of the agency, capital and depreciation expenses, and similar indirect costs. Morrison writes:

Although such costs do not appear in the operating budget of specific programs, they must be accounted for if such programs are to [be analyzed]. Once identified, they should be divided in an equitable way among the several service programs of an organization. Several reasonable methods serve to allocate such costs; let common sense be your guide.[26]

Zero-based budgeting

Zero-based budgeting, which has become popular in many governmental fiscal planning operations, has been viewed as a euphemism for "You're not getting a cent more in your budget than last year." Actually, it is a budgeting approach requiring that every program element and expenditure be reevaluated annually to determine its relative merit. Not intended as a replacement for traditional budgeting procedures, it forces decisions to be made on points such as these:

1. Is the department overstaffed at its current level?
2. Does the department continue to serve a useful purpose and function in the overall operation of the organization?
3. Should a certain program or programs be curtailed to fund an alternative, higher priority program?
4. Are available funds used to promote recreation goals and objectives or to promote an individual's whims?

Underkoffler points out that zero-based budgeting forces a department to make a case for its entire appropriation request each year, just as if the programs and projects were entirely new. Rather than merely modifying the previous year's budget or justifying only the increases, managers must start anew:

They must develop the rationale and determine the resources required for alternative levels of service. Accordingly all programs, old and new, including various levels of service, are assessed equally for placement in the final budget.[27]

In implementing zero-based budgeting, it is necessary to determine decision units—the basic activity or group of programs about which the department must make decisions. Appropriate alternative service levels for each package of services (including programs and maintenance) are determined with detailed statements that include information such as (1) the goals of the alternative programs; (2) their scope of operations; (3) the required level of performance by personnel; (4) the required funding; (5) anticipated revenues and participation or other outcomes; (6) relationship of program elements to other department functions; and (7) probable consequences of not funding either the total or the partial package.

Teams of managers, budget analysts, and other employees are put to work on defining alternative service levels for each of the functions. As an example, Singleton and others identify six service levels that would apply to a public-safety department:

Level 1. Basic patrol and preliminary investigation of major crimes
Level 2. Preliminary investigation of all criminal complaints; response to priority non-criminal calls
Level 3. Follow-up on all criminal and non-criminal calls; operation of jail and selective parking enforcement
Level 4. Increased parking enforcement; full-service response to non-criminal calls

Level 5. Additional patrols, school crossing guards (current level)

Level 6. Expansion of patrol, parking enforcement, and school crossing functions[28]

Higher levels of service in a recreation and park department's summer playground operation might be marked by (1) a greater number of playgrounds with full-time personnel during the summer; (2) a fuller weekly schedule or a longer season; (3) provision of additional trip programs or mobile recreation units; or (4) assignment of music, dance, or arts and crafts specialists to lead special activities or plan playground festivals.

As part of the zero-based budgeting process, it is necessary to determine the financial costs of each of the alternative service levels (including personnel, supplies and equipment, utilities, fringe benefits, and other expenses). The benefits or anticipated outcomes of each level of service are also determined. These, reviewed against the stated objectives of the department, are used to place the service package itself, along with the alternative levels, on a scale of priorities.

RANKING DECISION PACKAGES   To accomplish this, Edginton and Griffith[29] suggest the following steps:

1. Assemble the decision-making team. Users, civic officials, members of advisory committees, staff, and nonusers may be involved in this process.
2. Participants should fill out the decision package forms.
3. Brainstorming within the team should occur to establish criteria by which the decision makers might rank the packages. Examples of criteria that might be used are attendance, numbers served, user satisfaction, social values or purposes, anticipated revenues, and cost.
4. Next the criteria must be weighted; using a Likert-type scale, the decision-making team would vote on the relative importance of the different criteria to assign weights to them.
5. The team would vote, on a scale of 1 to 10, on how well each decision package meets the selected criteria; the mean score for each package would then be compiled. These would be multiplied by the weighting factor to obtain a cumulative score for each factor.
6. The packages would be placed in a ranked order based on their cumulative scores. Each package (or program element) would be priced according to both costs and anticipated revenues and would be approved, starting with the highest ranking packages, until the budget is used up. A cutoff line would then be established for approved packages. The full plan would then be reviewed with regard to its balance, demands on agency resources, and similar factors before final approval.

When done in a thorough and systematic way, zero-based budgeting is a complex operation that requires guidance from specialists skilled in its application. Some departments that are not able to apply the full method use it in a modified form, with a priority ranking of alternative decision packages.

OTHER COST-CUTTING MEASURES

In addition to the methods described thus far, leisure-service agencies have employed a number of other means of cutting costs or improving productivity. For example, some departments have focused on developing more effective time management by employees, hiring outside specialists for short periods to augment staff rather than hiring additional permanent employees, and reassigning staff members to maximize their contribution. Park and recreational facilities are being designed less expensively and with emphasis on making them maintenance free. In some cases, equipment is being rented rather than installed at the expense of the department. Volunteers are being used more heavily and creatively in a variety of roles.

In Ontario, Canada, the provincial park system has made use of a system of economizing called the "Hull method." Essentially, this consists of cutting a component or service back until problems arise and then "going back a few notches." In addition, Heit[30] points out that park managers have reduced park services related to firewood, garbage collection, cleaning, the length of seasons, greenhouse operations, and self-registration procedures.

Contracting approaches

Another specific method that has become increasingly popular in recent years as a form of cost cutting is contracting departmental functions out to other organizations, or *privatization* (assignment to the private sector), as it is sometimes called.

Obviously, many business transactions among both public and private agencies are carried out under written contracts. Most public agency contracts with other organizations fall into one of the following categories: (1) planning, design, or construction of capital facilities; (2) purchase of equipment, materials, and supplies; (3) arrangements for concessions, franchises, or leases of special types of service or facilities, such as food services or stadium operations; and (4) purchase of services, including the use of program activity specialists.

These contracts rarely involve the replacement of existing personnel. However, Paige writes that in the past, civil service employees in a number of states and cities

> looked at private contract services as a threat to job security. Employee organizations lobbied to enact protective measures and, subsequently, clauses were placed in charters or statutes were passed that restricted the use of private enterprise for any service regularly performed by Civil Service employees. These protection clauses are still in effect in many areas of the country.[31]

Within the present era of limits and in a more conservative political climate, the pendulum has swung, and many public agency functions are being carried out today by private contractors. Quinn and Cook describe this trend:

> The use of privatization as a vehicle for financing and operating public service facilities and systems has attracted growing interest in recent years. State and local government authorities have used privatization to develop, acquire and expand water and wastewater systems, solid waste/resource recovery projects, transportation systems, correctional facilities and parking garages. The primary benefit of these transactions has been cost savings to the public. . .[32]

Given the impact of Proposition 13 and the need to work with greatly reduced staffs and limited budgets, many California communities began to explore a much greater use of contract services. These have included the following aspects of park operations and recreation service delivery:

Training seminars
Parking lot staff
Special events coordinators
Minipark operation and maintenance
All accounting and bookkeeping services
Renovation and operation of tennis/racquetball facilities
Master planning
Architectural design
Construction management
Janitorial services
Turf maintenance
Operation of fee recreation programs
Sports officiating

New ventures into subcontracting were undertaken in both small and large communities. For example, when severe budget cuts threatened the survival of the Fair Oaks Recreation and Park District recreation program in Sacramento, two professional staff members formed their own private corporation and submitted a proposal to contract the recreation services from the district. Under the agreement, which was successfully carried out with an annual savings of over $50,000,

> the District provides facilities with their maintenance, while the corporation, Leisure Pro, Inc., provides the general recreation services [including] a complete range of programs for youth and adults, including sports, fee classes, special events, travel and concessions. The corporation is responsible for content and quality of programs, financial accountability, publicity, scheduling and, when needed, technical assistance. The District maintains its authority on fee levels and types of programs offered.[33]

On a larger scale the county of Los Angeles initiated a subcontracting program in the early 1980s that involved approximately $10 million of the department's activities over a 3-year period, with a projected savings of about $3 million. The functions included tasks such as golf course starter, security services, landscape maintenance, weed control, equestrian trail maintenance, trash pickup, and small equipment repair.

A U.S. Department of the Interior handbook on contract services in parks points out that private contractors usually have certain specific advantages that permit them to operate more economically than public agencies. These include:

> *Lower Personnel Costs.* Contractors do not need to conform to City pay scales. Contractors typically pay lower wages and provide fewer fringe benefits to their non unionized employees. Contractors often employ proportionately fewer supervisors and leadmen.
> *Fewer Regulations.* For example, commercial recreation firms may be able to earn added revenues through acting as travel agents or obtaining a license to sell beer.
> *Greater Flexibility.* Contractors are free of certain organizational contraints. Contractors have greater flexibility in managing both the size and distribution of the workforce to meet uneven work requirements. The contractor need not absorb the costs of underutilized staff.

Economies of Scale. Contractors are organized to do a specific function and can spread the capital costs of that function over a number of jobs. Contractors can more intensively utilize their equipment and are more likely to own up-to-date functional equipment. (Federal law provides that business operating equipment is eligible for 10% investment tax credit, applied as a direct reduction of current federal income taxes. This is an added incentive to the contractor to upgrade equipment).[34]

Donahue warns that several factors should be considered in making the decision to subcontract the functions of leisure-service agencies. It *can* work, he writes, if the following conditions exist:

1. Competent contractors are available in the marketplace. If contractors do not equal or exceed your own workers in technical ability or mechanization, you may find the product you buy is definitely substandard. A contractor who walks away from a job because it is not profitable can be a nightmare to replace in mid-season. Performance bonds can ensure completion of contracts.
2. The marketplace has enough firms to ensure a competitive price situation for an extended period of time. If only one firm can deliver a certain type of service you are at its mercy should it decide to increase prices. This is especially true if you get rid of specialized equipment and trained people in the conversion process.
3. You have the ability to write a contract that controls quantity, quality, and price of the work. Unmeasurable work standards, open-ended expense features, and a lack of quality standards can lead to constant combat over provisions of the contract, conflict that will ultimately only benefit lawyers. The work should not require such complex day-to-day work variation that no one can write an accurate list of duties that can reasonably dictate the work schedule.[35]

Paige agrees, pointing out that contract services in recreation and park agencies should be handled just as the recruitment and hiring process is carried on for key employees. Requests for proposals (RFPs) should be selectively distributed to qualified individuals or firms:

Fees become a factor in the selection process, but qualifications should be paramount. There are any number of methods to pay for services, including hourly charges, to a maximum; scope of services based on a specific budget; a retainer to cover basic services with hourly charges for expanded work; and others. The flexibility and effectiveness of contract services is limited only by the imagination of the people involved.[36]

Obviously, not all government services can or should be conducted by private contractors. There is a legitimate concern about the public department's losing control of its own operation and the negative impact on professionalism that might develop from excessive dependence on outside contractors to perform services. However, provided that the work can be legitimately done by private groups at a savings, with a precise definition of performance standards and the opportunity to evaluate these systematically, the shift to contracting is desirable. When the move is made to contracting, open bidding on contracts and careful supervision of performance will prevent graft or payoffs from the contractor to personnel in the public agency.

Cryder[37] stresses that when concession or lease agreements are under consideration, contracts must clearly specify the responsibilities of both agencies and particularly the standards of performance that must be maintained. Only if these conditions are met and if there is the opportunity for thorough, ongoing supervision, should concessions be approved.

Concession and leasing arrangements have had a long and successful history in national parks and other major outdoor recreation sites and appear to be an important way for municipal recreation and park departments to cut costs and operate more efficiently.

COMMUNITY UNDERSTANDING AND SUPPORT: NEW FUNDING SOURCES

The final aspect of innovative fiscal management that is discussed in this chapter is the need to explore all possible sources of grants, gifts, and other direct forms of financial assistance and to utilize resources within the community through synergetic program efforts. As indicated earlier, many federal and state grant programs that provided fiscal assistance during the 1960s and 1970s are no longer operative. Therefore leisure-service agencies must seek other forms of special assistance.

Funding assistance from foundations

Many governmental and voluntary leisure-service agencies have obtained assistance for facilities development or other special projects through foundations. Joyce defines the term "foundation" as

a nongovernmental, nonprofit organization having a principal fund of its own, managed by its own trustees or directors and established to maintain or aid social, educational, charitable, religious, or other activities serving the common welfare. It enjoys privileges with respect to taxation and continuity of existence not accorded to "noncharitable" trust funds.[38]

There are several different types of foundations: (1) *special purpose foundations,* created by will or trust instrument to meet a special charitable purpose; (2) *company-sponsored foundations,* tax-exempt nonprofit bodies legally separate from the donor company but with trustee boards that facilitate corporate giving; (3) *community foundations,* composite foundations usually set up as trusts, functioning under some form of community control to serve a given community or area; and (4) *family foundations,* usually established by a living person or family rather than by bequest to serve as a continuing vehicle for gift giving and as a means of reducing taxes.

The recreation and park department that seeks funding from foundations must approach the task in an intelligent and well-organized way. It is important to develop proposals that will clearly fit the general purpose of a foundation, that they will regard as significant and needed, that will be economical in terms of expected outcomes, and that do not represent already available services. Joyce stresses two key factors in gaining foundation approval. The first is the preparation and presentation through appropriate channels of a grants appeal specifically designed to meet the interests of a foundation. The second is to make appropriate personal contacts with the key people in the foundation to ensure a careful and fair consideration of the proposal.

The following strategies are suggested for recreation and park agencies that seek to develop grant proposals for foundations but may also readily be adapted to other types of fund-raising. They involve several steps.

1. *Establish a foundations committee.* The department should develop an ongoing, capable group of staff members and interested citizens—including businesspeople, professionals, and other individuals—who are willing to assist in this task. The committee must have a competent chairperson to lead its efforts.

2. *Prepare lists of foundations.* Several excellent sources are available in public libraries. These should be carefully analyzed to identify foundations whose purposes and past pattern of giving seem appropriate to the needs of the recreation and park department.

3. *Develop a proposal concept.* Foundations committee members consider possible approaches or concepts and select those with greatest potential value that might have specific appeal for appropriate foundations. At this point, they may sound out the foundation to determine its possible interest in the subject of the appeal, if personal contacts are feasible at this stage.

4. *Prepare a formal grant proposal.* Develop the grant proposal in written form. It should be brief and convincing, stressing the significance of the project or study to be funded. Elements that make a proposal effective are (1) demonstration of critical need; (2) innovative quality of the proposal; (3) availability of matching funds within department or from other sources; (4) social value to come from the proposal, including possible generalizability (findings or outcomes can be used elsewhere); (5) a precise statement of the budget; (6) identification of the personnel to be involved; and (7) a time frame or proposed schedule for the project.

5. *Present the proposal.* The grant proposal should be neatly packaged and sent by mail with an accompanying letter or delivered personally if personal contact has been developed.

6. *Follow through.* Shortly after the proposal has been sent—usually within 2 to 3 weeks—a meeting should be requested to discuss it. At this point, it is possible to present arguments supporting the proposal, to indicate a willingness to modify it or accept other suggestions of the foundation, and generally to work together to bring the proposal to the point of approval.

Developing acceptable proposals for foundations or government grants-in-aid programs is not a matter of impulsive, scattergun action. The process must be carefully thought out and systematically pursued. Recreation is not a high priority for most funding agencies. Therefore it must be linked, logically and strongly, to high-priority needs or program goals. For example, many funding programs for aging persons or youth offer an opportunity to link recreation with social, medical, legal, housing, counseling, or other forms of personal assistance.

The value of personal contacts in developing and submitting grant proposals cannot be overestimated. As suggested earlier, a preliminary meeting with foundation representatives can be used to determine their potential interest or gain an interpretation of their procedures or guidelines. Effective proposal writing requires special experience and know-how. Often large departments or agencies or city governments have grants officers who can assist in preparing proposals, who know individuals in funding organizations, and who are in a position to help guide a proposal along the track to serious consideration.

Grants are becoming more difficult to obtain, both from federal and state agencies and from foundations. The ''lead time'' from early application to final delivery has increased in many cases from about 9 months to about 1½ years. Many projects are rejected summarily. Those that are given consideration may have the requested amounts slashed by half or more. New criteria are being applied by many funding agencies, including considerations such as the following.

1. High priority is being given to proposals that come from more than one agency or sponsor. Pairs, trios, or even clusters of agencies, such as the municipal recreation and park department with the local Boys' Club and police department or a YMCA in concert with a YWCA, settlement house, or rehabilitation agency, are likely to find greater receptivity than would a solo project.

2. Grant applications must document that special populations were fully consulted about the proposal. Depending on the nature of the proposal, this might mean consultation and planning with the mentally retarded (or their families), youth groups, senior citizens, transient workers, ethnic minorities, residents of institutions, or similar populations.

3. Wherever possible, grant proposals should be designed to serve areas or residents with special needs. Thus target districts are ideally congested, central-city neighborhoods with high crime, welfare, and arson rates; such characteristics will increase the likelihood that a proposal will be approved.

4. There must be evidence that existing programs and facilities are being fully utilized and that the grant proposal is part of a systematic, carefully thought-out plan for upgrading recreation and park services in the community.

5. Municipalities or agencies applying for grants must be prepared to guarantee a substantial proportion—perhaps as much as 50%—of the total grant proposal. Very few 100% grants are now awarded. Furthermore, the municipality or agency is frequently asked to fund the entire sum initially on the premise that 50% reimbursement will be forthcoming in 3 to 6 months.

6. Grant application forms must be filled out in detail and in exact accordance with regulations. This often means that voluminous paperwork, amounting to 10 to 15 pages of detailed information, must be provided. In addition, the city or agency applying will be required to collect and submit payroll records, newspaper advertisements (to demonstrate affirmative action compliance), news clippings, activity reports, and various other records. At the end of a project, the accumulated records and reports are likely to approach a suburban phone book in thickness.

In working with a specialized grants expert who is in charge of submitting funding proposals, the mayor, city manager, department heads, and other administrators will often be called on to attend night meetings or sudden brainstorm sessions, fill out long forms, supply huge amounts of needed data, or provide other forms of cooperation. Woe betide the department head who causes a grant application to miss its submission deadline because of failure to produce the necessary information, or the bureaucrat who permits the grant officer to submit incomplete or erroneous data and risk rejection by the funding agency.

Despite all these difficulties, most recreation and park directors have little choice but to pursue all possibilities for federal, state, or foundation funding. To accomplish this, the creative manager will go far beyond the traditional or conventional approach of applying for grants, which consists of routine applications to advertised grants programs, with an easy surrender at the first refusal or obstacle. Instead, what might be called a guerrilla approach (involving a persistent, resourceful, determined attack) should be used, including elements such as these:

1. Beat the crowd, develop contacts, know about new grants before they are fully announced.
2. Visit grant headquarters, meet the key people, personalize your approach. Remember, they are bored by the mountains of paper which flood in on them.
3. Invite them to your city, and make the visit memorable; visit all sites.
4. Contact local political party leaders for assistance; seek industry and business people with high contacts.
5. In your presentations, use films, displays, large sketches, and graphics.
6. At first refusal or resistance, question why, and follow up; persist until successful.
7. If grant is awarded, get full newspaper coverage of it; have articles on it written for appropriate periodicals, and give the funding agency a huge "plug."[39]

Other fund-raising sources: business and industry

In addition to grants obtained from government and foundations, many leisure-service agencies have sought assistance from industry and business concerns in their communities. In the past, this effort tended to be approached as a charitable, small donation, just as a local merchant might be asked to put up some prizes for a tournament or contribute refreshments for a picnic.

Beginning in the mid-1960s, many municipal recreation and park departments began calling on major companies—such as soft drink and beer manufacturers or distributors, banks, insurance companies, airlines, department stores, or newspapers or television stations, for more significant forms of help. These took several forms: (1) outright gifts of money, land, or equipment; (2) cooperation in cosponsoring major events or ongoing programs; (3) business responsibility for maintaining or "adopting" specific facilities, such as parks or waterfront areas; or (4) providing expertise in the form of consultants, technical assistance, equipment, or other valued assistance to recreation and park agencies.

Today, the rationale underlying industry and business support of municipal recreation and park agencies is more clearly understood. The relationship between a successful business or industrial plant and a healthy, vigorous recreation and park environment is an important one. Business executives have come to recognize that a new plant or office turning out a fine product or service may fail because its environs are decayed and depressed. Shabby streets, loitering gangs, badly illuminated parking areas, and lack of sports facilities are some of the factors that can create a dangerous and unpleasant environment for employees. Such conditions can lead to walls covered with graffiti, broken windows, vandalized autos and trucks, and a high rate of pilferage and petty crime surrounding the plant or office. These conditions can result in increased operating costs and inevitable price rises or difficulty in retaining or attracting productive personnel.

The alert business executive recognizes that a healthy, vigorous, leisure-oriented society is the type of market environment in which products sell best. Communities that care for their streets and parks, schools, and hospitals and that manage their funds frugally are usually cities of high stability and low taxes. Many industrial concerns have therefore become more fully involved in recreation and park planning and program sponsorship. The small neighborhood park to be located just across the street from corporate headquarters is important, but so is the nearby golf course, sports field, ice rink, zoo, or civic auditorium. Employees and executives alike have become part of a cooperative relationship with recreation and park agencies and in so doing have helped public departments function more effectively at a time of fiscal austerity.

Many corporations today play a significant social role by "plugging" gaps in valuable public programs. Duwe sums up the trend:

> Across the country, the corporate sector is accepting such a role in community recreation and many corporations are even seeking worthwhile projects for funding. As one company president said, "In the past we have tended to be 'reactive' in making corporate contributions. We now intend . . . to be more 'proactive' in our giving."[40]

Numerous examples may be cited of both local businesses contributing to community recreation programs and national corporations sponsoring major sports competitions or subsidizing fitness facilities.

Sometimes the assistance takes the form of a special promotion or income-sharing venture. In Alamagordo, N.M., the Dairy Queen Company marketed a "Knockout Burger." For every burger sold on certain days, the city received a share of the profits, with money donated going to help build the city's amateur boxing program. McDonald's marketed a "McBike Burger," contributing 30% of the income from it to help the city construct a bicycle trail along a railroad right-of-way. Donations from business and industry in other cities have included $600,000 for a community center and ice rink, $70,000 for a park for special populations, and $175,000 for preservation of an "urban wilderness" area.

Gift catalogs

To stimulate giving, some departments have published *gift catalogs*. These are portfolios that itemize and illustrate the specific needs of the department in a solicitation of outright donations. The purpose, value, and cost of each item are listed, so that recreation and park departments or voluntary organizations can directly encourage private givers to make a contribution geared to their gift-giving capability or in line with their particular needs.

Dodge points out that gift catalog programs should seek broad-based support by providing opportunities for contributions of various sizes. He writes:

> An individual or corporation may provide a $100,000 donation for the construction of a new park, but a class of fifth graders may also contribute $10 to purchase bird seed for a nature center. Recognition of the importance of both gifts is fundamental to a successful long-term campaign, and, in fact, your local media may be more willing to focus a human interest story on the fifth grade's contribution and thus provide free promotion for your gift catalog program.[41]

Program cosponsorship

On the local level, many businesses or industries are playing an actual sponsoring or cosponsoring role in cooperation with recreation and park departments. New Rochelle, N.Y., a community of 70,000, offers several examples of how such assistance may be developed. For the past several years in New Rochelle, the Manufacturers' Hanover Bank of New York has provided financial backing for the Westchester Half-Marathon. In 1979, 4000 runners entered the race, making it the largest half-marathon in the nation and one of the most important East Coast races. Manufacturers' Hanover also provided funding for one of the first Parcourse exercise jogging trails in the East and has cosponsored basketball clinics for youth in the city in cooperation with the New York Knicks professional basketball team. Other manufacturers and companies have also jointly sponsored recreational activities of various types in the city.

Adopt-a-park programs

Corporate giving has in some cases involved a unique arrangement in which a company takes specific responsibility for helping maintain or operate a park it has "adopted." The East Bay Regional Park District in California embarked on a campaign to have major corporations underwrite costs of maintaining, operating, and improving a facility for at least 3 years. Under the adoption arrangement, the company and the district's staff consult to determine exactly what the funds should be used for and the corporation provides "hands-on" staff assistance in areas where its expertise would be especially helpful.

Full range of corporate assistance

Cryder[42] has developed a detailed statement of the various ways in which corporations are able to assist recreation and park departments. These include the following.

1. *Loaned executives.* The corporation could share its expertise in legal, financial, maintenance, management, engineering, and other technical matters with the park and recreation agency.
2. *Volunteer labor.* Employees, through employee associations, could volunteer time and talents to special projects benefiting the agency.
3. *Training.* The corporation might routinely invite park and recreation personnel to attend corporate training programs (especially management training).
4. *Efficiency analysis.* Drawing on in-house resources, the corporation could assist the agency in determining the most efficient operations and maintenance practices for existing areas and in planning for future low maintenance.
5. *Energy conservation.* The corporation could share its energy conservation program with the park agency and at the same time demonstrate to the community its lead in this area.
6. *Adjoining parkland.* At only incremental cost to itself, the corporation might have its staff maintain parkland adjacent to corporate land holdings.
7. *Professional services.* Many parks contract for services such as litter pick-up, security/firewatch, vehicle repair, plumbing, and electrical work. Corporations with extensive staff specialization in these services could extend or donate such services.

8. *Public relations.* Corporate expertise could help organize effective public relations for the park and recreation agency.
9. *Surveys/data management.* Corporations might share their extensive experience in data management with park administrators and might assist the park agency in evaluating its effectiveneess.

Other ways through which business and industry can assist recreation and park departments include lending equipment or allowing use of computer time, assisting with joint purchasing of bulk orders, donating used or recycled equipment, providing transportation opportunities to special groups, opening employee recreation facilities to the general public, helping with communications efforts, donating land to the recreation and park agency, auctioning off equipment or supplies that they no longer need and donating the proceeds, assisting with insurance coverage or consultation, providing "scholarships" to help disadvantaged community residents participate in programs, and paying for advertisements of jointly sponsored activities.

CORPORATIONS AS A MARKET   Seeing corporations only as a source of financial or technical assistance is short sighted. Recreation and park agencies should seek to be of service to *them,* as by helping with their employee recreation programs or providing leisure services directly. Crompton and Younger point out that these programs have traditionally been seen as the exclusive domain of individuals employed in what was known as "industrial recreation," now referred to as "employee recreation and services." Today municipal leisure-service agencies are beginning to move into this field of professional need:

> We believe that during the next few years, this corporate market will emerge as one of the field's most important client groups. Serving corporations enables recreation and park agencies to reach citizens who have never previously used their services and to develop additional citizen support. [If] recreation and park agencies offer direct service and foster direct relationships, they are likely to develop trust, understanding, credibility, and contacts upon which corporate donations depend.[43]

Crompton and Younger cite the example of the Johnson County, Mo., Park and Recreation District, which responded to a request in 1979 by the Bendix Corporation to assist in providing recreation for its employees. Four years later, the district had developed a corporate recreation program serving 15,000 employees of 84 different companies, with over 450,000 acts of participation a year. Based on findings of a needs assessment survey, each such program works through a recreation committee formed within the company and has several operational alternatives: (1) activity programs offered at company locations; (2) programs using public facilities leased by the Johnson County Park and Recreation District from local school systems; (3) company programs integrated with those offered to the general public; and (4) classes for employees at private facilities, such as tennis centers, bowling alleys, or ice rinks.

Program costs are generally shared by the participants and their companies, and revenues are deposited in a fiscally self-sufficient enterprise fund of the recreation and park district. As extensions of this effort, a number of major competitions have been developed among participating corporations, and 20 companies have joined together to finance a \$1.8 million recreation center on a time-sharing basis. Crompton and Younger conclude:

> In times of financial difficulty a corporate program offers a very cost-efficient way of reaching substantial numbers of citizens. Serving this market offers substantial return on effort invested to citizens employed by those companies, to the corporations, and to the recreation and park agency.[44]

Clearly, such efforts serve several different purposes. Not only do they result in greatly expanded recreational opportunities for citizens throughout the area, but they help bring about constructive relationships between the public recreation and park agency and the corporate and financial community.

Mobilizing total community support

In addition to working closely with corporations, managers should seek to involve as many community organizations and groups as possible in the overall operation of the public leisure-service agency.

USING "FRIENDS" ORGANIZATIONS   In some cases municipal recreation and park departments have been able to stimulate increased community support by mobilizing a wide range of private citizens, service organizations, business concerns, and other groups in a coordinated and continuing effort. San Francisco provides an interesting example. It became apparent in that city several years ago that the public's need for adequate recreation and park opportunities could *not* be met by taxes alone. A major support group that would bring together and channel a wide variety of agencies in the city was needed to obtain financial assistance and other important forms of backing for recreation.

To accomplish this, a tax-exempt organization known as Friends of Recreation and Parks was incorporated in 1971 in San Francisco. By 1973 after intensive membership drives, more than 350 individuals and companies had joined it. Annual dues ranged from \$5 to over \$1000. Caverly writes:

> Every major city has its neighborhood associations, citizens' groups, conservation clubs, and a myriad of hobby, craft, and cultural organizations. Most communities are blessed, too, with public-spirited citizens whose generosity makes possible additional beautiful parks and serviceable playgrounds. San Francisco is not unique in this respect. . . . What *is* unique is the collective backing of these groups and the coordination of their efforts. An important objective of the Friends is to obtain financial assistance from the business community, citizens, and organizations for worthy programs [and] to contribute to the burgeoning cultural and recreation climate of the city by sponsoring events such as opera concerts and field plays.[45]

The Friends of Recreation and Parks have raised substantial sums to support special recreation projects, have developed an Adopt-a-Park program, and have aroused widespread civic interest and support for the city's recreation and park system. A number of other municipal departments have used this approach with considerable success. In many cases they have also formed special foundations through which to channel funds and resources acquired through the "Friends" method.

GUIDELINES FOR DEVELOPING SUPPORT

Logical steps that public or nonprofit agencies should employ as they seek support and cooperation from the private sector include the following:

1. Defining goals and objectives of the fund-raising campaign, including an organized statement of acts to support the appeal and persuade potential donors or cooperating agencies to assist
2. Organizing to carry out the campaign: identifying available leadership, time, and money, which will be necessary to do it effectively
3. Carrying out an inventory of all needs and tasks to be accomplished: this includes dollars, materials, land, equipment, programs, expertise, and other resources for purposes such as operations, maintenance, programming, or general management
4. Identifying and analyzing all potential resources, including foundations, corporations, other community agencies, and individuals and matching the organization's specific needs with the resources that are most likely to be able to provide the needed assistance
5. Planning a direct approach to potential donors, which includes an initial publicity campaign, person-to-person contacts, including personal visits, presentations of brochures and requests, with follow-up calls and visits as appropriate

The following tactics illustrate one way of securing industry or business support for program cosponsorship:

1. Approach large, influential, or powerful companies first (those with the greatest resources and capability for providing substantial assistance).
2. Make the proposal a two-way street; offer *them* services, programs, or other forms of help. Repeat the offer genuinely. If asked for help, deliver generously and effectively.
3. Involve their personnel informally, in formal meetings, and through information contacts. Boost their egos.
4. Propose a cosponsored event in which *they* will want to be involved for public relations or other purposes. In it, utilize their personnel and talents, as well as your own.
5. Submit a *modest* budget, emphasizing your own in-kind contributions.
6. Plan carefully to *guarantee* success and favorable publicity; lavishly praise the company afterward.
7. Lay low for a time before approaching with new and more ambitious plan.

Whenever dealing with an industrial firm or other company, it is wise to make a preliminary study of their products and services, including a thorough tour of their plant. If appropriate, the agency can offer helpful merchandising ideas related to leisure services that might be part of their marketing operation. Building a bridge to city hall strengthens their sense of involvement and civic responsibility. Agency representatives should meet with company officials frequently. When presenting the proposal, they should make sure that it is highly professional and convincing.

Summary

To achieve a fiscally sound operation, leisure-service agencies of all types must embark on a process of strategic planning. This is far more than simply raising funds through increased fees, grants, or gifts. It requires analysis of the agency's fundamental philosophy and goals, a redefinition of priorities, and restructuring its organizational units and practices where necessary. At the heart of the process is the adoption of a vigorous marketing approach that ensures that programs and services are keyed to public needs or to the interests of whatever specialized constituency the agency serves.

Beyond this, a number of specific techniques for increasing productivity, cutting costs, and obtaining grants and gifts are described in the chapter. Ideally, all such elements are coordinated in a total fiscal plan that is then reflected in ongoing policies and procedures and that is regularly reviewed and modified to meet changing environmental conditions. The development of such a plan and the innovative fiscal methods it embodies is a key responsibility of leisure-service managers. In conclusion, it should be stressed that while most of the examples cited throughout this chapter are drawn from public recreation and park agencies, they certainly apply equally well to other types of leisure-service sponsors, such as voluntary, armed forces, campus, or employee recreation programs.

STUDY QUESTIONS

1. Select a single popular form of activity, such as health and fitness programming. With other students, examine the way it is offered in several different settings (public, YMCA, employee program, or profit-oriented health spa) from a marketing point of view. Report on and compare the approaches in each setting in the areas of product or service, target market, pricing, and presentation.

2. Carry out a cost-benefit analysis of several program elements in a college or university campus recreation program. These might include sports activities (intramurals and sports clubs), major entertainment and cultural events, and social clubs or events that are assisted by the institution. Based on the stated rationale for the campus recreation program, compare each of these activity categories in the areas of budget allocations, extent of participation, and measurable outcomes or benefits.

3. Hold an in-class debate on the issue of whether public recreation and park agencies should move more heavily into subcontracting direct program or maintenance functions with outside organizations or should limit such arrangements. Deal with productivity and fiscal benefits, as well as implications of the issue for the leisure-service profession.

Case 13   *Meeting the Marketing Challenge*

YOU ARE SEAN DALY, director of the health and physical recreation center of a large urban YMCA in a neighborhood with varied residential and business areas. Your exercise and physical fitness program has become very popular in recent years with the growth of public interest in fitness.

However, a new, privately owned health spa has just opened a few blocks away. It has a glamorous, high-tech design and all the latest equipment, including a swimming pool, Jacuzzi and whirlpools, flashy decorations, and rock music playing regularly, as well as a bar. You are certain that you will be losing many of your regular clients, who are style-conscious, up-scale yuppies (young urban professionals) and who are impressed by this facility and its "with-it" image and high-powered advertising.

From a marketing perspective, how can you meet this challenge?

Questions for Class Discussion and Analysis

1. The new commercial health spa is offering attractions with which you cannot compete. What can *you* offer that they cannot?
2. What target markets are open to you that might not be suitable for the new health spa? From a pricing and cost point of view, do you have an advantage?
3. Design a campaign intended to hold your present clientele against the challenge offered by this new competitor and to reach groups that you have not targeted in the past. Consider both program elements and ways of involving individuals and groups in the YMCA's fitness program.

Case 14   *Contracting the Greens: The Union Sees Red*

YOU ARE ISAIAH JEFFERSON, facilities manager of the South Wingate Special Park District. Your district operates three golf courses, which have traditionally barely paid for their own operation through greens fees.

With the present tight budget, you are unable to maintain the courses adequately or do the rehabilitation that you feel will be required soon. Therefore after considerble exploration, you have decided to subcontract the maintenance of the courses; the job can be done more efficiently and economically, you believe, than you could possibly do it yourself. Two large lawn and garden maintenance companies are interested in the contract and are preparing to bid on it.

If the plan goes through, you do not plan to fire any personnel. Instead, you will transfer them to other locations. However, since several of them are long-term employees and will retire soon, you probably will not replace them and will cut the maintenance staff through attrition.

While the plan makes sense from a fiscal point of view, there is strong labor union resistance to it. The head of the union, Fred Foley, is threatening to fight it in the newspapers and before the park district board and if necessary to call a "job action" to prevent it.

Continued.

Case 14
cont'd

Contracting the Greens: The Union Sees Red

Questions for Class Discussion and Analysis

1. What is the legal situation on this issue; does the park district have the right to subcontract this function? What other issues are involved in the decision? How would it affect the public?
2. How could you make the plan more acceptable to the union?
3. Identify the pros and cons of the plan that should be fully presented to the park district board. What would be its most serious disadvantages or possible negative outcomes? What would be its positive outcomes? Develop a fiscal plan showing the present operation and the way it would change if it were subcontracted.

REFERENCES

1. Bullaro, John J.: "The Business of Survival: Developing a Marketing Strategy," *Leisure Today, Journal of Physical Education, Recreation and Dance,* April 1982, p. 64.
2. Deppe, Theodore R., and Sharpless, Daniel: ". . . Financial Outlook," *Parks and Recreation,* July 1980, p. 52.
3. "Editorial: Faced with Constraints," *Recreation Canada,* Sept. 1980, p. 4.
4. Kemp, Roger, and Feliciano, Marty: "The Creative Management of Recreational Services," *Parks and Recreation,* Oct. 1982, p. 54.
5. Howard P. James, cited in Special Advertising Section, American Hotel and Motel Association, *Time,* May 7, 1984, n.p.
6. "Boating Bonanza," *USA Today,* March 29, 1984, p. B-1.
7. "Dirty Money in the Spotlight," *Time,* Nov. 12, 1984, p. 84.
8. Gray, David: "Managing Our Way to a Preferred Future," *Parks and Recreation,* May 1984, p. 48.
9. Rimer, Sara: "The Airline That Shook the Industry," *New York Times Magazine,* Dec. 23, 1984, pp. 18-19, 24, 28-30.
10. Kotler, Philip: *Marketing for Non-Profit Organizations,* Englewood Cliffs, N.J., 1975, Prentice-Hall, Inc., p. x.
11. Howard, Dennis R., and Crompton, John L.: *Financing, Managing and Marketing Recreation and Park Resources,* Dubuque, Iowa, 1980, William C. Brown Co., p. 320.
12. Kotler, *op. cit.,* p. 74.
13. *Ibid.,* p. 92.
14. Crompton, John L.: "Selecting Target Markets—A Key to Effective Marketing," *Journal of Park and Recreation Administration,* Jan. 1983, p. 8.
15. Sustronk, Hans: "Planning a Marina for Future Boating Demand," *Recreation Canada,* March 1980, pp. 8-11.
16. Matheusik, Mick R.E., and Mills, Allan S.: "Selection of Underwater Park Target Markets: A Canadian Example," *Journal of Park and Recreation Administration,* Oct. 1983, pp. 53-65.
17. Downs, Joseph P.: "Planning and Marketing: Two Keys to a Recreation Center's Success," *Parks and Recreation,* Oct. 1983, p. 31.
18. Crompton, John L.: "How to Find the Price That's Right," *Parks and Recreation,* March 1981, pp. 32-34.
19. Kozlowski, James C.: "GAO Recommends National Park Entrance Fee Increases," *Parks and Recreation,* Oct. 1982, p. 16.
20. *Ibid.*
21. Canham, Don: "Marketing: Key to Successful Athletic Programs," *U.S. Sports Academy News,* July-Aug. 1980, pp. 1-2.
22. *Productivity in the Changing World of the 1980s,* Report of the National Center for Productivity and Quality of Working Life, Washington, D.C., 1978, U.S. Government Printing Office, p. vi.
23. Judson, Arnold S.: "Forum: The Productivity Challenge," *New York Times,* Feb. 17, 1985, p. 3-1.

24. *Productivity in the Changing World of the 1980s,* *op. cit.,* p. 57.
25. Webster, William D., and Reich, Charles M.: "Benefit/Cost Analysis—Its Uses in Parks and Recreation," *Recreation Canada,* Jan. 1977, p. 26.
26. Morrison, Richard B.: "Cost-Effectiveness," *Journal of Physical Education, Recreation and Dance, Leisure Today,* April 1982, p. 53.
27. Underkoffler, Larry: "ZBB: Keeping Your Budget and Goals in Line," *Parks and Recreation,* Dec. 1979, p. 40.
28. Singleton, David, *et al.:* "Zero-Based Budgeting in Wilmington, Del." *Governmental Finance,* Aug. 1976, pp. 24-25.
29. Edginton, Christopher R., and Griffith, Charles A.: *The Recreation and Leisure Service Delivery System,* Philadelphia, 1983, Saunders College Publishing, pp. 203-207.
30. Heit, Michael: "Doing More with Less: The Ontario Provincial Parks Example," *Recreation Canada,* Sept. 1980, pp. 12-14.
31. Paige, Ronald F.: "Contracting for Services: A Valid Response to Fiscal Conservancy," *Parks and Recreation,* Nov. 1983, pp. 54-55.
32. Quinn, Kevin G., and Cook, Bryson L.: "Financial Management," *American City and County,* Feb. 1985, p. 20.
33. *Leisure Lines,* California Park and Recreation Society Newsletter, Oct. 1980, p. 1.
34. Heritage Conservation and Recreation Service: *Contract Services Handbook,* Washington, D.C., 1979, U.S. Department of Interior, p. 13.

35. Donahue, Ron: "Get More for Your Maintenance Dollar Through Contracting," *Parks and Recreation,* Feb. 1983, p. 43.
36. Paige, *op. cit.,* p. 57.
37. Cryder, Ralph: "Lease (Contracting) vs Self-Operations," Presentations at Fees and Revenue Management Workshop, California Consortium, Oakland, May 1980, pp. 1-2.
38. Joyce, Donald V.: "Foundation Funding . . . Where to Look," *Parks and Recreation,* Feb. 1974, p. 24.
39. Presentation by Joseph Curtis at Financial Assistance Institute, National Recreation and Park Association Congress, New Orleans, La., Oct. 1979.
40. Duwe, Michael J.: "Coaxing the Corporate Dollar," *Parks and Recreation,* Sept. 1981, p. 58.
41. Dodge, Rick: "Gift Catalogues: The Marketing Technique for New Revenue Sources," *Parks and Recreation,* Aug. 1982, p. 22.
42. Cryder, Ralph: "Private Sector Involvement Opportunities," 1980, Revenue Sources Management School.
43. Crompton, John L., and Younger, Leon E.: "What Are You Doing for Your Corporate Constituency?" *Parks and Recreation,* May 1983, p. 42.
44. *Ibid.,* p. 46.
45. Caverly, Joseph: "Friends of Recreation and Parks," *Parks and Recreation,* Jan. 1973, p. 77.

CHAPTER 12

"You are probably in the best industry in America," said Kentucky Governor John Y. Brown to the 1982 Congress for Recreation and Parks. "With logic, it should be the fastest growing industry in the decade of the 1980s. But your industry is one of the most competitive, and what you need to do in the decade of the '80s is to up sales," said the former fried chicken king. "You've got to promote."[1]

Public and Community Relations

*P*ublic relations represents one of the most important areas of concern for leisure-service managers. Unless they can get their message across to the public, as well as to the specific audience they serve, their efforts will be wasted, no matter how attractive a program they offer. It is not just a matter of "selling" a program or of "planting" publicity in a traditional press agentry sense. The task of public relations today is more broadly concerned with achieving public understanding and confidence and involves a two-way communication process.

Closely linked to public relations is the process of community relations, which includes a total effort to work closely with community groups and organizations, to obtain their understanding, support, and assistance, and to join forces with them in solving mutual problems. Community relations may include varied approaches such as developing neighborhood or center advisory committees or district councils, recruiting volunteers to assist in agency operations, and having synergetic relationships in cosponsored programming or other forms of coordination in community-based leisure service.

This chapter provides detailed guidelines for implementing both public and community relations in varied types of leisure-service organizations.

Goals of Public Relations

Public relations may be defined as a two-way relationship between organizations of various types and the public they serve, with three major purposes: (1) to disseminate information to the public, (2) to alter the public's belief and actions through persuasion, and (3) to attempt to coordinate the actions and attitudes of the public and the organization that seeks to serve it. In this context the term "public" implies both the diversified mass of people in the community at large (including specific target groups in this external audience), and internal constituencies or membership groups *within* a given organization.

Taking the public recreation and park field as an example, why is there a need for public relations? Certain prevalent attitudes enforce this need.

First, many individuals feel that public recreation is not really a necessity—that the public is able to meet its leisure needs independently. Associated with this is the view that public funds should not be spent on an amenity such as recreation.

Second, many persons have limited knowledge of the department's work and do not know about the wide range of services and programs it offers.

Third, by the very nature of recreation and park operations, there are frequent occasions in which individual citizens tend to be irritated, frustrated, or disappointed—sometimes to the point of generating an army of critics who speak out against recreational goals and programs. The father of the unsuccessful Little Leaguer, the mother of the youthful ice skater not included in the recreation department ice show, the resident whose house is damaged by a branch from a city-owned tree, or the patron who finds the door of a park toilet locked—all are potentially vociferous critics of the local recreation and park operation.

Therefore it is essential that administrators seek to reach the public at large with a continuing and comprehensive program of information that will bring about public understanding and goodwill and ensure support that is translated into votes, legislative action, contributions, support on annual budgets, participation in activities, and volunteer service. The specific goals of such a public relations program may be listed as follows:

1. To provide accurate information regarding the overall program and offering of the department to the general public to overcome misunderstandings, false impressions, or lack of information about organized recreation
2. To inform the general public specifically about the services, facilities, and programs offered by the department and to encourage their attendance and involvement
3. To specifically impress the public with the values and benefits achieved by the department and to bring about a sense of satisfaction that the tax dollar is being well spent in this area
4. To keep the public fully informed of all major plans or policies of the department (this may refer to special new programs, the acquisition or development of facilities, the imposition of fees, or the scheduling of seasonal programs)
5. To bring public attention to a specific project or program at a key time (this may involve a crash effort to publicize a new program or mass event and encourage large-scale participation, or it may consist of a press campaign to give out facts regarding a proposed bond issue for land acquisition)
6. To encourage public involvement in the program in the form of volunteer leadership, serving on councils or advisory groups, or making other contributions
7. To develop a fuller public understanding of the role of recreation and leisure in the lives of individuals and in community well-being: inevitably, the department is the major representative for this area of service and social concern
8. To help promote other forms of community involvement in recreation by encouraging the development of hobbies or the formation of new neighborhood clubs or interest groups
9. To develop channels for two-way communication with the public at large in the form of meaningful dialogs on community leisure interests and needs, problems and complaints, new proposals, and new forms of cooperative action between the department and community residents

A final purpose is to demonstrate to the public that its recreation and park department is dynamic and future oriented and that its methods include a constant search for new programs, techniques, vehicles, and concepts of recreation and leisure that will enrich community life. Similar purposes apply to other types of leisure-service sponsors, such as voluntary, private, commercial, armed forces, or employee recreation agencies.

Identifying Audiences for Public Relations

To achieve these goals, it is necessary for recreation and park managers to determine exactly which audiences they are trying to reach or involve through their public relations efforts. Generally, public relations may involve either a *shotgun* or a *rifle* approach. The shotgun sprays its message over a wide range without trying to identify any single group or tailor a specialized message. In contrast, the rifle is aimed at a specific audience with a message that is uniquely designed for it.

There are usually several audiences or publics that a leisure-service agency's public relations efforts must seek to reach. These include not only the public at large, but also specific segments of the public, which may be identified by age category (such as children, youth, or the aging) or by special characteristics (such as the handicapped, "singles" populations, or racial or ethnic minority groups). Public relations messages may also be aimed at civic, religious, political, industrial, labor, fraternal, and similar organizations in the community.

In addition to such "external" audiences, many leisure-service agencies must seek to reach their own "internal" publics or constituencies with public relations messages. For example, on a large military base, armed forces recreation managers must constantly communicate publicity about upcoming programs to uniformed personnel, civilian employees, and dependents. Employee recreation specialists must publicize their offerings to employees on all levels, and program directors of a large YMCA or YWCA must do the same to their membership to promote registration and participation in classes and special events. In a hospital, therapeutic recreation specialists have several audiences: (1) patients themselves, to encourage participation in general, nonprescribed activities; (2) members of treatment teams, such as occupational or physical therapists or other hospital administrators or staff personnel; and (3) families of patients and to some extent those in the surrounding community who might assist as volunteers or assist programs in other ways.

Channels for Public Relations

In a manual on private sector involvement, the U.S. Department of the Interior identifies many ways of reaching the public:

> The use of communications media can include television specials, particularly on public television; newspaper or magazine articles in State and national magazines or the Sunday supplements of newspapers; public service announcements; and news stories and interviews for radio, television, and newspapers. Attractive brochures are valuable in explaining the purposes of the program. Posters, bumper-stickers and other promotional devices might be used. Speeches to civic, school and other groups can be effective. Also, use of visual media, such as films, slides and pictures, can graphically demonstrate the need for gifts of

recreational and open space land. Special events, contests and gimmicks, such as dinners and walk-a-thons, may yield needed publicity.[2]

In general, public relations approaches may be divided into two categories: (1) *informational media,* which include direct channels for publicity such as newspapers, magazines, television and radio, or similar means of communication, and (2) *interpersonal links,* such as advisory committees or councils, task forces, public meetings or planning sessions, or less formal relationships between professional staff members and leisure consumers.

In planning the use of informational media, certain factors must be taken into consideration. The type and length of the message to be delivered, the purpose of the message, the specific audience to be reached, the time available to prepare and disseminate the message, and the funds available are all important elements. It is advisable to have both regularly scheduled outlets for public information and special types of releases or media to publicize events or programs that require separate intensive coverage.

USE OF PRINT MEDIA

Despite the popularity of television and radio, the simplest and most effective means of reaching large numbers of people is through print media, such as newspapers, brochures, and reports. Newspapers in particular are an inexpensive outlet for public relations, and can provide sustained coverage of a program or activity and immediate and timely means of transmitting information from day to day. In addition, newspaper editors are usually receptive to printing news of popular interest, particularly when it contains elements of human interest.

The process of press relations is a key aspect of effective public relations, since most people's attitudes regarding any department or program are formed by reading newspapers, watching television, or listening to radio news. Scherer writes:

> Public relations has sometimes been called "press agentry" with a conscience. For example, publicity that makes false or misleading claims obviously does an organization more harm than good. Conscientious public relations, on the other hand, is introspective before it rushes into print. It has been proven many times that some of the most beneficial press releases are those that are never issued—because someone thought a second time. Conversely, a dramatic, thoughtfully-planned, well-timed, accurate and targeted press release can clarify the position, plans or programs of an organization and win it friends.[3]

When a recreation and park manager has news of interest to the local newspaper, one of these basic approaches should be used:

1. Prepare a news release and mail or deliver it to the editor. If possible, address it to the editor by name.
2. Call the newspaper and talk to the appropriate editor or reporter, summarizing the information briefly. The editor or reporter will indicate whether it would be best to have a release prepared or whether the details should be given over the telephone and the story written in the newspaper office. It may be appropriate to send a reporter out to conduct an interview.
3. Arrange a news conference and invite interested reporters and editors. This device

should be used sparingly; it is best to save it for really important stories that justify calling such a meeting at a time and place of your own choosing.

Guidelines for preparing newspaper releases

There are several sections of most newspapers that can be used for printing recreation and park releases. These might include general news sections, editorial pages, letters to the editor sections, columns, calendars of public events, or special departments such as sports or women's activities.

Newspaper stories should be prepared with the following guidelines in mind:

1. Newspaper copy should be kept simple, factual, and straightforward and should avoid editorializing. It should consist of short, easy to read paragraphs, with the first paragraph (the lead) including all relevant information, such as who, what, when, where, and how.
2. Whenever possible, the release should be limited to one page, with the most important information covered in the early sections and the least important in the later copy, since it is usual editing practice to cut copy or type at the end of a story.
3. In preparing stories, an attempt should be made to feature a prominent or interesting individual or group of people, since readers are generally interested in reading names with whom they may identify or who lend importance to an article.
4. Material should be neatly typed, with adequate margins, headings, and sources given where necessary. The name of the department and the name, address, and telephone number of the person responsible for issuing the release should be printed at the top of the sheet.
5. Copy should be submitted with plenty of lead time to be easily edited and prepared for the printer. It is important to know the deadline of the newspaper to which you are submitting copy and to meet it with a comfortable margin.

In general, the key factor in obtaining newspaper coverage of departmental events or news is maintaining a positive and cooperative relationship with the newspaper editor and staff. This means that whenever news breaks occur or interviews are held, information should be given fully and honestly, and reporters should be treated with respect and consideration. Information should never be distorted or exaggerated. When reporters cover stories or events, they should be assisted with transportation, special briefings, or facilities to make their job easier.

It is helpful to have contacts and cultivate useful outlets for news publicity, but it is also essential to be able to produce newsworthy copy. This means that, whenever possible, events should be produced or scheduled that *are* interesting, colorful, of human interest, and worthy of newspaper space.

Magazines

Many of the same guidelines apply to the preparation and placing of articles in magazines. Although it is seldom possible to place articles or releases in national publications unless the story is particularly exciting or unusual, it *is* often possible to have material accepted by local, regional, or state publications.

There are special publications that reach municipal officials, recreation and park professionals, planners, or personnel specialists. Other publications are geared to those concerned with rehabilitation, aging, or different population groups. Some magazines are designed to promote tourism and accept articles on interesting events or facilities. Others are concerned with specific interests, such as sports, hobbies, cultural activities, or travel. Generally, magazine articles must be longer and written with greater style or flair than newspaper stories.

Picture stories tend to find a market more easily than written articles without illustrations. It is often helpful to query the editor of a magazine first about his or her interest in a particular story before writing and sending it.

This valuable medium is underused because administrators seem to think that good magazine articles just happen. Experience indicates that the vast majority of talented recreation and park staff personnel have little awareness of or inclination toward the specialized field of magazine writing. One or more individuals should be designated as article writers and given full support and encouragement if articles are to be produced and marketed.

Newsletters and brochures

These are prepared by most departments on an annual or seasonal basis to present attractive descriptions of their programs. They may range from simple mimeographed or photo-offset handouts of a page or two to elaborate four-color brochures. Generally, such brochures include a description of all major locations where programs will be held and a listing of program activities to be offered during a given season.

They should usually include the following:

1. The name of the sponsoring department and its administrator or key staff, the names of board members, and the names of key municipal officials
2. The major citywide office and telephone numbers and other district or area offices where information or permits may be obtained
3. A listing and brief description with a map of all major park centers, pools, and similar facilities; in a large community with many facilities, this may appear in a separate directory or guide map
4. A listing of major activities offered on a citywide basis; this might include separate groups for each age level, special events, leagues and tournaments, courses, or other services
5. A listing of fees or charges for each activity where applicable
6. A brief statement of the philosophy or purpose of the department

Such brochures may be distributed in mailings to organizations, officials, members of committees, or citizens, by house-to-house delivery, by having them available at all offices and centers, by distribution through parent-teacher associations, churches, civic clubs, or similar groups, and by mailings to a special list of those who have indicated interest or been involved in previous programs.

Since such newsletters or brochures represent a major way in which most individuals come in contact with the department and gain an impression of it, they should be colorful, crisp, and attractive. At the same time, having them too thick and elaborate may give the impression of being overly lavish and cause taxpayer criticism.

Some departments print thick and detailed brochures (as an exception to the above recommendation) that have the appearance of a newspaper supplement, particularly to give full information about programs during an upcoming season (e.g., a summer brochure or a fall-winter brochure). In some cases, as in Dade County, Fla., these may actually be published as an insert in the daily paper or as the major feature in the weekly magazine section of the Sunday newspaper, thus reaching all newspaper readers in the area.

TELEVISION AND RADIO

These popular media provide an important means of reaching the public directly with spur-of-the-moment news and with direct coverage of actual recreation events. They are useful in reaching all age groups and making a strong public relations impact. Television time, in particular, is often difficult to obtain. Therefore it is necessary to identify the types of programs that may be likely to use recreation announcements or cover important or interesting citywide events. These include:

1. *News programs.* These may provide direct coverage of events, interviews with personalities, or similar features.
2. *Commentator programs.* These may occasionally deal with recreation topics such as entertaining human interest features.
3. *Spot announcements, to be used during programs that list community events.* All stations and channels are required to carry a specified amount of public service programming, and this may be used for recreation announcements.
4. *Interviews and talks.* These are given by department members, participants, or interesting leaders.
5. *Regular departmental programs.* In some cities, special time is set aside at least once a week for news of the department to be given. Just as there is a sports broadcast or a weather forecast, so may there be a recreation broadcast.
6. *Panel discussions.* These may be scheduled on topics of general concern, such as new and interesting kinds of programs, the leisure needs of different groups in the community, or environmental problems related to recreation and parks.

The key factor in securing effective television and radio coverage is the ability to provide timely, interesting, and professionally prepared program materials. If the department prepares its own scripts, they must be done expertly and up to the standards of the network or station. In general, radio time is more available than television time. In attempting to get coverage on the picture medium, it is important to ask questions such as:

Is television the *right medium* for your message?
Do you have something to *show* as well as *tell?*
Can you reach the right *audience* at the right *time?*
Can you properly use *expensive* television time?
Can you *entertain* as you *inform?*
Do you have *time* to spend on a *good* production?
Usually it is not difficult to get spot announcements used on television and radio.

However, more extensive coverage will require developing a contact with the local station director.

MOTION PICTURES

Many municipal and county recreation departments have prepared their own audiovisual materials as means of reaching community groups, professional associations, or other special audiences with information about their department. Generally, a motion picture may simply be sent to a requesting group for a specified showing date and thus may reach many civic groups, service clubs, schools, or other organizations during the course of a year.

Usually a motion picture is fairly expensive to make; a professionally filmed and edited color 16 mm film is likely to cost at least several thousand dollars. Therefore it is important to receive volunteer assistance or the help of community groups wherever possible in making a motion picture about the recreation and park department. Frequently, a professional camera operator or editor will be willing to lend his or her services as a contribution to the community.

Local colleges often have courses in filmmaking and will assist in actual coverage, editing, and providing the use of equipment, which would be extremely expensive if rented. It is important to map out the script carefully in advance and to have a thorough review of all plans for the film, although it is possible simply to shoot a random selection of footage over a period of several months and then edit it into an interesting, colorful, and lively film.

As in the case of a brochure, a film that sells the message of a municipal recreation and park department should include coverage of the governing structure and organization and goals of the department. It should be visually oriented and should give major emphasis to action and interesting events. The film that consists primarily of the departmental administrator standing deadpan before the camera making a speech is not likely to be asked back for a reshowing.

If part of the film shows the department's administrator or supervisor making a presentation about the department, this should be kept brief and lively, using visual aids, such as charts, pictures, maps, and similar materials.

A film should attempt to give a professional, colorful, and positive picture of the department, including its major features and special events, its rationale and contributions to the community, and the new directions it is pursuing. As much as possible, it should avoid events or other elements that might tend to date it in the viewer's eyes; clothing and hairstyles are likely to do that in any case.

SLIDE TALKS

Slide talks represent a less expensive but effective means of reaching an audience with colorful and convincing pictures and accompanying descriptions of a recreation and park department's program. It is a good idea to have a department photographer or a skilled volunteer regularly shoot pictures of special events, facilities, and other features that make good presentations. These may then be assembled easily into an effective slide presentation. If thoroughly familiar with the material shown, the speaker need only put the slides into the correct order and then can speak extemporaneously about them. If several speakers are to use the slides, it is a good idea to prepare a script in which each slide is numbered and the accompanying text typed out.

Slides offer a lively, interesting, and flexible way of entertaining an audience with a recreation and park department presentation. Despite the reputation that family slide showings may have gained, slides are *not* necessarily dull if the picture and accompanying talk are good.

Since slides are much less expensive as a publicity medium than films, they may be designed to meet special purposes, such as showing to parents' groups to promote a summer camp program and encourage recruitment, promoting interest in doing volunteer work in the department, gaining support for a proposed new facility or bond referendum for land acquisition, or encouraging job applications for summer positions among high school or college students.

SPEAKERS

It is also possible for a department to assign its supervisors or leaders to making presentations to community groups, clubs, leagues, or other organizations. In some cases a department actually maintains a speakers' bureau, although this is not common. When it *is* done, it is crucial that the speaker have a fresh and interesting message to deliver rather than overfamiliar, tired material.

EXHIBITS AND DISPLAYS

This provides an excellent means of informing the public about the work of a department. Since recreation itself is composed of so many varied kinds of hobbies and activities, it is possible to develop extremely interesting and unusual kinds of exhibits and displays to entertain and inform the public. These might include:

1. *Exhibits.* Art shows, science displays or fairs, photography exhibits, craft exhibits and sales, hobby shows, nature exhibits, and similar presentations can show the products of recreation programs carried on in the department. They may also include illustrated talks or demonstrations of skills, such as glassblowing or work at the potter's wheel.

2. *Special events.* These may include play days, drama festivals, dance performances, aquacades, or similar showings. The purpose is not so much to entertain an audience as to give a picture of the work of the department.

3. *Displays or demonstrations.* These may be given in varied settings. Central points in shopping malls may be used for demonstrations when large crowds will be there. Schools, libraries, municipal buildings, and hotel or theater lobbies are all places where recreation exhibits or displays may reach large numbers of viewers. One city constructed a giant greeting card, welcoming visitors, and placed it on display in its civic plaza; it was submitted as an entry to the *Guinness Book of World Records* to establish a record for its size and weight.

4. *Action demonstrations.* Demonstrations should be well publicized and given in central locations to draw substantial numbers of viewers. In some cities a large plaza in the downtown business district or in front of the city hall may be used to

show interesting activities during lunch hours when crowds of employees throng the streets.

As a single example, many local recreation and park agencies, professional societies, and other leisure-service groups have used the "Life. Be in it" theme to promote festivals and demonstrations, communitywide parties, Special or Golden Olympics, sales of "Life. Be in it" merchandise, games fairs, "whistle-stop relays," community "paint-ins" or "bike rodeos," or a host of other events. These serve to promote not only the local leisure-service agency, but also the basic pro-recreation message of the campaign.

TOURS AND OPEN HOUSES

The open house or tour is an excellent way of showing officials, parents, local residents, service clubs, PTA members, newspaper reporters, state or county authorities, or other interested groups exactly what is going on in a department.

Guided tours or open houses are usually scheduled at the time of dedication of a new facility, the beginning of a seasonal program, or other occasion that shows the department in a favorable light. They should be carefully planned, with attention given to the following elements:

1. Preliminary planning of the area or activity to be shown, with a schedule showing what points are to be visited at various times throughout the event
2. Arrangements for guides, organizing the visitors into groups, rest stops, seating arrangements, briefing sessions, and transportation
3. Preparation of a mailing list and invitations, mailing, and if advisable direct follow-up by television
4. Preparation of a tour outline, including the itinerary, program, list of those making the tour, schedule, and similar details
5. Last-minute check of all elements involved in the tour or open house and reminder of all invited participants; pretour publicity in newspapers or other media
6. After the event, thank-you notes to all involved and follow-up publicity

ANNUAL REPORTS

A comprehensive report may be published each year by the department and officially submitted to the mayor or city manager, the city council, the recreation and park board, and other municipal authorities.

Annual reports may be addressed solely to such individuals or may be designed to reach the public at large. In the latter case they are likely to be less detailed and more like a brochure in appearance, with photographs and illustrations, colorful layouts, and informal style. Prepared in this way, annual reports may serve as useful public relations tools and should be widely distributed. Normally, annual reports include the following elements:

1. Departmental address and board and staff roster, with or without photographs of key individuals
2. Opening messages, which may be from the mayor, chairperson of the recreation and park board, or administrator of the department

3. Table of contents and acknowledgments of appreciation to those individuals or organizations that served the department during the year
4. Organization chart
5. Financial report, consisting of a simple statement of the authorized budget and sums actually spent; this may include summaries of past and future or predicted budgets
6. A report of physical resource development and the major facilities operated by the department, as well as acquisition, maintenance, or refurbishment projects carried out during the course of the year
7. Report of attendance and participation in programs, usually done by major department divisions or types of activities

Annual reports may deal with a specific theme or have a feature story describing some of the outstanding accomplishments of the department during the course of the year. In general, they should be professionally laid out with contrast, balance, and interest and should make generous use of visual devices to explain the material and attract the eye.

Need for Quality and Creativity

For many years it was considered acceptable for recreation professionals to prepare printed fliers, newspaper stories, cardboard posters, and an occasional radio announcement, all done routinely and with little flair, to herald new programs, special events, or significant developments in recreation and park operations.

Although all of these are valid public relations tools and must be used today as in the past, it must be recognized that a much more sophisticated public is now on the receiving end of department communications. Today many persons make fine home sound movies, use kinescope equipment for filming events, and are much more sensitive and responsive to sound-recording gear.

Recreation and park executives must therefore keep in mind the plethora of communications equipment and message flow with which they must compete. This imposes the need for promotional materials to be of the highest quality possible and geared to reaching appropriate audiences at suitable levels of interest.

CREATING OTHER PUBLIC RELATIONS OPPORTUNITIES

The alert recreation and park manager will seek out many special opportunities throughout the year to provide helpful information or services that contribute to the public relations impact of his or her department and lend themselves to press or television coverage. Examples of such opportunities include:

1. Carrying out a special beautification project at several key entrances to the city with a clear identification of the department of recreation and parks as the city agency responsible for the effort
2. Making special awards with newspaper or other media coverage to:
   a. Most attractive gas stations
   b. Greatest number of new trees planted (on church sites, hospital grounds, etc.)

    c. Outstanding Boy or Girl Scout troop for urban beautification projects
    d. Volunteer leaders with outstanding records
    e. Winners of window box or front lawn garden competitions
3. Sponsoring special Family Day once a year, when any family group may enter all recreation facilities or programs without charge
4. Using press or television to issue important statements (warnings, suggestions, offers of help, etc.) to the public, such as:
    a. Danger of mushy ice on ponds and lakes in spring
    b. Urging homeowners to reforest their city by tree planting
    c. Encouraging family recreational activities
    d. Suggesting and assisting neighborhood recreation events and forming of neighborhood associations
    e. Providing advice, clinics, or contests on home and community gardens
    f. Condemning vandalism as a waste of taxpayer's money
    g. Providing warnings against July Fourth fireworks accidents or Halloween excesses or sponsoring safe holiday activities
    h. Urging public to use care and caution in swimming, boating, and fishing
5. Selecting a junior commissioner of recreation and parks for a day or a week; put him or her in the commissioner's place to tour facilities, run meetings, and deal with real problems, with the press close at hand

Often municipal departments use novel ways of sending out messages to the public or sponsor unique events as a way of attracting public interest. For example, the Raleigh, N.C., Department of Recreation and Parks issues regular, detailed reports to the public on the progress of major capital projects, such as golf courses, swimming pools, or skating rinks. They find the public tends to be more supportive when it is kept in close contact with each such project.

The Boston Park and Recreation Department enlisted the entire city in an urban reforestation program by calling it *Plantree* and pointing out that the city was "going bald." More than $100,000 was raised from private industry to plant thousands of new trees in parks and on school and hospital grounds.

In Atlanta, one full evening at the new Omni Stadium was used to display the talents of participants in Atlanta Recreation and Park Department programs before a live audience of 50,000 and a regional television audience of several million.

Other types of agencies have also developed unusual approaches in their public relations efforts. For example, the Department of Human Kinetics (Health, Physical Education, and Recreation) at Rutgers College in New Jersey initiated an unusual program in cooperation with a merchants' association at a major shopping center in the central New Jersey area.

> The mall was chosen because shopping centers provide a convenient and appropriate forum for rapid and efficient distribution of information to many people. It is not uncommon for more than 100,000 people to pass through a suburban mall during Saturday shopping hours. In addition, most merchants' associations have developed formal advertising programs with local newspapers and thus can provide for a substantial amount of publicity for programs which they cosponsor.[4]

Community play facilities. *Upper left,* Playground equipment firms like Gametime U.S.A. design new settings for creative play used in many public parks. The Oakland County, Mich., Parks and Recreation Commission has a wide variety of special facilities, including a mobile "puppet wagon" *(upper right),* platform tennis center, *(lower left),* and two-tiered golf driving range *(lower right).*

The Menlo Park Merchants' Association agreed to cosponsor a community affairs program with Rutgers, with the focus on promoting health, fitness, and recreational activities for all segments of the community. It was based on a series of fast-moving, action-oriented stage shows performed each hour of the day, involving activities such as table tennis, disco dancing, square dancing, tumbling, and trampolining, accompanied by day-long exhibits on fitness, nutrition, first aid, recreation and leisure opportunities, and other informational materials. Thousands of spectators were reached through this program, which also included promotional materials for Rutgers College.

Guidelines for Public Relations

To ensure that public relations efforts are carried out systematically and on a planned basis, it is helpful to have at least one staff member assigned to this function on a regular basis. This person should enjoy public relations work and have a knack for it. Such an individual constantly sees and uses public relations opportunities, and is always working at picture taking and mounting, tape recording, assembling window displays, writing releases, and printing, letters, or painting publicity posters or arranging to have these produced.

To help this individual, the department should have a kit of equipment and supplies readily available for public relations purposes. This kit might include:

1. Public-address system—a portable amplifier and speakers (at least 30-watt output) light enough to be handled by one person—man or woman; also a phonograph turntable or tape deck
2. Cameras—three different kinds are useful: (1) a 35 mm still camera; (2) a press-type Graflex, which produces an excellent glossy print for newspaper or display use; and (3) a 16 mm movie camera for making department films of events
3. Poster materials—colored ink markers, pens, rulers, and plastic letter stencils and guides; a good supply of mimeograph and construction paper; drawing boards and tag boards; and a uniform poster made in quantity with about a fifth of its space devoted to a colorful heading identifying the department and the rest open for special announcements, photographs, or other use
4. Display complex—a homemade or purchased portable display complex, consisting of combinations of folding tables, hanging panels, and lights, which may easily be disassembled, moved, and set up for display purposes in city hall, banks, restaurants, shopping malls, or conferences and training meetings
5. Worktable and hardware—a study worktable, at least 4 by 6 feet, with needed scissors, paper cutting blade, staplers, and similar office tools, along with an adjacent steel filing cabinet offering organized storage of papers, booklets, and department public relations materials

Overall Approach to Public Relations

The previous section of this chapter dealt with various types of media used to reach the public with messages. Equally important are the direct ways in which a department has daily contact with residents.

For example, all individuals visiting a department office or telephoning should be treated with promptness, courtesy, and efficiency. Complaints regarding programs or facilities, from whatever source, should be received with serious attention and should be processed through appropriate channels without delay. The suggestions of participants or other residents should be solicited at all times.

Whenever assistance of any kind is given to the department by an individual or organization, this should be promptly acknowledged. All members of the department should conduct themselves with appropriate deportment, dress, and general appearance in their contacts with the public.

Buildings, offices, facilities, equipment, and vehicles should all be carefully and attractively maintained and when suitable should have departmental insignia or other identification signs to promote public awareness of the department.

Recreation administrators and supervisors, in particular, should seek to become widely acquainted in the community; it is desirable to become active in civic groups, service clubs, and similar organizations.

The administrator should visit and chat with the heads of major business firms, colleges, hospitals, and other organizations in the area about the philosophy and programs of the recreation and park department, the needs of the city, and other relevant concerns. He or she should *not* ask for direct support at early meetings but should attempt to build a cooperative relationship first before developing the possibility of such ventures. The administrator may offer to assist the company or other institution in improving its own recreation or sports program, including assistance with facilities planning or renovation, advice on activities and special-interest groups, or even the loan of films, books, equipment, or special facilities. Such tangible help is a sound public relations step and frequently makes the business firm or agency a permanent and enthusiastic ally.

The administrator should be prepared to accept speaking and panel assignments frequently and willingly at civic or religious organization meetings in the community and should present a clear and positive picture of the recreation and park department and its program.

The department should prepare and distribute pamphlets giving details of seasonal programs (activities, schedules, dates of registration, locations, and fees) in a thorough, timely, and attractive form. Many residents hang or tack such brochures next to their telephones for ready reference. Some communities use brochures to include general information about public offices and services, including the names and telephone numbers of city officials and departments, special services (such as senior center clubs, health services, or suburban minibus program schedule), and similar materials.

The department's office should be bright, cheery, and businesslike, with colorful decorations, neat housekeeping, and a ready and responsive receptionist. Dreary surroundings or a rude, uncommunicative staff person can seriously damage citizen goodwill. In general, all recreation and park personnel must stress the department's role in assisting, guiding, and helping people find and enjoy their own recreation rather than seeking to structure all program opportunities. They should constantly stress positive, constructive human relations, healthy and enriching leisure experiences, and the building of close ties with the community.

Finally, the most professionally produced newspaper releases, films, or guided tours will accomplish little if the program they represent is not an effective one. The best public relations medium is the satisfied user. Actions speak louder than words, and the ultimate basis for an effective public relations program is an imaginative, well-attended, and successful variety of activities enjoyed by all age groups and citizens of all backgrounds throughout the year.

EVALUATING THE PUBLIC RELATIONS PROGRAM

Given this, it becomes appropriate to take a hard look at the specific elements in the public relations program to make sure that they are doing the best possible job of promoting a favorable image of the department and gaining community support and involvement. The following questions may be raised in carrying out such an evaluation:

Are there effective and well-produced brochures and pamphlets to inform the public of the program during the course of the year?

Is maximum possible use being made of the public media, such as newspapers, television, and radio?

Is information regarding the program disseminated both regularly and on special occasions to promote or publicize unique situations or events?

Has consideration been given to the use of films, slide talks, speakers, or open houses or tours?

Has the responsibility for public relations been assigned to a competent individual or office within the department, or is it everybody's business?

Are adequate funds provided to carry out this function?

A departmental committee may be established to examine the overall problem of public relations and determine exactly what views the public holds of the recreation and park department. It should make proposals for improving the public relations efforts of the department and should be made responsible for following through on them.

Finally, it is essential that public relations be viewed as a two-way street. It does not just consist of passing out information. It is also a matter of listening to what the community has to say about its offerings and redesigning its program on the basis of this information. Ultimately, the total problem of maintaining an effective community relations program becomes a vital aspect of public relations.

Community Relations

A key responsibility of leisure-service managers is to establish an effective community relations process that has two basic elements: (1) to involve community residents and groups in meaningful ways, particularly in planning, decision making, and volunteer forms of participation and (2) to join with other organizations to coordinate or cosponsor a variety of needed programs and services.

WORKING WITH COMMUNITY GROUPS

Citizen input is an essential part of community relations. This may take several forms. One of the most common is to develop advisory committees that provide information on user needs and preferences or positions on issues facing the leisure-service agency. Public understanding and support for programs may be enhanced as members of the public are educated through involvement in such groups. However, the way in which they are formed and used is critical to their success. Schultz writes:

> No agency can be isolated in the community and remain effective, and professionals realize that advice is valuable to any manager. Advisory groups have served park and recreation agencies well, guiding the planning of programs and mobilizing support at the same time. Those groups serving as permanent committees or temporary ones must be established and involved in an honest and open way. Enough examples exist of poorly used groups and their unfortunate repercussions to advise against using these valuable bodies in less than a candid fashion. An example, perhaps, is when an agency has a referendum planned and enlists the help of ''concerned'' citizens to work for their cause. Their expertise and input are not the focus; rather, they are used as ''workers'' to get the issue passed.[5]

To avoid situations in which advisory groups perform ineffectively, Schultz urges that their functions be clearly delineated and that their members be carefully selected to ensure diversity of representation. Meetings should be carefully planned, and professional staff representatives should not dominate the citizen representatives on the advisory groups with their status or expertise. Schultz suggests:

> Caution those attending to listen far more than they talk. Encourage questions related to points made by individuals. Be sure, however, that the questions are positive, information-seeking questions, rather than judgmental or threat-laden ones. Listening and questioning are two ways of impressing on an advisory group that they are being involved honestly and that opinions offered will be heard and respected.[6]

In addition to such groups, many urban recreation and park departments establish actual councils on three levels: neighborhood, district, and citywide. They have the following makeup and functions.

Neighborhood or community center recreation council

A neighborhood or community center recreation council is usually formed on a neighborhood basis to support the efforts of a large community center and athletic complex. It may consist primarily of members of the center, parents, local businesspeople, and similar individuals. Its function is usually twofold: to assist in planning programs or schedules, usually on an advisory basis, and to help in carrying them out by providing volunteer assistance, raising funds, or providing supplies and equipment.

District recreation and park council or committee

A district recreation and park council or committee is a somewhat comparable type of organization intended to assist in the operation of recreation and park programs within a larger area of the city. Normally it is concerned with total needs and programs in the district. It is composed of representatives of major community organizations, such as PTA's, Boy and Girl Scouts, churches, service clubs, labor organizations, and businesspeople's and homeowners' associations. It is concerned with assisting and guiding overall program and facility development. It may help to raise special funds, promote special programs, or provide political support for the department when needed.

Citywide council or committee

In addition to recreation and park boards or commissions, which are usually based on legal authority and have a formal status within the governmental structure, many different types of citizen groups promote park and recreation programs on the citywide level. These include recreation councils, councils of social agencies, recreation and park associations, conservation clubs, or special committees and task forces.

Whenever possible, each of these types of organizations should be broadly diverse in its representation. All age groups should be represented, including youth and the aged. Various racial, ethnic, and religious groups should be well represented, and other municipal agencies, such as the schools, youth service boards or commissions, or police departments and housing agencies, should be represented. Collectively, such agencies help ensure that government has a clearer vision of the needs of the people and that the process of representative democracy is really at work.

In addition to advisory councils or committees, many public recreation and park agencies make use of citizen input or interact with other community organizations in various ways. These include the following: (1) use of volunteers either as individuals or in groups, such as neighborhood groups or informal organizations concerned with particular recreational activities or needs; (2) cooperation with citizens' groups that assist in the development or maintenance of facilities, sponsoring or cosponsoring ongoing programs, or help organize special events; and (3) varied forms of coordination or cooperation with other public or private agencies.

Role of Volunteers

Leisure-service agencies are increasingly recognizing the importance of volunteers in their programs. The recreation movement was borne on the backs of volunteers shortly after the turn of the century and heavily supported by them through World War II.

Even after the blossoming of the recreation profession in the 1950s and 1960s, with college curricula and advanced degrees and more effective professional organizations, the volunteer remained the prime "foot soldier" of the movement. PTA recreation programs, Little League and Pony League Baseball, Pee Wee Hockey, Pop Warner Football, Biddy Basketball, the scouting movement, and a host of other youth activities, as well as programs for the aged and the disabled, were all based on the availability and eagerness to serve hundreds of thousands of adult volunteer coaches, managers, instructors, chaperones, drivers, fund raisers, and general duty people. Both men and women served in these roles, but often the motivation began with women, who tended to be more concerned with family and neighborhood needs.

Under the impact of the women's liberation movement, a subtle change occurred. Women of all ages were reassured that their skills and services were not merely appendages to the cultural and business communities and that they had in fact valuable and needed talents that were directly convertible to careers, income, and standing. The vast pool of middle-income wives and mothers who had done the telephoning, letter writing, chauffeuring, program leadership, or chaperoning on thousands of volunteer projects began to dry up. Former office workers began polishing up their typing and secretarial skills and studying the want ads. Women with college degrees returned for graduate work, and others went back to complete their degrees, usually with a practical eye to job opportunities. Voluntarism was no longer as respectable as it had been, and with the rapid growth of the working woman population, this source of enthusiastic assistance began to dissolve for many social-service agencies.

Today as the economic crunch has compelled many public agencies to cut back on projects and prune their staffs, there is a new emphasis on the smaller, close to home, low-budget operation that can flourish with volunteer help. Volunteers are again being sought—this time through neighborhood organizations and committees that are eager to improve their communities and fight urban blight. More systematic and thorough supervision is being given to volunteers, along with the opportunity to work on truly meaningful projects. Volunteers are being invited to training sessions and refresher courses for regular staff members. Hours are being tailored to meet the work schedules or lifestyle needs of volunteers, and insurance plans are being developed to protect both the volunteer and the agency from liability suits.

As a consequence, increased numbers of volunteers—both men and women—are today becoming meaningfully involved in the work of community recreation agencies. They are being treated with increased courtesy and dignity and are often assigned a fuller degree of responsibility and autonomy than in the past.

As documentation of the importance of volunteers in recreation and park service today, the following examples shows what they can accomplish:

> A community center operated for seniors by the Department of Parks and Recreation in Eugene, Oregon, uses approximately 200 volunteers a year at a value of some $100,000 in volunteer services.
> During a recent fiscal year, 62,421 volunteers in Baltimore County, Maryland served 77 different recreational programs for a total of 856,664 hours.
> During a recent ten-month period, some 1,670 San Leandro, California volunteers donated almost 19,000 hours of labor to the Recreation Department—all under the coordination of one staff person.[7]

COMMUNITY INVOLVEMENT IN SPORTS PROGRAMS

As indicated earlier, many organizations such as Little League or Pop Warner Football provide extensive sports programs for youth. In addition, in many communities, independent parents' groups or coaches' associations organize and direct team sports competition for children and youth in cooperation with public recreation and park departments. For example, in the northeastern section of Philadelphia, a sprawling area of the city with over 400,000 residents, dozens of adult-run youth organizations conduct leagues and tournaments in the major team sports using city-owned facilities. Involving approximately 10,000 children, the volunteer leaders of these groups provide programs that the public recreation agency simply could not because of limited staff resources. However, the city assists these groups by providing them grants of $1000 to $1500 each, to an annual total of approximately $110,000 for the entire city.[8]

PARK MAINTENANCE BY COMMUNITY GROUPS

In a growing number of cities, neighborhood associations have assumed responsibility for maintaining parks and other outdoor recreation facilities, in some situations on a contractual basis and in others as a purely volunteer arrangement.

In Seattle, for example, a unique plan has been developed that delegates routine park maintenance to neighborhood workers hired by a number of neighborhood associations under contract with the city's Park and Recreation Department. Funding is provided from the city's general fund; however, so economical is the approach that some 30 neighborhood parks throughout Seattle are mowed, swept, and trimmed on a "bottom-line" budget that would ordinarily pay for about four full-time park maintenance personnel. In addition to cutting costs and providing employment in low-income, racially mixed neighborhoods, this plan has helped to stimulate "pride of ownership" attitudes among Seattle residents in the neighborhoods involved and serves as a desirable form of community relations.

In New York City, a group of neighborhood residents have built and maintained a unique recreational sports field known as the Asphalt Green using the site of an abandoned city-owned asphalt-mixing plant. Constructed and maintained almost entirely with private funds—raised through door-to-door campaigns, benefits, and from foundations—the Asphalt Green provides the only grass playing field on Manhattan's East Side, serving dozens of youth sports leagues. The building has also been remodeled and today houses extensive indoor activities.

PROGRAMMING FOR THE DISABLED

In many communities, citizens' groups join together to provide needed recreation programs for special populations, such as the mentally retarded, blind, or physically disabled. These may take the form of continuing programs over a period of time or single events, such as Special Olympics or similar competitions or community celebrations involving special populations.

COMMUNITY DEVELOPMENT TRENDS

Individual and group volunteer efforts represent more than simply a way to compensate for inadequate funds on the part of public leisure-service agencies. Instead, they illustrate the trend in many cities and smaller communities toward citizen participation in the process of government or in taking responsibility for improving living conditions in their own neighborhoods. Tindell points out that such citizen-professional partnerships are part of the overall "community development" movement that has been expanding since the 1960s. She writes:

> Providing opportunities for people to get together to fulfill socialization needs and achieve community goals can have important economic, educational, political, and individual [values] as well. Community development may embody a myriad of processes and activities, depending on the needs of a particular group of people. . . . As part of the individual human growth process, community development can serve as a means of . . . creating social cohesion within individual neighborhoods . . . achieving administrative efficiency and responsiveness in delivery of municipal services; broadening democratic par-

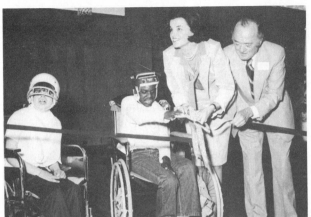

Programs for the disabled. *Above,* San Francisco Mayor Diane Feinstein cuts the ribbon at the opening of a new Recreation Center for the Handicapped facility. *Center,* SOAR (Shared Outdoor Adventure Recreation) offers boating and winter sports for the handicapped in Portland, Ore. *Below,* Nepean, Ont., Canada, sponsors integrated adult fitness activities for disabled and nondisabled participants.

ticipation in urban political parties and voluntary associations; building strategies and action for neighborhood improvement and empowerment; providing an avenue for democratic participation. . .[9]

Coordination and Cooperation among Agencies

On a broader scale, the community relations effort of public recreation and park departments involves another important responsibility: the effort to coordinate all community organizations that provide recreational facilities and programs. As pointed out earlier, school boards in many cities either provide facilities for use by the municipal recreation and park department or offer programs of their own (although this practice has declined steadily). Other agencies providing recreation include libraries and museums, police departments, housing authorities, and youth boards or commissions. In addition, voluntary agencies, service clubs, colleges and universities, religious organizations, and antipoverty councils provide extensive programs in many cities. In some cities there is a considerable duplication and overlap of services in some neighborhoods, whereas in others, there are marked shortages of programs and facilities.

The obvious solution is to develop joint planning and cosponsorship arrangements among all agencies to ensure adequate coverage of the community's needs. In Washington, D.C., for example, the city recreation department not only operates extensive programs using public school facilities but is also responsible for coordinating the use of such facilities by other community groups through a permit system. Instead of resisting such uses, the school system encourages them; many principals believe that neighborhood attitudes are more favorable toward schools that offer recreation programs and that problems of security are thereby minimized.

However, there continue to be numerous problems with respect to interagency cooperation. Park and recreation administrators complain that custodial charges for using school buildings are frequently extremely high. Policies regarding such arrangements vary from school to school, often depending on the attitudes of individual principals. In some cities, park and recreation administrators report that, although they are generally able to make use of schools, high school gymnasiums are often unavailable because of school sports programs during the afternoon.

COOPERATION BETWEEN RECREATION DEPARTMENTS AND SCHOOLS

Since such problems exist, it is helpful to examine in detail certain communities where cooperation between recreation and park departments and school systems has been fully developed. Two examples are Spokane, Wash., and San Diego, Calif.

In Spokane, a coordinating committee was formed consisting of two members of the school board, two members of the park board, the superintendent of schools, and the park director. The primary purpose of this committee is to coordinate the use of park and school facilities by the community and to work together on planning, with the interests of both school and park departments fully considered.

School facilities are planned with the cooperation of the Park Department to provide adequate community centers for recreational use in nonschool hours. Playgrounds are placed immediately adjacent to schools whenever feasible. A systematic interchange of facilities between the two agencies ensures maximum public use at all times.

In San Diego, the city and school district have entered into a contractual agreement for the joint operation of school facilities. School facilities serve as community centers. According to the terms of the contract, the school district makes all playgrounds, classrooms, auditoriums, cafeterias, gymnasiums, storage rooms, and other special facilities available to the municipal recreation department as needed, and recreation facilities are made equally available to the schools.

In a number of Canadian cities, similar policies prevail. The Vancouver, B.C., Board of Parks and Recreation, for example, has developed a number of year-round, full utilization complexes built adjacent to secondary and elementary schools. These include facilities such as indoor swimming pools, community meeting rooms, health and welfare centers, playing fields, teenage lounges, and similar areas.

Hafen points out that many problems occur when two different agencies attempt to use the same facility. When verbal agreements are relied on, what happens when there are later misunderstandings? Who should cover expenses of utilities, custodial expenses, or breakage? What happens when school facilities are not in proper order when classes begin the next morning? He suggests these guidelines to prevent such problems:

> There should be written policies that clearly indicate the responsibilities and rights of each agency. These should be signed by key officials representing both the recreation and park department and the school board.
>
> It is advisable to hold periodic conferences of school officials, recreation administrators and interested cities to assist in maintaining a cooperative relationship. A joint committee should be established as a steering body to regulate, evaluate, and establish policies and to assist in the planning of new facilities.
>
> Community use of school facilities must not interfere with the ongoing school program.
>
> When policies and standards are established, both school and community officials must abide by them. No individual may enforce his own policies in opposition to official agreements.
>
> The process of making facilities available to community groups (public or voluntary) should be as simple as possible and based on a clear order of priority.
>
> Rental fees should be established and publicized, along with other policies dealing with hours that school facilities are available, what types of activities may or may not be conducted in school facilities, regulations regarding smoking and drinking, and assignment of costs of heating, lighting, and maintenance during community use.
>
> Policies should clearly outline the community group's responsibility with respect to cleaning up after use or payment when damage is done to facilities or equipment.[10]

These and similar joint use policies are often spelled out in precise detail in contracts between public recreation and park departments and school boards or in policy manuals of school districts.

An excellent example of such cooperation may be found in Maryland, where the Maryland School Community Centers Program was established to promote school use for recreation and adult education during the early 1970s. Over a 10-year period with state funding assistance, this program resulted in over 140 different categories of classes, workshops, and recreational activities, with more than 10 million individual registrants during the period. Mangum[11] points out that a key factor in the Maryland program's success was that it promoted regular, continuous interchange between school and community recreation agencies, with joint planning and cooperative programming that reduced competitiveness and duplication in many sponsored activities.

COMMUNITY SCHOOLS

Another aspect of such cooperation has involved the community school movement. This is based on the concept of providing educational, recreational, and other social services within a single major facility. Programs are jointly planned and operated, with facilities designed and built expressly for this purpose.

Since the late 1950s, hundreds of cities across the nation have experimented with community education centers. These community schools are open 12 months of the year, 7 days a week in many cases, and 14 hours or more a day if needed. They are designed to blend community life with the academic function and environment of the school. They extend the school's task around the calendar to areas such as youth enrichment, recreation, adult education, and the solving of community problems.

There is a growing conviction among educators, urbanologists, recreation authorities, and other civic leaders that schools cannot remain merely centers of academic instruction. Instead, they must become centers of community life, with a meaningful impact on social problems. By deliberate design, they should deal effectively with issues such as delinquency, illiteracy, school dropouts, poverty, poor health, unemployment, civil rights, neighborhood strife, and family disintegration. In addition to the daytime academic programs, community schools should provide social, cultural, recreational, and vocational experiences for all neighborhood residents.

In some cases departments of education themselves have taken a major responsibility for conducting large-scale programs of recreation and allied social services. A number of major regional centers have been established around the United States with the assistance of the Charles Stewart Mott Foundation to promote the establishment of effective community school programs.

PARTNERSHIP FOR PEOPLE: PORTSMOUTH, VA.

In other cities, community relations approaches have taken different forms. In Portsmouth, Va., for example, the Parks and Recreation Department has encouraged the formation of 13 neighborhood organizations called Recreation and Parks Forums. These groups help to plan and approve the overall municipal budget for recreation and parks and have

> agreed to raise a share of the costs themselves. The forums select improvements to be made to existing locations and are given an "allowance" to spend on making them. They even match city monies to build new playgrounds and purchase new equipment.[12]

Portsmouth's "Partnership for People" has been nationally acclaimed, winning recognition such as the All-American City Award, the National Gold Medal for Excellence in Parks and Recreation Management, and the National Conference of Mayors Volunteer

Program Award. Within a single year, it was able to accomplish the following:

1. A 352% increase in the number of programs offered in the city; athletic teams increased by 51%
2. More than 1000 citizens involved in the forums as members, officers, and committee members; approximately 235,000 volunteer hours donated to recreation services, an average of more than 2 hours for every person living in the city
3. City recreation equipment budget reduced by more than 60%; projects, totaling $110,000, built using matching city and community raised funds

In a later year, the forums raised more than $100,000 to supplement the city's recreation budget, with other organizations, such as civic leagues, athletic associations, and service clubs, chipping in an additional $200,000. Monies are made available to each of the 13 community forums to upgrade existing facilities; more than 200 projects have been selected and initiated during the 2 years since the program began. One of the unique elements of this operation is that rather than have low-income neighborhoods depend on their wealthier neighbors, several of the most distressed areas of Portsmouth became leaders in organizing programs and raising funds.

Cooperation with the Private Sector

Several of the programs described in this chapter are excellent examples of *synergy;* that is, the process under which two or more organizations join forces to accomplish tasks that could not be done through their individual efforts. Increasingly, the leisure-service field is experimenting with varied forms of synergy between public and private or commercial leisure-service agencies.

A key example of this type of arrangement is the concession/lease contract described briefly in Chapter 8. This approach helps provide revenue-producing park facilities without the necessity for operations and maintenance costs and in some cases without capital expenditures. It produces nontax money that can be used to help support other non-revenue-producing recreational facilities or programs, and it can be used on any facility to which fees and charges may be applied. Allen writes:

> In effect, private enterprise leases public park land for between 20 and 25 years during which it constructs, operates, and maintains a specified facility. The lease provides safeguards for both the community and the entrepreneur so that: the facility is an asset to the park in which it is placed; it is properly maintained; it conforms to standards for safety and the handicapped; it provides for equitable lease monies to the community; and it stipulates the disposition of the facility at the end of the lease.[13]

The advantages of such arrangements to both the public and private agencies are obvious. For the public department, a high-quality facility is developed and operated for a period of years, providing a fair financial return to the municipality and becoming its property after a set period, according to a frequently used arrangement. For the commercial organization, there is no need to secure expensive land or meet difficult zoning requirements, and although a lease fee is paid, it often is less than property taxes would be on a strictly private development.

In some cases the public agency builds the shell of a facility and turns it over to the lessee, who is responsible for supplying interior fixtures, fittings, and furnishings. In others, as in the case of a number of large sports stadiums, the municipality puts up the initial sum to build a new facility.

A frequent arrangement is one under which the governmental agency makes a substantial initial investment to stimulate further investment or revenue. For example, in Grand Prairie, Tex., the city passed a $1.6 million bond issue and loaned the money to Lion Country Safari, Inc., to assist that organization in locating a new safari park within the city boundaries. The first revenues received by the park each year from admissions are used to repay the bond debt.

In some cases a major leased facility will be developed from scratch within a large public park. In the city of Fountain Valley, centrally located in Orange County, Calif., a parcel of approximately 120 acres was carved out of a larger regional park and put up for concessionaires' bids to develop and operate a major public golf course under a 30-year lease. At no expense to the county an 18-hole regulation course was developed complete with pro shop, clubhouse, and coffeeshop, at a cost of more than $1 million. The taxpayers of Orange County now receive combined tax and income from this concessionaire totaling $100,000 per year.

It is essential that such public-private contracts contain clear safeguards to the municipality or county government, including clauses dealing with appearance and cost of facility lease length and final ownership, responsibility for utility costs, annual cost of lease, sharing of existing park facilities, sign control, operation standards, use of facility for municipal programs, and similar elements.

OTHER EXAMPLES OF SYNERGY

Numerous other illustrations of synergy between different types of leisure-service agencies may be cited.

In the therapeutic recreation field, for example, Riveredge Hospital, a private psychiatric hospital in Forest Park, Ill., has developed a shared services program with the West Suburban Special Recreation Association (WSSRA), a jointly sponsored program of several suburban communities. Beginning in an effort to better serve the hospital's patients in their return to the community, both agencies committed themselves to developing better linkages between community-based programs and clinical treatment centers. The shared services program included several elements: (1) use of varied community facilities for hospital-sponsored programs and vice versa; (2) patients' participating in WSSRA programs; (3) new discharge options, in which Riveredge patients nearing discharge participated in community programs as volunteer recreation aides; and (4) post-discharge integration of patients into community programs.[14]

Armed forces recreation programs provide excellent examples of facilities sharing. To illustrate, Seymour Johnson Air Force Base near Goldsboro, N.C., has developed synergetic relationships with many community, educational, social-service, and professional organizations in its area. Fig. 12-1 demonstrates the interchange of facilities, programs, services, and personnel centering around the base and resulting in a considerable savings for all agencies concerned.[15]

	Seymour Johnson AFB		Community, state, private agencies	
	Provides	Uses	Provides	Uses
Pools	●	●	Seyboro Swim Team	Seyboro Swim Team
Golf course	●			High school
Ball fields	●			Junior high school
Gyms		●	Junior high school	
Bleachers	●			Goldsboro P & R Dept.
Chairs		●	Goldsboro P & R Dept.	
Toy repair	●			Salvation Army
Water safety		●	Red Cross	
Entertainment	●			Senior citizens
Nature trails	●			Boy Scouts
Interns		●	Colleges and universities	
Hospital	●			Special Olympics
Hobby shop	●			Wayne Community College
Classes and seminars		●	Wayne Community College	
Big Brothers/Big Sisters	●			Elementary schools
Theater arts			Community Arts Council	
Running track		●	Junior high school	
Recreation center	●			N.C. Recreation and Park Society
Volunteers in education	●			Local School System Society

FIG. 12-1   Examples of cooperation between community and Armed Forces. (From Moler, S.H.: Parks and Recreation, June 1983, p. 35.)

Similarly, numerous examples may be cited of the joint use and fiscal support of recreational programs and facilities by municipal recreation and park authorities and voluntary community agencies, such as the YMCA, YWCA, or Boys or Girls Clubs. In Peterborough, Ont., Canada, for example, the municipal government gave substantial funding to the Peterborough YMCA to support capital additions and building improvements. The facility was then leased to the city for 25 years, with the agreement that the YMCA would operate it, with considerable joint programming and improved access to the YMCA for all community residents.

Summary

This chapter provides guidelines for the conduct of public relations operations and gives numerous examples of trends in community relations activities. Its message throughout is that a fragmented leisure-service field is not functional today. Instead, agencies of all types must coordinate their efforts and cooperate in identifying and meeting public needs for constructive recreation programming.

Most of the examples cited in the chapter deal with public recreation and park departments. However, it is obvious that voluntary, private, commercial, and other types of leisure-service organizations *must* promote their programs effectively if they are to be successful. Indeed, for many types of agencies, such as major companies, recreation itself serves as a useful medium of public relations by providing or subsidizing programs under leadership for various community groups. It should be a key responsibility of managers, who are in a position to see the big picture, to promote such concepts and initiate policies that will encourage their staff members to develop innovative practices in public and community relations.

STUDY QUESTIONS

1. Plan a major recreational event for a public or voluntary agency, such as a communitywide celebration. Outline a public relations campaign designed to promote it, including specific examples of television spot announcements, news releases, or other "action" forms of promotion.

2. Develop a movie script designed to present a leisure-service agency or program in a favorable light and educate its various publics about it. Indicate its purposes, major content areas, and strategy for having it produced. Finally, prepare several sample sections of the script, including both the scenes that will be shot or included, and dialog or commentary.

3. Analyze the community relations needs of an armed forces base, a voluntary agency, or similar leisure-service organization. Then identify a set of strategies for meeting these needs through specific projects involving joint planning, interchange of facilities or staff, or similar synergetic activities between this agency and other community-based organizations.

Case 15   *Sexual Abuse of Children: A Critical Concern*

YOU ARE MARGARET EVANS, owner-director of a privately operated day camp program. In addition to your adult professional staff, which functions year-round, you hire a number of high school juniors and seniors for expanded programming during the summer months.

You have just heard from the chief of police that some parents have accused your staff members of sexually abusing their children. Rumors are flying, and a number of parents have also called you angrily, threatening to withdraw their children. The camp is on the brink of disaster.

You go to the police station, where several parents are meeting with the chief. It turns out that one assistant counselor, a high school junior male student, is the focus of all the charges. It is claimed that he made physical overtures to a 10-year-old girl camper while on an overnight camping trip. The police have questioned him and are conferring with the district attorney's office about whether charges should be filed.

Questions for Class Discussion and Analysis

1. In light of this emergency, which is the only such episode in the 15 years of the camp's existence, what would be your best action from a public relations point of view?
2. Your staff manual explicitly states that counselors will be fired for drinking or drug use on the job and contains rules against counselors driving alone with children in their cars. However, there is no direct statement regarding sexual abuse of children, since such a problem had never occurred. How should you deal with this problem in the future?
3. Examining your hiring and supervisory practices, is there anything you could have done to prevent this incident from occurring or to nip it in the bud before it became a serious problem?

Case 16   *Captain Fuller Takes a Hard Line*

YOU ARE MARIA GONZALEZ, civilian recreation director at a naval air station close to a small coastal community, Port Jeffries, with a population of about 7500.

While Port Jeffries has a few small parks and outdoor recreation areas, it has no indoor recreation facilities or organized leisure programs. You have therefore interchanged the use of facilities with them; they use your swimming pools, gymnasium, and crafts shops, and you use their sports fields for your intramural programs. You also have welcomed a local Catholic Youth Organization (CYO) to participate in some of your activities for children and youth; several dependents of personnel on your base belong to the CYO, and this seemed like a good thing to do.

A new base commander has taken over, Captain Don Fuller. He is determined to run a tight ship at the naval air station and cut costs, doing away with all extraneous programs and services. As part of this policy, he has asked you to set up a system

Continued.

Captain Fuller Takes a Hard Line

of fees, under which all outside groups would be required to pay to use the base facilities. After conferring with Port Jeffries officials and the director of the CYO, you report to Captain Fuller that they would be unable to pay the fees and could no longer use the base facilities. If they were then barred, probably they would no longer let the base's sports programs use their facilities or welcome them to any of their activities.

Captain Fuller is not upset by this. He feels that the air station will have a more efficient and economical recreation program without "outsiders" involved. However, you know that general policy in the armed forces is to encourage cooperative relationships with community residents and organizations.

Questions for Class Discussion and Analysis

1. How can you make your case more strongly to Captain Fuller? If you challenge him or try to get input from "higher ups" in the system, will you risk your own security as a civilian employee?
2. Is there any constructive way you can use community people in this process? From a "dollars and cents" perspective, what is your strongest argument? Develop a plan to deal with the problem.

REFERENCES

1. Life. Be In It: A Merchandising Natural, *Parks and Recreation,* Nov. 1983, p. 32.
2. Heritage Conservation and Recreation Service: *Private Sector Involvement Workbook,* Washington, D.C., Oct. 1979, U.S. Department of Interior, p. 6.
3. Scherer, Daniel J.: "Establishing Local Press Relations," *Parks and Recreation,* Oct. 1967, p. 36.
4. Feigley, David A.: "Public Relations Program for a Shopping Mall," *Journal of Physical Education and Recreation,* Jan. 1980, p. 28.
5. Schultz, Joe: "The Use and Misuse of Advisory Committees," *Parks and Recreation,* Jan. 1983, p. 64.
6. *Ibid.,* p. 65.
7. Heritage Conservation and Recreation Service: *Volunteer Handbook,* Washington D.C., 1978, U.S. Department of Interior, p. i.
8. Cooke, Russell: "Sports Clubs: When They Play, Nobody Loses," *Philadelphia Inquirer,* Feb. 13, 1983, p. 41.
9. Tindell, Jane: "Expanding Citizen-Professional Partnerships: Grass Roots Community Development of Leisure Opportunity," *Journal of Park and Recreation Administration,* Jan. 1984, p. 65.
10. Hafen, William J.: "Written Guidelines to Clarify a Dual Role," in *Leisure Today: Selected Readings,* Washington, D.C., 1975, American Association for Leisure and Recreation.
11. Mangum, Barry D.: "Cooperation at Work in Maryland," *Parks and Recreation,* Sept. 1981, p. 68.
12. Greiner, James: "A 'Proposition 13' That Works *for* Recreation," *Parks and Recreation,* June 1979, pp. 29-30, 57.
13. Allen, Stewart E.: "Public-Private Cooperation," *Parks and Recreation,* July 1980, p. 44.
14. Laudick, Bonnie, McGovern, John, and Cosgrove, Susan: "Linking the Hospital and the Local Recreation Agency," *Parks and Recreation,* April 1982, pp. 44-45, 67.
15. Moler, Stephen H.: "Military and Civilian Cooperation—A Case Study," *Parks and Recreation,* June 1983, p. 35.

CHAPTER 13

Once the piece of flammable foam rubber was ignited, the fire spread quickly. Within a few moments, it had shot up a wall and across the ceiling. The smoke went everywhere— thick, black smoke . . . and was aided by four fan units that ventilated it through the Haunted Castle with alarming and ultimately fatal speed. The horrible panic was played out without two safety items that many people would have assumed were there: smoke detectors and fire sprinklers.

When the May 11 fire ended inside the Haunted Castle of the amusement park and firefighters dug through the rubble and charred wood, they found something they had never expected to find—the bodies of eight teenagers who . . . had been unable to escape. The firefighters were so shocked that they first mistook the bodies for fallen mannequins.[1]

Risk Management and Security Control

A sturdy 7-year-old is climbing high on a jungle gym in a neighborhood playground. As she reaches out to the rung above, her hand slips. She falls head first, hitting the blacktop below with a sickening thud. Within moments, the shrill siren of an ambulance is heard, racing toward the playground.

A human tragedy? Yes, and also a constant managerial concern for recreation and park practitioners. The risk of injury and the possibility of negligence suits pose a threat for leisure-service managers in agencies of every sort. This chapter is concerned with accident prevention and emergency procedures, together with the need to maintain security controls that will prevent vandalism or other illegal activity in recreation and park settings.

Need for Risk Management

The need for effective risk management has become evident to leisure-service managers in various settings. As more and more people have visited large national or state parks, forests, and recreation areas, the risk of injury or death from environmental hazards has grown greatly. Falls off cliffs or from horseback, bites from poisonous snakes or attacks from other dangerous animals, exposure to boiling springs or similar hazardous attractions, deaths from freezing, heatstroke, or similar dangers must be guarded against. Controls that will protect participants from their own ignorance of the natural environment or from behavior that *invites* injury or death, such as unsafe boating practices, must be instituted.

In the urban setting, accident prevention and the development of effective safety practices are equally important. Poorly maintained or dangerous equipment in parks, playgrounds, or athletic complexes, as well as inadequately supervised activities, may lead to serious injury or death. Activities such as the use of playground equipment, swimming, archery, riflery, skateboarding, and team sports have this potential. Even in community center buildings, unsupervised play may lead to serious injury. Amusement parks have recently become a special area of concern, since a number of serious accidents have occurred in such settings.

Both to protect participants and staff members and to minimize the risk of lawsuits, which are becoming increasingly common and costly today, recreation and park managers must have well-organized programs of risk management and accident prevention, as well as appropriate follow-up procedures to be carried out when injuries occur.

A second important concern, which also deals with the protection of participants and staff, is vandalism prevention and law enforcement. Vandalism is commonly thought of as the deliberate damaging or theft of buildings, equipment, supplies, or other physical aspects of the facility. However, it also refers to any sort of antisocial behavior in parks and other recreation settings, including theft, assault, arson, or other forms of negative or destructive behavior. This may range from juvenile gangs extorting money from other children or deliberately setting park structures on fire to organized looters stealing from automobiles in wilderness camping grounds. Park and recreation managers have found it necessary to develop more sophisticated approaches to educating the public in appropriate environmental values, as well as guarding against criminal acts through strong law enforcement measures.

Scope of Physical Risk in Outdoor Recreation

In 1978, 190 visitor fatalities and 2483 visitor injuries occurred within the National Park System. Measured against the 283 million visitors recorded in the same year, this amounts to an accident frequency rate of 0.067, translating to one fatality per 1.5 million visitors. In the same year, 1505 National Park Service employees were injured, with a total cost to the government (including workers' compensation, pay continuation, replacement of damaged equipment or property, and tort claims) of about $5 million.[2]

More than 1 million injuries a year occur in high school and college sports programs. According to the U.S. Consumer Product Safety Commission, close to 1 million injuries each year are related to public playground equipment. In a recent year an estimated 93,000 emergency room visits to hospitals occurred.[3] Other statistics on drownings in pools and similar accidents underline the need to develop effective risk management and accident prevention programs in recreation settings.

REASONS FOR THE ACCIDENT RATE

One important reason for the increase in serious injuries in outdoor recreation is the much greater volume of park visitors and outdoor recreation involvement. Blauvelt writes with special reference to the National Park System:

> In the early days of the National Park System, the environment was relatively slow-paced with the typical park visitor coming to sightsee and to enjoy the beauty and tranquility of the park resources.
>
> However, today, because of the increase of leisure time and the increasing accessibility of most park locations, parks are undergoing a future shock syndrome. Items such as high-velocity speedboats, motorized water skis, hang gliders, trail bikes, motorcycles, snowmobiles, remote-controlled model airplanes, and recreational vehicles—all of which utilize technological advancements—have increased accidents and incidents in parks significantly.[4]

A clear picture of the nature of accidents and their causes is essential. An analysis of the frequency and severity of accidents for specific parks would take into account factors such as (1) regional and park-specific differences based on the type of park management philosophy dictated by enabling legislation, (2) the number of people using the park, and (3) the types of activities engaged in by the using public. To develop standards for determining whether accident rates are within "acceptable" levels (recognizing that a certain number of accidents will inevitably occur because of natural hazards and the nature of activity), Davis[5] recommends psychological studies of user attitudes and monitoring of accident patterns in different types of park settings to develop a normative picture of accidents and their causes.

Developing Risk Management Plans

Simply developing safety procedures or inspecting equipment is not sufficient. Instead, Nilson and Edginton argue that a comprehensive risk management plan that systematically attacks each level of the problem is essential. They define risk management as "a management tool that is directed toward reducing or preventing financial loss resulting from handling risks associated with operation of a park and recreation department."[6]

Such losses may include loss of property through fire, vandalism, theft, or natural disasters; claims from persons injured as a result of presumed negligence of the leisure-service agency; costs associated with medical or indemnity payments for injured employees through worker compensation; or reduced public or membership confidence and a damaged image because of avoidable accidents. The potential loss must include the total impact of a serious injury on victims and their families.

Nilson and Edginton[7] suggest a model of the risk management process, which involves five stages: (1) identifying *sources of potential risk,* such as programs, facilities, leadership or supervisory practices, or participant behavior; (2) identifying actual *risk occurrences* and agency policies for handling them through records, interviews, and questionnaires; (3) evaluating the *probability of accidents* occurring in given programs or sites and their probable degree of severity; (4) determining appropriate *methods of handling risks* by taking steps to avoid them entirely, or reduce or transfer liability for them; and (5) developing *risk control processes* through educational programs, safer work or program procedures, better supervision and inspection, and similar activities.

Ewert[8] describes risk management plans as involving an initial determination of the degree of possible risk, the decision to proceed with or terminate a hazardous program activity, and the development of appropriate ways of modifying or controlling an activity to reduce risk levels.

Accident Prevention and Control Procedures

In practical terms, five specific guidelines are essential to the reduction of accidents and the management of risks in any recreation setting. A discussion of each follows.

SYSTEMATIC REPORTING AND RECORD KEEPING

As already indicated, records are necessary to maintain an accurate picture of trends in accident locations or "trouble spots" and their causes. Frequencies that go beyond normal or predictable accident rates will become evident and call for corrective action. Furthermore, if control techniques are effective in reducing incidents, record keeping will reveal such improvements.

It should be noted that, while this is a logical process, it cannot be totally effective in preventing a ''freak'' accident (one that may occur extremely rarely and thus have no record of frequency of occurrence, and yet when it occurs is devastating in its effects). For example, the capsize of a heavily overloaded fishing boat in a storm with the resultant loss of many lives may happen very infrequently and thus not appear in systematic reporting records. Yet, extreme care must be taken to prevent such accidents.

FACILITIES INSPECTION AND HAZARD ABATEMENT

In a playground setting, facilities inspection would include all equipment, such as slides and swings or climbing equipment, to ensure that it is in good working condition and not hazardous in any way. In a park setting it might involve all areas imposing special risks. Speed limit signs, rock slide warnings, barriers, thin ice warnings, or similar prohibitions should be posted to protect participants against natural hazards. In urban parks and recreation facilities, architectural features such as walks, steps, buildings, and other structures must be inspected regularly. Poor visibility, inadequate barriers or walls, accessible high-voltage transmission lines, inadequate storage facilities for flammable liquids, low clearance, blocked exits, or poorly marked emergency circulation routes are examples of problems that must be identified and corrected.

A classic example of inadequate inspection is the major fire that occurred in the Haunted Castle of a crowded New Jersey amusement park in May 1984, in which eight teenagers were killed. According to newspaper accounts, a foam rubber ''crash pad'' attached to a wall caught fire when a youngster lit a cigarette lighter to see where he was in the almost totally darkened facility (a strobe light that provided partial illumination was not working).[9] The lack of smoke detectors, sprinklers, alarm signals, or other safety measures is believed to have contributed to the tragedy. If the Haunted Castle had been classified as a permanent structure, it could not have passed safety code inspections. However, because it consisted of a series of trailers, it was not required by township authorities to undergo such inspection.

PARTICIPANT SAFETY PROCEDURES

There should be a regular, consistent approach to providing all participants with an understanding of the inherent risks in outdoor recreation participation, whether active or passive. They must be helped to understand the nature of the risks that are involved, unsafe acts and their consequences, and hazards to be avoided. This can be done through posted rules, briefing sessions held in campgrounds, regular supervision and warning by rangers, or similar methods. Strict policies for boating practices, for example, should be enacted and enforced.

In playgrounds or other urban recreation settings, leaders and supervisors should consistently teach safety awareness and should reinforce this with thorough supervision and enforcement of rules.

STAFF TRAINING AND GOAL SETTING

Risk management can be effective only if all staff members are aware of it, familiar with important safety and accident prevention principles, and committed to maintaining a safe environment and program. This can best be done if safety and accident prevention are made important items in staff orientation and training and if they are reinforced in meetings, evaluations, and other management procedures.

Staff members should be involved in setting safety goals and objectives, developing reporting and recording systems, and protecting both the public and themselves. It should be noted that employees may run a higher risk of injury than visitors because they are in the recreation setting on a full-time basis and because they must become involved in emergency or lifesaving procedures, such as fire fighting or rescue operations.

EMERGENCY PROCEDURES

First aid, accident, and other emergency procedures should be clearly laid out and known to all employees. In community centers, fire alarm procedures and building evacuation should be practiced at regular intervals. On playgrounds and in other outdoor recreation areas, there should be precise directions for handling physical injury, sunstroke or heatstroke, drowning, or similar accidents.

In facilities that cover large areas in which the risk of injury is substantial, such as mountain-climbing territory or ski slopes, there should be regular patrol procedures, arrangements to monitor the progress of climbing teams, and the capability for reaching and evacuating the injured in case of avalanches or other emergency situations through the use of casualty sleds or snowmobiles.

In facilities that may hold many participants or spectators, such as theaters, stadiums, dance halls, bowling alleys, or skating rinks, a public-address system to make emergency announcements, an alarm system, telephones to summon assistance, and other means of communication are desirable. Evacuation or escape routes for visitors and employees and access for vehicles such as fire trucks, ambulances, or tow trucks should also be kept clear.

Staff members should be given instructions regarding appropriate public relations procedures after an accident or other emergency situation. After the New Jersey Haunted House fire, the county prosecutor and reporters said they had been ''abused, stonewalled and misled'' by the amusement park's owners, operators, and representatives. According to newspaper accounts, the park reopened in a ''carnival atmosphere'' the day after the fire.[10] Apparently no effort was made to communicate helpfully with the families or provide solace for them. Clearly, emergency procedures in any leisure-service agency should include consideration of appropriate public relations policies after serious accidents or injuries.

First aid supplies and arrangements for transportation should be available in all settings. Today, many departments include cardiopulmonary resuscitation (CPR) and Heimlich maneuver training as part of emergency procedures or first aid training courses. Christiansen concludes that park and recreational facilities planners and managers

> must incorporate these safety and emergency provisions in their physical and administrative plans for the welfare of recreationists and employees in park areas. These considerations are both preventive and reactive. While hazard control and safety planning attempt to pre-

vent accidents, contingency support facilities, procedures and personnel training for emergency situations are also essential parts of a park plan.[11]

Specific Areas of Safety Concern

Several specific areas of recreational participation are now examined. The first of these involves water safety.

WATER SAFETY

With more deaths attributable to drowning than any other cause in major outdoor recreation areas, a high priority must be placed on water safety knowledge and behavior. The National Park Service has assigned staff members to appear on radio and television and visit schools and community organizations to present vital water safety messages. Warnings and information are included in park brochures, and dramatic posters are located in numerous park sites. Some parks have experimented with prohibiting the sale and consumption of alcoholic beverages within their boundaries, since liquor and drugs are major contributing factors in many cases of drowning.

Organizations such as the U.S. Coast Guard, Power Squadron, and the American Red Cross seek to promote boating safety. They urge recreational boaters, for example, to carry out safe fueling practices, obey the rules of the road, wear flotation gear, carry other needed equipment including compasses and signaling equipment, know distress signals and weather warning signals, and follow guidelines for waterskiing.

Swimming pool management

Of comparable importance in preventing drownings is setting up an effective plan for staffing, maintaining, and monitoring swimming pools. Since personnel at most public swimming pools are college students or teachers working on a part-time or seasonal basis, it is important that they be given a 2-day orientation, during which period each manager and guard should present proof of his or her water safety instructor certification or other required licensing.

Emergency phone numbers and step-by-step procedures should be gone over at this time, and lifeguard procedures and responsibilities should be thoroughly reviewed. Many departments use the orientation period to give CPR training. Other guidelines to maximize safety include (1) keeping rescue equipment on hand, such as ring buoys or long poles; (2) use of polarized sunglasses and umbrellas to reduce glare and eyestrain for lifeguards; (3) practice in changing chlorine tanks and monitoring pool chemical balance; and (4) regular inspections and routine safety procedures that are rigidly enforced.

Dressing rooms or lockers should be kept clean, dry, and in good repair, with all outside areas free of broken glass and litter. Fences should provide a good obstacle against intruders. If necessary, additional supervision or regular patrols will ensure that pools are not being used surreptitiously at night.

Pool managers should regularly watch or check lifeguards to make sure that they are carrying out their duties responsibly. Schedules should be posted for lifeguards, giving exact periods for patrolling the perimeter of the pool, sitting on towers, and taking breaks.

Guidelines for lifeguard selection and training

Lifeguards represent the key element in preventing accidents and in providing rescue and first aid to victims when accidents occur. To avoid being found negligent in the case of a drowning or other serious accident, all recreation agencies with pools must employ qualified aquatic staffs. However, given the variable quality of instruction in lifesaving and lifeguarding, standard certificates of course completion, even from recognized national organizations, do not guarantee that potential pool employees are capable lifeguards.

Andres therefore suggests that, although certificates of course completion may be required as a prerequisite to employment, performance testing should also be used. In addition, it is desirable for lifeguards to hold valid certificates in first aid and CPR.

Once lifeguards have been hired, on-the-job training should be carried out.

> Each guard must be taught to distinguish between distress and drowning situations as well as where they most frequently occur and how they may be prevented. In addition, emergency procedures, rules, special equipment and first aid techniques must be overlearned so that each member of the lifeguarding team can work efficiently and effectively.[12]

Up-to-date emergency procedures for handling suspected spinal cord injuries (which may arise from diving accidents) and the use of oxygen delivery resuscitation equipment should be presented. Continual in-service training should ensure that essential job-related skills are practiced and that all needed equipment is readily accessible and in good working order. Finally, rules of conduct for swimming patrons should be conspicuously posted and enforced consistently, both to prevent accidents and to maintain a sanitary and healthy pool environment.

Thanks to effective pool supervision by qualified lifeguards and more widespread swimming instruction, drownings have declined from 10.2 per 100,000 in 1900 to 3.4 per 100,000 today. Only 10% of drownings occur in pools owned and operated by states, counties, municipalities, schools, colleges, and voluntary groups, which collectively serve the largest number of swimmers.

Supervision of beaches

Supervising surf beaches is a more complex and difficult assignment because of the scope of responsibility and the natural environment in which the lifeguard must operate. D'Arnall[13] describes the great number of variables that affect surf lifeguarding and suggests that, before a marine lifeguard supervisor can even begin to set policies and outline procedures for operating any surf beach area, the beach area under consideration must be thoroughly analyzed, including the following factors: (1) nature and magnitude of environmental hazards, (2) extent of beach usage, (3) seasonal and year-round weather conditions, (4) types of aquatic activities engaged in by the public, and (5) financial capability of the operating agency.

Based on this information, it is possible to make decisions about equipment and facility needs, personnel assignments, and training programs. Generally, marine safety authorities agree that training a swimmer to be a lifeguard is more feasible than training a lifeguard to be a swimmer. D'Arnall points out that, unlike pool lifeguards, surf lifeguards must be able to swim long distances at a good rate of speed under adverse surf or weather conditions.

A frequent practice in employing surf lifeguards is to give applicants a physical qualification examination to select those with acceptable swimming ability. Candidates passing this hurdle are then given a comprehensive basic training program

> designed to educate them in all phases of a surf lifeguard job, ranging from basic rescue procedure and medical aid to communications and special operating procedures. Following the training program, all applicants must participate in an oral board examination during which lifeguard supervisors and personnel experts determine each applicant's motivation, attitude, and general fitness for service.[14]

PLAYGROUND SAFETY

As previously indicated, a major area of concern to recreation and park managers is accident prevention in children's playgrounds. A key factor is the type of playground equipment used, since poorly designed, located, or maintained equipment frequently is the cause of serious injuries. Certain pieces of equipment are generally viewed as more risky; a recent 3-year study of playground equipment by the British Standards Institution revealed that falling from or being hit by swings accounted for 30% of playground injuries; jungle gyms were responsible for 26%; and slides were associated with 20%.[15]

Numerous professional or safety-related organizations have developed guidelines for the design of playground equipment to minimize such risks. The British study, for example, developed a design code intended to minimize potential hazards dealing with materials and components, such as exposed surfaces, protective rails, and clearances between parts, particularly swinging, rocking, and rotating items.

Particularly when children with physical or emotional disabilities use a playground, it is important that careful leadership be used to ensure that they have the most favorable possible learning experience and that accidents be prevented.

Examples of guidelines for playground safety appear in the boxes on pp. 341 and 342. Fig. 13-1 provides a sample accident report form.

OTHER AREAS OF SAFETY CONCERN

Many other specialized areas of concern regarding safety and accident prevention might be cited. Three such examples are briefly cited: (1) those dealing with a particular type of facility (such as amusement parks), (2) those dealing with a type of activity (such as skateboarding), and (3) those dealing with natural hazards (such as lightning and heatstroke).

Amusement parks

Thrill seekers by the millions visit amusement parks for the express purpose of being terrified by dangerous rides. *U.S. News and World Report* commented that in the mid-1980s at the 100th anniversary of the modern roller coaster, people were flocking to

GUIDELINES FOR PLAYGROUND SAFETY

General Safety

1. Safety is a basic consideration in playground and pool operation and the well-managed recreation facility is a safe place for people to play.
2. Remember that *all* accidents have a cause and might have been prevented. Prevention of accidents is one of the basic rules of first aid training.
3. Be sure that you are a safety-conscious person yourself and that you attempt to instill this attitude in others through your safety program.
4. All staff members at pools or playgrounds should know the procedure for handling cases involving serious accidents or injuries. Discussion of these procedures should take place in one of your first staff meetings.
5. Each playground and pool should have a listing of emergency numbers near their telephone, if they have one. Included should be the Fire and Police Departments and the Central Office. Playgrounds that do not have telephones should have access to two or more telephones within the immediate neighborhood.
6. Know the location of your first aid kit and keep it well stocked. Brush up on your first aid methods.
7. Be sure that all staff members are aware of the areas on a park or playground where accidents generally occur. (Please check list on Guides to Safety to help your program of safety.)

Playground Safety

1. Check apparatus and equipment daily. If it is not in working condition or is dangerous, place it OUT-OF-ORDER and notify the office immediately.
2. Teach children the correct methods of using the apparatus and insist that they be followed.
3. Prepare, post and enforce simple rules of safety for your playground.
4. Know where accidents are liable to happen and be alert to these areas.
5. Enforce ordinances involving dogs and the riding of bicycles on the playground to the best of your ability.
6. Motor scooters and other types of motorized vehicles are not allowed on parks or playgrounds. Contact police at once if this occurs.

Slides

1. Do not permit crawling or running up slides.
2. Do not allow children to stand up when sliding down.
3. Do not permit children to slide down backwards.
4. Do not permit hanging of feet over sides when sliding.
5. Caution children to observe that all persons are clear of the chute before they slide.
6. Do not permit wrestling on the ladder. See that they wait their turn.
7. Generally do not allow children over 12 years of age to use slides.

Continued.

GUIDELINES FOR PLAYGROUND SAFETY—*continued*

Seesaws

1. Do not allow children to jump or slide off while another person is up in the air on the other end.
2. Do not permit bumping seesaws on the ground.
3. Caution children to keep their feet from under the board at all times.
4. Do not permit standing on seesaws.

Swings

1. Do not allow more than one person on a swing at a time.
2. See that persons use swings that are for their size.
3. Caution children about standing in swings and do not allow jumping from swings.
4. Caution children about running in front of swings.
5. Do not allow children to run under swings when they are pushing another person.
6. Do not permit children to climb on swings.

Climbing Apparatus

1. Do not allow children to stand on top of any climbing equipment.
2. Caution children about holding onto horizontal ladders, chinning bars and jungle gyms with both hands.
3. Do not allow overcrowding.
4. Be sure that persons who are waiting, stand far enough away so that they will not be struck by the feet of a swinging child.
5. Do not allow pushing, shoving, or dangerous stunts.

From *Recreation Leader's Manual,* Oklahoma City, Okla., Department of Parks and Recreation.

"monster roller coasters with such names as the Beast, Colossus, King Cobra, the Cyclone and Mister Twister. Some traverse as much as 4 miles of steep, curving, looping track at speeds up to 70 miles per hour."[16]

Citing a number of cases of fatal accidents, in which people were hurled from bobsleds or roller coasters or gondola cars broke loose, the magazine points out that only 25 states have laws regulating the safety of amusement parks. Ride owners in most states are not required to have a special license and often operate with limited insurance coverage. The problems are of three types: (1) park visitors try to show off for their friends, change cars, walk along tracks, or dismount too quickly; (2) operators lock safety devices too hastily, thereby hitting riders on the hand or head; and (3) equipment malfunctions occur. Often local and state authorities are concerned about such problems but hesitate to crack down on amusement parks, which pay high taxes.

Skateboard safety

Skateboarding has become a popular and accessible activity, with elements similar to both skiing and surfing and yet far less expensive for participants of various ages.

Public Recreation Commission
2 S.E. Eighth Street
Evansville, Indiana

Accident report form

1. Name_____Address_____ _____
2. Location_____Sex: M_____; F_____; Age_____
3. Time accident occurred: Hour_____a.m.;_____p.m.;_____Date_____
4. Place of accident: Building_____Playground_____Beach_____
   Swimming pool_____Camp_____Elsewhere_____
5. Witnesses: Name_____ Address_____
                Name_____ Address_____
                Name_____ Address_____

Nature of injury   Description of accident
6. Abrasion _____   Bruise _____   How did accident happen? What was patron doing? Where was
   Amputation_____ Burn _____   patron? List specifically unsafe acts and unsafe conditions existing.
   Laceration _____ Cut _____   Specify any tool apparatus, equipment involved. Give your opinion
   Concussion _____ Sprain_____   as to cause of accident.
   Fracture _____
   Scratches _____   _____
   Puncture _____   _____
   Other (specify)_____   _____
Part of Body Injured   _____
   Ankle _____   Face _____   _____
   Finger_____   Foot _____   _____
   Scalp _____   Nose _____   _____
   Tooth _____   Leg _____   _____
   Wrist _____   Knee _____   _____
   Elbow_____   Eye _____   _____
   Back _____   Arm _____   _____
   Hand _____   Other_____   _____
7. Leader in charge when accident occurred_____
                                              (enter name)

Immediate action taken
8. First aid treatment   _____   By (name)_____
   Sent home   _____   By (name)_____
   Taken to hospital   _____   By (name)_____
   Contact emergency vehicle_____   By (name)_____
   Were parents notified: Yes____No_____
Location   Remarks
9. Athletic field_____ Game room_____   What recommendations do you have for preventing other
   Auditorium _____   Home ec _____   accidents of this type?
   Locker room_____   Pool _____   _____
   Playground _____   Beach _____   _____
   Craft room _____   Camp _____   _____
   Gymnasium _____   Stairs _____   _____
   Corridor _____   Showers _____   _____
                          Other _____   _____

This report must be sent to office within 24 hours after accident.

Signed: Director_____

       Leader _____

FIG. 13-1   Accident report form, Public Recreation Commission, Evansville, Ind.

There are believed to be more than 20 million skateboarders in the United States today, and the annual manufacture of skateboards has been estimated to be a $1 billion business annually, with numerous commercial and some public facilities specially designed for this activity. Skateboarding is a relatively high-risk activity. In a recent year an estimated 106,000 victims sought treatment in hospital emergency rooms because of skateboarding accidents, and skateboarding was the cause of 25 deaths between 1975 and 1977.

In many areas skateboarders have come into conflict with pedestrians, cars, bicycles, and the police, with riders on downtown sidewalks or streets occasionally being cited for "reckless skateboarding." Some communities have banned skateboarding in specific locations, and others prohibit it entirely.

In recognition of the popularity of the activity, a substantial number of skateboard parks have been developed by commercial or public agencies in recent years. A skateboard park, writes Della-Giustina, is a

> winding course of curved banks and straight-aways that is supervised to keep young skateboarders away from dangerous hillside streets, highbanked concrete river beds, parking lots, and empty swimming pools.[17]

Even in such settings there is a considerable risk of injury, since skateboards have no braking or steering equipment and must depend solely on body movements by the rider to stop and steer the skateboard; furthermore, one of the challenges of this activity is to do difficult or dangerous stunts. To prevent injuries, parks that are affiliated with the American Skateboard Association require participants to wear knee and elbow pads and helmets. Track monitors are on hand to prevent horseplay or dangerous moves that could endanger the skater or other participants.

Other hazards: lightning and heatstroke

For managers who administer outdoor recreation and park facilities, it is essential to recognize thunderstorms and lightning as important safety hazards. More than 100 lightning fatalities occur each year, with many of these in park settings. Thunderstorms are more frequent in summer than in winter, with 70% of all deaths and injuries from lightning occurring in June, July, and August. Of all lightning deaths reported over the past 20 years in the United States,

> a federal survey found that 26 percent of the victims were in open fields, ballparks or playgrounds. Fifteen percent were people standing under large trees, which is a poor idea in a thunderstorm. Twelve percent were boating, fishing or swimming, five percent were playing golf, and six percent were driving farm tractors or heavy equipment.[18]

Staff members should be made familiar with appropriate safety procedures to protect both themselves and recreation participants from lightning. For example, at the first sound of thunder, swimming pools should be immediately cleared. First aid training should include guidelines on reviving lightning victims, who may not have been struck directly and killed, but who may be in temporary shock and require immediate mouth-to-mouth or cardiopulmonary resuscitation to start their heart and lungs working again. Many victims who appeared dead from lightning have been revived by immediate first aid procedures.

Another weather-related hazard is that of hot weather, which may cause heat exhaustion, cramps, or strokes in both active participants and recreation and park employees. Griffin[15] points out that hot weather, coupled with even moderate work or recreational physical activity, may cause such problems. Among the factors to be considered are (1) *acclimation,* since even healthy and well-conditioned individuals who are suddenly exposed to heat stress may develop abnormally high body temperatures, pounding heart, and other signs of heat intolerance; (2) *surface area–to–weight ratio,* since obese or stocky individuals run a greater risk of succumbing to heatstroke, especially if unacclimated and unfit; (3) *age,* since older individuals are less able to compensate for heat loads; and (4) other factors such as the need to maintain a healthy water and salt balance and to avoid excessive intake of alcohol before exposure to severe heat conditions.

Appropriate measures that will help protect employees or recreation participants include adjusting work schedules and postponing physically demanding but nonessential tasks during extremely hot periods. Managers should try to identify air-conditioned areas near work or recreation sites. Such buildings, which may be public or commercial facilities, should be used in case of emergencies, since it has been shown that recovery from heat stress occurs more rapidly in air-conditioned rest areas.

Prevention of Vandalism and Crime in Recreation Settings

Vandalism and the prevention and control of antisocial behavior represent related aspects of management responsibility, particularly in large recreation and park departments or commercial recreation organizations.

Clearly, damage to buildings, plants, and equipment beyond the normal wear-and-tear of daily operations is a serious problem for many recreation and park agencies. A research team that conducted a major study of vandalism for the city of Boston concluded that it was costly

> not only in dollars spent on maintenance, repair and replacement, but also in terms of lowered staff morale and, perhaps most important of all, in facilities which have been made less attractive to the public.[19]

The deliberate defacement or destruction of property is only part of the problem facing park and facility managers today. Theft, mugging, and other forms of criminal behavior have become increasingly common in recreation and park facilities of every type. Years ago, campers and backpackers felt confident that they could trust their neighbors in the wilderness and could leave their possessions at campsites for long periods of time without risk. Today the situation is quite different; in Yosemite National Park in California,

> groups of what are known as ''car clouters'' have been found moving through crowded campsites and trailheads, seeking loot from campers' tents, cars and recreational vehicles. A few of these criminals, according to some rangers, are traveling from park to park, attracted by what one ranger called ''the real easy pickings.''[20]

In many urban communities, park benches, fountains, lights, and other fixed pieces of equipment are regularly demolished. Park buildings are broken into, ravaged, and not infrequently set on fire. Playgrounds and miniparks are often dominated by alcoholics or drug addicts or by youthful gangs that extort money from other children and frighten away law-abiding would-be park users. Graffiti and broken windows are commonplace.

Perry identifies a number of distinct categories of such antisocial forms of behavior that affect recreation and park agencies:

1. Disorderly or disruptive behavior, often associated with excessive alcohol consumption; inappropriate activities or violation of park rules, including use of illegal drugs
2. Crimes against property, including vandalism directed against buildings, grounds, equipment, and other structures or damage to vehicles, which may include arson
3. Larceny, involving theft of tools, equipment, picnic tables, and similar equipment or burglary, involving break-ins of park offices and administrative buildings
4. Muggings and physical or sexual assaults, including frequent crimes against children

Perry points out that when problems of crime begin to escalate, a "fear syndrome" takes over and "many park users will become discouraged and apprehensive. Families and elderly persons may avoid the parks, allowing a small user segment to dominate. Outdoor areas will then cease to provide service to the general community."[21]

Obviously, recreation and park departments are not the only agencies to suffer from such problems. However, because they tend to operate so many separate, isolated facilities that are difficult to patrol and oversee and that are normally open and available to the public, problems of vandalism and crime prevention are particularly acute for them. Punitive or defensive reactions, such as reliance on security guards, surveillance, or police dogs or demands that the police and courts be harsher on violators who are arrested, rarely succeed in stopping vandalism and park crime.

GUIDELINES FOR IMPROVING SECURITY AND PREVENTING VANDALISM

As the Boston vandalism study suggests, there should be a comprehensive and coordinated plan of attack. This plan has three elements: (1) understanding the problem by gathering full information about vandalism and other antisocial acts, (2) reviewing alternative methods of dealing with the problem, and (3) devising and putting a strategy into action.[22]

Understanding the problem involves gathering as complete a picture as possible of current conditions. Focusing specifically on property-directed vandalism, for example, it would be essential to carry out a systematic observation and inspection of recreation and park settings and review vandalism reports and statistics of facility repair and equipment replacement. In this way an accurate picture of current levels, types, and locations of vandalism could be drawn.

All personnel should be required to file damage reports, using a standardized form that details the nature and extent of the damage, as well as other pertinent information. This encourages maintenance personnel and supervisors to note vandalism immediately and act on it rather than accept it as inevitable. It also should have the effect of speeding up requests for repair, which in turn helps prevent the buildup of minor damage and the creation of an atmosphere in which facilities are more seriously vandalized. Finally, it helps to provide the raw data necessary for a clearer understanding of the problem and its financial costs.

A second stage of analysis is to examine individual cases selectively throughout a recreation and park system. It will involve a review of condition and damage reports, site observations, and interviews with staff members and possibly participants, nearby residents, and community leaders or businesspeople.

A number of specific approaches may be used to prevent or control vandalism, including the following:

1. Planning and design of facilities geared to minimize damage or misuse
2. More efficient and prompter maintenance and repair to prevent damaged structures or equipment from remaining in such condition over a period of time, which tends to encourage additional vandalism
3. Improved staffing and supervision of facilities and fuller programming and scheduling of areas and facilities
4. A positive program of community relations that will develop support and cooperation in preventing vandalism

Many agencies attempt to reach neighborhood youth with educational efforts designed to discover vandalism or enlist their help and that of their parents in protecting facilities. When citizens take a direct responsibility for helping to operate and maintain facilities, and large numbers of residents of all ages are involved in meaningful programs, vandalism is much less likely to occur. For example, the city of Mississauga, Ont., Canada, established a task force on vandalism to determine how to reduce the level of deliberate destruction and related crimes in community facilities. Representatives of numerous organizations developed a report with a series of 14 recommendations, which led to the formation of a special community group called Counter-Act to carry on this fight. Among the recommendations, which were designed to work through the school system, were the following:

1. To sponsor a student awareness program, using available films and other visual aids, to impress on the student body the impact vandalism has on their community
2. To develop an incentive program, in which a special fund would be established to be used for student activities in certain schools, provided that vandalism did not otherwise deplete the available money
3. To hold a student poster contest in elementary schools emphasizing the need to control vandalism
4. To install improved lighting and electronic detection devices in areas heavily damaged by vandals
5. To hold meetings with residents in areas surrounding facilities that were threatened by vandalism, to enlist their support[23]

A local newspaper and shopping mall in Mississauga, in cooperation with the city's Recreation and Park Department and the Counter-Act organization, sponsored major cleanup days in which hundreds of children and adults collected litter in several city parks. Collectively, these efforts heightened public awareness of the problem and had a major impact on the community.

Use of Rangers and Park Police

The overall problem of law enforcement extends beyond the need to prevent deliberate damage to recreation areas and facilities. It involves the need to prevent theft, arson, personal assaults, and other crimes in any recreation setting, from secluded wilderness sites to crowded urban areas.

One of the most active security forces to have developed sophisticated techniques in this area has been the U.S. Park Police, administered by the National Park Service, which provides law enforcement in urban national parks in Washington, D.C., New York City, San Francisco, and many other cities.

> Policing of these areas is accomplished by the use of horse-mounted officers, motorcycles, scooters, helicopters, boats, dogs, and foot patrols. Parks in urban areas require a specially sensitive type of police officer who is able to adapt readily to the needs of the park visitor, and on the other hand, act firmly but with courtesy to those who attempt to violate the law. Officers must easily adapt from dealing with hard-core criminals to assisting people in need.[24]

Officers frequently sponsor Special Olympics programs or work with juvenile authorities and the courts in helping youthful offenders redirect their energies into more socially constructive areas. Well-trained dogs are used by both the U.S. Park Police and their counterparts in Canadian national parks; the Royal Canadian Mounted Police has a professional K-9 division. They are extremely helpful in curbing criminal activity and as part of search and rescue teams.

TWO-WAY RANGER RESPONSIBILITY

In national and state parks, rangers (or their counterparts under other job titles) have a number of functions that extend beyond the prevention and control of criminal activity. Essentially, their task is to protect the natural environment against heedless or deliberate abuse by park visitors and to protect park visitors against the hazards that may exist in wilderness or natural settings. Wade writes:

> Visitors frequently come to wilderness-type areas ignorant of the hazards they might encounter. Too often they are unprepared to deal with even minor emergency situations and they know little about preventing emergencies. They over-estimate their own knowledge, skills, and abilities, and under-estimate the potential effects of nature.[25]

To carry out their work effectively, park law enforcement personnel must tread a delicate line between carefully supervising park visitors and permitting them spontaneity of action and the sense of independence, self-reliance, and discovery that should characterize the outdoor-recreation experience.

For several decades the law enforcement function of park police and rangers was relatively informal in many major federal and state parks. However, as attendance and problems of visitor control increased, the problem of "people management" grew rapidly. Given this situation, many park management authorities have developed extensive and sophisticated training programs in visitor protection and law enforcement. In Illinois, for example, the role of the game warden has changed. Today they are known as "conservation police officers," and must have 14 weeks of training at the department's Law Enforcement School, followed by 9 months as trainees in the field, where they gain skills in enforcing the state Fish and Game Code, the Boat Safety and Registration Act, the Snowmobile Act, and other regulations and laws of the state park system.

Harmon[26] sums up the overall process of park law enforcement, including five key steps. These are:

1. To recruit and train competent personnel experienced in and responsible for various specialized duties
2. To provide organization and training of personnel to deal with varied emergencies and challenges as they may occur—including ongoing in-service training in methods of law enforcement, first aid, and similar functions
3. To promote the safe design and construction of facilities; while law-enforcement personnel are not usually involved in this process, they can contribute helpful information at the planning stage to prevent problems that may occur later
4. To provide a sound public relations and interpretive program, in order to give the park visitor a high-quality experience in the natural environment, improve the public image of the park system, and familiarize visitors with the rationale underlying park regulations and ecologically sound use of the park setting
5. To carry out fair and thorough enforcement of the rules, with emphasis on a positive and pleasant approach to the public, stressing education and helping to build positive attitudes, rather than a punitive or threatening approach

Although the emphasis in this concluding section of the chapter has been on larger national and state park systems and the role of law enforcement personnel in them, many of the same principles also apply in community settings. Vandalism and crime prevention are based on working with people, and sound human relations will help control many of the problems that exist in this area of recreation and park management. Patience, diplomacy, and resourcefulness are keys to success in most such situations.

A new concept of using park rangers has been developed in many cities. Young men and women of high school or college age are recruited on a seasonal or part-time basis and are trained to carry out a number of functions involving interpretation, staffing facilities, overseeing park areas, and providing general control and security, short of actual law enforcement powers. By patrolling wide-ranging outdoor spaces and developing favorable contacts with park users, these young rangers are able to supplement the formal park police or other law enforcement personnel and perform tasks that do not require armed intervention.

Summary

One of the most important functions of leisure-service managers is to ensure that participation in recreation and park facilities and programs is as safe as possible, that natural hazards and program-related accidents are avoided, and that controls over vandalism and other forms of criminal behavior are maintained in the leisure setting.

The logical solution to solving such difficulties is to develop plans for risk management or control of vandalism and crime. The extent and nature of the problem must be assessed, appropriate methods for dealing with it must be selected, and these must be put into action, with careful supervision and systematic evaluation. Policies, procedures, and appropriate assignment of personnel play a role in this effort, along with community relations and educational efforts that get at the roots of the difficulty and help remove its causes.

STUDY QUESTIONS

1. Select a major type of facility that presents a fairly high degree of accident potential, such as a ski center, a sportsman's center (with rifle and pistol ranges and similar elements), or a riding facility. Develop in outline form a risk management plan for this facility, including elements such as an assessment of present practices and accidents, needed policies, and a manual for staff training.

2. Select a single type of outdoor activity with a high risk potential, such as hang gliding, white water canoeing, or similar adventure program focus. Debate the appropriateness of a public or voluntary agency sponsoring outings featuring such an activity.

3. With other students, conduct a survey of vandalism in several nearby cities or towns or county or park district agencies. Prepare and deliver in class a comparative study of the extent and nature of the problem, measures used to prevent or control it, and their apparent degree of success.

Case 17   *Rocky Times With the Rock Festival*

YOU ARE FRED MILLER, the recreation and park director in a small oceanfront community. For the past 8 years, you have sponsored a rock festival each Easter week. Generally, community merchants have favored this, since it brings the area publicity and visiting college students have filled the motels and patronized the restaurants in town.

Increasingly, however, motorcycle gangs have been coming to the festival, and creating problems of drinking, drugs, and fighting with local high school boys. Many of these attending also sleep out on the beach, which creates problems of safety and sanitation. The local Chamber of Commerce is still in favor of continuing the annual rock festival, although the town board is leaning toward discontinuing it.

The police chief feels that his force is too small to supervise the event properly. However, since several members of the force gain substantial income from the overtime hours they put in during the week, he is reluctant to call for an end to the rock festival.

Questions for Class Discussion and Analysis

1. Weighing the pluses and minuses, is this program worth continuing? As recreation and park director, what do you see as the key arguments on each side?
2. Is there any good way to control the misbehavior that has been occurring? What other resources could you draw on to manage the program?

Case 18   *Sports Injuries—Reducing the Risk Factor*
cont'd

YOU ARE SUZANNE BROCK, employee recreation director for a large manufacturing company. In cooperation with the municipal recreation deparment, you have traditionally cosponsored a major youth football program, ending in a well-attended elimination tournament.

This program has always resulted in good publicity and community relations for your company. However, a number of minor injuries have occurred in the past, and this fall two serious injuries resulted in negligence suits.

The problem is that while you are a cosponsor of this program, you have little control over it. Most of the planning and management is done by the municipal recreation department, and the coaching is done by parents. They are fanatically determined to win and have encouraged or permitted certain risky forms of play such as "spearing," as well as excessive drilling on very hot days, occasionally resulting in heat exhaustion.

You do not want to end your company's participation in this program because it is basically worthwhile and provides excellent publicity. However, you cannot afford further risks of expensive liability claims.

Continued.

Case 18 cont'd	*Sports Injuries—Reducing the Risk Factor*

Questions for Class Discussion and Analysis

1. What is inherently weak in your sponsorship role? How could it be strengthened?
2. Draw up a risk management plan to control the youth football program, reduce the possibility of further serious injuries, and provide fuller protection against lawsuits.

REFERENCES

1. Bissinger, H.G.: "Fire's Legacy: Legal Issues and Confusion," *Philadelphia Inquirer,* May 20, 1984, p. 1-A.
2. Doerr, Kay: "Accident Analysis—A Statistical Survey of Park and Recreation Accidents," *Trends,* Winter 1980, p. 27.
3. Gold, Seymour M.: "Risk Management in Public Playgrounds," *Journal of Park and Recreation Administration,* July 1983, p. 2.
4. Spivey, Leroy B.: "National Park Service Approach," *Trends,* Winter 1980, p. 4.
5. Davis, William W.: "Safety/Accident Control Programs in Parks and Recreation," *Trends,* Winter 1980, p. 22.
6. Nilson, Ralph A., and Edginton, Christopher R.: "Risk Management," *Parks and Recreation,* Aug. 1982, p. 34.
7. *Ibid.,* p. 36.
8. Ewert, Alan: "The Decision-Package: A Tool for Risk Management," *Parks and Recreation,* April 1982, pp. 39-41.
9. Bissinger, *op. cit.,* p. 26-A.
10. Weiner, Tim: "In the Fire's Aftermath: A Dearth of Information," *Philadelphia Inquirer,* May 20, 1984, p. 27-A.
11. Christiansen, Monty L.: "Planning and Design for Safety and Emergency Provisions," *Trends,* Winter 1980, p. 13.
12. Andres, Frederick F.: "Swimming Pool Lifeguarding," *Journal of Physical Education and Recreation,* May 1979, p. 41.
13. D'Arnall, Douglas G.: "Supervising a Surf Beach," *Journal of Physical Education and Recreation,* May 1979, p. 44.
14. *Ibid.*
15. Council for International Urban Liaison: "New Safety Standards to Decrease British Playground Hazards," in *Urban Innovation Abroad,* Washington, D.C., July 1980, p. 1.
16. "When Parks' 'Scare Rides' Run Wild," *U.S. News and World Report,* Aug. 20, 1984, p. 66.
17. Della-Giustina, Daniel: "Skateboard Safety," *Journal of Physical Education and Recreation,* June 1979, p. 48.
18. Griffin, Donald J.: "Hot Weather: An Insidious Health Hazard," *Parks and Recreation,* June 1980, pp. 67-68, 70.
19. *Managing Vandalism: A Guide to Reducing Damage in Park and Recreation Facilities,* Parkman Center for Urban Affairs, and Boston Park and Recreation Department, May 1978, p. 8.
20. Kotkin, Joel: "Crime Rate Outstrips Growth of U.S. Park Tourism," *Philadelphia Inquirer,* Dec. 24, 1978, p. 18-E.
21. Perry, Michael J.: "Strategies for Combatting Crime in the Parks," *Parks and Recreation,* Sept. 1983, p. 50.
22. *Managing Vandalism, op. cit.,* pp. 12-32.
23. Scott, Ian W., and Franks, Vivian: "Vandalism: It's Nothing to Smile About," *Recreation Canada,* Dec. 1979, pp. 21-23.
24. Langston, Robert E.: "U.S. Park Police Meet Urban Challenge," *Trends,* Fall 1979, p. 25.
25. Wade, J.W.: "Law Enforcement in the Wilderness," *Trends,* Fall 1979, p. 13.
26. Harmon, Larry C.: "How to Make Park Law Enforcement Work for You," *Parks and Recreation,* Dec. 1979, p. 20.

CHAPTER 14

Generally, the law balances the burden of precaution against the foreseeable risk of serious injury in establishing liability for negligence. If the foreseeable risk of serious injury is great, public agencies will be expected to be more demanding and stringent in their maintenance and safety procedures. On the other hand, agencies are not the insurers of safety for users of their facilities. In other words, public agencies do not have a duty to compensate every person injured on the premises. Liability presumes negligence, a failure to adhere to the standard of care required by law.[1]

Legal Aspects of Recreation and Park Management

*I*nseparable from the function of risk management is the issue of liability and the need to develop policies and procedures that help protect an agency from expensive lawsuits. This in turn is part of the broader topic of legal aspects of recreation and park management.

This chapter examines several key concepts of liability and related managerial concerns: (1) guidelines for establishing contracts and other legal constraints or commitments of recreation and park agencies; (2) affirmative action and related legal issues affecting the personnel management process; (3) the responsibility for provding nondiscriminatory programs with full access to potential participants; (4) basic guidelines affecting law enforcement practices; and (5) the need for familiarity with the various laws that empower various types of leisure-service agencies to operate or that limit the roles they may legitimately play.

Liability as a Management Concern

Certainly liability is one of the most important issues affecting leisure-service managers today. The term "liability" is commonly used to describe the situation in which an individual or organization is subject to lawsuit because of failure to carry out certain responsibilities as required by law or within a contractual agreement. Graham and Klar define it as

> a concept that infers the existence of certain responsibilities between two or more persons (individuals, corporate structures, associations, and all legal entities). This concept further implies that any person failing to properly and adequately fulfill his or her responsibilities because of *negligence* must provide compensation to those affected by such failure.[2]

The most dramatic and threatening aspect of liability today lies in the growing number of lawsuits directed at public, commercial, and other leisure-service agencies for injuries incurred while taking part in programs or while on their premises. Lawsuits have become a "way of life," writes van der Smissen, and

> the recreation and park field is certainly a prime target. The future of legal liability as a determinant of recreation and park services is inextricably intertwined with economics, operations, and social values. While lawsuits are commonplace in metropolitan areas for recreation and park professionals, a lawsuit filed against a medium or small local government is still a major and traumatic event.[3]

TYPES OF LIABILITY

There are several different types of liability. In *criminal liability,* government may bring an individual to court because of an alleged criminal act, such as assault or burglary. In *liability based on violation of civil laws,* such as health and safety codes or civil rights laws, government may sue or enjoin an individual or organizations. The two types of liability of greatest concern in the leisure-service field are *tort liability* and *contractual liability.*

Tort liability

A tort is a legal wrong committed on a person or property outside of a contractual relationship. It may involve either (1) a direct violation of some legal right of the individual or (2) the infraction of some public duty or responsibility, by which the individual suffers special damages.

Intentional torts, such as assaults, fraud, libel, or slander, are classified as criminal and may result in payments being awarded by the court to the individual who has suffered the tort, as well as possible imprisonment. Unintentional torts are those that have been caused by negligence and customarily call for the payment of actual damages to the wronged person by the wrongdoer.

Under the law, those subject to lawsuit for negligent action resulting in a tort may include the corporate entity itself, such as a corporation or owner, individual board members or trustees, managerial personnel, and those directly responsible for leadership within a program. In the past, most government agencies and their employees were immune from such claims under the doctrine of ''sovereign immunity.'' This principle held that the state (or local governments as subdivisions of the state) was not liable for injuries resulting from the negligence of its employees or other agents. Courts held that tort liability could not be maintained against local governments unless specifically provided for by an act of legislation.

Since the early 1960s, a number of state legislatures have abrogated the principle of ''sovereign immunity'' by enacting statutes that place responsibility for participant safety directly on the agency conducting the program. In California, for example, a clause was added to the state government code that states, ''A public entity is liable for an injury proximately caused by an act or omission of an employee of a public entity within the scope of his employment.'' Similar statutes have been enacted in over 30 states, and although there is considerable variation with respect to the liability of agencies for different types of programs or services, it must be considered that there is no absolute defense against possible lawsuits for injury. Recreation and park departments must therefore seek to avoid such claims by preventing possible charges of negligence in their operations and developing sound defenses against such claims.

CONCEPT OF NEGLIGENCE

Negligence is the key element that must be proved satisfactorily before an individual or agency can be held legally responsible for unintentional torts that have resulted in injury to others. Leighty writes:

Negligence is generally considered to be the omission by an individual to do something which a "reasonable man" would do under similar circumstances; conversely, negligence may be the act of doing something which a reasonable and prudent man would not do. The standard used to determine negligence then, is the behavior of "a reasonable and prudent man."[4]

Beyond this rather general concept, several more specific elements must be proved before a claim for injury or other loss based on negligence can be won. These include (1) *duty,* defined as an obligation under the law requiring the agency or individual to conform to an approved standard of conduct or behavior to protect others against unreasonable risks; (2) *breach,* defined as failure to conform to the required standards; (3) *proximate cause,* defined as a reasonably or sufficiently close causal connection between the conduct of the agency or individual and the resultant injury or loss to another; and (4) *damages,* defined as actual loss or injury to the interests of another.

A number of other circumstances may support a claim for negligence. These include improper performance or lack of appropriate care; dangerous circumstances or conditions; an unreasonable degree of risk in the situation because of the likelihood of the action of third persons or inanimate forces; the use of dangerous devices or instrumentalities by persons incompetent to use or care for them properly; failure to give adequate warning or to keep persons out of danger zones; failure to inspect and repair areas or equipment as needed; or failure to control third persons who by reason of some incapacity or abnormality one knows to be likely to inflict harm on others.

EXAMPLES OF CLAIMS AGAINST RECREATION AND PARK AGENCIES

Because of the very nature of recreational participation, there are many circumstances under which recreation and park agencies are likely to be sued by injured participants or facilities users or their families.

In a relatively high-risk activity, such as skiing, the assumption is that participants must have a reasonable awareness of the risk factor and the sponsoring agency is not responsible for an injury caused by chance or natural circumstances. However, if the agency has not properly groomed the slope, permitting skiers to become caught in hidden undergrowth and seriously injured, or if it has not provided adequate supervision or has permitted other dangerous circumstances to exist, it may be found guilty of negligence. Obviously, highly dangerous activities require more intensive care and higher standards of supervision than others, subject to the "reasonably prudent" guideline.

Claims that have been made in recent years have included a great variety of accidents. A 15-year-old football player suffered paraplegia when struck in the chin during a drill in which two players facing each other several yards apart were instructed to hit head on. Responsibility for paying the $750,000 settlement was divided between the helmet manufacturer and the school coaches who allegedly taught head blocking and tackling. A huge affirmed judgment, $4.58 million, was awarded to a quadriplegic 18-year-old who struck his head on the 8-foot bottom of a pool after diving from a newly installed aluminum springboard that violated local specifications.

Frakt cites other cases:

Recent cases in which there have been substantial settlements or favorable judgments for plaintiffs involve obviously predictable hazards and injuries: a toy rocket launcher that took out a child's eye with impact "greater than a BB gun" ($100,000); a trampoline accident resulting in paralysis from the armpits down ($575,000); a snowmobile with alleged sharp protuding metal brackets (trial ordered), etc.[5]

In a series of articles regarding the liability of recreation and park agencies for accidents occurring in their facilities or programs, Kozlowski cites examples of cases stemming from playground games such as "crack the whip" or defective conditions in park or playground maintenance. In each situation the specific conditions surrounding the accident determined whether suits against municipalities were successful or were rejected by the courts.[6,7]

Numerous other cases involve injuries after falls from swings or after trespassing in fenced recreation areas; being blinded by a golf ball in flight; falling off a bluff despite warning signs and trenches designed to keep out intruders; and irreversible brain damage after almost drowning in swimming pool programs run by Ys and other agencies. In some cases claims for the effects of the physical injury itself are accompanied by claims for psychological trauma, fright, humiliation, and other forms of pain and suffering. Loss of future earnings may lead to substantial additional sums.

Frakt[5] points out that many recreational injuries, particularly those involving violent or contact sports, are attributable to the failure of safety equipment such as helmets or roll bars. One problem, he suggests, is that such equipment often encourages individuals to take risks and extend their performance beyond what might normally be considered prudent. Other injuries stem from the use of recreation products that are inherently dangerous, do not have adequate safeguards, or break down because of built-in defects or weaknesses.

In addition to such cases, settlement-eager plaintiffs may seize on varied opportunities such as the following. A woman leaving a quiet recreational bridge instruction session turns her ankle on the stairway and sues the recreation department, claiming that the stairs were poorly lit. A man completing an evening of woodworking finds his automobile damaged and holds the department responsible for not providing better supervision in the parking lot. A mother whose child was sickened by candy or fruit collected at a community Halloween parade and party sues both the recreation department and the cosponsoring Lions Club.

PERSPECTIVE ON LIABILITY CLAIMS

Despite the preceding examples, leisure-service agencies must not become so fearful of lawsuits that they are unwilling to offer any activity that might lead to negligence claims. Frakt[7] points out that over the past several years the annual number of reported appellate court decisions awarding damages in cases arising from parks and recreation, as well as sports and games activities, is on the average no more than a dozen. It is highly unlikely that there are as many as 50 such cases a year with final settlements or awards of $100,000 or more, and these for the most part involve crippling injury or death. Frakt summarizes major cases as involving one or more of the following overlapping elements:

1. High-risk activities which by their nature involve the possibility of serious injury, such as football, diving, or trampolining
2. Man-made or substantially man-altered activity sites, such as prepared ski slopes, swimming areas, or athletic fields with hidden holes or concealed sprinklers
3. Activities involving machinery or complex gear, such as snowmobiles, dune buggies, football helmets, or other complicated equipment
4. Inadequate professional supervision, particularly of children, and failure to use or understand approved emergency or first-aid techniques, or to live up to approved national or local standards or regulations for equipment and personnel

Prevention of Negligence Liability Claims

As Chapter 13 points out, the best defense against accidents and potential lawsuits is a systematic program of risk management. This would include elements such as careful selection and placing of playgrounds and sports areas and equipment; thorough, regular inspection of all facilities with repair or replacement of defective items when needed; elimination of antiquated or dangerous facilities; and careful maintenance of signs, fences, or other barriers to keep trespassers out of dangerous areas or from entering them at improper times.

Other important factors include the safety education of the public at large and particularly of participants, with emphasis on the appropriate ways in which to carry on activity and the risks and dangers to be avoided. Linked to this is the employment of supervisory and leadership personnel who are highly skilled and qualified in the activities they direct and who also are alert to safety needs and competent in emergency and first aid methods.

Elements in Defense of Liability Suits

A number of specific strategies may be used to resist the plaintiff's claim of negligence or limit the money awarded by a jury or agreed on in negotiation as damages.

CONTRIBUTORY NEGLIGENCE

Contributory negligence is an act of negligence on the part of the plaintiff that is at least partially responsible for the accident and the damages suffered. Approximately 20 states currently recognize the concept of contributory negligence, and in some cases it has been used to absolve the defendant of liability. If the sponsoring agency or individual shares a portion of the negligence, although there may be a finding for the plaintiff, the fact of contributory negligence is likely to result in considerably reduced award of damages. The extent to which one party or the other held the major responsibility for the negligence that caused the accident is likely to affect the sums awarded.

ASSUMPTION OF RISK

Assumption of risk is a defense strategy based on the argument that the plaintiff knowingly and willingly entered into an environment or activity where the potential for injury was great. It is particularly appropriate for high-risk recreational activities in which it can be shown that a plaintiff was fully aware of the dangers inherent in an activity such as mountain climbing or skydiving and yet chose to participate. It is therefore desirable for agencies to be able to document that they have warned their clientele of the potential risks in an activity.

UNAVOIDABLE ACCIDENT

An unavoidable accident is one in which an "act of God" or other unusual natural circumstance, such as a strong gust of wind, sudden swarm of bees, or the like, was the direct cause of the mishap. If the accident was caused in this way rather than the result of negligence, it would not normally be the basis for awarding a settlement.

WAIVERS

Many public and commercial recreation agencies require participants to sign liability waivers, under which participants state that they will not hold the department or other organization resonsible for accidents that may occur. This is invalid in the case of children, who cannot legally sign away their right to sue, and it is also generally ineffective for other age groups. Instead, van der Smissen suggests that participant acknowledgments that describe the nature of the activity to be engaged in, as well as its potential risks, and in which the participant agrees to obey all established rules and guidelines, are a more useful approach. In case of a later lawsuit, the defendant may use such agreements as evidence of contributory negligence if the plaintiff did not follow the agreed-on rules.[9]

Other Aspects of Liability

The overall problem of negligence liability is complex and involves many other legal concepts and considerations that cannot be dealt with here in detail. There is, for example, the concept of "attractive nuisance," which involves maintaining a facility that by its very nature tends to invite trespassers and provides a possible setting for serious accidents. For years, a distinction has been made between "government" and "proprietary" functions, with those that are proprietary in the sense that substantial fees may be charged and a possible profit cleared being less likely to be protected against lawsuit. Today this distinction is not as useful or valid as in the past.

The question of who is liable for injuries and who may be sued is also complicated. As indicated earlier, these individuals or agencies may include the municipal government itself, the department, its board members, executives, supervisors, other professional staff members, and in many cases independent contractors such as concessionaires or outside maintenance or repair companies involved in the facility.

To deal with questions of liability, it is essential that competent legal counsel be retained and that guidelines be formulated under legal advice, not only for the operation of programs and facilities but also for emergency procedures, including public relations *after* an accident. If the principles suggested throughout this chapter are scrupulously followed, they should keep lawsuits to a minimum. However, it is obvious that despite all precautions that can possibly be taken, some injuries will inevitably occur, particularly in active sports programs and adventure and high-risk activities. Even under the best of circumstances, many of these will lead to lawsuits—some justified and some simply because our society is attuned to litigation and seeking financial redress whether justified or not. Given this circumstance, adequate insurance coverage must be maintained.

Liability Insurance

Many county or municipal governments have blanket liability insurance coverage that protects all departments under a single "umbrella" policy. In other cases separate departments or agencies believed to have a significant negligence claim risk are empowered to purchase their own policies at appropriate levels of coverage and at premiums they assume within their own budgets.

Certain national companies specialize in this type of coverage. Since rates vary greatly, it is wise to get a number of quotations before purchasing coverage. Epperson[10] points out that, since demand for insurance for private or commercial organizations is relatively new, with limited claims data on which to base premium levels, some companies may refuse to offer them such policies or may charge excessively high rates. It should also be recognized that one or more claims or verdicts against a leisure-service agency may cause a company to raise its premiums sharply or even cancel its coverage, making it all the more necessary to prevent possible claims and protect one's "insurability."

SPECIAL COVERAGE ARRANGEMENTS

In cases in which individual employees of a recreation and park department are operating within the scope of a court-determined proprietary function, they may be protected against negligence suits by the overall agency coverage. However, if the municipality itself is held immune, the employee is more likely to be held personally responsible for negligence claims and lawsuits. Under such circumstances, departments may indemnify their employees and take out policies that protect them against claims. Employees may also wish to take out personal liability insurance policies for additional protection, which may be made available through a group-coverage plan.

In addition to overall coverage, some organizations take out special short-term policies for trips or other special programs involving risk, making this coverage available for participants at their own expense, usually at a minimal cost.

RISING COST OF INSURANCE

With the steady increase in lawsuits and expensive verdicts of all sorts, insurance premiums have risen dramatically over the past several years. As a vivid example, Ventura County, Calif., saw its premiums climb from $130,000 to $904,000—an increase of over 600%—within a 12-month span. In some cases agencies find it extremely difficult to get a company to offer coverage at *any* rate because insurers may find themselves overextended, vulnerable, and unwilling to take on new responsibilities.

Self-insurance

A growing number of municipalities are resorting to self-insurance, in which the city government sets aside in its annual budget a specific sum of money, perhaps $500,000 for cities whose population is under 50,000 or $1 million for cities up to 200,000 in population. This money is earmarked for court settlements but is meanwhile banked at the maximum rate of interest. Obviously, the government is gambling that no catastrophic losses will be incurred during the first year or two. If the municipality can keep judgments down for a few years while making new payments each year and accruing substantial interest, it emerges the winner. Having saved annual premiums of perhaps $250,000, the city still has most of its capital reserve earning interest. It is now prepared to cover a major award or two if necessary, so it makes sense to continue the practice of self-insurance.

Contractual Liability

In addition to tort liability, which includes negligence injury claims, an important area of concern for recreation and park managers is contractual liability. In simple terms, this refers to legal claims that may be made, leading to a condition of liability based on charges of failure to perform as contracted. Lawsuits are usually concerned with the performance of services or the provision of a given product and seek monetary damages.

Leisure-service agencies may be involved in various contracts with concessionaires, construction or maintenance companies, vending machine operators, utilities companies, cosponsoring organizations, transportation carriers, designers and planners, manufacturers and suppliers, and a host of other companies or individuals. Whenever there is an agreement to provide a product or service along with some form of "consideration" (bargained exchange), there is a contract.

Guadagnolo points out that contract law is regarded as the most complex area of law and therefore that the recreation and park manager must

> seek legal assistance in reviewing or drafting contractual agreements. A close scrutiny of the document by the manager is needed in order to be certain that all possible eventualities are covered within.[11]

Within any given area of performance, it is essential that important elements be spelled out as precisely as possible. For example, in a concessionaire agreement, elements to be covered in a contract would include the length of the arrangement with exact dates on which given actions are to take place; the responsibility of both parties for providing, inspecting, or maintaining equipment; standards of performance; possible charges for costs arising from maintenance or vandalism; nature of advertising or public relations; nature of payments based on flat annual fees, percentage of sales, or net profit; and all other important aspects of the agreement.

Traditionally, contracts have been written in "legalese," meaning highly technical words, often based on ancient usages that are likely to be incomprehensible to the contracting parties and must be interpreted for them by lawyers. Today, there is a movement toward the use of plain language in contracts, which has been spearheaded by lawyers, consumer advocates, educators, and others. This concept has already been adopted by law in a number of states, particularly in relation to consumer contracts. Till and Gargiulo write:

> This premise, when operational, mandates that existing highly technical legal words and phrases in contracts be replaced in rewritten contracts with plain words and that long, multipart sentences be replaced with [a series of] shorter sentences. In other words, contracts should be written in words that the average user of the document can reasonably be expected to understand.[12]

Although they cannot unilaterally determine that all contracts into which they enter will be written in this way, recreation and park managers would be wise to urge their lawyers to frame contracts in this fashion—subject to the willingness of other parties in the agreement. This will make the exact obligations and specifications of contracts clearer to them without legal interpretation and will make it easier for them to adhere to the exact arrangements that have been agreed on and to require the same of others.

LIMITATIONS ON AGENCY FISCAL PRACTICES

In many areas, recreation and park managers do not have the *right* to enter into certain kinds of contracts because of legal restrictions. For example, Chapter 11 described the trend in many public leisure-service agencies toward leasing public property to private operators as a way to maximize revenue returns with minimum investment risk or capital commitment. Kozlowski points out that such innovative leasing arrangements between the public and private sectors appear likely to continue because of increased costs of acquisition, construction, operation, and maintenance and budget limitations among public recreation and park departments. However, he also points out that, lacking a specific grant of authority from the state, municipalities and counties do not generally have the power to lease their property to private persons.

The ultimate decision whether to lease, he writes, will depend on a careful analysis of the municipal charter, ordinances, regulations, state enabling statutes, and court decisions in a given jurisdiction, as well as possible restrictions in the deed of a property. Questions must be asked, such as these:

1. Is there a specific grant of authority, state statute, or charter provision that expressly permits leasing public recreation facilities to private operators?
2. Does the lease conform in writing to the provisions of the state statute or municipal charter, particularly as it relates to lease extensions and public advertising/bidding requirements?
3. Do the written lease provisions ensure the availability of the facility to the public on an equal basis with other groups?
4. Is the lease consistent with and in furtherance of public use and enjoyment of the recreational facility?
5. Does the lease conform to the meaning and intent of any restrictions imposed on the grant of the property to the public?
6. Would a concessionaire's license to operate a facility be preferable to a lease?

7. Does the lease permit the city a high degree of control regarding rules and regulations for public or private use of the recreational facility?
8. Given charter provisions and court interpretations in a particular jurisdiction, does the city operate the facility in a proprietary or a governmental capacity?
9. Is the facility being leased because it has become inadequate or unsuitable for its intended public use; has the intended public use been abandoned?[13]

Similarly, other new fiscal practices of public recreation and park departments may violate existing legal codes. Kozlowski cites the example of such departments selling goods and products as part of a trend toward merchandising leisure-related services and making profits to be pumped back into programs and facilities. He comments that "entrepreneurial ardor" must be tempered by an understanding of state laws regulating public sector involvement in the marketplace. The general legal principle in this area is that without "express legislative authority from the state, a municipality has no power to engage in any independent business enterprise or occupation usually pursued by private individuals [or] to expend tax funds for a private enterprise that does not primarily promote public purpose."[14]

Among issues that have come before the courts with respect to this principle have been lawsuits related to the right of city-owned recreation complexes to sell alcoholic beverages, operate public ambulance services in competition with private firms, or purchase a large man-made lake to sell hydroelectricity from its power plant and on which· to operate a recreational and tourist business. The question of what constitutes rational or justifiable public purposes is constantly being redefined in an era of changing socioeconomic conditions; there is no simple rule of thumb to determine what sorts of "private" enterprises a public agency may undertake.

Personnel Management and the Law

Guadagnolo[15] points out that both public and commercial recreation enterprises have become subject to an increasing number of federal and state regulations affecting personnel management, as well as other ordinances or procedural guidelines that are based on existing laws or court decisions regarding personnel. These include varied management concerns such as policies and practices in the area of wages and hours, employee benefits, worker's compensation, safety and health, employees' personal rights, and civil service procedures.

Hiring, firing, and promotional practices are probably the most troublesome areas, since the need for careful observance of affirmative action has compelled administrators to use extreme care in personnel management.

AFFIRMATIVE ACTION REQUIREMENTS

Title VII of the Civil Rights Act of 1964 prohibits federal, state, and local government agencies, as well as unions, employment agencies, and other related groups, from discriminating against employees or potential employees on the basis of race, color, religion, sex, or national origin with respect to hiring, firing, transfer, promotion, salary levels, or apprenticeship or other training programs. Later presidential executive orders extended its regulations against discrimination to federal government contractors and subcontractors and in effect to all organizations receiving federal funds to support their programs.

The Equal Employment Opportunity Act of 1972 amended Title VII by expanding its coverage of governmental agencies and educational institutions and to private companies with more than 15 employees. Based on these laws, government, educational, and other social-service organizations are required to maintain accurate records of their employment actions and practices, to file detailed annual reports dealing with the sex and ethnic background of their employees, and to develop affirmative action plans that list their employment policies and specific objectives designed to promote employment and promotion of minority groups. In general, agencies must seek to develop work forces that reflect the makeup of the available population.

Given this background, it is essential that leisure-service agencies, along with other types of public, voluntary, commercial, and educational institutions, seek to overcome past patterns of discrimination and diversify their work forces as vigorously as possible. Guadagnolo suggests a number of strategies:

> These include: seeking referrals from their existing employees; using private employment agencies in an attempt to reach qualified candidates; newspaper advertisements; and recruitment at colleges and universities. Other nontraditional approaches which may be pursued include using minority oriented media to publicize position opportunities, contacting various civic and social organizations representing the minority community, or notifying schools with substantial minority representation.[16]

Although enforcement of federal or state antidiscrimination laws has been inconsistent and clear guidelines regarding what constitutes acceptable compliance have not been established, most government agencies have moved ahead to develop and carry out affirmative action plans.

To avoid possible charges of discrimination, managers must be cautious to observe recommended guidelines and procedures, particularly in the hiring process. They typically may *not* ask questions that seek to learn an individual's nationality or family origin, type of military discharge, marital status or number of dependents, arrest or criminal conviction record, religious background, general medical condition or physical disabilities, race or color, or similar information. Although it is possible to gather relevant information in a number of these areas, it is not legal to do so in ways that appear simply to seek out derogatory information or that might provide the basis for discriminating against an individual.

Based on such regulations, agencies should carefully review their application forms and the procedures used in interviews and other employee selection processes to ensure that they conform to legal requirements. Particular emphasis is being given today to varied forms of sexual discrimination; numerous organizations have been successfully sued for past discrimination against women in their hiring or promotional practices. Furthermore, women are bringing charges of sexual harassment, that is, on-the-job superiors making sexual overtures to them and threatening or actually carrying out retaliatory actions if they refuse to comply.

FIRING PRACTICES

Apart from the issue of possible discrimination, firing practices have become complex from a legal point of view. In many government agencies or other large enterprises that are unionized, employers must show just cause before terminating an individual's employment and must follow required procedures for documenting the person's failure to perform, holding conferences with the person, and placing the person "on warning."

In most private concerns the right to fire an employee was generally available to employers with few restrictions until the mid-1970s. Since then, however, numerous court decisions have placed various restrictions on firing. For example, an employer may be sued for wrongful dismissal, if the reason for firing had to do with the employee's serving on a jury, filing for worker's compensation, protesting against the employer's violation of an earlier promise, or reporting that the employer had not followed required safety and health practices.

OTHER LAWS AFFECTING EMPLOYMENT PRACTICES

Recreation and park managers must also be familiar with other important pieces of legislation that affect employment practices.

The Federal Labor Standards Act includes minimum wage and maximum hour regulations that must be observed. The National Labor Relations Law and a number of subsequent amendments, including the Taft-Hartley and Landrum-Griffen acts, provide stipulations with regard to labor union practices. For example, agency or company managers may not interfere with the employees' rights to form or join labor unions or bargain collectively; on the other hand, unions may not coerce or threaten employees to build or maintain their membership.

As in the case of legal liability, this is a complex and diversified area of concern. In many units of local government and many voluntary or commercial organizations, personnel managers are employed who are expert in various aspects of the law, including affirmative action, and who guide policy in such matters.

Programming and Access for Special Populations

Closely linked to the problem of affirmative action related to employment is the need to program and provide access to facilities for all populations, regardless of sex, age, race, socioeconomic status, or physical or mental ability. Until recently, there was comparatively little concern about blacks or other ethnic or racial minorities in public recreation programs; they often were limited to restricted and inadequate facilities by either law or community custom. Similarly, many recreation programs have been designed to attract and involve men and boys and have tended to slight the needs of women and girls. The mentally and physically disabled have typically been excluded from programs or have been served in limited and restricted ways.

The 1960s and 1970s will probably be recognized as years in which tremendous changes occurred toward ensuring equality and opportunity for all segments of society. Numerous federal and state laws have sought to ensure equal opportunity for special populations in our society, and community recreation and park programs have been required to comply with both the spirit and the letter of these laws.

Despite widespread initial resistance to civil rights statutes regarding desegregation of public recreation facilities such as parks, playgrounds, golf courses, swimming pools, and beaches, particularly in southern states, in general there has been a positive transition, and many such facilities are successfully integrated today.

Regarding gender, many schools, colleges, and recreation and park departments have greatly expanded their sports programming to include girls' and women's activities. Lawsuits have compelled organizations such as Little League baseball to admit girls as players. Through continuing legal claims based on Title IX of the Educational Amendments Act of 1972, this trend will clearly continue in the years ahead.

With respect to programming for the physically and mentally disabled, the Education for the Handicapped Act of 1975 (P.L. 94-142) has focused national attention on the need to improve educational and other rehabilitative programming for disabled individuals. Other federal laws, such as the Architectural Barriers Act of 1968 (P.L. 90-480) and the Rehabilitation Act, Section 504, of 1973 (P.L. 93-112), require that all public or voluntary agencies receiving federal funding be fully accessible to special populations.

Clearly, an important responsibility of all recreation and park administrators is to promote programs serving the full population range and involve the disabled themselves, as well as their representatives or advocates, in planning and implementing such programs. For both legal and moral reasons, such efforts should be given the highest priority. However, this does not mean that all special populations can or should be "mainstreamed" in the sense that they are fully integrated with nondisabled populations. Often their degree of disability makes this impractical; they would be unable to carry on the activity successfully, and other participants would strongly resist their involvement. The appropriate solution is to integrate the disabled fully where this can be done and, if not, to develop specially modified, segregated programs.

EXCLUSION OF NONRESIDENTS

An issue related to access concerns the exclusion of nonresidents by communities or park districts. Whereas in larger cities individuals are generally permitted to use all facilities (for example, swimming pools, golf courses, museums, or parks) without having to demonstrate residence in the city, this is not the case in smaller communities or suburbs within metropolitan areas. There—particularly for desirable facilities such as parks, lakes, swimming pools, beaches, or athletic areas—the practice has developed in recent years of requiring would-be users to prove their residence, often by use of a special card or laminated "leisure pass."

This has become a matter of legal concern; in a number of large metropolitan districts, civil rights groups have contended that policies excluding nonresidents represent a deliberate effort to keep racial minorities or disadvantaged urban residents out of suburban parks and recreation areas.

Clearly, this will continue to be a legal issue, particularly in suburban communities surrounding large central cities. It is less troublesome in county or large park districts that serve more extensive areas, including many disadvantaged populations. In a number of such suburban areas, however, recreation and park authorities were reluctant to apply for federal grants in aid for land acquisition and facility development during the 1960s and 1970s, if it meant that they would be required to permit nonresidents to enter their facilities.

Kozlowski[17] points out that ordinances may not arbitrarily, oppressively, or unreasonably discriminate against nonresidents; such ordinances would unconstitutionally deny them the equal protection of the law. However, municipal regulations that exclude nonresidents from public recreation facilities are not necessarily unconstitutional. Public safety and health, for example, have been cited as reasonable causes for excluding nonresidents. In addition, court decisions have supported the right of government agencies to impose different fee scales on residents and nonresidents, provided that there is a rational basis for doing so.

PRIVATE CLUBS

Numerous social or luncheon clubs in larger cities have been subjected to suit by women to permit their admission and have gradually begun to do so. The argument has been that such clubs are typically used by leading business executives or other professional or members of the city "establishment" to discuss business plans or other important concerns, and not to admit women as members (a traditional pattern in the past) is to exclude them from an important area of economic life and career opportunity. Similarly, suit has been brought against fraternal or service clubs in some cities that have excluded blacks as members to compel them to cease this practice. As a result, some such clubs have lost their tax-exempt status, and others have opened their membership to include formerly unwelcome minority group members.

Law-Enforcement Policies and Practices

A final important area of legal concern in leisure-service agencies is their ability to enforce law and order and protect both their visitors and their facilities from criminals, vandals, or other lawbreakers. As indicated in Chapter 13, this is a mounting problem, particularly in agencies whose facilities cover a large geographic area.

One issue has involved the right to free speech and assembly as it applies to the granting of permits for public "protest" meetings or parades that seek to use park areas. Another legal issue has revolved around the right of individuals to privacy and freedom from unwarranted surveillance, particularly as it affects park users in park-owned cottages and lodges or tents, campers, or mobile homes. Searches for drugs, liquor, or other contraband materials must be carried out within the constraints imposed by general constitutional rights and also laws of the individual states or legal precedents governing law enforcement activities. Leighty[18] points out that lawful arrests may be made on probable cause without a warrant and that reasonable searches may be made of the arrested individual's person and surroundings.

Law-enforcement officers within recreation and park areas must be familiar with "search and seizure" procedures, the use of roadblocks, the so-called Miranda warning requirements when suspects are apprehended, and other constitutional principles. It should be stressed that whereas laws and regulations vary from state to state, the basic principles do not, and all who exercise enforcement powers must be familiar with them.

As a general policy, the orientation and training of law enforcement employees should include these guidelines. Many communities or park districts send representatives to regional law enforcement institutes or workshops cosponsored by the National Recreation and Park Association and leading universities to provide a thorough grounding, as well as "refresher" information in this area.

Summary

This chapter has presented a number of important areas of concern for managers with respect to issues such as avoiding costly negligence litigation, understanding contractual liability, current limitations on agency fiscal practices and leasing operations, affirmative action and other legal aspects of personnel management, access for special populations, and problems dealing with law enforcement practices.

Since the practice of law is a sophisticated and complex field with many subspecialties, most leisure-service managers will not develop a high degree of expertise in it. However, they should be aware of the general guidelines affecting their policies and practices in the management functions and should be careful to follow approved procedures or guidelines at all times. Beyond this, they should read articles on legal aspects of recreation and park management in professional periodicals, attend workshops or seminars, and above all rely on qualified counsel for advice as new issues or problems appear.

STUDY QUESTIONS

1. Examine the problem of liability based on negligence in the operation of playgrounds and athletic fields in a public recreation and park department. Develop a summary statement regarding the factors leading to the judgment of negligence and then prepare a set of operational guidelines to reduce the possibility of successful liability claims or lawsuits against the agency.

2. Take a specific type of legal problem affecting public leisure-service departments, such as (1) policies leading to the exclusion of nonresidents or the handicapped from programs and faciliues; (2) issues regarding personnel management, including hiring, promotion, and firing; or (3) problems of law enforcement in public facilities. Examine the literature on this issue, possibly including a search for relevant cases and precedents, and outline principles based on your findings that are appropriate for your state and type of agency.

3. Prepare a unit on legal aspects in recreation and parks that might be part of an in-service training program for leaders in a leisure-service agency.

Case 19   *You're Not a Feminist—But. . .*

YOU ARE DONNA PARTRIDGE, a middle-level manager within the operations division of a large theme park. You have had several years' experience in similar programs in smaller commercial recreation settings, working with packaged tour groups and family-oriented programming.

After 3 years at the park you feel that you have done well and have received excellent evaluations. However, during this period you have remained at the same job level, while several men with less experience have been promoted past you. Although salaries are confidential, through a close friend in the personnel office you find out that you are being paid less than men in comparable positions.

You are not a feminist and take pride in handling your own problems, as well as in being able to compete with men on equal terms. However, this apparent discrimination enrages you. You make an appointment to talk to the company personnel director, Al Bevins. He is pleasant but not helpful. "Several factors go into the promotion process and salary determinations," he says. "Don't quote me, Donna, because I'll deny it and it's your word against mine. But these men support families. You do not, and you have a husband with a good job. That's part of our thinking."

Questions for Class Discussion and Analysis

1. If you were Donna, recognizing that you cannot prove that Al Bevins admitted the company's discriminatory policy based on gender, how could you make a strong case that the policy *did* discriminate?
2. What is the law in this area? How could it be pursued in legal terms?
3. If you chose not to take legal action but to fight the case within the company, what would be your best strategy? How could you avoid compromising your career by fighting too aggressively for your rights? Would this be possible?

Case 20   *Race and Recreation*

YOU ARE LUCILLE CRANE, a member of the board of a nonprofit community association within the Springdale Heights area of the city. In the past, there were no blacks or Hispanic residents in Springdale Heights because of unspoken policies of real estate offices in the area that regarded this as a racially "closed" community.

Today there are a few minority group families in Springdale Heights, and the number is growing. However, since your membership system works by having members propose new members, who must be approved by a majority of the members, no black or Hispanic families have yet been invited to join the association. This means that they cannot use your swimming pool or tennis courts or take part in other social events unless they are specially invited.

A faction of younger white families in Springdale Heights have indicated that they want more racial diversity in the community and in the recreational facilities and programs. They intend to propose minority group members, and if they are unable

Case 20 cont'd   Race and Recreation

to gain sufficient support, they intend to initiate a lawsuit designed to remove the tax-exempt status of the association.

Questions for Class Discussion and Analysis

1. As a member of the community association board who has not taken a stand on this issue in the past, what do you see as the moral issues involved?
2. From a legal perspective, research the law to determine the precedents and whether you can be compelled to open the membership in this way.
3. When the issue comes before the board, what position do you intend to take? How will you justify it?

REFERENCES

1. Frakt, Arthur S., and Rankin, Janna S.: *The Law of Parks, Recreation Resources, and Leisure Services,* Salt Lake City, 1982, Brighton Publishing Co., p. 105.
2. Graham, Peter J., and Klar, Lawrence, R. Jr.: *Planning and Delivering Leisure Services,* Dubuque, Iowa, 1979, William C. Brown Co., pp. 278-279.
3. van der Smissen, Betty: "Where Is Legal Liability Heading?" *Parks and Recreation,* May 1980, p. 50.
4. Leighty, Leighton L., in Lutzin, Sidney G. (Editor): *Managing Municipal Leisure Services,* Washington, D.C., 1980, International City Management Association, p. 106.
5. Frakt, Arthur: "Putting Recreation Programming and Liability in Perspective," *Parks and Recreation,* Dec. 1979, pp. 45-46.
6. Kozlowski, James C.: "Two Cases of ''Crack The Whip'' Playground Liability," *Parks and Recreation,* Jan. 1984, pp. 28-30.
7. Kozlowski, James C.: "Liability for injury-causing conditions in parks," *Parks and Recreation,* Sept. 1983, p. 28.
8. Frakt, *op. cit.,* p. 44.
9. van der Smissen, *op. cit.,* p. 51.
10. Epperson, Arlin F.: *Private and Commercial Recreation,* New York, 1977, John Wiley & Sons, Inc., pp. 213-214.
11. Guadagnolo, Frank, in Howard, Dennis R., and Crompton, John L.: *Financing, Managing and Marketing Recreation and Park Resources,* Dubuque, Iowa, 1980, William C. Brown Co., p. 180.
12. Till, Paul, and Garguilo, Albert: *Contracts: The Move to Plain Language,* New York, 1979, American Management Association, pp. 5-6.
13. Kozlowski, James C.: "Leasing Public Facilities to Private Concerns: Some Legal Checkpoints," *Parks and Recreation,* May 1982, p. 61.
14. Kozlowski, James C.: "Municipal Competition with Private Enterprise must Satisfy Public Purpose Test," *Parks and Recreation,* Dec. 1982, p. 18.
15. Guadagnolo, *op. cit.* pp. 163-170.
16. *Ibid.,* p. 165.
17. Kozlowski, James C.: "Validity of Non-Resident and Other Discriminatory Regulations in Municipal Recreation," *Parks and Recreation,* March 1982, pp. 28-34.
18. Leighty, *op. cit.,* pp. 113-115.

CHAPTER 15

Evaluation is an essential aspect of systematic program design. Systems-designed programs have built-in evaluation potential. By stating goals and objectives in behavioral language, and then logically designing a program to accomplish them, evaluation becomes simple compared to other approaches. It is relatively easy to determine whether goals have been met, or the degree to which the program has succeeded, when data are collected daily and analyzed periodically.[1]

The Controlling Function

Evaluation, Management Information Systems, and Computers

Within every field of leisure service, there is growing awareness of the need to develop meaningful standards and quality controls and measure the extent to which programs have achieved their stated objectives. This process is commonly referred to as evaluation; it provides a means of documenting the outcomes of organized recreation service and lending credibility to an agency's performance.

This chapter presents evaluation as an element in the control function held by leisure-service managers. It defines evaluation, presents several methods of carrying it out, and shows how agencies, programs, personnel, and participants may be evaluated, with special emphasis on the use of computers and electronic data processing.

Evaluation Defined

Evaluation is carried on within many types of organizations—governmental, business, educational, and social service. It is the process of determining the extent to which an agency has achieved its stated objectives. In the field of recreation and parks, it might be used to measure the overall performance of an organization or determine its worth based on widely accepted standards.

In an era of budget cutting and increased demand for accountability, it is essential that community agencies document the outcomes of their programs. Woo and Farley write:

> Ongoing evaluation of past policies and commitments is critical because public funding is shrinking and the era of cutback management has arrived. . . . Evaluation provides information that documents, supports and makes public programs accountable to their constituency.[2]

However, evaluation must not be perceived as a means of automatically justifying a program. Evaluation is essentially a form of applied, practical research and like other forms of research, it does not seek to ''prove'' a case. Instead, the evaluator asks a series of questions and gathers evidence as systematically and objectively as possible to determine whether agency goals have been met and appropriate professional standards of practice have been achieved. If evaluation is performed honestly, it may well yield negative rather than positive findings.

Evaluation should be regarded as part of the ''control'' function of managers. It involves continual monitoring, reporting, and evaluating, with corrective measures or fresh action taken when necessary to improve performance.

GOALS OF EVALUATION

The overall goals of evaluation in leisure-service agencies are the following[3]:

1. To determine how effective an agency is in meeting its stated objectives
2. To provide comprehensive information about the full range of its achievements and outcomes, as well as possible areas of weakness or inadequacy
3. To measure the quality of an agency or program, based on accepted standards and criteria
4. To appraise the quality of specific aspects of an agency's operation, such as the performance of staff members or the effectiveness of given policies or procedures
5. To provide feedback for improving programs while they are being carried on or direction for future operations

MODELS OF EVALUATION

Howe,[4] Rossman,[5] and others have identified a number of complex contemporary models of evaluation. In practical terms, these may be described under three major headings: (1) evaluation designed to measure the *effectiveness of programs* in meeting their stated goals and objectives; (2) evaluation designed to measure the overall *quality of programs,* based on professional standards and criteria; and (3) evaluation designed to measure the *level of satisfaction of program participants.* It may also focus on specific elements such as personnel, facilities, or other agency practices or resources.

Summative and formative evaluation

In the past, evaluation was primarily thought of as *summative:* that is, carried out at the end of a program to measure its success or failure and make recommendations for the future. Today much evaluation is *formative,* with continuous monitoring of a program while it is being planned and implemented. Evaluation does not ask only whether objectives *have been* met but whether they are *being* met. It is used to determine whether the plan is working properly or should be modified at once.

Process and preordinate models

Another distinction may be made between *process* and *preordinate* models of evaluation. Rossman defines these:

> Process models delineate a set of steps and procedures to be used in conducting an evaluation without identifying the judgment criteria to be used in making judgments of worth. Preordinate models provide a process and specify the judgment criteria to be used in determining the worth of a leisure program.[5]

In other words, some evaluation models involve the application of standardized instruments, such as checklists, rating scales, or questionnaires. Others begin with a process, in which the agency's staff determine exactly why they need to carry out an evaluation, the kinds of information that will be required, and the best way to gather it. No one approach is correct for all situations, and both are often used in evaluating an agency.

Some types of evaluation may be required as part of funding or accreditation processes. For example, agencies that receive grants to carry out demonstration projects or provide special social services often must include an evaluation component in their proposals or contracts. Hospitals and other treatment centers may be evaluated as part of the accreditation process, just as college and university recreation and parks curricula are.

Depending on the purpose of the evaluation process and the type of agency or program under examination, any or all of these approaches may be used. Several examples of evaluation procedures and instruments are presented in this chapter, followed by general guidelines for effective evaluation.

Methods of Agency Evaluation

In evaluating community leisure-service agencies, several different methods may be used, including: (1) self-study, or study by a visiting team of experts, using rating forms with recommended standards criteria as a basis for making judgments; (2) evaluation carried out through a computer-based systems approach, which uses methods such as management by objectives, planning-programming-budgeting systems, or cost-benefit analysis; (3) evaluation that measures the agency's success in achieving its objectives; and (4) surveys or questionnaires of participants and staff members, linked with actual observation of programs and analysis of records and reports.

NATIONAL RECREATION AND PARK ASSOCIATION EVALUATION AND SELF-STUDY APPROACH

The first approach is outlined in a manual published by the National Recreation and Park Association (NRPA),[6] *Evaluation and Self-Study of Recreation and Park Agencies: A Guide with Standards and Evaluative Criteria.* This document, which is an improved version of an instrument originally developed by the Great Lakes Standards Committee, includes 35 standards (major guidelines for effective practice) and 140 criteria (substatements that provide a basis for judging performance on each of these standards). These are used in measuring the effectiveness of a department in six major categories: (1) philosophy and goals; (2) administration; (3) programming; (4) personnel; (5) areas, facilities, and equipment; and (6) evaluation.

To use this manual, a study team must systematically observe a municipal recreation and park department in action, holding interviews and gathering varied forms of data to determine whether the agency is living up to recommended practices. In scoring the final report, it is possible to obtain figures through which a given department may be compared with other agencies. However, this is not the major purpose of the evaluation; rather, it is used chiefly to provide a profile of strengths and weaknesses within each administrative category and thus to indicate the need for improvement where it exists.

To illustrate the nature of such instruments, Fig. 15-1 presents one standard from this instrument and its criteria. Each of the 35 standards in the document follows a similar format.

To interpret the scores on each of the standards, a profile may be drawn that graphically shows the relative performance of the agency. After the scores are computed,

	Is criterion met?					
	Yes	Almost	To some degree	No	Does not apply	Comments
Standard 30. Volunteers Volunteers should be utilized in the program. (If volunteers are not utilized, check "no" column in shaded area and go to standard 31).	▨	▨	▨	▨	▨	
Criteria						
a. There should be a special orientation program for volunteers.						
b. Volunteers should be given supervisory visits and conferences, as well as in-service training.						
c. There should be a selection process for volunteer leadership with a written selection procedure.						
d. Volunteers should be utilized for leadership, financial drives, promotion, clerical services, advisory councils, etc.						
e. There should be an on-going and enthusiastic recruitment program for volunteers.						

FIG. 15-1   Example of standards and criteria for agencies. (From van der Smissen, B., editor: Evaluation and self-study of public recreation and park agencies: a guide with standards and evaluative criteria, Arlington, Va., 1972, National Recreation and Park Association.)

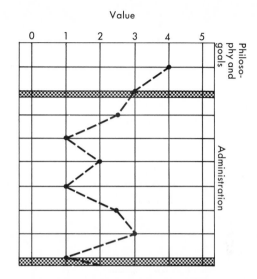

Standard

1. Philosophy

2. Goals

3. Organizational structure

4. Administrative manual

5. Cooperative community planning

6. Cooperative operations agreements

7. Financial administration

8. Public relations

9. Service statistics

FIG. 15-2   Standards profile (partial presentation). (From van der Smissen, B., editor: Evaluation and self-study of public recreation and park agencies: a guide with standards and evaluative criteria, Arlington, Va., 1972, National Recreation and Park Association.)

each standard is located on the scale, and a broken line is drawn to connect the dots, presenting a picture of the agency's strengths and weaknesses (Fig. 15-2). Based on this, the evaluation report indicates areas of positive and negative performance and serves as the basis for remedial action.

Agency evaluation in other areas of service

In addition to public leisure-service organizations, other types of recreation sponsors use similar approaches to evaluation. For example, the National Council on the Aging has published a detailed manual on the operation of senior centers, which may be used in the systematic evaluation of such agencies. In the area of therapeutic recreation, Berryman and associates[7] developed a manual to evaluate recreational services in residential institutions as part of a 3-year study supported by the U.S. Children's Bureau. This document provides a method of evaluating a total program by applying 55 different standards grouped under several major categories. The standards relate to categories such as philosophy and goals; administration; personnel; programming; areas, facilities, and equipment; and evaluation and research. In turn, each standard is supported by several illustrative criteria that represent desirable program practice, and a department is judged on the basis of the degree to which it follows these practices and thus meets the recommended standard of performance.

Self-study process

Manuals of the type just described provide useful instruments for agency self-studies, as well as for the evaluation by teams of outside experts. Evaluators also use several other techniques, such as interviews with staff members and participants, examination of records and reports, direct observation of programs and facilities, and critical measurement of the outcomes of programs through a variety of means.

EVALUATION OF SPECIFIC PROGRAMS

A second important aspect of evaluation in leisure-service agencies involves the appraisal of specific programs. These might be as broad as a major area of service, such as creative arts or sports and games, or as narrow as a single course, workshop, or special event.

For example, the Boys' Clubs of America encourages local clubs to carry out systematic studies of their operations and of different categories of program service. Stressing the need for rigorous and regular evaluation, the national organization states:

> Although an evaluation may be highly organized and formalized and include all aspects of a program, it may also be limited to one particular phase. . . . It may also be used as a guide to the establishment of programs in new Boys' Clubs or for expanding and improving the operation of existing ones.[8]

Guidelines presented in the Boys' Clubs evaluation manuals outline desirable practices actually found in many clubs, as well as the opinions of many administrators and board members. In the program evaluation manual, for example, 50 or more practices are suggested for each of the program categories: (1) arts and crafts, (2) citizenship education, (3) cultural programs, (4) game rooms, (5) guidance program, (6) health program, (7) organized small groups, (8) physical program, and (9) special events.

Example of program evaluation: National Youth Sports Program

A specific example of an evaluation form developed to review the work of agencies contracting to provide programs under special funding is shown in Fig. 15-3.[9] This is a section of the instrument used to evaluate summer youth sports programs conducted by colleges and universities throughout the United States under the sponsorship and coordination of the National Collegiate Athletic Association (NCAA) with funding appropriated by Congress through the Community Services Administration (CSA). The section shown deals with the element of *project schedule*. The other sections are *institution, participants, activities, enrichment program, nutrition, medical services, staff, project organization,* and *coordination*. A maximum number of 180 points may be given to any summer program that is evaluated. Depending on the number of points awarded, a college or university may be approved unconditionally for funding in the following summer, approved conditionally, or disapproved.

Other methods of evaluating specific programs

A number of other methods exist for evaluating specific programs, including both major program units or continued activities and individual classes, tournaments, or other

```
            National Youth Sports Program   NCAA/CSA
          Section of Evaluation Form:   Project Schedule


                                                    Points
     Item                                           available

     1.  Meets minimum:  5 weeks, 5 days per           2
         week; or 6 weeks, 4 days per week
     2.  Exceeds number of funded days                 1
     3.  Provides minimum of 2 hours of sports         2
         activity per day
     4.  Provides 3 hours of sports activity           1
         per day
     5.  Provides 4 hours of sports activity           1
         per day
     6.  Majority of enrollment before summer          2
         project begins
     7.  Staff orientation and briefing before         2
         summer project begins
```

FIG. 15-3   Sample evaluation form. (From National Youth Sports Program: Manual of directions
for project evaluation, Washington, D.C., 1984, National College Athletic Association.)

events. These consist of the following: (1) systems-based, goal achievement models; (2) participant-based evaluation; and (3) staff-based evaluation processes.

SYSTEMS-BASED, GOAL ACHIEVEMENT MODELS

This method seeks to determine, as precisely as possible, whether stated objectives of the program were achieved. It assumes that objectives were clearly defined as part of the program-planning process and that they lend themselves to precise measurement. Gunn and Peterson point out that effective systems-designed programs require that a basic evaluation plan be developed before the program is set in motion. The plan not only should state the exact objectives of the program but should indicate what information must continually be recorded and the forms needed to gather and record that information:

> Most evaluations deal with the same basic questions: Was the program effective? Why did we get the results we did? How can we improve the programs? . . . Were the activities appropriate? Were the interaction techniques appropriate? Was the program implemented as designed? Each of these questions can be relatively easy to answer when information directly related to each is systematically collected throughout the program's operation by the individuals conducting the program.[10]

This approach to program evaluation is often linked to a *discrepancy evaluation* process that compares the program's processes and outcomes (as designed in its original plan) with what actually occurs. The gap between the two, or discrepancy, identifies the extent to which the program has been effective and provides the basis for making recommendations for future change. Kennedy and Lundegren write:

> By adapting the techniques of systems analysis, it is possible to construct a standard adequate for use in program evaluation. Such a standard defines the intent of a program by describing expected *inputs* (what will go into the program—people, resources, etc.), *processes* (the activities and operations which will take place), and *outputs* (the changes or products which should emerge), and charts their interrelationships.[11]

PARTICIPANT-BASED EVALUATION

Participant-based evaluation relies on the judgment of the participants. Using survey forms, questionnaires, or personal interviews, participants may be asked to indicate their level of satisfaction with the overall program, as well as to rate leadership, facilities, fees, schedule, or similar elements. Such forms typically follow a Likert scale format, in which the respondents are not simply asked to reply "yes" or "no" but rather are given a range of possible replies to each question on a four- or five-point scale. They may also be asked to indicate what they saw as the strengths and weaknesses of the program using an "open-end" question format and to make suggestions that would improve it.

Participants may be hesitant to criticize the program because they do not wish to harm the practitioners responsible for it. In the same vein, many professionals are extremely apprehensive when their programs are being evaluated because negative ratings may harm their job security or advancement potential. It may be helpful to indicate that evaluation findings will not be used in this way but rather to determine the strengths and weaknesses of the program and develop recommendations for improving it in the future.

Separate program events should be evaluated on the basis of their success, using criteria such as how well planned they were, how smoothly they went, how attendance met expectations or compared with past events, or the degree to which they have met goals and objectives that were established for them. It is desirable to have a regularly used evaluation form, which is routinely filled out by supervisors, staff members, or participants, after such events. In departments that sponsor in-service training workshops, for example, it is highly desirable that participants be asked to evaluate the value of each element of the workshop, as well as the leadership provided.

Evaluation of Personnel

Personnel evaluation is a part of supervisory responsibility in leisure-service agencies. It is too often neglected or done sporadically by recreation and park managers. It is essential that supervisors regularly rate subordinate employees on criteria such as personality traits, degree of responsibility, enthusiasm, initiative, human relations skills, appearance, specific job-related skills, and overall level of performance during the time period. Such rating scales are most effective when they deal concretely with traits or characteristics that are relevant to the job situation and when they involve gradations of

PERFORMANCE STANDARDS	RESOURCE DEVELOPMENT DIRECTOR
Planning and Organizing:	Develops through plans and carries out assignments effectively and creatively. Is able to adjust plans and special events to meet unexpected deadlines.
Adaptability to Work Situation:	Works effectively within framework of agency, using initiative to do job in creative ways. Maintains composure under pressure. Exhibits good self control under adverse circumstances.
Knowledge of Program:	Excellent knowledge and understanding of program, policies, and procedures.
Resourcefulness:	Is gaining excellent knowledge of community resources for funding and ability to use them appropriately. Is very thorough, and has used seminars and training sessions very effectively.
Use of Department Handbooks and Manuals:	Has used all Center written and printed materials very well. Has excellent ability to upgrade them. Has shown interest in history, philosophy, and goals of the Center.
Quality and Quantity of Work:	Consistently accepts responsibility for quality and quantity of work produced. Establishes and maintains higher standards of expectations.
Delegation of Authority and Responsibility:	Defines and delegates authority and responsibilities commensurate with worker's capacity. Accepts responsibility for authority delegated.
Decision Making:	Makes sound, effective decisions. Able to analyze complex issues and problems and render a good decision. Accepts responsibility for decisions made.
Communication:	Communicates effectively with all levels of staff and individuals, and groups of varied backgrounds. Is able to inspire and stimulate groups to help us. Oral and written communications are clear and concise. Uses appropriate channels to relay suggestions and complaints.

FIG. 15-4   Sample of 6-months evaluation. (From Supervisory personnel evaluation form, San Francisco, 1984, Recreation Center for the Handicapped.)

response, such as *excellent, good, fair,* and *poor* or *always, frequently, sometimes,* and *never.*

Personnel evaluation should be directly shared in a nonthreatening way by supervisors and subordinate employees, with a full discussion of the individual's strengths and weaknesses, as well as a specific plan for upgrading performance in the time period ahead. It should be a two-way process, with both individuals sharing their view of the work experience and coming to a mutual agreement about the goals that need to be set.

EXAMPLES OF PERSONNEL EVALUATION INSTRUMENTS

Two examples of evaluation instruments that focus on specific areas of the staff member's performance follow. The first, Fig. 15-4, is used by the Recreation Center

Name			Establishment no.						
Present position (organization title)		How long	Increment date						
Location	Department		Unit						
Initial employment date			Payroll no.						
Reporting officer		Department head							

Part A—Primary functions and responsibilities List the primary functions and responsibilities of this employee's present position. Evaluate how well he is performing each of them in terms of actual results achieved:	Outstanding	Superior	Fully satisfactory	Acceptable	Entry/marginal
1.					
2.					
3.					
4.					
5.					
6.					
Overall performance Based on the above ratings, how do you evaluate this employee's overall performance?					

FIG. 15-5   Sample appraisal form for managerial employees. (Courtesy City of Edmonton, Can.)

for the Handicapped in San Francisco to measure an employee's performance after the first 6 months of work. It requires the evaluator to write a detailed analysis of the employee's work under a number of major headings related to job responsibility. It shows how, instead of simply using a rating form that requires the supervisor to assign a score to a subordinate's performance in different job areas, a descriptive approach may be used to present a fuller picture. The example presented here has been taken

PART B   QUALITATIVE PERFORMANCE FACTORS

IN THE LIGHT OF THE PRIMARY FUNCTIONS AND RESPONSIBILITIES YOU HAVE EVALUATED, DESCRIBE HOW YOU WOULD RATE THIS EMPLOYEE IN TERMS OF THE FOLLOWING FACTORS:

  I. KNOWLEDGE

      A. Professional/technical know-how, on-the-job.

 II. MANAGERIAL/SUPERVISORY PROFICIENCY

      A. Planning (Setting objectives, foreseeing contingencies, etc.)

      B. Organizing work (Making assignments, schedules, establishing priorities, etc.)

      C. Personnel Management (Finding, placing, directing, motivating, developing staff)

      D. Control (Reports, records, expenses, measuring results, etc.)

      E. Communications (Written, oral; timeliness, appropriateness, feedback)

      F. Problem-Solving (Investigation, analysis, decision-making, "business sense," etc.)

III. PERSONAL QUALITIES (Habits)

      A. Appearance (Dress, manner, poise, self-assurance)

      B. Energy (Drive, ambition)

      C. Adaptability (Flexibility, versatility, mobility)

      D. Initiative (Ingenuity, self-reliance, self-starting)

 IV. MAJOR STRENGTHS: Describe this employee's major assets, strengths, and abilities in the light of their relationship to the foregoing and to the requirements of his present position:

  V. AREAS REQUIRING IMPROVEMENT: Describe the areas requiring improvement in this employee's performance in his present position:

PART C   DEVELOPMENT PLANS:

Indicate below your plans to bring about improvement in those areas indicated above. For each subject, indicate by priority, the type of plan or plans, that you intend to employ and the tentative timetable for action. Use the appropriate numbers provided below.

FIG. 15-5—cont'd

from an actual evaluation report; the name of the employee has been deleted.

The second form, Fig. 15-5, is used to evaluate managerial employees in Edmonton, Alb., Canada. The key element in this approach is that the supervisor is required to identify at least three high-priority areas in which the employee must be encouraged to improve performance during the work period ahead and to suggest appropriate methods, such as directed self-study, formal courses, counseling, or outside seminars or clinics,

Priority	Subject	Type of plan(s)	Tentative timetable			
			Begin: mo.-year		End: mo.-year	
1						
2						
3						

Subject

1—Managerial techniques

2—Supervisory techniques

4—Personal facts or habits

5—Communication skills

6—Technical knowledge or subject
matter (specify type)

7—Other (specify)

Type of plan

1—Directed self-development
(reading, self study, etc.)

2—In formal training—(ed. dept.
courses)

3—Outside educational programs
(seminars, courses)

4—Counseling, coaching

5—On-the-job training

6—No plan at present

Comments:

FIG. 15-5—*cont'd*

to help bring about this improvement. In the actual instrument, sufficient space is allowed after each of the items to permit detailed written responses.

In the Edmonton personnel evaluation system, the employee and the supervisor discuss the appraisal in detail, and both individuals sign the report. In a separate, confidential statement, the supervisor indicates his or her view of the employee's promotional potential, the type of responsibilities the employee is best suited to handle, and whether the supervisor is prepared to accept the individual for continued employment at this level of employment.

General Guidelines for Evaluation

In carrying out the evaluation process leisure-service managers should observe the following guidelines.

ASSIGNING RESPONSIBILITY

If evaluation is to be carried out in a responsible and thorough way, it should be assigned as an important responsibility to a specific staff member. This individual will be expected to work with other employees on all levels and assist in the development of evaluation and planning workgroups or committees, to both carry out the regular evaluation process and undertake specific short-term evaluation projects or studies.

DEFINING GOALS AND PRIORITIES

At an early stage the individual who is responsible for coordinating evaluation efforts should meet with others to determine the goals of evaluation within a given agency or department and identify the level of priority or need for evaluation of different elements in the program. It is important to determine both short- and long-term goals.

Based on this preliminary analysis, it will be possible to establish a plan for ongoing evaluation of personnel, events, participants, facilities, or the overall agency, with a timetable and a clear statement of the staff resources that will be required to carry it out. Some evaluation efforts may be done routinely without any special investment of time or money. Others may require special expertise, data analysis, or other expenses and therefore call for special authorization.

EVALUATORS

Some forms of evaluation are normally carried out by regular employees of an agency, who are on the job and in a position to observe programs, participants, or other personnel. Others are best conducted by outside experts, brought in for this purpose.

Making use of regular members of a department's staff has the obvious advantage of being less expensive than hiring outsiders; it is also more convenient, since they are already familiar with the program that is to be evaluated. On the other hand, "insiders" may be biased or self-protective and may not be able to make completely honest observations and judgments.

Outside experts are likely to be more specifically knowledgeable in a given area, since it is possible for a department to choose highly qualified specialists to perform evaluations. They also are more likely to be impartial and objective in their judgments than regular employees of an agency. In some cases they may be obtained without charge or at little cost from nearby colleges and universities, appropriate government agencies, neighboring communities, or similar sources.

INSTRUMENTS AND PROCEDURES

A variety of different instruments and data-gathering procedures may be used according to the type of evaluation being done. Such instruments or procedures seek to gather relevant information in a standardized, objective way. They may be of the following types: (1) closed-end checklist forms, with essentially "yes" or "no" responses possible; (2) rating scales that have several possible responses to each question according to degree of positive or negative response or other variations; (3) open-end questionnaires that permit a free or unstructured response; or (4) combinations of any of these.

Closed-end forms

Closed-end forms typically require only a "yes" or "no" answer. Possible questions, for example, that might appear in an evaluation form appraising department personnel policies would be:

Is there a department personnel manual?	Yes_____	No_____
Are newly hired personnel given a formal orientation to the agency?	Yes_____	No_____
Are there written job descriptions and qualification standards for employment?	Yes_____	No_____

Rating scales with variable responses

Rating scales may ask for a response along a range from high to low or may also ask for responses indicating frequencies or similar information. Examples of rating scales that examine programs would be:

Please rate the degree of community interest and support to your playground program.
☐ Excellent ☐ Good ☐ Fair ☐ Poor
Maintenance services provided to your facility were: ☐ Excellent ☐ Good ☐ Fair ☐ Poor

Questions that ask for variable responses might include items such as the following:

Average daily attendance on your playground is: ☐ under 50 ☐ 51-75 ☐ 76-100 ☐ over 100

Open-end questionnaires

An open-end questionnaire permits a free or unstructured response. For example, a questionnaire on vandalism might ask respondents to describe the extent to which vandalism is a problem in their facilities and how they have attempted to control it.

• • •

In general, *closed-end* instruments are useful for obtaining exact responses to queries or forcing respondents to choose from possible answers that are given to them and thus gathering data that may easily be tabulated in separate categories. Although *open-end* questionnaires cannot be summarized as easily, they tend to yield more detailed and varied information.

Other data-gathering methods may include direct observation, photographing participation, interviews with staff members or participants, and examination of records and reports.

Records and reports are helpful in providing useful quantitative information about participation, personnel performance, or other subjects being evaluated. However, they tend to be limited to the bare facts and not to give underlying causes or factors.

GOALS AND OBJECTIVES

Some evaluative procedures simply seek to gather general descriptive information about the performance of an agency or program. Others measure its success in achieving concrete goals and objectives. If objectives are to be useful in evaluating agencies or programs, it is important that they be clearly defined in the early stages of the planning process. They should be highly specific in identifying people, places, time periods, and quantifiable outcomes. In the case of behavioral objectives or performance measures, they should also describe the exact way in which tasks or skills will be performed.

ANALYSIS AND CONCLUSIONS

In any process of evaluation, it is not enough simply to gather information about the performance of a staff member or participant or about facilities, budget, or administrative processes in an agency. Such information must be examined in the light of appropriate standards or expectations and must result in a set of conclusions or recommendations.

ESSENTIAL PURPOSE OF EVALUATION

The key purpose of evaluation is *not* simply to provide a score with respect to the success or quality of any individual or program. Instead, it is to give a picture of strengths and weaknesses that can be used to bring about improvement. To the extent to which specific standards or objectives are not being met, it permits an agency or supervisor to pinpoint steps that must be taken to upgrade professional performance.

Evaluation must be continuous and systematic. It is not just something that happens once or twice a year or only at the end of programs. Programs and activities should be evaluated while they are in process and at their conclusion, and staff members should be regularly observed in action and given feedback that will be helpful to them in improving their performance. Used in this way, evaluation will contribute significantly to an organization's productivity and will improve the quality of service, as well as document the contribution it is making in objective ways.

Need for Efficient Management Information Systems

Evaluation both depends on and contributes directly to an efficient *management information system*. This term refers to the manager's need for a comprehensive body of data that tells how the agency's resources are being utilized, what the nature of participation is, what the costs of different programs are, what kinds of problems (such as vandalism or accidents) affect the system and at what costs, and similar information.

In part, the management information system is developed through the intelligent use of manuals, records, reports, and forms, which help provide control for agency operations and ensure that policies are correctly followed.

USE OF MANUALS, RECORDS, REPORTS, AND FORMS

Manuals are booklets or printed guidelines that are used to give the vital facts of an organization to its staff and that present in concise, up-to-date, and accurate form the policies they must follow or the schedules, responsibilities, and methods that contribute to efficient program operation.

Records consist of various types of information kept on file, usually in the agency's central office, relating to several important areas of management responsibility: (1) legal authorization, charter, ordinance, or other laws bearing on the agency's existence and function; (2) official statement of philosophy and management policies; (3) minutes of board or commission meetings and actions; (4) maps, blueprints, and lists of properties and facilities owned by the department; (5) personnel records, including applications, regular evaluation reports, statements of personnel actions, and commendations for past and present employees; (6) budgetary and financial records; and (7) program records, brochures, reports, and a wide variety of other administrative information, such as public relations releases or clippings, intradepartmental and extradepartmental communications, permits and reservations, contracts and bids, and similar printed materials.

Reports are descriptive summaries that are submitted internally within an agency or prepared for submission to a governing board or council, the community at large, an organization's membership, or other higher authority. They may be as narrow in scope as the weekly report of a playground or community center, which summarizes attendance, program activities, and special incidents or events. They may be as broad as the annual report of an organization, which sums up its total accomplishments during the year, including revenues and expenditures, major program elements, participation totals, facilities development, and similar elements. Internally, they are a form of management mechanism; externally, they are often used for public relations purposes.

Forms are the means through which reports of various kinds or requests for funds, equipment, material, facilities, transportation, or other assistance are made. By outlining exactly the type of information that must be provided, they provide a precise, systematic record of many happenings or transactions within the department. In addition, they ensure that policies are carried out correctly by mandating that certain actions receive official approval by the appropriate administrator or supervisor.

Collectively, manuals, records, and forms are essential to the properly managed recreation and park department or agency. They are part of efficient office management and ensure that employees are given appropriate information to help them perform their jobs properly. They help the manager carry out his or her tasks effectively and provide needed backup information. However, they also represent an ever-present danger. The tendency to require reports, memoranda, requisitions, and other forms of written communication—usually in triplicate—sometimes results in a situation in which an agency winds up swimming in paper. Staff members can be kept so busy filling out and shuffling documents that they have little time to do their jobs. Therefore the intelligent administrator will keep manuals, records, and forms to a minimum, using or requiring only data that are absolutely essential.

One way in which data may effectively be organized and interpreted is through the use of electronic data processing. In all forms of research, for example, computers provide an invaluable means of organizing data, compiling and tabulating a wide range of facts, determining their meaning, and providing in-depth understanding of their relationships. Thus computers have become a key tool in carrying out evaluation and in performing other forms of applied research within an organization. However, their uses in leisure-service agencies, as in many types of governmental, business, or educational and social-service institutions, have become far greater.

GENERAL ROLE OF COMPUTERS

In describing the functions of computers in organizations, one must recognize the powerful forces that have transformed our society and economy in recent years. The first "megashift"—and the most powerful one according to John Naisbitt—has been the transformation that has occurred from an *industrial* to an *informational* economy. He points out, for example, that in 1950 only about 17% of the working population held information jobs, while in the early 1980s over 65% held such positions:

> Most Americans spend their time creating, processing, or distributing information. For example, workers in banking, the stock market, and insurance all hold information jobs. . . . Professional workers are almost all information workers—lawyers, teachers, engineers, computer programmers, systems analysts, doctors, architects, accountants, librarians, newspaper reporters, social workers, nurses, and clergy. . . . In our new society, the *strategic* resource is information. Not the only resource, but the most important.[12]

In his visionary book *The Third Wave,* Alvin Toffler agrees, pointing out that the key to this revolutionary advance has been the computer. He writes that computers were still a scientific curiosity in the early 1950s, with their combination of electronic memory with programs that enabled the machine to process the stored data. Gradually, moviemakers, cartoonists, and science fiction writers began to use computers, with massive concentrations of superhuman intelligence, as symbols for the future. In the 1970s, Toffler writes, fact outraced fiction:

> As miniaturization advanced with lightning rapidity, as computer capacity soared and prices per function plunged, small, cheap, powerful mini-computers began to sprout everywhere. Every branch factory, laboratory, sales office or engineering department claimed its own. So many computers appeared, in fact, that companies sometimes lost track of how many they had. . .[13]

To illustrate the speed of change in this field, McCann points out that ENIAC, the first fully electronic computer, weighed 30 tons and required complete rewiring for each program run. The first "micro" was developed in the early 1970s. It weighed about 30 pounds, calculated 20 times faster than ENIAC, and cost only $400. She writes, "Had the automobile developed at the same rate as the computer . . . a car comparable to the Rolls Royce would cost $2.75, average three million miles per gallon, and would be powerful enough to propel the Queen Elizabeth II."[14]

At every level, computers have entered our lives, ranging from the most trivial to the most profound functions. *U.S. News and World Report* points out that in the 25 years since artificial intelligence (AI) began, computers have gone from playing chess games to mimicking human expertise in complex fields such as assembly line scheduling, advanced missile guidance systems, and computer design: "Technology is changing the computer from a fantastically fast calculating machine to a device that can see, touch, smell, recognize spoken commands and answer in plain 'English'. . . ."[15]

Within the home, computers are gradually shifting to tasks such as the regulation of room temperatures, controlling lights, and activating security systems. Videotex systems permit people to use television sets, telephones, and computers to shop and pay bills electronically, tap into reference and referral services, and take advantage of popular home computer programs such as games and foreign language instruction. Henderson and Bialeschki estimated that 1 million persons owned low-cost "user friendly" computers in the mid-1980s, with many recreational as well as work-related uses:

> catalog ordering, activity planning, home library and educational use, cooking and nutrition monitoring, paying bills, reading newspapers and books, tax and health record keeping, and home maintenance, safety, security, and environment systems. . . .[16]

On every level, computers are being used today in the business and professional world, with tasks ranging from making out payrolls or keeping stock inventories to piloting sophisticated aircraft or predicting earthquakes and tornadoes. While few authorities believe that artificial intelligence will replace human brainpower in the foreseeable future, *U.S. News and World Report*[17] concludes that the development of the computer is certain to change civilization by at least as much as the invention of the printing press 500 years ago.

COMPUTER PROCESSES AND APPLICATIONS

It is not necessary to understand the scientific basis of computers or their mechanisms to learn how to use them. Instead, it is important to understand the concepts of "hardward" and "software" and how to select and use them. The term "hardware" refers to the computers themselves, which are of two major types: (1) the large mainframe computers that are located in central places in government, business, or university offices, but that have satellite locations where individuals may use them and (2) smaller microcomputers or word processors for personal, home, or office use. The larger computers are capable of much more sophisticated analysis and storage abilities, while the smaller ones are useful in more basic kinds of calculations or data storage.

The microcomputer may be defined as an electronic unit of equipment that stores, manipulates, and presents information rapidly. It is one of five elements that comprise a microcomputing system and may be described as the "brains" or "inner workings" of the system. However, it cannot function without one or more of the following: keyboard, disc drive, monitor, and printer. Beeler describes these as follows:

> A *keyboard* is very similar to a typewriter keyboard. It contains the letters, numbers, characters, and symbols of a typewriter. . . . The keyboard's purpose is to enter information and commands into the microcomputer.
> The *disc drive* transfers information into the microcomputer. A cassette recorder may also be used for this purpose.
> The *monitor* resembles a television set and is used to exhibit information and commands [as a] visual display.
> The *printer* is used to produce a "hard" [printed] copy of the results of microcomputing. Letterhead paper, mailing labels, dittos, roll paper, and typical computer paper may be used. . .[18]

The term "software" refers to portable programs, usually on discs, that are inserted into the computer and then provide the formula through which data may be analyzed. Typically, software programs such as the Statistical Package for the Social Sciences (SPSS), Statistical Analysis System (SAS), and FORTRAN Library Program are used with mainframe computers. Many other software packages have been developed for use with microcomputers, and those who become expert in using them can also develop their own programs.

There are essentially three stages of computerized data processing. The first, called the *input* stage, involves communicating to the computer what it is to do. Input may be in the forms of paper tape, punched cards, magnetic tape, a teletype keyboard, or some other device. The second stage is the *processing* stage, in which the machine analyzes the data or presents it in formats that have been programmed. The third stage is *output,* which is presentation of the product, either on a screen for direct visibility or by computer printout sheets that are fed out with immense speed.

Computer languages

A number of user-oriented programming languages have been developed, each for a specific purpose or type of use, which are then translated into language that is intelligible to the machine. These include: BASIC (Beginners All-Purpose Symbolic Instruction Code); COBOL (Common Business Oriented Language), chiefly used for business applications; FORTRAN (Formula Translation); ALGOL (designed primarily for international applications); SCAT and INTERACT, used in monitoring psychological experiments; and numerous others.

So complex is the computer field in the different types of machines, systems, languages, and programs that it often is initially threatening to potential users. Sharpless comments:

> The decision process (whether and how to use computers) is fraught with hazards. . . . The case histories of park and recreation agencies seeking computer support are full of incidents in which service bureaus provided poor service, computers arrived late, programs did not run properly, and so on. There is much to be learned from studies on computers gone awry. . .[19]

For various reasons, many practitioners resist the use of computers. Ewert comments that despite the benefits to be gained by computer use, many professionals appear to fear them. Individuals who lack computer knowledge see this complex new technology as a symbol of unwanted change within the workplace and often resist its implementation. Ewert writes:

> Negative reactions to computer augmentation include *aggressive behavior* (actually sabotaging the equipment or software), *protective behavior* (projecting all failure onto the computer), and *avoidance behavior* (deliberately avoiding or ignoring information provided by the computer).[20]

Underlying these reactions are elements such as staff members fearing that they will be displaced by computers or that they will be unable to gain the skills necessary to use them effectively. Sometimes employees feel powerless, meaningless (reduced to the role of machine attendant), or normless (with the machine receiving the credit for successes at the job). Rather than seeing the computer as a useful tool, they may see it as a problem-generating machine, with the potential for creating stress, anxiety, and alienation.

Use of computers in leisure-service management

It is likely that such concerns were responsible for the relatively slow and limited acceptance of computers in leisure-service agencies for functions other than routine inventory processing, payrolls, or other rudimentary tasks.[21] By the mid-1980s, however, Stuyt and Siderelis reported that the use of microcomputers by recreation and park agencies had grown dramatically. Typically, they are being used in the following operational functions: word processing, budgets, registration, management, inventory, maintenance, payroll, personnel, finance, and research. An important trend noted by Stuyt and Siderelis[22] was the growing linkage of microcomputers and mainframe computers for data processing functions.

Numerous examples of different uses of computers in leisure-service management are now presented. These include: (1) use of computers to analyze community surveys, needs assessments, or similar research data; (2) planning, scheduling, and registering varied types of program activities and keeping records of participation; (3) counseling clients or developing treatment plans in therapeutic recreation programs; and (4) developing systematic maintenance plans and using the computer to assign personnel, determine priorities, and monitor outcomes.

Needs assessments and constituency surveys

Numerous leisure-service agencies use computers to carry out systematic studies of community recreational needs and interests or to survey their constituencies (memberships) or target populations. These may range from marketing surveys of visitors to theme parks or random samplings of families in selected large cities to comprehensive community planning studies that examine leisure behavior.

Constituency studies are conducted in various ways. One approach has been to use computers to analyze the residential location and demographic characteristics of community residents using a particular facility. For example, some recreation and park districts have developed electronic monitoring systems under which each participant who uses a major park or other facility has a plastic registration card that must be slipped into a sensing device at the entrance to the facility. The participant's residence and other relevant information are electronically recorded; with this device it is possible to tell at any time *how* facilities are used (age, neighborhood, or other characteristics of users) or *what* use is made of recreation resources by people from any particular neighborhood.

As an example of such data-gathering procedures, the town of Ramapo, N.Y., uses a plastic photo identification card for admission to certain facilities. It has Hollerith coding to facilitate computer analysis of attendance data and provides information on sex, age group, geographical residential area, type of membership (seasonal or daily), and similar information. When the card is put into the sensor, the correct fee is indicated to the gate official. As a planning mechanism used during a recent summer, this device gathered evidence that the major users of the town's swimming pool were mothers and preschool children. There were few male adults except on weekends and few teenagers. Based on data gathered, the Ramapo Recreation and Park Commission was able to justify a strong need for a second pool and develop precise guidelines for its construction: a larger deck area, a women's bathhouse, and a kiddie pool.

In the National Parks of Canada, visitor survey forms and checklists have been used to determine the volume and type of traffic, the place of origin, the location of accommodation, and the length of stay in the region. For example, the Park Visitor Survey Questionnaire used in Kejimkujik National Park in Nova Scotia (Fig. 15-6) gathers comprehensive information regarding visitors' trip plans, nature of vehicle or shelter, preferred facilities or accommodations, and similar data. Because of the bilingual nature of the Canadian population, it is printed on one side in English and the other in French.

Cheek[23] describes a Computer-Oriented Recording and Processing System (CORPS), which was developed to handle information conversion from a large sample of visitors to U.S. Army Corps of Engineer facilities. Using CORPS, it was possible for a research team to interview more than 30,000 visitors and analyze the results within a moderate time span. It is the researchers' opinion that with minor modifications a similar approach will work for practically any situation in which recreational and park visitation information is needed.

The survey form presented a simplified way of measuring the patterns of recreational behavior of visitors to water recreation sites, including: (1) visitor characteristics, including numbers and home county; (2) day use activities, such as boat or bank fishing, hunting, skiing, pleasure boating, picnicking, swimming, or sightseeing; and (3) boat characteristics, such as length and horsepower. It was deliberately designed to be convenient for easy transfer to computer cards.

Planning, scheduling, and registering program activities

Increasingly, computers are being used in the process of developing and implementing program activities in leisure-service agencies. As indicated, they are extremely useful in assessing participant needs and interests. They may also be used to analyze preferences with respect to fees and charges, appropriate times for scheduling, and similar factors that affect the planning process. Furthermore, they are helpful in developing mailing lists of participants, needed program resources, or other elements that are part of the planning process. Raiola and Sugarman, for example, describe the use of computers in planning outdoor recreation activities for Maine college students. The students themselves developed programs that included

> an inventory program for the outdoor recreation equipment room, a computerized mailing list, and a section on state canoeing areas for an existing program on rock-climbing sites and day climbing areas. Using a menu-planning program, students can select the desired menu, input the number of people, and end up with the correct amount of each ingredient. Survival and decision-making simulation activities permit students to make mistakes without jeopardizing themselves or their groups.[24]

Some investigators have explored the use of computers in therapeutic recreation. Berryman and Lefebvre[25] and Peterson[26] have developed systems-based methods of identifying patient or client needs and capabilities and designing individualized treatment plans. Similarly, Compton and Price[27] have developed the Linear Model for Individual Treatment in Recreation (LMIT), a detailed model for planning, implementing, and evaluating program services for individual clients. While widespread use has not

1973 Park visitor survey handback questionnaire

Parks Canada   Parcs Canada   Kejimkujik National Park   No 03262   Job no. [0] [4] [8]

Please answer all of the following questions

1. How long do you plan to be away from home on your trip?
   └─┘ Number of nights

2. How long did your party stay in this park on this trip?
   Number of hours
   └─┘ (If you did not stay overnight) or └─┘ Number of nights

3. If you stayed overnight away from home on this trip, please indicate

Inside the park		Rest of trip to date	
└─┘ Tent	└─┘ Tent trailer	└─┘ Tent	└─┘ Tent trailer	└─┘ Rented cabin
└─┘ Self-contained (camper truck)	└─┘ Other	└─┘ Self-contained (camper truck)	└─┘ Commercial house-keeping cottage	└─┘ Private home or cottage
└─┘ Cabin trailer		└─┘ Cabin trailer	└─┘ Hotel or motel	└─┘ Other

4. Where is your present home located?

_____ And _____ Or _____ [ ][ ][ ]
Town or city   Province or state   County other than Canada/U.S.A.

5. Which one type of overnight accommodation would you prefer to use in or near this national park? (check one only)

☐ 1. Privately operated campground fully serviced (sewer connections, toilets, showers, food concessions, etc.)

☐ 2. Privately operated campground semi-serviced (toilets, small food concessions, etc.)

☐ 3. National park campground fully serviced (sewer connections, toilets, showers, food)

☐ 4. National park campground semi-serviced (toilets, firewood)

☐ 5. National park campground unserviced or primitive

☐ 6. Rented cabin—no housekeeping

☐ 7. Commercial cabin—housekeeping

☐ 8. Hotel or motel

☐ 9. Private home or cottage

☐ 10. Other (please name)

6. Did you experience any difficulty in finding campground accommodation within the park? (please check all that apply)

1. ☐ No difficulty   2. ☐ Forced to arrive early (before 3 p.m.)   3. ☐ Campgrounds full—camped in park's overflow accommodation   4. ☐ Campgrounds full—will look for accommodation outside the park   5. ☐ Other

7. How many times did your party use each of the following park facilities on this visit to the park?

└─┘ Picnic area	└─┘ Day use area	└─┘ Exhibit	└─┘ Unguided hiking trails
└─┘ Viewpoints	└─┘ Campgrounds	└─┘ Personal contacts with naturalist	└─┘ Guided walks
└─┘ Serviced beach	└─┘ Wilderness campground area	└─┘ Exhibit trailer	└─┘ Self-guided interpretive trails
└─┘ Unserviced beach	└─┘ Outdoor theatre	└─┘ Information bureau	└─┘ Canoe routes
└─┘ Boat launching, mooring or docking site			└─┘ Fishing areas

8. Which, if any, would you have used if had been available in this park?

☐ Boat tours   ☐ "Bike-only" access campgrounds   ☐ Motor boating

☐ "Boat only" access campgrounds   ☐ Cycle trails   ☐ Other (name)

9. If you have any comments you would like to make on your visit to this national park, please make them below:

_____

_____

As you leave the park, please deposit this card in the box located at the park exit. Thank you.
If you are unable to deposit this card, please mail to: Chief, Planning Division, National Parks Service, 400 Laurier Ave. West, Ottawa, K1A OH4

Official use only
☐ Deposit box   [ ]☐ Day [0]☐ Month [1]   ☐ Mail-back   Francais au verso

NPC518K (4-73)

FIG. 15-6   Visitor survey form, Kejimkujik National Park, Can.

yet been made of computers in such programs, this is likely to occur in the years ahead.

In addition, computers themselves are becoming part of the programs provided in some therapeutic recreation settings. Bleland[28] comments that computer and video games may have considerable appeal for clients and that other applications in education, rehabilitative home and work environments, and security are useful for therapeutic recreation professionals working within a holistic framework.

Bleland also describes ways in which microcomputers may be used by the aged or physically disabled persons in security and monitoring functions to control locks and windows in their homes through emergency call systems, for medication reminders, and in similar uses. Therapeutic recreation specialists who offer activities in daily living (ADL) programs should become familiar with computer capabilities in such areas in planning treatment programs.

Computer technology is extremely helpful in the registration process and in scheduling program activities. Foss describes the use of computers as a management resource to improve organizational efficiency in the San Mateo, Calif., Park and Recreation Department. The city has decentralized its registration operation for an extensive network of recreation classes offered in its four major recreation centers by providing staff training and terminal installation at each center to provide instant communication capability:

> The . . . system, connected to the city's IBM 38 Main Frame, allows staff to access and manipulate information on any class or activity in the data base. Through the new system, mail-in preregistration processing time has been cut by 75 percent. Direct entry at the satellite locations provides immediate information on the status of the 400 classes conducted quarterly and eliminates delays on transfer and refund transactions.[29]

As another example, VersaForm, a versatile data base management system, was used to register contestants and schedule and keep records for the 1983 Maryland Senior Olympics, involving several hundred older men and women in 33 different sports events. McLaughlin and Morgan report:

> The automated registration system not only saved the Senior Olympics Commission time and money, but also provided information that had not been available during the first three years of the program. Reports that took several days to prepare manually were generated by VersaForm only minutes after data from the last registration form were entered into the automated registration system.[30]

In addition to such program uses, computer systems are being used to develop user profiles to facilitate individualized program advisement for potential participants in urban settings and make possible phone-in registrations and other convenient procedures. Such a system has been developed as a cooperative project of the Environment and Behavior Research Center of the University of Massachusetts and the Department of Parks and Recreation in Hartford, Conn. An information data bank is being developed that will quickly and easily help community residents become more aware of leisure opportunities in the urban environment and will match their interests to available resources.

Program planning has also been greatly facilitated by computer applications. Theobald states:

A computer program can be written to describe the physical characteristics of . . . facilities, the participation rate at each facility, and the carrying capacity of each. The program then simulates the flow of participants into and out of the facility, keeping track of average numbers, overcrowding, and even the duration of individual participation. The program can simulate inclement weather and traffic hazards, and the researcher can observe the resulting facility use.[31]

Maintenance operations, in particular, which lend themselves to precise and objective definition of tasks to be performed and which have clearly measurable outcomes, are also being approached by many departments through computer-based systems planning.

Computer analysis has also been used in other leisure-service settings, such as college and university recreation programs. The intramural sports program at Brigham Young University, for example, must organize, schedule, and track as many as 500 bowling teams, 700 to 900 basketball teams, and more than 500 flag-football teams at different times of the year, along with over 55 other sports. Scheduling several hundred games a week, recording scores, registering forfeits, defaults, team-power ratings, and similar data created a statistical nightmare for the coordinating staff until a feasibility study was conducted by the university's computer department, which resulted in the development of a COBOL program and the placement of a computer terminal in the intramural office, with access to an IBM 360 computer.[32]

The computer is used to schedule all events and also to provide an instantaneous check of each student's eligibility status, identification of officials and evaluation of their performance, and complete history of each team's record. It also produces team game sheets, with full game statistics. This method is obviously useful not only in the scheduling process, but in overall planning of the intramural program, developing staff assignments, and evaluating the entire operation.

In summary, Howe points out that computer use may range from the most simple and repetitive tasks, such as inventory control or payroll operations, to much more complex tasks that assist in the guidance and control of leisure-service organizations. Indeed, throughout the entire programming cycle—including needs assessment, program planning, implementation, evaluation, and modification or revision of program elements—computers provide invaluable assistance. She writes: "Finally, in terms of cost effectiveness, the use of a computer as a decision-making tool may help management to determine the most economical number of programmatic offerings, their diversity, the use of personnel, scheduling, and so on."[33]

She also points out that a basic problem with computers is that smaller and less expensive microcomputers cannot meet the full range of needs in the programming cycle, and thus more expensive and elaborate hardware is required to perform all the functions just described. Beyond this, until recently there were few appropriate, standardized software packages designed for moderate-sized park and recreation departments. Farrell comments that as needs become more highly specialized, useful software may not be available. Some practitioners attempt to write their own programs. In her view this is not a realistic option for most practitioners:

If you are not currently a programmer, then a major time commitment is required before you can begin to help yourself with usable programs. . . . . Learning to program at the level of sophistication required in the operation of a professional office would demand at least full-time programming study for one year. At a time when universities are producing tens of thousands of computer science graduates each year, release time costs seem unreasonable.[34]

Instead, there is the option of employing a skilled specialist to write the needed program or, as is the case in most agencies, seek out the available software on a ready made basis.

Selection of software

Sharpless[37] comments that a popular axiom in computer circles is "software dictates hardware." This means that buyers should first look for computer programs that will accomplish the work desired and then select a computer that will run the programs. A number of recreation and park agencies, he writes, have developed computer programs for purchasing, maintenance, registration and reservations, and similar uses. For example, he describes a number of "canned" programs designed for leisure-service agencies that are available through a Seattle clearinghouse, Marketing Computing, Inc., a North Carolina firm, Management Applications, Inc., and others. One company, A.E. Klawitter and Associates, of Glenview, Ill., has developed a number of software programs concerned with local government and specifically with recreation and park systems.

NRPA computer software directory

More than 740 software programs for recreation and park use have been cataloged in the National Recreation and Park Association's newest publication, *Computer Software Directory for Recreation and Park Agencies.** The directory does not contain the actual software programs; instead, it is a compact listing of such programs used by leisure-service agencies across the country. In addition, a detailed listing of computer resources and references was published in *Parks and Recreation* in November 1984.

Without question, computers represent an important thrust in leisure-service management today and will become increasingly useful in planning, decision making, problem solving, fiscal management, maintenance operations, and similar services. However, Beeler points out that although the "brains" of a computer system may "seem impressive and have extensive capabilities, they are literally useless without human intervention. A microcomputer is never better or worse than a user."[38]

Moreover, computers can never make independent judgments, but must be programmed to make judgments according to predetermined criteria. They cannot define values; this function is reserved for people. To the extent that recreation and park management is concerned with human outcomes and rooted in the base of constructive human relations processes, electronic data processing, and indeed all forms of evaluation, planning, and research must be regarded as tools and not masters.

---

*Available to NRPA members for $12 per copy and to nonmembers at $15. Those wishing to order should write to NRPA, Publications Center, 3101 Park Center Dr., Alexandria, VA 22302. Enclose a check for the appropriate amount, plus postage of $1.25 for orders up to $25; $2 for orders of $25.01; and $3 for orders up to $75, or call (703) 820-4940. Prices are as of 1984 to 1985.

Summary

This chapter has been concerned primarily with the process of evaluation as a key element in leisure-service management. It defines evaluation and shows the need for assessment of agency or program quality and success in achieving objectives. It presents the key goals of evaluation and describes several approaches to carry out agency or program evaluation.

The chapter then presents numerous examples of methods used to evaluate agencies, specific programs, and personnel. After offering guidelines for evaluation, it broadens the discussion to the overall management information system as an aspect of management. It describes the growing role of computers and electronic data gathering in organizing and analyzing data of all kinds and then presents recent trends in the use of computers in recreation and park agencies. These include the increased use of computers in program planning, implementation and scheduling, and maintenance and fiscal operations.

STUDY QUESTIONS

1. Have members of the class divide into small groups to develop appropriate instruments for evaluating community recreational facilities, such as senior centers, aquatic complexes, or similar structures. With the permission and cooperation of the directors of these centers, they may then actually carry out the evaluation as a field assignment.

2. Develop, present, and compare forms to evaluate personnel using guidelines found in the chapter. Combine the best elements of forms presented by several students, arriving at a final version.

3. Invite as a guest speaker a recreation and park administrator who extensively uses computers in varied agency functions to conduct a workshop in computer applications in leisure-service management.

REFERENCES

1. Gunn, Scout Lee, and Peterson, Carol Ann: *Therapeutic Recreation Program Design: Principles and Procedures,* Englewood Cliffs, N.J., 1978, Prentice-Hall, Inc., p. 70.

2. Woo, Judith, and Farley, Michael: "Portland's Program Planning and Evaluation Model," *Parks and Recreation,* April 1982, p. 50.

3. Mobily, Ken, and Iso-Ahola, Seppo: "Mastery of Evaluation Techniques for the Undergraduate Major," *Leisure Today, Journal of Physical Education and Recreation,* Oct. 1980, p. 32.

4. Howe, Christine: "Current Strategies for Evaluating Leisure Programs," *California Parks and Recreation,* April/May 1981, pp. 22-24.

5. Rossman, J. Robert: "Theoretical Deficiencies: A Brief Review of Selected Evaluation Models," *Leisure Today, Journal of Physical Education and Recreation,* Oct. 1980, pp. 43-45.

6. van der Smissen, Betty (Editor): *Evaluation and Self-Study of Public Recreation and Park Agencies: A Guide with Standards and Evaluative Criteria,* Arlington, Va., 1972, National Recreation and Park Association.

7. Berryman, Doris L. (Project Director): *Recommended Standards with Evaluative Criteria for Recreation Services in Residential Institutions,* New York, 1971, New York University School of Education.

8. *Program Evaluation in A Boys' Club,* New York, National Manual of Boys' Clubs of America, n.d.

9. National Youth Sports Program: *Manual of Directions for Project Evaluators,* Washington, D.C., 1984, National Collegiate Athletic Association.

10. Gunn and Peterson, *op. cit.*, p. 70.

11. Kennedy, Dan W., and Lundegren, Herberta: "Application of the Discrepancy Evaluation Model in Therapeutic Recreation," *Therapeutic Recreation Journal,* 1st Q. 1981, p. 27.

12. Naisbitt, John: *Megatrends: Ten New Directions Transforming Our Lives,* New York, 1984, Warner Books, pp. 4-5.

13. Toffler, Alvin: *The Third Wave,* New York, 1981, Bantam Books, Inc., p. 169.

14. McCann, Rebecca: "Communications Are the Goal in Computer World," *Parks and Recreation,* Nov. 1984, p. 33.

15. "Machines that Think: They're Brewing a Revolution," *U.S. News and World Report,* Dec. 8, 1983, p. 59.

16. Henderson, Karla, and Bialeschki, M. Deborah: "A Computer in Every Home: Implications for Future Recreation and Leisure," *Leisure Today, Journal of Physical Education, Recreation and Dance,* April 1984, p. 49.

17. "Machines that Think," *op. cit.*

18. Beeler, Cheryl S.: "Taking the Byte out of Micro Computers," *Parks and Recreation,* Nov. 1984, p. 29.

19. Sharpless, Daniel R.: "Navigating the Computer Maze Successfully," *Parks and Recreation,* May 1983, p. 38.

20. Ewert, Alan: "Employee Resistance to Computer Technology," *Leisure Today, Journal of Physical Education, Recreation and Dance,* April 1984, p. 34.

21. Dunkel, Margot S., and van Doren, C.S.: "Computers," *Parks and Recreation,* Oct. 1974, p. 42.

22. Stuyt, Jeff, and Siderelis, Chrystos: "The 1983 National Survey of Computers in Parks and Recreation," *Parks and Recreation,* Nov. 1984, p. 36.

23. Cheek, Don L.: "Visitor Surveys: A Snap with a Computer," *Parks and Recreation,* April 1982, p. 55.

24. Raiola, Ed, and Sugarman, Deborah: "Bits/Bytes and Outdoor Wilderness Recreation," *Leisure Today, Journal of Physical Education, Recreation and Dance,* April 1984, p. 59.

25. Berryman, Doris L. and Lefebvre, Claudette: "A Computer-Based System for Comprehensive Activity Analysis and Prescriptive Recreation Programming for Disabled Children and Youth," in van der Smissen, Betty (Editor): *Indicators of Change in the Recreation Environment—a National Research Symposium,* University Park, Pa., 1975, Penn State HPER Series.

26. Peterson, Carol A.: "Applications of Systems Analysis Procedures to Program Planning in Therapeutic Recreation Service," in Avedon, Elliott M.: *Therapeutic Recreation Service,* Englewood Cliffs, N.J., 1974, Prentice-Hall, Inc., p. 131.

27. Compton, David M., and Price, Donna: "Individualizing Your Treatment Program: A Case Study Using LMIT," *Therapeutic Recreation Journal,* 4th Q. 1975, pp. 127-134.

28. Bleland, Robert M.: "The Therapeutic Recreation Professional: Microcomputer Applications," *Leisure Today, Journal of Physical Education, Recreation and Dance,* April 1984, p. 52.

29. Foss, Karen: "San Mateo's Recreation Registration System," *Leisure Today, Journal of Physical Education, Recreation and Dance,* April 1984, p. 58.

30. McLaughlin, Jo H., and Morgan, John M.: "No Longer Handmade: Automating Registration," *Parks and Recreation,* Nov. 1984, p. 44.

31. Theobald, William F.: *Evaluation of Recreation and Park Programs,* New York, 1979, John Wiley & Sons, Inc., p. 118.

32. Holley, Bruce: "Computer Coordination for Campus Intramurals," *Leisure Today, Journal of Physical Education, Recreation and Dance,* April 1980, p. 20.

33. Howe, Christine: "Let Your Computer Do the Calculating," *Parks and Recreation,* Jan. 1982, pp. 71-72.

34. Farrell, Pat: "Computer Literacy: What Does It Mean?" *Leisure Today, Journal of Physical Education, Recreation and Dance,* April 1984, pp. 54-55.

35. Sharpless, *op. cit.*, p. 39.

36. Beeler, *op. cit.*, p. 60.

CHAPTER 16

It is our deeply felt belief that the key factor in motivation, productivity, profit and successful management is the individual. No matter what the job, the work situation is always the same: a private encounter between the individual and his or her task. Any change which influences this central relationship for the better can—and will—be truly significant in terms of corporate results.

That is the essence of back-to-basics management. There are dozens and dozens of books available on management principles, motivation, productivity, understanding how corporations function and hints on how to get along in the corporate structure. But [we] firmly believe there is much more to successful managing than principle, theory and the "bottom line." We believe that people are the "X" factor.[1]

The Effective Manager

Having examined other important aspects of leisure-service management in depth, we now focus on its *most* important concern: the men and women who hold key administrative or advisory posts in recreation and park agencies. What does it take to be an effective leader of others and provide inspiration and direction to one's organization—be it a government bureau, business, hospital, private membership organization, or non-profit agency?

This chapter presents perspectives on the effective manager. It begins with a discussion of the qualities, areas of knowledge, and skills of the successful manager and then examines a number of organizational roles and processes, dealing with some of the challenges of practical politics and interpersonal relationships and presenting guidelines for executive self-management. It concludes with a summary of the need for continuing professional development and growth and the critical need to be able to live in the "future tense"—dealing with tomorrow's problems and possibilities rather than yesterday's.

Qualities and Skills Underlying Managerial Success

What traits are typical of successful managers? Must the manager possess that unique combination of prescience, chemistry, dynamism, perception, and judgment that is often associated with leading business or government executives, or is he or she one of the many who display an impressive array of physical attributes, fine speech, and polished skills, but who lack drive and initiative? The characteristics of the successful manager could be the most important message of this book for the reader in understanding effective management.

Successful managers come from diverse backgrounds and have widely varying personalities. Obviously, factors such as intelligence, motivation, willingness to work hard, and planning are predictive of success in managerial positions. However, in a study of 95 graduates of a leading American university, many of whom became top-ranking government officials, business executives, or professionals, it was found that only two traits in adolescence were useful in predicting success in adult life: being "well integrated" and practical and organized. Positive personal adjustment, the ability to overcome barriers, personal warmth and generosity, and the ability to play and enjoy long and imaginative vacations were characteristics of those who were high achievers in their careers.[2]

Peter Drucker, a leading consultant to American business firms, comments that success in managerial positions is not the result of any single basic personality type. Instead, it is the result of a complex of habits or practices of self-management in effective executive behavior, many of which are described throughout this chapter. James Hayes, president of the American Management Association, points out that successful managers tend to rank high in a number of competencies, which may be placed in clusters under headings such as knowledge, entrepreneurial, intellectual, and socioemotional.

Of these, the *entrepreneurial* cluster contains two important competencies: efficiency orientation and proactivity.

> *Efficiency orientation* tell us that managers have a continuing interest in doing things better, and accomplishing them with the most productive combination of resources. The *proactivity* competency is responsible for initiating action—to write a proposal, initiate a project, call a meeting.[3]

The *intellectual* cluster includes logical thought, conceptualization, and diagnostic use of concepts. Effective managers must think methodically in terms of systems and cause-and-effect relationships.

> *Logical thought* is essential to placing events in meaningful sequences, while *conceptualization* helps managers assemble information or apparently unrelated events into meaningful patterns. *Diagnostic use of concepts* involves the ability to fit existing situations of decisions into known theories or models.[3]

The *socioemotional cluster* places emphasis on competencies related to *self-control, spontaneity, perceptual objectivity, accurate self-assessment,* and *adaptability.* Although not all successful managers possess these competencies in equal degrees, it is clear that they all contribute significantly to supervisory or administrative performance.

Mescon and associates challenge the assumption that being a successful entrepreneur necessarily means that a person would be a good manager. An imaginative, daring, or creative business innovator may be too independent or aggressive to function well within an organizational structure. They write:

> Such characteristics as taking personal risks, responding to financial opportunities, and willingness to put in long, hard hours at work that make a person a great entrepreneur do not necessarily enable that person to effectively *manage* the organization as it grows larger. Some entrepreneurs simply may not have the ability or inclination to perform the managerial functions of planning, organizing, motivating, and controlling effectively.[4]

Many young managers in business appear to be bringing subtle but important changes to the concept of what individuals working their way up the corporate ladder should be like. Apparently, for such young men and women, deference to superiors and other tried-and-true ways of getting ahead are low priorities. Instead, such managers want their work to be stimulating and meaningful and are prepared to challenge authority and make their views strongly known. One personnel director comments, "The old master-servant concept that existed for many years just isn't here any more. Young managers today don't look to their job for life fulfillment, and they don't look to their boss as a role model."[5]

For many people on the way up in large organizations, conformity and concern about security are no longer important. Instead, one consulting psychologist for businesses comments: "These young people can't be managed by power, by status or by fear. Good management has to be more participative, allow for more communication."[6]

Other characteristics of effective managers appear to be that they are aggressive, think positively, are optimistic, and are able to rebound from adversity and overcome serious personal problems. According to the Cox Report, a recent study of successful business executives, attitude is a key predictor of success and can help "make or break" one's career.

> The right kind of attitude makes it possible for you to learn from failures. It keeps you from feeling unfairly treated and instead helps you mobilize formidable energy into constructive efforts. . . . More than 90 percent of all executives say they can advance their careers measurably by thinking positively, thinking optimistically, being perceptive, and being persuasive with their coworkers. . . . Also let it be said that there is a place for idealism in corporations. . . . Half of all executives believe that idealism has had a positive impact on their careers.[7]

Finally, there is widespread agreement that successful managers must be forceful and proactive. Ostro comments:

> The leader or administrator must be a *doer,* not a posturer. When the going gets tough, he must be ready to roll up his sleeves and take command. . . .
> Decisiveness is also essential. A good leader doesn't shrink from decision-making, but he also subscribes to the democratic process. He involves his staff in decisions, and delegates extra responsibilities to capable and interested subordinates. . . . However, never abdicate responsibility and authority. Always be the unifying and cohesive force. . . . Everyone wants to be liked, but it is better to be strong-minded and run a tight ship than to be thought of as "a nice guy without a backbone."[8]

VALUE SHAPER

Probably the most important trait that managers should possess is the ability to lead and inspire others. Chester Barnard, a noted authority on business management in the 1930s, stressed that the chief executive's role was to harness the social forces in the organization, to shape and guide values. He described good managers as "value shapers concerned with the informal social properties of organization [in contrast to] mere manipulators of formal rewards and systems, who dealt only with the narrower concept of short-term efficiency."[9]

In their analysis of successful American companies, *In Search of Excellence: Lessons from America's Best-Run Companies,* Peters and Waterman discuss Barnard's argument that organizational values and purposes are defined more by what executives do than what they say: "Values are clear; they are acted out minute by minute and decade by decade by the top brass; and they are well understood deep in the companies' ranks."[10] Managers must also have a clear sense of the *whole* organization and be able to provide strong leadership on many levels, stressing both the day-by-day operations and the long-range achievement of economic or other organizational goals.

TECHNICAL EXPERTISE

Beyond such important qualities, successful managers must also possess technical expertise. This does not mean that they must be experts in every specialized area of recreation and park management. However, they must know enough to be able to judge when tasks are being performed properly and take corrective action when necessary. They must also be able to employ consultants who *are* highly skilled specialists and take advantage of their in-depth expertise in planning, programming, maintenance, and similar functions.

Ideally, the successful leisure-service manager will be knowledgeable in both theoretical and practical areas of concern. One important priority is theoretical: the process of determining what provides pleasure and healthy social outcomes for community residents in their leisure time. The manager must also deal with concrete factors such as payrolls, annual budgets, fees and charges, blueprints, and earth-moving machines. The administrator must face city councils and the demands of neighborhood associations, as well as a host of other problems large and small in which knowledge and experience are essential for success.

ORGANIZATIONAL ROLES OF MANAGERS

In addition to their more obvious professional responsibilities, effective managers recognize that they must play the following symbolic roles within organizations:

1. *Actor.* This term is intended in two senses: (1) the administrator must *act* rather than be passive and (2) must be acutely aware of the *image* he/she portrays on the public stage and must consciously present himself/herself in positive and effective ways.
2. *Catalyzer.* The administrator must be a person who makes things happen, who brings diverse individuals and groups together and who facilitates community processes and programs.
3. *Disciplinarian.* It is the responsibility of the administrator to make sure that others in the organization obey its policies and carry out their assigned functions.
4. *Friend.* In addition to his/her professional functions, the effective executive is also a friend in that he/she may have a close and warm personal relationship with many of his/her coworkers.
5. *Guardian.* The administrator must guard and husband the resources of his/her department, both in the sense of physical resources and public funds and as far as its reputation is concerned.
6. *Innovator.* The effective manager must be a person who can create new ideas and projects or who is receptive to the innovative ideas of others.
7. *Model figure.* The administrator must be able to define the fundamental values and objectives of the department and must personally command respect and support; he/she should be able to serve as a model for others in the department.
8. *Spokesperson.* In both a literal and figurative sense, the administrator speaks for the department in the press and other media, at city council meetings and similar events, and in all public interchange.

9. *Technician*. Finally, in many practical ways, the manager must be a master of the practical processes of management and must be skilled at carrying them out directly or supervising subordinates in them.

As they fulfill these varied roles, managers realize that they have separate sets of responsibilities: (1) to themselves, in the sense that they must satisfy their own professional values and personal needs in both financial terms and job satisfaction; (2) to the community at large or to the specific population served by their agency; (3) to the owners—the municipal government, the board or commission, the trustees, or others to whom they are responsible; (4) to the recreation and park profession in representing its interests, goals, values, and standards of ethical practice; (5) to their coworkers in municipal government or the voluntary agency or therapeutic field and to employees in their own departments; (6) to those who participate directly in sponsored programs; and (7) finally, to the overall society and (particularly for park managers or resource planners) to the environment in the sense that their departments must follow policies that preserve and enhance rather than destroy or abuse nature.

Ideally, effective managers are able to recognize and blend these separate sets of responsibilities in a harmonious way. A key aspect of this process involves the ability to work effectively with people.

HUMAN RELATIONS SKILLS

Earlier chapters in this book describe current trends in personnel-management theory. Managers should encourage interpersonal and interdivisional communication, create an atmosphere of trust and high morale, and encourage the kinds of self-motivated work attitudes that make for maximum job performance. The manager's ultimate purpose is to develop a work force that is "turned on," excited about its mission, and committed to productive performance. In a discussion of the success of Japanese companies that have established plants in the United States, Peters and Waterman present this argument:

> The productivity proposition is not so esoterically Japanese as it is simply human . . . loyalty, commitment through effective training, personal identification with the company's success and, most simply, the human relationship between the employee and his supervisor.[11]

At its highest point the manager provides leadership that James McGregor Burns refers to as "transforming." Leaders and followers raise one another to higher levels of motivation and morality:

> Transforming leadership is dynamic leadership in the sense that the leaders throw themselves into a relationship with followers who will feel "elevated" by it and often become more active themselves, thereby creating new cadres of leaders.[12]

This influence does not result from the sheer power or magnetism of the leader's personality. Instead, psychologist David McClelland suggests that the leader arouses confidence in subordinates by strengthening and inspiring *them*. By creating a sense of believability (it *can* be done) and excitement, the leader helps them feel capable of accomplishing whatever goals they have established in common.

NEW MODELS OF "POWER" STRATEGIES

Some writers have promoted an image of successful executives as individuals who know how to exploit organizational power ruthlessly in advancing their own careers. For example, in the popular book *Power! How to Get It, How to Use It,* Korda advises executives to practice a "power gaze" in front of a mirror, learn to pick the power seats at meetings, and cultivate an air of mystery. Some of Korda's specific suggestions to would-be executives include:

> *Shaking things up below.* About one such executive, someone said: "He likes to stir the pot to show he owns the spoon." An effective strategy.
> *When to offer your opinion.* Be silent, impassive, alert, visible until everyone else has spoken his piece—then fire away, in complete safety.
> *The miracle word.* "No." Every time you say it, your power increases.
> *Hysteria as a source of power.* Most people will do anything to avoid a scene.
> *Don't cross your legs.* Plant your feet firmly on the floor. This projects an aura of solid power.
> *Speak low,* to make others lean forward to hear what you have to say.[13]

As an example of a highly successful executive who brings an aura of aggressive confrontation to work, Jack Tramiel, the newly appointed chairman of the Atari Corporation is described as the most feared and respected leader in the computer industry. Firing and rehiring executives, alienating distributors, and squeezing suppliers have been his customary tactics in staging assaults on competitors in the home computer field. Tramiel agrees with this characterization, saying "I believe business is war. Give me any competitor—I am prepared to knock him out."[14]

The concept of business as war is accepted by many authorities. In a recently published book, *Corporate Combat,* a former Assistant Secretary of the Army, William Peacock, makes the case that executives can learn much about running a successful enterprise by looking at the principles that have guided victorious military campaigns down through history. He concludes that these principles, which deal with massing one's forces against the enemy's weakness, being clear on your goals, and taking the offense with simple, direct strategy, underlie all successful organizational efforts:

> Through history, armed conflict has produced in a Darwinian sense a set of basic principles that provide an excellent checklist for any type of competition, especially business. While the stakes may not be life or death as in war, we in business are fighting in a "zero sum" game for things that are very dear to us—the livelihood of our stockholders, our employees and our families, to say nothing of our own integrity.[15]

In contrast, many authorities would make the case that the best way to achieve success today in public service organizations is through a cooperative "win-win" strategy rather than a "dog-eat-dog" approach. For many, Korda's "power game" advice to managers is unsound and even repulsive, with its implication that the best way to reach and hold power is by manipulating others through bullying and intimidation. They regard the openness, fairness, and trust implied in McGregor's Theory Y as essential to managerial success.

In sum, it is important that managers strive to break away from traditional or rigid models of organizational management. Such approaches, with hierarchical chains of command and narrowly defined and task-centered roles, often make it difficult to respond creatively to new challenges. Formal reliance on decision making at the top and a restricted flow of communication limit the success potential of executives. On the other hand, innovative managers tend to be far more flexible in their structures, roles, and decision-making procedures.

Knowles[16] points out that good managers are people centered and caring, more informal and trusting. They have a willingness to risk and learn from errors. They recognize that an important function of management is to release the energy and creativity of subordinate personnel.

According to Zemke, the attitudes of low- and moderate-achieving managers differ greatly from those of high achievers in personal beliefs about people.

> Low achievers are characterized by pessimistic outlooks and a basic distrust of both the intent and competence of their subordinates. High achievers, on the other hand, display virtually no distrust and seem, on the whole, to view their subordinates optimistically, expecting not only that they would do their best but that their best would be of high quality.[17]

Particularly in public recreation and park departments, it is helpful for managers to be vigorous, active, and colorful and be able to project a positive and strong image for their departments. Under pressure, they must demonstrate courage, resourcefulness, intuition, and—above all—consideration. Staff and line personnel will perform at a superior level if they are following a strong and thoughtful leader. This is particularly true in moderate-size and large departments where intimate, day-to-day contacts are impossible. Charisma, a difficult to describe aura that surrounds exciting leaders and public figures, is simply a combination of these leadership qualities in one dynamic personage.

People who are moving into management roles must develop an appropriate level of assertiveness, based on strong feelings of self-confidence and the ability to deal directly and openly with others. They must learn to say no when necessary and give negative feedback without feeling guilty. Many companies and other organizations sponsor assertiveness training workshops for their supervisory personnel to strengthen them in these areas.

Intelligent Decision Making

A critical quality of the successful manager is the ability to make sound decisions. Mescon and associates write:

> One operates as a manager only either when making organizational decisions or implementing them through other people. Decision making . . . is integral to every managerial function. It pervades virtually everything a manager does to formulate and attain objectives in an organization.[18]

A decision may be viewed as a choice between alternatives. Although decision making was discussed earlier in this text as an aspect of the planning process, with emphasis on the use of systems models, it will be considered here as a key element in the personal effectiveness of managers. Drucker comments:

> Effective executives do not make a great many decisions. They concentrate on the important ones. They try to think through what is strategic and generic, rather than "solve problems." They try to make the few important decisions on the highest level of conceptual understanding. . . . They want to know what the decision is all about and what the underlying realities are which it has to satisfy. They want impact rather than technique, they want to be sound rather than clever.[19]

He goes on to suggest three basic points that are important in the decision-making process.

1. Problems should be understood as being primarily generic—that is, part of a typical pattern and subject to solution through the application of a rule or principle. Only a few problems are unusual enough to require original analysis and fresh decision making.

Since this is the case, the intelligent executive does not attempt to develop fresh, imaginative solutions for every problem that comes across his or her desk. Rather, the manager's energies are given to developing sound principles of administration and attempting to apply them where possible rather than to solve many problems with different solutions.

2. A second important element in decision making is to determine the boundary conditions of the decision. What goals must it achieve? What conditions must be satisfied? Objectives must be determined in advance and reasonable assurance gained that the decision will achieve them.

3. It is essential, Drucker believes, to start out with what is right rather than what is acceptable. Ultimately, compromise may be necessary, but concern at the outset about anticipated obstacles and objections tends to negate positive, clear action.

Organizational decisions with which managers may deal cover a wide range of possibilities, including both those that are programmed by existing policies or regulations and others that are unprogrammed and require fresh decision-making approaches. Feldman and Arnold indicate that they deal with "issues, problems, policies, or practices of the organization [that] can vary from the trivial (e.g., which brand of paper clips to order), to the highly consequential (e.g., whether to open a new plant or launch a new product line)."[20]

The decision-making process involves the same kinds of steps that are found in planning processes, including the identification and selection of appropriate alternative courses of action. They may be performed on varied levels of importance. Jubenville[21] identifies four such levels:

1. *Primary decisions*—strategic decisions made in determining long range direction the agency will follow and which give direction to the organization and fulfill its goals
2. *Problem-oriented decisions*—decisions made through careful analysis of specific problems, often involving the determination of policies needed to overcome challenges and achieve stated objectives
3. *Task-oriented decisions*—decisions made at lower levels of management, to im-

plement earlier primary decisions, and part of operational planning and program implementation

4. *Reflex decisions*—routine decisions on minor operational procedures, based on normal management approaches, without requiring special decision-making consideration

Not all decisions flow from the departmental executive or divisional manager. In many cases lower-level personnel make quick decisions on the job. Some, however, must be "pushed up" to supervisors for resolution or approval, just as supervisors find it necessary to clear more critical decisions with *their* administrators. More difficult problems may require that an agency administrative head seek the advice or approval of a governing board, particularly when questions of public support on controversial matters are involved.

MANAGER AS STRATEGIST

Beyond the ability to make wise decisions based on the kinds of processes just described, the effective manager must be capable of strategic planning and policy making. Mescon and associates write:

> Strategies are broad decisions to act and to allocate resources in certain ways in order to attain objectives. . . . A strategy is typically formulated by top management and chosen from among major alternative ways of achieving the organization's objectives. [It] restricts the organization's effort to a single, general line of action but still allows considerable discretion.[22]

Tactics are short-range strategies designed to meet immediate challenges and are often developed and implemented by middle-level managers. Both long-range strategies and tactics are designed to achieve objectives within the framework of the agency's capability, the needs of its consumers or participants, and environmental factors such as social or economic conditions or competing organizations.

Strategic management often requires internal reorganization rather than simply new programming or consumer relations approaches. For example, Tichy suggests that a manager might have such tactical concerns as:

> Should we centralize or decentralize?
> Should we launch a company-wide "quality of work" program or not?
> Should we individualize or [make] collective the incentive system?
> Should we attempt to do a better job of relating business strategy to organization design?[23]

Managing strategic change may require creative new solutions to controversial issues regarding the agency's role or the types of program services that should be offered. This must be done in a coherent, integrated way rather than with a piecemeal, scattered process that responds to emergencies as they arise. Gray provides an overview of strategic planning that sums up the manager's task:

> In its simplest form, strategic planning consists of an environmental scan to identify major trends, issues, problems, and opportunities; identification of a preferred future for

the agency; an audit of the agency's resources to identify strengths and weaknesses; formulation of strategies to attain the preferred future; and implementation of the strategies. This process of identifying a preferred future and working backward to design strategies to achieve it is a substantial departure from traditional planning.[24]

MEETING THE CHALLENGE OF PRACTICAL POLITICS

Strategic planning and problem solving cannot be carried on in a vacuum. Often leisure-service managers must deal with conflict situations or sharply opposed community groups or value systems. They must be able to meet the challenge set by practical politics, either in a governmental situation or in the voluntary, therapeutic, or other type of agency in which they hold responsibility. The term *practical politics* may be interpreted in various ways. To some it refers to the need to deal with political officials, neighborhood organizations, legislators, or state and federal departments in constructive and professionally sound ways to gain support for the department. To others it suggests that the department head sacrifices professional ideals to the demands or pressures of harassed politicians.

If they are too expedient, "practical politics" players are likely to be losers in the long run. Recreation and park managers who yield to political pressures at every turn, hire strictly on the basis of party affiliation, and give top priority to those neighborhoods that vote "right" are not true professionals. They cannot provide a full measure of service to the overall community, tend to be regarded as politically partisan, and are subject to swift dismissal when elections bring a turnover in party power.

In other types of leisure-service agencies, although political parties may not be involved, other factional pressures or interpersonal conflicts may create problems for managers. Board members or trustees may seek to influence hiring decisions or other business relationships in favor of their friends or relatives. As previous chapters have shown, hiring standards in recreation and parks are often ambiguous or lack strong professional criteria. To improve the work of their departments and strengthen professionalism within the recreation and park field, managers, both as individuals and through their professional societies, must give full support to processes such as certification, registration, and accreditation of college and university programs of professional preparation that will ensure a higher caliber of individuals at work in the field.

To be respected and maintain their credibility, recreation and park managers must consistently meet commitments and back up statements, promises, or threats, whether made in public or private; act in predictable rather than irrational or "on-again, off-again" ways; follow a legitimate and carefully articulated philosophy of recreation and public service; and encourage the airing and sharing of dissent.

EFFICIENT ORGANIZATIONAL GUIDELINES

Beyond these general qualities and behavioral styles, it is essential that effective managers be efficient and well organized. They must have developed routines and procedures that work and achieve maximum productivity within their agencies or service units. McMaster[25] suggests the following steps that supervisors must carry out if their goal is to "manage for results." They relate specifically to organizing work within the organization and supervising personnel who carry out assigned functions.

1. Identify and complete an inventory of all segments of work (programs, functions, subfunctions, activities, and transactions) necessary before an organization be established successfully, or an existing organization can be examined and improved.
2. Identify the relative importance of activities, and determine which may be eliminated or cut back without serious impact on the agency's performance.
3. Develop the most practical organization structure, with appropriate definition of goals, objectives and policies for each unit and assigned tasks.
4. Measure work, set performance standards and correlate workload and staffing allocations on a logical basis.
5. Identify, prepare and implement a program of training and staff development that will enable employees to perform current assignments better, expand their capabilities into other areas, and encourage the most capable to progress on the career ladder.
6. Establish and maintain a project and filing system which will ensure a systematic means of scheduling and controlling work; review all directives, forms, reports and other "paperwork" requirements, to determine whether they are needed and fulfil their function efficiently.
7. Solve problems scientifically and present solutions to management in effective briefs or through concise and convincing memos.
8. Appraise employees regularly for the purpose of helping them improve their work performance; provide management recognition and rewards as appropriate, and take necessary action against substandard or uncooperative employees.

Providing Creative Leadership

In their fascinating study of outstanding corporations, *In Search of Excellence,* Peters and Waterman[26] identify attributes that characterize innovative and successful concerns and that clearly reflect the creative leadership of their top executives. These attributes include the following:

1. They have a *bias for action,* for getting on with it. In many of these companies, the standard operating procedure is "Do it, fix it, try it."
2. They are *close to the customer.* They learn from the people they serve; they provide unparalleled quality, service, and reliability—things that work and last. They listen to those they serve, intently and regularly.
3. They encourage *autonomy and entrepreneurship.* Innovative companies foster creative, risk-taking leadership throughout their organizations, and support good tries. They follow the commandment: "Make sure you generate a reasonable number of mistakes."
4. *Productivity through people* is their keynote; they treat rank-and-file employees as the key source of quality and productivity gains. They avoid "we/they" labor attitudes.
5. They typify *hands-on, value-driven* management. They believe that basic philosophy of an organization—carried out daily in practice—is more important to its

success than its technological or economic resources or organizational structure.

6. They *stick to their knitting,* by focusing on the kinds of products and services they do well and are appropriate for them, rather than strive for a "conglomerate" approach.

7. Their organizational structures are *simple and lean,* with very clearly defined lines of authority and responsibility, and small numbers of top-level corporate staff.

8. Finally, they have *simultaneous loose-tight properties,* in the sense that they encourage both centralization and decentralization. They maintain strong central controls over their key values and thrusts, while promoting autonomy and delegation of authority in many other ways.

While these attributes were found in business concerns, they also apply to other types of organization and therefore should be seriously considered by leisure-service managers.

EFFECTIVE SELF-MANAGEMENT

Research has shown that successful managers possess a core of habits or practices that contribute to their overall performance. These practices can be learned and should become firmly ingrained in the day-by-day behavior of the individual. They are within the grasp of any reasonable capable supervisory or agency administrator and add immeasurably to the manager's overall effectiveness.

Effective managers know where their time goes

The use of time is a key factor in an administrator's effectiveness. Many managers are harassed, under constant demands and torn among responsibilities, and they use their time in a variety of nonessential ways. Often they have a "disorganized plan of work, inadequate scheduling of tasks, unwanted interruptions, and overburdensome paperwork." To overcome such problems, Virgilio and Krebs[27] suggest the following steps:

1. *Make a list.* Each day, list tasks to be done in order of importance; complete high-priority tasks first.

2. *Analyze tasks.* Break down more complex tasks into smaller units, so that tasks can be completed in increments and progress is made.

3. *Reduce procrastination.* Resist the temptation to put things off; tackle them today.

4. *Get organized.* Organize your work space, filing materials and other work materials systematically to provide ready access and convenient work procedures.

5. *Be willing to say no.* Be prepared to resist unnecessary tasks; do not accept new responsibilities unless they are critical and can be fitted into your work schedule.

6. *Avoid the paper avalanche.* Set aside regular time each day to deal with memos, requests, and correspondence. Discard nonessential items, reroute others, and be prepared to delegate appropriate tasks to others. Make sure they are dealt with and not simply set aside to pile up.

7. *Develop a support system.* Make sure that you use available human resources around you, to absorb part of your load and share varied responsibilities.

Managers are often their own slave drivers. Gherman points out that we are all acutely aware of time and often let it dominate our lives. We speak of "taking," "stealing," "losing," "gaining," and "killing" time. We regard it as a substance to be bought, sold, manipulated, and structured. Our sense of pressure caused by demands on our time and deadlines that must constantly be met creates stress and anxiety. Gherman suggests that the following questions can be used to indicate stress:

> Do you rush your speech? Hurry or complete other people's speech? Hurry when you eat? Hate to wait in line? Never seem to catch up? Schedule more activities than you have time available? Detest "wasting" time? Drive too fast most of the time? Often try to do several things at once? Become impatient if others are too slow? Have little time for relaxation, intimacy or enjoying your environment?[28]

It is important for persons under stress to understand how they are letting their pace of living and attitudes toward time create tension and undermine their effectiveness on the job. The guidelines suggested earlier will help overcome some of the practical difficulties people make for themselves. Beyond these steps, managers need to develop a more measured, comfortable, and realistic approach to their lives and to accepting obligations and responsibilities. In the long run they will be more productive.

One way to accomplish this is to divide tasks into three levels of priority: A, of greatest benefit to the agency; B, of medium benefit; and C, of low benefit. These may provide a basis for scheduling, with A tasks having precedence and performed during "prime time", either early in the day or when the manager tends to be most productive.

In time management, it is necessary to limit interruptions that cut into the period in which concentrated work is required. One simple means for the manager to ensure periodic opportunities for quiet thinking and planning is to arrange a comfortable retreat (a hotel room, university lounge, isolated classroom, unused summer cottage, or similar location) where there will be tables, chairs, space—and privacy and quiet. The secretary is asked not to call this location except for the most extreme emergency. Needless to say, the manager is not to be visited by other staff persons unless they have been asked to join in a thinking and planning session.

Effective executives focus on outward contribution

Drucker points out that the prime focus of the executive should be on achieving results rather than on the effort expended.

When the manager focuses on the way his or her own contribution can affect the overall performance of the department, the executive turns away from a concern with his or her own narrow skills or those of subordinates and looks at the entire organization and its purpose. The manager is minimally concerned with techniques and tools and maximally concerned with impact and accomplishment.

Effective executives build on strengths

Executives must make use of all the resources available to them, their ultimate superiors, and their entire staff. Although they cannot overcome weaknesses, they can make them irrelevant. In assigning subordinates, for example, the administrator should ask, "What *can* they do well?" and then make sure that they are productively used in such roles.

Jobs *should* be made big and challenging, so that all employees have the opportunity to use their talents to the fullest and grow within the organization. This implies that they must know that the executive is fully receptive to their creative efforts.

Effective executives do first things first

The successful administrator concentrates on the few major efforts in which superior performance will produce key results. Such concentration is essential because there are so many possible tasks demanding the attention of the typical executive in government or business. In Drucker's view:

> The more an executive focuses on upward contribution, the more will he require fairly big continuous chunks of time. . . . Yet, to get even that half-day or those two weeks of really productive time requires self-discipline and an iron determination to say "No."[29]

CONTINUED PROFESSIONAL DEVELOPMENT

An important element in professional growth and success is the manager's effort to remain "on top" of the field and improve his or her competencies through continuing education. This may be accomplished in many ways through various professional interchanges, reading, entering graduate degree programs in colleges and universities, attending special seminars or workshops, or participating in conferences sponsored by professional societies on the state, regional, or national level.

Many organizations publish magazines, texts, and manuals and sponsor special short-term courses that develop management and supervisory skills. These tend to be general and geared primarily to use by business executives and middle management personnel. However, some are specifically designed for managers of charitable, religious, cultural, social-service, governmental, educational, and health-related organizations. Others, particularly those cosponsored by the National Recreation and Park Association in cooperation with colleges and universities, focus on the direct needs of recreation and park managers, in areas such as revenue source management, executive development, or law enforcement.

In many cases, state society conferences, which are more accessible to most recreation and park practitioners than national meetings, have excellent programs that promote ongoing professional development. Attending such sessions can be extremely valuable for the continued professional development of leisure-service managers. The benefits will be greatest if practitioners plan to maximize the value of the conference for themselves. Banes[30] suggests that preregistering and making early reservations for housing, special events, and travel, along with a preliminary plan for attending meetings or participating in meetings and updating oneself on the latest trends, will help professionals make the most of such opportunities. Beyond this, the following guides are useful: (1) become quickly familiar with the nature of the conference badge identification system and the layout of meeting spaces; (2) be early to sessions and make a point of meeting those from other agencies or communities rather than your "homefolk"; (3) be an active participant in meeting people and attending social functions; and (4) keep notes, gather available materials, and follow up on the conference by preparing reports, presenting findings at local meetings, or developing objectives based on conference learnings.

Supplementing such processes, subscribing to relevant newsletters or other publications in recreation and park management, and maintaining an up-to-date professional library will be invaluable in continued executive development. In addition, hundreds of cassette tapes recorded at these conferences deal with subjects ranging from law enforcement, facility maintenance, and grantsmanship to issues dealt with at special branch sessions or research symposia. These may be purchased by those unable to attend such professional meetings.

As a final characteristic, the effective manager is not satisfied with success in the present. Instead, he or she recognizes that success in the present is just that and that as Naisbitt states in *Megatrends,* we live in an era of unprecedented change:

> The social upheavals of the late 1960s, and the quieter changes of the 1970s . . . paved the way for the 1980s—a decade of unprecedented diversity. In a relatively short time, the unified mass society has fractionalized into many diverse groups of people with a wide array of differing tastes and values, what advertisers call a market-segmented, market-decentralized society.[31]

Managing in the Future Tense

Without question, the quality that distinguishes *outstanding* leisure-service professionals from others who are respected and capable is their ability to be creative, open, and responsive to the crucial social challenges of the present day. They are able to develop exciting and innovative programs and concepts, to see beyond the traditional, and to envision new roles and solutions for recreation and parks. We live in an era of immense change in technology, international affairs, social values and relationships, medicine, education, population trends, family life, career choices, business practices, mobility—and leisure.

SERVING A CHANGING CONSUMER

A key example of the need to shift to the future tense lies in the recreation professionals' awareness of present-day consumers of public and voluntary agency recreation services. Too often, they tend to assume a constituency unchanged from the 1950s or 1960s. Magazines, textbooks, and college courses often portray the typical family as consisting of Mom, Dad, and three or four children living in a neat, landscaped frame house on a tree-lined street. Dad is the full-time breadwinner, while Mom fills her daytime hours with volunteer work for the church, PTA, or League of Women Voters. Not so!

More than half of American married women today hold full- or part-time jobs. Women have actively entered dozens of trades and professions that were almost closed to them just 10 or 15 years ago, as law enforcement personnel, fire fighters, airplane pilots, professional auto racers, financial consultants, and in numerous other roles.

Beyond this, there have been radical changes in family and neighborhood structures. The number of single-parent households has risen sharply as a result of divorce and separation, as well as children born to unwed mothers, adoptions by single parents, or combinations of these factors. Households frequently consist of two men or two women living together or children living with adults who are not blood relatives. Halfway houses, group homes, and homes for the mentally retarded or otherwise handicapped individuals dot many once homogeneous communities.

All this has changed the face and posture of recreational services consumers. The recreation and park agency must be keenly aware of the different life-styles and needs of potential participants. Physically disabled or mentally ill persons, prison returnees, children without parents, refugees from foreign countries—all these and many more "atypical" individuals are present in many neighborhoods and demand that the contemporary park and recreation planner plan actively to serve a changing constituency. Facilities, programs, and leadership must be adapted to the varied needs and time constraints of such consumers.

This trend should in no way militate against maintaining a high priority on conventional and traditional activities designed for the typical nuclear family. To the contrary, such families need wholesome and challenging activities more than ever before, and public, voluntary, and commercial agencies must meet this critical need. However, it means that the homogeneity of past recreation constituencies no longer exists. A growing number of individuals and groups who pose new challenge for service must be given a full measure of consideration by leisure-service planners and managers.

Leisure-service managers in any sector of the diverse leisure-service field must be able to grow and to develop significant programs that meet the changing needs of their own field—be it armed forces, corporate/employee, commercial, or therapeutic recreation service. As they do so, they must be able to demonstrate accountability and justify their existence in economic terms, whether through cost-benefit analysis or by bringing in substantial revenues through self-sufficiency strategies. At the same time, however, they should follow philosophical beliefs and values that enable leisure-services participants to make a meaningful contribution to changing community life-styles.

Many other critical issues face leisure-service managers today. In forecasting a recent Recreation and Park Congress, Mobley[32] concluded that leisure in the twenty-first century will require a new breed of futuristic thinkers who are able to plan creative, meaningful experiences. Although it is essential to conduct programs and manage agencies to serve today's clientele, it is also imperative to carry out innovative planning for the future. Toffler supports this view, stressing that it is essential to be *visionary,* to *anticipate the future,* to *speculate* about it, to *be ready* for it before it confronts us with seemingly unanswerable challenges. He writes:

> Instead of deriding the "crystal-ball gazer," we need to encourage people, from childhood on, to speculate freely, even fancifully, not merely about what next week holds in store for them but about what the next generation holds in store for the entire human race. We offer our children courses in history; why not also courses in "Future," courses in which the possibilities and probabilities of the future, are systematically explored, exactly as we now explore the social system of the Romans or the rise of the feudal manors?[33]

MEETING THE CHALLENGE OF CHANGE

The challenge of change is intimidating for some. The idea of radical change in society, the abandonment of old standards and patterns, seems to lead to ambiguity and uncertainty in the recreation and park movement as in many other areas of human life or community service. Yet Gray points out that change may also represent new possibilities for those in the leisure-service field. He writes:

> Change brings crisis *and* opportunity. In periods of rapid change, reforms are possible that could never be accomplished in periods of stability. Flexibility, recognition of opportunity, escape from pessimistic thinking, and leadership are required to respond to this period. Now is the time to escape yesterday's success and bring our dreams into reality.[34]

Ultimately, the most successful leisure-service managers will be those who are able to *shift into the future tense,* who are able to read and understand social change as it occurs rather than to resist it, and who can anticipate clearly the leisure-related needs of their communities and regions. Recreation and park managers must be trendsetters and not simply followers of the traffic flow. Only under this kind of creative and imaginative leadership will the broad field of leisure service be able to establish itself fully as an integral part of community life and a valued government function. This then is the ultimate challenge facing recreation and leisure-service managers both in the present and in the decades that lie ahead.

Summary

This chapter sums up the essential personal qualities and areas of technical expertise of successful managers. It makes clear that managers must be aggressive and ambitious, but that they must also be sensitive to others and able to weld their staff members into a unified, cooperative whole. Shaping values and unifying and inspiring organizational effort represent their most important thrust.

Different approaches to management are examined, including "power" strategy models, effective decision-making processes, and ways of meeting the demands of practical politics. It is essential that managers employ efficient organizational methods in in-house systems that achieve results with maximum economy and productivity. At the same time, managers must encourage innovation and risk and be prepared to experience failures in the drive for success. Eight attributes of highly successful companies are summarized as presented by Peters and Waterman in the best-selling *In Search of Excellence.* These offer clues to the management of leisure-service agencies of all types.

The chapter concludes with a discussion of self-management methods and the need to be able to manage "in the future tense" as societal change continues to bring new challenges to the leisure-service field.

STUDY QUESTIONS

1. Identify an effective manager you have known and do a personality profile on this individual, emphasizing his or her qualities that led to on-the-job effectiveness. Share these profiles in class discussion and identify the key elements that appear most frequently.

2. Prepare a report on *Megatrends, In Search of Excellence,* or one of the other books cited in this chapter. Based on your readings, list key implications for management in leisure-service agencies.

3. Examine your own life from an "effective self-management" perspective. Recognizing that you face the same challenges that agency managers do in planning, organizing, motivating, and controlling your personal and school or work lives, identify your strengths and weaknesses and define specific objectives that will help you become more effective.

REFERENCES

1. Culligan, Matthew, Deakins, Suzanne, and Young, Arthur: *Back-to-Basics Management: The Lost Craft of Leadership,* New York, Facts on File Publishers, 1983, p. vii.
2. Vaillant, George E.: *Adaptation to Life,* Boston, 1977, Little, Brown & Co.
3. Hayes, James L.: "How I Can Do a Better Job as a Manager," *Management Review,* Feb. 1980, pp. 2-3.
4. Mescon, Michael H., Albert, Michael, and Khedouri, Franklin: *Management: Individual and Organizational Effectiveness,* New York, 1981, Harper & Row, Publishers, p. 28.
5. "The 'Me Generation' in the Executive Suite," *U.S. News and World Report,* March 9, 1981, p. 71.
6. *Ibid.,* p. 72.
7. Cox, Alan J.: *Report on the American Corporation,* New York, Delacorte Press, 1982, pp. 309-310.
8. Ostro, Harry: "What Makes One Leader More Effective Than Another?" *Scholastic Coach,* Sept. 1983, p. 4.
9. Peters, Thomas J., and Waterman, Robert H. Jr.: *In Search of Excellence: Lessons from America's Best-Run Companies,* New York, 1982, Warner Books, p. 6.
10. *Ibid.,* pp. 97-98.
11. *Ibid.,* p. 39.
12. Burns, James McGregor: "What Makes You a Leader?" in Kraus, Richard G., Carpenter, Gaylene, and Bates, Barbara J.: *Recreation Leadership and Supervision: Guidelines for Professional Development,* Philadelphia, 1981, Saunders College Publishing, p. 77.
13. Korda, Michael, cited in Kelly, Joe: *How Managers Manage,* Englewood Cliffs, N.J., 1980, Prentice-Hall, Inc., pp. 86-87.
14. Richards, Evelyn, and Greer, Jonathan: "Business is War for 'General' Tramiel," *Philadelphia Inquirer,* Dec. 1, 1984, p. 8-D.
15. Peacock, William E., cited in "Competition in Business Has Much in Common with War," *U.S. News and World Report,* Feb. 7, 1985, p. 68.
16. Knowles, Malcolm: *The Modern Practice of Adult Education,* New York, 1970, Association Press.
17. Zemke, Ron: "What are High-Achieving Managers Really Like?" *Training/HRD,* March 1979, p. 36.
18. Mescon, *op. cit.,* p. 165.
19. Drucker, Peter F.: *The Effective Executive,* New York, 1967, Harper & Row, Publishers, pp. 113-114.
20. Feldman, Daniel C., and Arnold, Hugh J.: *Managing Individual and Group Behavior in Organizations,* New York, 1983, McGraw-Hill Book Co., p. 332.
21. Jubenville, Alan: *Outdoor Recreation Management,* Philadelphia, 1978, W.B. Saunders Co., pp. 29-30.
22. Mescon, *op. cit.,* p. 219.
23. Tichy, Noel M.: *Managing Strategic Change,* New York, 1983, John Wiley & Sons, Inc., p. 4.
24. Gray, David: "Managing Our Way to a Preferred Future," *Parks and Recreation,* May 1984, p. 47.
25. McMaster, John B.: *Optimum Management,* New York/Princeton, N.J., 1980, Petrocelli Books, Inc., pp. 2-3.
26. Peters and Waterman, *op. cit.,* pp. 13-16.
27. Virgilio, Stephen J., and Krebs, Paul S.: "Effective Time Management Techniques," *Journal of Physical Education, Recreation and Dance,* April 1984, pp. 68-69.
28. Gherman, E.M.: "Win Your Battle With the Clock," *Nation's Business,* March 1982, p. 90.
29. Drucker, *op. cit.,* pp. 100-101.
30. Banes, Robert E.: "Getting the Most Out of a Conference," *Parks and Recreation,* Sept. 1978, pp. 41-42.
31. Naisbitt, John: *Megatrends: Ten New Directions Transforming Our Lives,* New York, 1982, 1984, Warner Books, p. 260.
32. Mobley, Tony A.: "A Look at the Future Through the Lens of Today," *Parks and Recreation,* Sept. 1979, p. 26.
33. Toffler, Alvin: *Future Shock,* New York, 1971, Bantam Books, Inc., p. 424.
34. Gray, *op. cit.,* p. 47.

Bibliography

Bannon, Joseph J.: *Problem Solving in Recreation and Parks,* Englewood Cliffs, N.J., 1981, Prentice-Hall, Inc.

Bannon, Joseph J.: *Leisure Resources: Its Comprehensive Planning,* Englewood Cliffs, N.J., 1976, Prentice-Hall, Inc.

Carpenter, Gaylene M., and Howe, Christine Z.: *Programming Leisure Experiences: A Cyclical Approach,* Englewood Cliffs, N.J., 1985, Prentice-Hall, Inc.

Chubb, Michael, and Chubb, Holly R.: *One Third of Our Time? Introduction to Recreation Behavior and Resources,* New York, 1981, John Wiley & Sons, Inc.

Christiansen, Monty I.: *Park Planning Handbook,* New York, 1977, John Wiley & Sons, Inc.

Colgate, John A.: *Administration of Intramural and Recreational Activities,* New York, 1978, John Wiley & Sons, Inc.

Culligan, Matthew, Deakins, Suzanne, and Young, Arthur: *Back-to-Basics Management: The Lost Craft of Leadership,* New York, 1983, Facts on File Publishers.

Curtis, Joseph E.: *Recreation: Theory and Practice,* St. Louis, 1979, The C.V. Mosby Co.

Doell, Charles E., and Twardzik, Louis F.: *Elements of Park and Recreation Administration,* Minneapolis, 1979, Burgess Publishing Co.

Edginton, Christopher R., Compton, David M., and Hanson, Carole J.: *Recreation and Leisure Programming: A Guide for the Professional,* Philadelphia, 1980, Saunders College Publishing.

Edginton, Christopher R., and Griffith, Charles A.: *The Recreation and Leisure Service Delivery System,* Philadelphia, 1983, Saunders College Publishing.

Edginton, Christopher R., and Williams, John G.: *Productive Management of Leisure Service Organizations,* New York, 1978, John Wiley & Sons, Inc.

Farrell, Patricia, and Lundegren, Herberta M.: *The Process of Recreation Programming: Theory and Technique,* New York, 1984, John Wiley & Sons, Inc.

Feldman, Daniel C., and Arnold, Hugh J.: *Managing Individual and Group Behavior in Organizations,* New York, 1983, McGraw-Hill Book Co.

Frakt, Arthur S., and Rankin, Janna S.: *The Law of Parks, Recreation Resources, and Leisure Services,* Salt Lake City, 1982, Brighton Publishing Co.

Gibson, James L., Ivancevich, John M., and Donnelly, James H. Jr.: *Organizations: Behavior, Structure, Processes,* Plano, Texas, 1982, Business Publications, Inc.

Godbey, Geoffrey: *Recreation, Park and Leisure Services: Foundations, Organization, Administration,* Philadelphia, 1978, W.B. Saunders Co.

Graham, Peter J., and Klar, Lawrence R. Jr.: *Planning and Delivering Leisure Services,* Dubuque, Iowa, 1979, William C. Brown Co.

Hjelte, George, and Shivers, Jay S.: *Public Administration of Recreational Services,* Philadelphia, 1978, Lea & Febiger.

Horine, Larry: *Administration of Physical Recreation and Sport Programs,* Philadelphia, 1985, Saunders College Publishing.

Howard, Dennis, and Crompton, John: *Financing, Managing and Marketing Recreation and Park Resources,* Dubuque, Iowa, 1980, William C. Brown.

Jubenville, Alan: *Outdoor Recreation Management,* Philadelphia, 1978, W.B. Saunders Co.

Knudson, Douglas M.: *Outdoor Recreation,* New York, 1984, Macmillan Publishing.

Kraus, Richard G.: *Recreation and Leisure in Modern Society,* Glenview, Ill., 1984, Scott, Foresman & Co.

Kraus, Richard G.: *Recreation Leadership Today,* Glenview Ill., 1985, Scott, Foresman & Co.

Kraus, Richard G.: *Recreation Program Planning Today,* Glenview, Ill., 1985, Scott, Foresman & Co.

Kraus, Richard G.: *Therapeutic Recreation Service: Principles and Practices,* Philadelphia, 1981, W.B. Saunders Co.

Kraus, Richard G., Carpenter, Gaylene, and Bates, Barbara J.: *Recreation Leadership and Supervision: Guidelines for Professional Development,* Philadelphia, 1983, Saunders College Publishing.

Lundegren, Herberta M., and Farrell, Patricia: *Evaluation for Leisure Service Managers: A Dynamic Approach,* Philadelphia, 1985, Saunders College Publishing.

Lutzin, Sidney G. (Editor): *Managing Municipal Leisure Services,* Washington, D.C., 1980, International City Management Association.

Mescon, Michael H., Albert, Michael, and Khedouri, Franklin: *Management: Individual and Organizational Effectiveness,* New York, 1981, Harper & Row Publishers.

Naisbitt, John: *Megatrends: Ten New Directions Transforming Our Lives,* New York, 1984, Warner Books.

National Park Service: *Marketing Parks and Recreation,* State College, Pa., 1983, Venture Publishing, Inc.

Niepoth, E. William: *Leisure Leadership: Working with People in Recreation and Park Settings,* Englewood Cliffs, N.J., 1983, Prentice-Hall, Inc.

Pestolesi, Robert A., and Sinclair, William A.: *Creative Administration in Physical Education and Athletics,* Englewood Cliffs, N.J., 1978, Prentice-Hall, Inc.

Peters, Thomas J., and Waterman, Robert H. Jr.: *In Search of Excellence: Lessons from America's Best-Run Companies,* New York, 1982, Warner Books.

Peterson, Carol Ann, and Gunn, Scout Lee: *Therapeutic Recreation Program Design: Principles and Procedures,* Englewood Cliffs, N.J., 1984, Prentice-Hall, Inc.

Rodney, Lynn S., and Toalson, Robert F.: *Administration of Recreation, Parks and Leisure Services,* New York, 1981, John Wiley & Sons, Inc.

Russell, Ruth V.: *Planning Programs in Recreation,* St. Louis, 1982, The C.V. Mosby Co.

Sessoms, H. Douglas: *Leisure Services,* Englewood Cliffs, N.J., 1984, Prentice-Hall, Inc.

Sessoms, H. Douglas, and Stevenson, Jack L.: *Leadership and Group Dynamics in Recreation Services,* Boston, 1981, Allyn & Bacon, Inc.

Shivers, Jay S.: *Leisure and Recreation Concepts: A Critical Analysis,* Boston, 1981, Allyn & Bacon, Inc.

Shivers, Jay S.: *Recreational Leadership: Group Dynamics and Interpersonal Behavior,* Princeton, N.J., 1980, Princeton Book Co. Publishers.

Theobald, William F.: *Evaluation of Recreation and Park Programs,* New York, 1979, John Wiley & Sons, Inc.

Tichy, Noel M.: *Managing Strategic Change: Technical, Political, and Cultural Dynamics,* New York, 1983, John Wiley & Sons, Inc.

Toffler, Alvin: *The Third Wave,* New York, 1981, Bantam Books, Inc.

Weiskopf, Donald C.: *Recreation and Leisure: Improving the Quality of Life,* Boston, 1982, Allyn & Bacon, Inc.

Periodicals Related to Recreation and Park Management

American City and County, Berkshire Common, Pittsfield, MA 01201.

California Parks and Recreation, California Park and Recreation Society, 1400 K St., Suite 302, Sacramento, CA 95814.

Campground Management, 500 Hyacinth Pl., Highland Park, IL 60035.

Camping Magazine, American Camping Association, Bradford Woods, IN.

Club Operations. 495 Westport Ave., Norwalk, CT 06856.

Employee Services Management, National Employee Services and Recreation Association, 2400 S. Downing, Westchester, IL 60153.

Executive Fitness, Rodale Press, Inc., 33 E. Minor St., Emmaus, PA 18049.

Journal of Leisure Research, National Recreation and Park Association, 3131 Park Center Dr., Alexandria, VA 22302.

Journal of Park and Recreation Administration, American Academy for Park and Recreation Administration, HPER 133, University of Indiana, Bloomington, IN 47405.

Journal of Physical Education, Recreation and Dance, American Alliance for Health, Physical Education, Recreation and Dance, 1900 Association Dr., Reston, VA 22091.

Management Focus, Peat Marwick, 345 Park Ave., New York, NY 10154.

Leisure Commentary and Practice, North Texas State University, Box 5344, Denton, TX 76203.

Managing the Leisure Facility, Billboard Publications, Inc., Box 24970, Nashville, TN 37202.

Parks and Recreation, National Recreation and Park Association, 3131 Park Center Dr., Alexandria, VA 22302.

Parks and Recreation Resources, Mahoph Publishing, Inc., Box 1304, E. Lansing, MI 48823.

Public Management, International City Management Association, 1120 G St., NW, Washington, DC 20005.

Recreation Canada, Canadian Parks/Recreation Association, 333 River Rd., Vanier City, Ont.. Canada KIL 8B9.

Resort and Commercial Recreation Newsletter, Resort and Commercial Recreation Association. Frigg Island, SC 29920.

Therapeutic Recreation Journal, National Therapeutic Recreation Society, 3131 Park Center Dr., Alexandria, VA 22302.

Training: Magazine of Human Resource Development, Lakewood Publications, 731 Hennepin Ave., Minneapolis, MN 55403.

Trends, Park Practice Program (National Recreation and Park Association and National Park Service), 3131 Park Center Dr., Alexandria, VA 22302.

Author Index

A

Albert, Michael, 110, 144, 402, 407, 409
Allen, Larry, 104-105
Allen, Stewart A., 325
Annison, Michael, 14
Andres, Frederick F., 339
Argyris, Chris, 30
Arnold, Hugh J., 4, 114, 125, 142, 145, 409

B

Bannon, Joseph J., 13, 42, 58, 152-153
Barnard, Chester, 403
Beech, S.A., 146
Beeler, Cheryl S., 390-391, 397
Benedict, Judith S., 257
Benest, Frank C., 12
Berryman, Doris, 377, 393
Bialeschi, M. Deborah, 390
Bleland, Robert M., 395
Brademas, James, 123-124
Brightbill, Charles K., 3
Buechner, Robert D., 160-161
Bullaro, John J., 9, 268
Burns, James McG., 405

C

Caverly, Joseph, 294
Chambliss, George, 93-94
Cheek, Don L., 393
Christiansen, Monty L., 337-338
Christie-Mill, Robert, 119
Cleaver, Vicki, 157
Clegg, Charles C., 93-94
Cole, Robert, 51-52

Colgate, John A., 262-263
Compton, David M., 204-205, 393
Conway, K.L., 186-187
Cook, Bryson L., 284
Cox, Alan J., 403
Crompton, John L., 18, 173, 229-230, 238, 272, 275-277, 293-294
Crossley, John, 259
Cryder, Ralph S., 97, 100, 188, 286-287, 292-293
Culkin, David, 159-161

D

D'Arnall, Douglas G., 339-340
Dattner, Richard, 190
Davis, William W., 334-335
Della-Giustina, Daniel, 344
Deppe, Theodore R., 269
Desaulniers, Connie, 119-120, 129
Dodge, Rick, 291
Doerr, Kay, 334
Donahue, Michael, 186
Donahue, Ron, 188, 286
Donnelly, Kevin, 176
Downs, Joseph P., 276
Drucker, Peter, 402, 408, 413-414
Duwe, Michael J., 291

E

Eckhoff, Harry C., 179
Edginton, Christopher R., 47, 50, 60-61, 79, 90, 151-152, 204-205, 237, 242, 283, 335
Eisenhart, Henry, 157
Ewert, Alan, 335, 391

F

Farley, Michael, 373
Farrell, Patricia, 205, 396-397
Fayol, Henri, 23-24
Feigley, David A., 312
Feldman, Daniel C., 4, 114, 125, 142, 145, 408
Feliciano, Marty, 270
Fisher, Carl, 185-186
Foley, Jack, 12
Foss, Karen, 395
Frakt, Arthur S., 354, 357-359

G

Gherman, E.M., 412-413
Gibson, James L., 45-46
Glover, James M., 95
Gobar, Alfred J., 259
Gold, Seymour, 189-190, 334
Goode, Virginia, 52
Graham, Peter J., 94, 134, 219, 355
Gray, David E., 50-53, 271-272, 409-410, 417
Griffin, Donald J., 344
Griffith, Charles A., 60-61, 79, 283
Grossman, Arnold, 157-158
Guadagnolo, Frank, 362, 364-365
Gulick, Luther, 23
Gunn, Scout Lee, 372, 379

H

Hanson, Carole J., 204-205
Harmon, Larry C., 349
Harris, R.W., 186-187
Hatcher, Marilyn, 143-144
Hauser, R.C., 184-185
Hayes, James L., 402
Haywood, Lloyd A., 157-158
Heisel, W.D., 162
Heit, Michael, 284
Henderson, Karla, 52, 390
Herzberg, Frederick, 39-40, 146
Hines, Thomas I., 257
Hjelte, George, 3, 236
Howard, Dennis, 18, 159-161, 238, 272

Howat, Gary, 149
Howe, Christine, 374, 396

I

Iso-Ahola, Seppo, 374

J

Jasulak, Neil, 193-194
Johnson, Norman S., 250
Johnson, Richard, 44
Jordan, Joe, 182
Joyce, Donald V., 87
Jubenville, Alan, 408-409
Judson, Arnold S., 279-280

K

Kemp, Roger, 270
Kennedy, Bruce, 198
Kennedy, Dan W., 380
Kershaw, Frank E., 179
Kershaw, Warren M., 178
Khedouri, Franklin, 110, 144, 402, 407, 409
Klar, Lawrence R., Jr., 94, 134, 221, 355
Knowles, Malcolm, 407
Korda, Michael, 406
Kotler, Philip, 272-274
Kozlowski, James C., 277, 358, 363-364, 368

L

Lamke, Gene, 143-144
Landahl, William, 148
Landeck, Bonnie, 326
Laufer, Arthur, 44
Lefebvre, Claudette, 393
Leighty, Leighton L., 356-357, 368
Lewin, Kurt, 30, 35
Likert, Rensis, 30, 80
Lippitt, Ronald, 30
Locke, Edwin, 40
London, Manuel, 149
Lundegren, Herberta M., 205, 380
Lutzin, Sidney G., 61

M

Mangum, Barry D., 324
Maslow, Abraham, 30, 38-39

Matheusik, Mick R.E., 275-276
Mayo, Elton, 29-30, 35
McCann, Rebecca, 389
McChesney, James C., 96-97, 100, 131-132
McClelland, David, 39, 405
McGovern, John, 326
McGregor, Douglas, 30-31, 36-37
McLaughlin, J.H., 395
McMaster, John B., 95, 410-411
Mescom, Michael H., 37, 39, 110, 144, 402, 407, 409
Meserow, L. Hale, 244
Meyer, Harold D., 3
Mills, A.S., 186-187, 275-276
Mobily, Ken, 374
Mobley, Tony, 416
Moler, Stephen H., 327
Morgan, John M., 395
Morrison, Richard B., 281-282

N

Naisbitt, John H., 389, 415
Neal, Larry L., 146
Nilson, Ralph A., 50, 335
Nogradi, George S., 149

O

Ostro, Harry, 403
Ouchi, William, 52
Owens, Rhodell, 184

P

Paige, Ronald F., 284, 286
Peacock, William, 406
Perry, Michael J., 345-346
Peters, Thomas J., 403, 405, 411-412
Peterson, Carol, 47-48, 372, 379, 393
Pompel, David T., 244
Price, Donna, 393

Q

Quinn, Kevin G., 254

R

Raiola, Ed, 393
Rankin, Janna S., 354

Reich, Charles M., 244, 281
Ribble, Jon, 179-180
Rodney, Lynn S., 3, 23, 240
Roethlisberger, Fritz, 29-30, 36
Rosenberg, De Anne, 124
Rossman, H. Robert, 242, 374

S

Scherer, Daniel J., 304
Schultz, Joe, 317
Seid, Bradford, 117
Shank, Patricia, 158
Sharpless, Daniel, 269, 391, 397
Shedlock, Robert, 193
Shivers, Jay S., 3, 236
Siderelis, Chrystos, 392
Smith, Joseph A., 250
Smith, Michael P., 82
Spivey, Leroy B., 334
Sternloff, Robert E., 185
Stone, Robert, 241
Storey, Edward H., 61
Stuyt, Jeff, 392
Sugarman, Deborah, 393
Sustronk, Hans, 275

T

Tappley, Richard, 96-97, 100
Taylor, Frederick, 21-22
Theobald, William F., 395-396
Tichy, Noel M., 86, 409
Tindell, Jane, 320, 322
Toffler, Alvin, 389, 416
Torgerson, Paul E., 20-21

U

Underkoffler, Larry, 282
Urwick, Lyndall, 23

V

van der Smissen, Betty, 355, 360, 373-375
Vance, Bill, 190-191
Vroom, Victor, 40

W

Wade, J.W., 348
Waterman, Robert H., Jr., 403, 405, 411-412
Weber, Max, 22-23
Webster, William D., 281
Weinstock, Irwin T., 20-21
White, Ralph, 30
Williams, John G., 47, 146, 151-152, 237, 242
Woo, Judith, 373

Y

Yorks, Lyle, 151
Yoshioka, Carlton F., 50
Young, Ken M., 104-105
Younger, Leon E., 293-294

Z

Zemke, Ron, 407

Subject Index

A

Access of disabled to facilities, 182-184; *see also* Therapeutic recreation service, facilities in

Accident prevention, 182-183, 333-345; *see also* Risk management; Water safety

Accountability in recreation agencies, 9-10; *see also* Cost control; Evaluation in recreation and parks; Productivity

Accounting in fiscal management, 251-254

Accreditation of professional preparation curricula, 120-121

Acquisition of recreation and park properties, 176-178

Activities in recreation programs, 211-212

Administration in recreation and park agencies, 3; *see also* Managers, role of, in leisure-service agencies

Administrative positions, 112-114
  in structure of recreation agencies, 63-83

Adopt-a-park programs, 292

Adventure playgrounds, 190-191

Adventure recreation; *see* High-risk recreation

Advisory groups, 317-318

Age group needs, 231, 377; *see also* Elderly; Youth, problems of

Aging; *see* Elderly; Senior centers

Air-supported structures, 191

American Association for Leisure and Recreation, 120-121

American Red Cross, 338

Amusement parks, 340, 342

Annual reports, 310-311

Aquatic facilities, 192-194, 217

Aquatic programs, 211

Aquatic safety, 338-340

Armed forces recreation, 75, 77, 303, 326-327, 329
  fiscal practices in, 241-242, 263
  fitness emphasis in, 189
  personnel openings in, 115-116
  philosophy and goals of, 90-91

Arts and crafts, 211

Asphalt Green in New York City, 320

Assessment of participants' needs and interests, 208-209

Athletic programs, marketing of, 277-278; *see also* Sports; Youth, sports for

Atlanta, Ga., Department of Recreation and Parks, 312

Atlantic-Richfield Company, 230

Auditing, 251-254

Authority
  delegation of, 41-42, 69
  levels of, 68
  as management principle, 35

B

Balance sheets, 253

Beach supervision, 339-340

Beatty Memorial Hospital, Westville, Ind., 129-130

Behavior modification, 148-149

Behavioral science management approach, 35-43

Boards and commissions, 65-57, 138-139

Boating, 270, 275-276, 338

Bonds as revenue source, 255-256

Boston, Mass., Department of Parks and
Recreation, 312, 345
Boy Scouts, 63, 129
Boys' and Girls' Clubs, 63-64, 66-67, 74-75,
116-117, 181, 239, 278
Brigham Young University, 396
Budgets in recreation and parks, 201-202,
236-251, 279; *see also* Accounting in
fiscal management
preparation of, 245-248
Bureaucracy in management, 22-23
Burnout, 158
Business; *see* Commercial recreation; Industry,
relations of public agencies with

C

Calgary, Alberta, Can., 160, 193
California, recreation and parks in, 258-259,
284-285, 292, 294-295, 326
Campus recreation, 130, 174, 201, 262-263,
277-278, 393-394, 396
Canada, recreation and parks in, 64, 71-72,
75, 136, 159-160, 184, 191, 193, 261,
270, 275-276, 321, 323, 327, 347-348,
382-384, 393-394
Capital budgets, 244
Catholic Youth Organization, 329-330
Centralization of authority, 68-69
Certification, 120-121
Challenges facing leisure-service managers,
11-15
Chesapeake, Va., sports programs in, 173
Chicago Park District, 218-219
Civil service, 114-116, 121
Classification systems in personnel
management, 111-114
Coaching as supervisory function, 147-148
Commercial recreation, 75, 77, 264, 340, 342
employment in, 117-120
facilities in, 174, 176, 196-198
Communication process, 42-43
Community centers, 179-180
planning for, 170-172, 276
schools as, 324
Community recreation programs, guidelines
for, 209
Community relations, 6, 316-329

Compensatory policies for special populations,
259-260, 325
Computers in management, 154-156, 388-398;
see also Electronic data processing
Concessions, 260-261, 325
Conflict resolution, 154-156
Contingency approach to management, 37-38
Continuing education, 120-121
Contributory negligence, 359
Controlling function in management, 372-398
Controls on agency expenditures, 249-251
Cooperation between agencies, 64, 131, 322-
329
Coordination function of public agencies, 206-
207
Cosponsorship of programs, 292-294
Cost control, 179, 250-251
Costa Mesa, Calif., 179-180
Cost-benefit analysis, 244, 281-282
Councils for neighborhoods or community
centers, 317-318
Counseling as supervisory function, 147-148
Creativity in leadership, 411-417
Crime in parks, 188, 195, 334
Critical path method, 48-49
Cultural programming, 231; *see also* Arts and
crafts; Dance; Drama; Music

D

Dade County, Fla., 168
Dallas, Tex., recreation in, 74-75, 93-94
Dance, 211-212
Decision making, 51-52, 153-155, 407-409
Decision packages in budget planning, 282-
283
Delegation of authority, 69, 152-154
Demographic changes in society, 8; *see also*
Families in modern life; Special
populations
Design of recreation and park facilities, 178-
184
Detroit, Mich., recreation programs in, 219-
220
Diagraph, 228-229
Directing function in management, 110-139
Disabled, facilities for, 182-184, 195-196; *see
also* Therapeutic recreation service

Disciplinary action, 132-133, 138

Discrepancy evaluation model, 379-380

Disney World, 75, 77-79, 134, 151, 162, 197

Division of labor, 24-25, 68

Drama, 211

E

East Bay Regional Park District, Calif., 292

Ecological recovery sites, 191-192

Economic influences on leisure service, 8-10, 269-272

Economics Research Associates, 258

Edmonton, Alberta, Can., recreation and parks in, 380-382

Education for leisure, 207

Elderly, 260, 377; *see also* Senior centers; Senior citizens

Electronic data processing, 9-10

Electronic entertainment, 10-11

Emergency procedures, 337-338

Employee recreation programs, 195, 234, 262, 293-294, 351-352

Employee-oriented supervisory style, 145-155

Employment in leisure-service agencies, 111-121

Enabling laws, 62

Environmental issues in recreation and park management, 10, 89, 107, 198-199

EPCOT Center, 77-79, 162, 197

Equal employment opportunity, 125; *see also* Legal aspects of recreation management

Equity in planning facilities, 173

Equity theory of motivation, 40

Evaluation
  of personnel, 133
  of public relations process, 316
  in recreation and parks, 6, 372-387

Evansville, Ind., Public Recreation Commission, 343

Expectancy theory of motivation, 40

Expenditures on recreation, 1-2, 270; *see also* Economic influences on leisure service; Revenue sources

Experiential training, 130

F

Facilities in recreation and parks, 5, 46, 168-203, 206, 214, 326-327, 336-338, 345-347; *see also* Community centers; Concessions; Maintenance of facilities; Parks

Fair Oaks, Calif., subcontracting in, 285

Fairfax County, Va., Park Authority, 276

Families in modern life, 113, 415-416

Family program emphasis, 231

Fees and charges, 257-260

Firing procedures, 366

First aid, 337

Fiscal management, 5, 268-298, 361-364 budgets and, 236-267

Fiscal pressures, 8-9, 201-202, 269-270

Fitness program emphasis, 77-78, 189, 194-195, 211, 230, 321

Flextime, 150

Formal management processes, 28, 60, 69, 71

Formats for program planning, 215-216

Forms in agency management, 388

Foundations, 261, 264, 287-290

Fountain Valley, Calif., 326

Frederick County, Md., Outdoor School, 220-221

Free-form agency structure, 82

Friends organizations in recreation and parks, 294-295

Function-based budgets, 240-241

Funding of recreation programs, 214; *see also* Budgeting in recreation and parks sources of, 254-264, 287-295, 324-325

Future as focus of recreation managers, 271-272, 415-417

G

Gambling as recreational activity, 107-108

Games, 211, 225-226; *see also* Sports

Gift catalogues, 291-292

Gifts and bequests, 261, 290-293

Girl Scouts of U.S.A., 63, 67, 100-102, 217

Goals
  as basis for evaluation, 379-380
  of public relations, 302-303
  in recreation and park agencies, 5, 87-92, 209-210

Golf courses, 179
Governance of leisure-service agencies, 58-83
Graft, 250
Grand Prairie, Tex., 326
Grants, as revenue source, 257, 287-291

H

Haunted Castle fire, 332, 336-337
Hawthorne studies, 29-30
Hazards in recreation settings, 336, 344-345;
    see also Risk management
Health spa, 77
Hearings for budget approval, 248
Hedonism in modern life, 10-11, 89
Hershey Youth Sports Program, 189, 231
Higher education in leisure-service
    management, 120-121
High-risk recreation, 334-335, 340-344, 357-
    360
Hobbies, 212
Home rule legislation, 63
Honeywell Corporation, 189
Horizontal organization structure, 27
Human relations era in management, 29-30,
    36-37
Human relations skills, 405-407
Human service programming, 8, 89, 207,
    212, 231
Huntington Beach, Calif., 195

I

Impact fees for developers, 255
Industrial humanism, 30-31
Industry, relations of public agencies with,
    290-295; *see also* Cooperation between
    agencies; Funding, sources of
Informal management processes, 28-29, 60,
    69, 71, 79-80, 82
Innovative fiscal management, 268-298
In-service education, 126-131, 135, 336-337
Insurance, 361-362
Interview methods, 124
Intramurals, 396; *see also* Campus recreation;
    Sports

J

Japanese management approaches, 50-53
Job classification systems, 111-114
Job enrichment, 149-150
Job satisfaction, 53, 143-144
Johnson Air Force Base, N.C., 327
Johnson City, Mo., Park and Recreation
    District, 293-294
Joseph P. Kennedy, Jr., Foundation, 264
Juvenile delinquency, 188

K

Kansas City, Mo., 213
Korea, military recreation in, 75, 77

L

Labor unions, 158-162, 366
Law enforcement, 6, 188-189, 345-351, 368-
    369
Leadership
    in program planning, 214
    quality of, 405
Leadership positions, 112-114
Leasing of recreation and park areas, 177,
    325-326, 363-364
Legal aspects of recreation management, 6,
    61-63, 125, 245, 354-370
Leisure
    education for, 207
    trends in participation in, 1-2, 10-11
Leisure pools, 193-194
Liability, 6, 333, 335, 351, 354-363
Lifeguard training, 339-340
Lighting of recreation and park facilities, 195
Line functions in management, 27-28
Linking-pin structures, 80
Local recreation and park agencies, 61-63
Los Angeles, Calif., recreation and parks in,
    64, 194, 196, 285

M

Machine model of management, 21-22
Maintenance of facilities, 5, 46, 168-169,
    179-180, 184-188, 320

Management
  contracting of, 188; *see also* Privatization
  contrasted with administration, 3-4
  by objectives, 193-194
  traditional concepts of, 18-28
Managers
  effectiveness of, 400-417
  functions of, 4-6, 60-61
  qualities of effective, 401-417
  role of
    in facilities development, 168-202
    in fiscal management, 236-298
    in leisure-service agencies, 1-15
    in public relations, 311-316
Management information systems, 6, 387-398
Management science, 35-54
Manuals in recreation and park agencies, 131-132, 387-388
Marina maintenance, 187
Market segmentation, 275-276
Marketing in recreation and parks, 5, 9, 89, 272-278
Maryland, school-community centers in, 323-324
Matrix organization structure, 80-82
Mechanized recreation, 334
Membership in clubs, 368
Mental activities, 212
Michigan State University, 119
Military recreation; *see* Armed forces recreation
Milwaukee, Wis., goals of recreation in, 90
Minorities and recreation service, 8
Mississauga, Ontario, Can., 347
Mobile recreation units, 191
Models, use of, in management theory, 47-49
Modular organizations, 80
Montreal, food concessions in, 261
Mt. Kisco, N.Y., 64
Mt. Sinai Hospital, N.Y., 222-234
Municipal leisure-service agencies, 61-63
Music, 211

N

Nassau County, N.Y., Department of
  Recreation and Parks, 98-100, 122-123

National Collegiate Athletic Association, 378-379
National Council on Accreditation, 120-121
National Council on Aging, 377
National Employee Services and Recreation Association, 121
National Institutes of Health Hospital, 126
National Park Service; *see* United States National Park Service
National Recreation and Park Association, 14, 120-121, 159, 170, 230, 369, 375, 397, 414
National Therapeutic Recreation Society, 120
National Youth Sports Program, 378-379
Nature centers, 192, 221
Needs assessment, 382
Needs hierarchy, 38-39
Negligence, 356-360
Neighborhood planning methods, 170-172
Nepean, Ontario, Can., 321
Network models in systems planning, 47-49
New Mexico state parks maintenance, 187
New Rochelle, N.Y., 293
New York City recreation facilities, 320
New York State Recreation and Parks Society, 113-114
Nova Scotia, Can., 394

O

Oak Park, Ill., 100-101
Object classification budget, 241
Objectives in leisure-service agencies, 91-94
Oklahoma City, Okla., Parks and Recreation Department, 341-342
Old Country at Busch Gardens, 119-120, 129, 197, 227
Omaha, Neb., Department of Parks, Recreation and Public Property, 71-72
Ontario, Can., 284
Open space, protection of, 198-199
Operating budgets, 244
Operations management, 44-49
Organizational commitment, 149
Organizational development, 5
Organizational roles of managers, 404-405, 410-411

Organizational units, budgeting for, 241
Organizations, structure of, 26-28, 36, 58-83
Orientation of employees, 126
Outdoor recreation, participation in, 1-12,
211, 221, 270, 321, 333-334, 393-396

P

Palo Alto, Calif., 192
Parcourse facilities, 195
Park rangers, 114-115, 347-349
Parks; *see also* Facilities in recreation and
parks; Maintenance of facilities
beauty of, 184-185
maintained by community groups, 320
uses of, 188-190, 392-394
Participants in recreation activities, 22, 214
Participative management approaches, 51-52
Pasadena, Calif., joint program sponsorship
in, 64
Penetanguishene, Ontario, Can., Mental
Health Centre, 136
People Express Airlines, 273
Peoria, Ill., Park District, 123
Performance budget, 242
Personnel
evaluation of, 380-384
management of, 5, 110-139
policies for, 131-134, 159-162, 364-366
scheduling of, 98-99, 150-151
selection and hiring of, 122-125
Peterborough, Ontario, Can., YMCA, 64, 327
Philadelphia, Pa., Recreation Department,
195, 319
Philosophy of recreation service, 7-15, 88-91
Physical fitness; *see* Fitness program emphasis
Piersol Rehabilitation Center, Philadelphia,
Pa., 91
Planning
for programs, 208-216
for recreation and park facilities, 169-176
Planning process, 103-106
Planning-Program-Budgeting Systems (PPBS),
49-50
Playboy Club, 225-226
Playgrounds
accidents on, 333-334, 340-342, 358

Playgrounds—cont'd
design of, 189-191
programming for, 224-225
Point Mallard, Ala., Aquatic Center, 192-193
Police power of states, 61
Police in recreation and parks, 368-369; *see
also* Law enforcement
Policies of leisure-service agencies, 95-103,
210
Politics in recreation and parks, 102-103, 125,
310, 321
Portsmouth, Va., Parks and Recreation
Department, 324-325
POSDCORB, 23
Power
sources of, 41-42
strategies for obtaining, 406-407
Poverty areas, 188-189, 260
President's Council on Physical Fitness and
Sport, 230
Pricing methods, 258-259, 276-277
Privatization, 188, 284-287
Problem solving, 153-155; *see also* Decision
making
Productivity, 278-281, 411-444
Professional identification, 162-163, 414-415
Professional societies, 95; *see also* National
Recreation and Park Association
Program Evaluation Review Technique
(PERT), 48-49
Programs
budgeting for, 242-243
development of, 208-216
life cycle of, 229-230
planning and implementation of, 5
structure of, 226, 228
Public relations, 6, 300-330, 337
print media in, 304-307
Publicity, 304-310
Purchasing procedures, 250

Q

Quality circles, 51-52
Quality-of-life approach to leisure service,
89

R

Racial minorities and recreation opportunity, 366-368, 370-371; *see also* Poverty areas; Special populations
Raleigh, N.C., Department of Recreation and Parks, 312
Reading, Pa., Recreation and Park Department, 127
Records, 387-388
Recreation and park agencies
    local, 61-63
    public, 65-66, 95-96, 375-377
Recreation program development, 204-235
Recruitment of personnel, 122, 135
Registration, 120, 395-396
Reinforcement theory of motivation, 40-41
Religion and program policies, 101-102, 107-108
Reports, 387-388
Research; *see* Evaluation in recreation and parks
Resort recreation facilities and programs, 196-198, 225-226
Revenue sources, 241, 254-266
Revere, Mass., employment of senior citizens, 136-137
Risk management, 6, 332-351, 357-360
Riveredge Hospital, Ill., 326
Rock festival, 351
Rotation of job assignments, 150-151
Rutgers College, N.J., 312, 314

S

Safety factors in facilities development, 182-183; *see also* Risk management
St. Louis, Mo., Veterans Administration Hospital, 115
San Francisco Recreation Center for the Handicapped, 67, 75-76, 175, 321, 381-382
San Francisco Recreation and Parks Department, 295-296
San Jose, Calif., parks maintenance in, 186-187
San Mateo, Calif., computer use in, 395

Scalar principle, 25
Scheduling of recreation programs, 215-216, 218-226
School use for recreation, 174, 322-324; *see also* Campus recreation
Scientific management theory, 20-28
Seasonal scheduling, 219-220
Seattle, Wash., Park and Recreation Department, 320
Self-management, 413-414
Senior centers, 107-108, 181-182, 377
Senior citizens, 136-137
Senior Olympics, 395
Sesame Place, Pa., 197, 213
Sexism in management, 53, 133, 364-368, 370
Sexual abuse of children, 329
Sexual behavior, trends in, 13
Shared Outdoor Adventure Recreation (SOAR), 80-82, 321
Skateboard safety, 342-344
Ski center managers, 119, 274
Skid Row Park, Los Angeles, 196
Skinny-dipping as policy issue, 234-235
Social factors affecting leisure-service management, 7-14
Social recreation, 212, 216
Society of Park and Recreation Educators, 120-121
Software in computer use, 390-391, 395-397
Span of control, 25-26, 68-69
Special populations, 259-260, 366-368, 415-416; *see also* Therapeutic recreation service
Spokane, Wash., Park Board, 70-71, 322-333
Sports, 189, 211, 218-219, 230-231, 275-276, 378-379, 396
    injuries in, 334
Staff
    functions of, in management, 27-28
    training of, for safety, 336-337
Standards approach
    in facilities planning, 170-171
    in maintenance, 186-188
State laws on recreation, 61-62

Strategies for fiscal survival, 270-272; *see also* Innovative fiscal management
Strikes, 159-160; *see also* Labor unions
Subcontracting of recreation functions, 284-286, 297-298
Supervision in personnel management, 111-114, 126, 135-136, 143-158
Surveys, 392-394
Synergy
   in facility operations, 198
   in grant applications, 289, 326-327

T

Taxes as revenue source, 254-256
Television
   as leisure outlet, 10-11
   as public relations medium, 307-308
Temple University, Philadelphia, Pa., 118, 130
Theme parks, 120-121
Theory X, 36-37
Theory Y, 36-37
Theory Z, 52
Therapeutic recreation service, 47-48, 65, 67, 80-82, 118, 212, 303, 320, 326, 393, 395
   facilities in, 174-175, 183-184
   funding for, 263-264, 266-267
   goals of, 91
   in-service training in, 129-130
   in Veterans Administration, 115
   volunteers in, 136
Time management, 384
Toronto, Can., 184, 191-192, 261, 275
Tort liability, 356
Tourism, 2, 196-198, 270
Transactional analysis, 152
Trips and outings, 216

U

United States Air Force, 326-327
United States Forest Service, 64
United States National Park Service, 64, 114-115, 277, 334, 345, 348
United States Navy, 115-116, 241-242, 250-252, 329-330

United States Veterans Administration, 65, 115
Unity of command, 25
University of Michigan, 277-278
Urban Parks and Recreation Recovery (UPARR) Program, 136
Urban planning in recreation and parks, 169-176
Urban problems, 188-190

V

Values in recreation and leisure, 10-11; *see also* Philosophy of recreation service
Vancouver, British Columbia, Can., 71-72, 75, 159-160, 191, 261, 323
Vandalism, 334, 345-349
Vertical organization structure, 27
Voluntary and nonprofit organizations, 63; *see also* Boy Scouts; Boys' and Girls' Clubs; Girl Scouts of U.S.A.; YMCA; YM-YWHA; YWCA
   employment policies in, 116-117
   facilities planning in, 174, 181, 195
   funding for, 261-262
Volunteers in leisure-service agencies, 134-136, 212, 318-319, 324-325

W

Waivers, 360
Washington, D.C., Recreation Department, 322
Water play parks, 193, 197, 227
Water safety, 338-340
Wave pools, 192-193
Wheelchair Olympics, 183
Women; *see also* Sexism in management
   changing role of, 415-416
   as participants in recreation, 2
   recreation opportunities for, 366-368
   role of, as volunteers, 318-319

Y

Yosemite National Park, 345
Young Men's Christian Association (YMCA), 63-64, 117, 262, 297

Young Men's and Young Women's Hebrew
    Association (YM-YWHA), 138-139,
    220, 222
Young Women's Christian Association
    (YWCA), 63
Youth
  problems of, 13
  sports for, 189, 318-319, 379

Z

Zero-based budgeting, 282-283
Zoos, 194, 259